I0819621

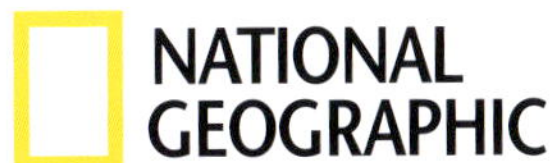

THE PHOTOGRAPHS

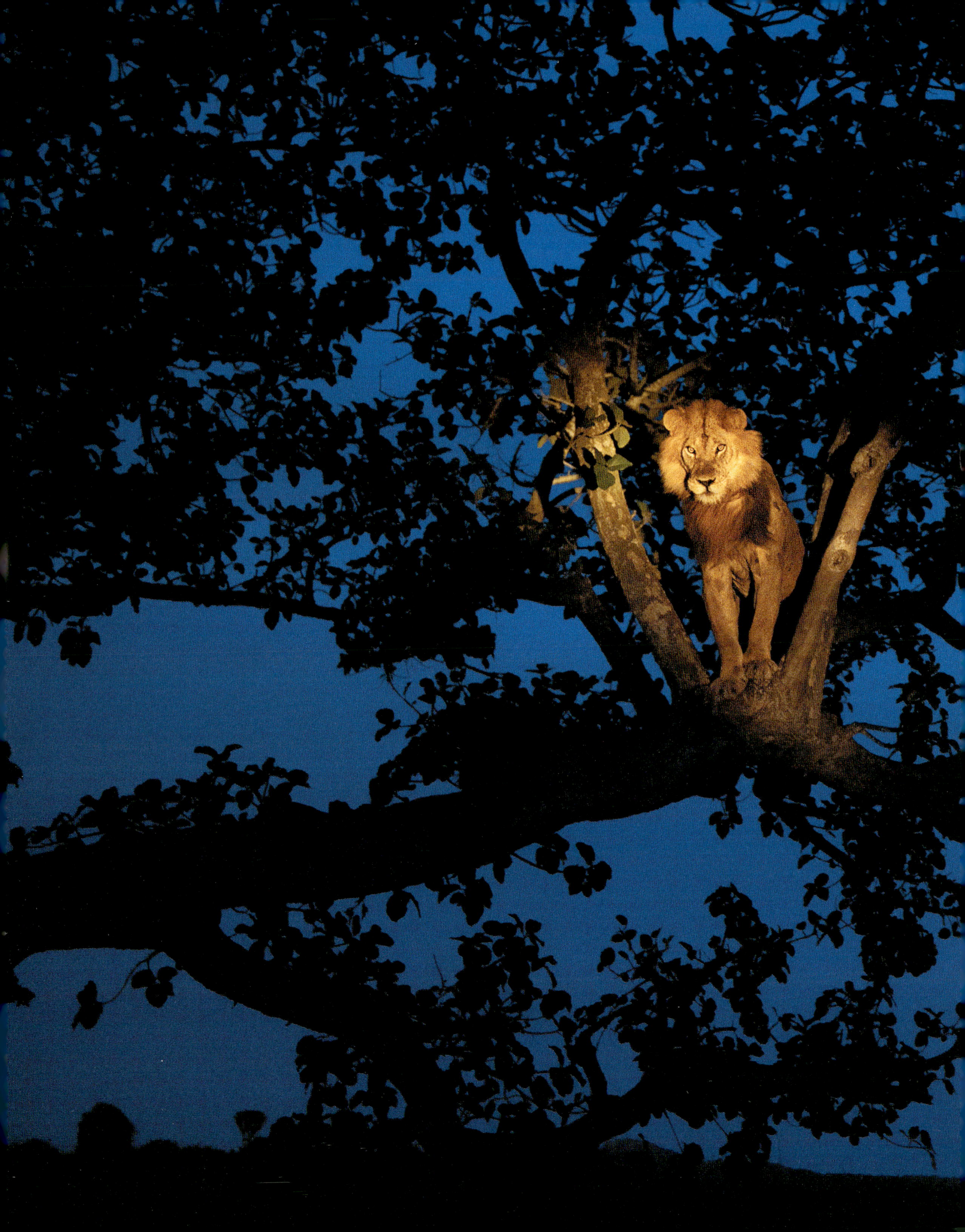

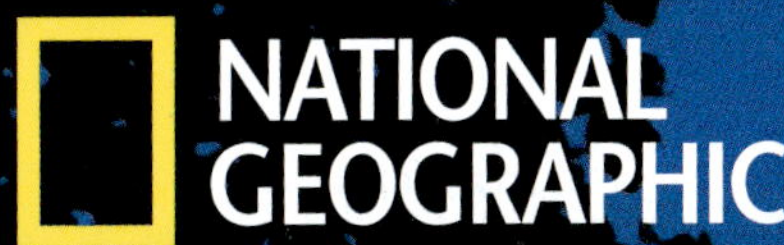

THE PHOTOGRAPHS

ICONIC IMAGES FROM NATIONAL GEOGRAPHIC

FOREWORD BY JIMMY CHIN
TEXT BY CATHY NEWMAN

NATIONAL GEOGRAPHIC
WASHINGTON, D.C.

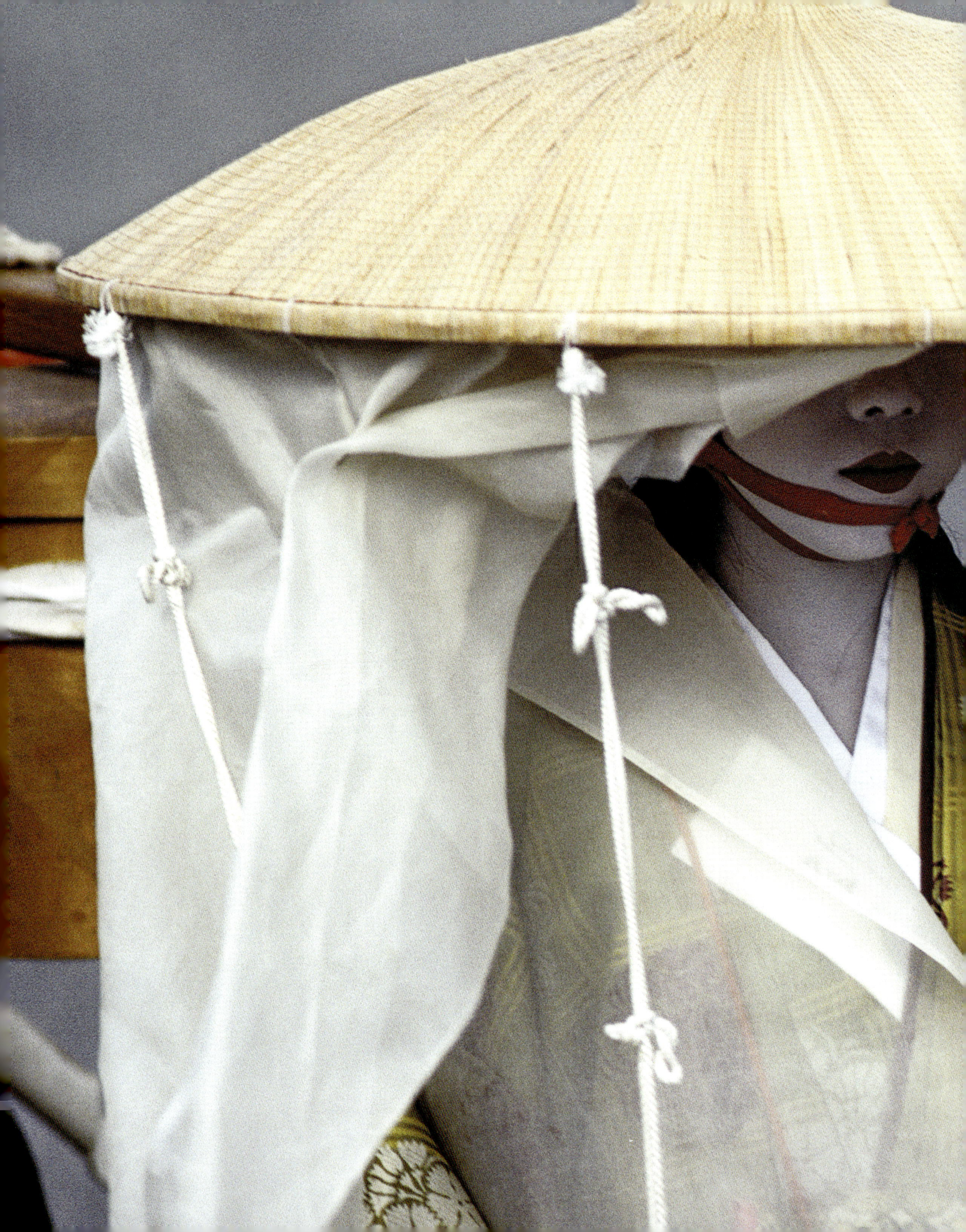

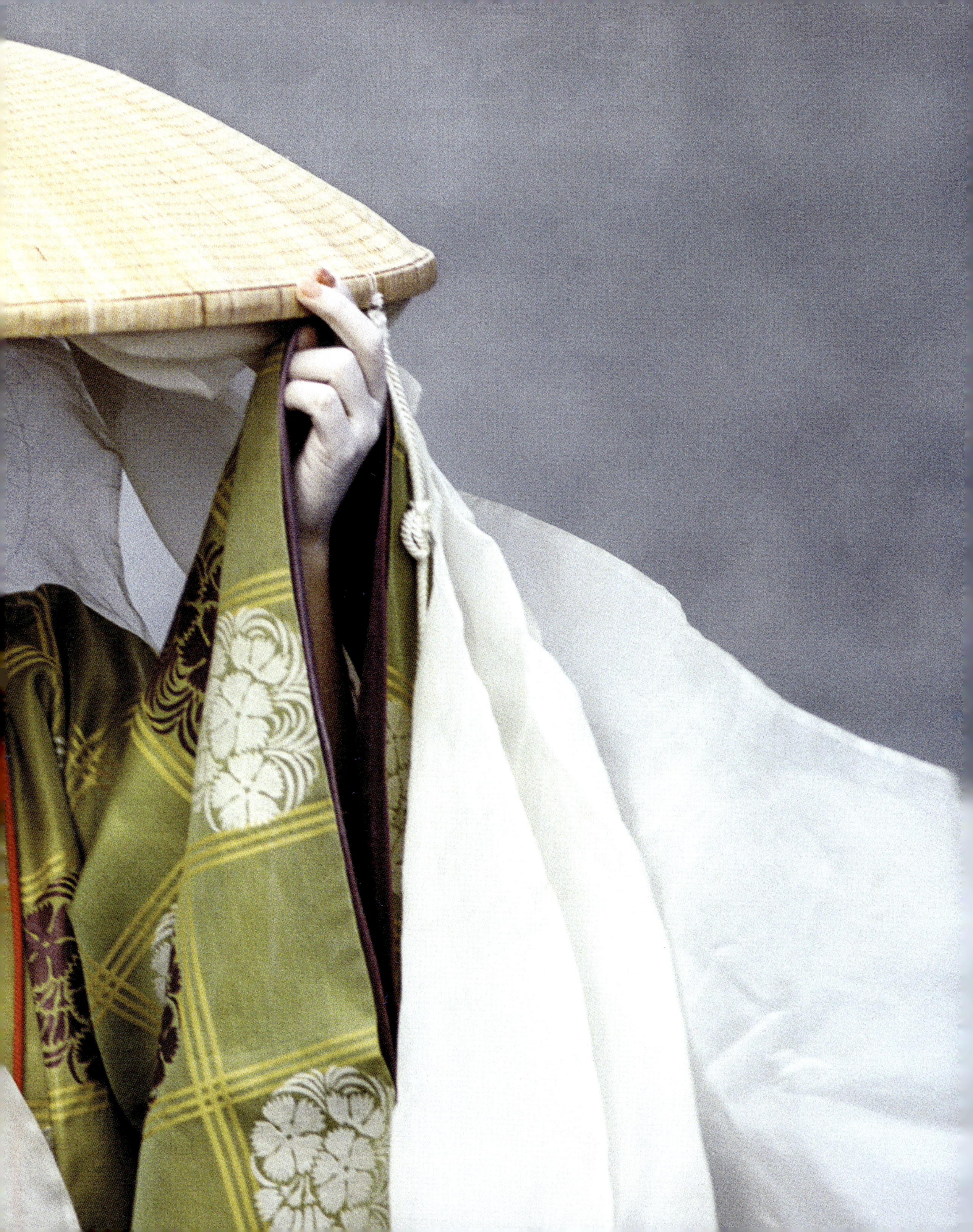

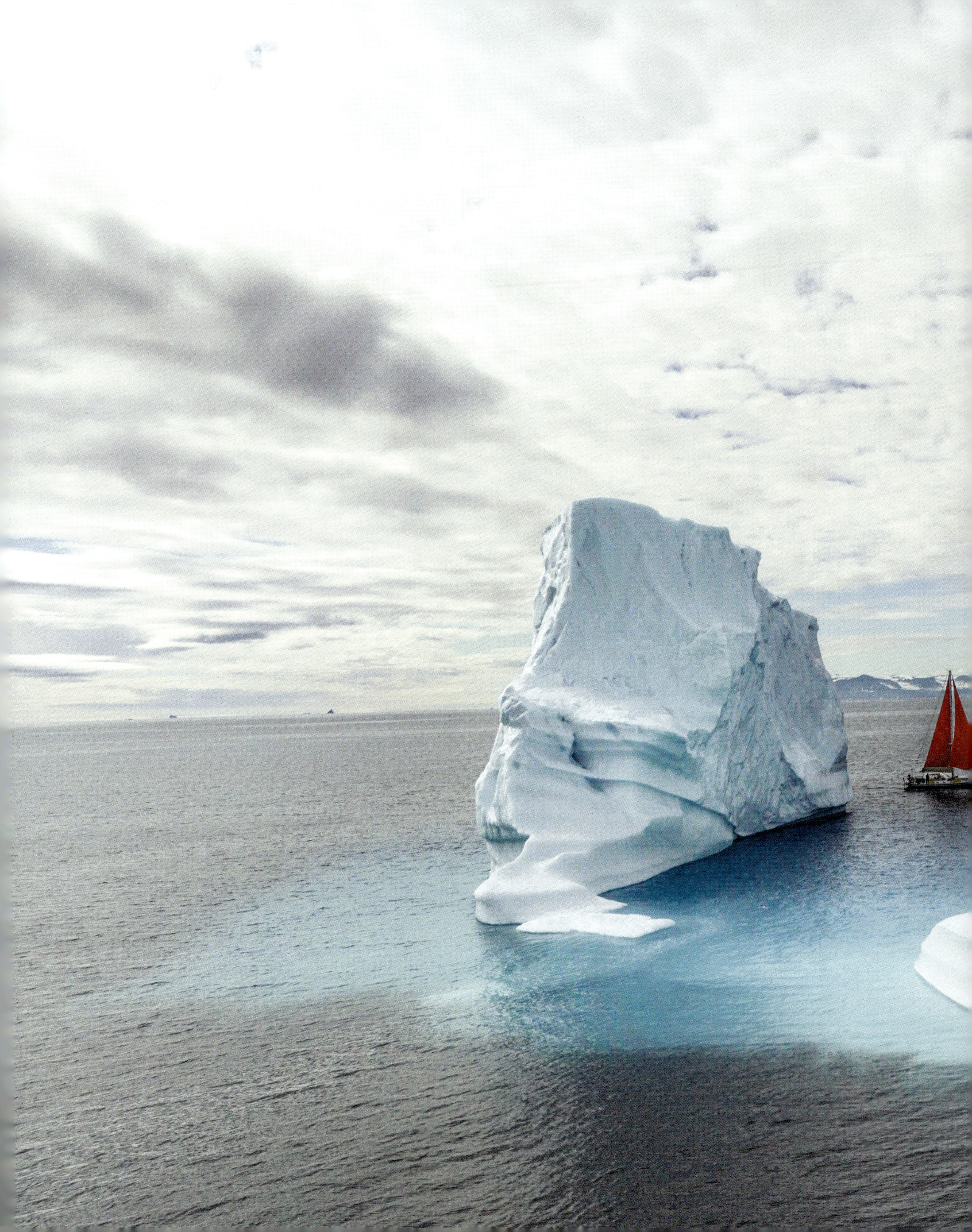

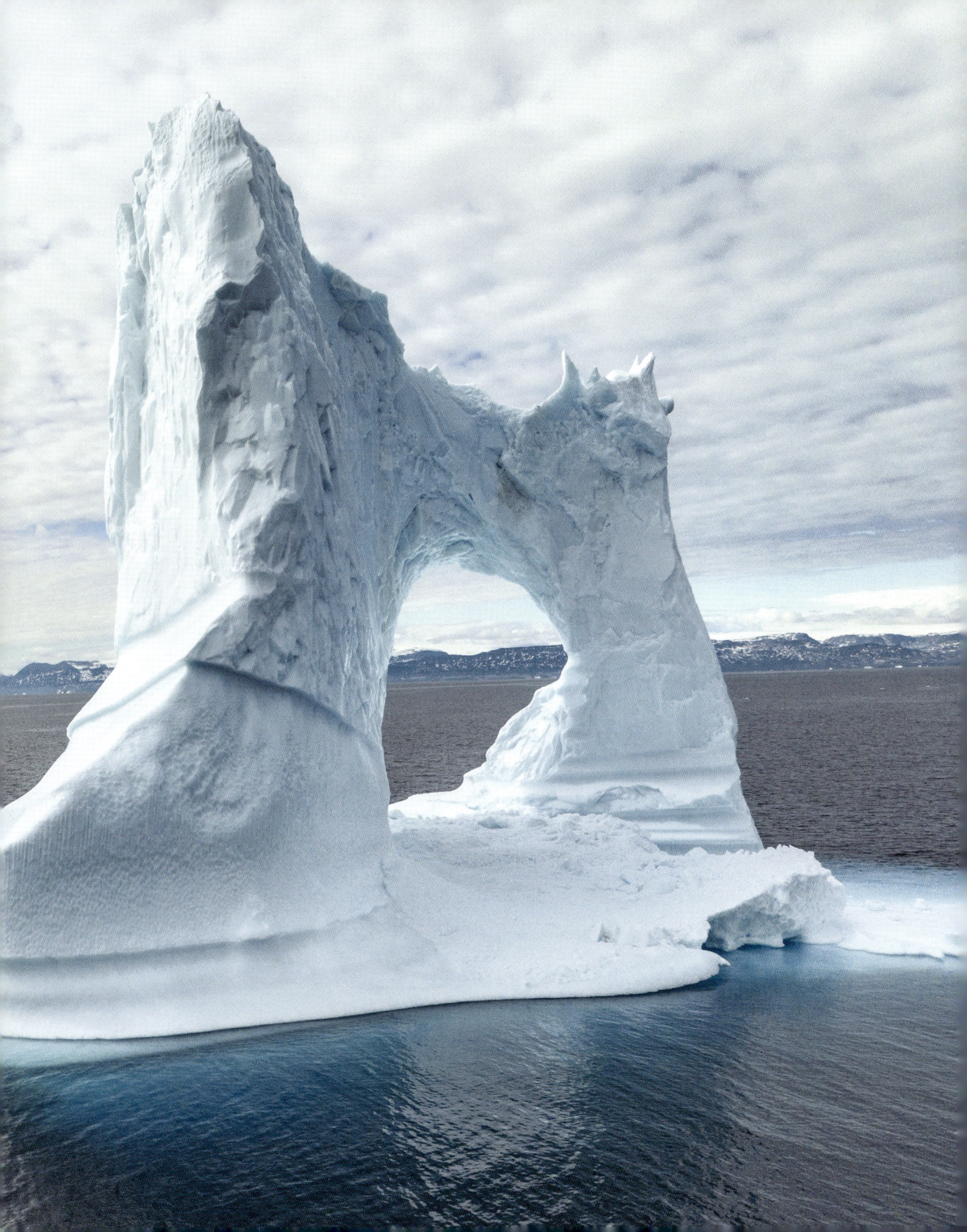

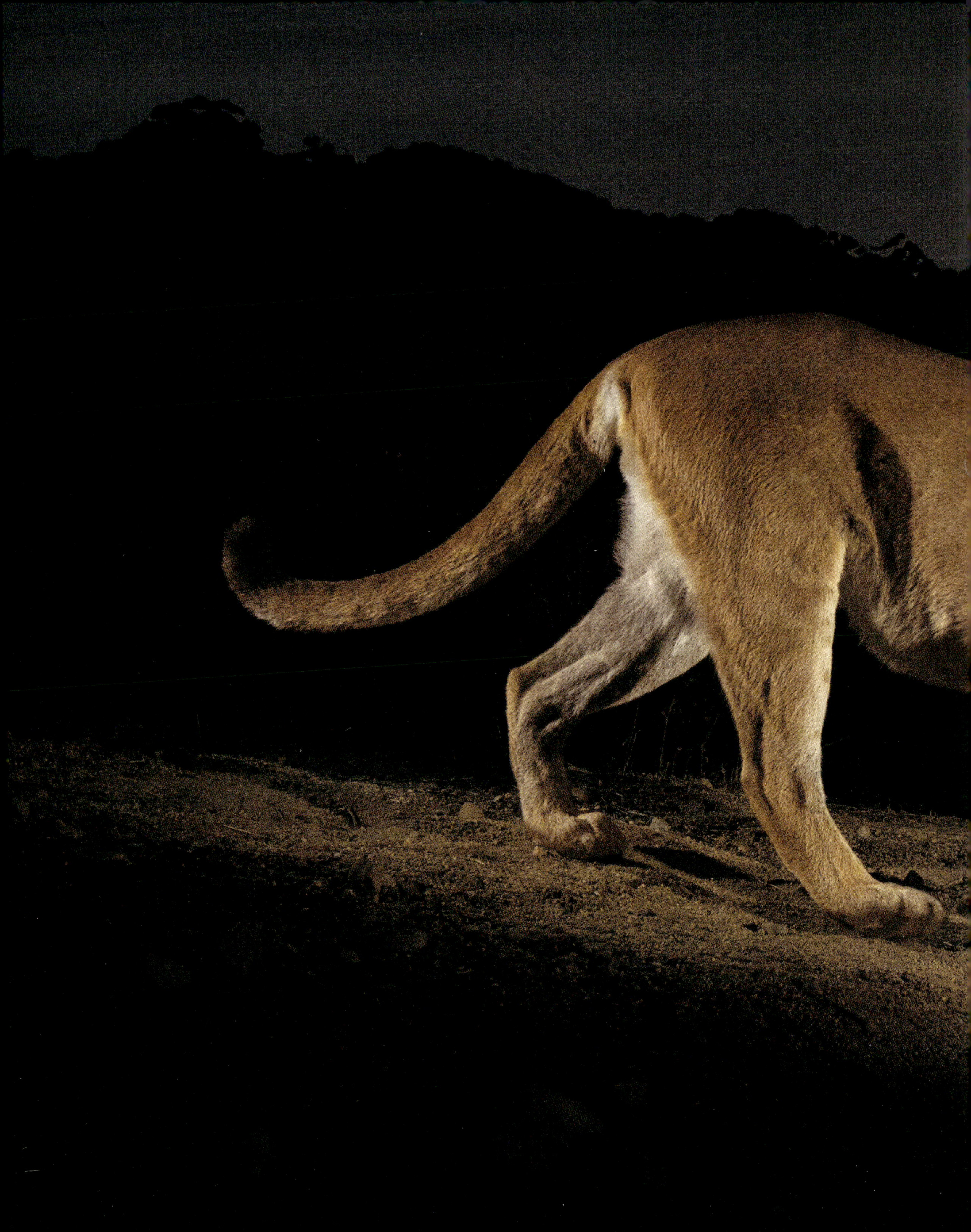

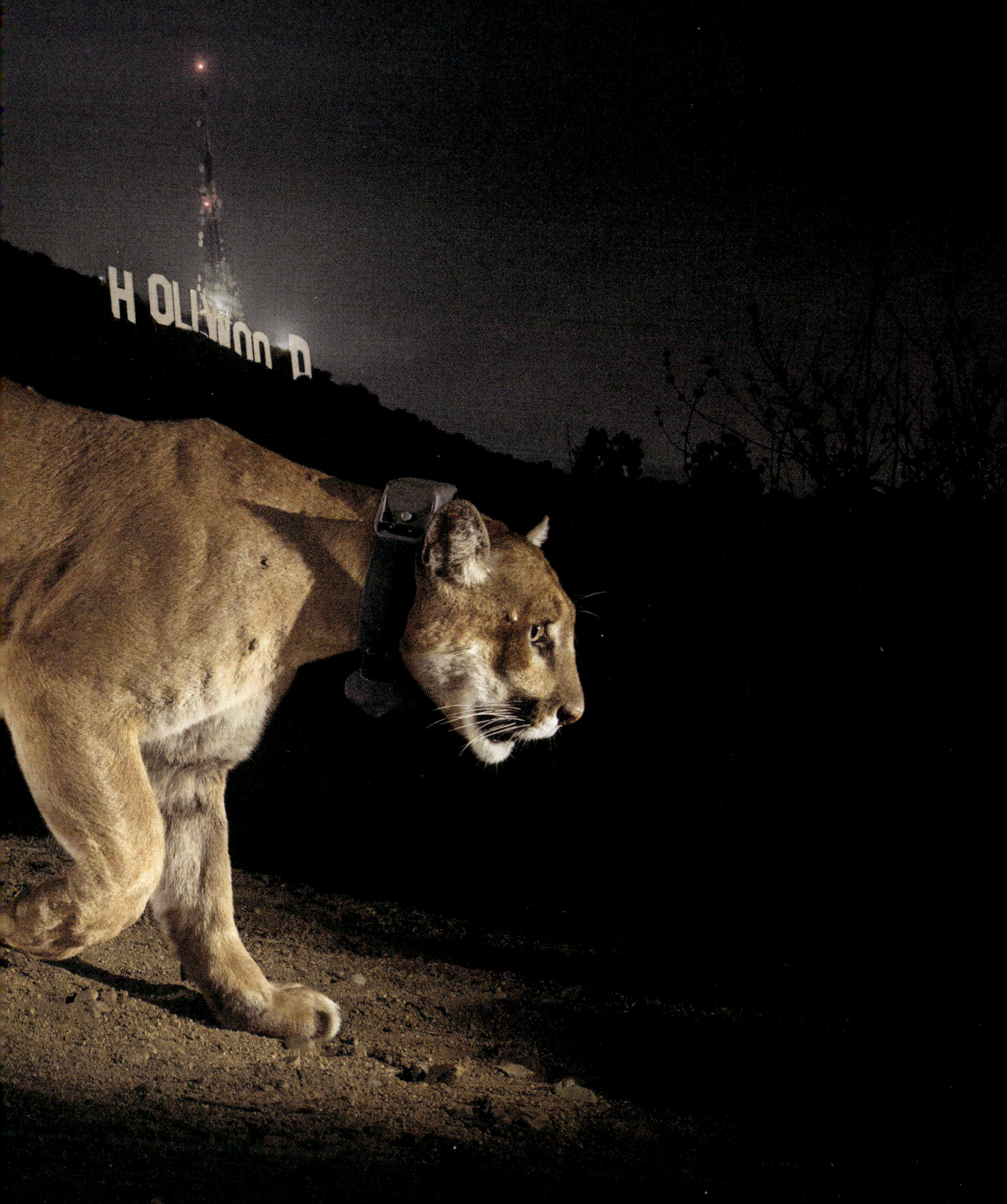

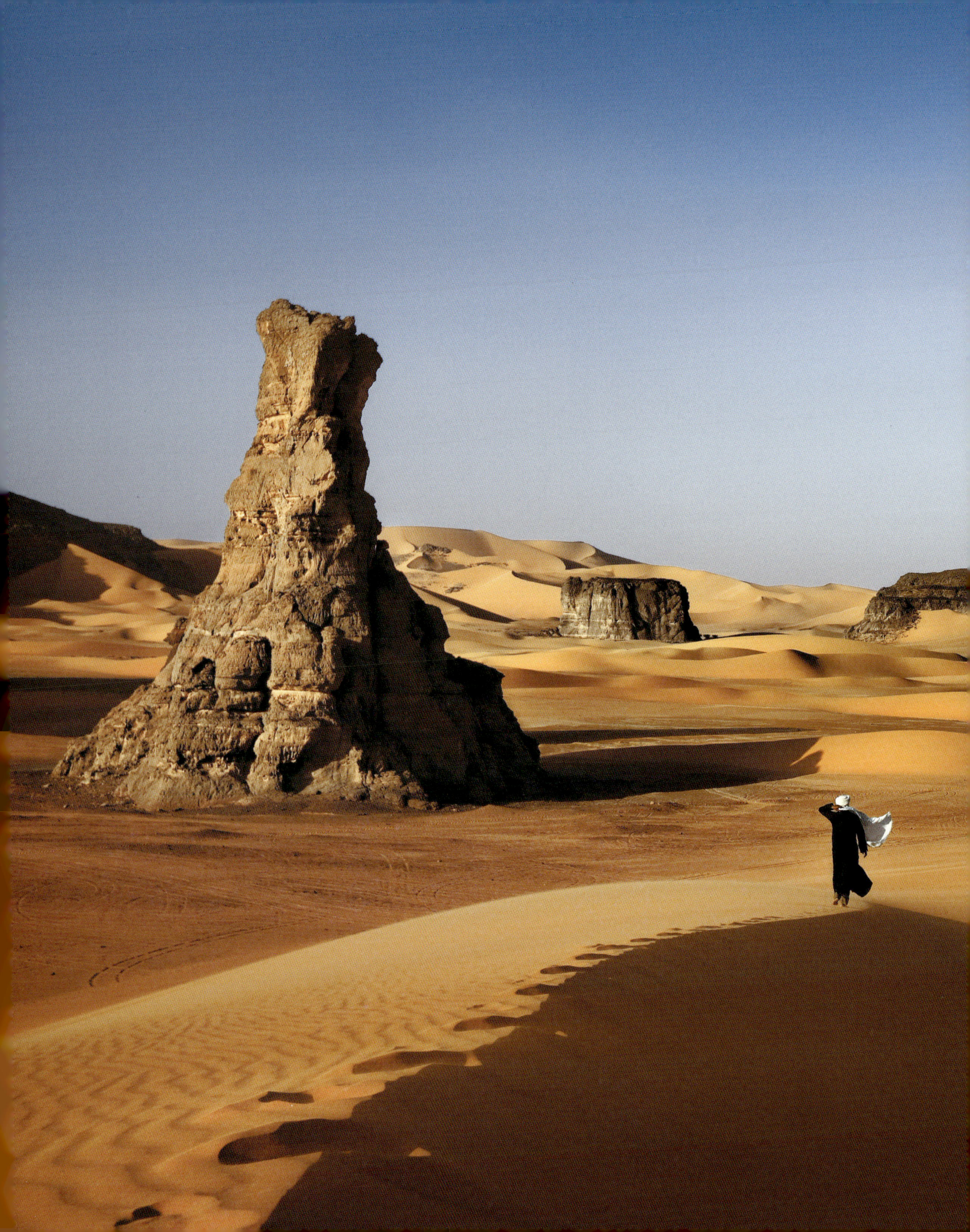

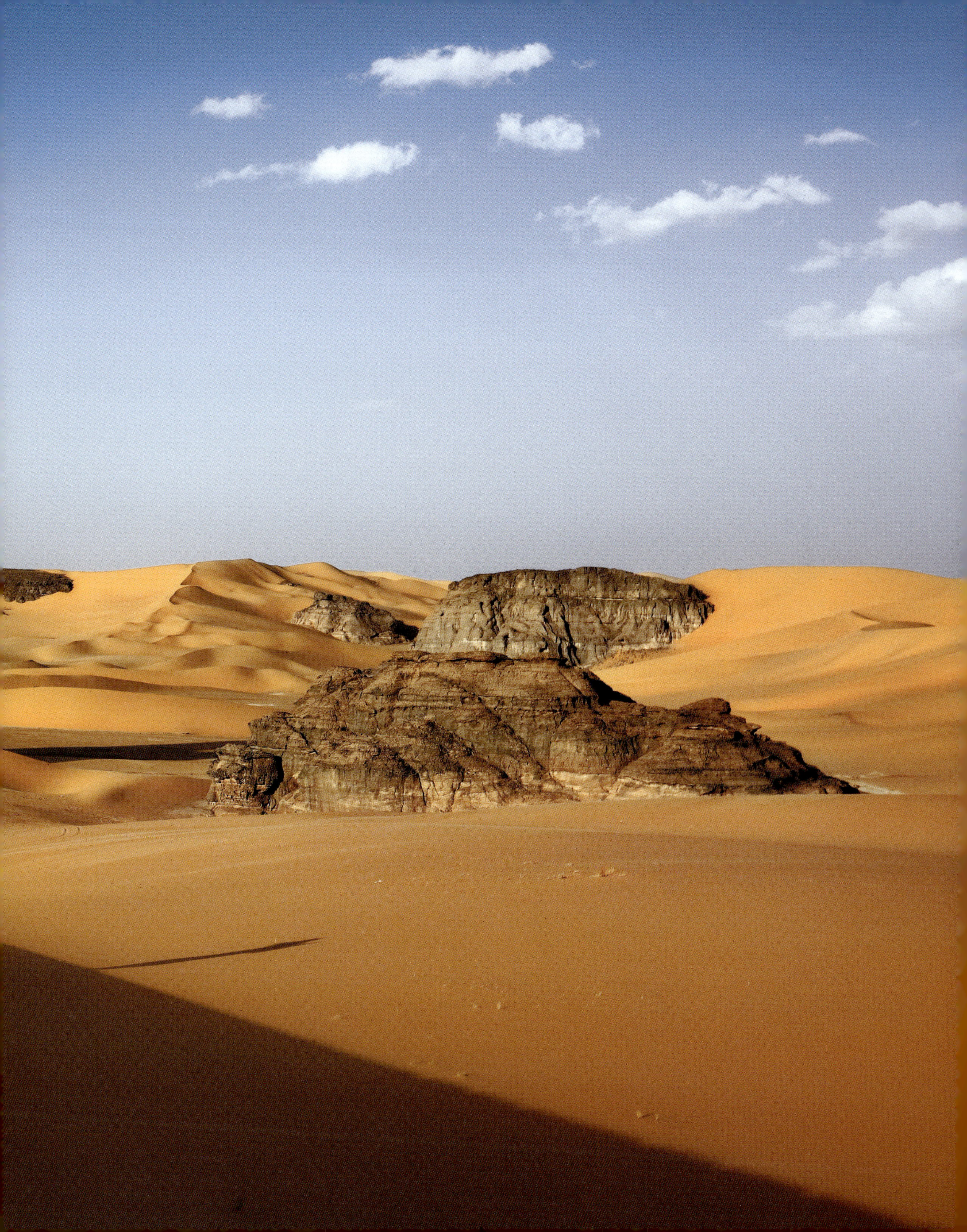

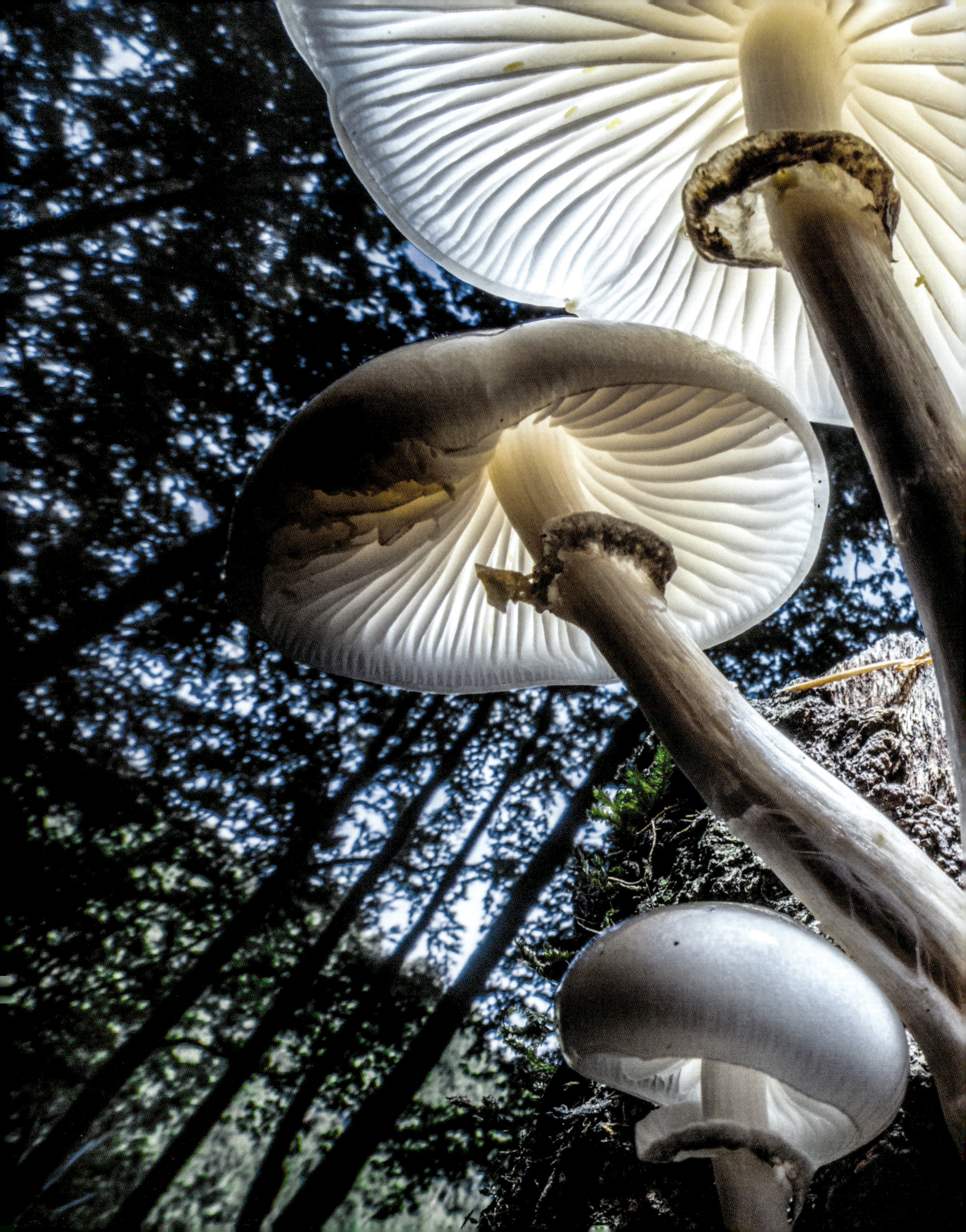

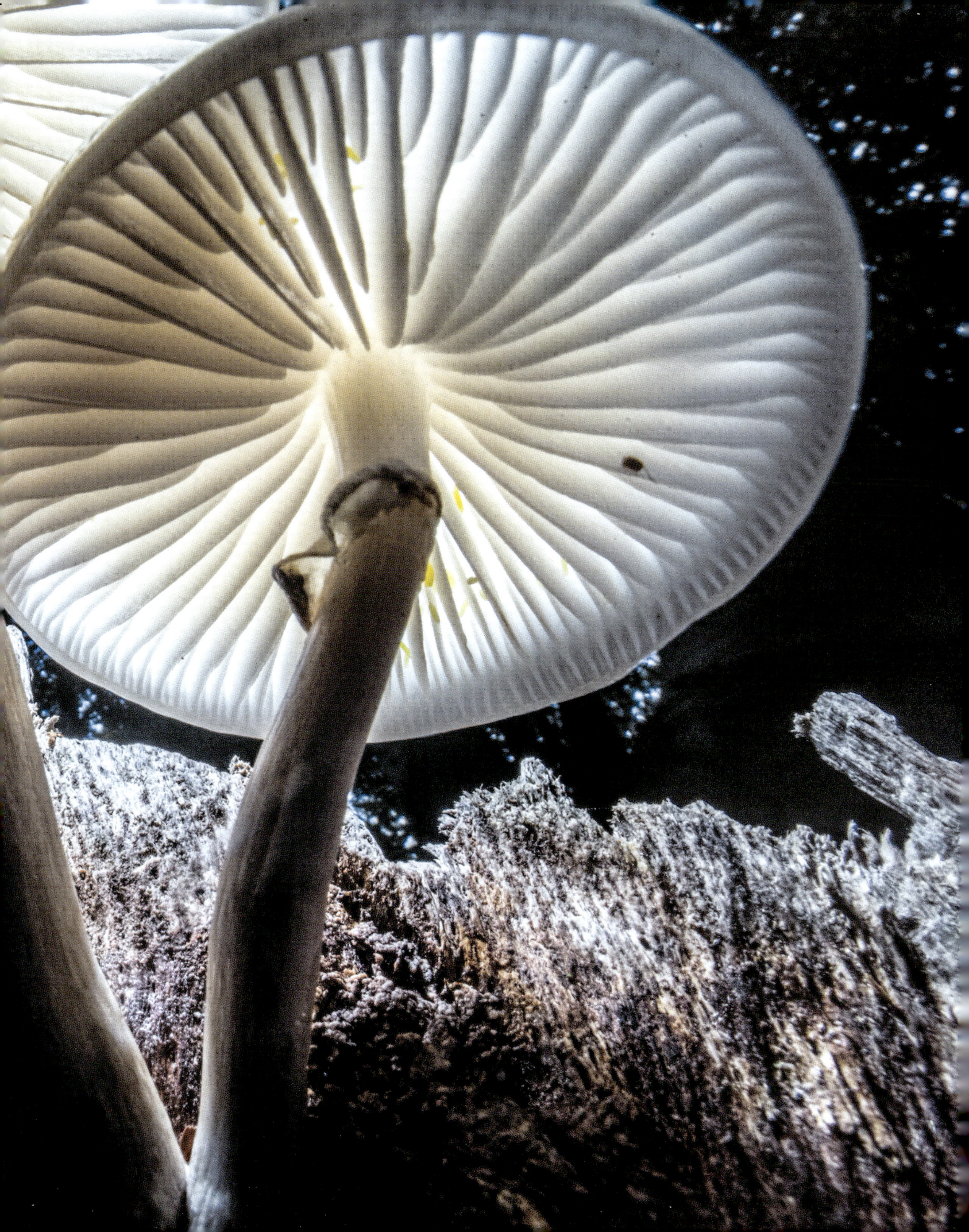

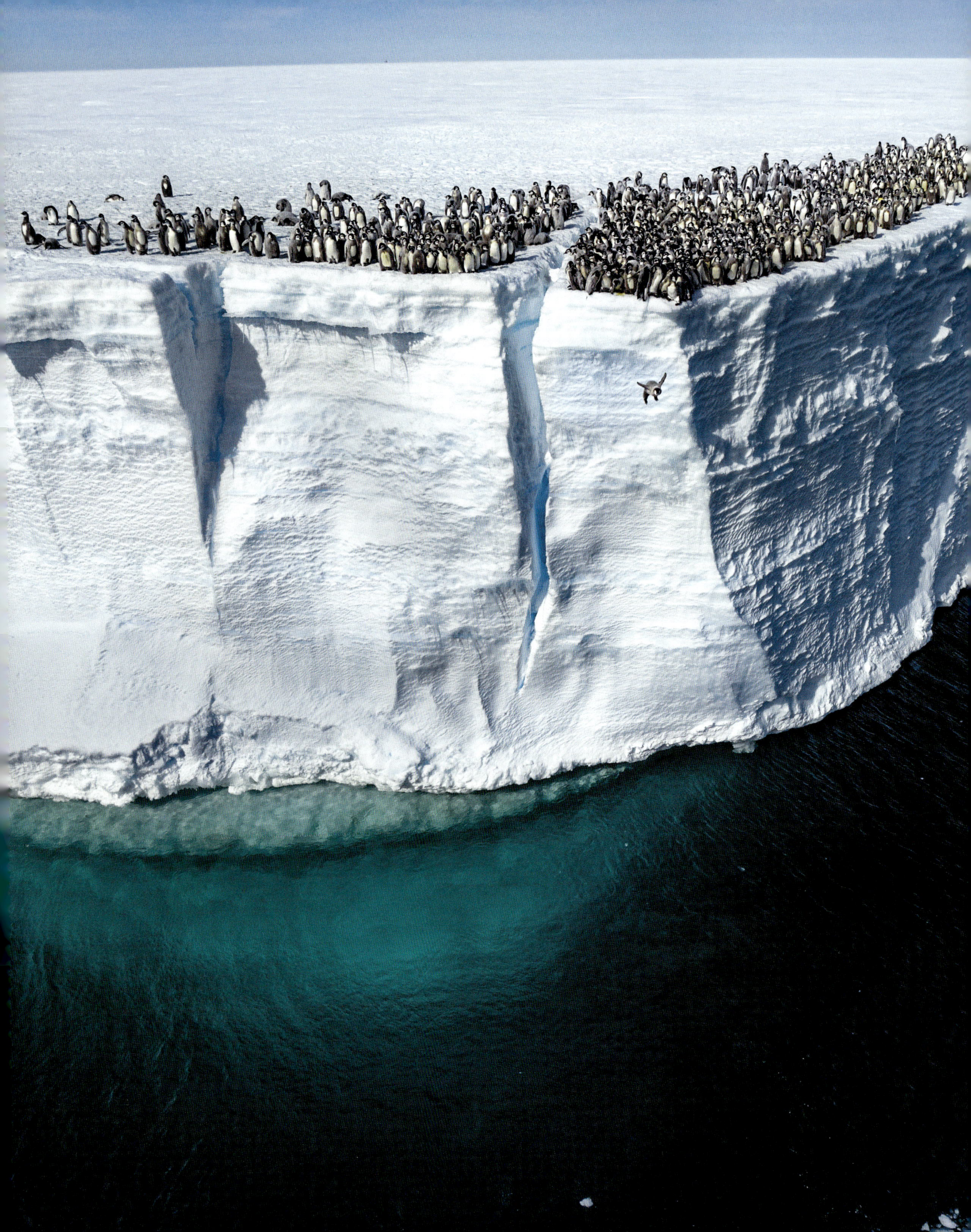

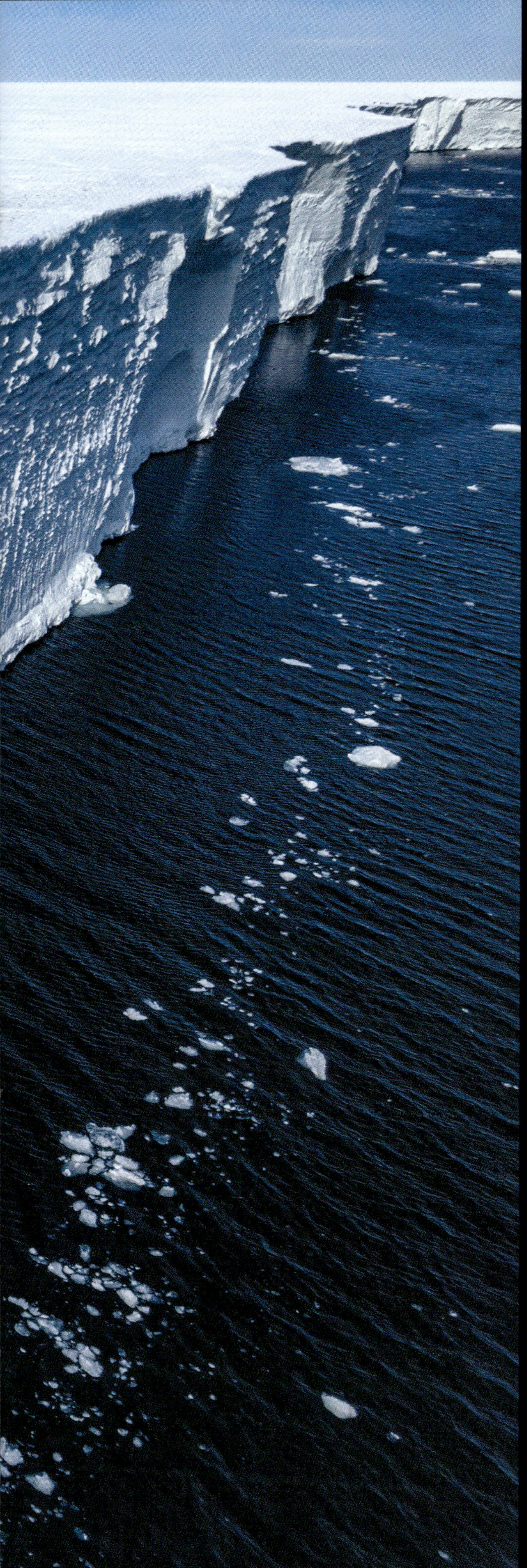

CONTENTS

OPPOSITE: **BERTIE GREGORY, 2024** For its first swim, an emperor penguin chick jumps into Antarctica's Atka Bay. *PAGES 2–3:* **JOEL SARTORE, 2010** Spotlit by wildlife biologists, a lion wakes up in Uganda's Queen Elizabeth National Park. *PAGES 4–5:* **JODI COBB, 1995** A geisha walks in Kyoto's annual Festival of the Ages. *PAGES 6–7:* **RENAN OZTURK, 2022** Tracing an 1847 voyage to the Northwest Passage, the expedition ship *Polar Sun* navigates the icebergs off Greenland's west coast. *PAGES 8–9:* **STEVE WINTER, 2013** A hidden camera captures P-22, a male cougar in Los Angeles. *PAGES 10–11:* **BRENT STIRTON, 2011** A Tuareg—a descendant of North African caravanners—strolls Tassili-n-Ajjer, a mountain range in Algeria's Sahara. *PAGES 12–13:* **AGORASTOS PAPATSANIS, 2024** Between one and three inches tall, porcelain mushrooms "tower" from a beech tree on Greece's Mount Olympus.

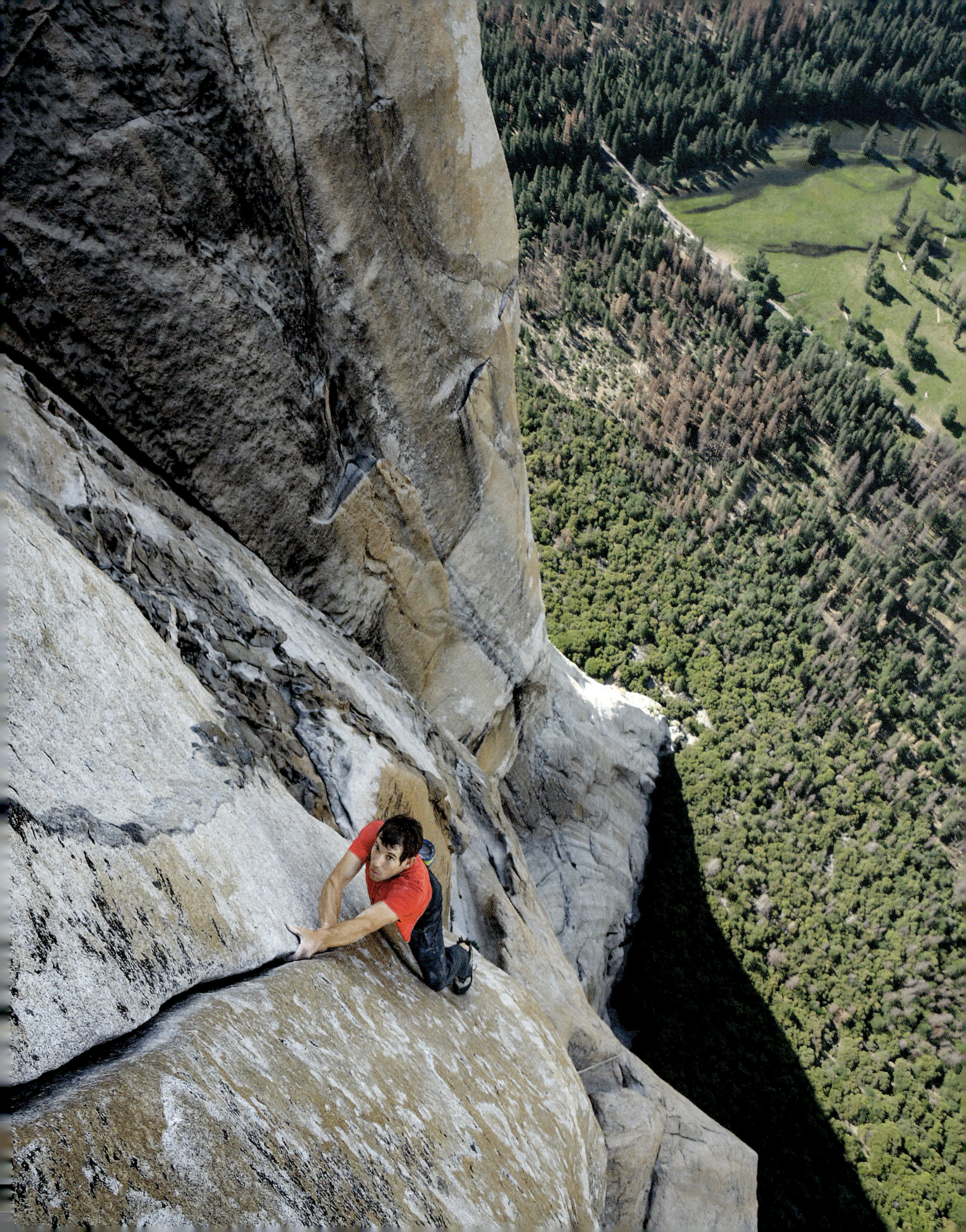

FOREWORD BY JIMMY CHIN

SUMMITING

MANY THINGS I'VE DONE REQUIRE METICULOUS PREPARATION. But some things in life are not—and never can be—planned.

I never really thought about being a photographer; it just happened. As a young man, I spent a lot of time climbing in Yosemite National Park, where a good friend who was hoping to be a photojournalist showed me how to use his camera. He invited me to make a picture with it—and as it turned out, that one frame got sold. I think I must have been paid $500. So I used the money to buy a camera of my own. I was in my early 20s and figured that all I needed to do to survive was to take one good picture a month. That says something about how raw and naive I was back then.

It was only later—much later—that I came to truly understand the serious commitment and time that professional photography demands. My appreciation broadened and deepened as I came to know some of the photographers you'll meet in the following pages. To learn how to recognize that instant when the light slants just right on a wall of ice, or the moment when a shadow lingers on a tent, was not a matter of taking just one good photograph a month.

As a mountain climber, I am attuned to ascend. So it makes sense that I attained my professional summit as a photographer when I was published in *National Geographic* for the first time. I was part of an expedition that crossed the vast alpine steppe of the 17,000-foot-high Chang Tang plateau in Tibet; one

JIMMY CHIN, 2017
Without any ropes to support his 2,900-foot climb, Alex Honnold makes the first ever "free solo" ascent of Yosemite National Park's El Capitan.

IN SHARING THESE TALES, WE OPEN THE DOOR TO A WORLD THE READER MAY NOT OTHERWISE EXPERIENCE.

of my pictures from that trip, which ran in the April 2004 issue, depicts a fellow traveler and one of the foremost adventure photographers of our time—my hero, Galen Rowell.

You could rightly say that Galen, who shot 11 stories for the magazine, invented a genre of adventure photography in which the photographer both documents and participates. As a result, the experience involves not just reading about a mountain but feeling it at gut level. The images telegraph a powerful you-are-there immediacy; the story crackles with vibrancy; excitement spills over the page. In sharing these tales, we open the door to a world the reader may not otherwise experience.

Galen's first story in *National Geographic* was about Yosemite, where I first fell in love with the act of capturing an image. He died in a plane crash soon after the Tibet expedition. It was a loss I felt in my bones. And along with the heaviness of that grief came responsibility. The torch, I realized, had been passed to me.

I've been part of the National Geographic family ever since.

JIMMY CHIN, 2017
Climber Alex Honnold (in red) navigates the southwest face of El Capitan with a companion in Yosemite National Park.

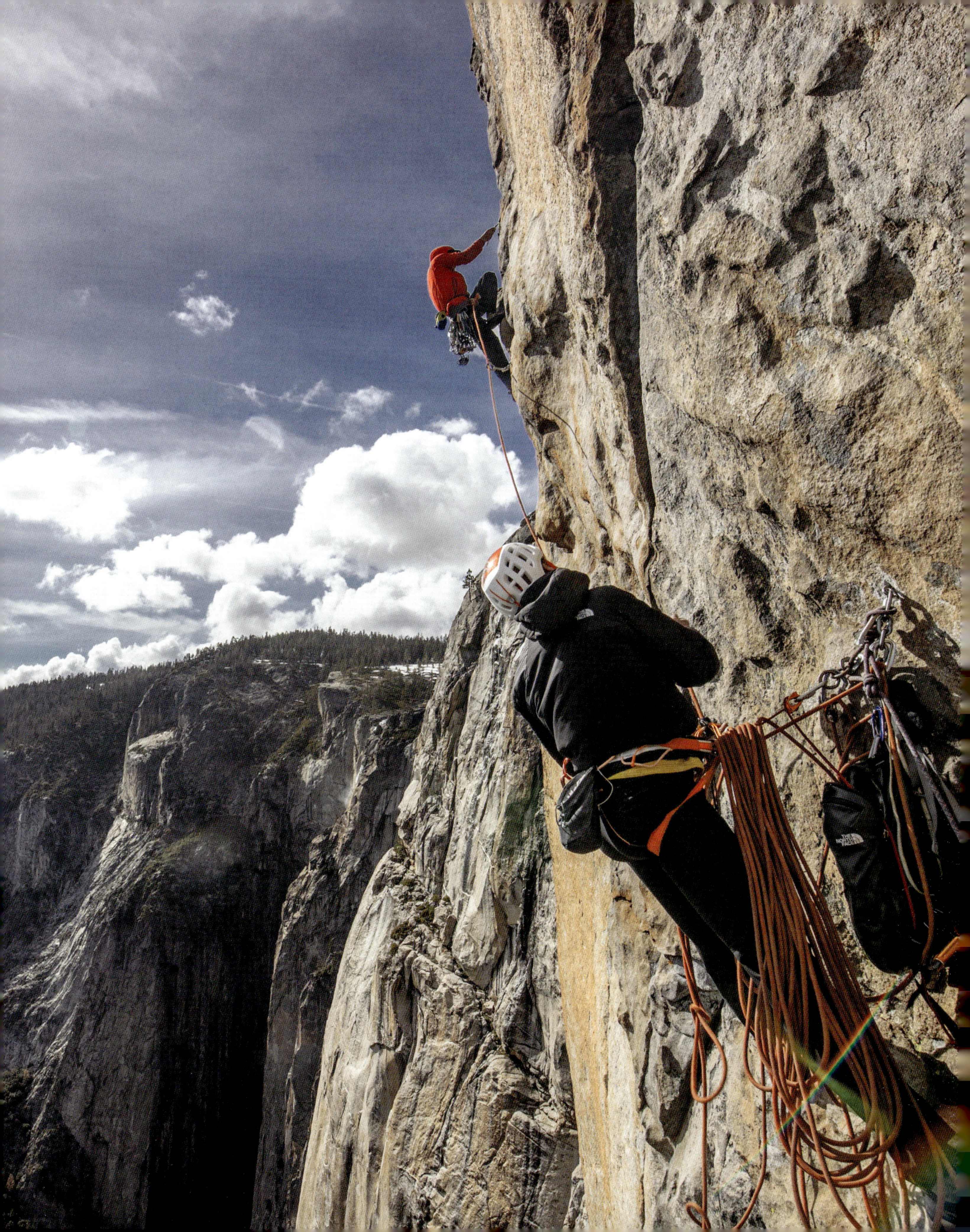

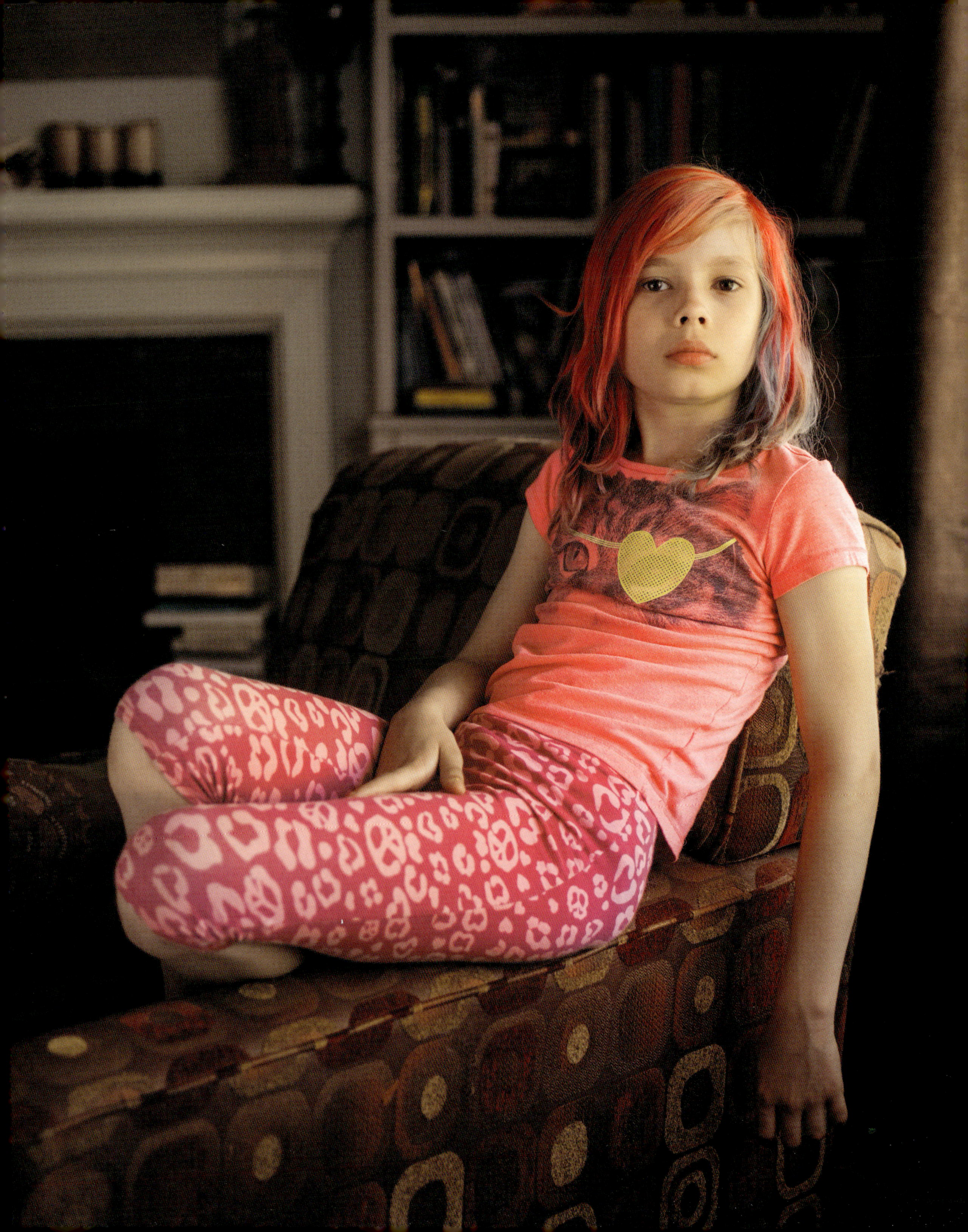

DRAWING WITH LIGHT

THE EXCELLENCE OF THE IMAGE IS THE HALLMARK of National Geographic. Photographs are the organization's most immediate and striking medium of communication with its global audience, and have been ever since Gilbert H. Grosvenor, the magazine's first full-time editor, ran 11 pages of photographs of Lhasa, Tibet, in 1905.

Though the first photograph in the otherwise black-and-white monotony of text that characterized *National Geographic* in its early days had appeared 15 years earlier, in 1890, those images from Tibet's forbidden city caused such a stir that people stopped Grosvenor (or GHG, as he was known both personally and professionally) on the street to offer congratulations. The following year, he devoted an entire issue to wildlife (74 images, with only four pages of text!), thereby establishing photography as the magazine's center of gravity.

The impact was dramatic. Photography jolted circulation—or membership, as it was then known—into fast-forward; it leaped from 3,000 to 20,000 in two years. By 1908, more than half the pages of the magazine included photographs, setting its trajectory for decades to come.

Long before the far reach of the world was accessible to anyone with a plane ticket, television, or internet connection, the magic carpet of the photographic image carried readers across oceans and continents, to mountains, deserts, glaciers, savannas, and forests, allowing access to "the world and all that's in it," as a catchphrase of the publication famously put it.

ROBIN HAMMOND, 2016
Nine-year-old Avery Jackson, the first transgender person to appear on the cover of *National Geographic* magazine, in Kansas City, Missouri

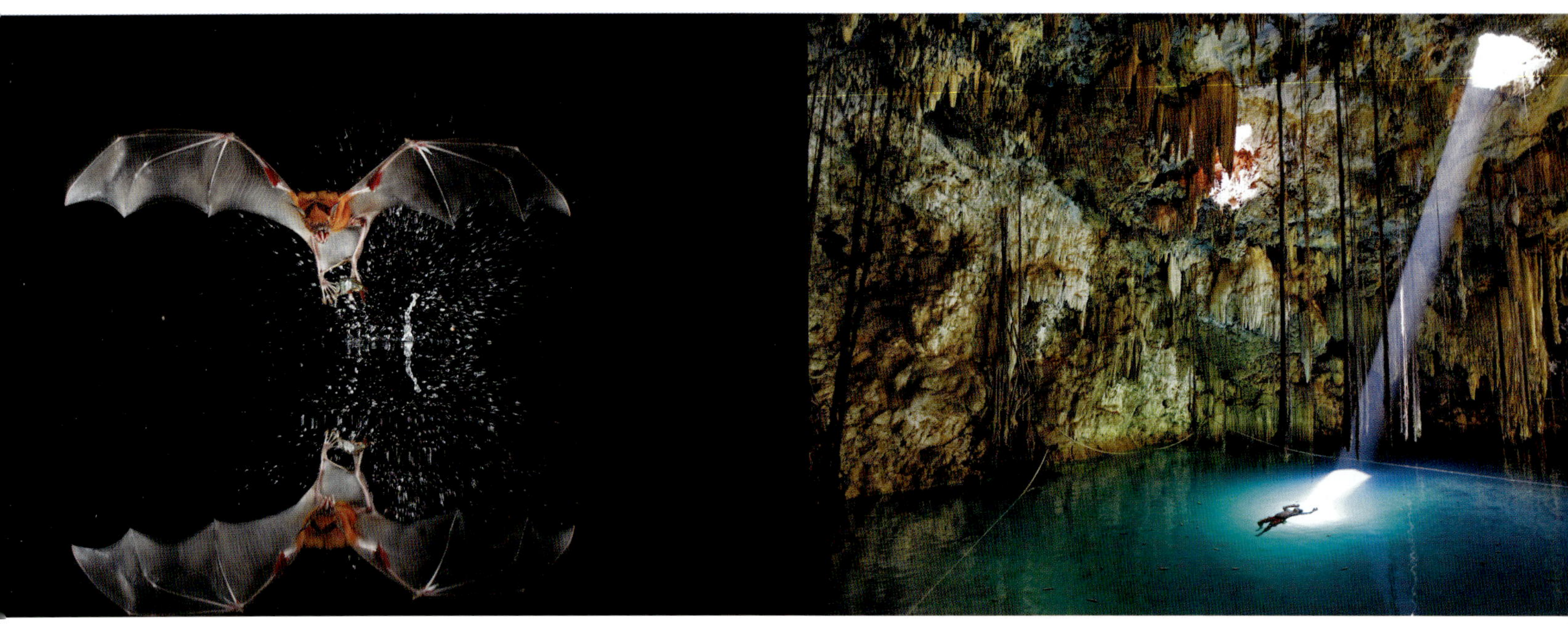

ABOVE LEFT
CHRISTIAN ZIEGLER, 2007
A bulldog bat attacks a fish in Panama's Barro Colorado Island. Its echolocation is sensitive enough to detect the fish's fin breaking the water's surface.

ABOVE RIGHT
JOHN STANMEYER, 2010
The Maya believed that natural sinkholes like this one—the Xkeken cenote, located in Mexico's Yucatán—led to the underworld.

The brotherhood of the camera in the magazine's first century was exactly that—a boys' club. But so was the National Geographic Society (the magazine was its official journal), founded in the mahogany-, leather-, and cigar-smoke-filled rooms of Washington, D.C.'s Cosmos Club in 1888 to "increase and diffuse geographic knowledge."

Well into the 1950s, a National Geographic photographer would set off on a foreign assignment armed with letters of credit. The trip might commence with a crossing on a luxury liner. Along with cameras and film (in earlier years, glass plates), he—and it was always a he—prepared for any contingency up to and including a coronation by packing black tie. (Joseph Rock, sent to cover China in 1922, even carried his own linen, tableware, and portable bathtub.) Standard operating procedure was "take all the time you like as long as you come back with the story." Photographer Volkmar Kurt Wentzel, assigned in 1946 to cover India, stayed for two years.

In the 1980s, the rosy *National Geographic* stories of the past, like 1947's "Scintillating Siam" and 1960's "Salzkammergut, Austria's Alpine Playground," yielded to a sometimes darker but authentic narrative that confronted the realities of the world. The change began under Editor in Chief Gilbert M. Grosvenor—a photographer himself—who opened the magazine's pages to the coverage of subjects like pollution and apartheid in South Africa. It continued in successive decades with reporting on thorny, difficult subjects, like Jodi Cobb's story on human trafficking, Saumya Khandelwal's story about the safety of women in India, and Lynsey Addario's feature on Ethiopia's civil war, along with extensive coverage

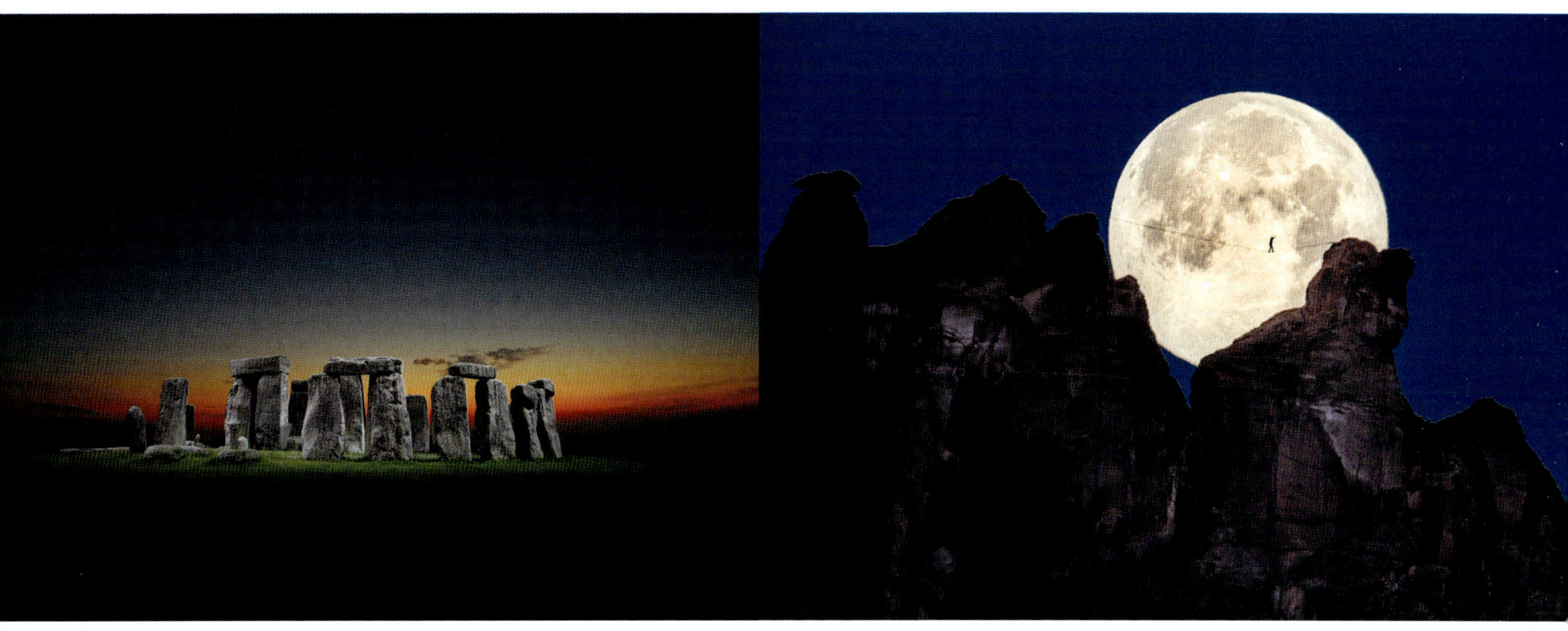

ABOVE LEFT
REUBEN WU, 2021
Drone lights and multiple exposures help capture sunset at Stonehenge, Wiltshire, England.

ABOVE RIGHT
RENAN OZTURK, 2020
Slackline artist Andy Lewis suspended between two peaks, in Moab, Utah

of environmental challenges and the ongoing commitment to conservation exemplified by photographers like Joel Sartore, Brian Skerry, and Brent Stirton.

Today, in addition to the print magazine, stories are spread across multiple platforms: television, feature films, books, and digital and social media. "Photographers are used to pulling out a smartphone to shoot video to capture behind-the-scenes moments, which social media audiences love," notes Sadie Quarrier, *National Geographic*'s editorial director of integrated storytelling and former director of photography. "Some of our photographers even double as filmmakers, and pull off the high-wire act of shooting, directing, or appearing as on-screen talent for TV in addition to producing stills of the highest quality. So before field time even begins, we think about our different audiences and plan where and how best to use the assets we gather."

From a technological standpoint, the most important milestone for the National Geographic photographer in the 21st century is arguably the shift to digital photography. At the beginning of 2005, 85 percent of published photographs were shot on film. At the end of that year, the obverse was true: More than 85 percent were shot digitally. Now, practically all are.

Photographers shoot more because they can. Those enthralled by statistics should know that in 2023, more than two million images were made by 165 photographers in the field. Of those images, perhaps 850 were published. What distinguishes rejected frames from those published in the magazine? "Beyond the expected criteria for well-executed images—great light and strong composition—I look for unique moments that surprise, delight, and elicit a strong emotional response," says Quarrier. Most of all, she adds, it's about storytelling: "In an era when everyone is a photographer, a lot of people can take a single good frame. We pride ourselves on creating a compelling narrative."

But some elements in the odyssey of covering a story never change. The pressure to produce the best photographs imaginable is as relentless as ever—and more so with financial constraints wrought by the attrition of print at the mercy of a digital world. Photographers can no longer take as long as they like, though by the standards of other publications, field time and budgets at *National Geographic* are generous. The shift to a highly focused story with a narrative line helps, but coverage time, once measured in months—even years—is now measured in weeks.

Another thing: For most of the magazine's history, the photographer was a man. A 1967 photograph in the archives captioned "the greatest photographic team in the world" shows 25 suit-and-tie-wearing men surrounding the desk of then *National Geographic* editor Melville Bell Grosvenor, suggesting, as the late historian of photography Naomi Rosenblum observed, that "the universal language of the photograph upon which this publication (and others) depended was solely a contribution of the male eye and mind."

In the 1980s, after wrestling a half dozen cases of lighting equipment through a museum door in preparation for shooting artifacts, National Geographic staff photographer Sisse Brimberg was asked when the photographer would be arriving.

"She has arrived" was her terse reply.

These days, the ratio is more balanced. After four decades of shooting for the magazine, the reality, says Lynn Johnson, "is that women used to be invisible. Now, they are not."

Meanwhile, hazards large and small still await photographers in the field. Arrest and detention, elephant charges, radiation exposure, burning lava, and shark attacks still threaten—not to mention land mines, malaria, frostbite, and the tyranny of border officials. In 2020, a hazard emerged that no photographer was immune to: Covid-19. Sending one out to cover a story in a world where travel was at a standstill was impossible. In response, the magazine expanded its work with locally based photographers like Esther Ruth Mbabazi in Uganda, Rehab Eldalil in Egypt, Muhammad Fadli in Indonesia, and others to tell the stories in their own backyards. This shift expanded and incorporated a more diverse range of voices and continues as the trend to tell stories from the "inside" gains agency. "Covid's silver lining," Quarrier calls it.

Finally, there is the cold-sweat malady suffered by nearly every National Geographic photographer: "Did I get the shot?" Usually, they do. And those shots are more arresting, more moving, more telling because those wielding the camera are driven to make them so. The National Geographic photographer is a marathoner, not a sprinter.

The magazine's photographic vision, like the world it celebrates, has expanded as well. That new framework is encapsulated in the 2012 feature on the quest by the Kayapo, Brazil's most powerful Indigenous people, to save their Amazonian homeland from loggers, miners, and ranchers. The magazine assigned Martin Schoeller, best known for celebrity portraits found in museums and galleries, to photograph the story; because of his artistic and journalistic sensibility, we feel a bond across the distance of place and culture. We meet their gaze. We connect. The images are fresh, engaging, authentic: photography at its best.

It's about the light, of course: illumination, which incorporates an inner light as well. The word "photography" derives from a marriage of the Greek words for "light" and "drawing." It is an etymology, perhaps, instinctively felt by a reader who wrote to thank the magazine for sending "light to dark places."

And that says it all. For nearly a century and a half, the magazine has explored, explained, and, above all, *illuminated* the world for readers. Its photographers are ever committed to honoring the mandate laid down by the National Geographic Society's first president, Alexander Graham Bell, more than a century ago when, in 1902, he dispatched Gilbert H. Grosvenor to Martinique to cover the eruption of Mount Pelée. His instructions? "Give us details of living interest beautifully illustrated by photographs."

The National Geographic photographer in the 21st century is as likely a woman as a man, and hails from different countries and cultures that reflect the diverse world it is their mission to document. The steamship trunks, glass plates, and letters of credit are passé. The commitment, passion, and creativity endure.

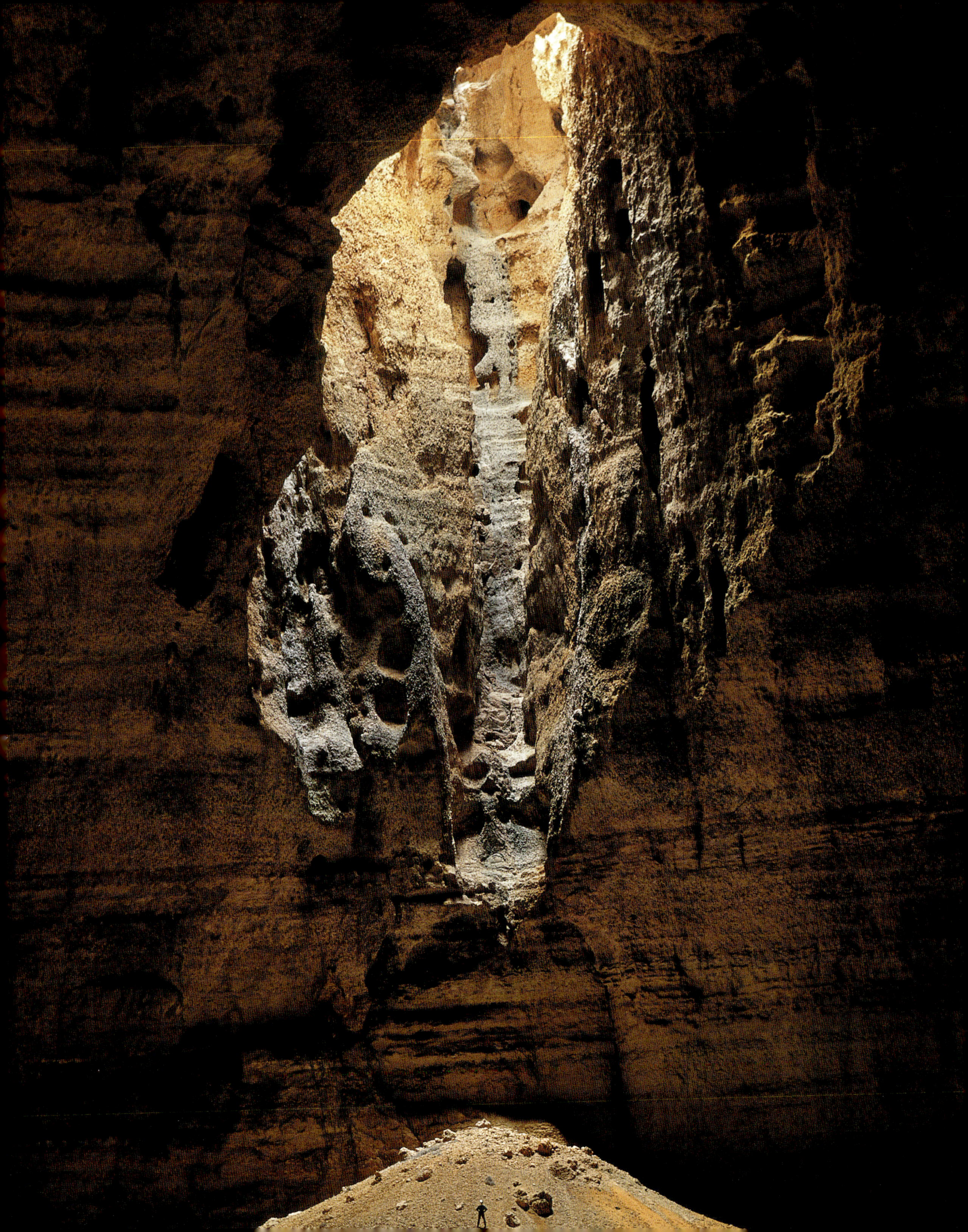

ADVENTURE & EXPLORATION

THE POWER TO

DISCOVER

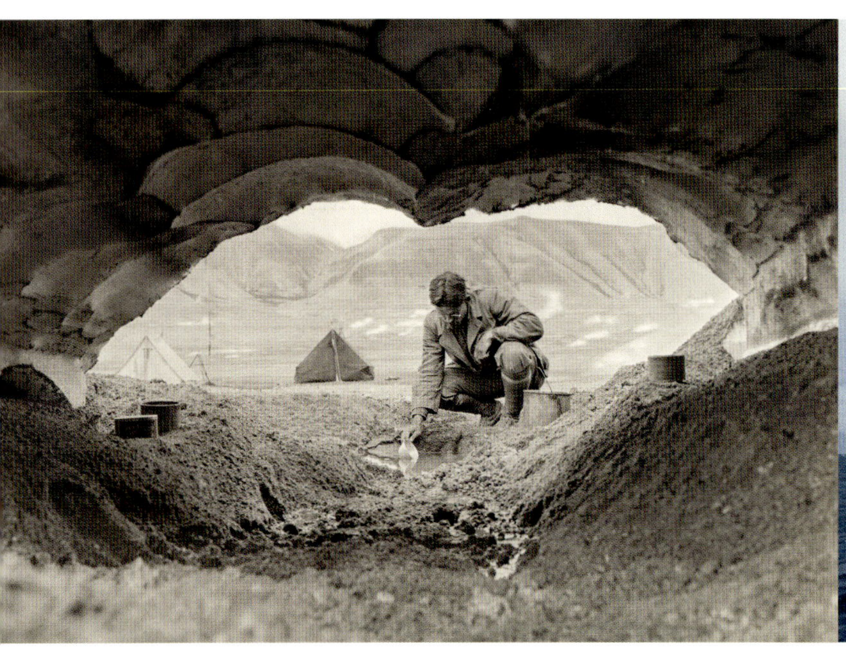

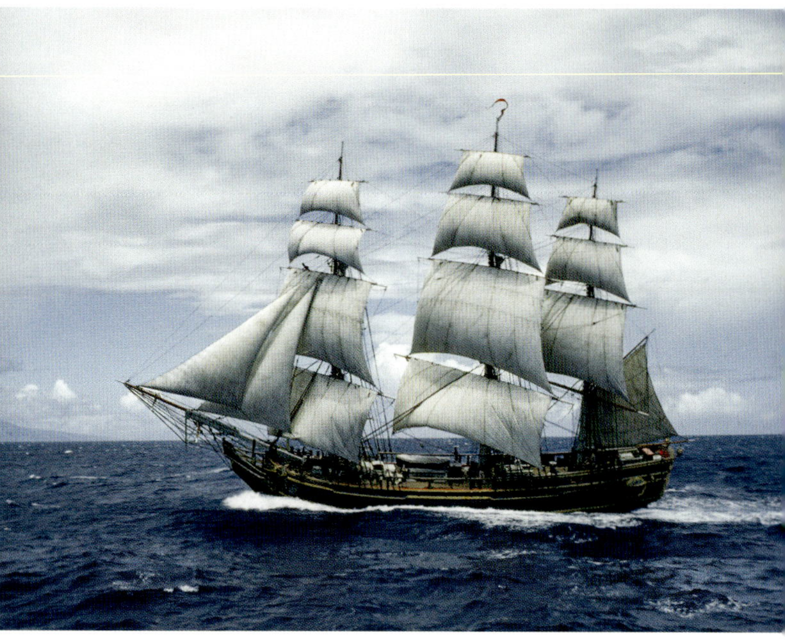

"BECAUSE IT'S THERE."

PAGE 26
STEPHEN ALVAREZ, 2003
One of the largest known cave chambers on Earth, Oman's Majlis al Jinn, dwarfs biologist Nancy Pistole.

ABOVE LEFT
EMERY C. KOLB, 1921
An explorer collects water from a snow cave in Alaska's Valley of Ten Thousand Smokes. A series of National Geographic expeditions brought attention to this region after the land was devastated by the 1912 Novarupta volcano eruption. Today, the valley is protected as part of Katmai National Park and Preserve.

ABOVE RIGHT
LUIS MARDEN, 1962
A replica of the HMS *Bounty* sails off the coast of Tahiti. The photographer was among the explorers who found the wreck of the *Bounty* in these very waters in 1957.

FROM THE BEGINNING, exploration has been a foundation of National Geographic. And we have the pictures to prove it.

"The greatest 'kick' a field man can have is to carry a million and a quarter members up onto a high mountain, show them the world and say, 'It's yours, in a way it could not be without me,'" Maynard Owen Williams wrote to editor Gilbert H. Grosvenor in 1929. Those words could serve as a mantra for the adventure photographers who would follow in his footsteps.

Williams, chief of the National Geographic Society's foreign staff, photographed the public opening of the tomb of Tutankhamun in 1923. He joins a host of explorers immortalized in the magazine, like Hiram Bingham, who excavated Machu Picchu, the Lost City of the Inca, and recorded the event with a panoramic camera in 1913; Geographic staffer Luis Marden, who found the wreck of the HMS *Bounty* off Pitcairn Island in 1957; and Bob Ballard, who discovered the graveyard of the *Titanic* near Newfoundland under some 12,500 feet of water in 1985. Staff photographer Emory Kristof used custom deepwater camera rigs to document the find.

Adventure and exploration stories that incorporate a cultural or scientific element—for example, Renan Ozturk's story on the last honey hunter of Nepal and Wes Skiles's exploration of deep underwater caves in the Bahamas—are the gold standard. Even so, there is still room for pure boundary-pushing adventure, like Alex Honnold's free solo climb of Yosemite's El Capitan, the basis for a magazine story and an Oscar-winning documentary.

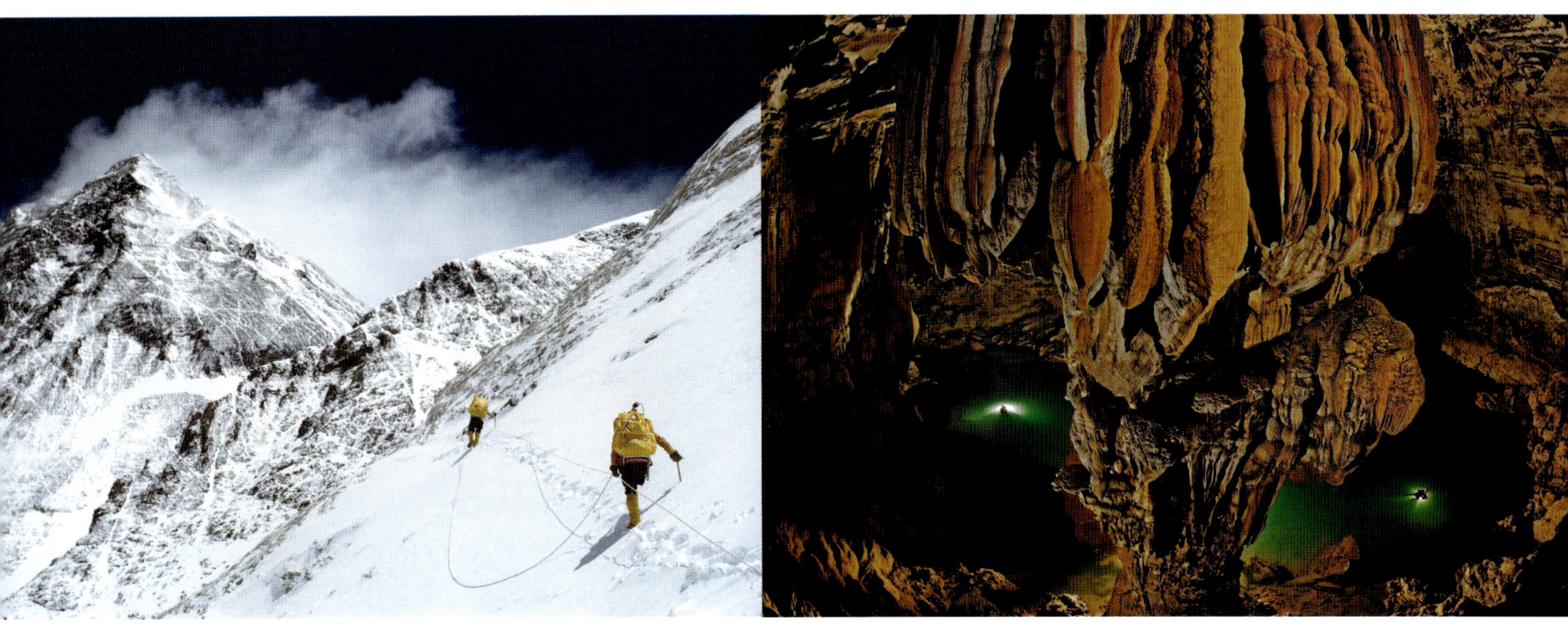

ABOVE LEFT
BARRY C. BISHOP, 1963
The first American team on Mount Everest treks toward the summit. A thousand men participated in this milestone expedition; six reached the pinnacle.

ABOVE RIGHT
CARSTEN PETER, 2010
A calcite flowstone column towers over explorers swimming in Vietnam's Hang Ken cave.

Risk is part of the equation. "Without the possibility of death, adventure is not possible," said Reinhold Messner, the first climber to summit Everest without oxygen.

"No other mammal moves around like we do," said Svante Pääbo, of the Max Planck Institute for Evolutionary Anthropology in Leipzig, Germany. "We push into new territory, even when we have resources where we are. Other animals don't do this ... There's a kind of madness to it ... We never stop. Why?"

"Because it's there," George Mallory said of Everest, the mountain that claimed his life.

"Exploration is an obsession. The more I discover, the more I want to know," said Meave Leakey, who spent decades in eastern Africa searching for clues to hominid evolution.

"It starts with an idea. And the idea becomes a vision," Messner explained.

Tremendous stamina is a requisite for adventure photographers. To photograph in the 24-hour darkness and minus 50°F temperatures of polar regions, Esther Horvath had to train to handle everything from falling into rough seas to polar bear encounters. Horvath, who documented the discovery of Antarctica explorer Ernest Shackleton's ship *Endurance*, finds the challenge exhilarating. "Searching and moving in the polar darkness has a certain mystery I'm drawn to," she says.

Madness. Obsession. A vision. And, simply, curiosity.

"Everyone is an explorer," Bob Ballard has said. "How could you possibly live your life looking at a door and not go open it?"

The photographers in the pages to follow have opened that door.

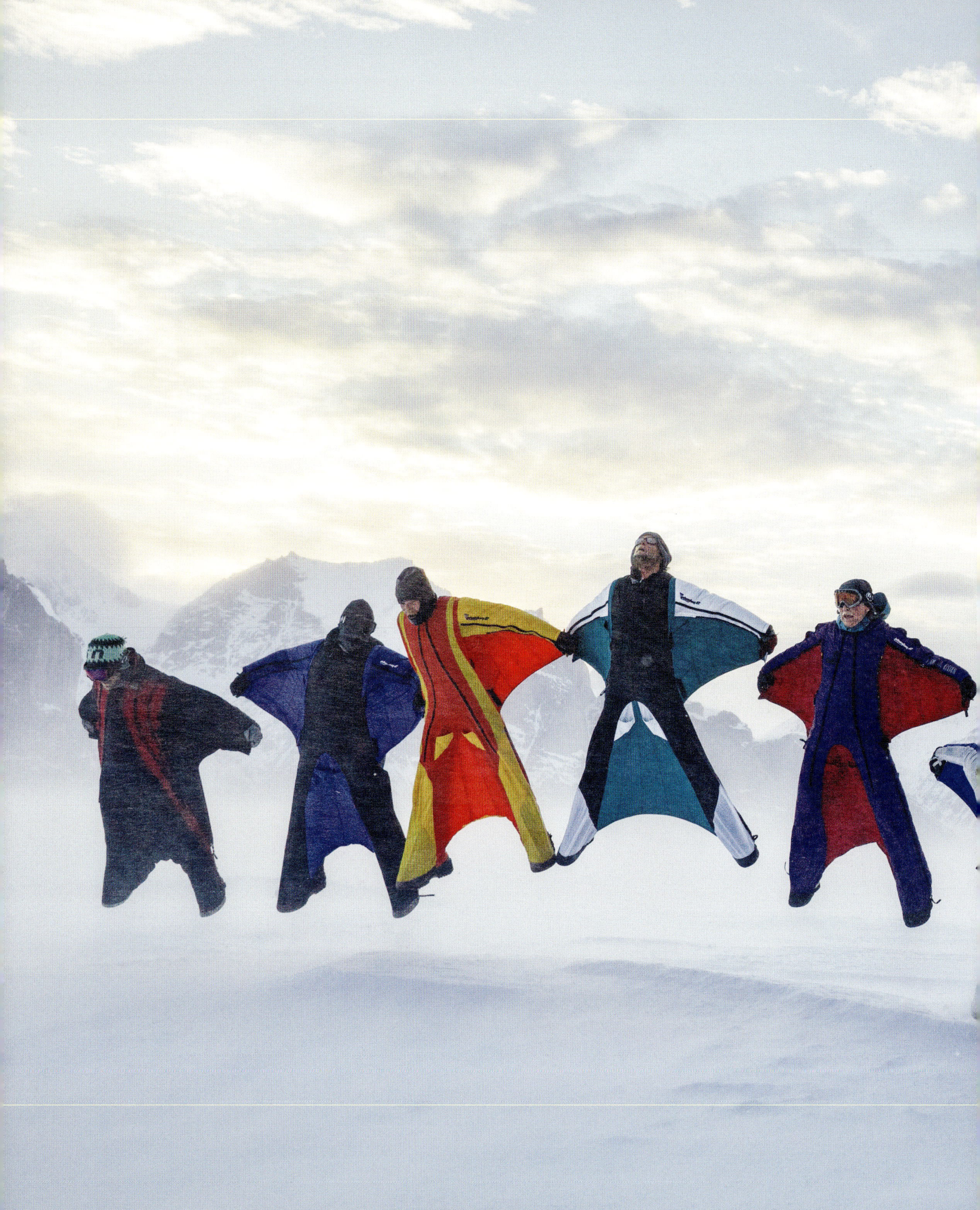

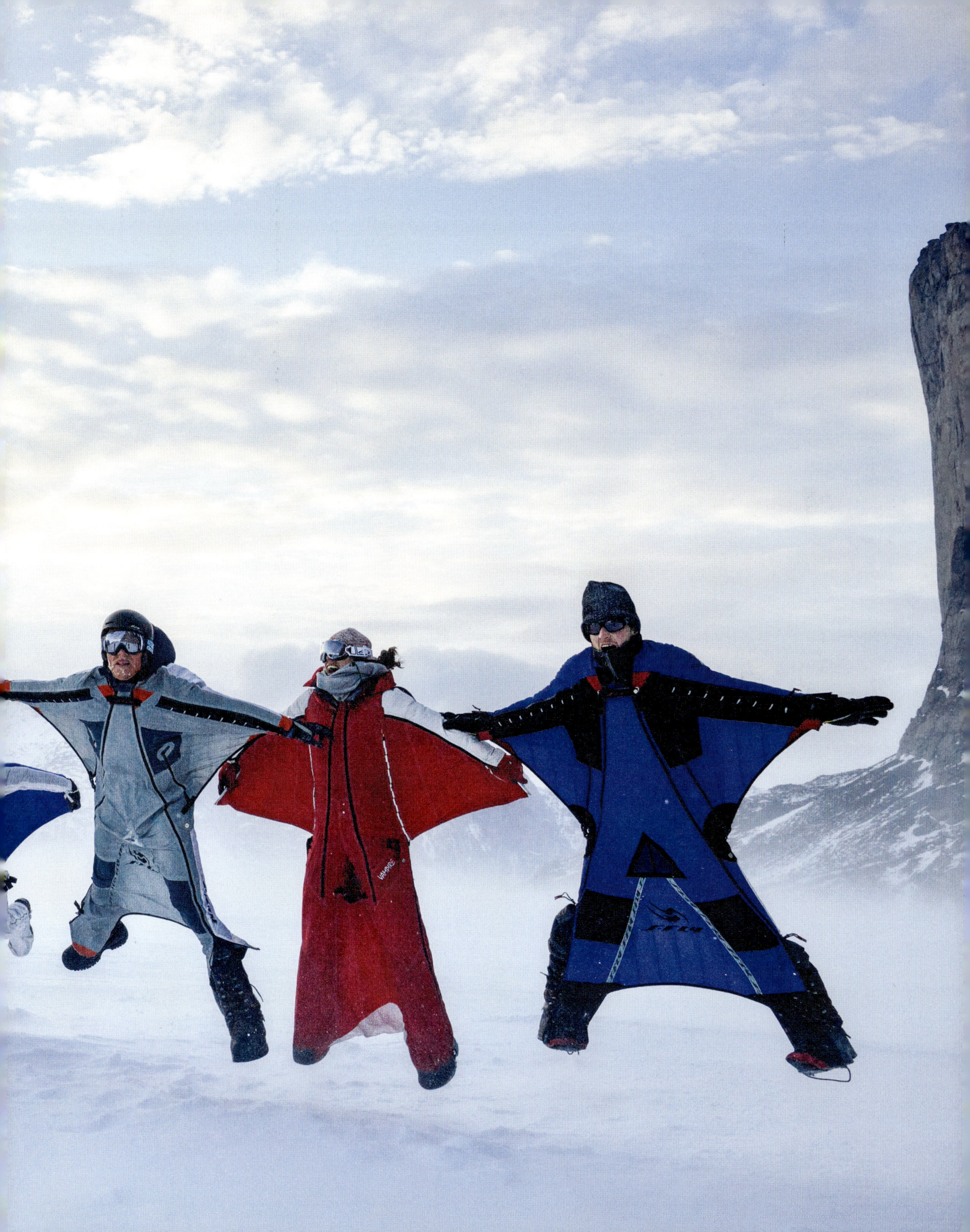
VAMPIRE

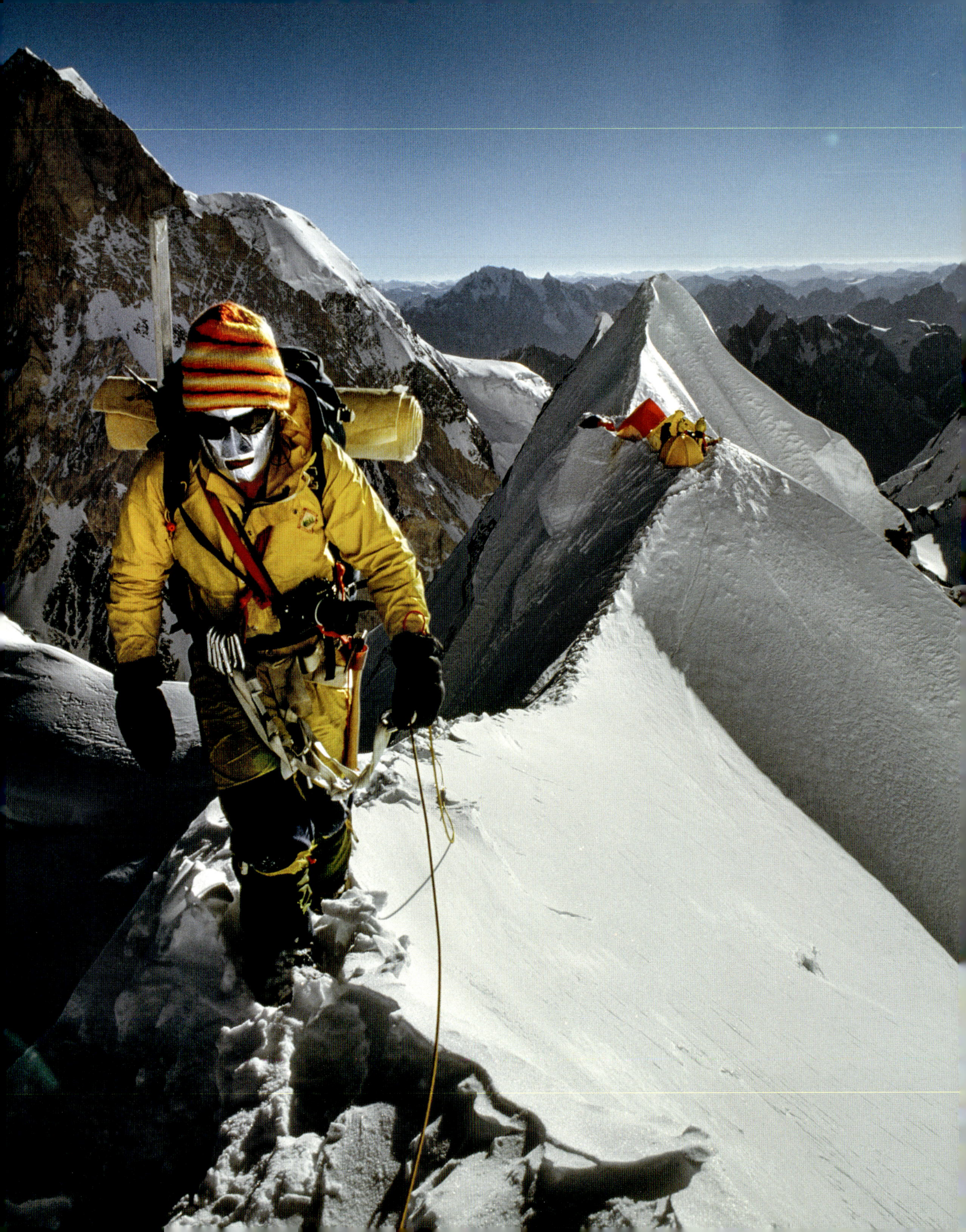

EXPLORATION IS AN OBSESSION. THE MORE I DISCOVER, THE MORE I WANT TO KNOW.

MEAVE LEAKEY, PALEOANTHROPOLOGIST

JOHN ROSKELLEY, 1979
With a metallic mask to insulate his face and reflect solar radiation, climber Rick Ridgeway treks toward Camp V on K2, the world's second highest peak. On this expedition, Americans would summit the mountain for the first time.

PREVIOUS PAGES
KRYSTLE WRIGHT, 2012
BASE jumpers test their wingsuits to see how far the wind can carry them backward on Baffin Island, Canada.

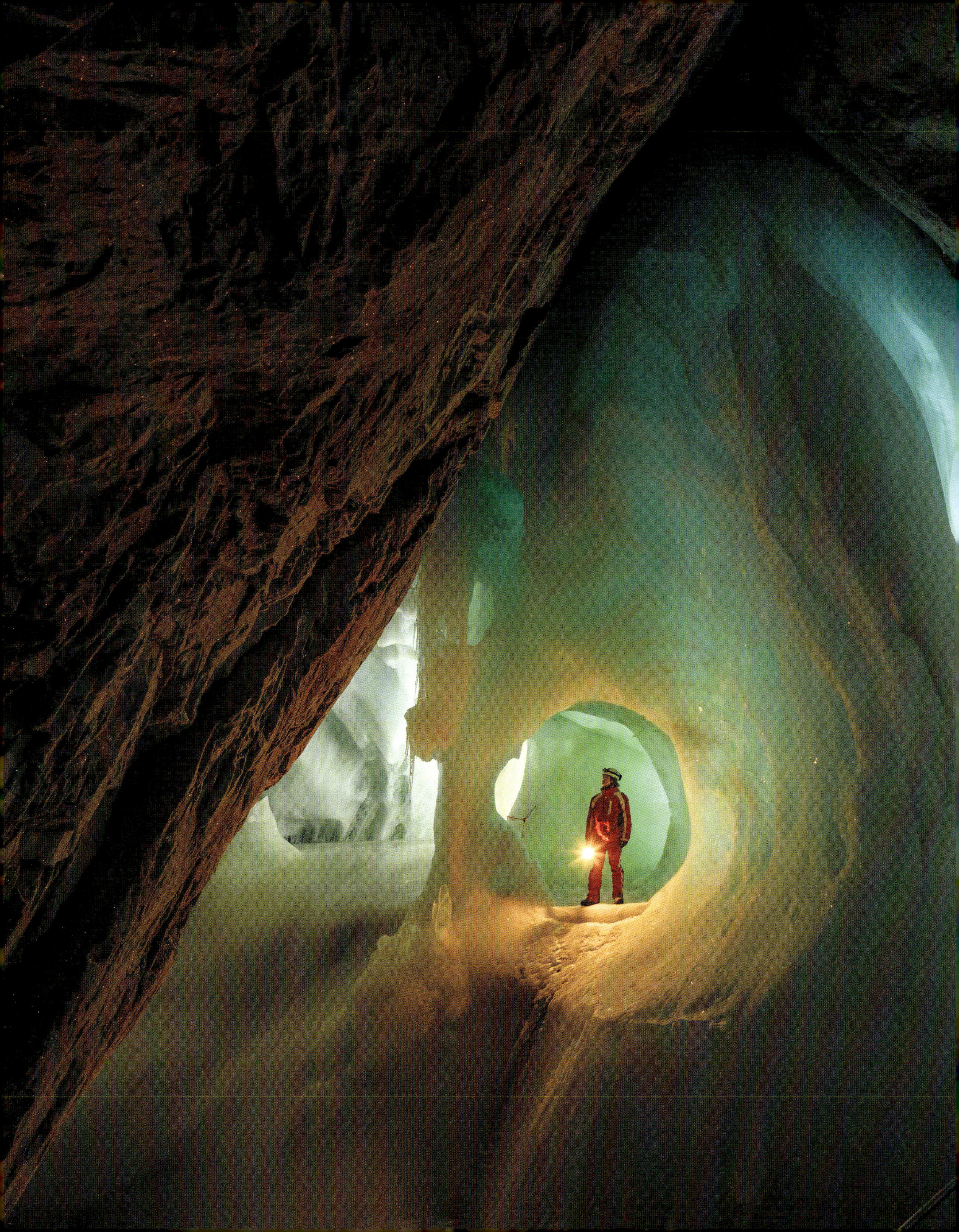

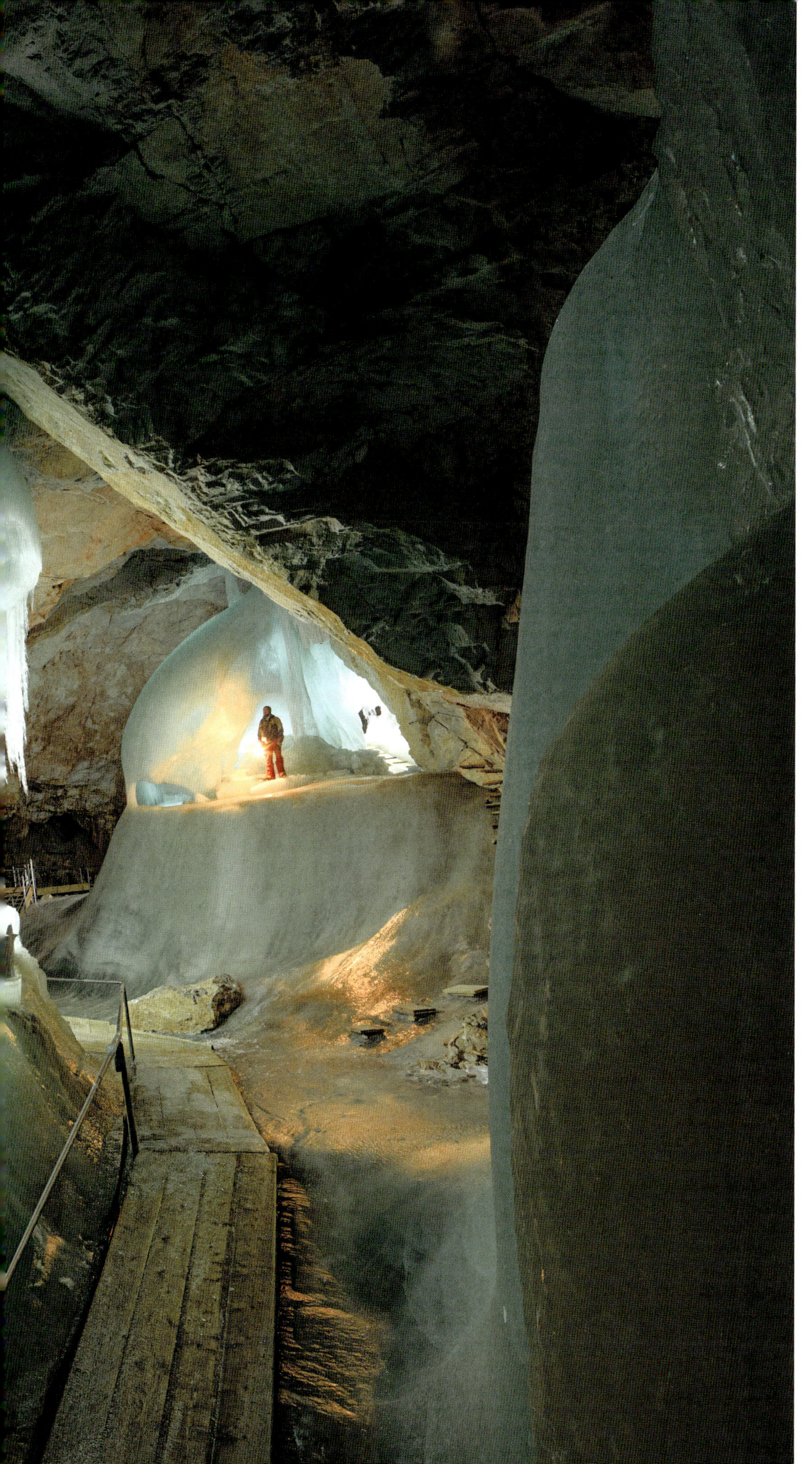

ROBBIE SHONE, 2021
Scientists navigate the ice-encrusted portion of the Eisriesenwelt cave system, which extends an astonishing 26 miles beneath the Austrian Alps. The area is under increasing pressure from climate change.

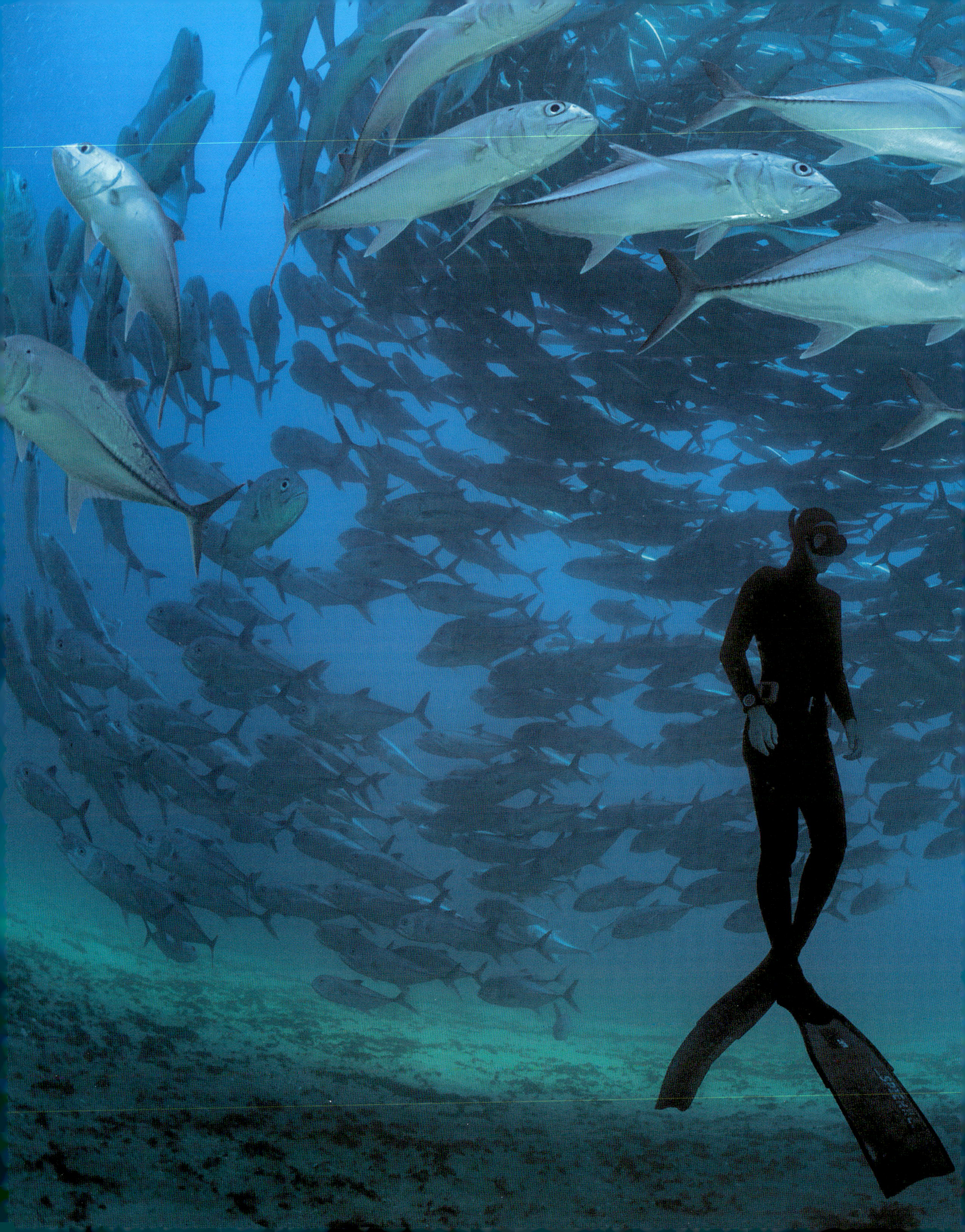

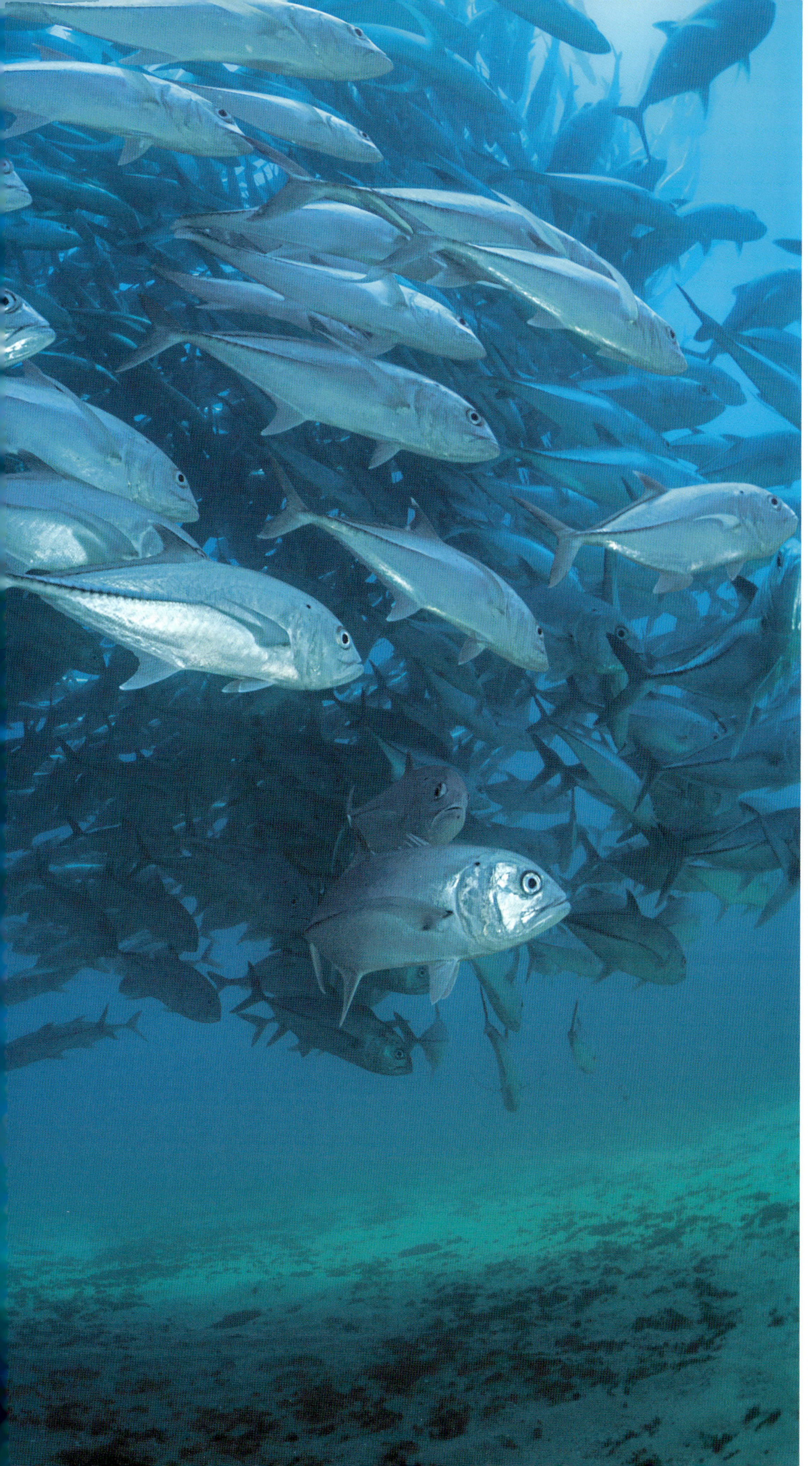

THOMAS P. PESCHAK, 2017
A free diver communes with bigeye trevallies—large marine fish found throughout the Indian and Pacific Oceans—in the Gulf of California near Cabo Pulmo. Biomass on this coral reef has increased almost threefold since locals and conservationists made the reef a no-take zone in 1995.

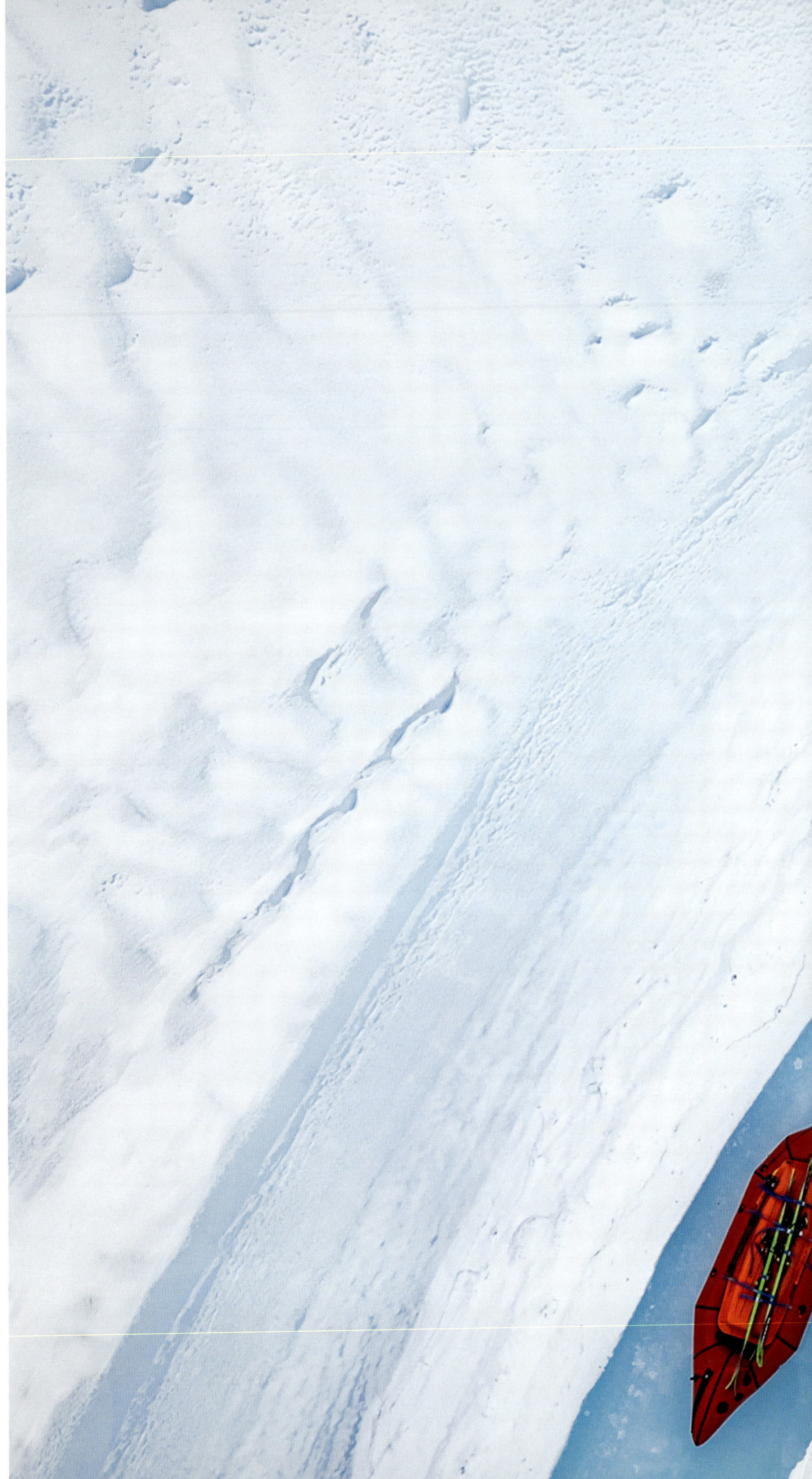

ERIK BOOMER, 2016
A drone captures Sarah McNair-Landry (right), the youngest person to travel to both the North and South Poles, as she traverses the Greenland ice cap—a feat she has accomplished five times.

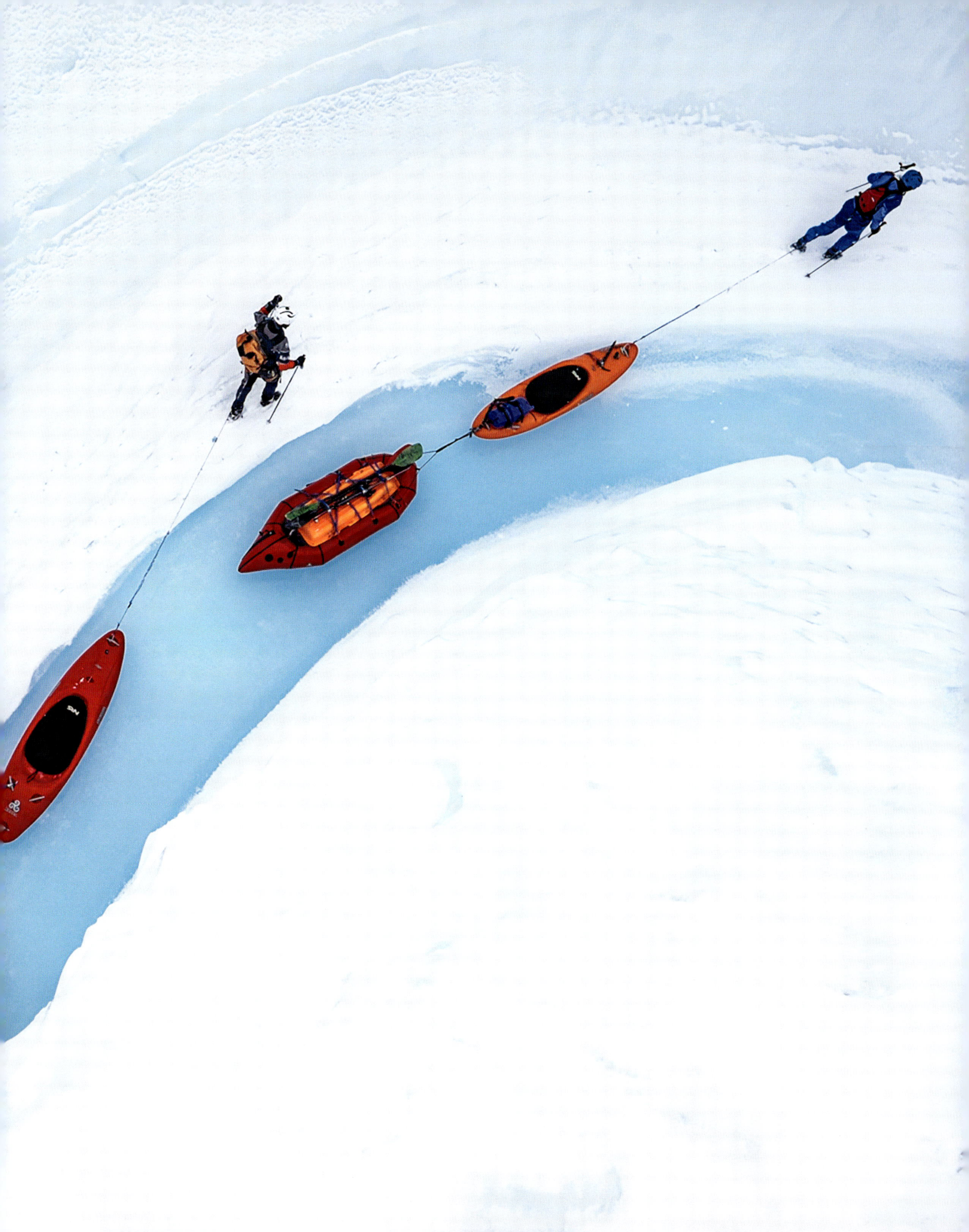

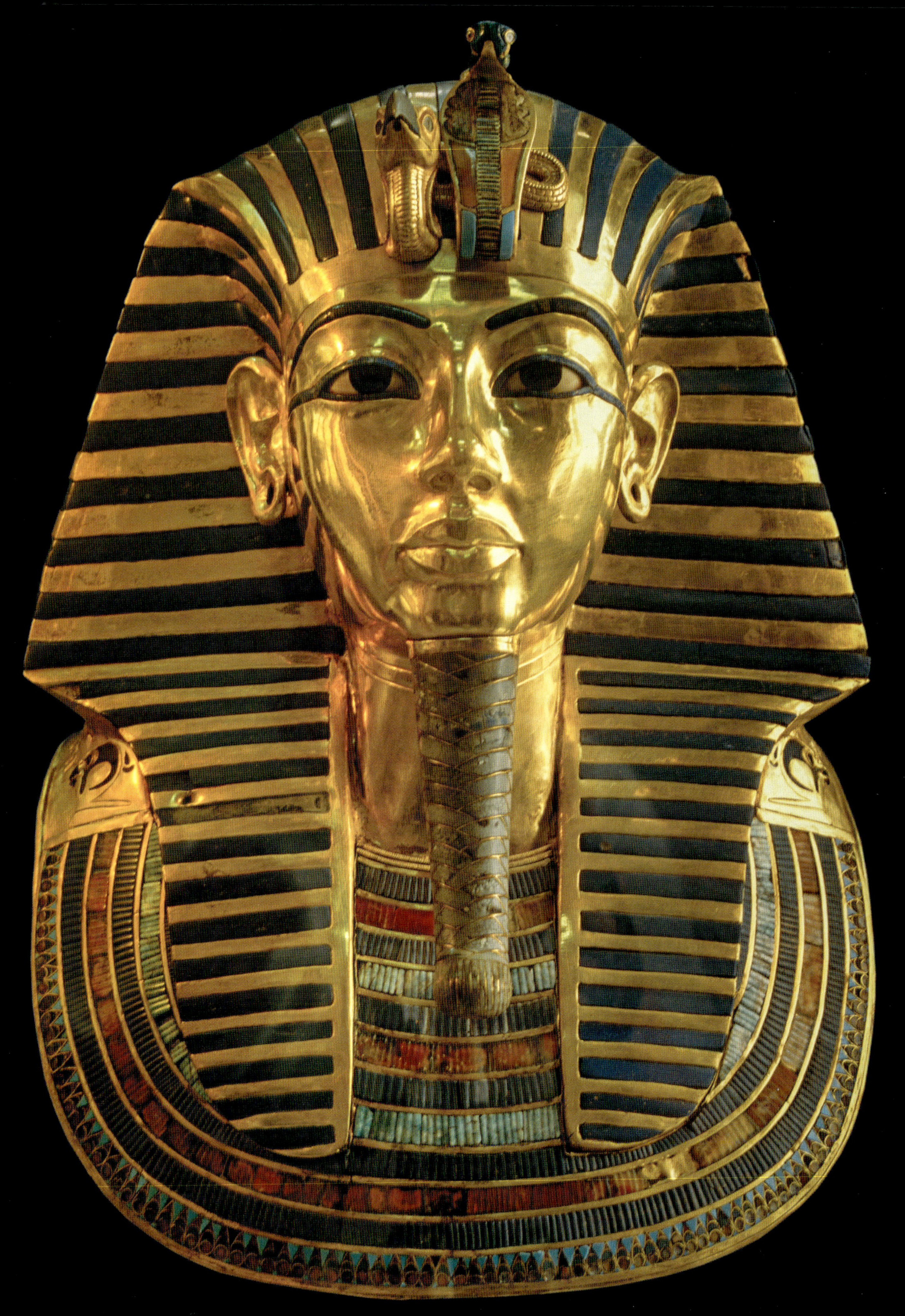

THERE IS DRAMA IN THE VERY AIR OF THE PLACE, AND I WANT TO BE THERE RECORDING IT FOR THE GEOGRAPHIC.

MAYNARD OWEN WILLIAMS, WHO PHOTOGRAPHED THE PUBLIC OPENING OF TUTANKHAMUN'S TOMB FOR NATIONAL GEOGRAPHIC IN 1923

KENNETH GARRETT, 2001
The death mask of teenage pharaoh Tutankhamun, discovered in 1922 by Egyptologist Howard Carter, is displayed in Cairo's Egyptian Museum. His final resting place is the best preserved pharaonic tomb ever found in Egypt's Valley of the Kings.

FOLLOWING PAGES
TOMÁS MUNITA, 2014
Bagualeros—cowboys who capture feral livestock—on an expedition in Patagonia, Chile

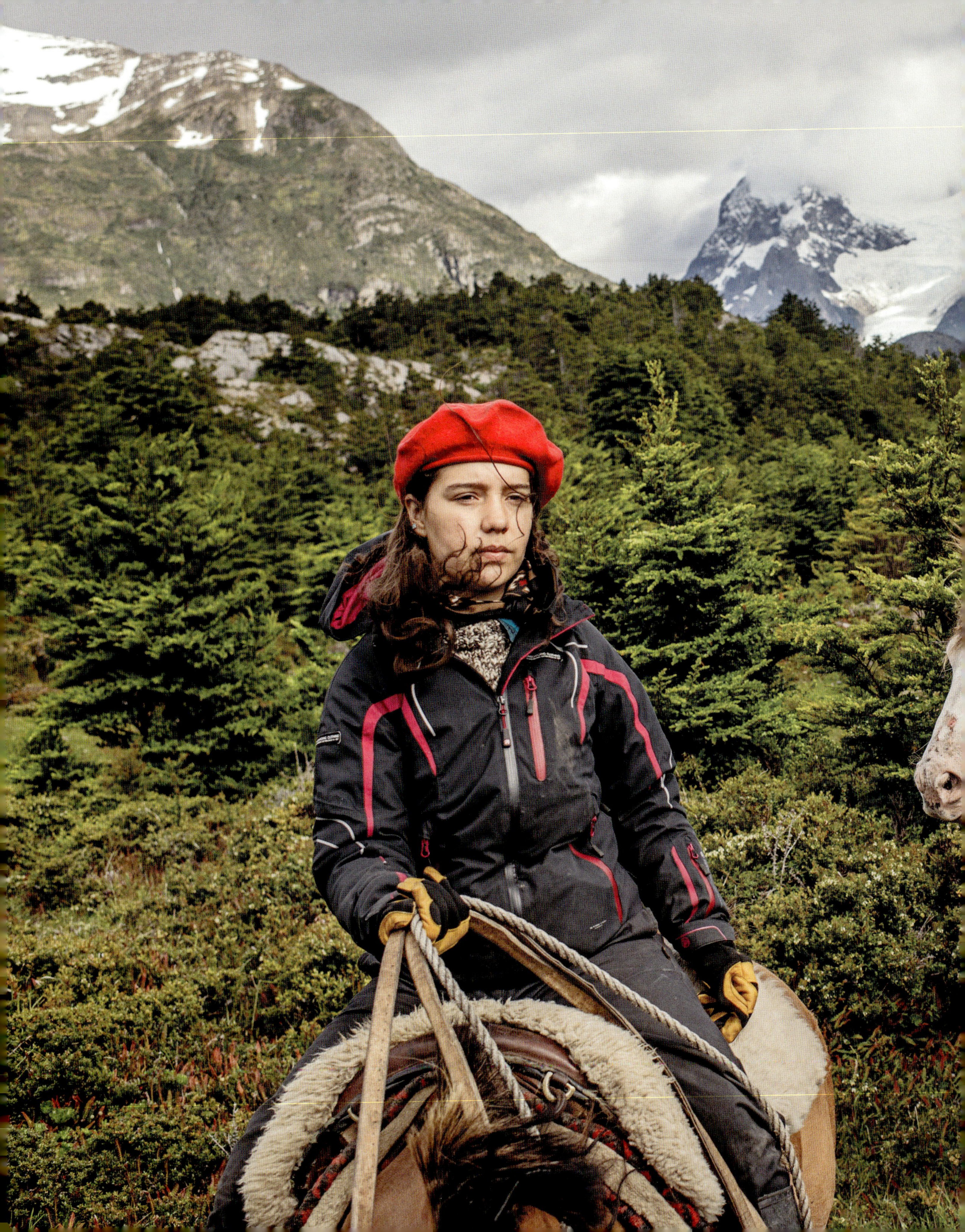

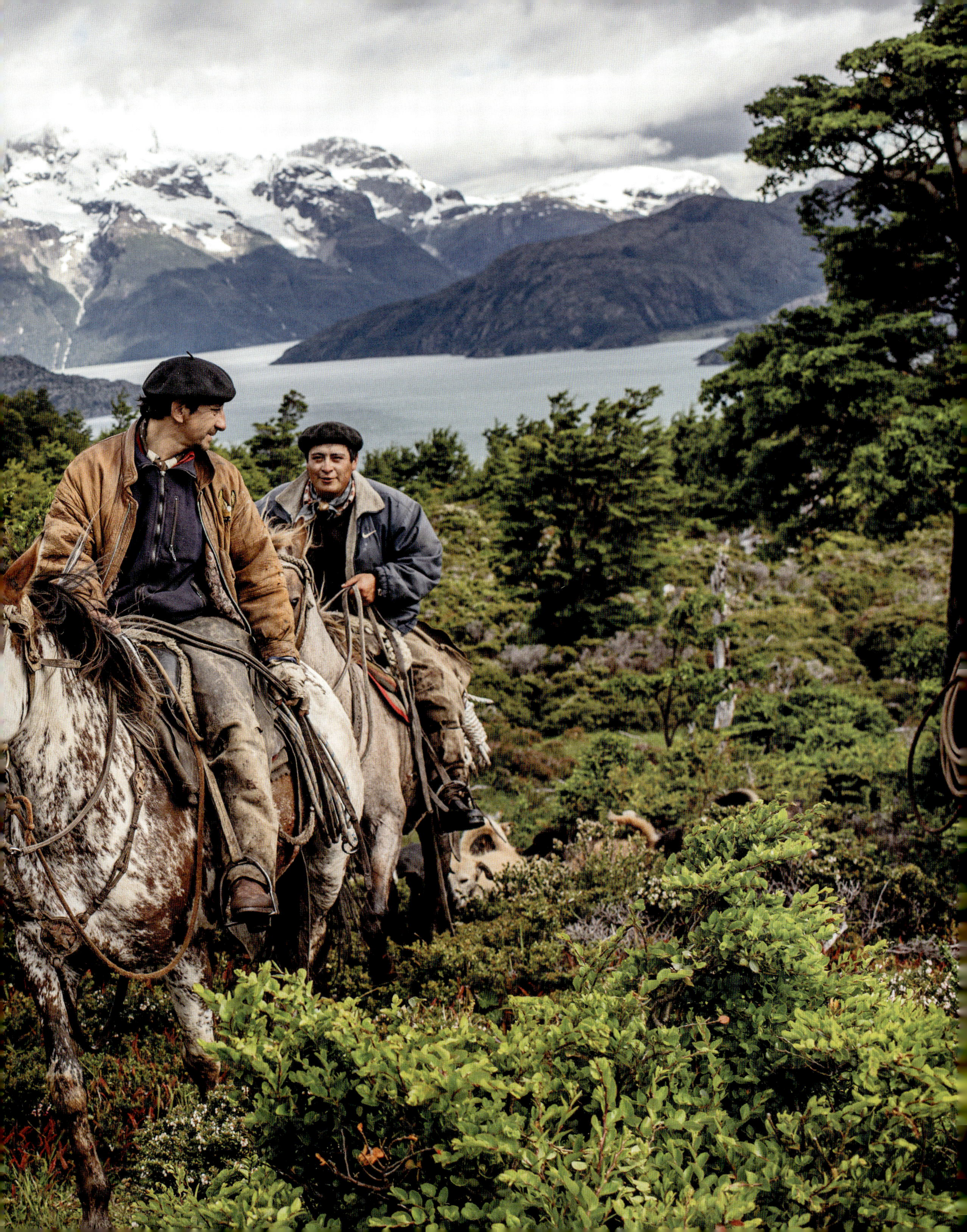

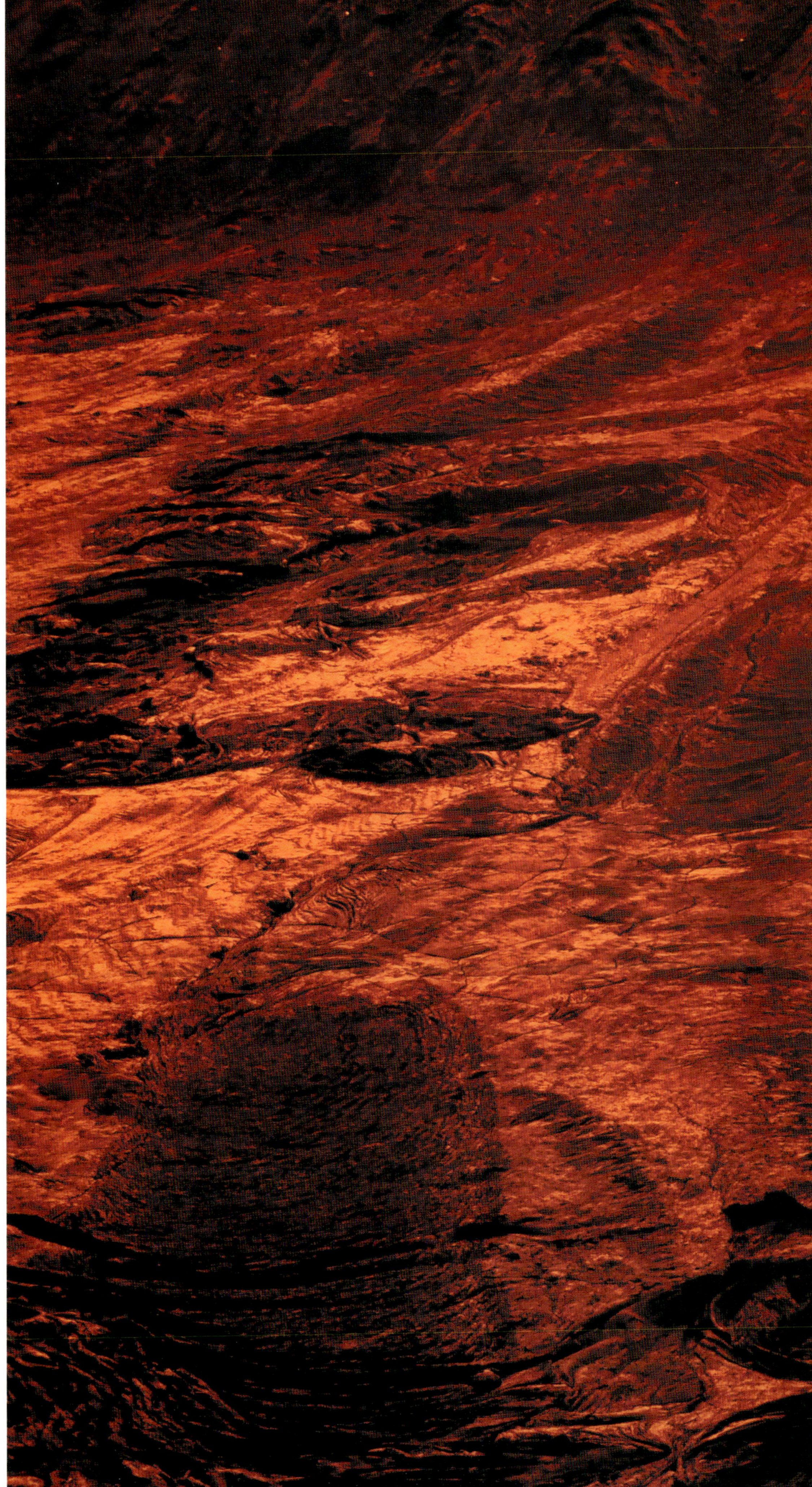

CARSTEN PETER, 2011
An expedition member walks on the cooled lava floor inside the Democratic Republic of the Congo's Nyiragongo volcano.

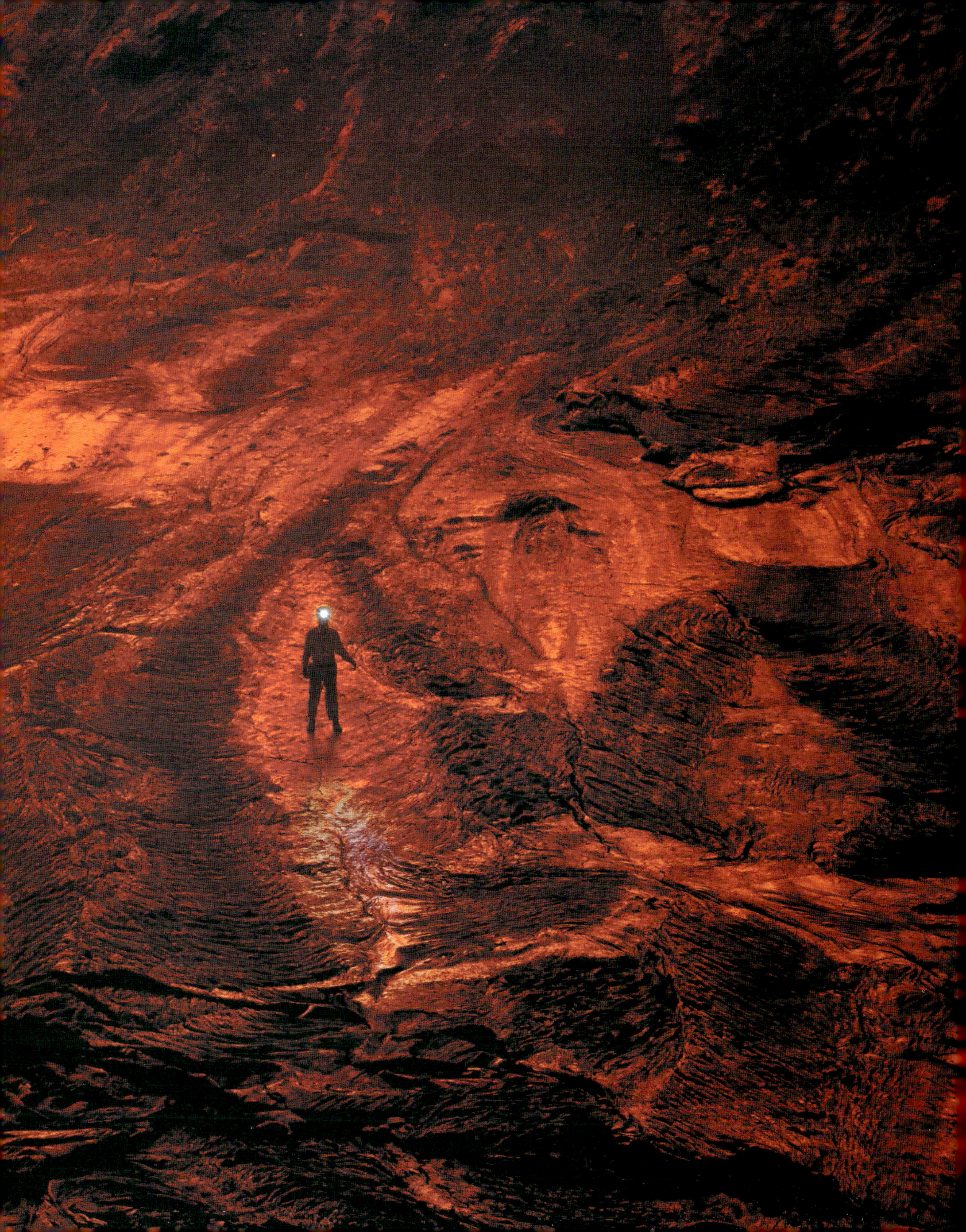

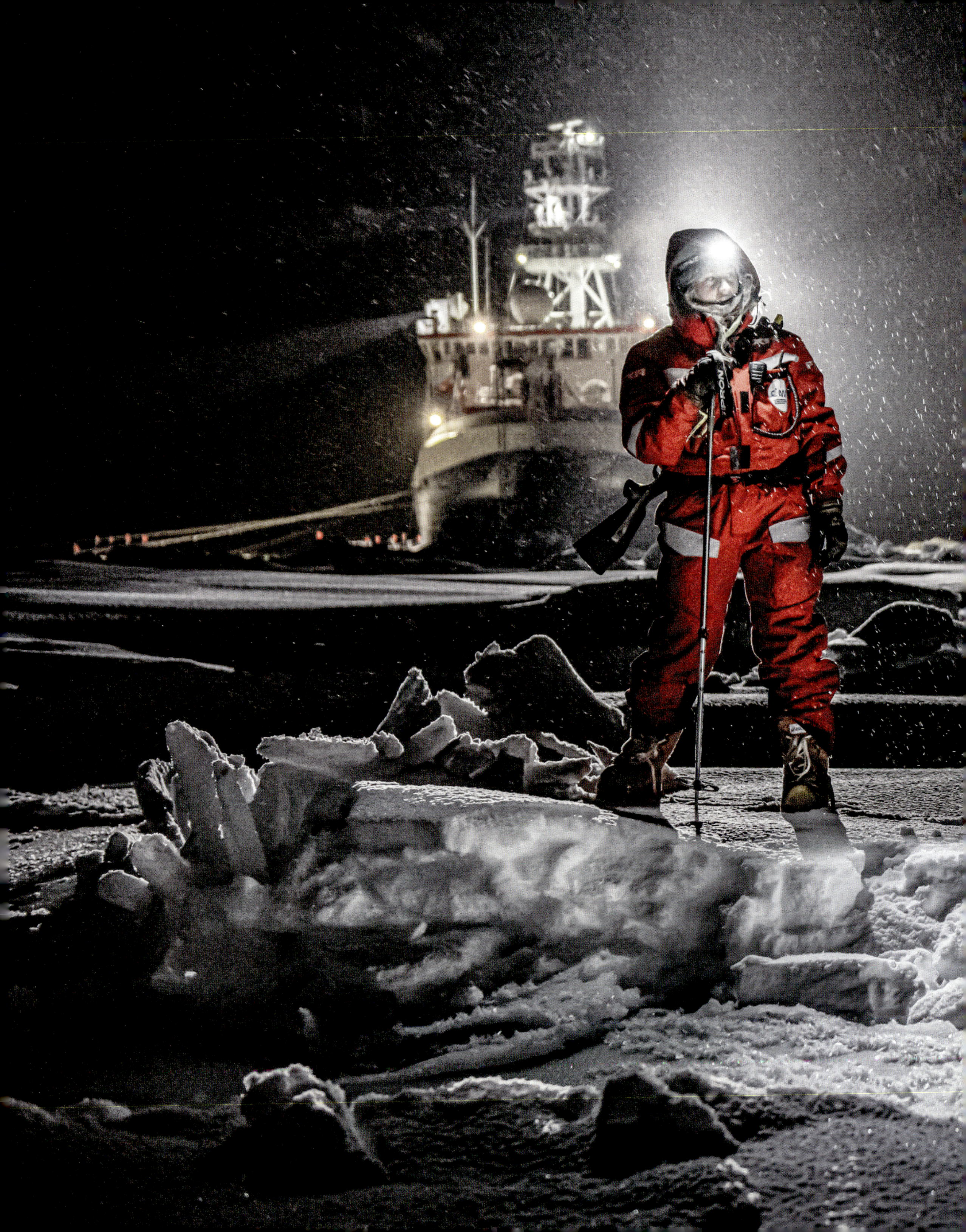

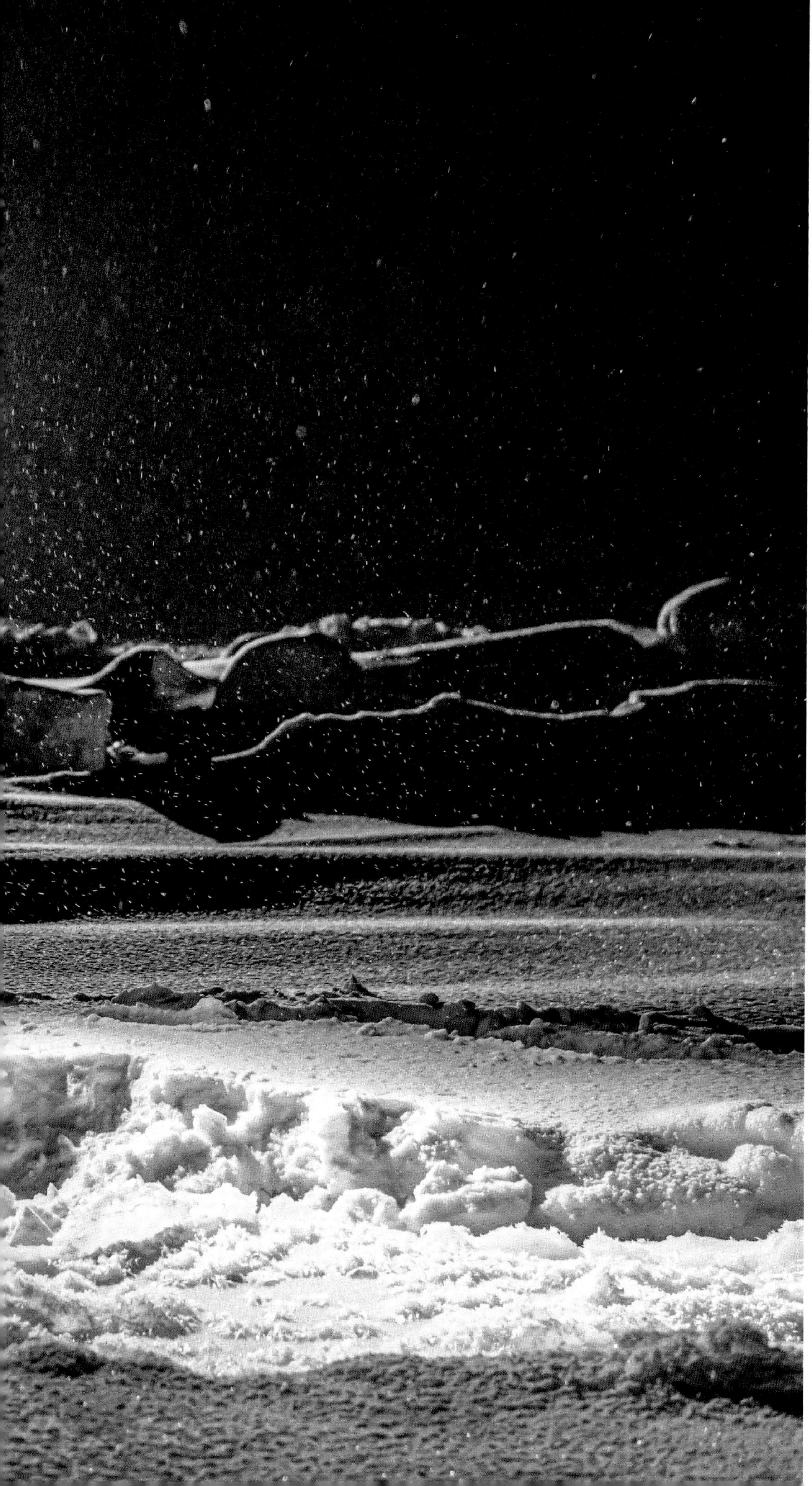

ESTHER HORVATH, 2019
A polar bear guard checks for safe passage across the sea ice during a 2019 scientific expedition in the Arctic Ocean.

BIOGRAPHY

JODY MACDONALD

FOR ADVENTURE PHOTOGRAPHER Jody MacDonald, when things are going wrong, they are going in the right direction. "I think about risk and failure differently than most people—I embrace them," she told Sadie Quarrier, editorial director of integrated storytelling, who describes MacDonald as "hard-core tough."

Comfort zones are to be avoided, MacDonald says, because "adversity is worth it." And in the course of her photographic career, she has dealt with plenty of that—from typhoid, staph infections, and shark attacks to getting sucked into a cloud while parasailing and enduring a 10-day storm in the Pacific that nearly took her ship's mast (chronic seasickness is part of her adversity list).

MacDonald, who was born in Canada but spent her early years in Saudi Arabia, is at home in the world—especially on its rough edges. Her photographs come from the richness of experiences like sleeping on top of Mauritania's iron ore train as it snaked through the Sahara, swimming in the warm waters of India's Andaman Islands with a four-ton elephant (one of her most famous images), eavesdropping on a humpback whale singing to her newborn in Polynesia, and paragliding in the Himalaya at 17,000 feet.

In addition to *National Geographic,* MacDonald has photographed for *Outside,* the BBC, and *Islands*. In 2023, *Men's Journal* included her in its article "The 45 Most Adventurous Women of the Past 45 Years."

"My greatest fear," MacDonald says, "is squandering my life."

OPPOSITE TOP
JODY MACDONALD, 2010
Accompanied by his mahout, or keeper, an Asian elephant walks the turquoise waters near Havelock Island (Swaraj Dweep) off the eastern coast of India.

OPPOSITE BOTTOM
JODY MACDONALD, 2015
Winds of 100 miles an hour whip up a sandstorm in the Mauritanian Sahara.

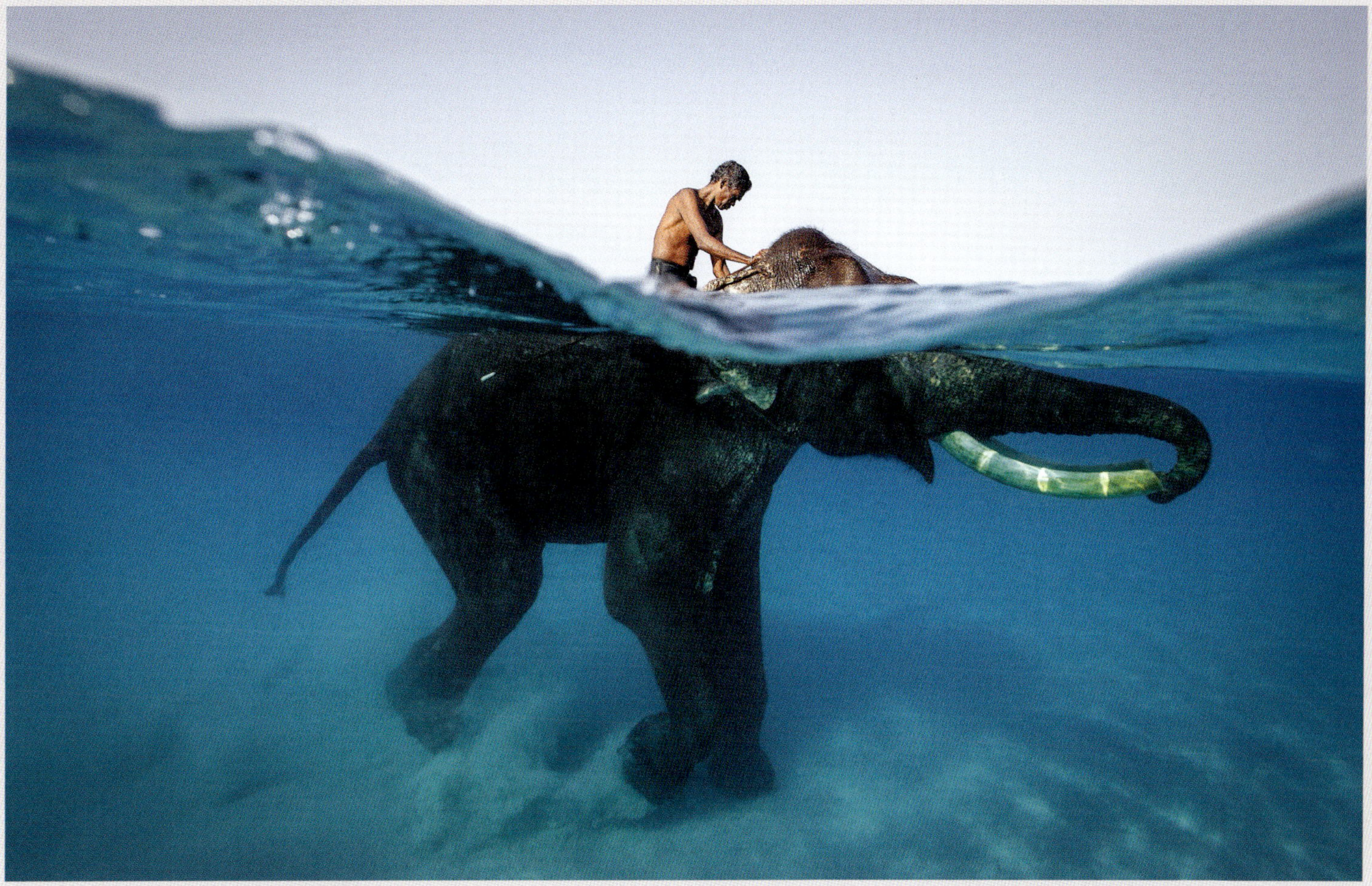

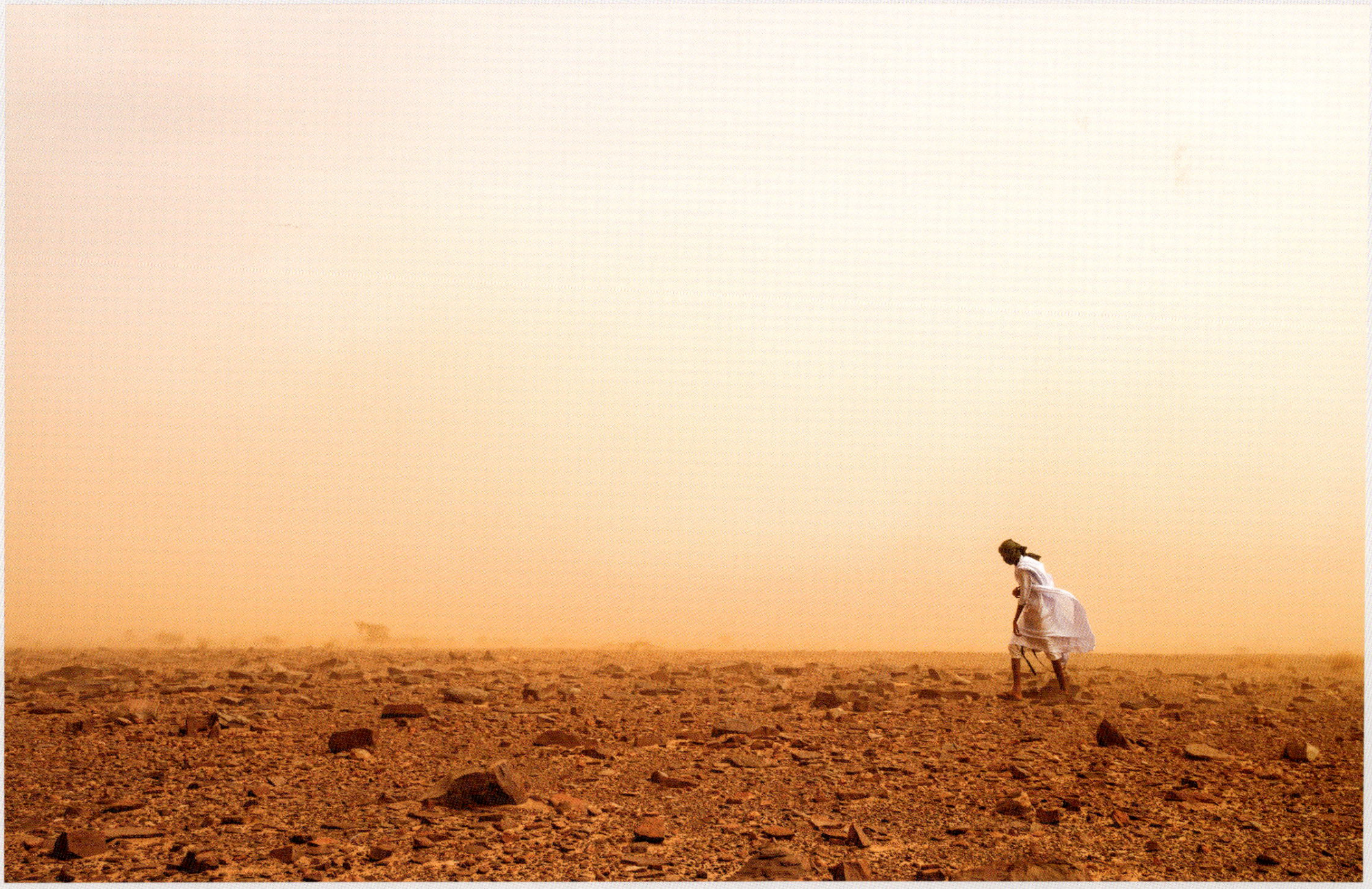

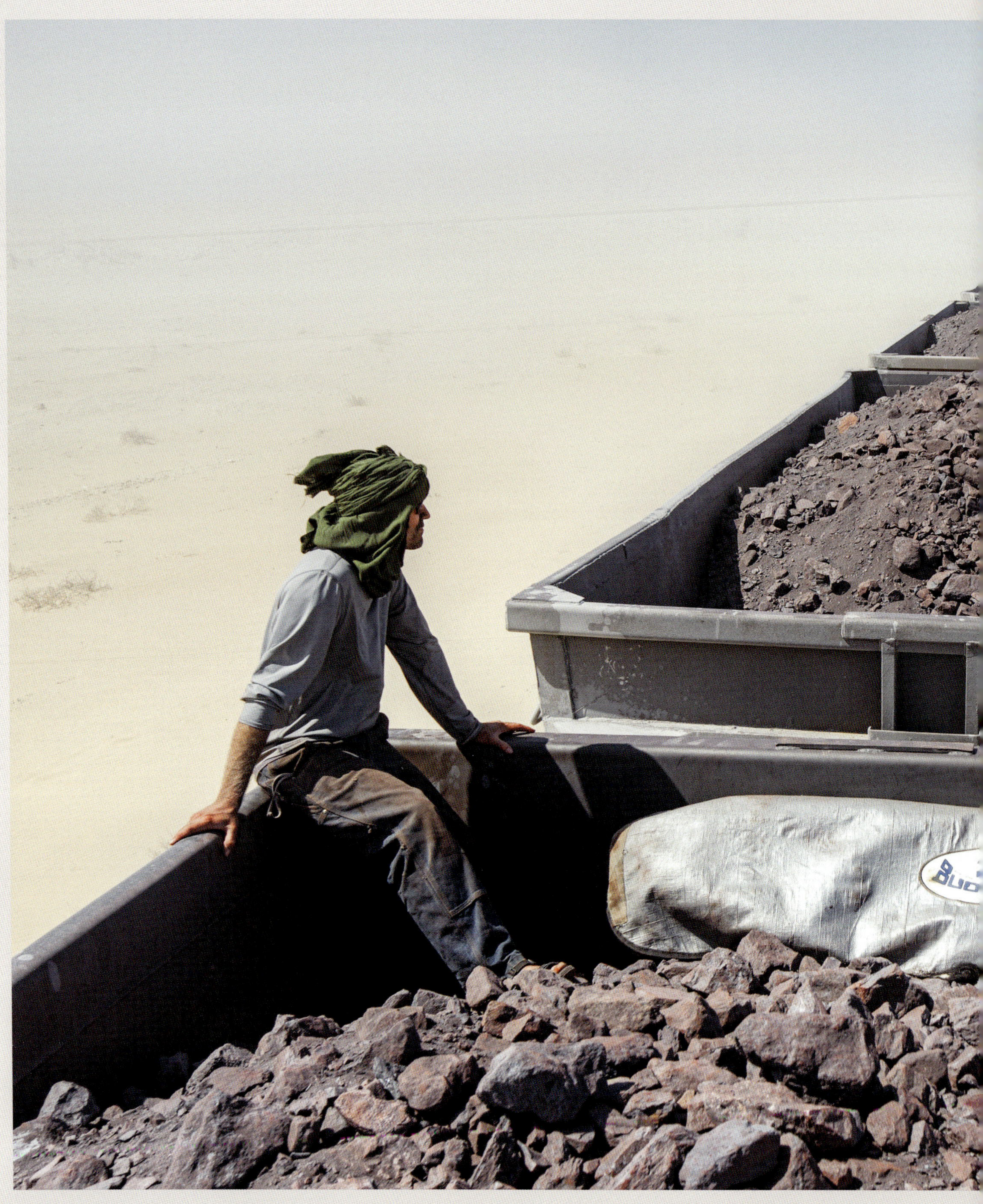

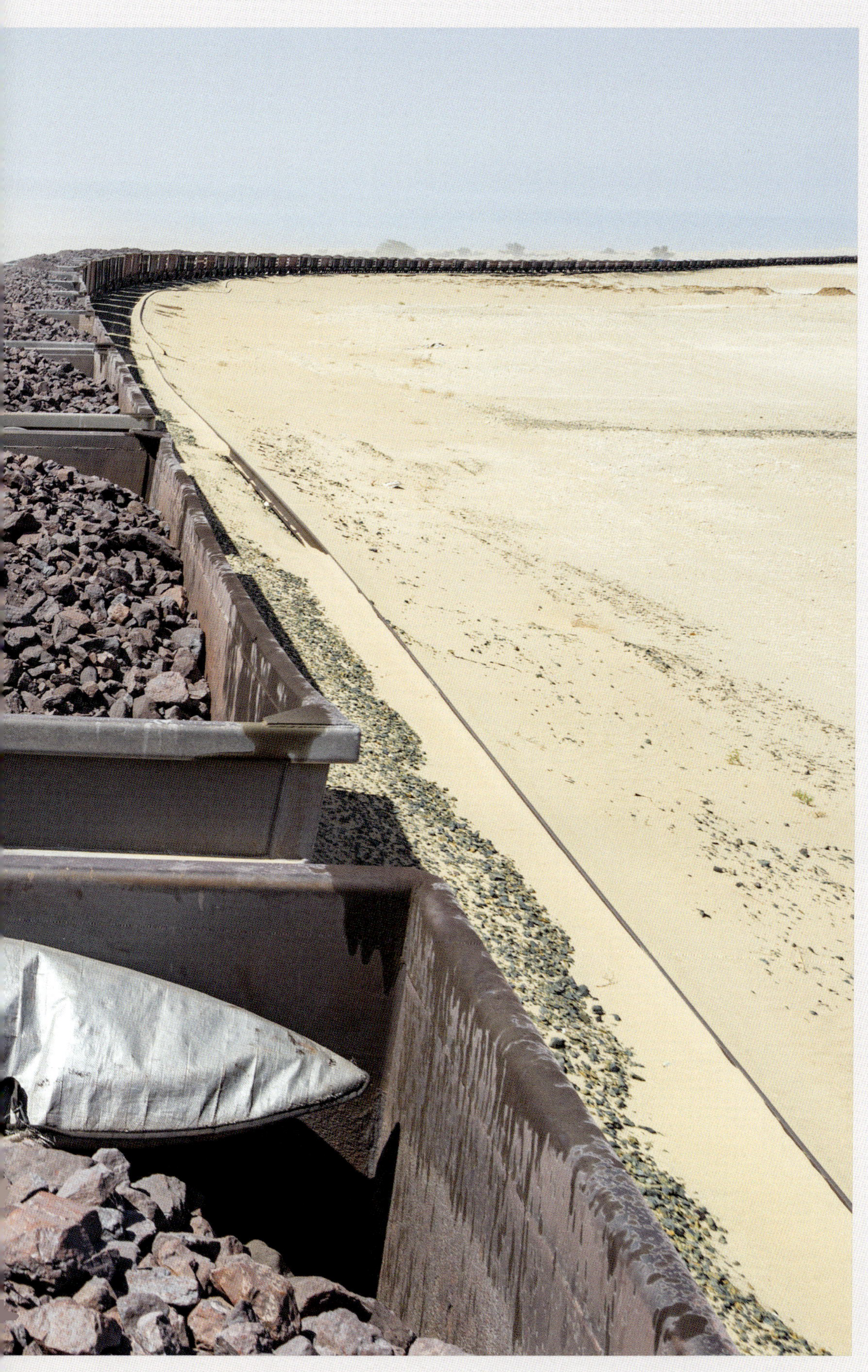

JODY MACDONALD, 2015
A train hopper catches a ride through the Sahara in Mauritania.

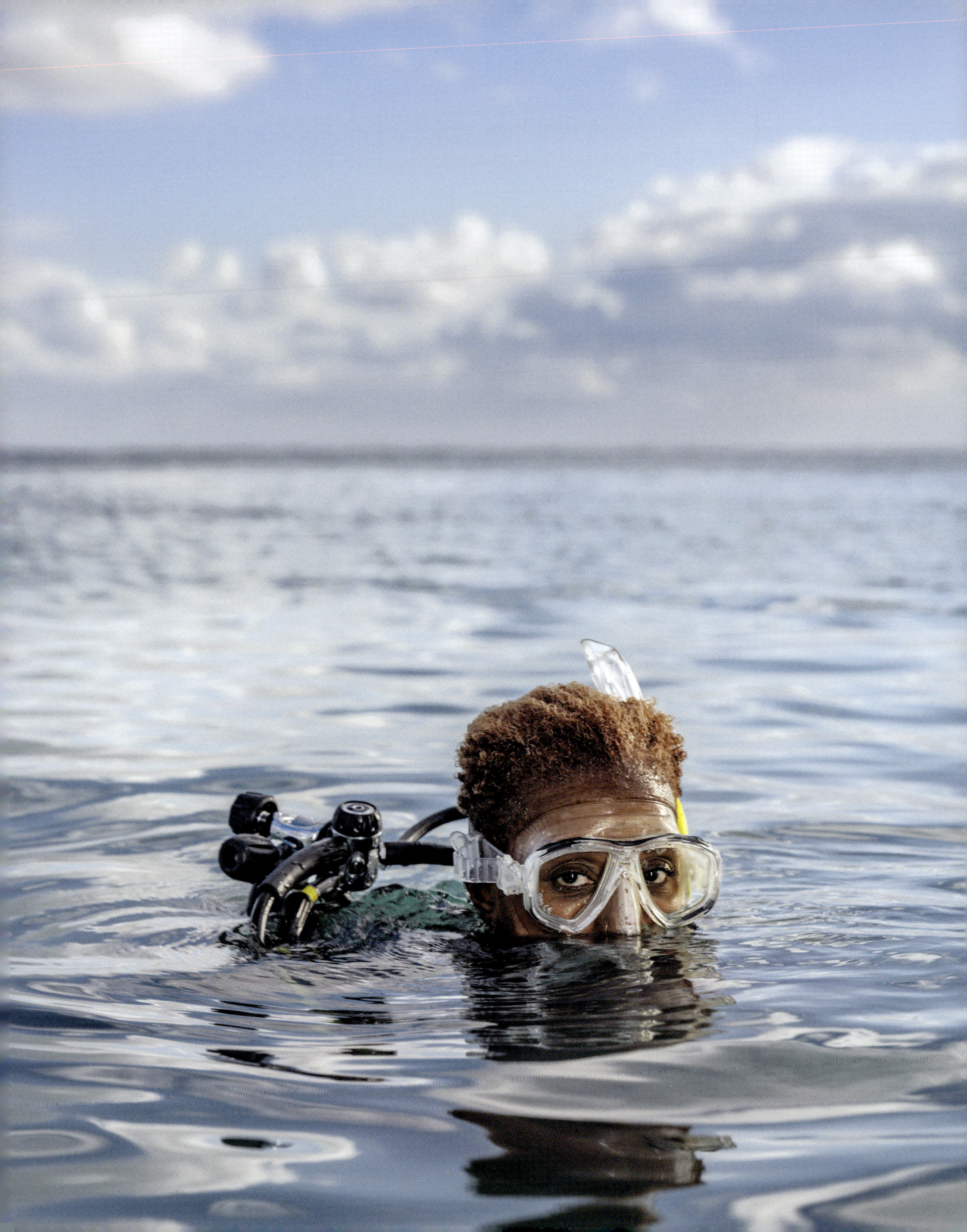

EVERYONE IS AN EXPLORER. HOW COULD YOU POSSIBLY LIVE YOUR LIFE LOOKING AT A DOOR AND NOT GO OPEN IT?

BOB BALLARD, UNDERWATER ARCHAEOLOGIST

WAYNE LAWRENCE, 2021
National Geographic Explorer in Residence Tara Roberts reports on shipwrecks that carried captive Africans during the transatlantic slave trade. Here, she dives the Florida Keys.

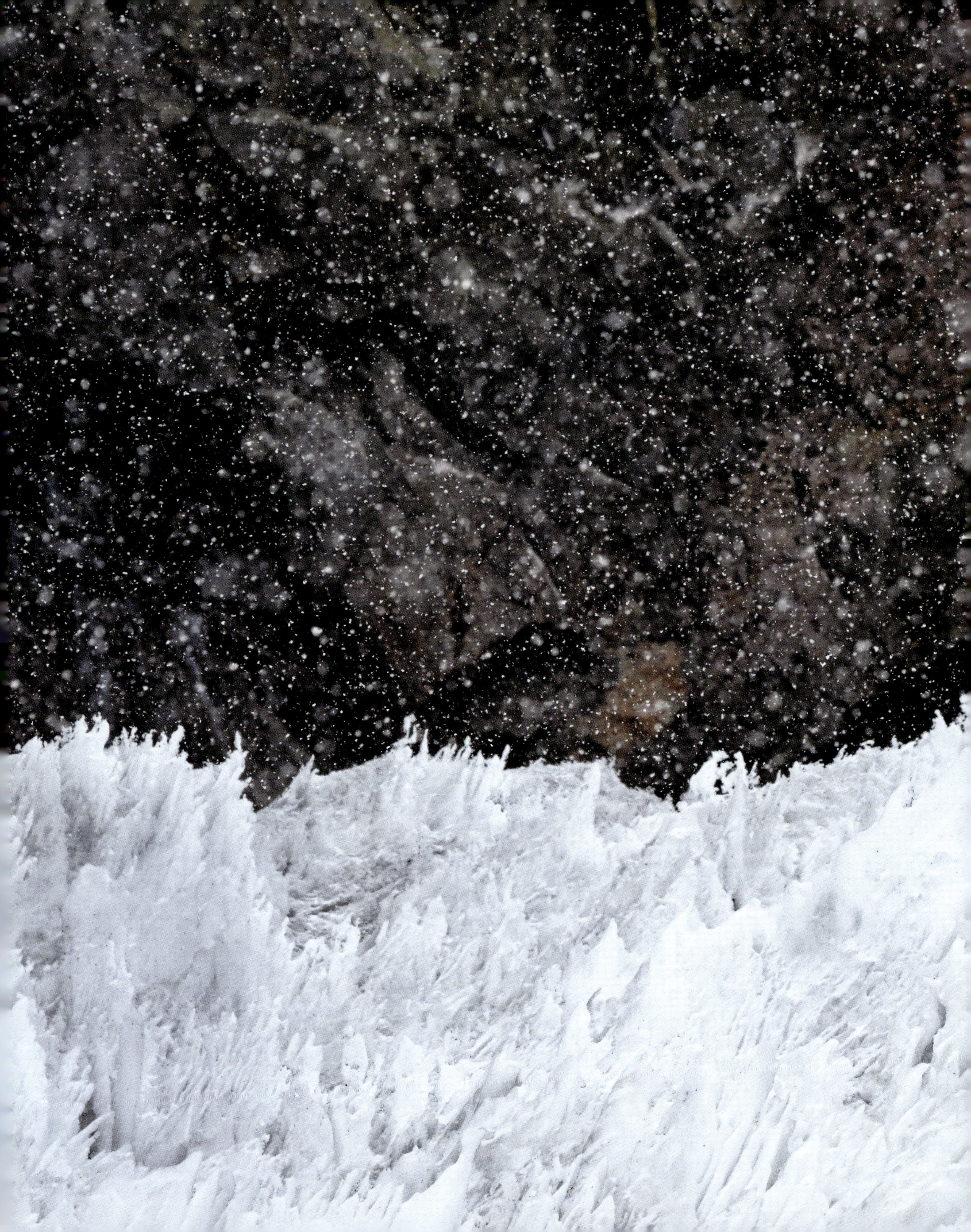

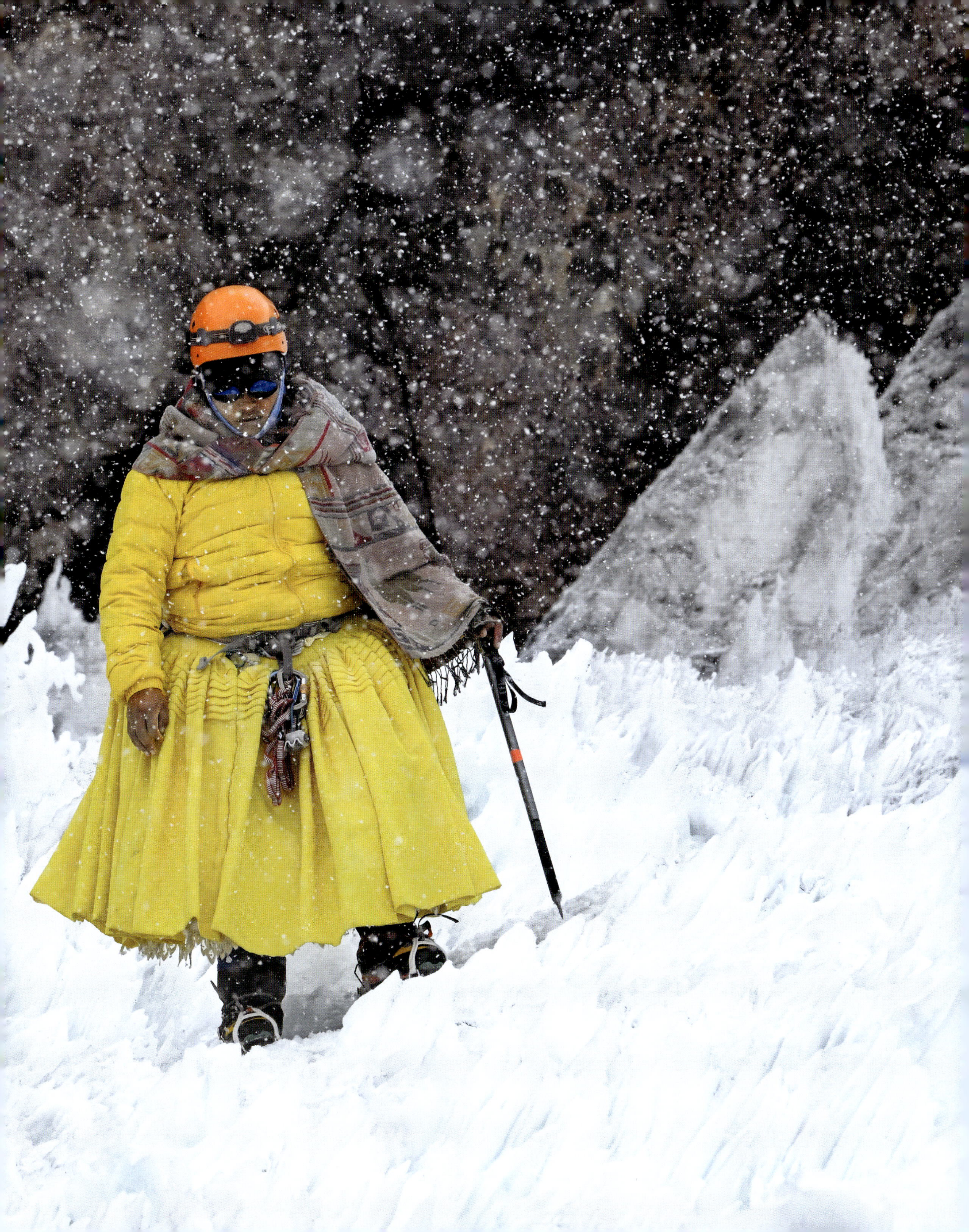

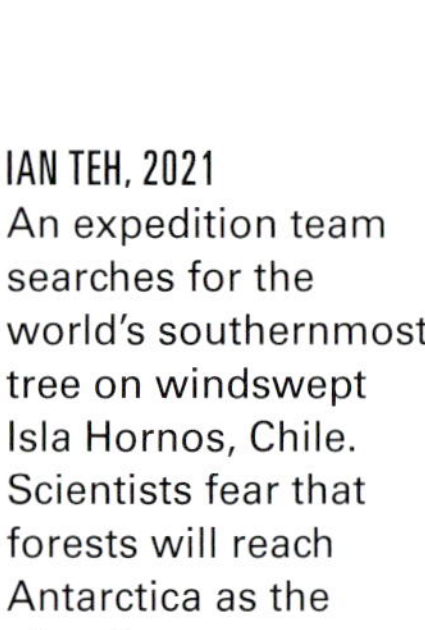

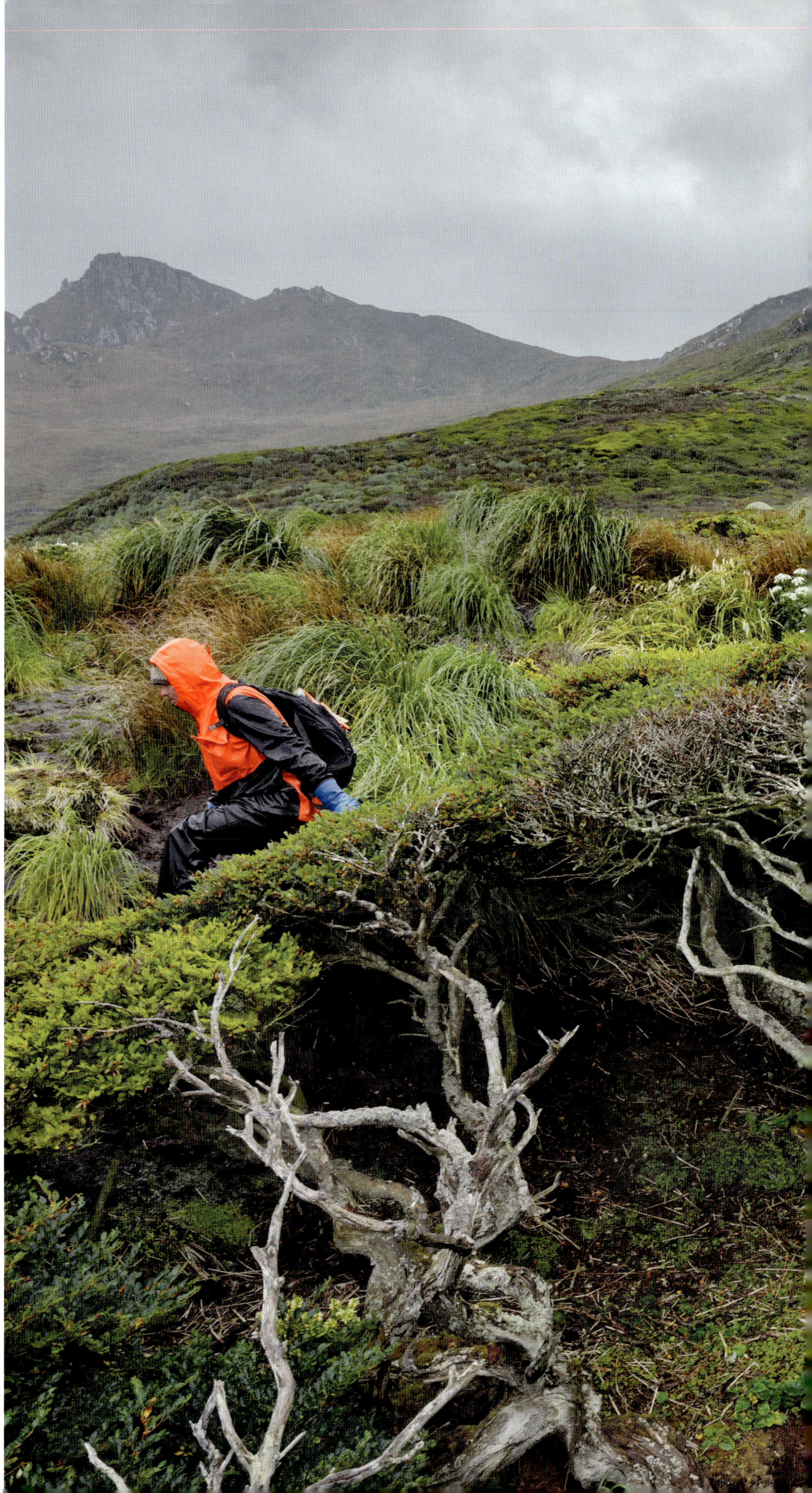

IAN TEH, 2021
An expedition team searches for the world's southernmost tree on windswept Isla Hornos, Chile. Scientists fear that forests will reach Antarctica as the planet warms.

PREVIOUS PAGES
THOMAS P. PESCHAK, 2022
A member of Bolivia's Aymara people accompanies a team from National Geographic to install a weather station atop Nevado Ausangate, a 21,000-foot peak in the Peruvian Andes.

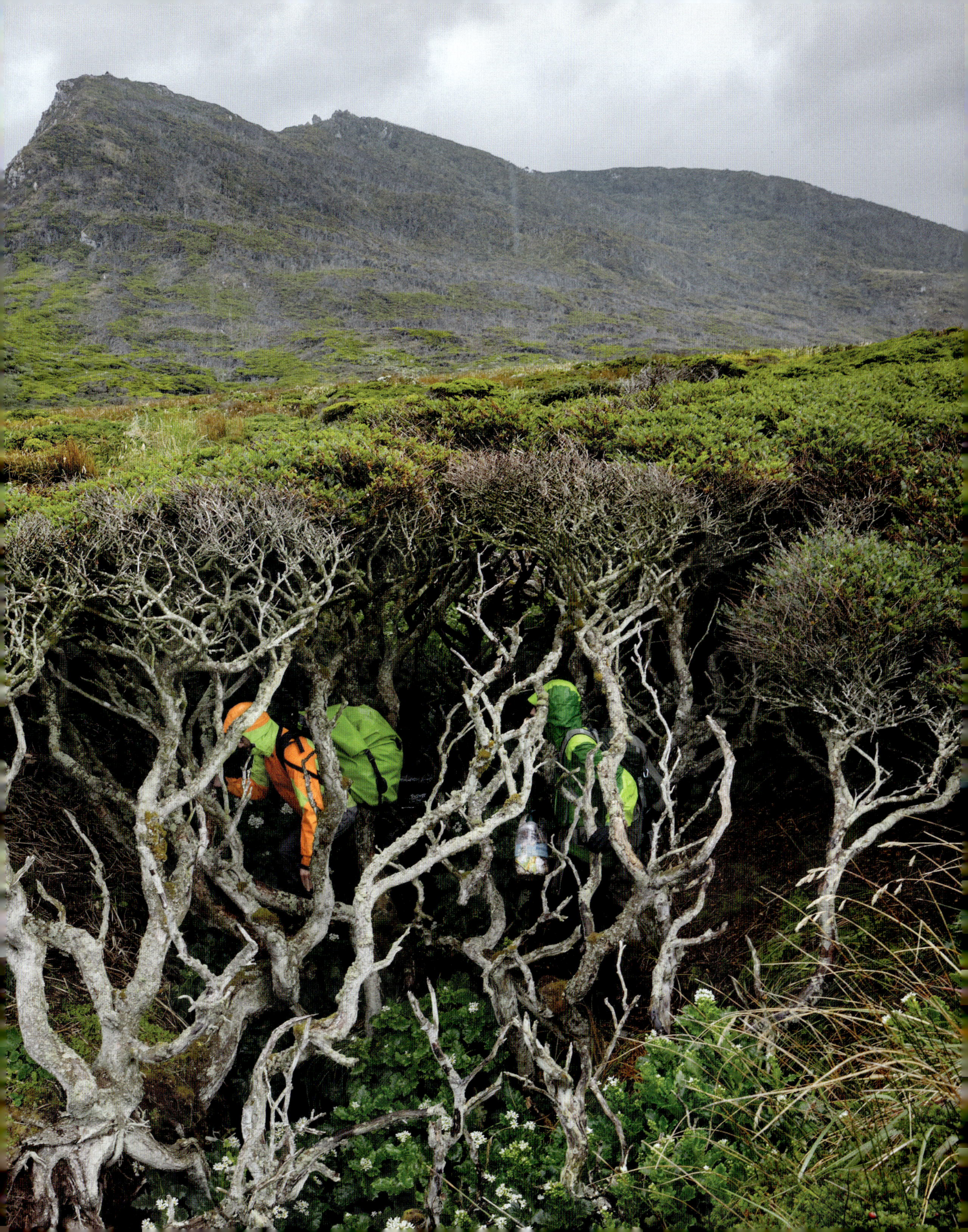

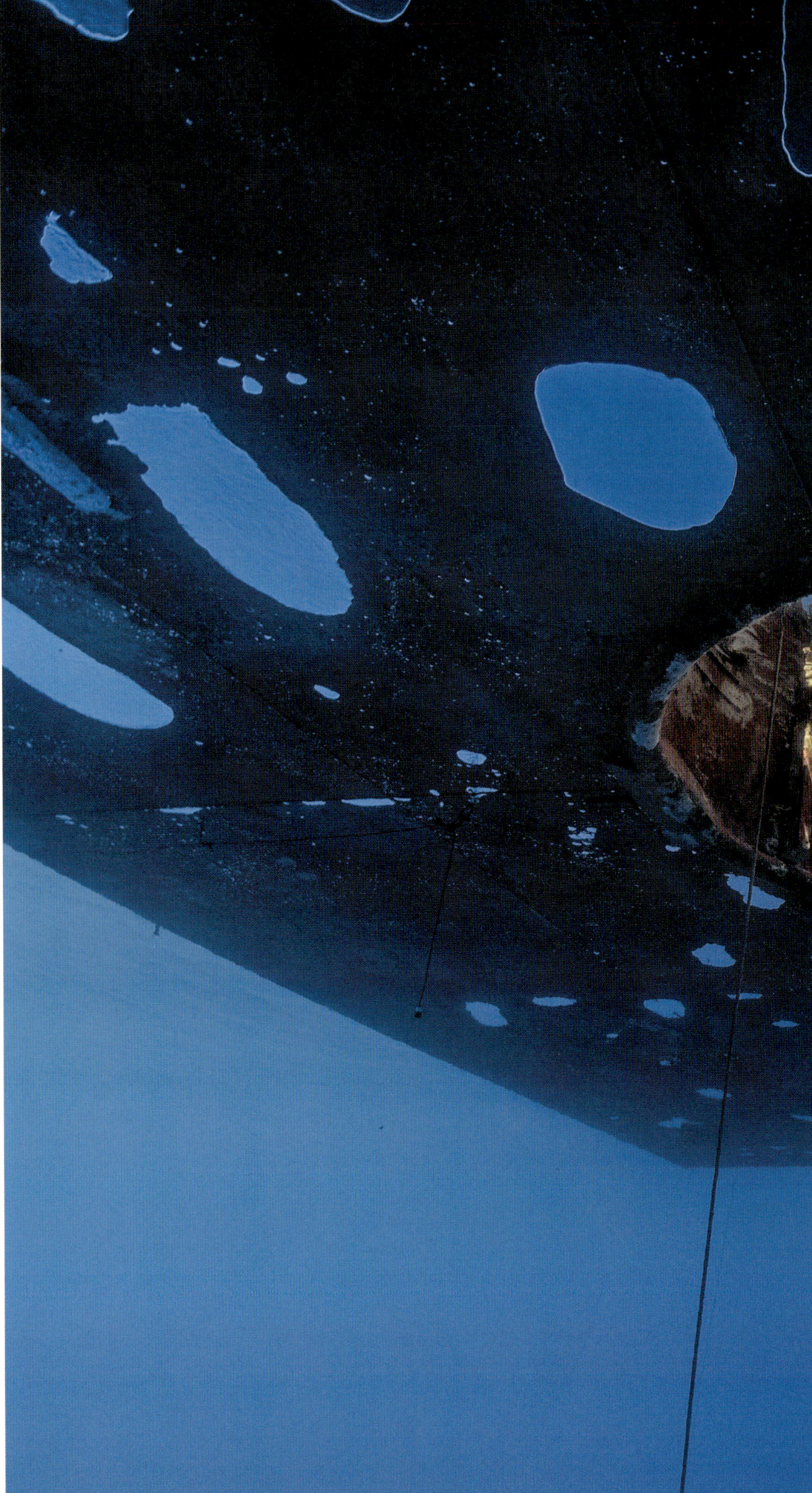

JORDI CHIAS, 2021
Crew member Cédric Gentil floats beneath an expedition barge in the Mediterranean Sea. He was part of a research team that lived in an enclosed, pressurized container for 28 days to continually dive the French Riviera, documenting unique cold-water reefs and evidence of human impacts.

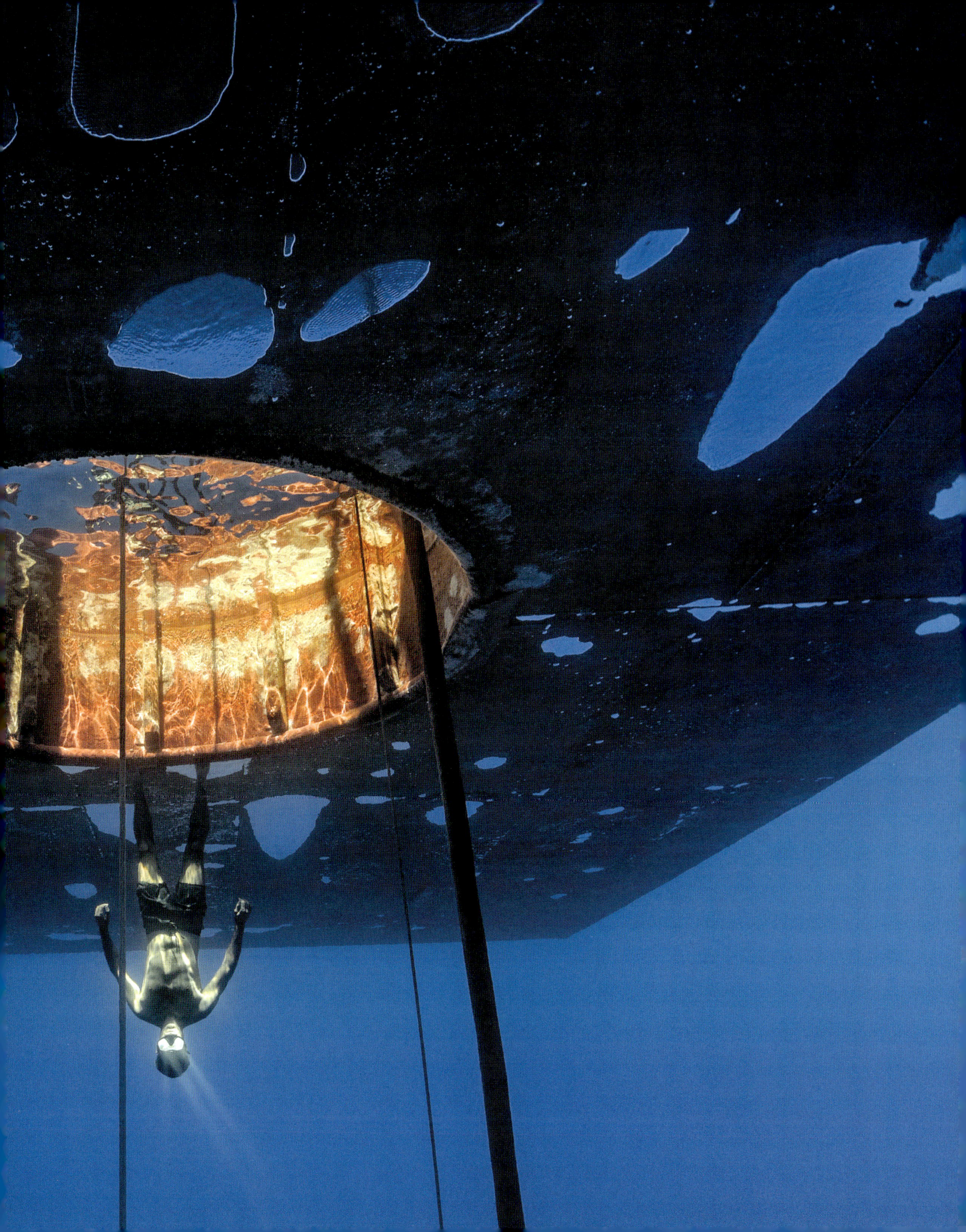

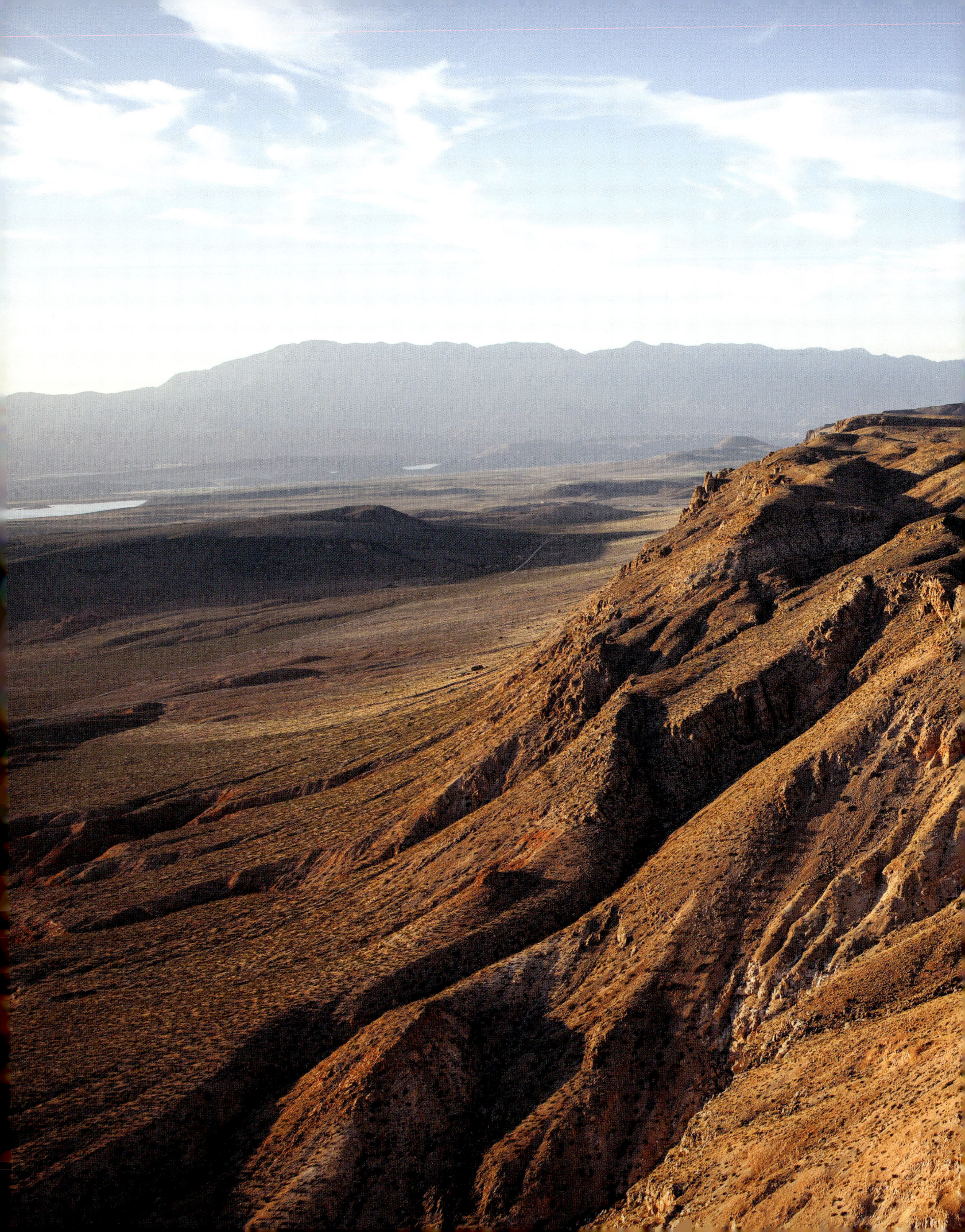

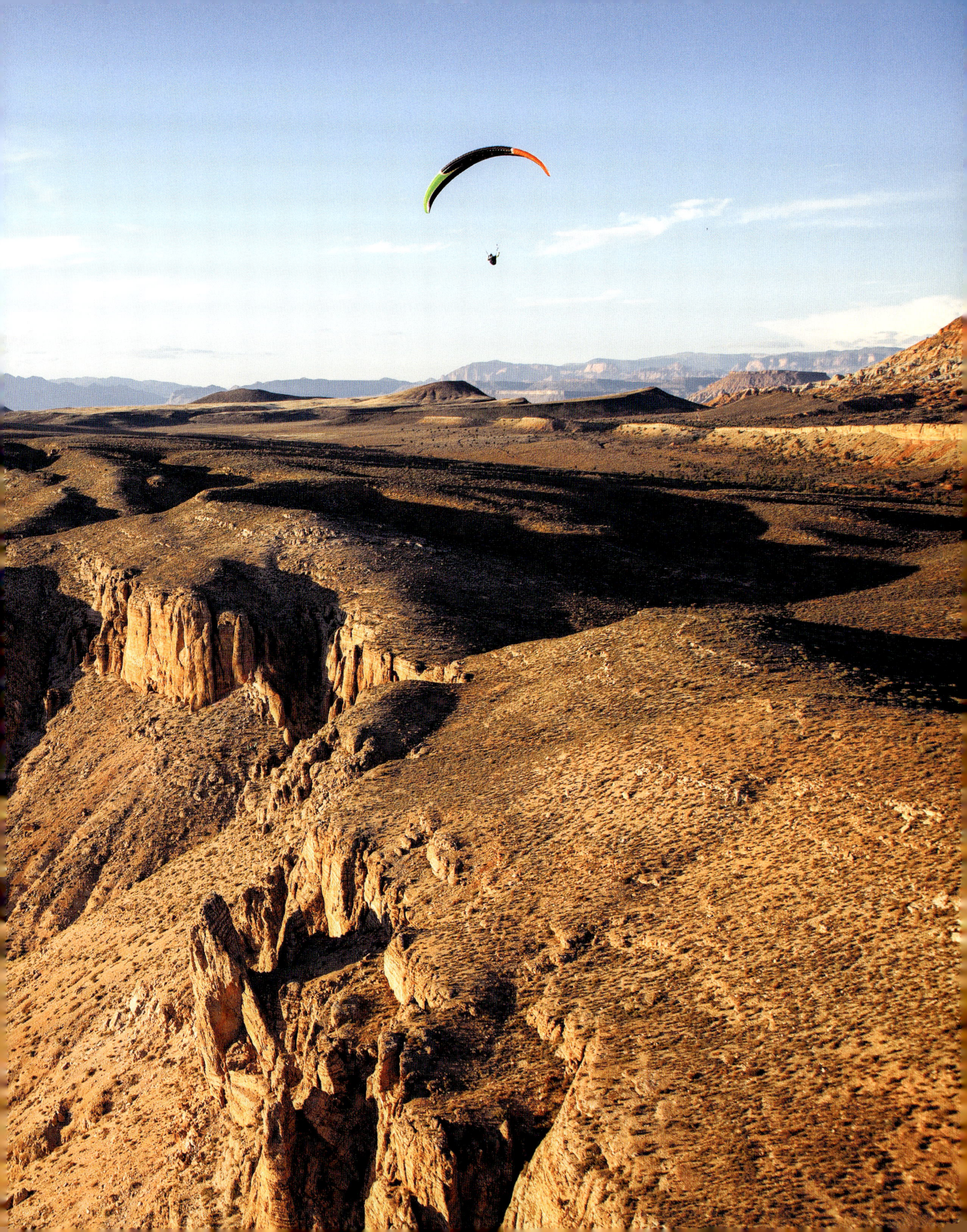

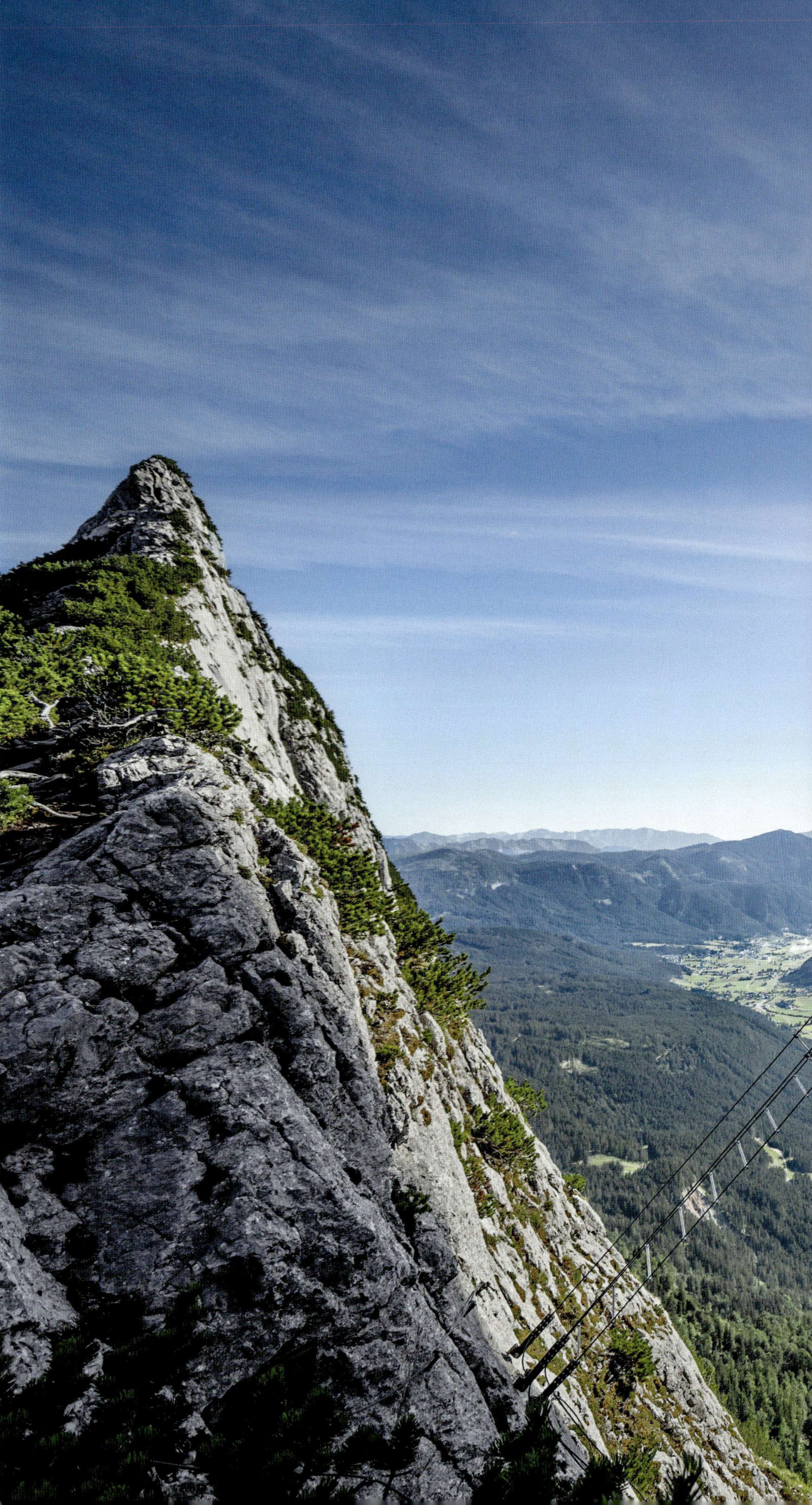

QUIN SCHROCK, 2021
A climber ascends the 130-foot-long Sky Ladder—also known as the "stairway to heaven"—on Austria's Grosser Donnerkogel mountain. The route was added to make the mountain more accessible to less advanced climbers.

PREVIOUS PAGES
JODY MACDONALD, 2013
A paraglider soars over southern Utah as part of a team attempting to fly 500 miles to Jackson Hole, Wyoming.

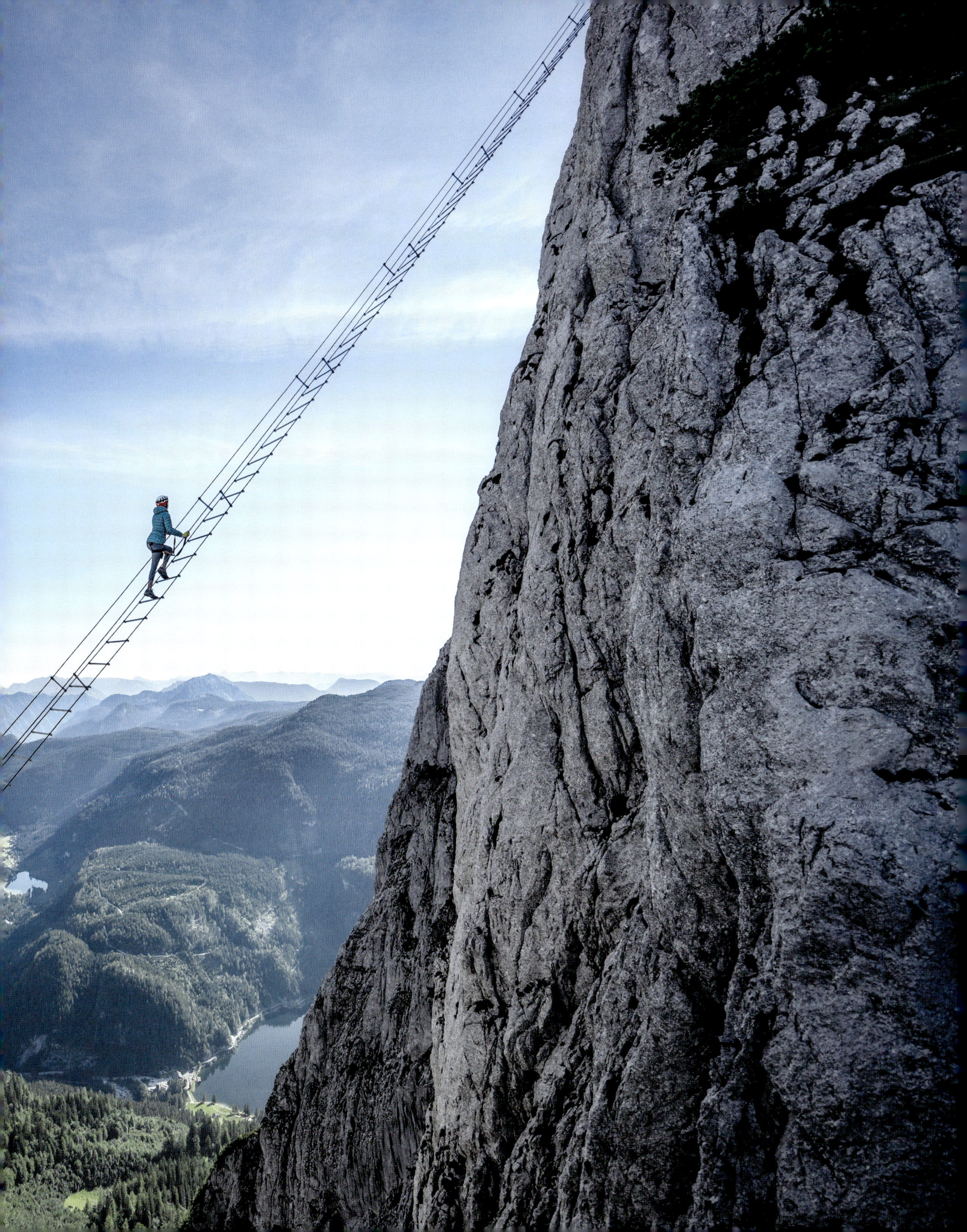

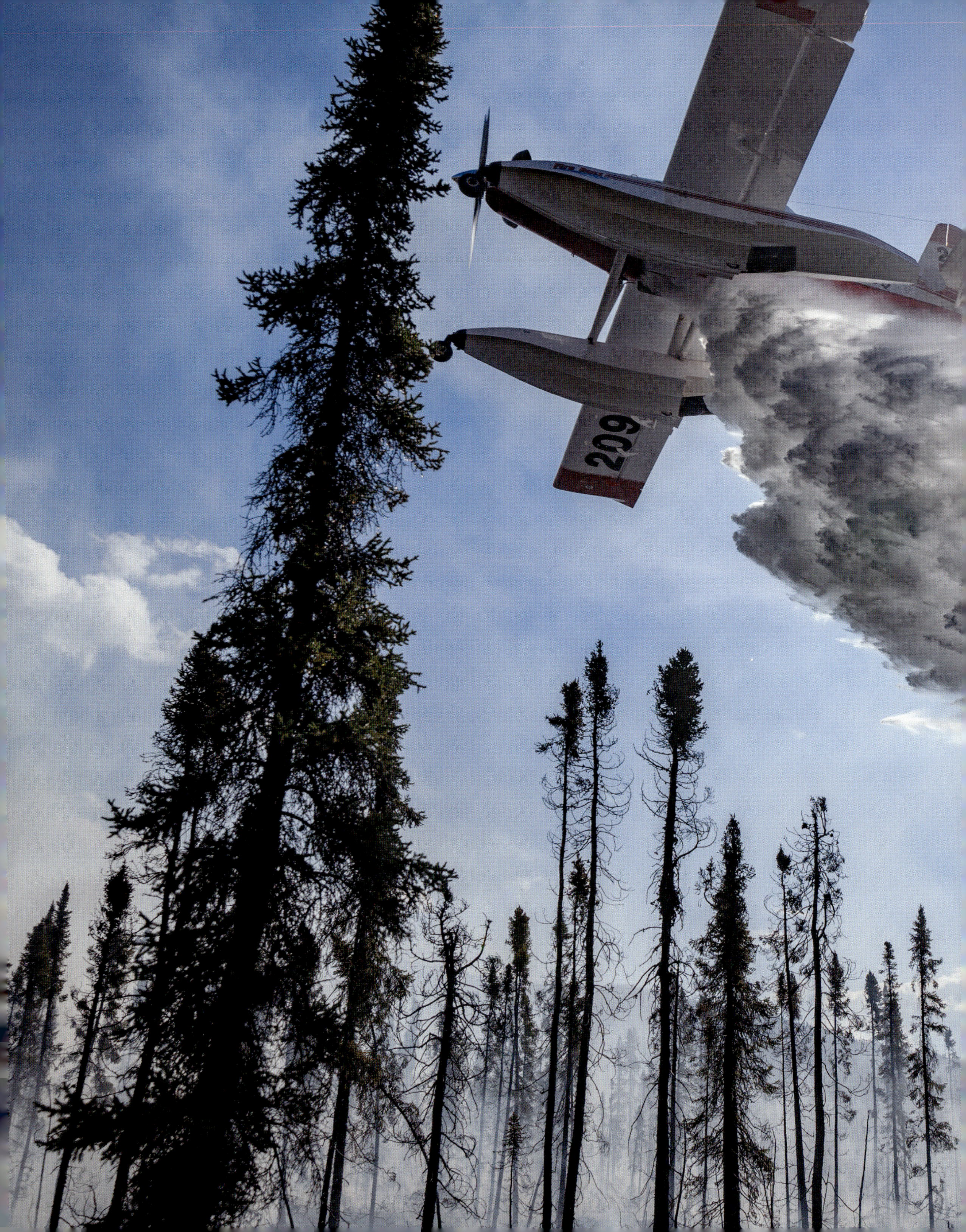
209

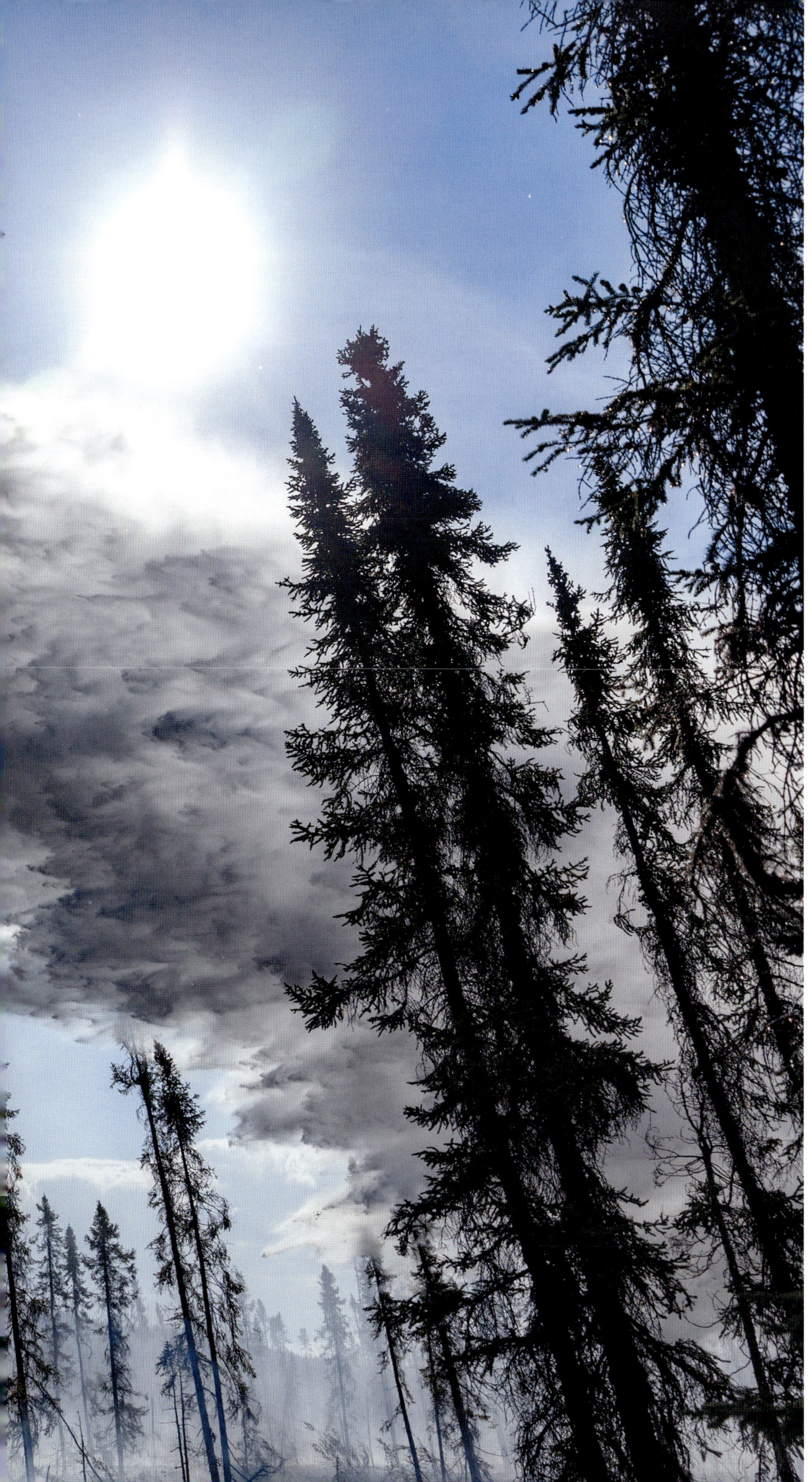

MARK THIESSEN, 2016
A Fire Boss plane dumps 800 gallons of water from its pontoons to aid a ground crew fighting a wildfire—the result of a lightning strike—in the Brooks Range, Alaska.

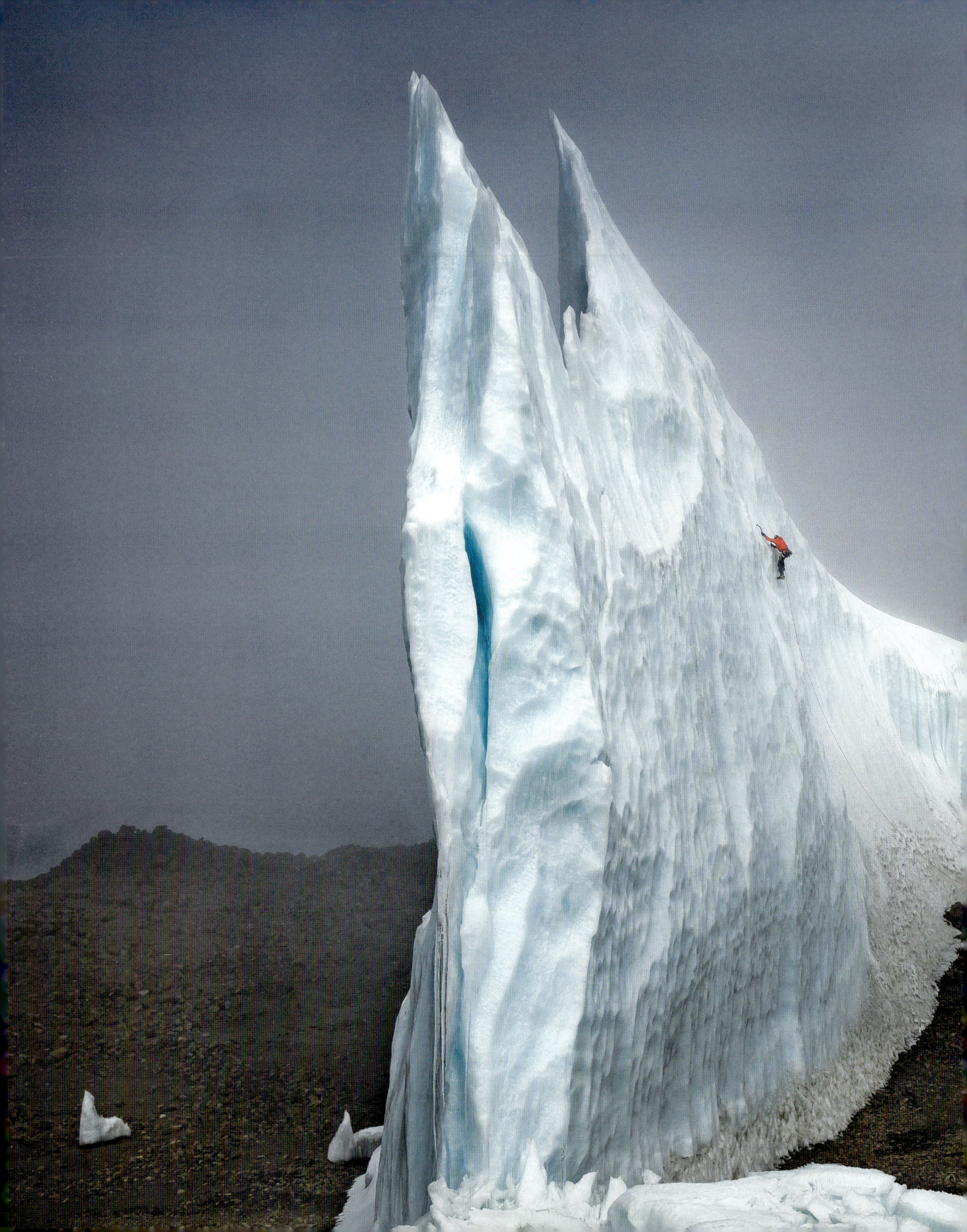

CHRISTIAN PONDELLA, 2020
A climber ascends a stand-alone tower of ice on Mount Kilimanjaro in Tanzania. Glaciers on the mountain's western side can rise 100 feet.

CARSTEN PETER

FOR CARSTEN PETER, a life on the edge—of a glacier in Greenland, an erupting volcano in the Canary Islands, a tornado in South Dakota—is a means to an end, not the end itself. Risk is to be managed; the point is to find out and be fascinated. "It's not like I'm actively looking for danger. I want to show people the wonders of nature," he explains.

That sense of curiosity has been embedded from the start. When Peter was 15, his parents drove him from Munich, where the family lived, to see Sicily's celebrated Mount Etna because he was infatuated with volcanoes. But to his disappointment, Etna was in a quiescent phase. Later, Peter experienced active volcanoes by descending into the craters themselves, where he would feel the rumble and pulse of the earth. "It's a magic place to be," he has said. But because of the danger—scalding lava, toxic gases—it's also "a big cat-and-mouse game where you don't want to be caught."

Peter's photography is also about problem-solving: how to light a cave interior; how to make pictures by the searing heat of a lava lake; how to address the condensation caused by changing temperatures in a cave. Then there are challenges like avoiding the debris of a volcanic eruption, eluding toxic gases—and navigating the unpredictability of a killer tornado. Peter spent 12 years tracking tornadoes with legendary storm chaser Tim Samaras, who was killed by a twister in 2013. Peter had been invited to join Samaras on that trip but was finishing a book and couldn't break away. "The cosmos shattered," he says of the tragedy that killed his close friend.

Peter has received many honors for his work, including the National Geographic Photographer's Photographer Award, two World Press Awards, and an Emmy. But in the end, it's not about accolades.

"The world is so big and these are such little corners I explore," he says. "But there is so much more." His quest continues.

OPPOSITE TOP
CARSTEN PETER, 2021
Molten rock rains down from La Palma's Cumbre Vieja ridge in the Canary Islands, after exploding nearly 2,000 feet into the sky.

OPPOSITE BOTTOM
CARSTEN PETER, 2021
The Cumbre Vieja eruption was one of the most destructive in 500 years for the Canary Islands.

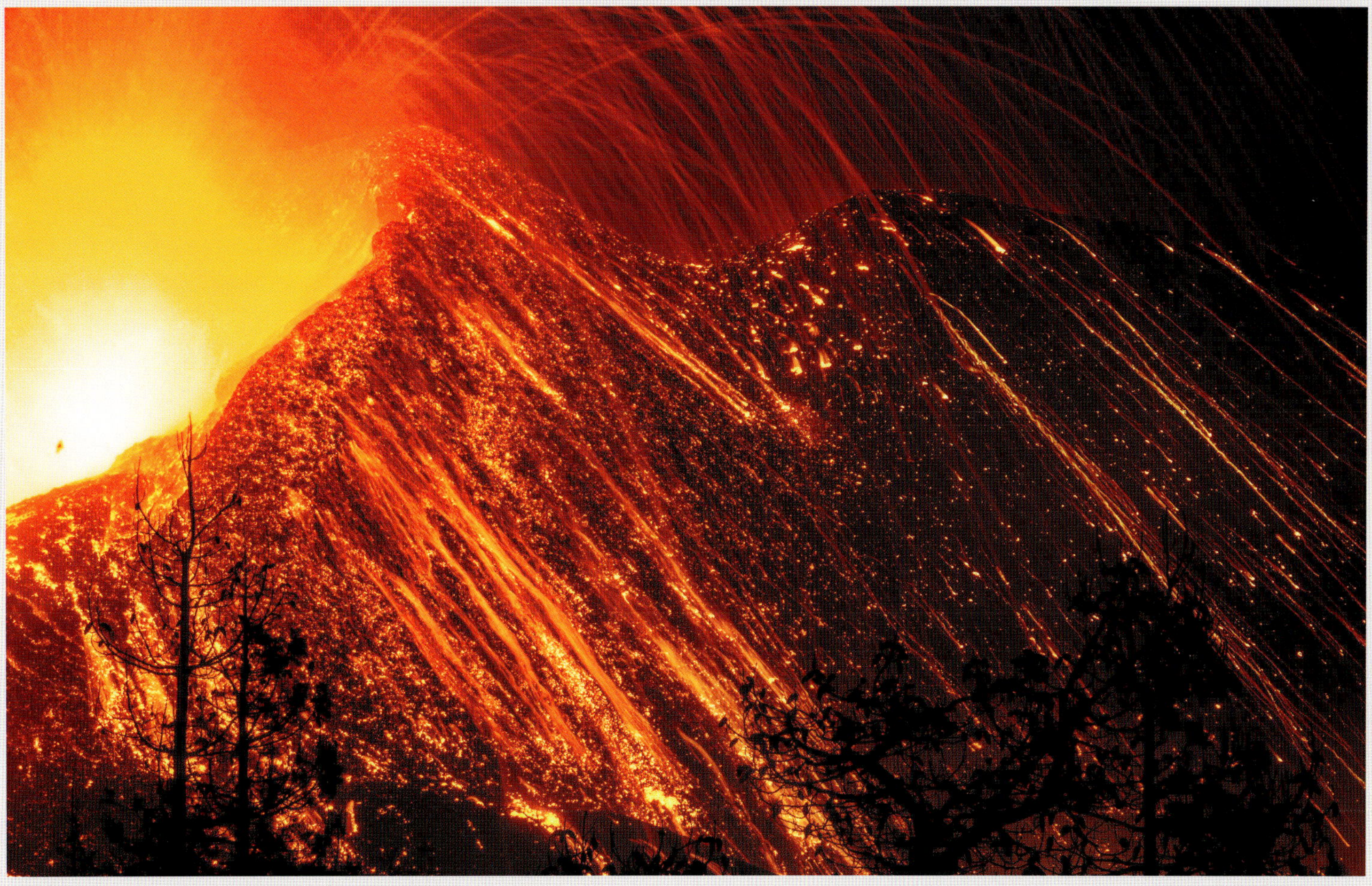

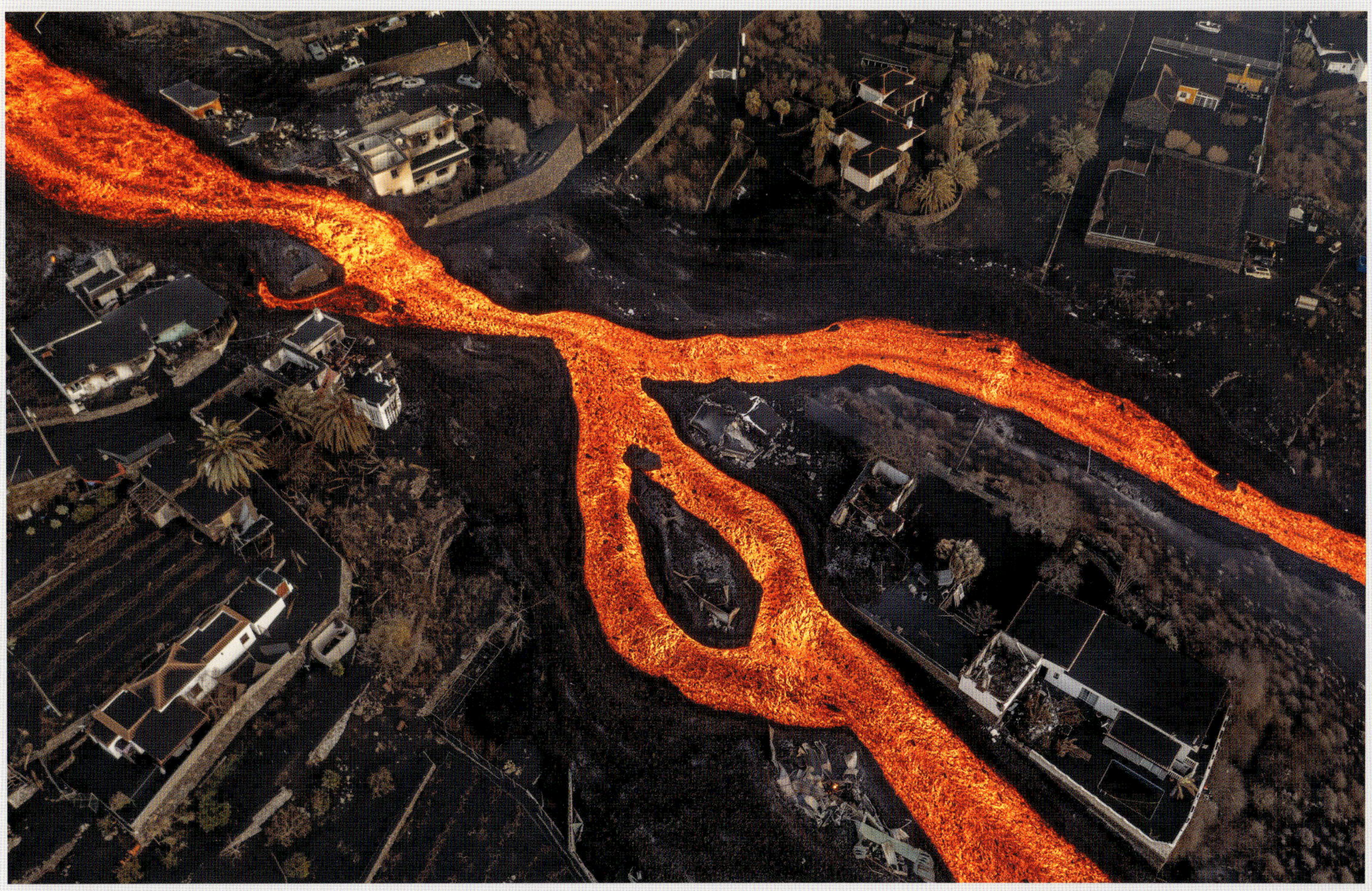

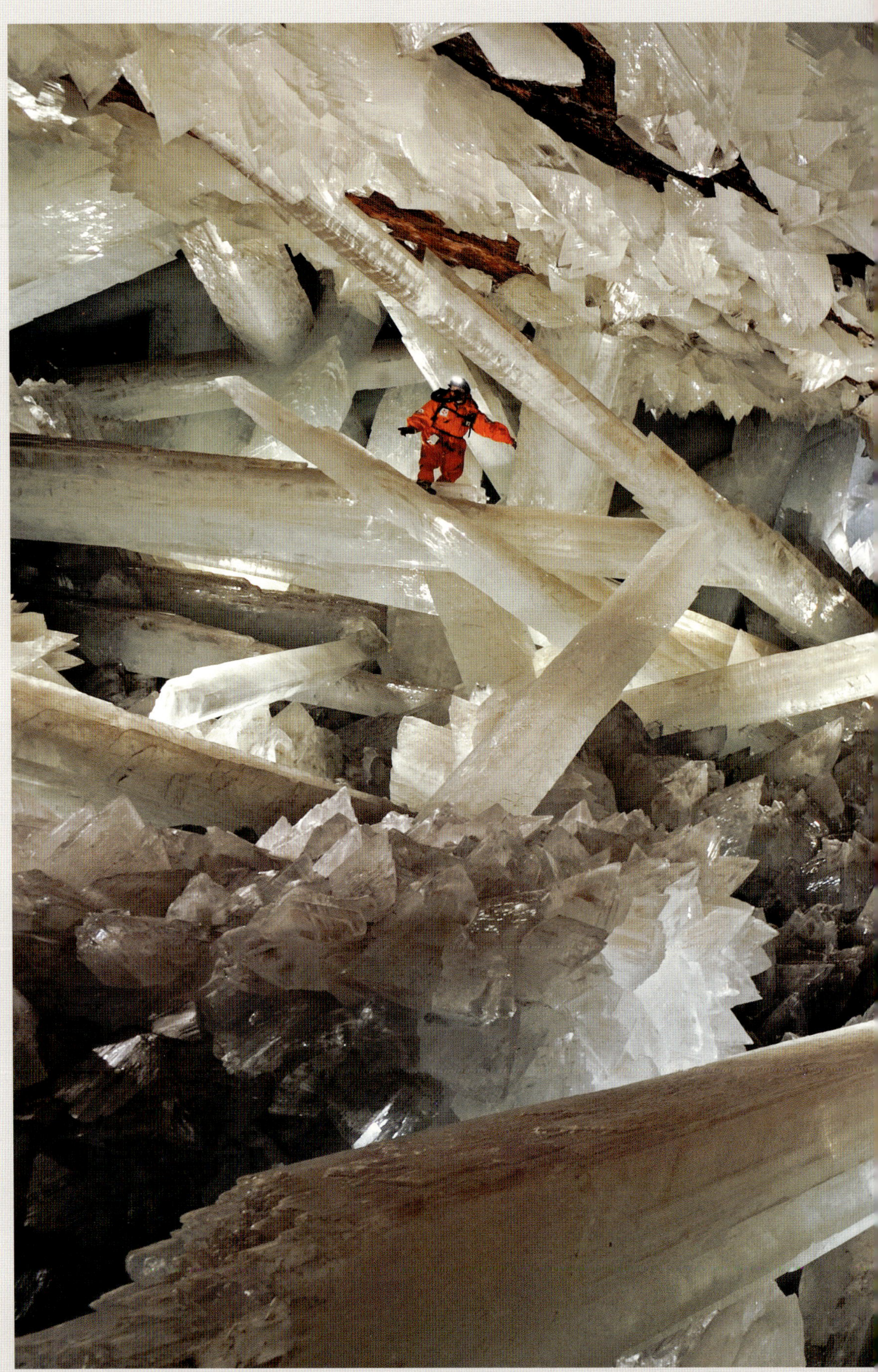

CARSTEN PETER, 2007
Intrepid explorers navigate enormous beams of selenite in Mexico's Cave of Crystals below the Chihuahuan Desert.

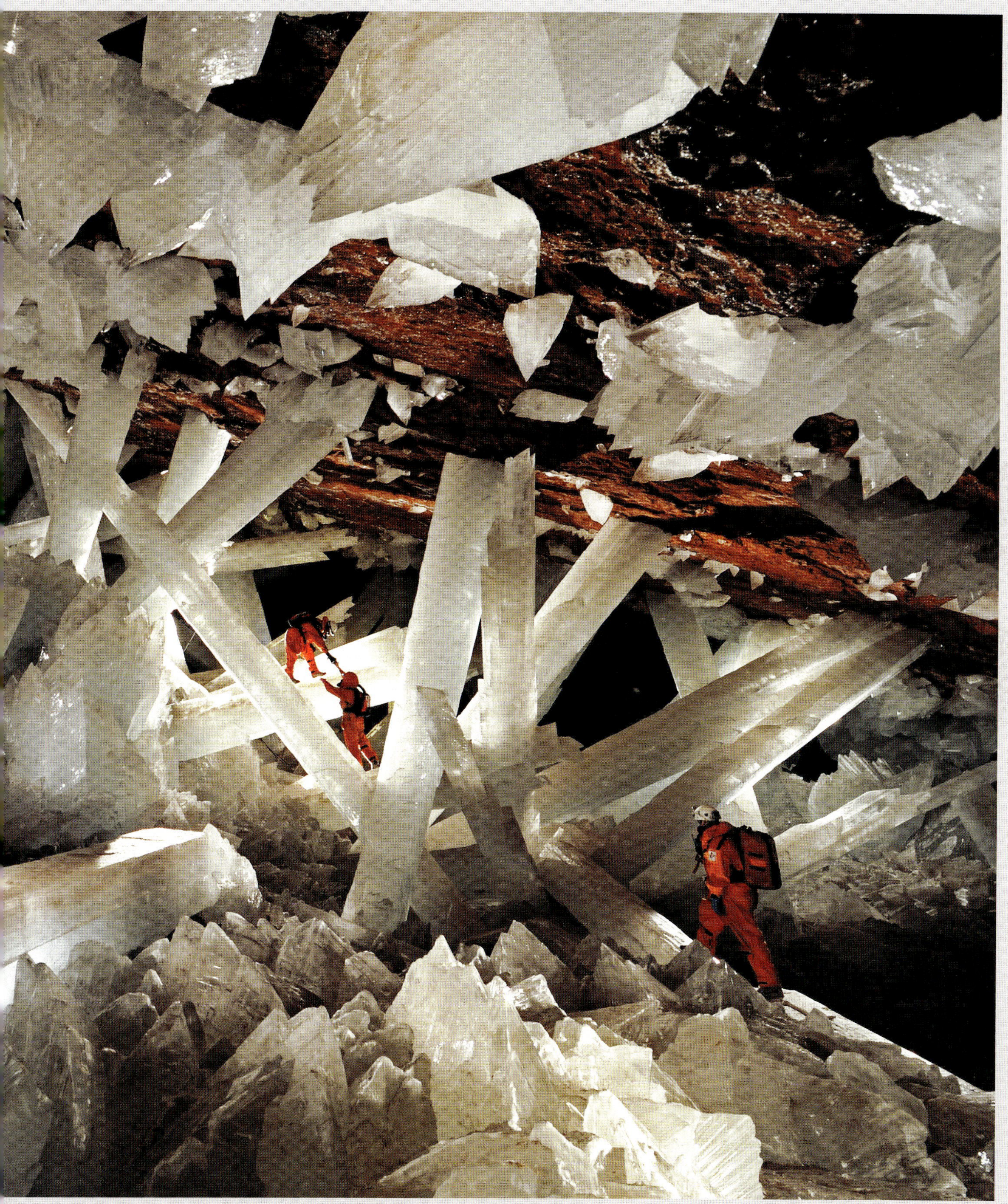

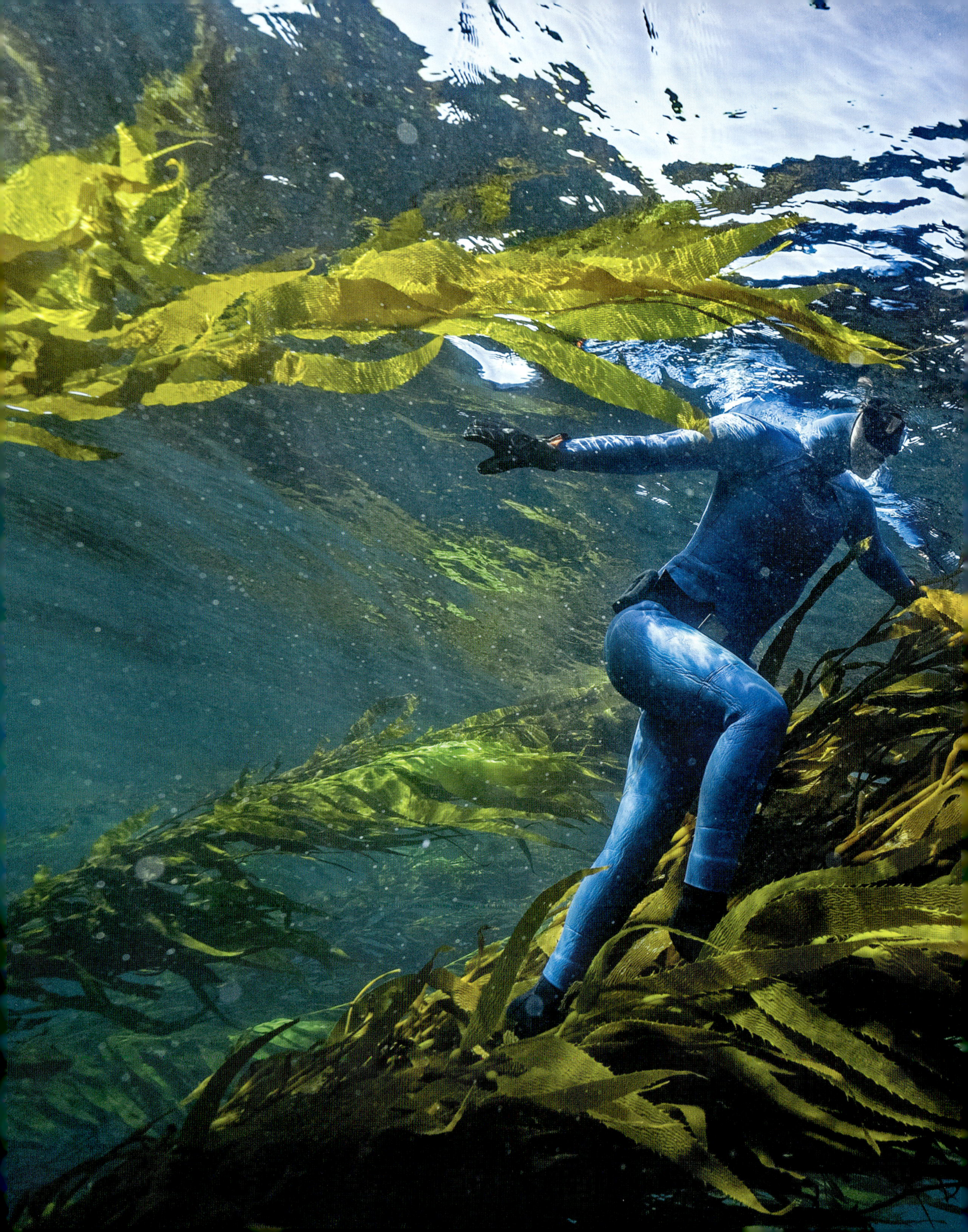

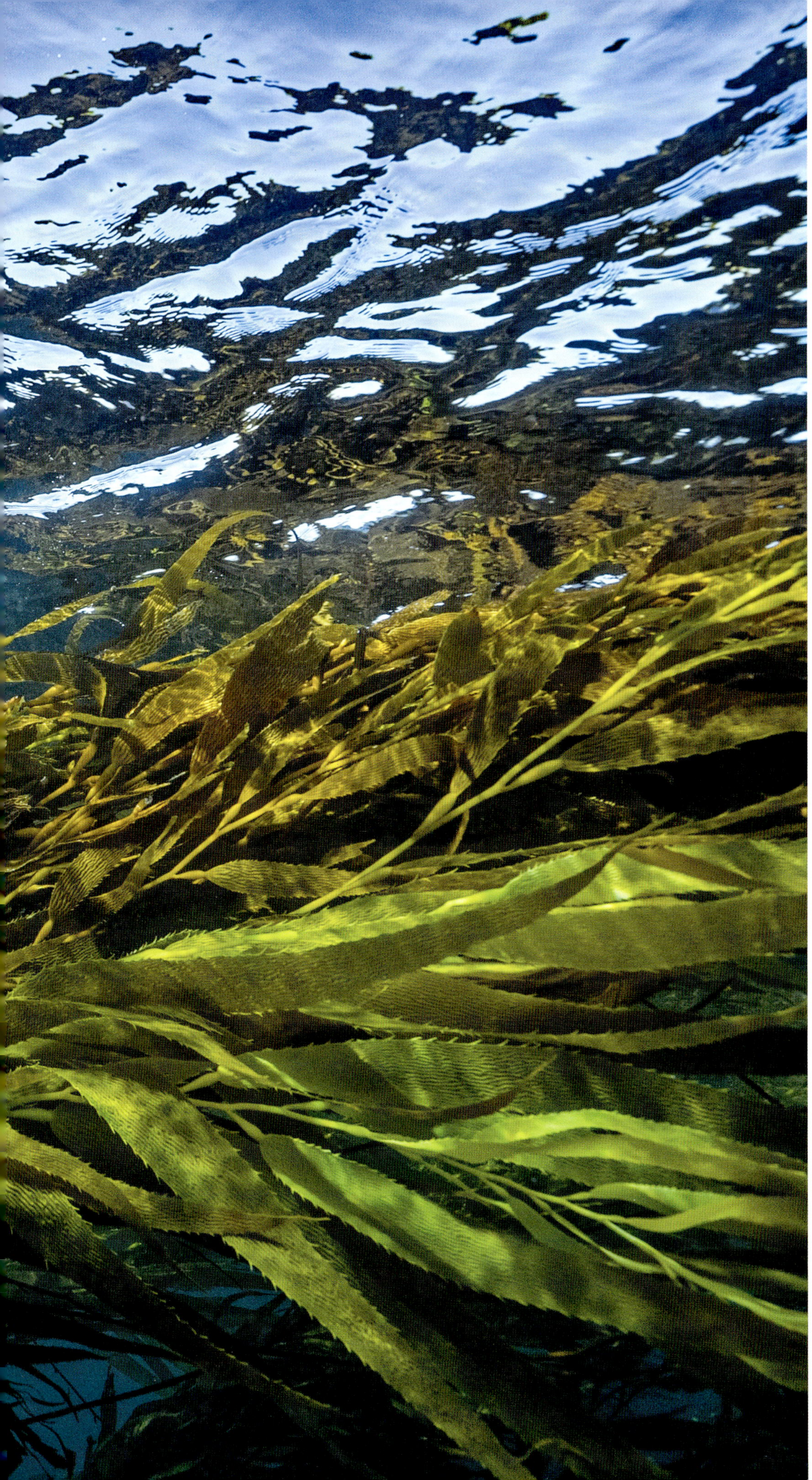

MARIA LAURA BABAHEKIAN, 2022
Camila Jaber, a Mexican free diver, explores an Argentine kelp forest to determine its potential as an air-cleaning carbon sink.

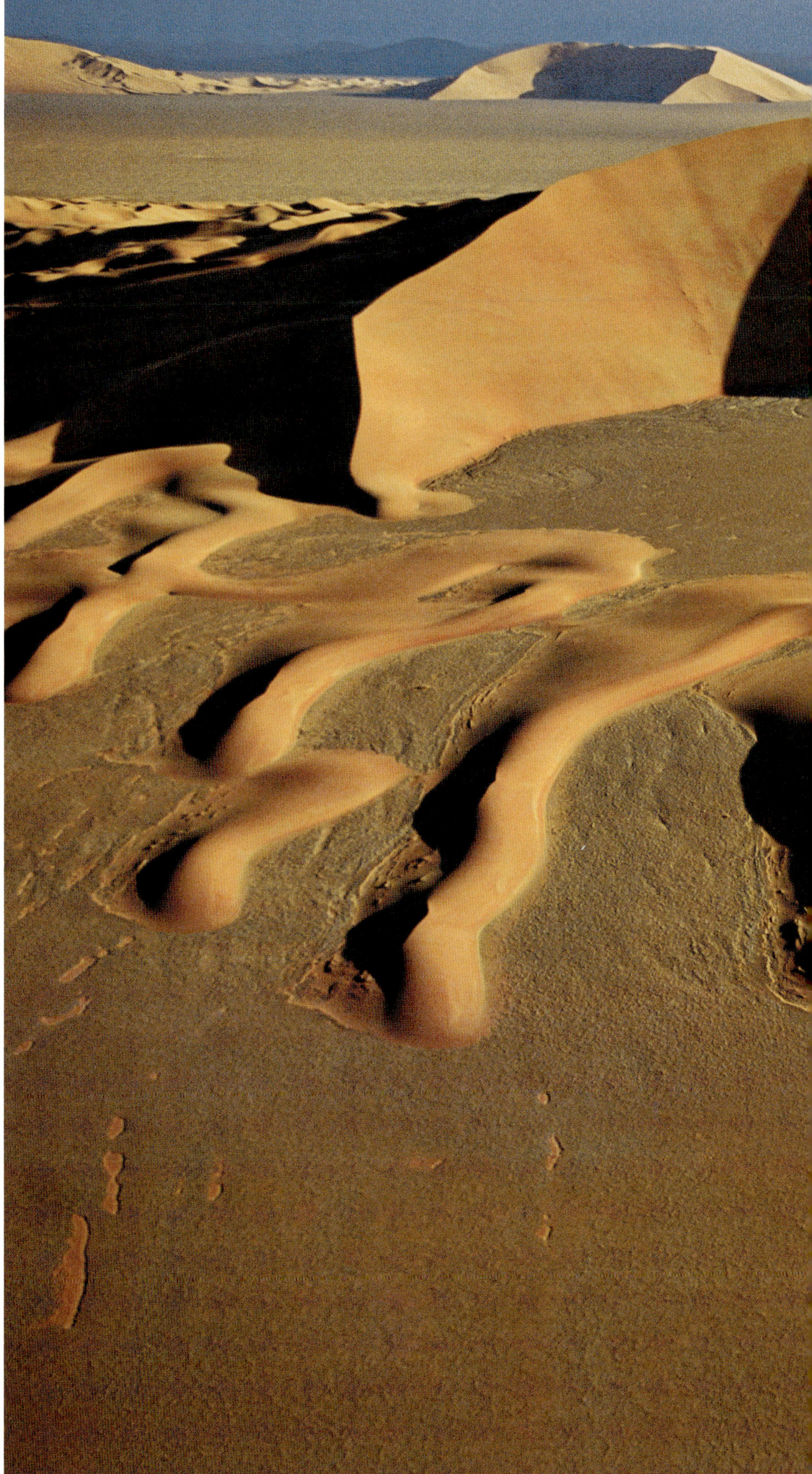

GEORGE STEINMETZ, 2012
A star dune towers over younger dunes in the Rub' al Khali, or Empty Quarter, a desert encompassing 250,000 square miles in the southern third of the Arabian Peninsula.

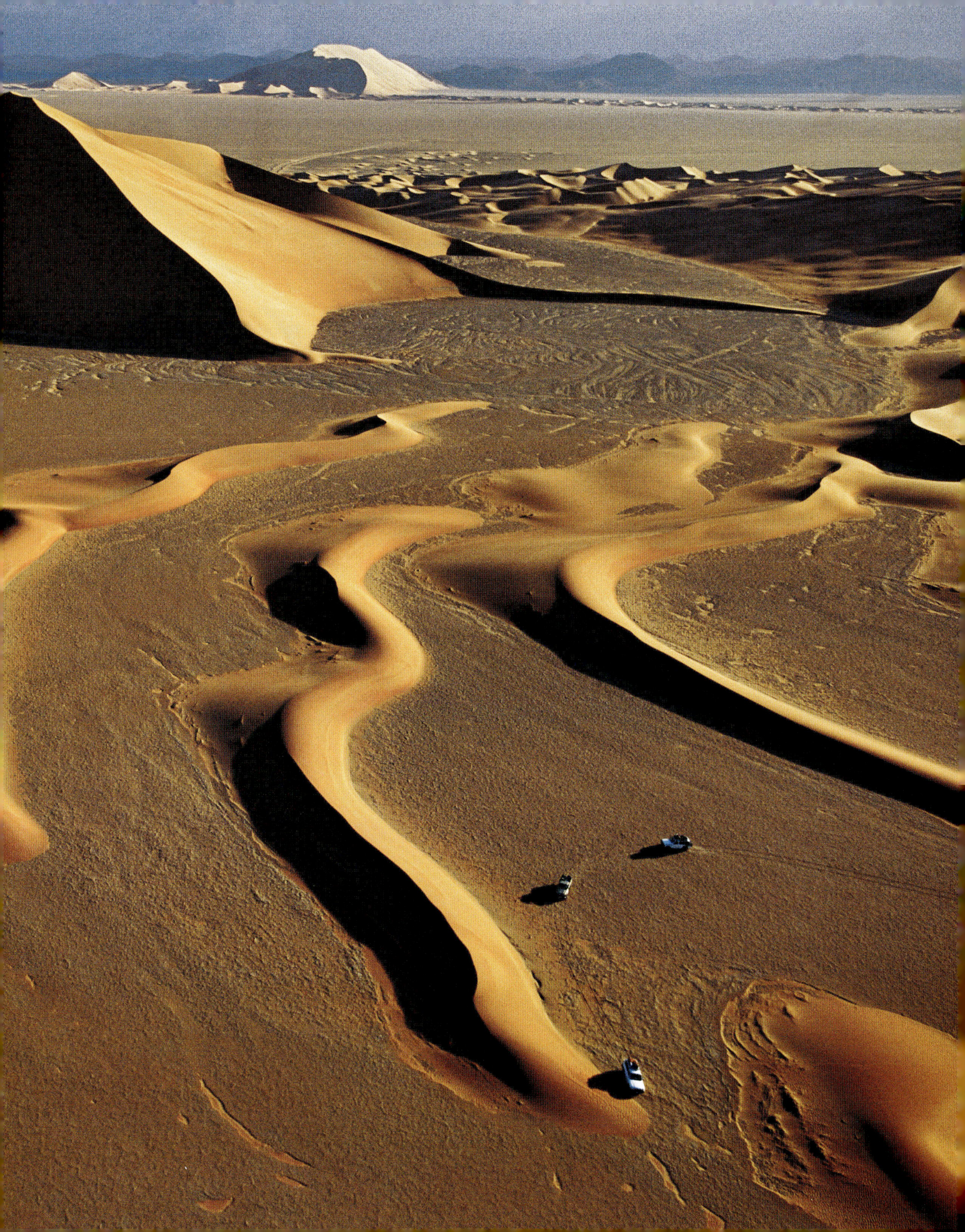

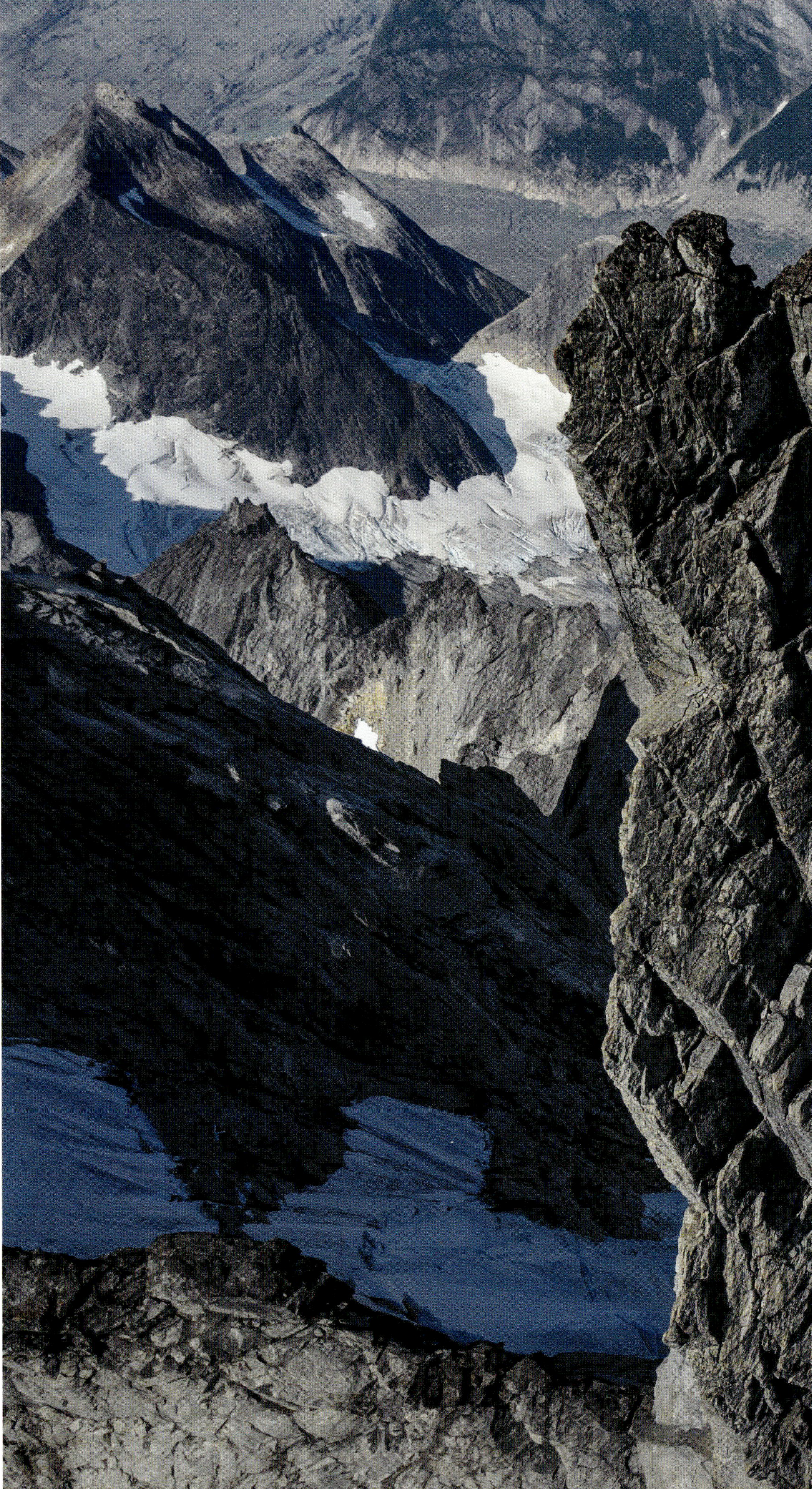

MATT PYCROFT, 2024
Climbers Tommy Caldwell and Alex Honnold ascend Cats Ears, a double tower on the west face of Devils Thumb in Alaska. This was the first of five summits they would attempt to traverse in a single day.

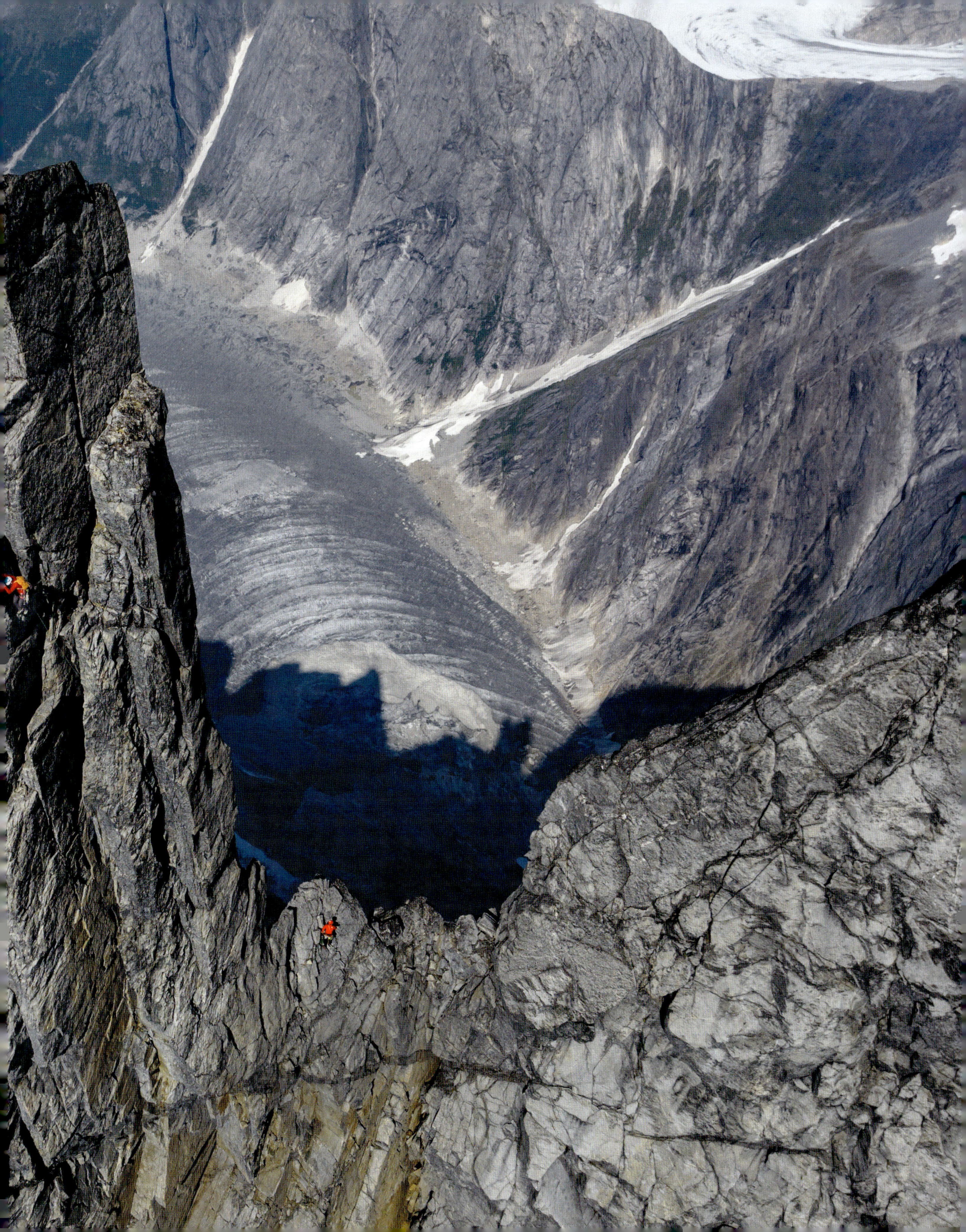

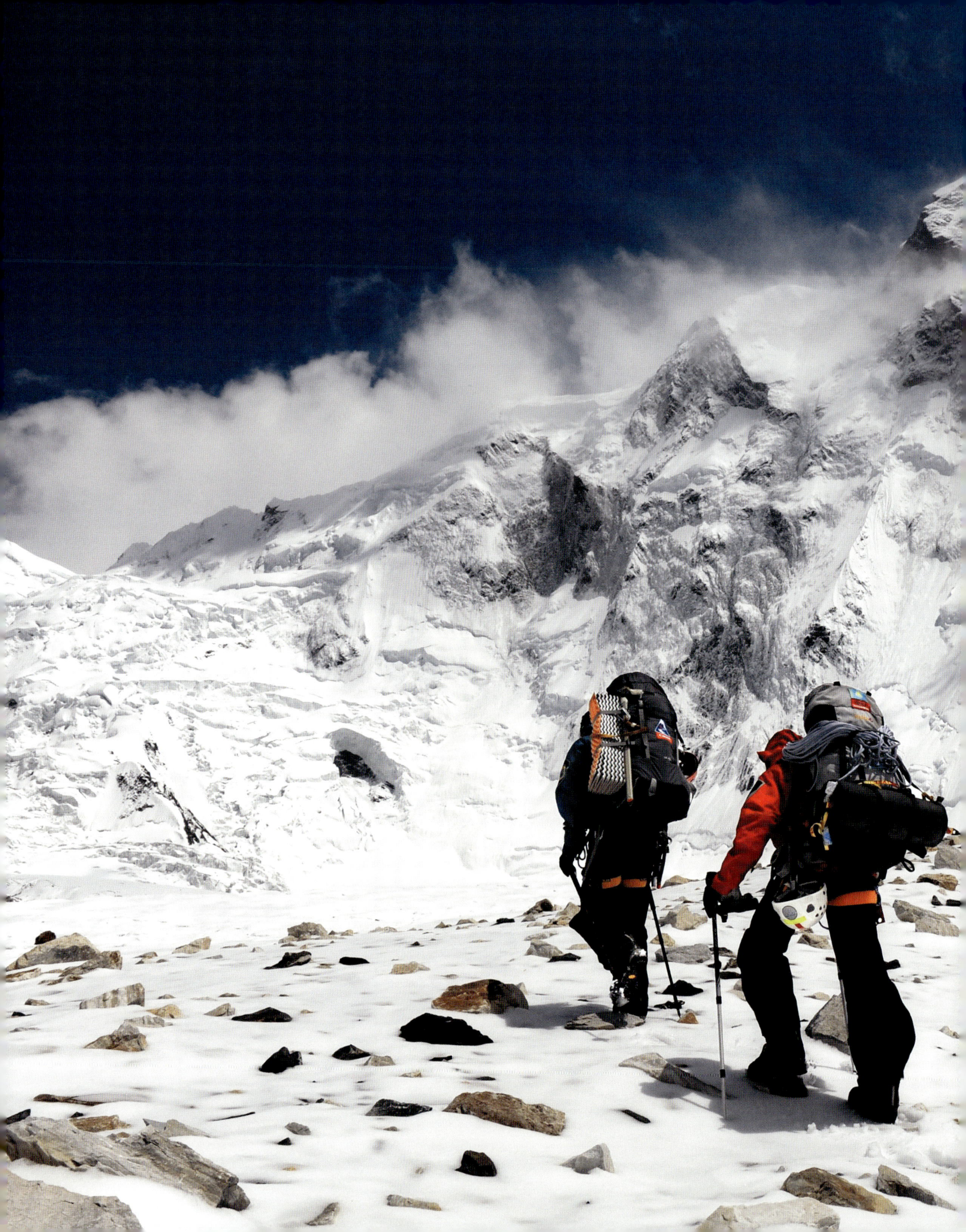

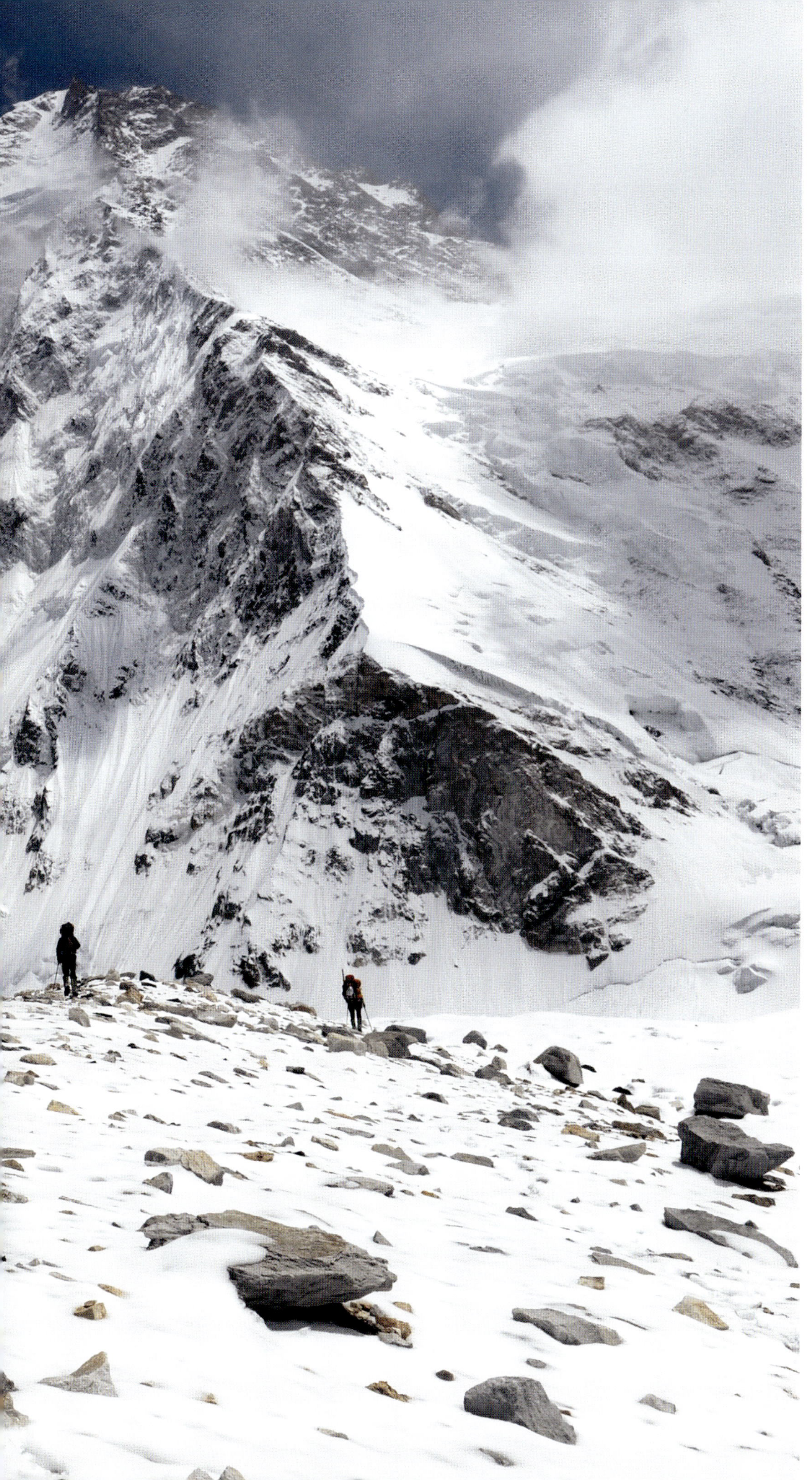

TOMMY HEINRICH, 2011
Climbers ascend the treacherous North Face of K2, the world's second highest mountain. On this climb, expedition leader Gerlinde Kaltenbrunner completed her quest to become the first woman to summit all 14 of the world's mountains higher than 8,000 meters in altitude without supplemental oxygen or high-altitude porters.

WITHOUT THE POSSIBILITY OF DEATH, ADVENTURE IS NOT POSSIBLE.

REINHOLD MESSNER, MOUNTAINEER

ROBERT E. PEARY, 1909

Although National Geographic initially ruled that the celebrated Arctic explorer Robert E. Peary—seen here in a self-portrait—was successful in his third attempt to reach the geographic North Pole in 1909, doubt shadowed its assessment. In 1988, National Geographic reexamined Peary's records and found his account to be inconclusive.

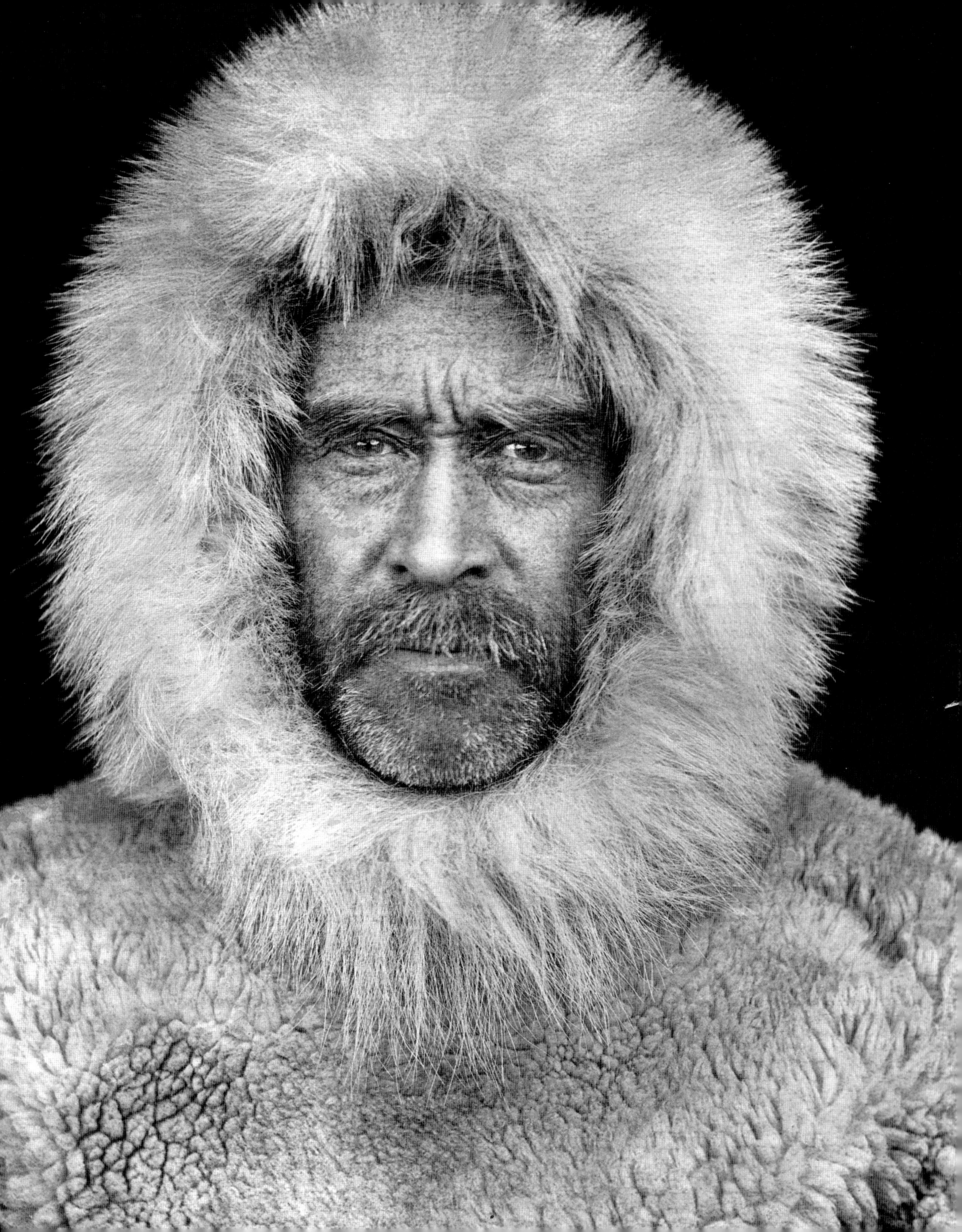

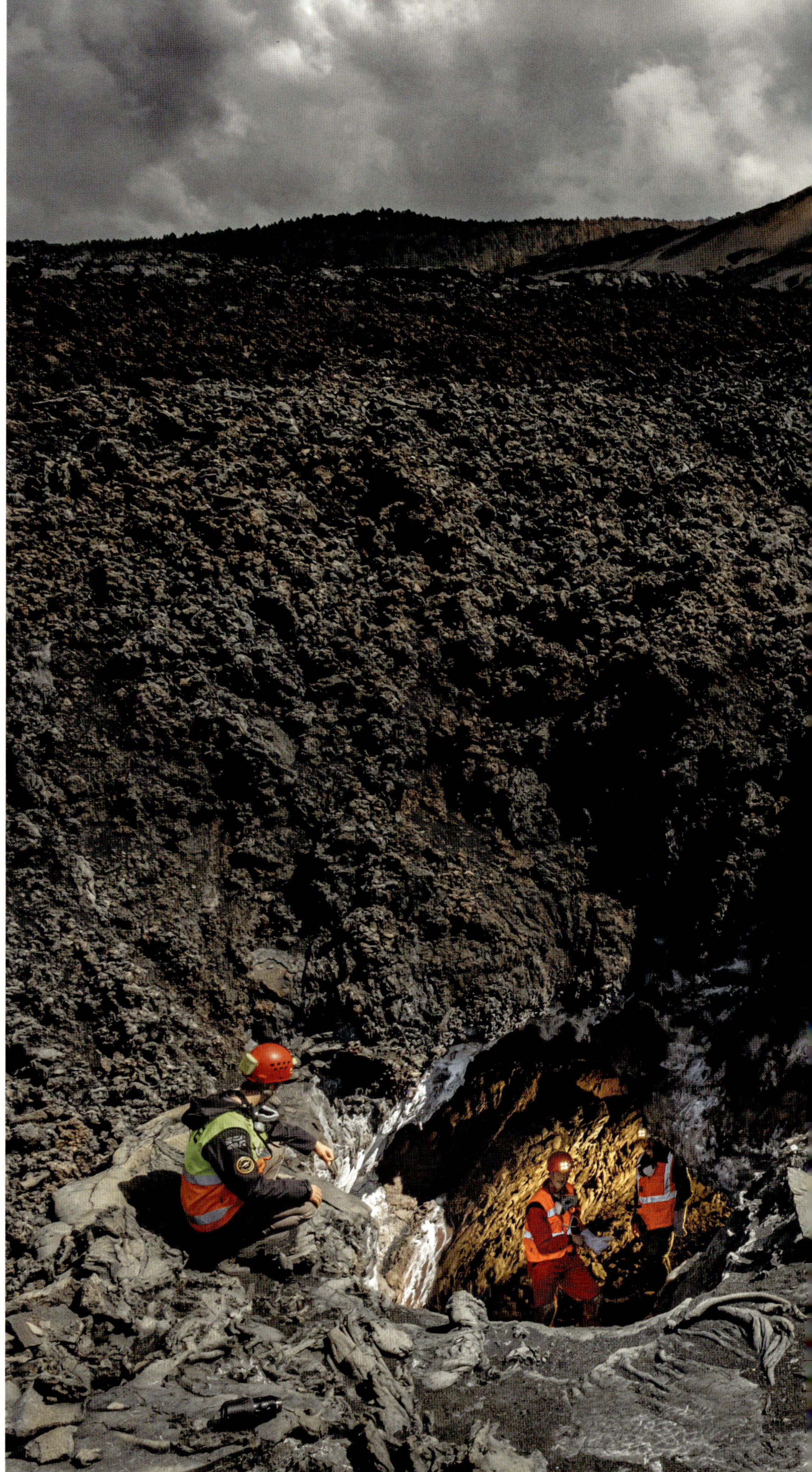

ARTURO RODRÍGUEZ, 2024
Cave specialists emerge from a lava tube produced by the Tajogaite volcano in El Paso, Spain. The tube opening registers about 140°F.

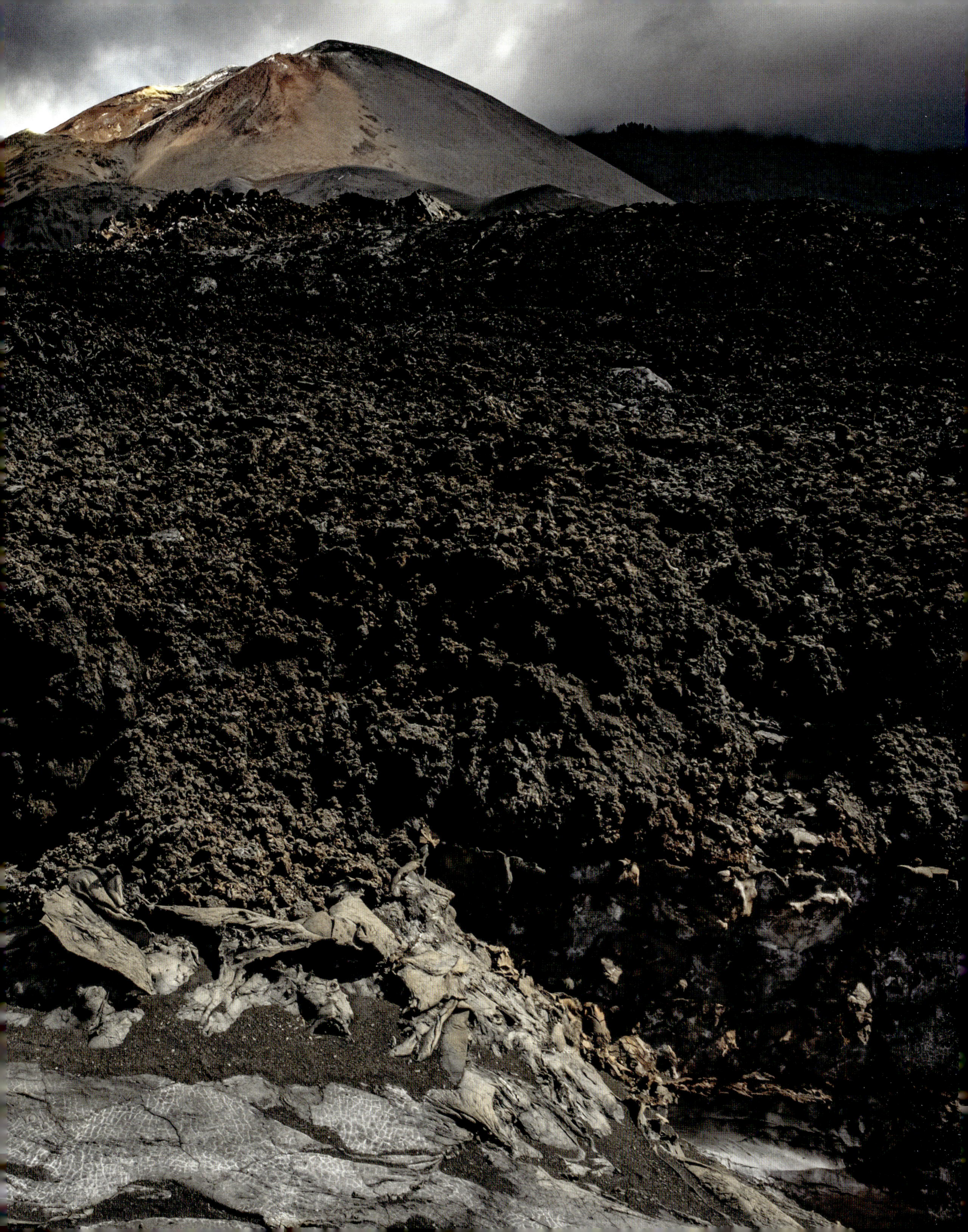

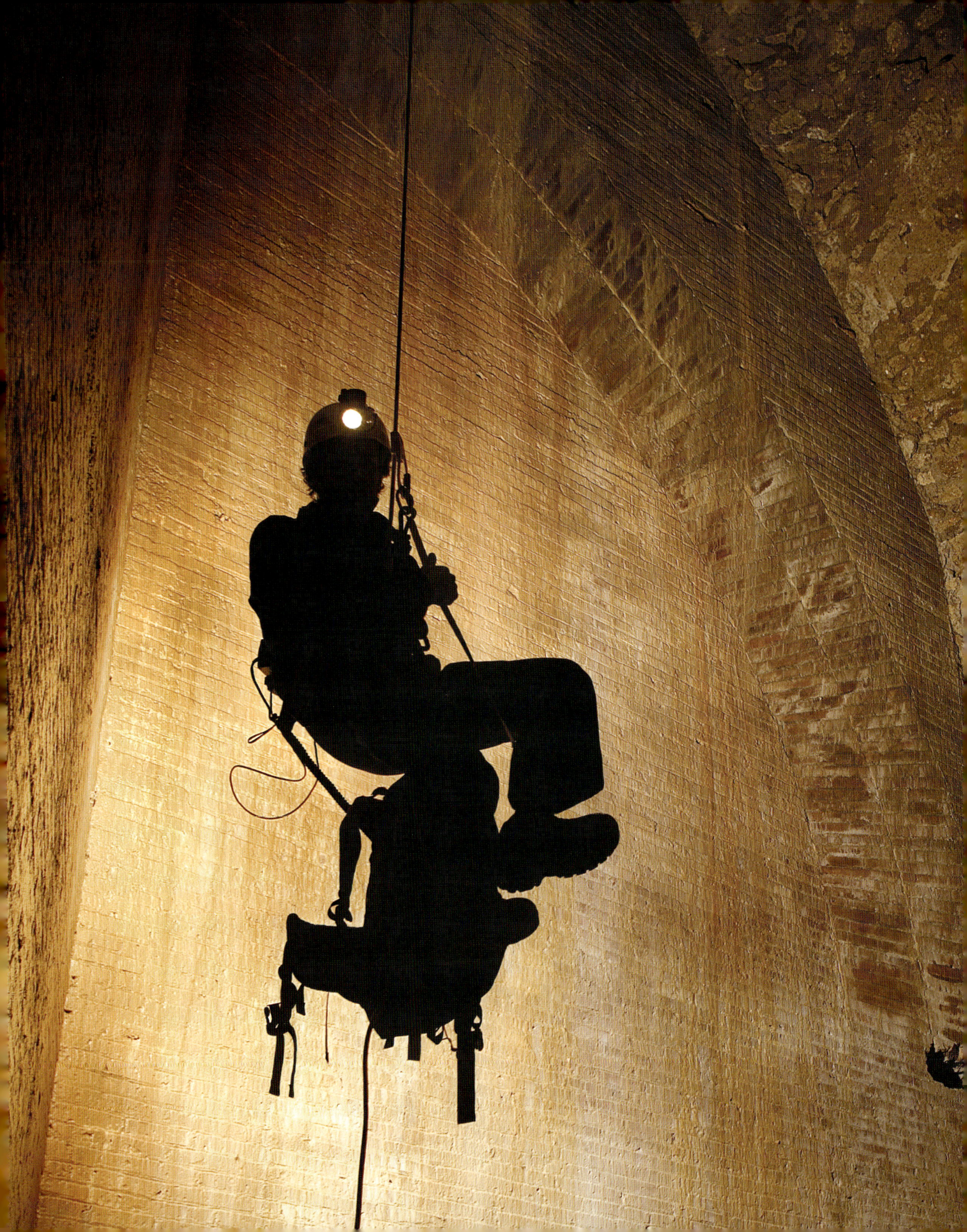

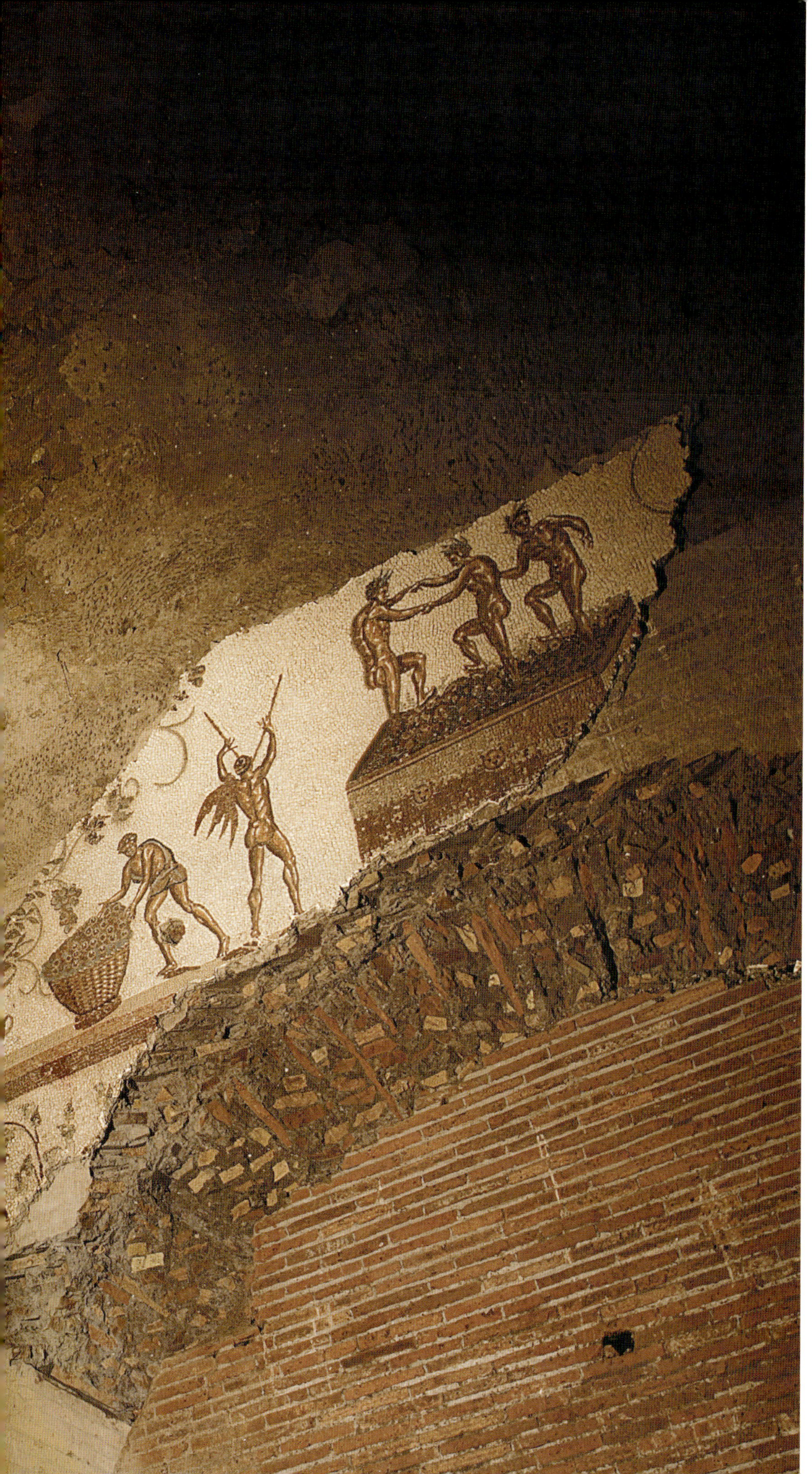

STEPHEN ALVAREZ, 2006
Two stories beneath a Roman hillside, urban speleologist Adriano Morabito examines a 2,000-year-old mosaic depicting a grape harvest. Researchers have found countless ancient artifacts while exploring Rome's centuries-old drainage system.

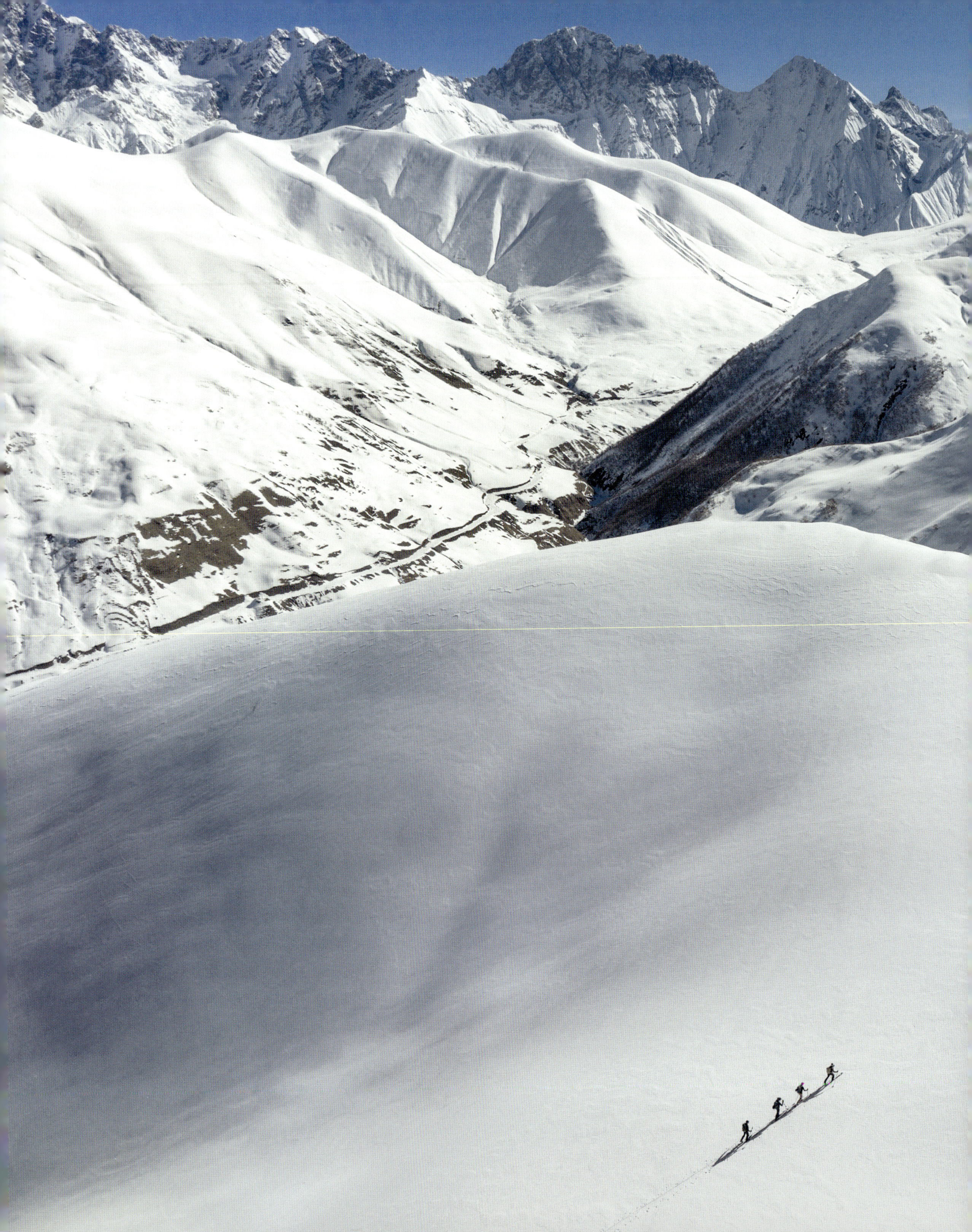

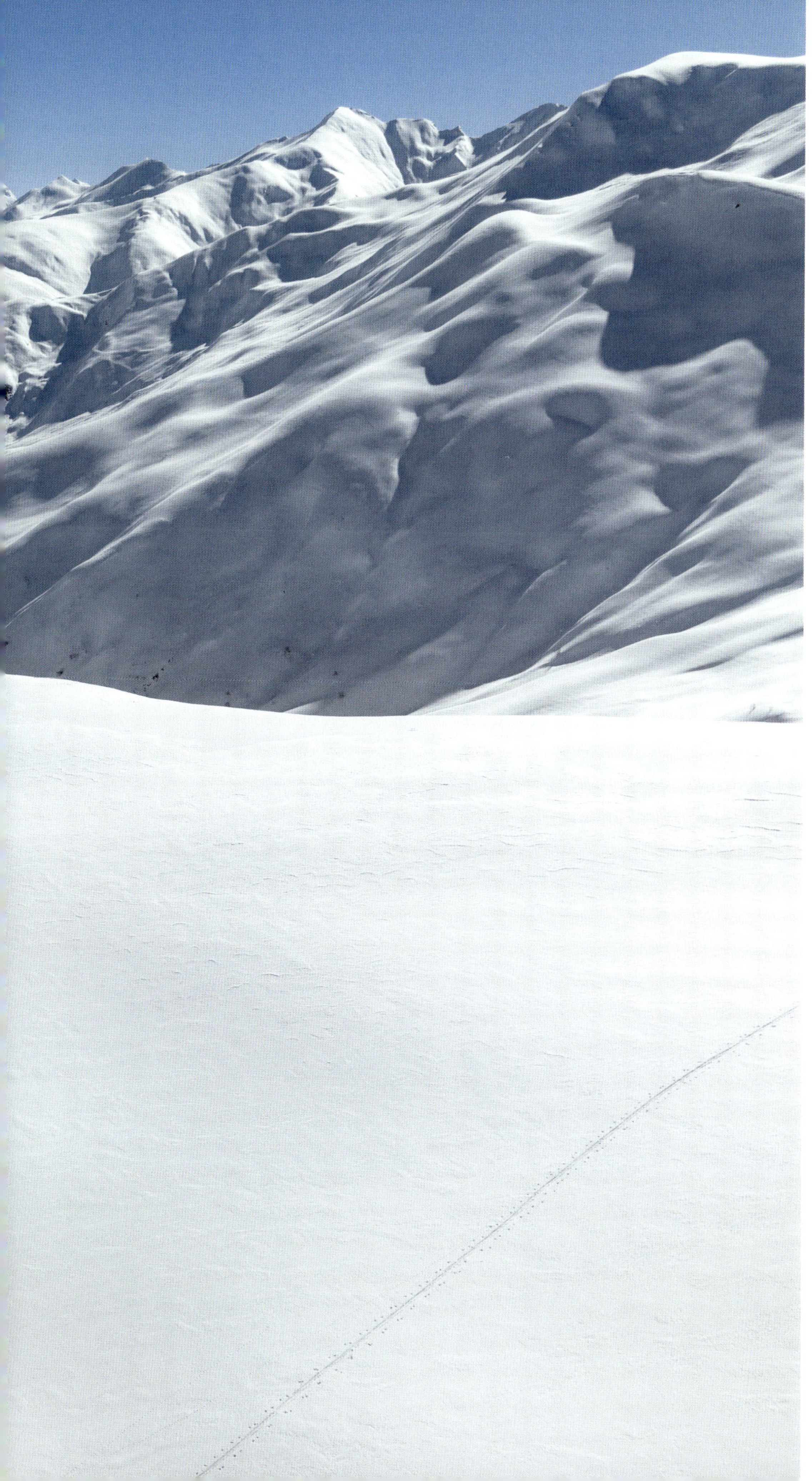

CIRIL JAZBEC, 2023
Backcountry skiers travel through Gvibari Pass in the Georgian Caucasus Mountains. The nearby village of Ushguli is the highest inhabited point in Europe.

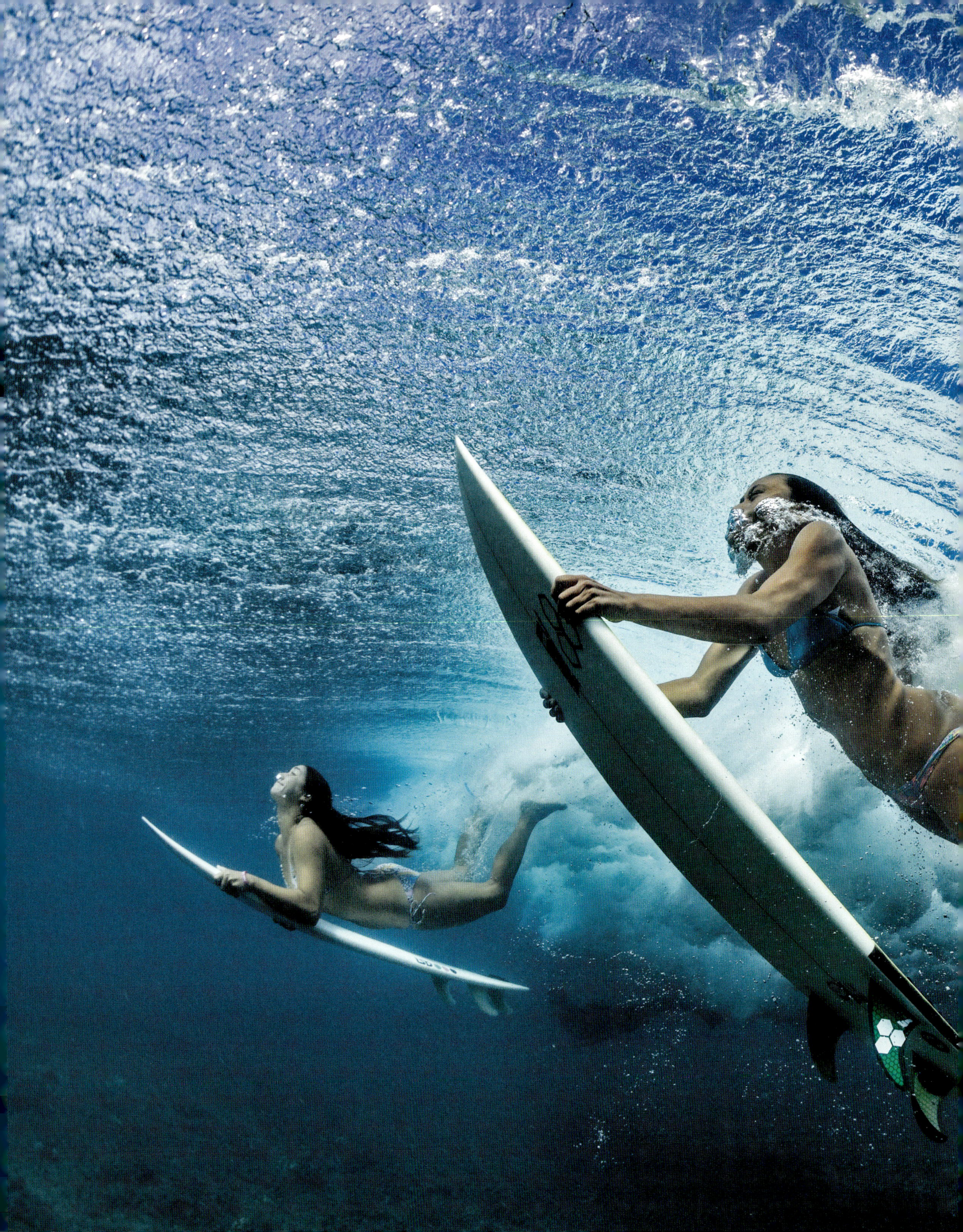

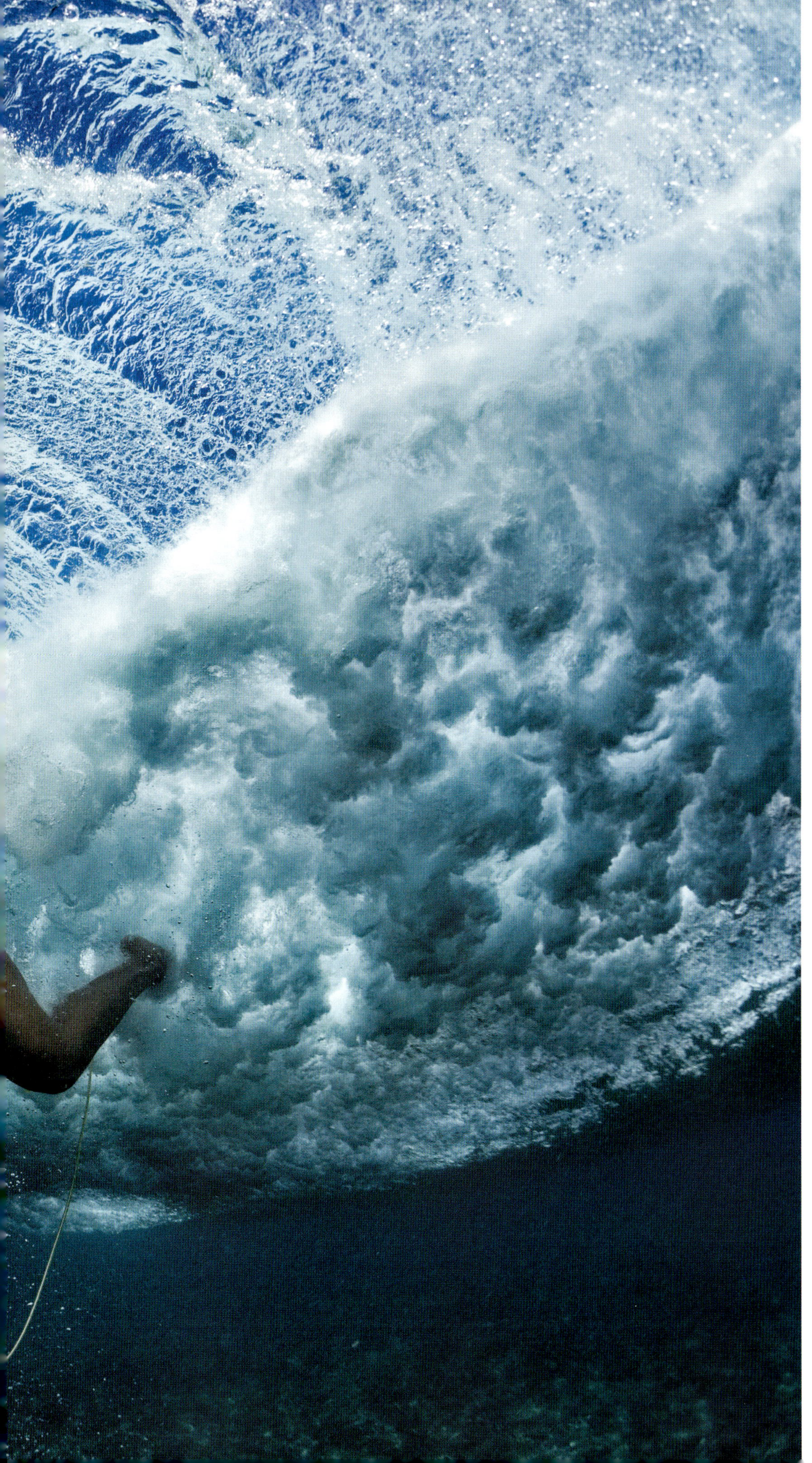

PAUL NICKLEN, 2013
Best friends and surfers Ha'a Keaulana (right) and Maili Makana dive under a wave near Makaha, Oahu, Hawaii.

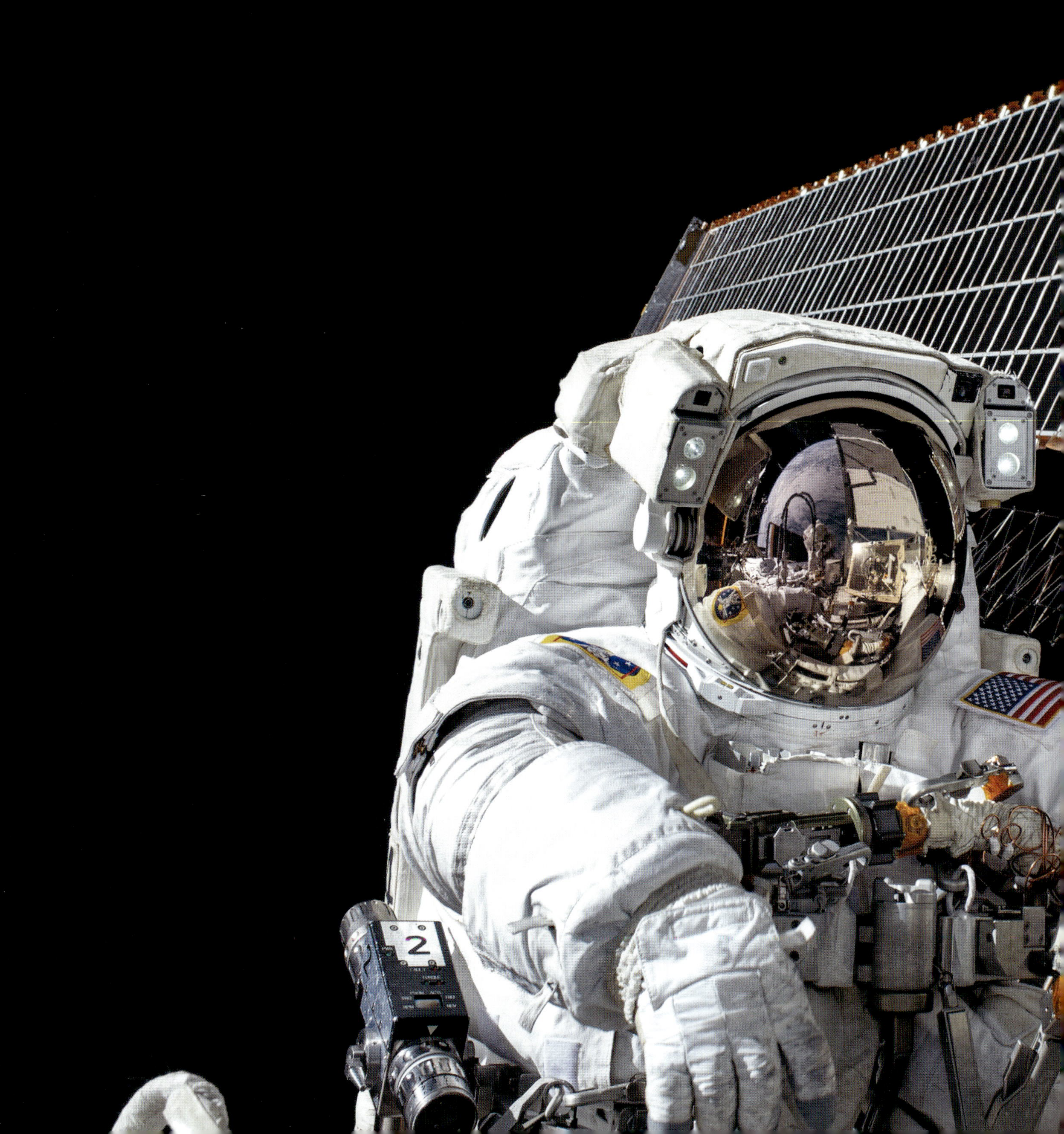
2

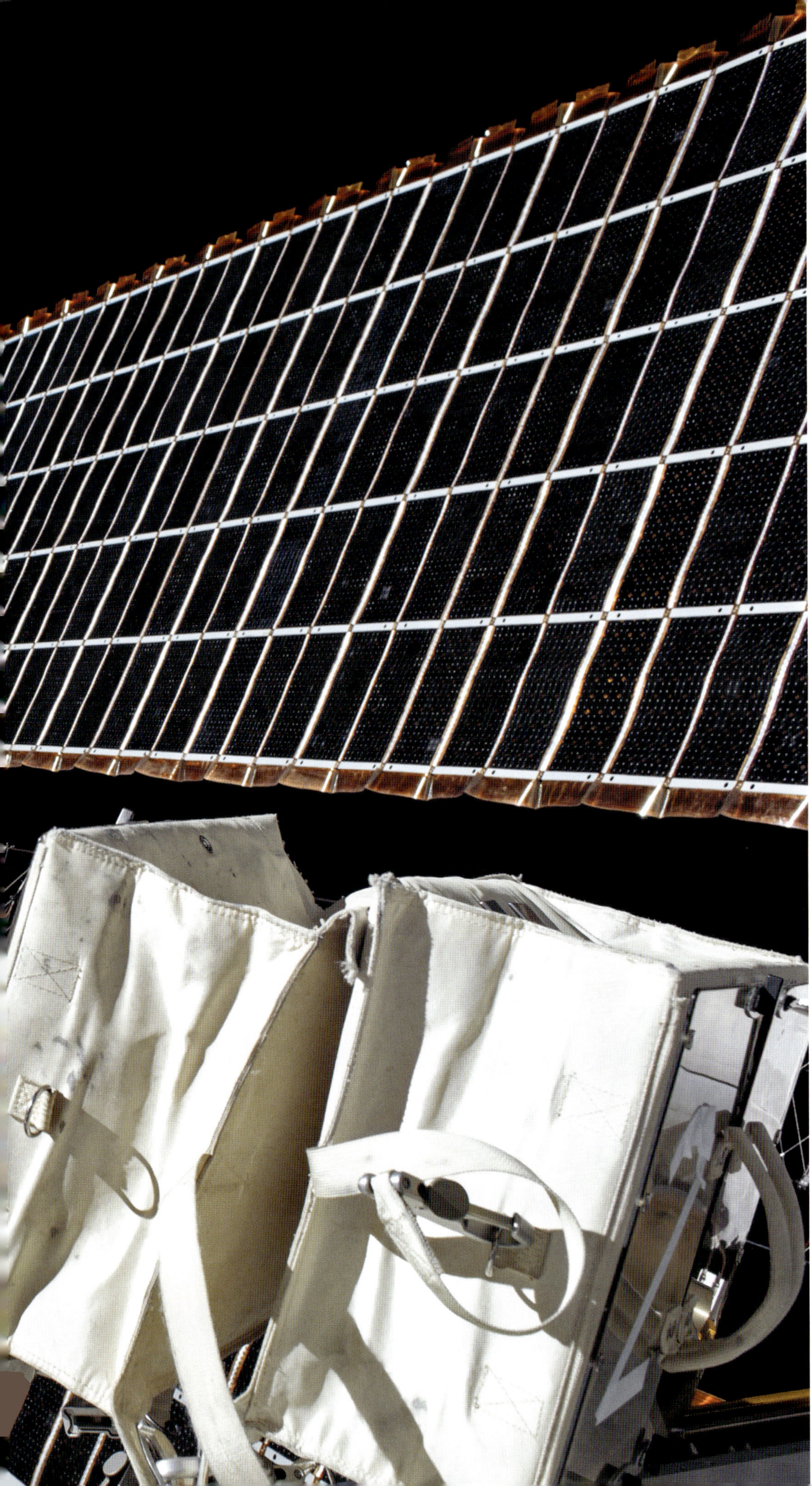

KJELL LINDGREN, 2015
Astronaut Scott Kelly, safely tethered to the International Space Station, reconfigures a cooling unit during a seven-hour, 48-minute space walk.

BIOGRAPHY

KEITH LADZINSKI

IN THE SPRING OF 1995, Keith Ladzinski used his earnings from a summer of mowing lawns to buy a secondhand camera, thereby planting the seeds of a career that would reach fruition as a National Geographic photographer.

His first subject was skateboarding. But with the Rockies practically in his Boulder, Colorado, backyard, it was no surprise that he soon turned to documenting rock climbing; the area is the epicenter of the sport. Climbing—his gateway to extreme sports and adventure photography—is, he says, a pursuit "where you look over the edge and feel your stomach drop in a great way."

In the years to follow, Ladzinski traveled all seven continents, "hoping to catch a moment of the sublime." He captured everything from the skeletal bones of blue whales in Antarctica; alligators in Florida's Everglades; the arthritic limbs of bristlecone pines, the world's oldest trees, in Nevada; killer tornadoes across the American Midwest; and China's karst rock formations.

The highest achievement for a photographer, says Ladzinski, is to be able to draw people into a story—to inspire them to learn and to feel passionate about an issue, and to engender understanding and respect for the planet. "The mark of any good photograph," he says, "is one that connects emotionally—be it awe, euphoria, or even sadness. A great photo leaves an imprint on us, allowing us to sit on a frozen microsecond in time and take in the nuance of the moment."

In addition to his National Geographic assignments—print, digital, video, and television—Ladzinski is a founding member of the SeaLegacy Collective. For his work as a documentary film director, he has received two Emmy nominations and five Telly Awards.

KEITH LADZINSKI, 2021
A researcher rappels along a towering ancient sequoia tree in California's Sequoia National Park.

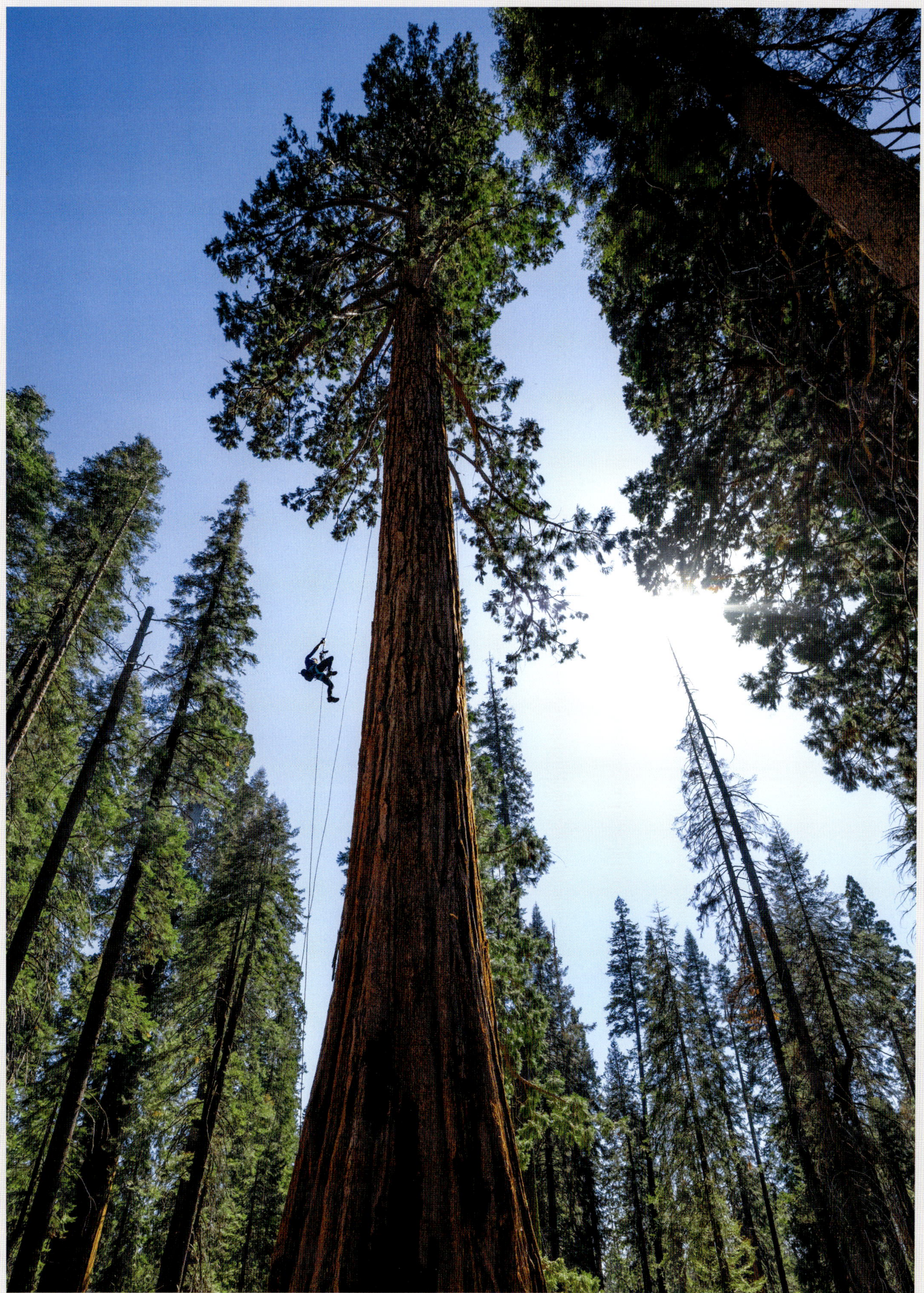

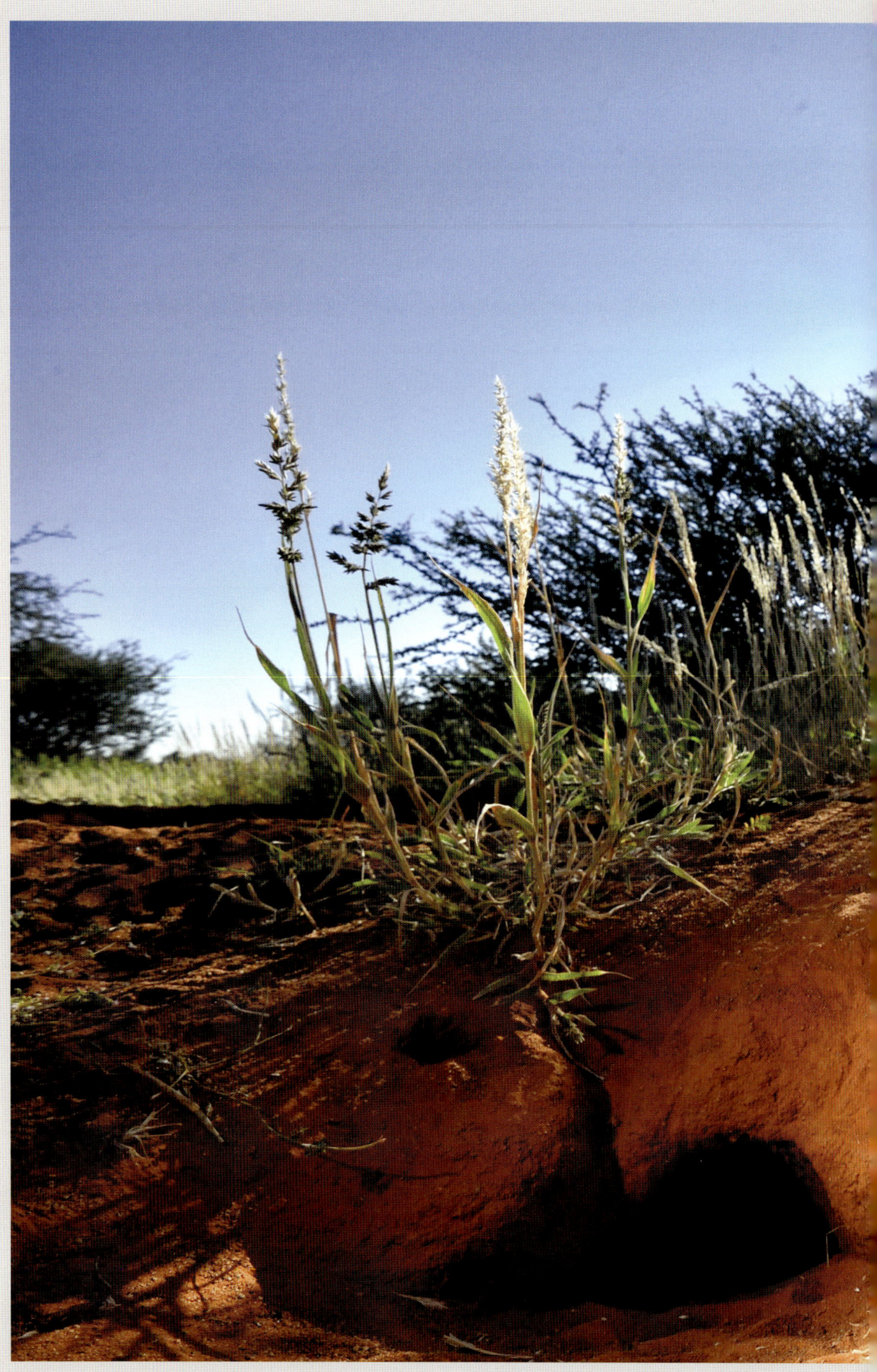

KEITH LADZINSKI, 2017
A meerkat keeps watch in southern Africa's Kalahari Desert.

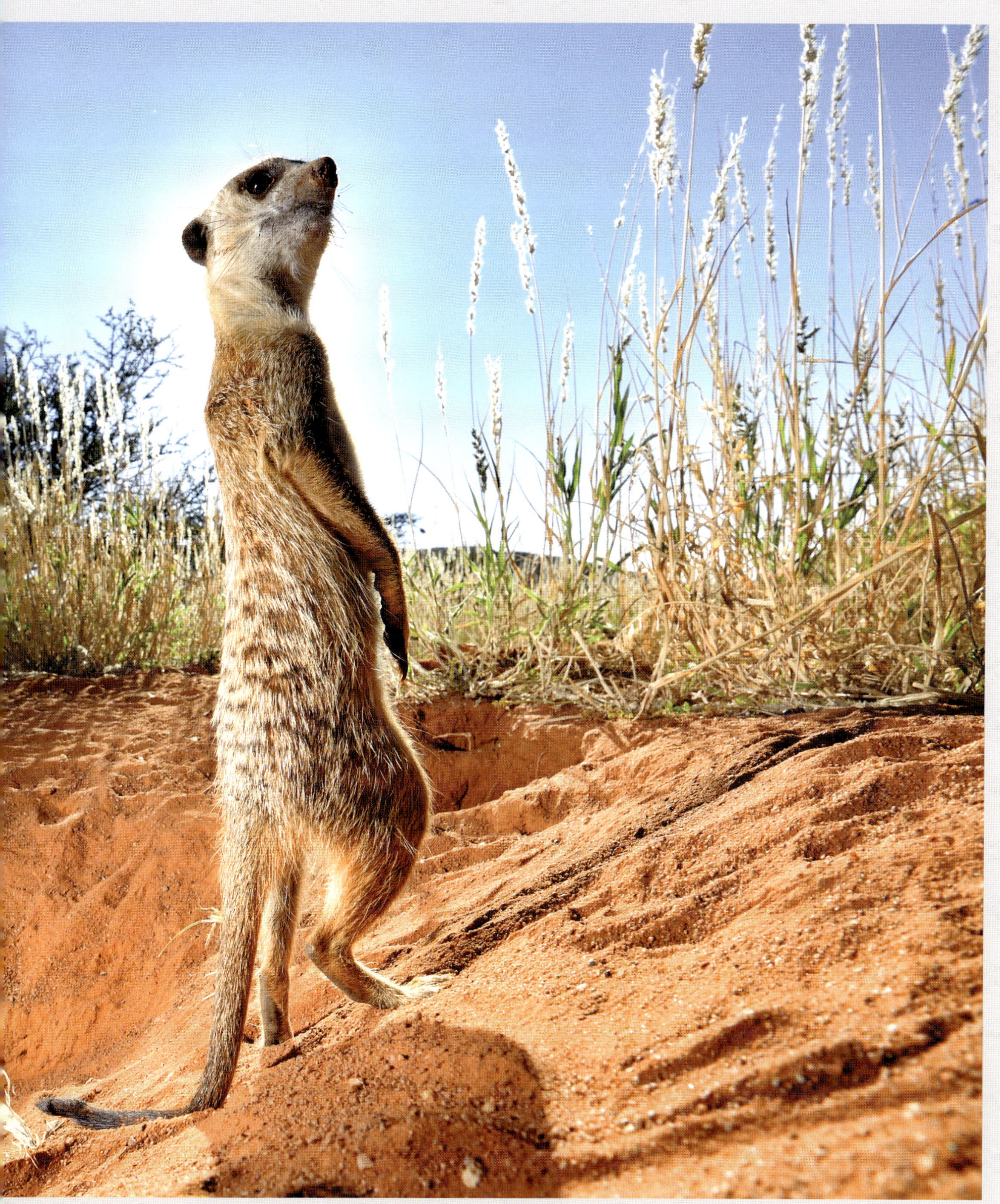

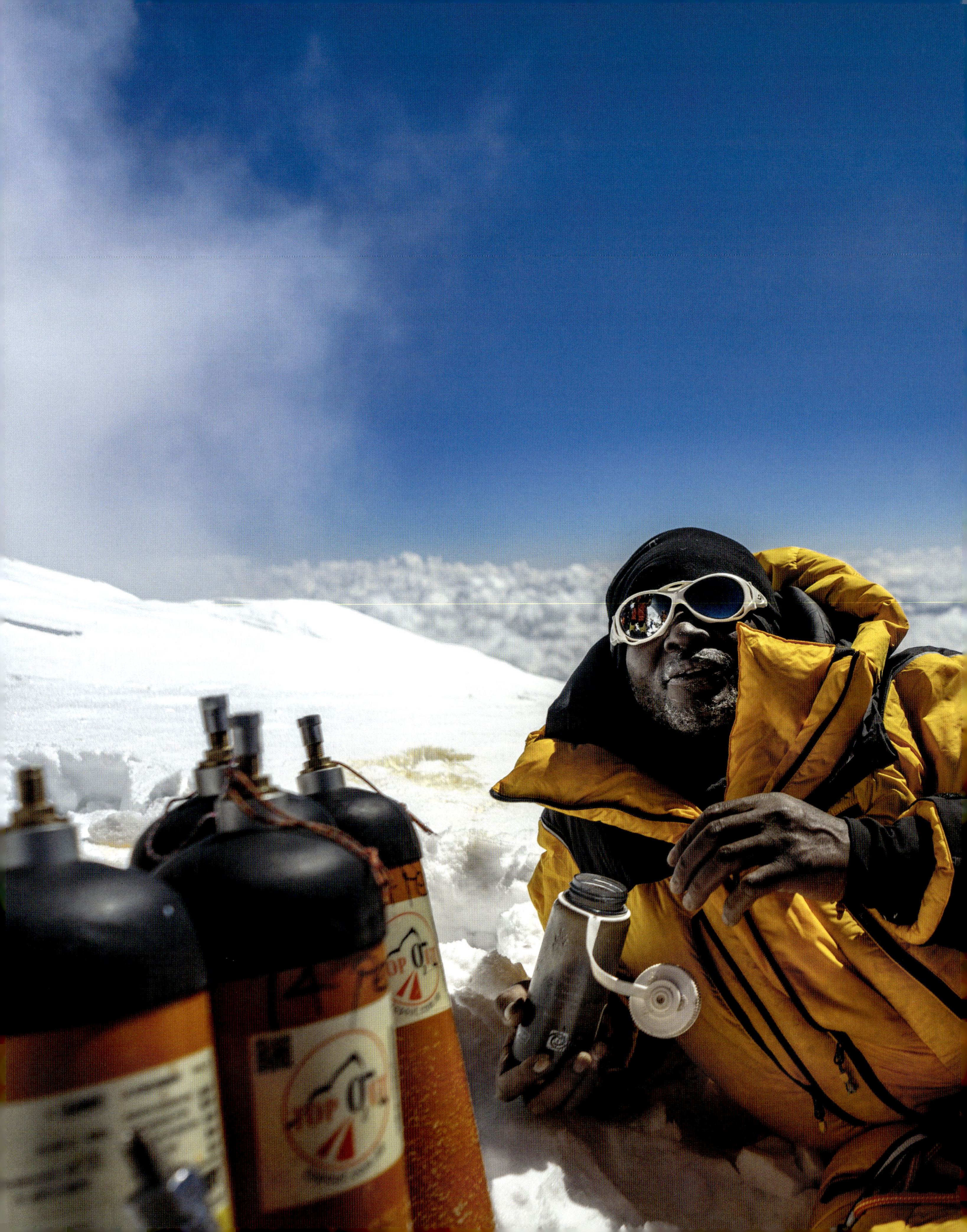

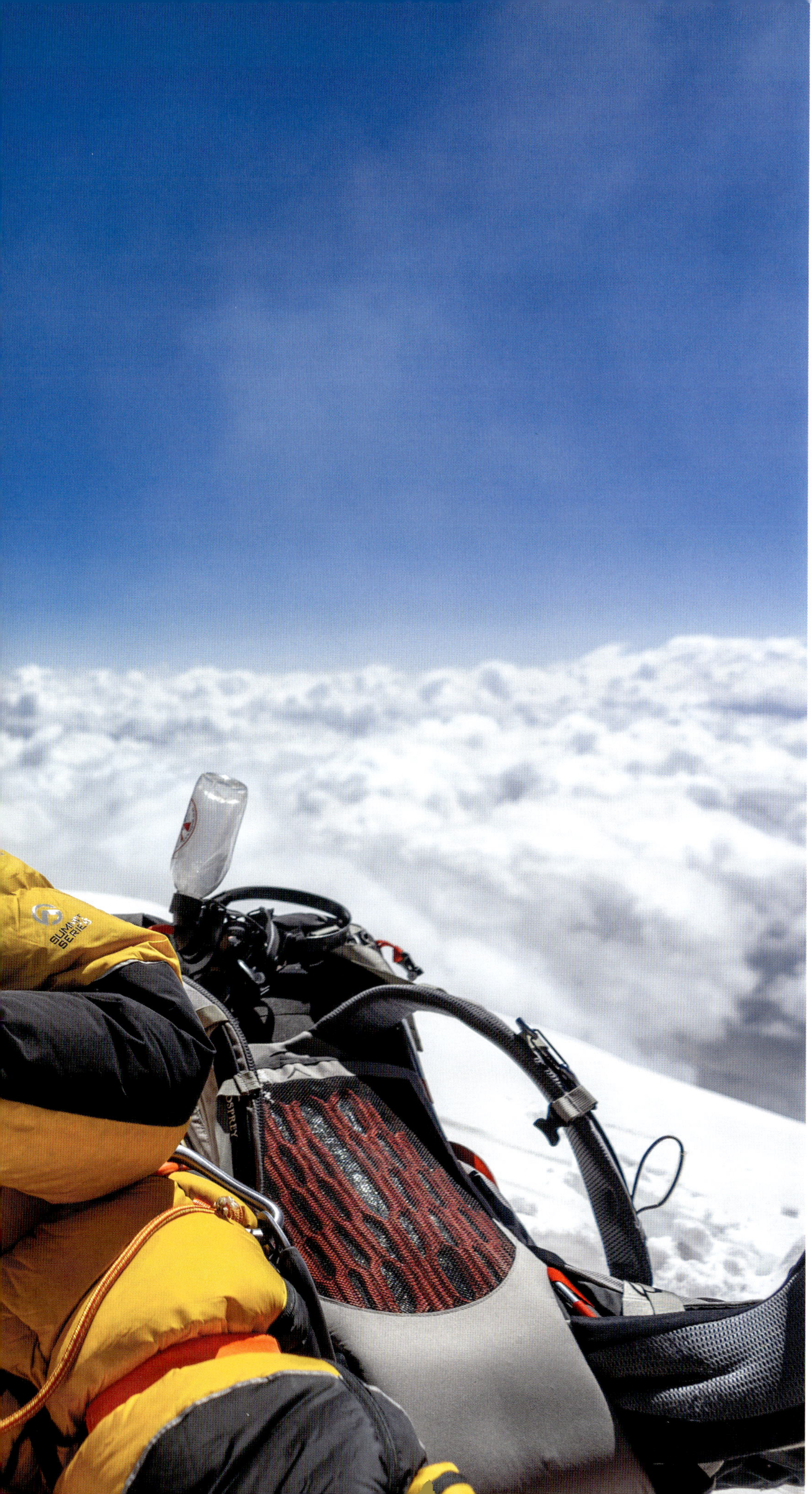

EVAN GREEN, 2022
James "KG" Kagambi, a member of the first all-Black expedition team to summit Mount Everest, pauses on the flat expanse of the mountain's Southeast Ridge, known as the Balcony.

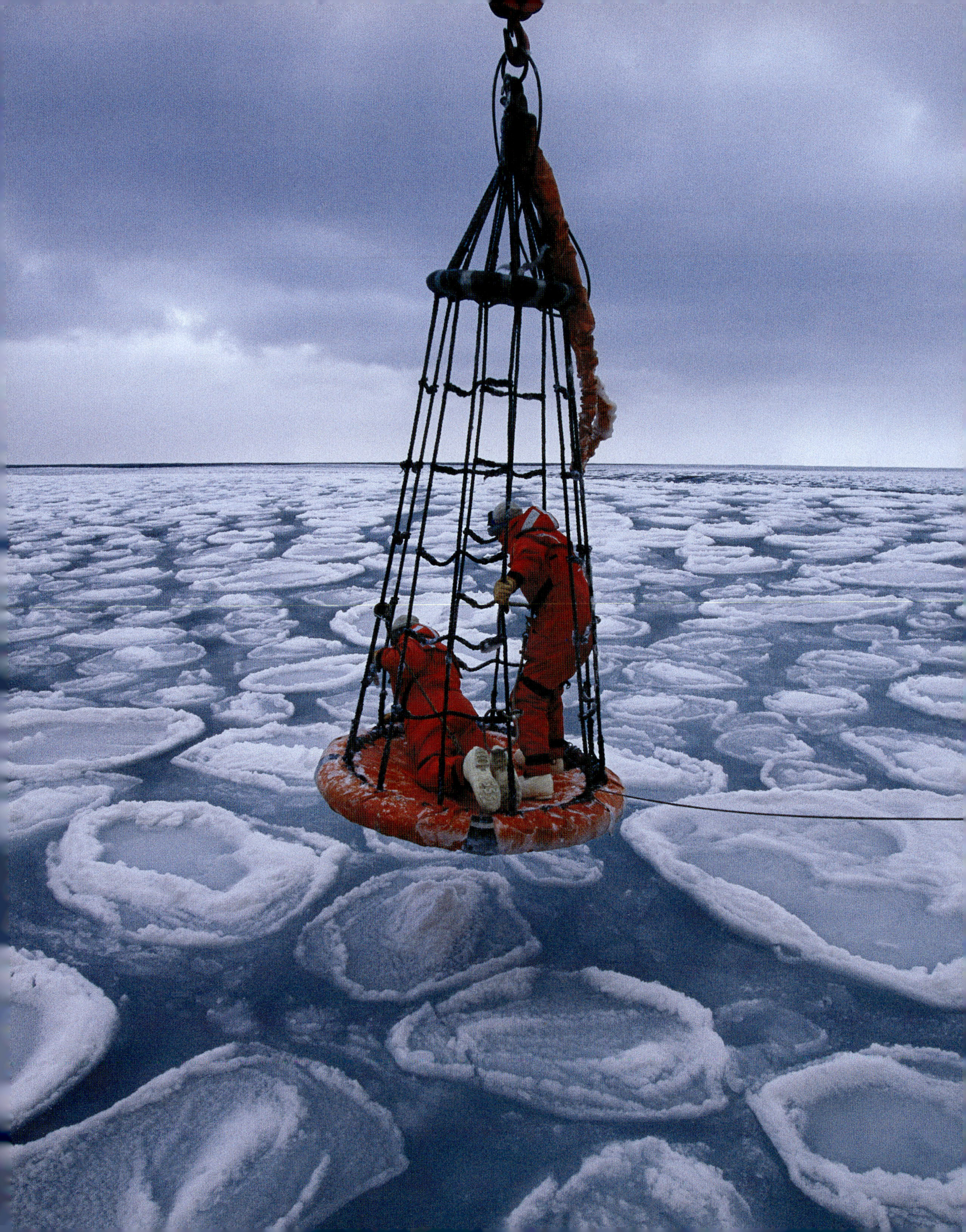

WE PUSH INTO NEW TERRITORY, EVEN WHEN WE HAVE RESOURCES WHERE WE ARE ... THERE'S A KIND OF MADNESS TO IT.

SVANTE PÄÄBO, GENETICIST AND NOBEL LAUREATE

MARIA STENZEL, 1996
Biologists search winter ice in Antarctica's Southern Ocean for life-forms, such as certain algae and mites, that are found only on the frozen continent.

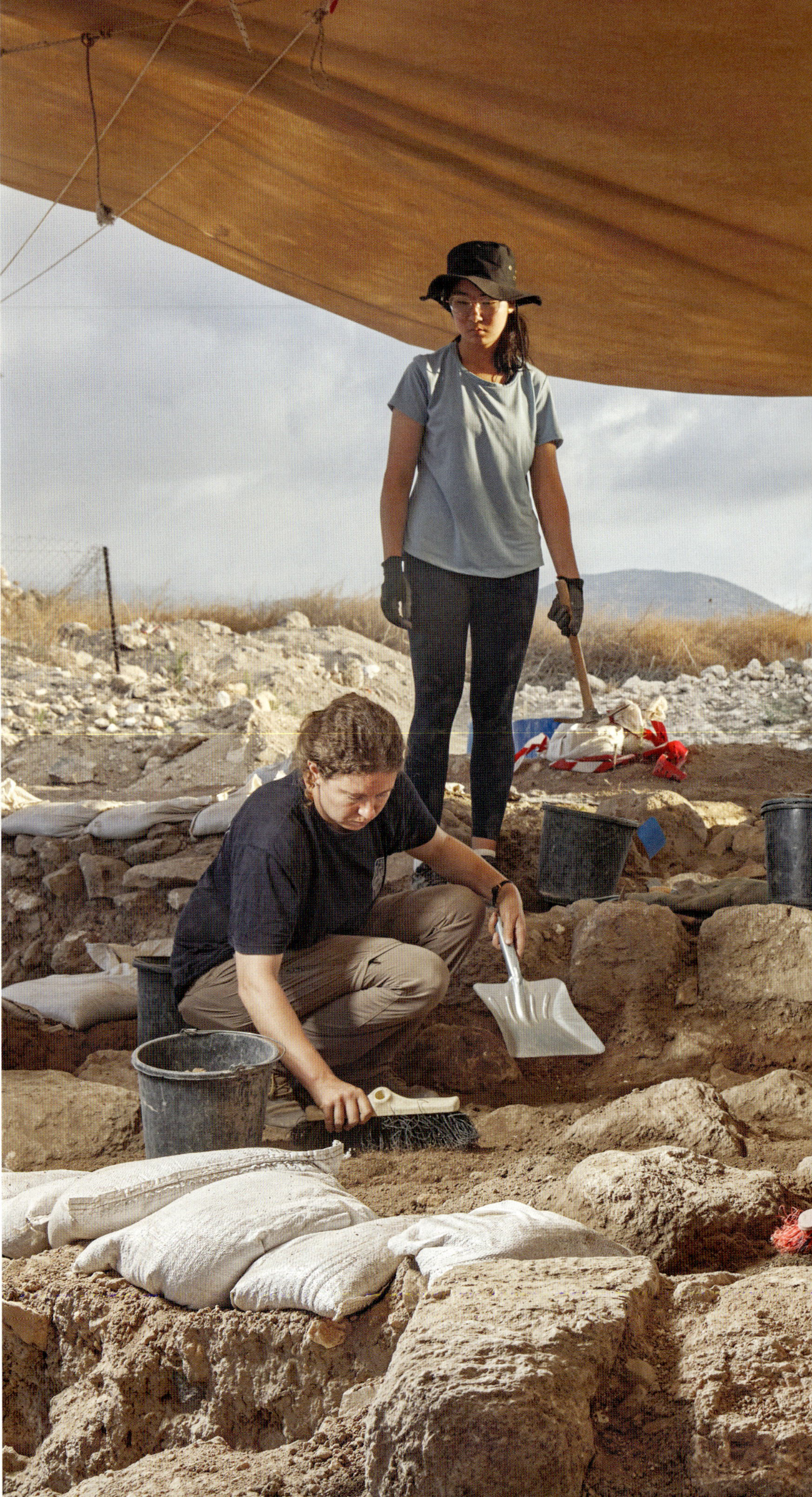

PAOLO VERZONE, 2023
Archaeologists excavate the ancient Jewish village of Huqoq in Israel, where they uncovered floor mosaics from a synagogue dating to the fifth century.

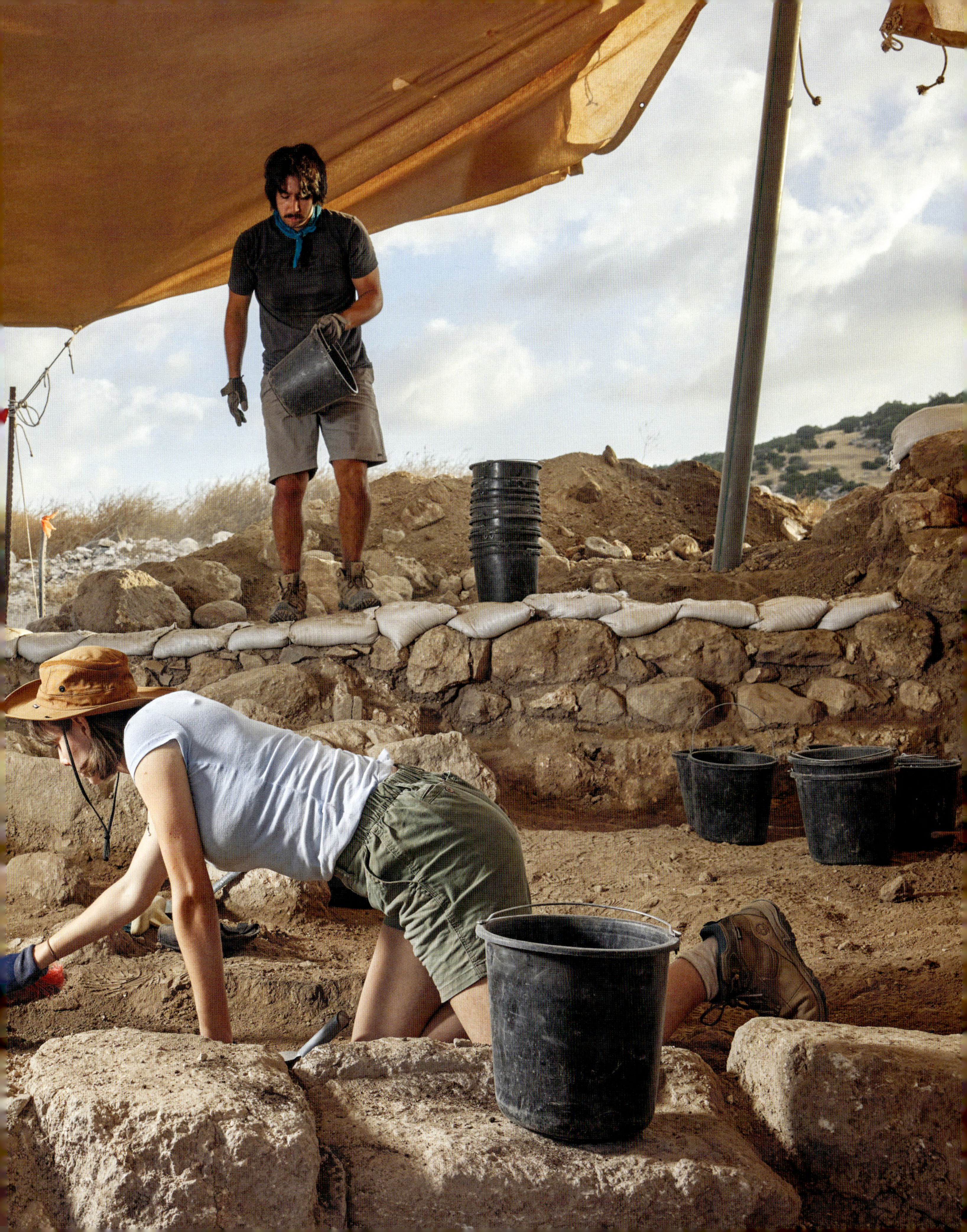

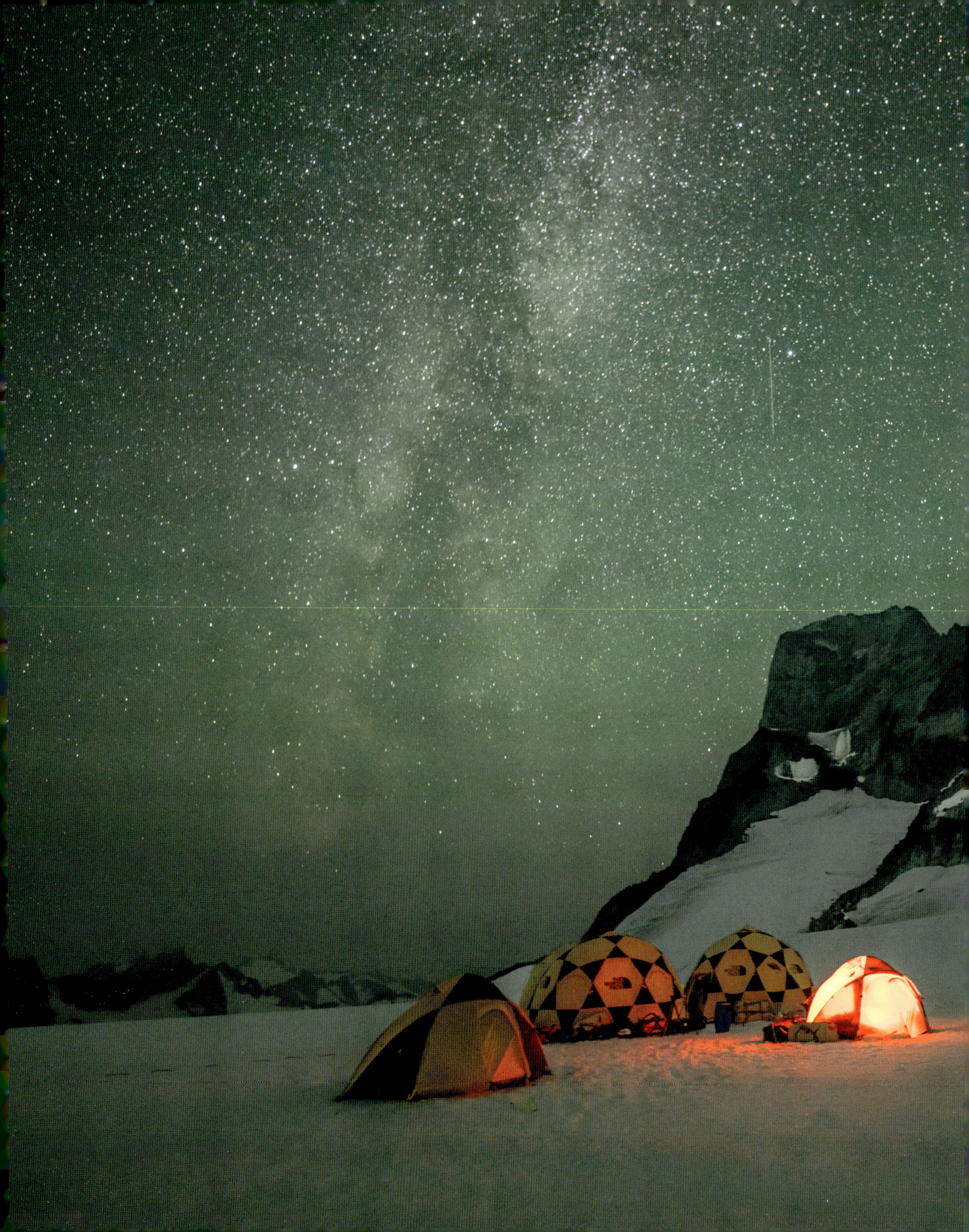

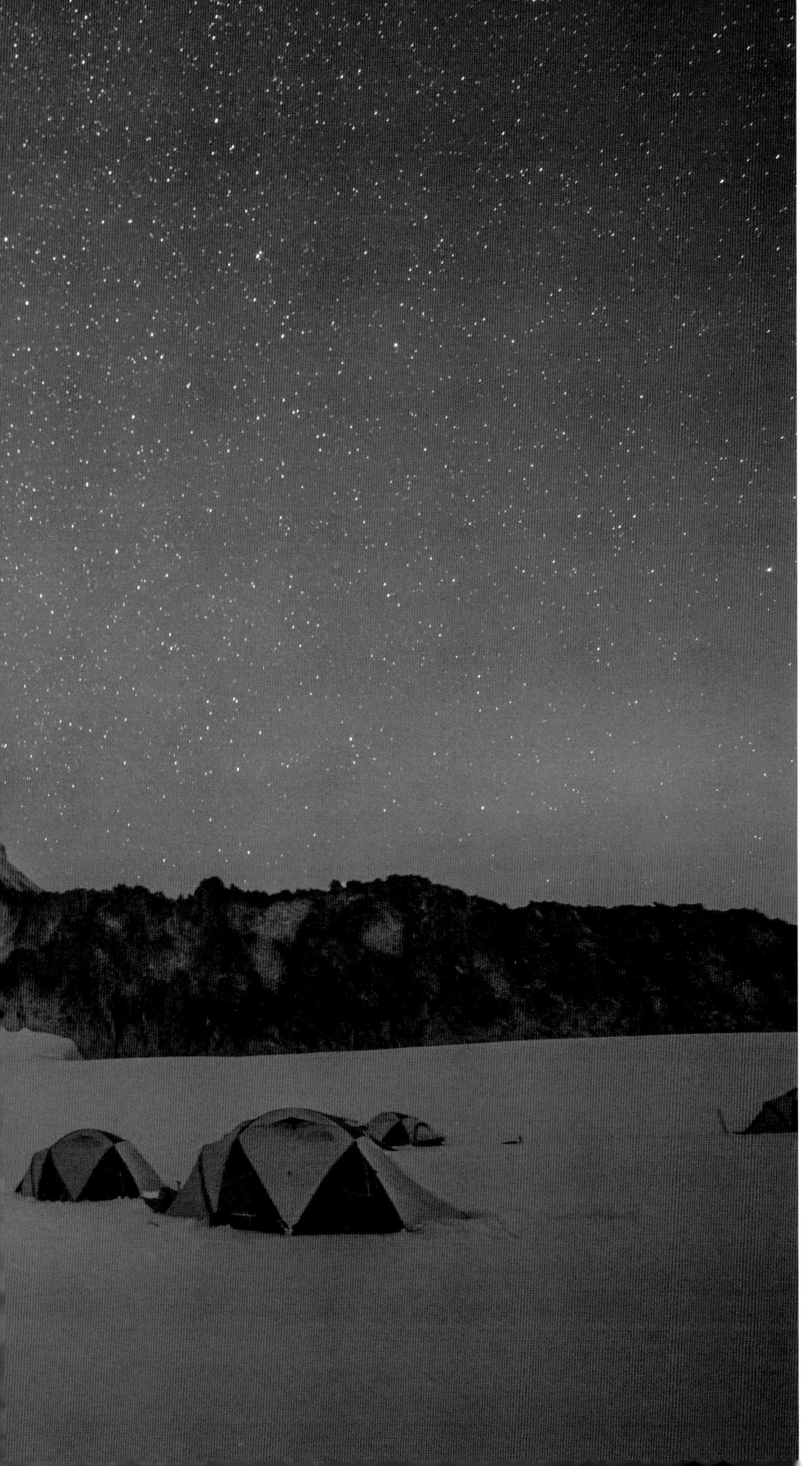

RYAN VALASEK, 2024
Climbers and crew make their base camp at Devils Thumb, Alaska. The following day, climbers Tommy Caldwell and Alex Honnold would summit the peak to conclude a 2,600-mile journey across North America.

FOLLOWING PAGES
EMORY KRISTOF, 1991
Shot two and a half miles beneath the surface of the Atlantic Ocean, under millions of tons of water, the rusted bow of the R.M.S. *Titanic* looms from the seafloor.

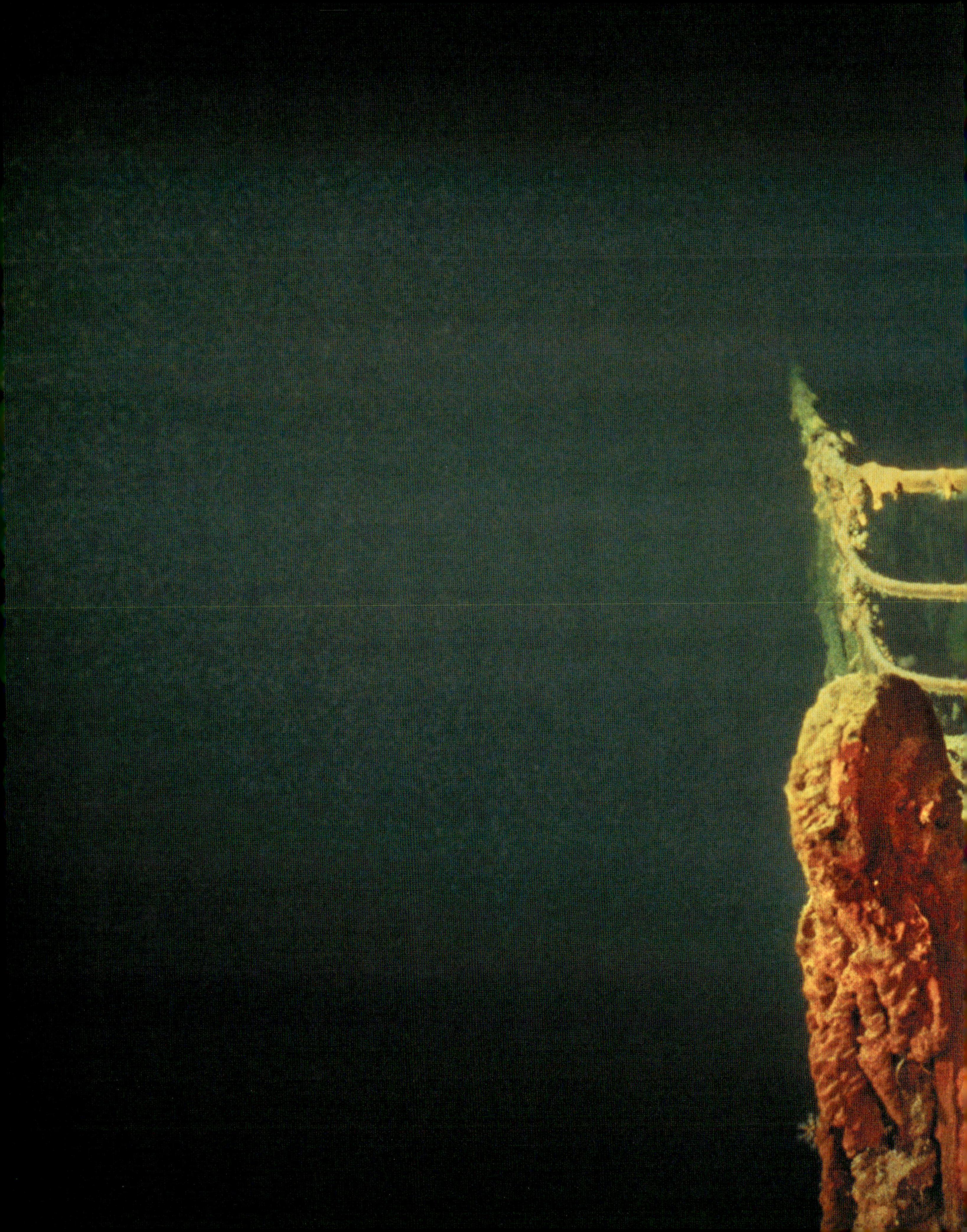

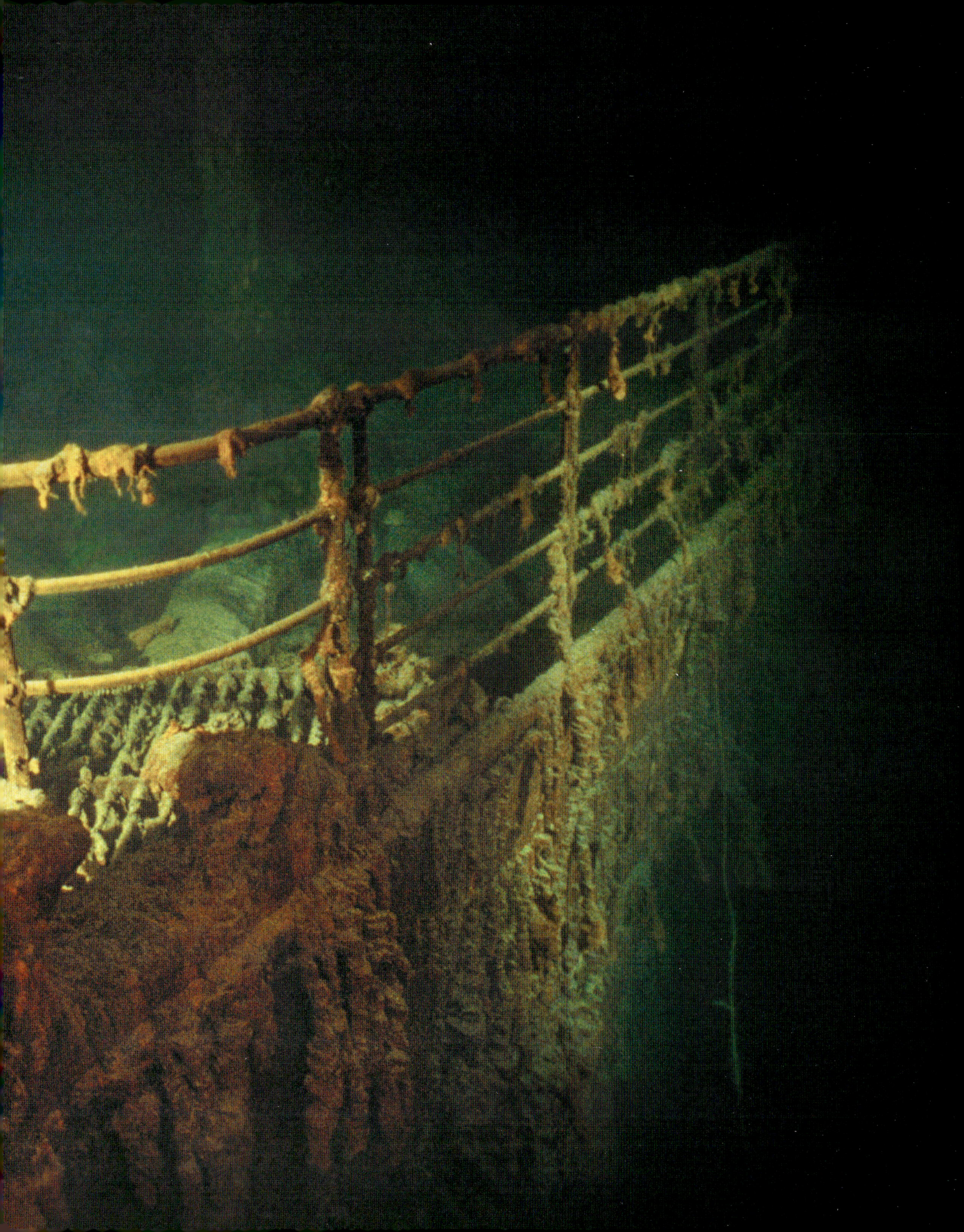

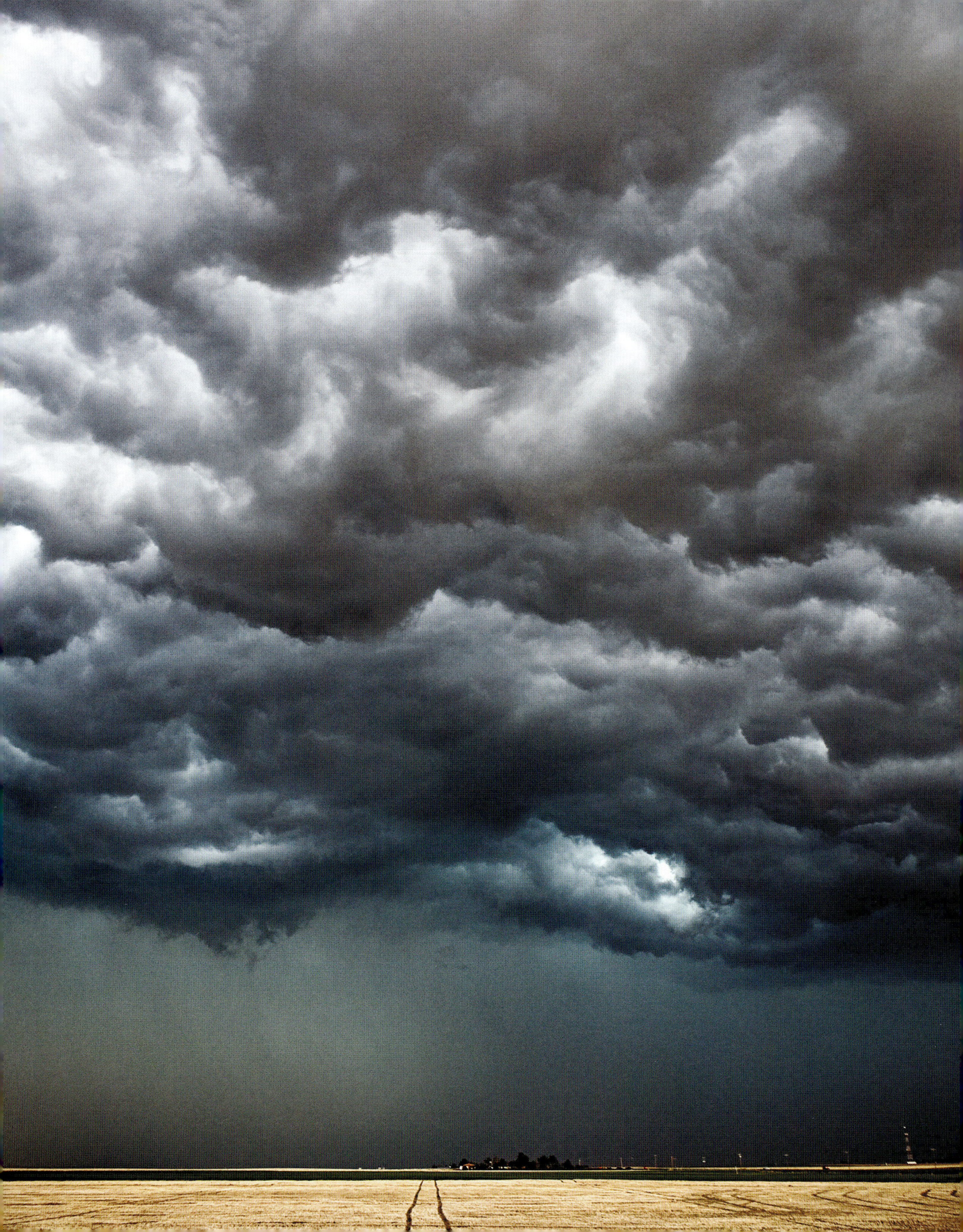

IN CONVERSATION WITH

CAMILLE SEAMAN

An unshakable belief in the interconnectedness of nature and humanity lies at the heart and soul of Camille Seaman's photography. Her images of icebergs are nothing less than portraits: unique, sculptural, shaped by their environment. The polar landscape Seaman is passionate about is a harbinger of climate change. "My job," she has said, "is to create a space, and if I've done my job right it will allow the viewer to formulate their own ideas and emotions about what I've shown them."

Storm chasing—another passion of Seaman's—comes with a different set of challenges and risks. But it springs from the same openness to adventure, along with a respect for the creative (and destructive) power of nature.

NATIONAL GEOGRAPHIC: Tell us about your childhood.

CAMILLE SEAMAN: My father is of Shinnecock and Montauk descent, and his family became the driving force of our upbringing. We spent a lot of time with my grandparents.

My grandfather would walk with me in the woods and introduce me to trees. He would show me how to clean fish, and we would plant the remains in the garden. He would explain that this fish not only feeds us, but it feeds the soil that feeds the plants. He was always talking about interconnectedness. He and my nana always told us that we were billions of years in the making, that we carried all our ancestors with us and had their wisdom with us. I always had that in my blood, in my body.

I was 13 when my grandfather died. That shook the foundations of the family, and I started down my punk rock road.

NG: Did that road lead to any kind of artistic expression?

CS: Drawing became one of my superpowers. By the time I got to high school, my mom and I were having a difficult relationship. My dad was remarried and had a new family. An aunt came to visit and found me drawing on the wall of the bedroom closet. Then she found me drawing on the underside of the dining room table. She said to my mom, "You should give that girl some paper!" I would sell those drawings at school for a couple of dollars. They helped me buy groceries to feed my brother and sister.

I left home at 15. My mom was getting more and more abusive, so I would rotate between couches of friends and family members. That allowed me to stay in school. I lied and said I was 16 to get a job at Woolworth's, and later at a one-hour photo lab.

NG: Was that your exposure to photography?

CS: It was part of it. I attended the LaGuardia High School of Music and Art, and they gave me a film camera and taught me how to use a darkroom. They said, "Go out and photograph your experience." And that probably saved my life.

The school required us to go to the museums of New York City every week, and the compositions began to fill my brain. I remember looking at Titian and Rubens and thinking, How are they doing that with paint? I had my own guard at the Metropolitan Museum of Art because I would get too close to the Monets.

NG: When did you begin exploring the world beyond New York City?

CAMILLE SEAMAN, 2008
"Tracks Through the Field": Angry storm clouds roil above a field in Kansas.

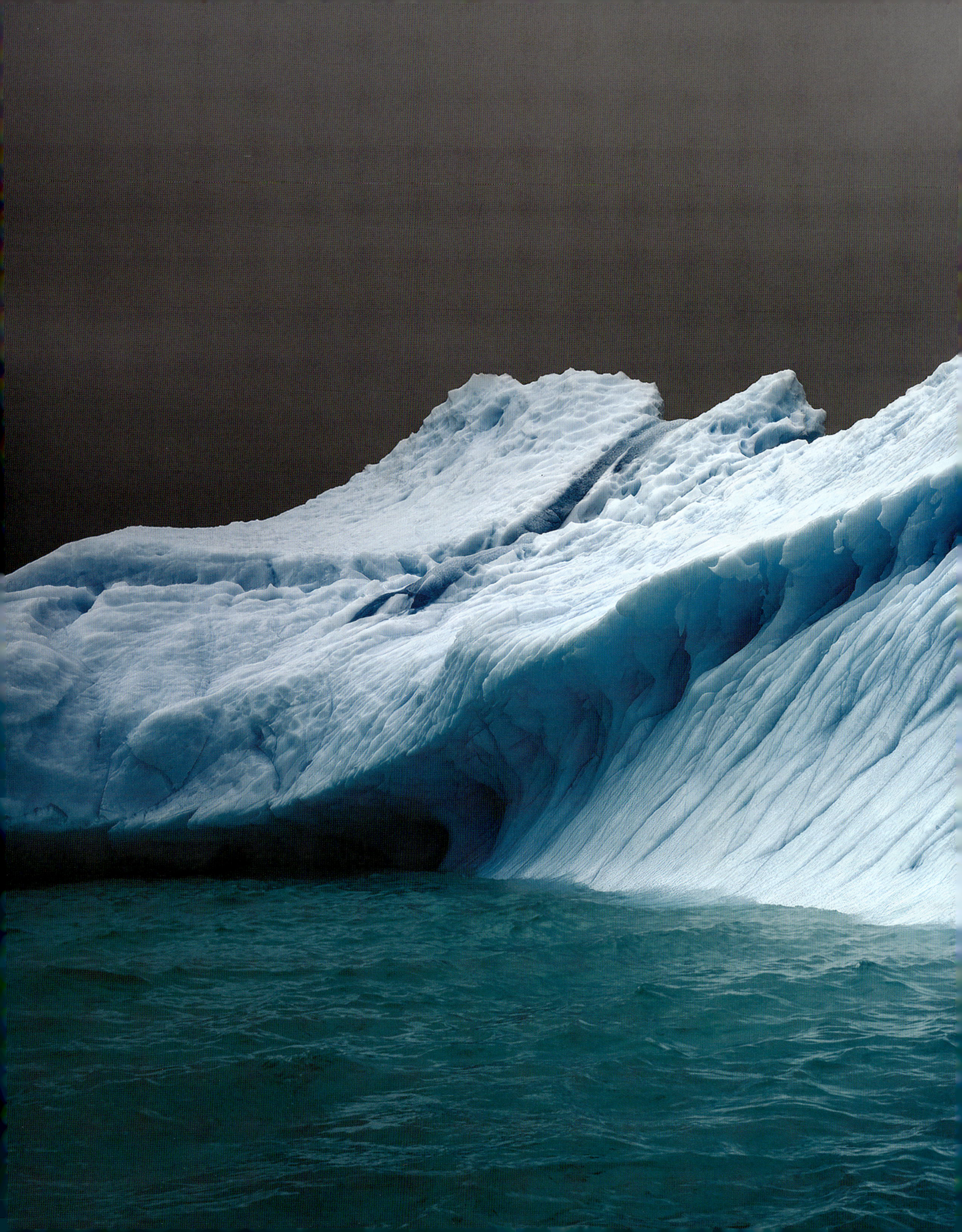

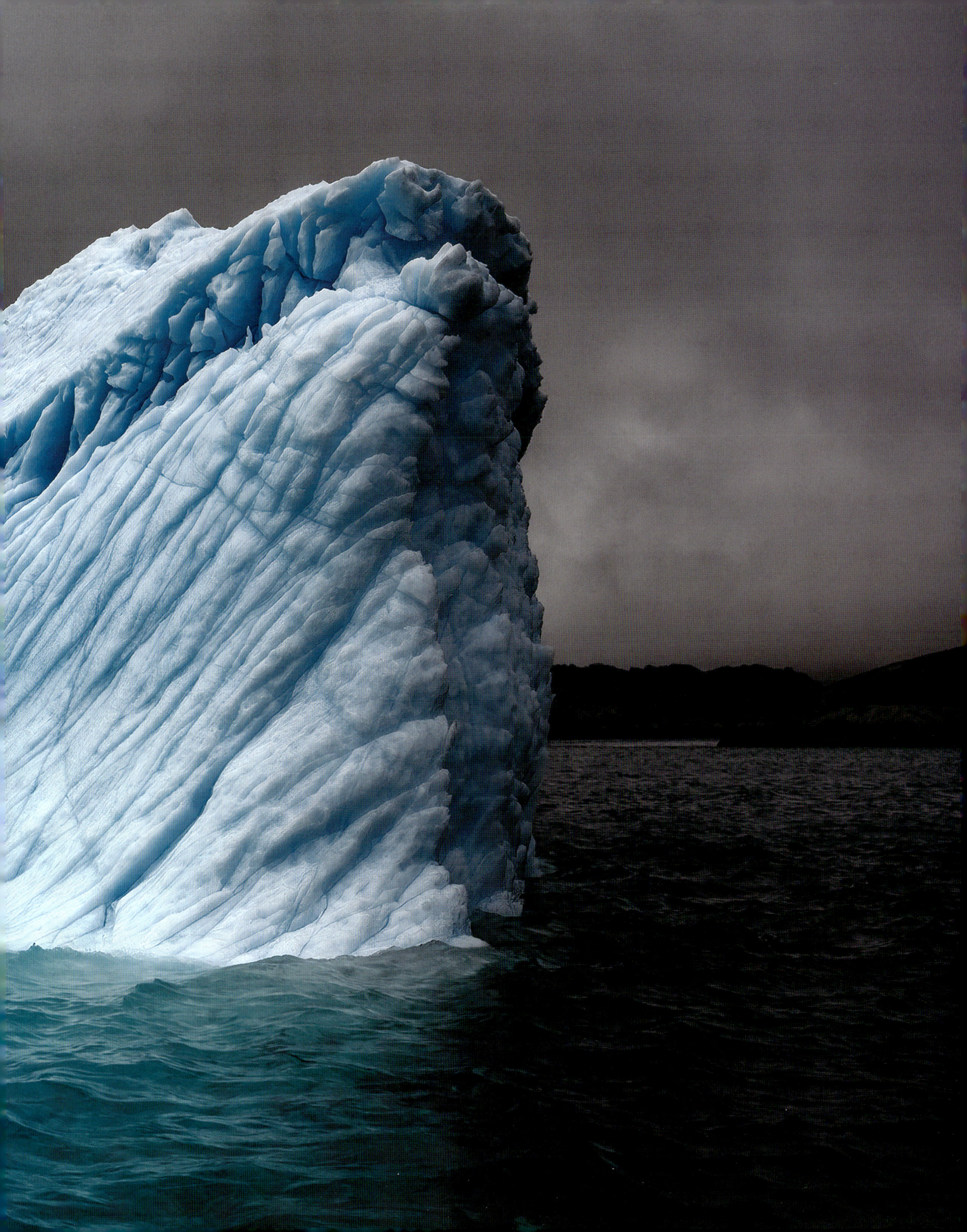

CS: After college, I was accompanying my boyfriend at the time on a business trip to L.A. when Oakland Airport announced that the airline had oversold our flight. They offered a free round-trip ticket to anyone who would give up their seat. I volunteered, and suddenly I had this free ticket to anywhere through Alaska Airlines. So I decided to go to a place in Alaska called Kotzebue, which was situated on the supposed Bering Land Bridge.

NG: Why there?

CS: If there's one thing about me, I am very curious. In our Native philosophy, we believe that only through what we call touching—actual experience—do you come to know anything. We say you must touch the four directions, so I was fully embracing that.

In Kotzebue, I ended up walking across the frozen sea ice by myself. It was this long horizon of ice, white in all directions. And I realized what my grandfather had taught me: that I am made of the material on this planet. That was profound because at the time—I didn't know it yet—I was three weeks pregnant with my daughter. I was awakening as an Earthling at the same time I was awakening as a mother.

NG: What does it feel like out on that terrain?

CS: It's an overwhelming sensation. When I experience these massive pieces of ice, I hear my grandfather's words: *These are your relatives. You are related to this water in the ice.* That's why I decided to photograph the ice as if I was making a portrait of it. I was trying to acknowledge all of the ancestors' water that was in it. There's a strange side effect to that: I remember every single iceberg I've ever photographed.

NG: Given that relationship, do you think your photographs can make a difference in how the rest of us see the polar landscape amid climate change?

CS: You catch me at an interesting time. I spent three and a half months this year in Antarctica, but when I left, it seemed pointless to continue going there. I don't feel I have made a difference. I don't feel that people are moving quickly enough in the direction that we need to be moving.

This is going to make me cry: I went back in 2022 to this glacier in Svalbard that I had not visited since 2011, only 11 years prior. And it was a gut punch; it looked like a ruined soufflé. In Antarctica, I see these glaciers have become more fractured, more unhealthy over the years. I called this season the "tour of death." We saw many dead animals, from birds to elephant seals to penguins. We visited an Adélie penguin colony in the Weddell Sea while it was 65°F. All of the little baby penguins—hundreds of thousands of them—were panting because it was so hot.

But I hope that my images don't monger fear. Change will never come through scaring people; you have to do it from love. You have to do it from beauty.

NG: Do you hold any sense of optimism?

CS: We have the ability to pivot, but I don't know if that can happen until enough people have a personal experience. The reality is, America is struggling against what I call pathological individualism. It's this idea that we find success all by ourselves, and we solve our problems without help. It's an illusion of separateness, and I think we need to cultivate a different story about ourselves and our planet.

NG: It's very important what you're doing. It reminds people of the purpose of living.

CS: I truly appreciate that, because I don't hear that very often. In 2018, I had a yard sale, and a man from China bought a bunch of my postcards. He held up my picture of the stranded iceberg and asked, "Did you take this picture?" I said yes, and he said, "When this picture was published, I cut it out of the magazine and put it on my wall. It's the reason I wanted to be a journalist, and that's why I've come to the United States." Then he gave me a hug. It's those rare times where I think, It's getting through.

NG: When did you start storm chasing?

CS: One afternoon I was vacuuming the living room while my daughter, who was almost eight years old, was sitting on the couch watching *Storm Chasers* on the National Geographic channel. She noticed me watching out of the corner of my eye, and she said, "Mom, you should do that."

So during a commercial, I googled "storm chasing," and this whole world appeared. I found one website that was super nerdy and had, like, lightning flashes across the screen. I wanted to go with that team. Through sheer luck, they had an opening for me to join them three days later.

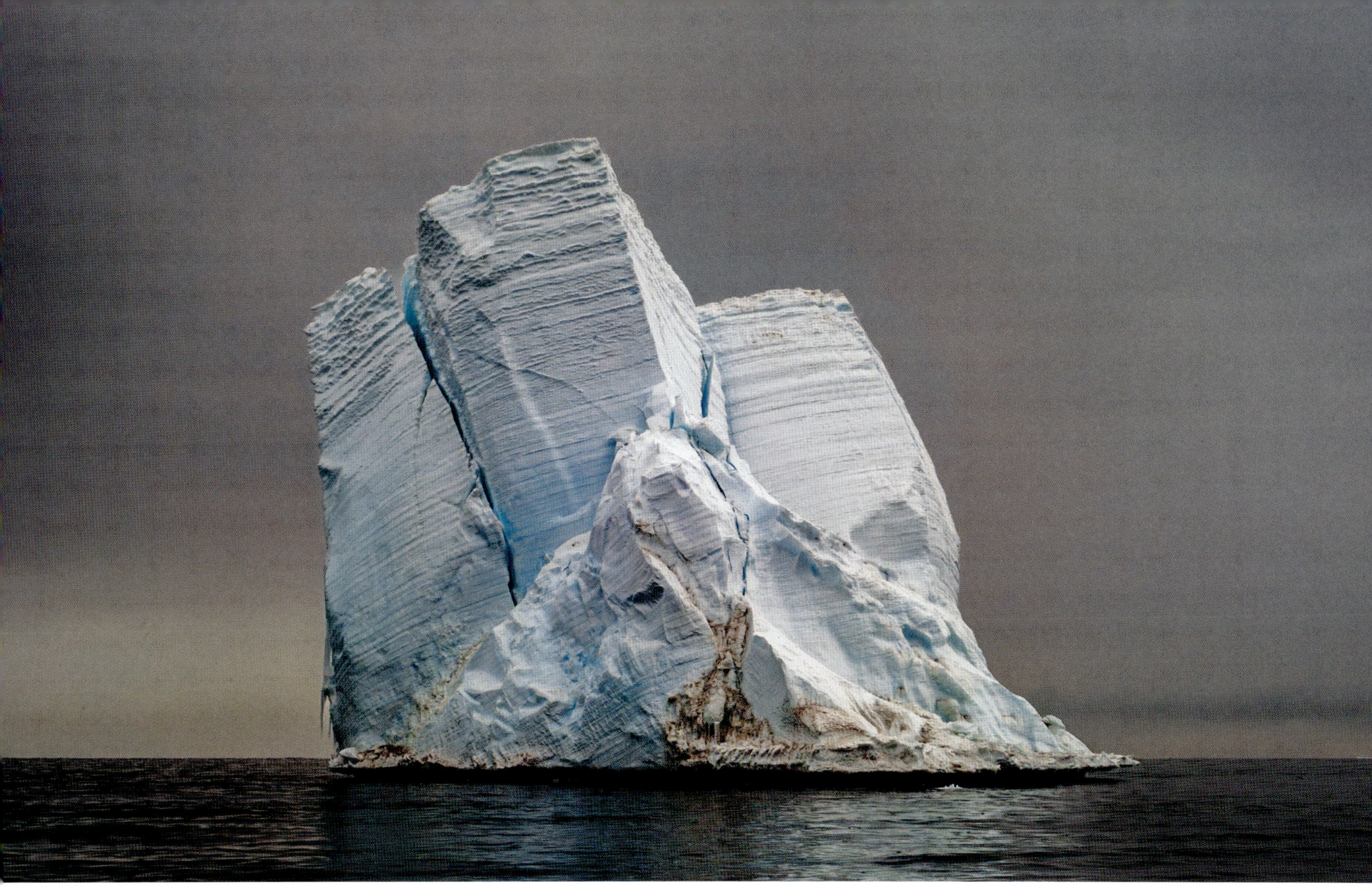

CAMILLE SEAMAN, 2006
"Stranded Iceberg" rests in the water off Cape Bird, the northwest extremity of Ross Island, Antarctica.

PREVIOUS PAGES
CAMILLE SEAMAN, 2008
"Breaching Iceberg" relinquishes its fresh water into the Greenland Sea.

NG: Explain your fascination with storms.

CS: I'm fascinated by the color and structures of their movement; it's sort of like a lava lamp. The smells are incredible—this warm, almost metallic smell. This is Shiva. This is destruction and creation in the same energy, the same vortex energy that builds our galaxy and probably the universe.

NG: Have you ever gone too far when you're chasing?

CS: You know, we call ourselves storm chasers, but every now and then we're the ones being chased. I was at the storm that killed Tim Samaras; his son, Paul; and Carl Young in 2013. I was just about a mile behind them with another team. Our team had a feeling that something wasn't right, so we turned the car around and found an exit point. It took seven hours of driving until we found safety. The next day we found out that Tim and the others had died. I saw that my daughter had texted me while I was out chasing: "Mom, are you OK?" It was the first time she had ever checked on me because she was afraid.

Nothing like a child will make you take fewer risks. The next year we tried chasing again, but we didn't have the same drive. We were hesitant, so we lost our edge. And it wasn't joyful anymore.

NG: Where is your curiosity leading you now?

CS: I'm trying to find things that we have forgotten that we should remember. I live in one of the oldest Viking areas in Denmark, so I've been spending time with people who try to keep the historic aspects of Vikings alive. It's fascinating. As someone who has gone so far to the ends of the earth, I've realized that when you come home, you realize there's an adventure right here too. You don't need to go so far to have an adventure and make a difference. And it's funny that it's taken me this big, long trip to end up back home.

For anyone reading this who wants to know how you start—well, you just have to have courage. You don't need to know where the road is going to lead or what's going to be on the other side. But you do need to have the courage to say, "I want to see it."

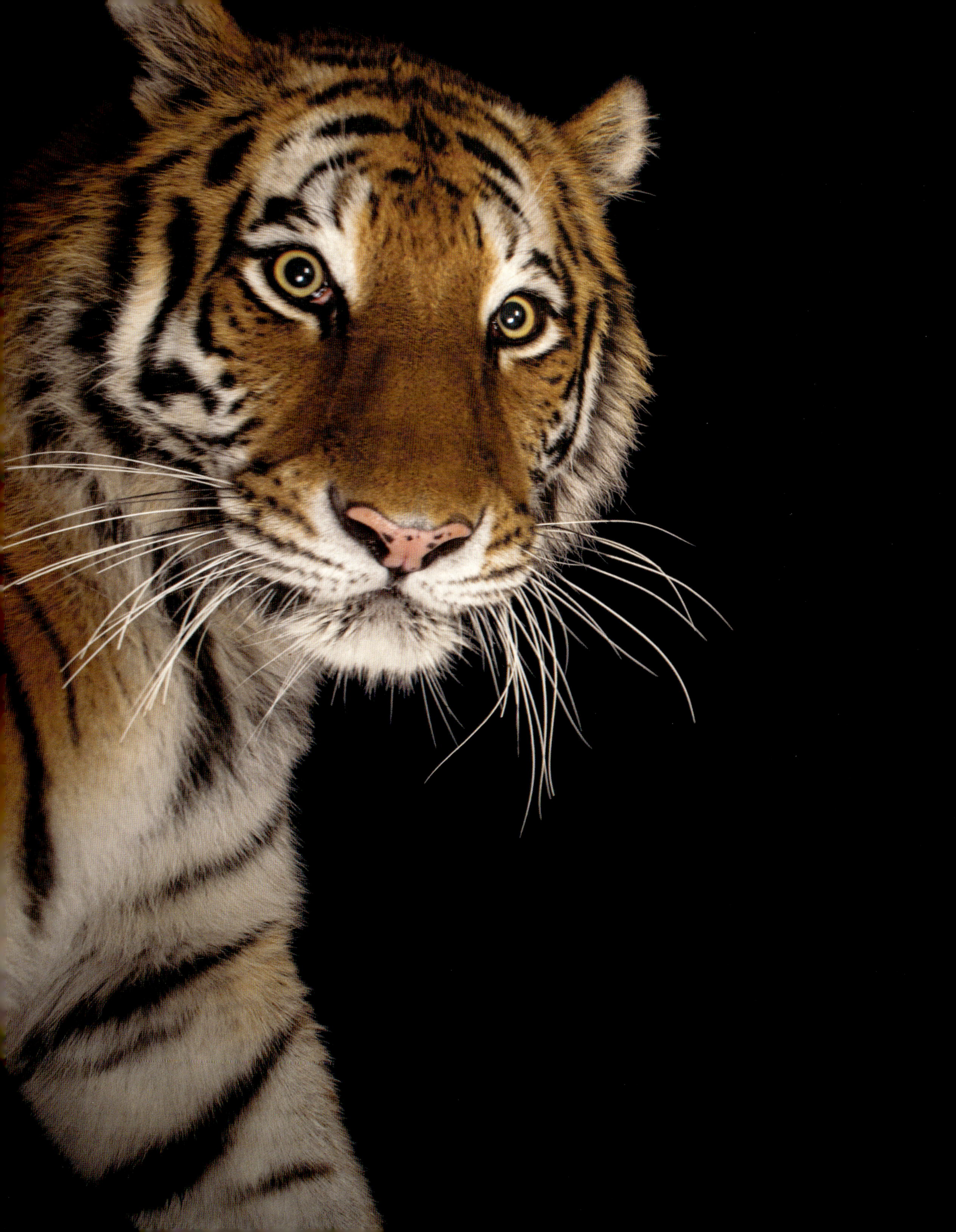

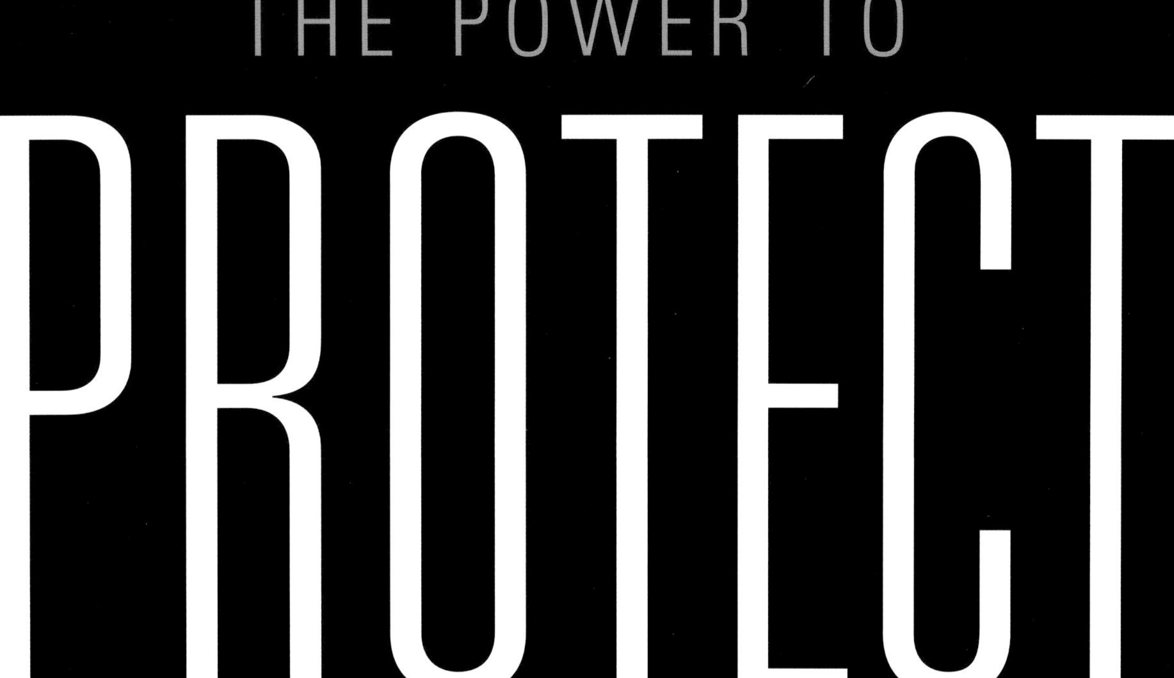
THE POWER TO
PROTECT

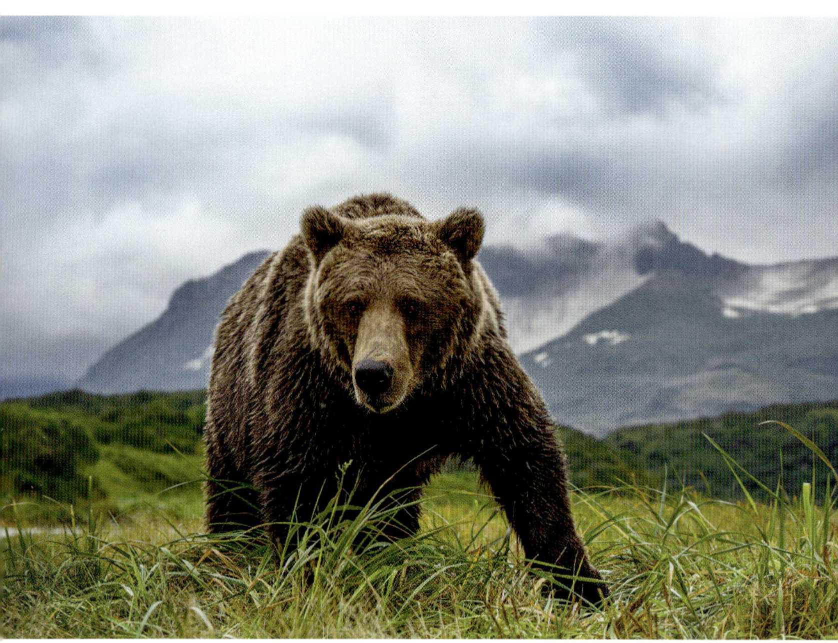

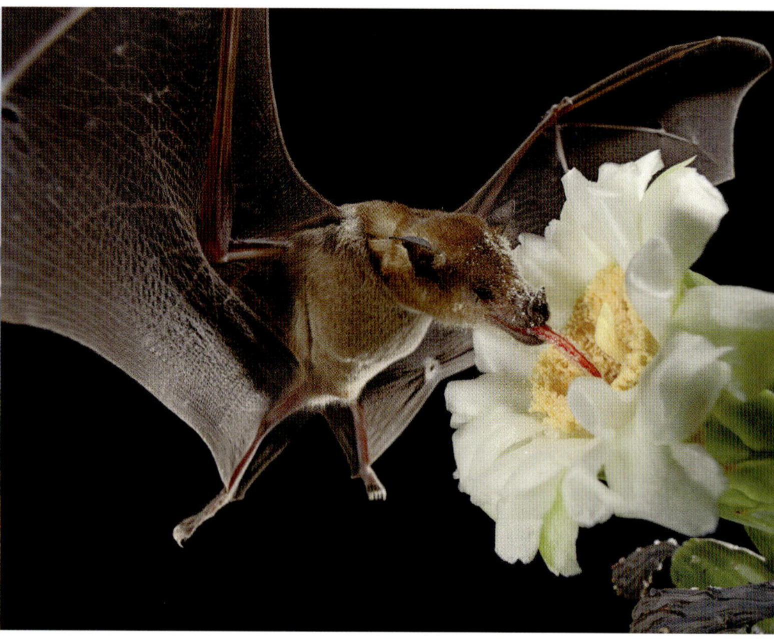

GOING WILD

WILDLIFE PHOTOGRAPHY IS NOT NINE-TO-FIVE WORK. You can't schedule an appointment with a tiger in the bush or a lion on the savanna. Forget cooperation with the subject; at best, it's a collaboration. Fieldwork can be measured in months or years, and, as a photo editor says, you have to go a little wild yourself.

National Geographic magazine's natural history coverage has shifted in the past three decades from a formulaic approach—which might have called for a portrait of an animal, obligatory photos of behavior, a landscape, and a field researcher—to a more comprehensive form of storytelling that makes conservation integral to the discussion. "Pure natural history is no longer the story," explains former deputy director of photography Kathy Moran. "You are not telling the whole story if you are not talking about the impact of climate change, overfishing, poaching, trophy hunting, or the challenges of sharing an environment with wildlife—as well as presenting possible solutions."

These stories are no less than epic narratives. And they matter. Who is the more effective conservationist, "polar-obsessed" photographer Paul Nicklen was once asked. The scientist or the photographer?

No contest, Nicklen answered. "We know ice is disappearing in the Arctic; if we lose ice, we lose polar bears," he said. "Maybe one hundred scientists will read a paper about polar bears. If you get one picture of a bear dying on the ice, that's all you need to know."

"Photographs drive home to our readers—in a way that words never can—that our choices have consequences," Moran adds. This is especially evident in photographer Brian Skerry's images portraying the plight of harp seals, the

PAGE 112
JOEL SARTORE, 2013
A female Amur tiger at the Cheyenne Mountain Zoo in Colorado Springs, Colorado

ABOVE LEFT
ACACIA JOHNSON, 2023
A brown bear in Alaska's Katmai National Park and Preserve, which boasts one of the densest brown bear populations in the world

ABOVE RIGHT
CHRISTIAN ZIEGLER, 2024
A lesser long-nosed bat drinks sweet nectar from a saguaro flower in Saguaro National Park, Arizona. The flower blooms only once, at night, and closes the next day.

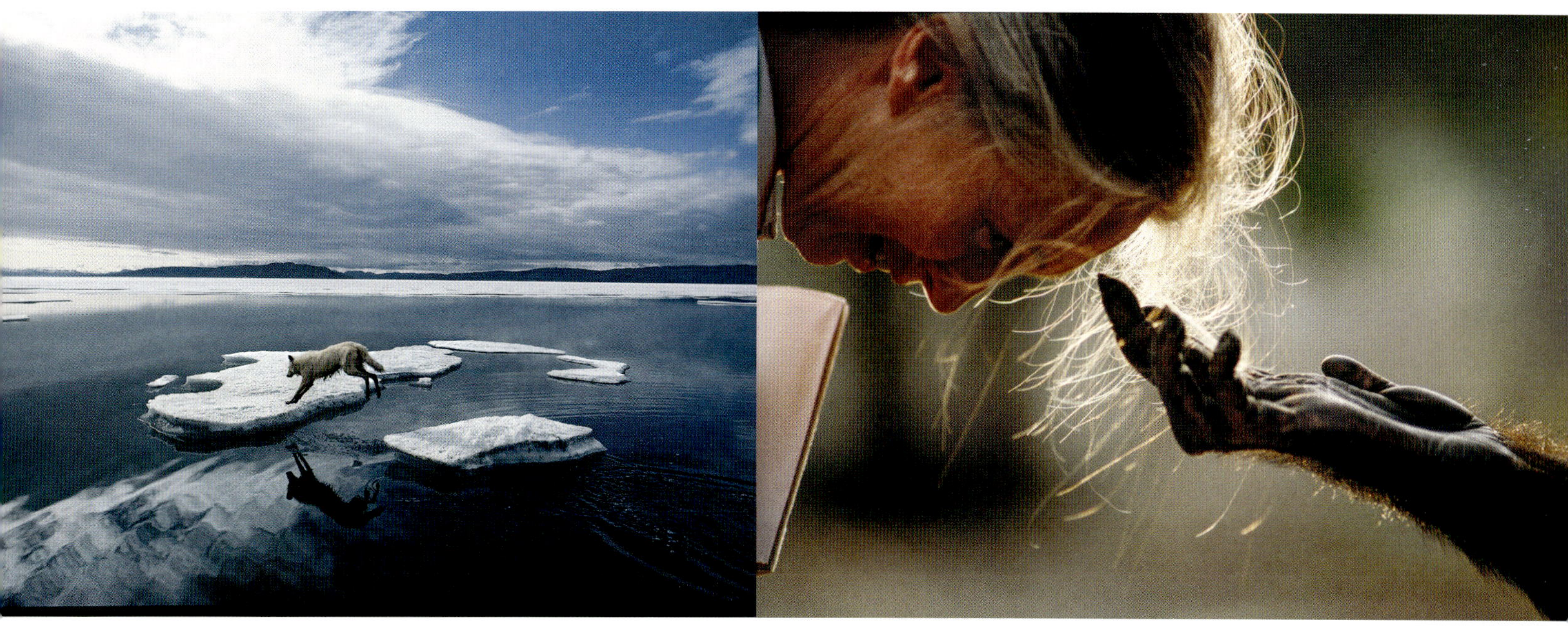

decimation of global fisheries, and the complex culture of whales. "Whether we wear harp seal fur, order the tuna dinner, or fail to consider whales as sentient creatures, our actions matter."

Most important, wildlife photography not only highlights and explains conservation issues; it provokes action. In 1999, Michael "Nick" Nichols began a 2,000-mile trek, or Megatransect, across Central Africa with scientist-conservationist J. Michael Fay to document Africa's last untouched wilderness. In 2002, his body of work inspired Omar Bongo, Gabon's president at the time, to set aside 11 percent of that country as protected land.

Other stories had similarly resounding impact. Photographer Brent Stirton and writer Bryan Christy's 2012 article on the ivory trade changed U.S. ivory import policy and prompted countries to burn elephant tusks to keep them off the black market. And in 2008, when he realized that research alone couldn't save the oceans, Enric Sala added photographer to his roles as marine biologist and conservationist when he established the National Geographic Society–funded project Pristine Seas. To date, it has inspired governments to set aside 2.5 million square miles of coastline and ocean in 26 marine protected areas. Photographer Steve Winter and journalist Sharon Guynup's reporting on captive tigers in the November 2019 issue led to the passage of the U.S. Big Cat Public Safety Act and helped convict a wildlife trafficker.

Small wonder underwater photographer David Doubilet calls natural history photographers the frontline reporters of the world. "The greatest story on earth is the Earth itself," he says. "It's all we have. There is no plan B."

ABOVE LEFT
JIM BRANDENBURG, 1986
A male Arctic wolf bounds across the ice floes on Canada's Ellesmere Island.

ABOVE RIGHT
MICHAEL NICHOLS, 1990
Jou Jou, an adult male chimpanzee, had been caged alone for an entire year when he reached out for connection with Jane Goodall at the Republic of the Congo's Brazzaville Zoo.

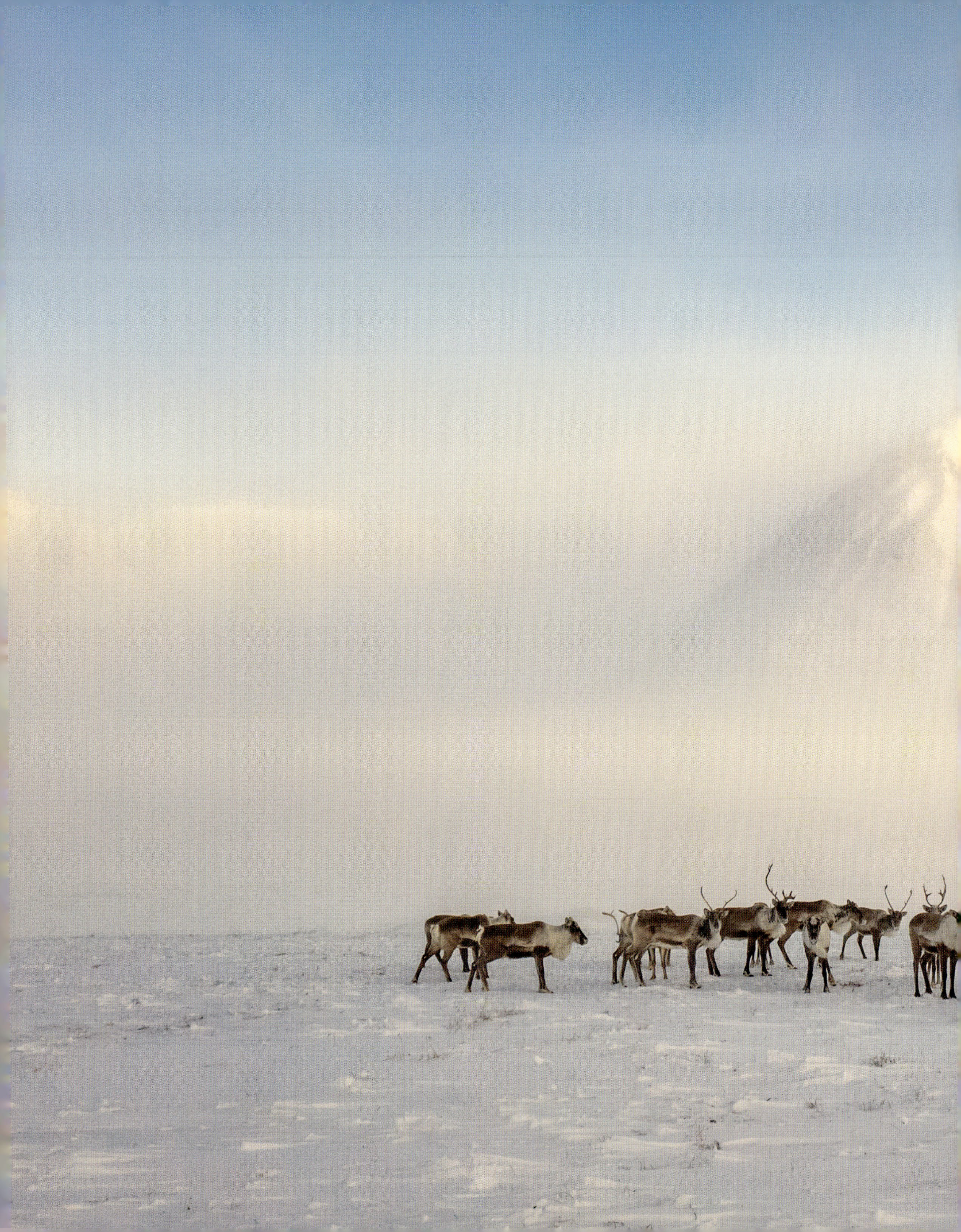

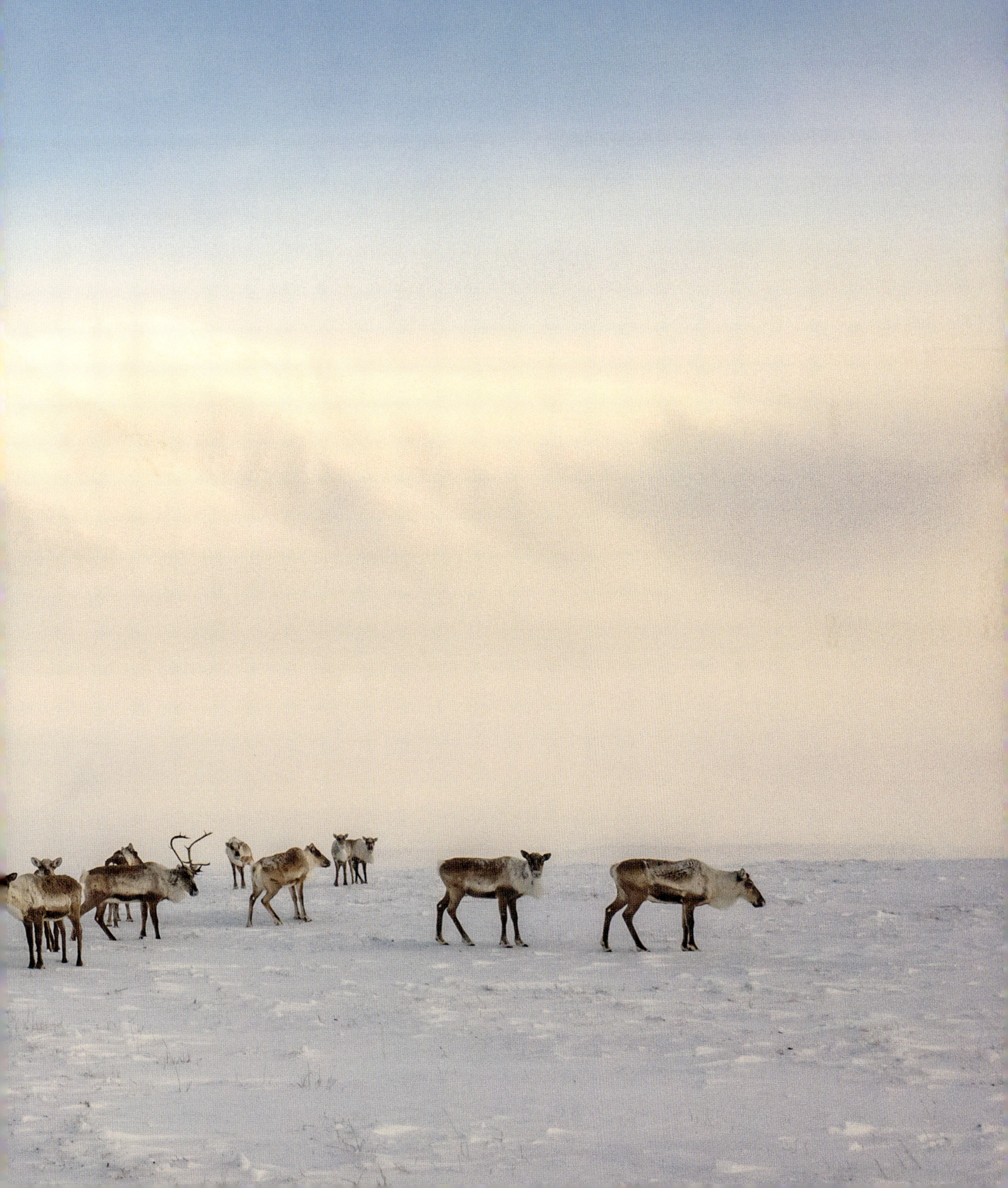

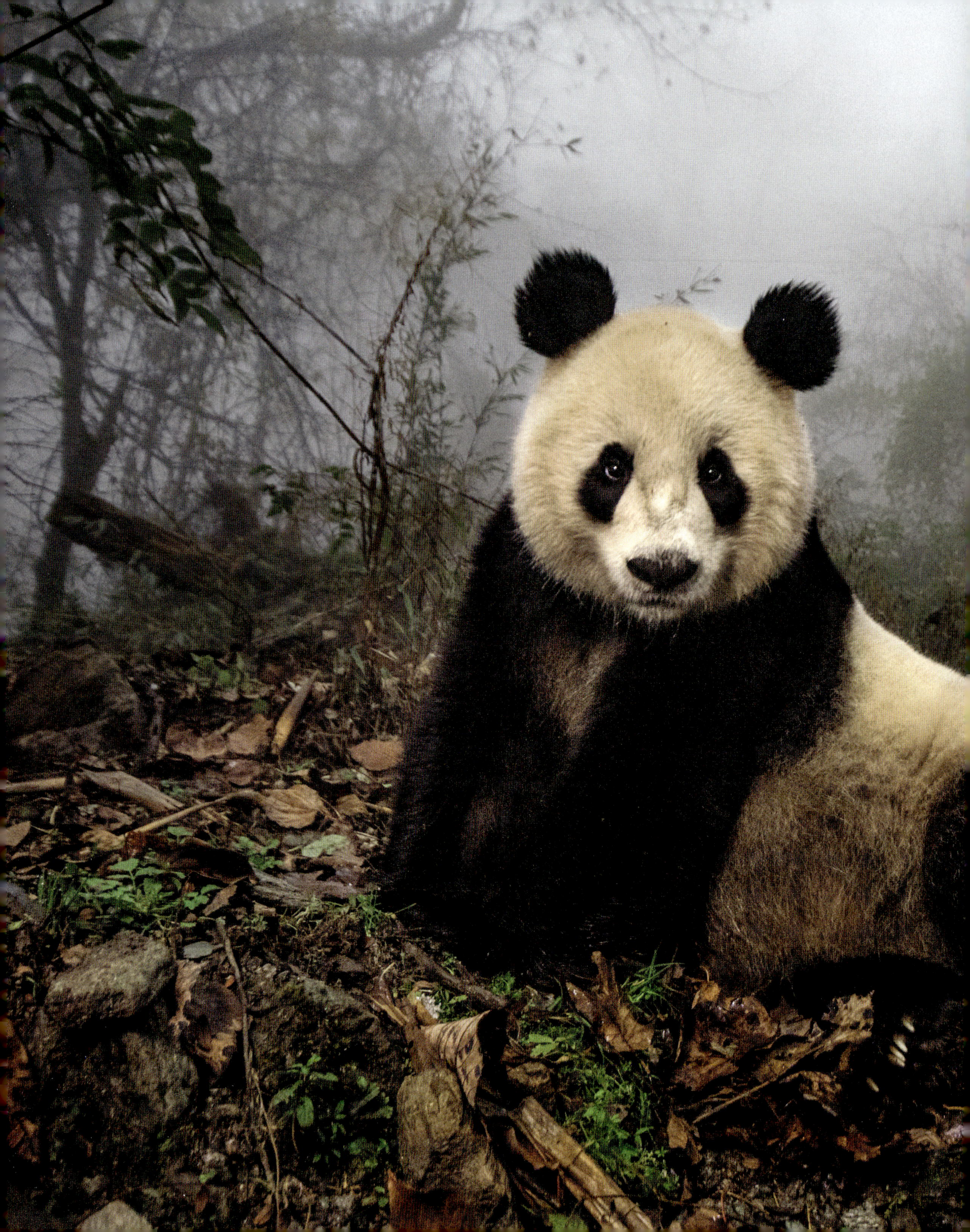

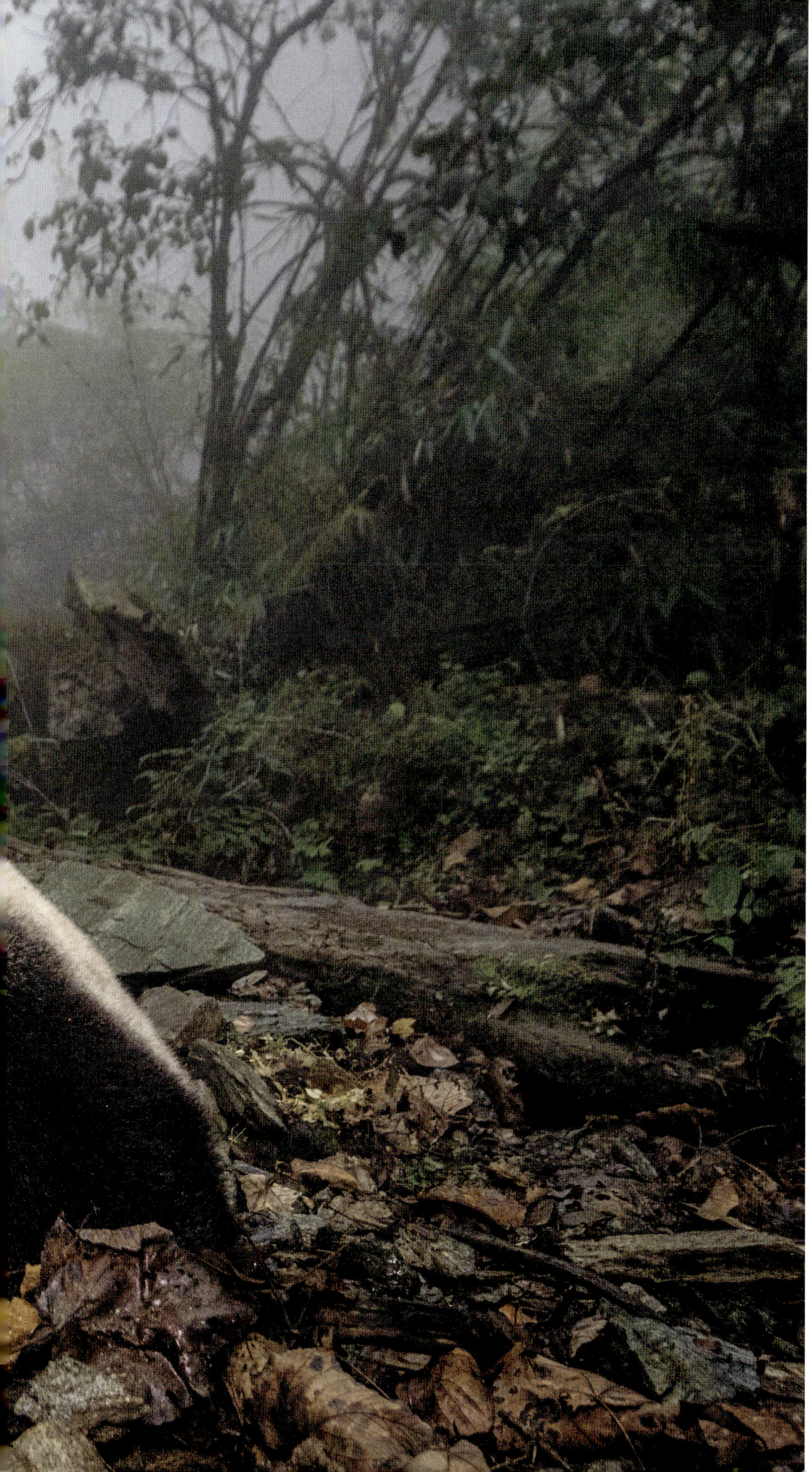

AMI VITALE, 2015
Ye Ye, a 16-year-old giant panda, in China's Wolong Nature Reserve. Her cubs are bred in captivity for reintroduction to the wild.

PREVIOUS PAGES
KATIE ORLINSKY, 2021
Caribou traverse the heart of Alaska's expansive Brooks Range.

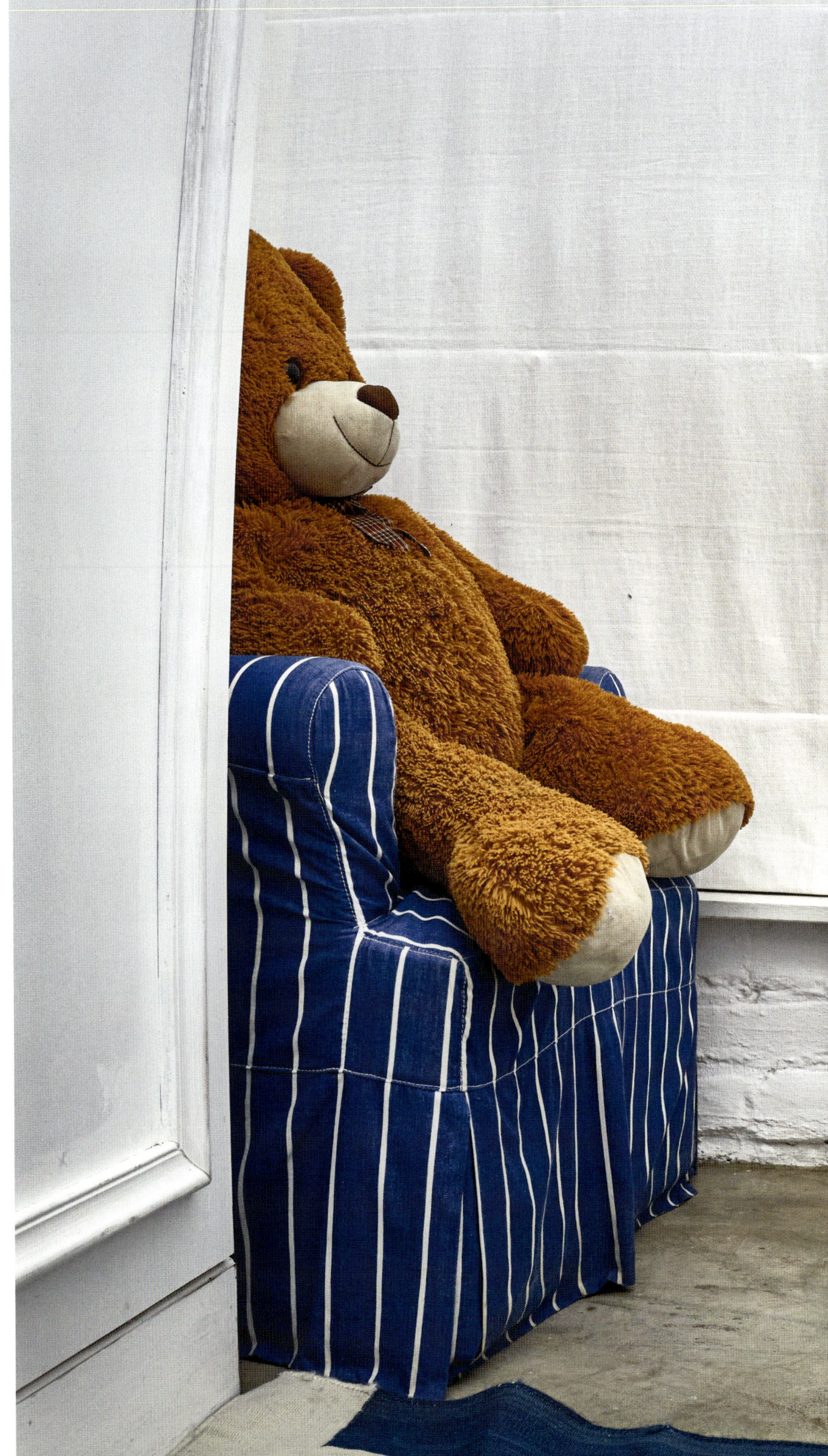

MÉLANIE WENGER, 2021
After becoming habituated to humans, an African penguin visits a guesthouse in Simon's Town, South Africa.

FOLLOWING PAGES
STEPHEN WILKES, 2016
A composite, stitched together from many photographs, captures the diversity of life around a water hole in Serengeti National Park in Tanzania.

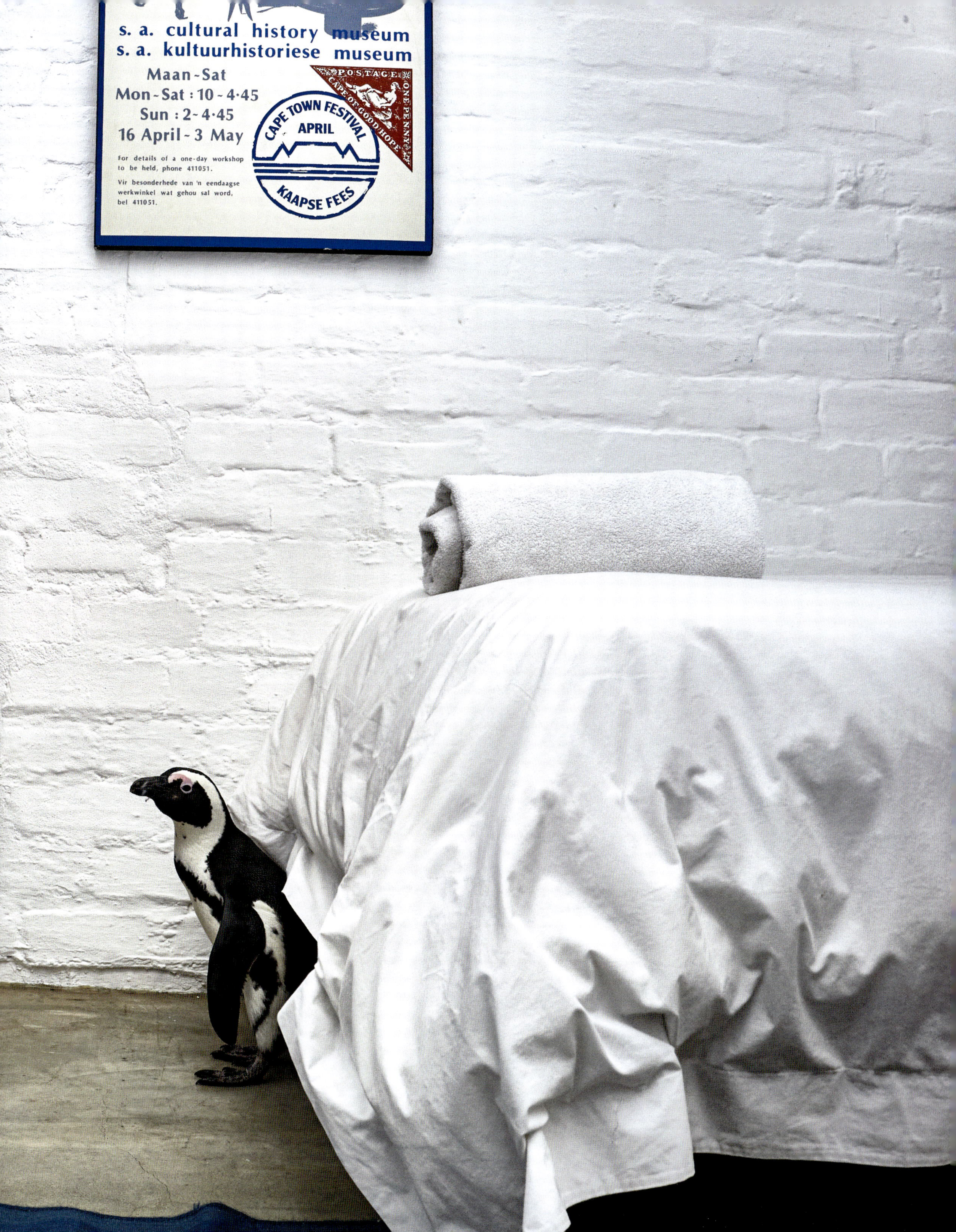
s. a. cultural history museum
s. a. kultuurhistoriese museum
Maan - Sat
Mon - Sat : 10 - 4·45
Sun : 2 - 4·45
16 April - 3 May
For details of a one-day workshop to be held, phone 411051.
Vir besonderhede van 'n eendaagse werkwinkel wat gehou sal word, bel 411051.
POSTAGE
CAPE OF GOOD HOPE
ONE PENNY
CAPE TOWN FESTIVAL
APRIL
KAAPSE FEES

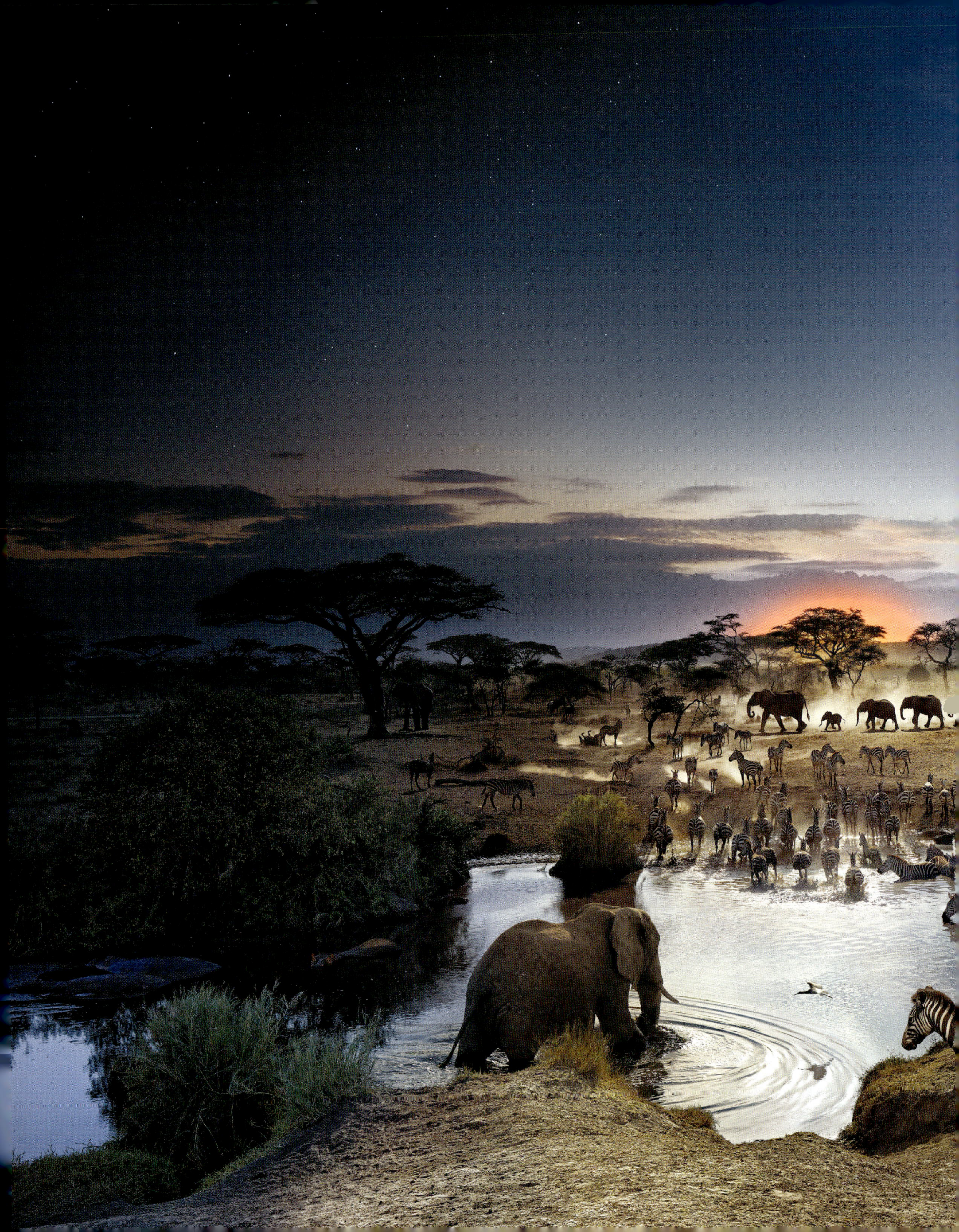

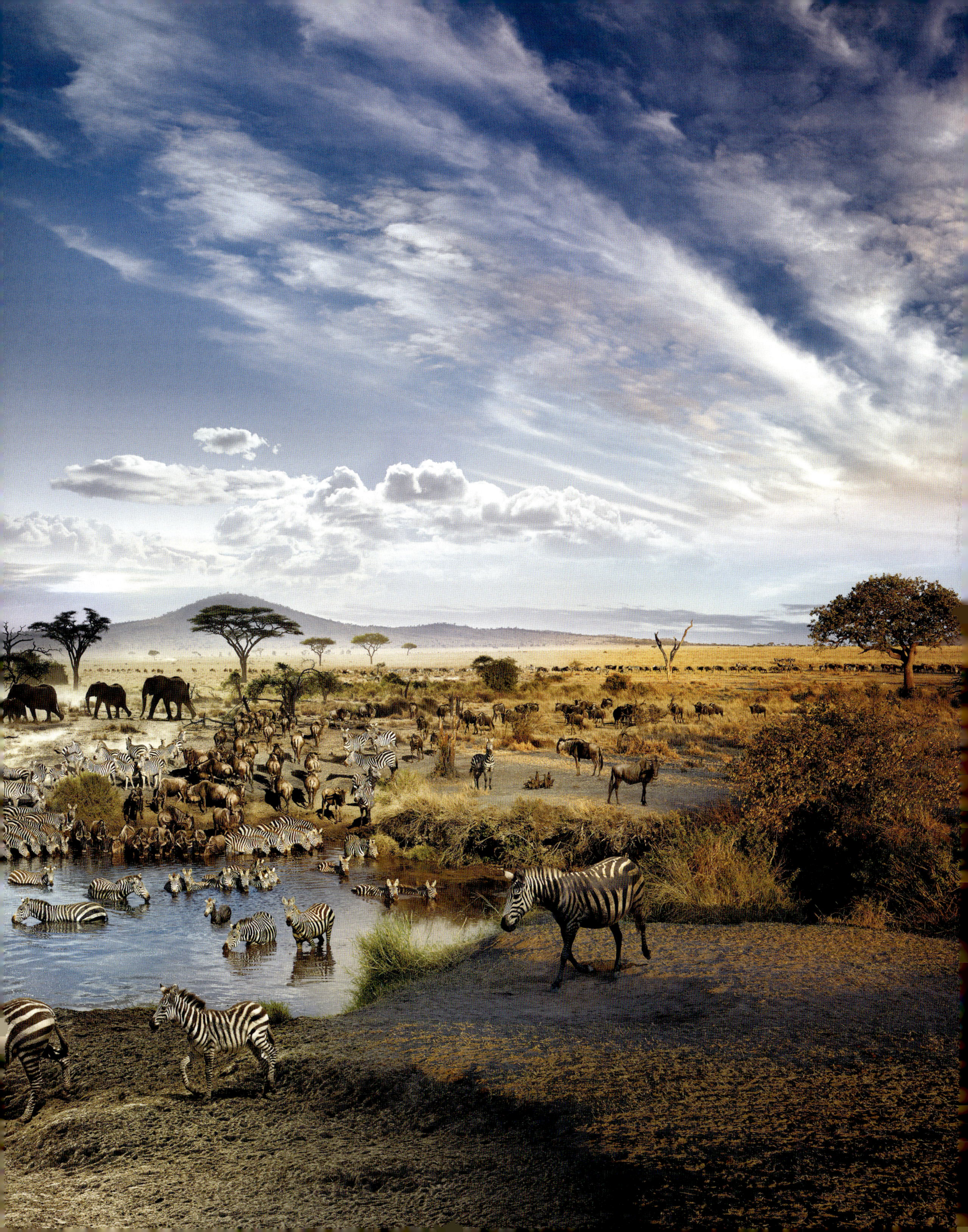

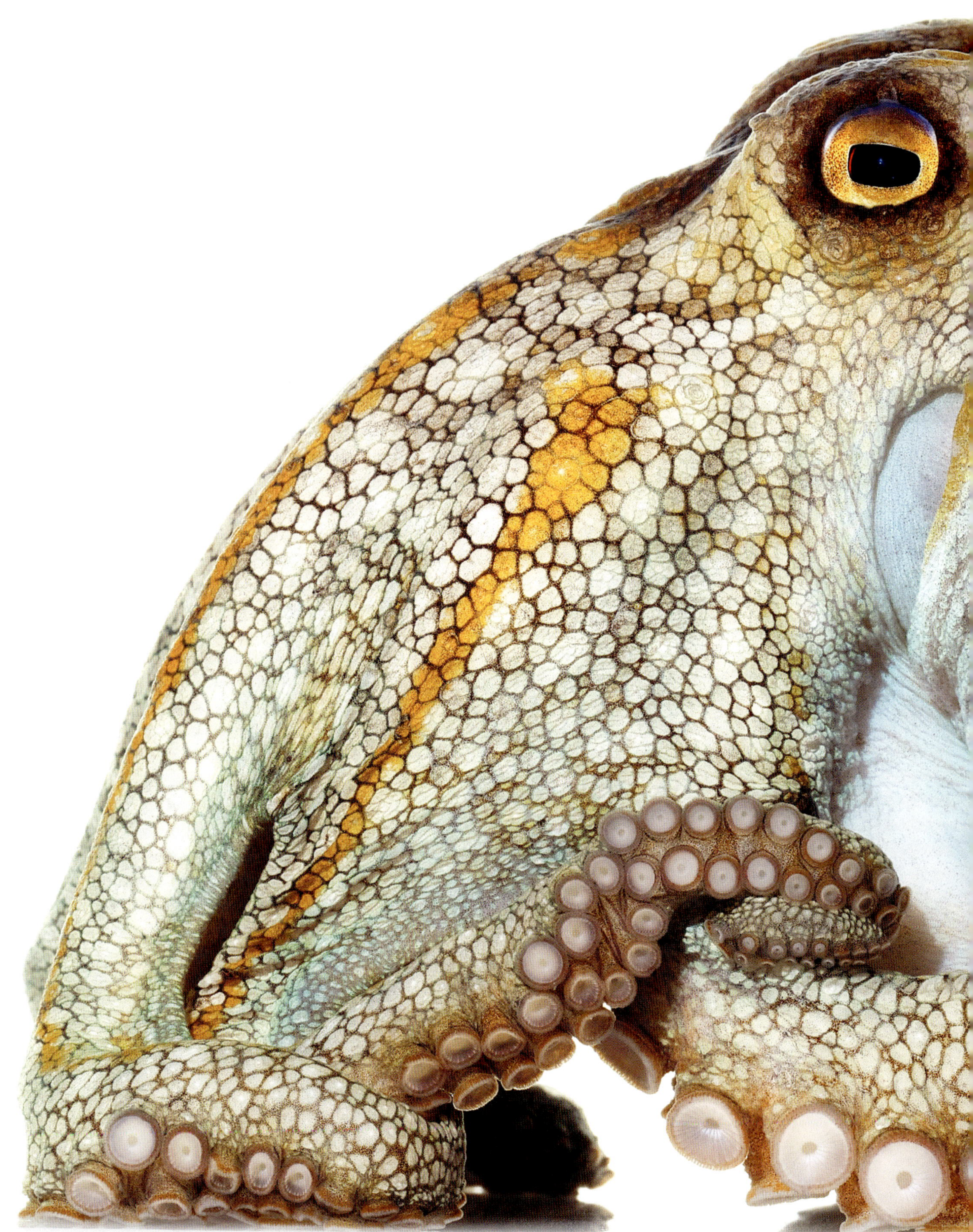

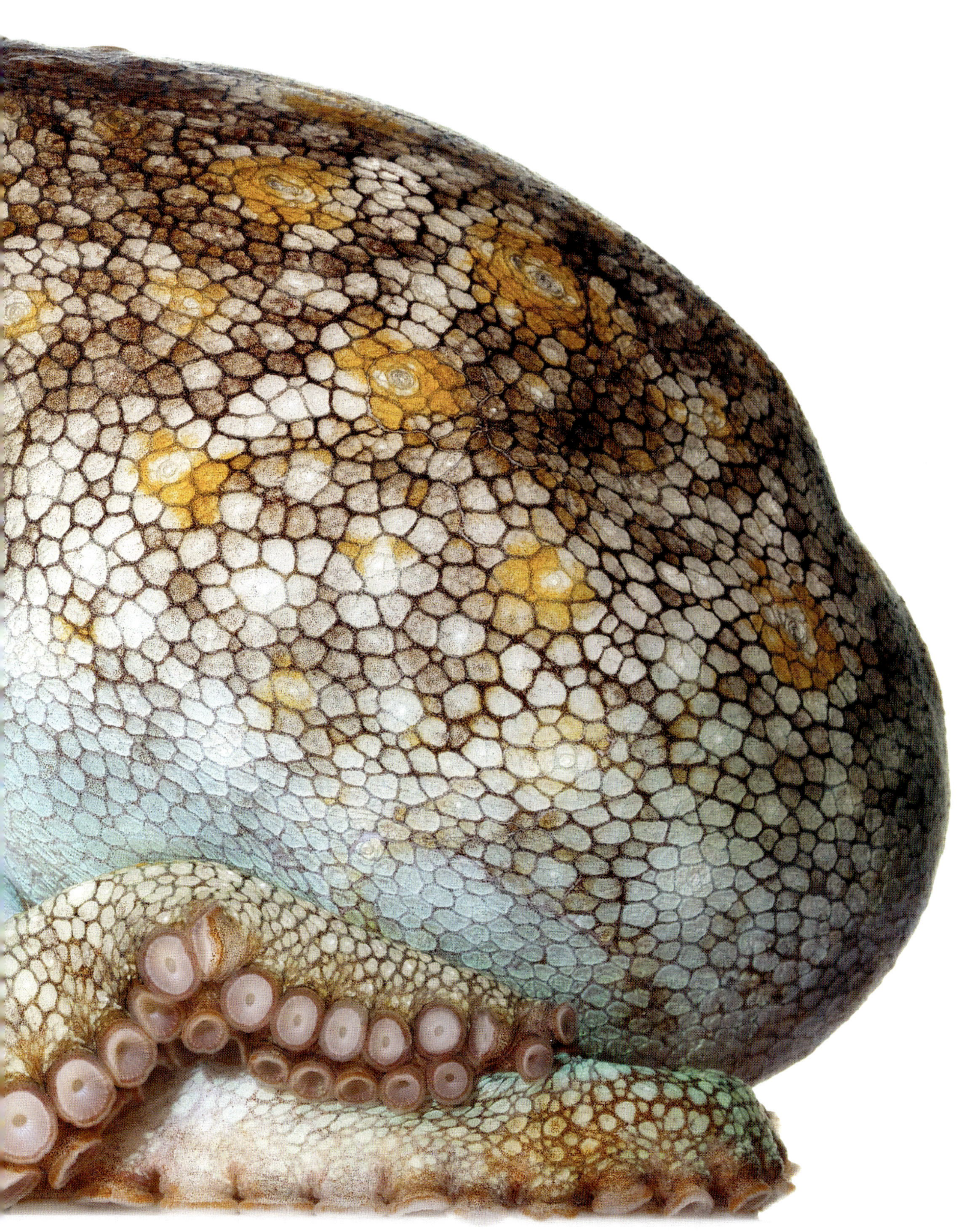

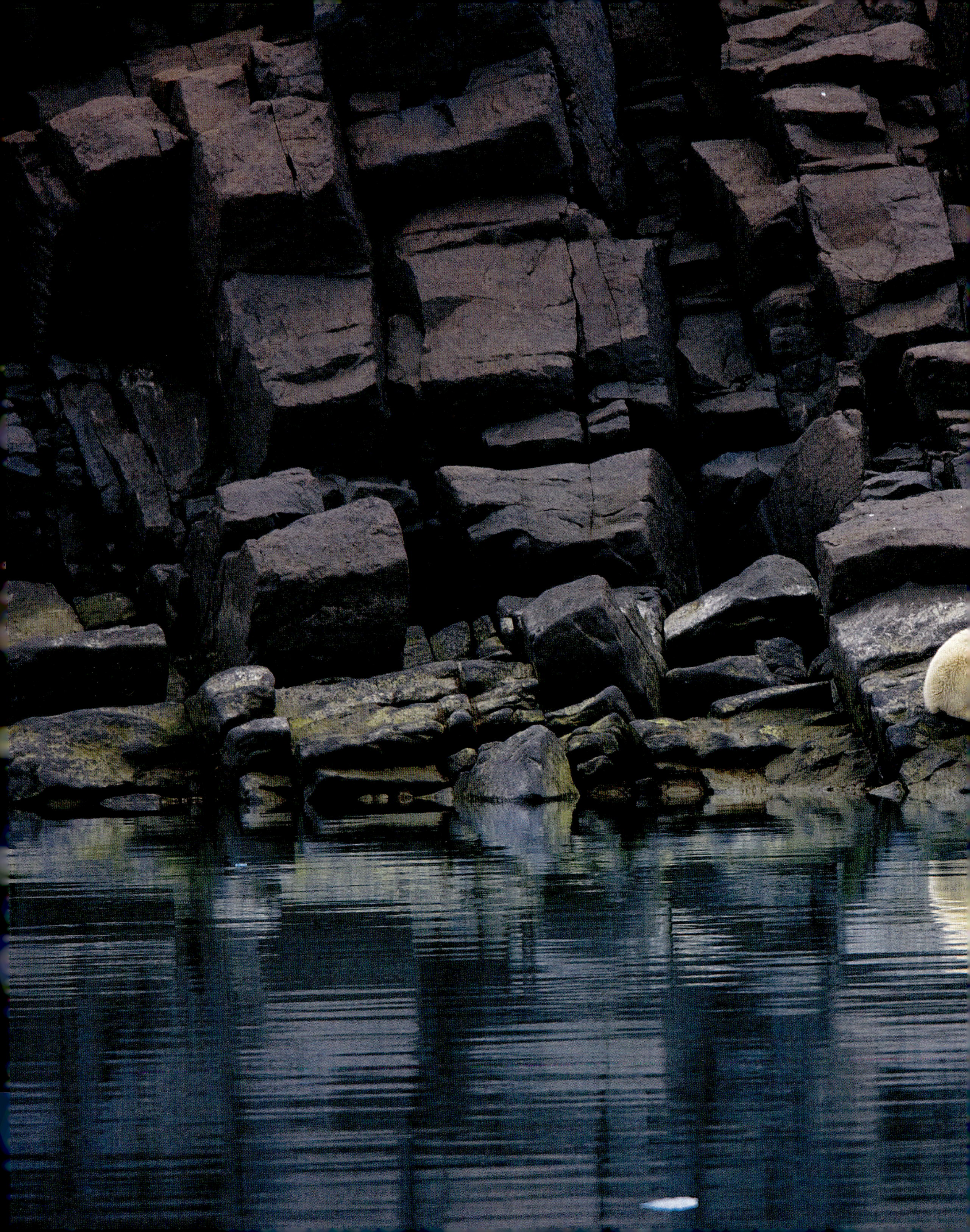

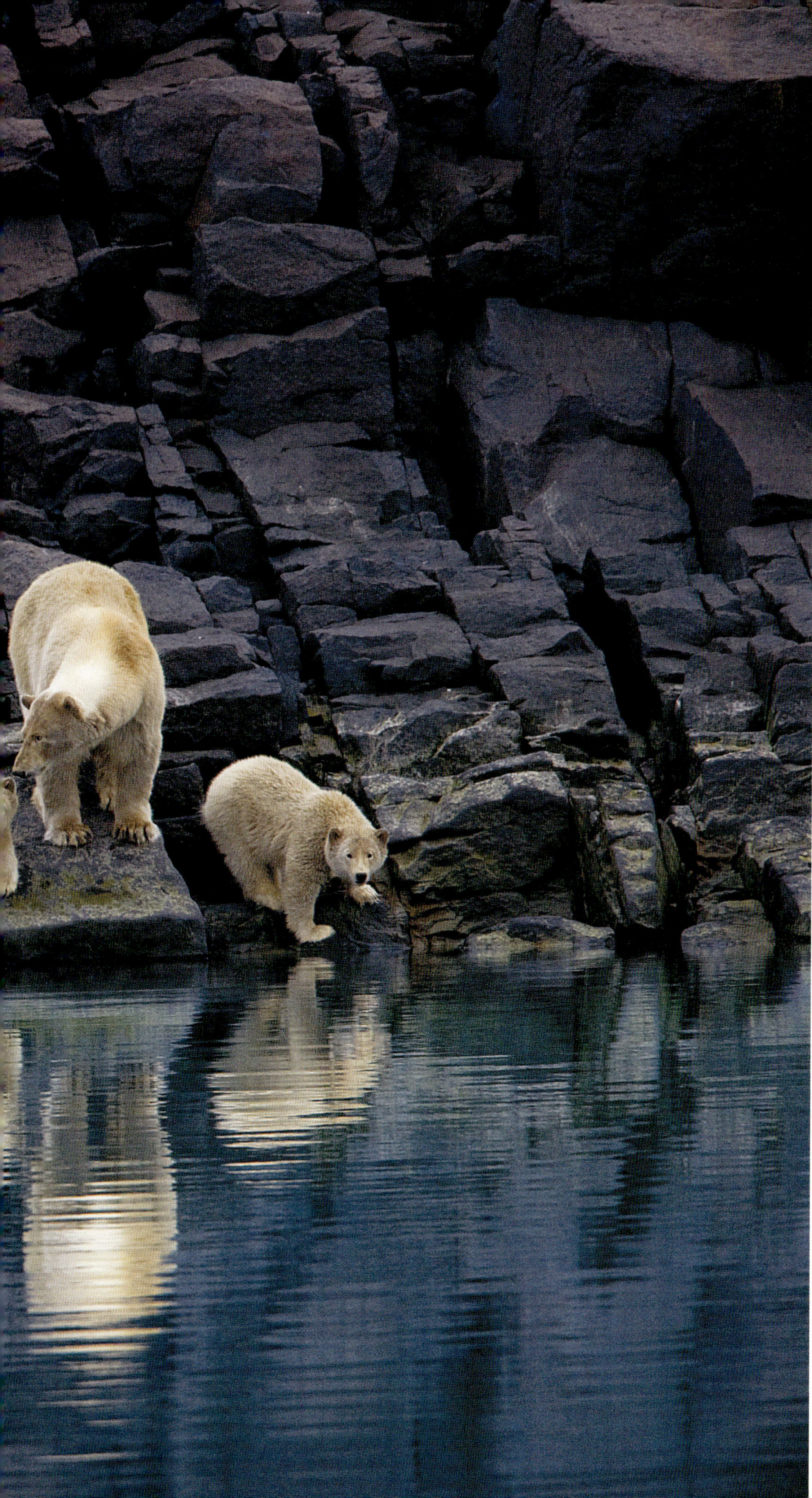

PAUL NICKLEN, 2007
A mother polar bear and her cubs must increasingly navigate a world without ice while hunting for food near Svalbard, Norway.

PREVIOUS PAGES
DAVID LIITTSCHWAGER, 2014
Stocky, with a large body and shortish arms, the pale octopus lives in the waters off southeastern Australia, where it emerges at night to feed on shellfish.

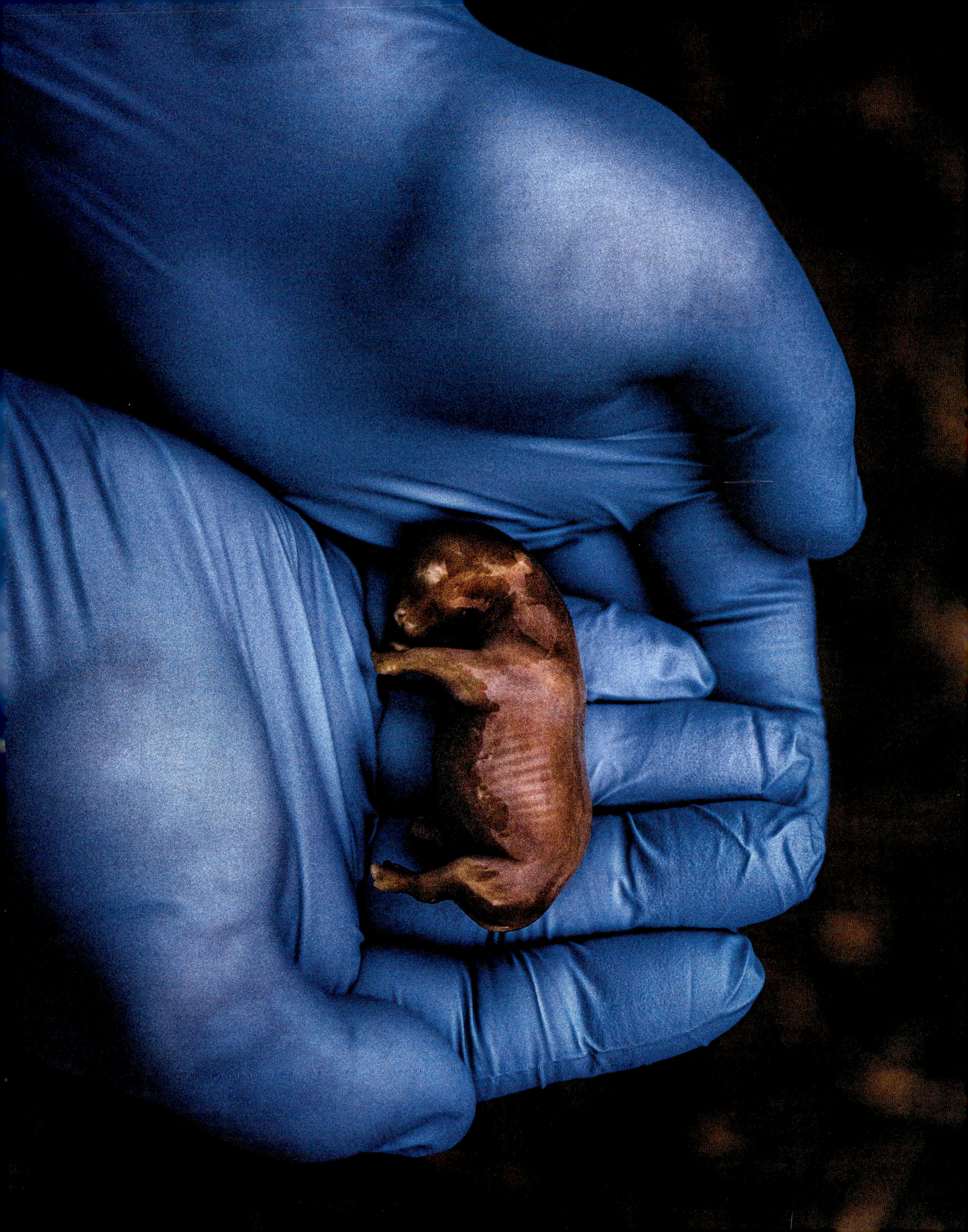

PHOTOGRAPHS DRIVE HOME TO OUR READERS—IN A WAY THAT WORDS NEVER CAN—THAT OUR CHOICES HAVE CONSEQUENCES.

KATHY MORAN, *NATIONAL GEOGRAPHIC* MAGAZINE PHOTO EDITOR, 1990–2021

AMI VITALE, 2024
A scientist holds the 70-day-old fetus of a rhino conceived through in vitro fertilization in Nanyuki, Kenya.

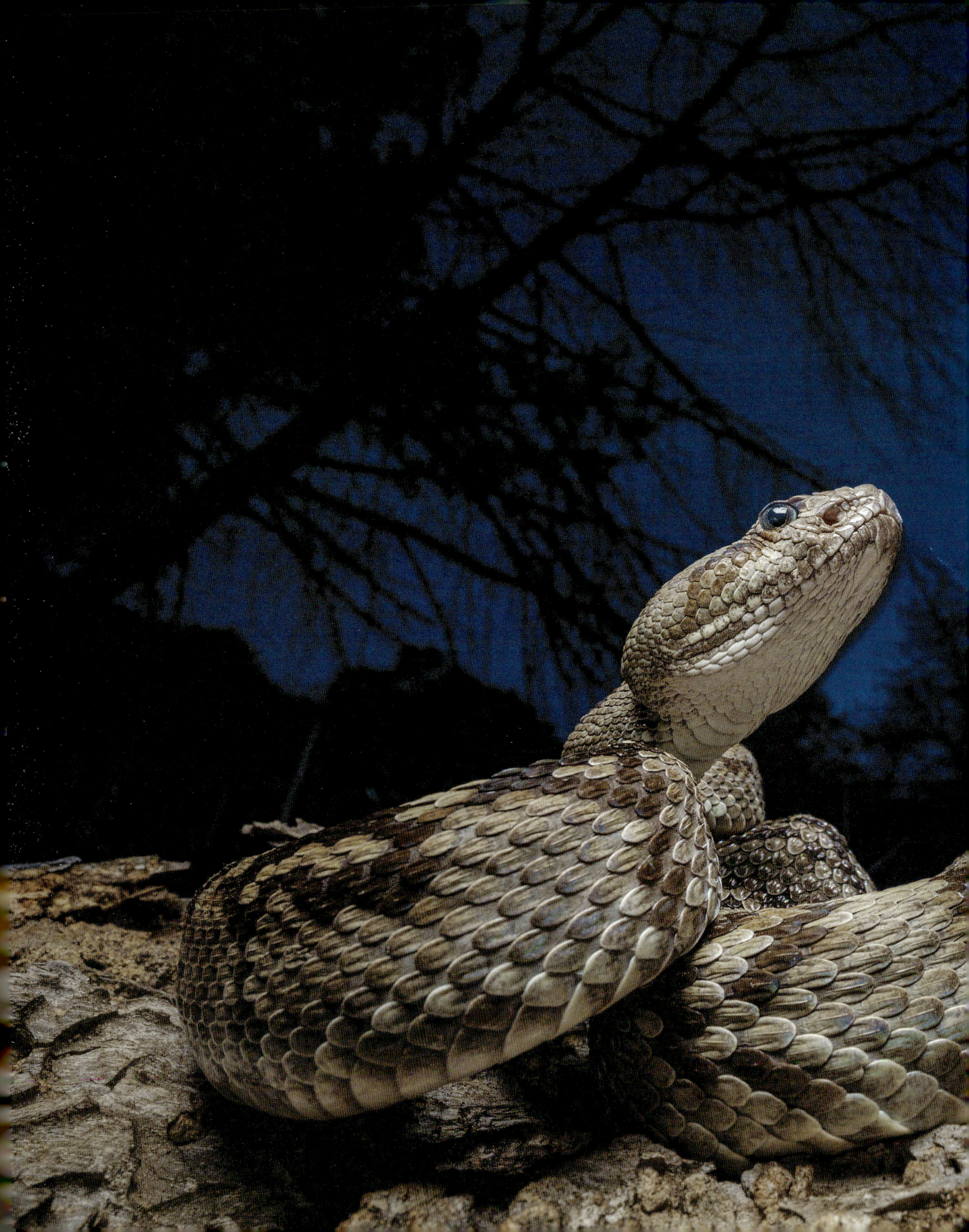

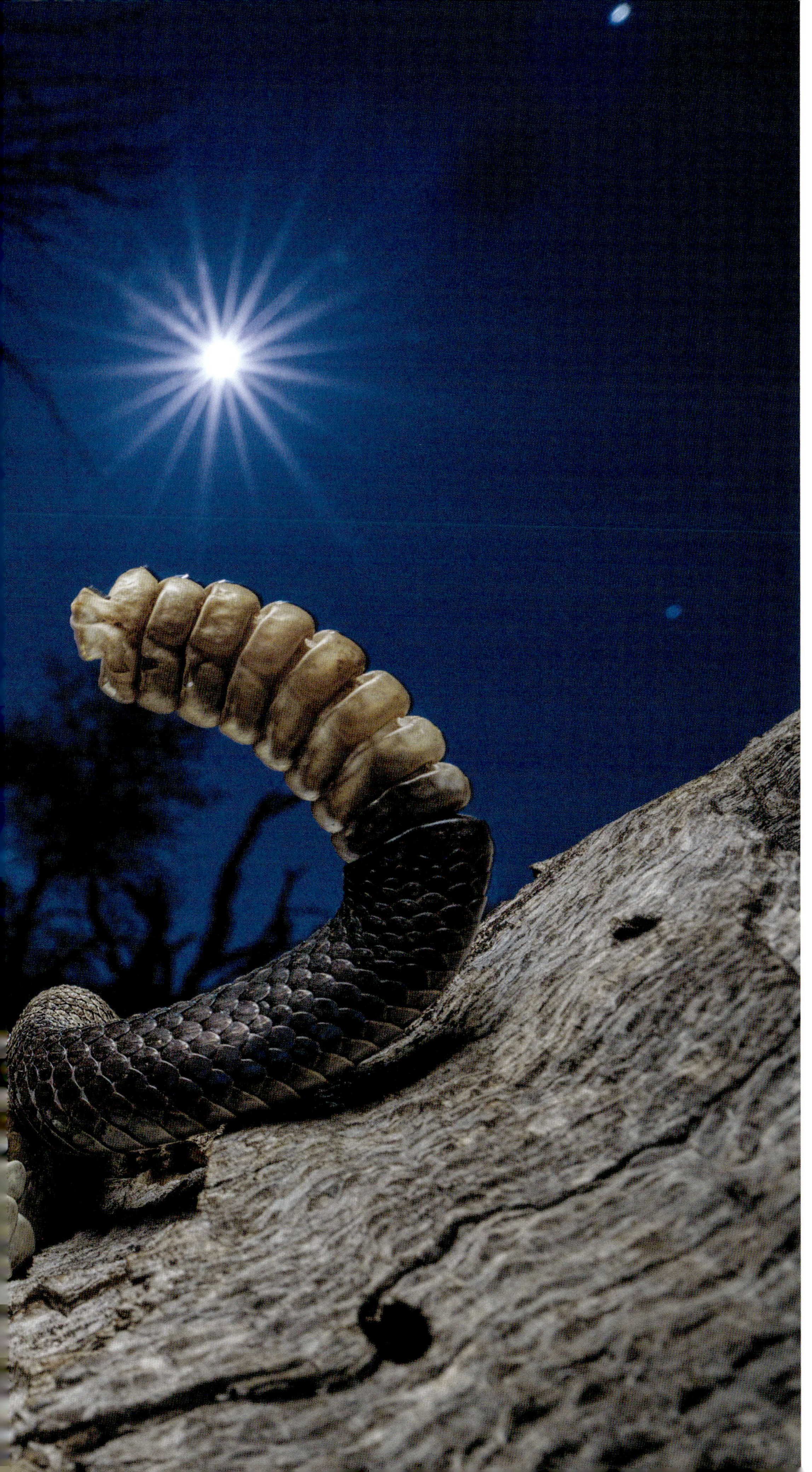

JAVIER AZNAR GONZÁLEZ DE RUEDA, 2021
An eastern black-tailed rattlesnake in Texas's Davis Mountains. These snakes' venom has been employed for medical use, including Covid-19 research.

FOLLOWING PAGES
CHRIS JOHNS, 1996
A lion patrols the Nossob riverbed, part of South Africa's Kalahari Gemsbok National Park.

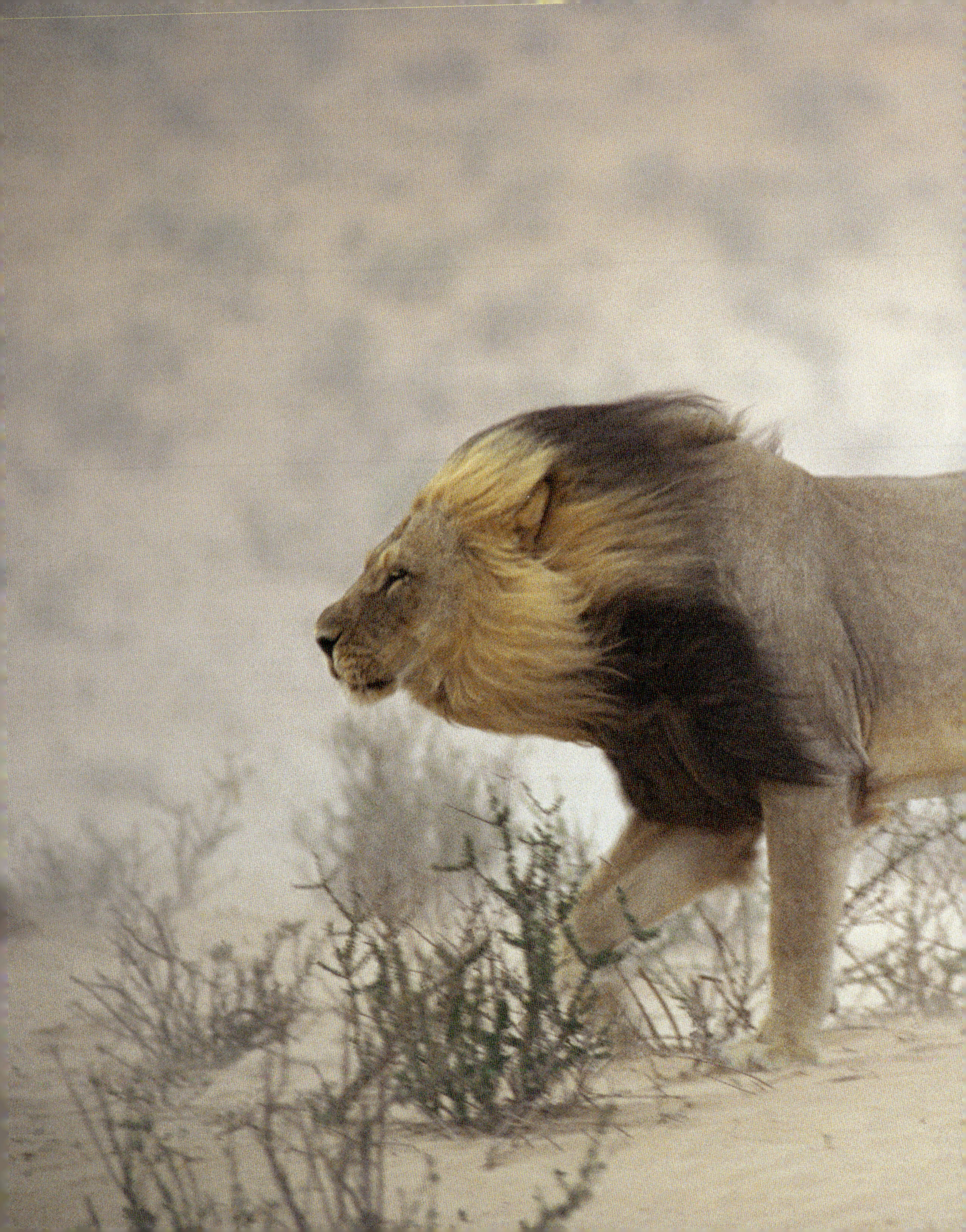

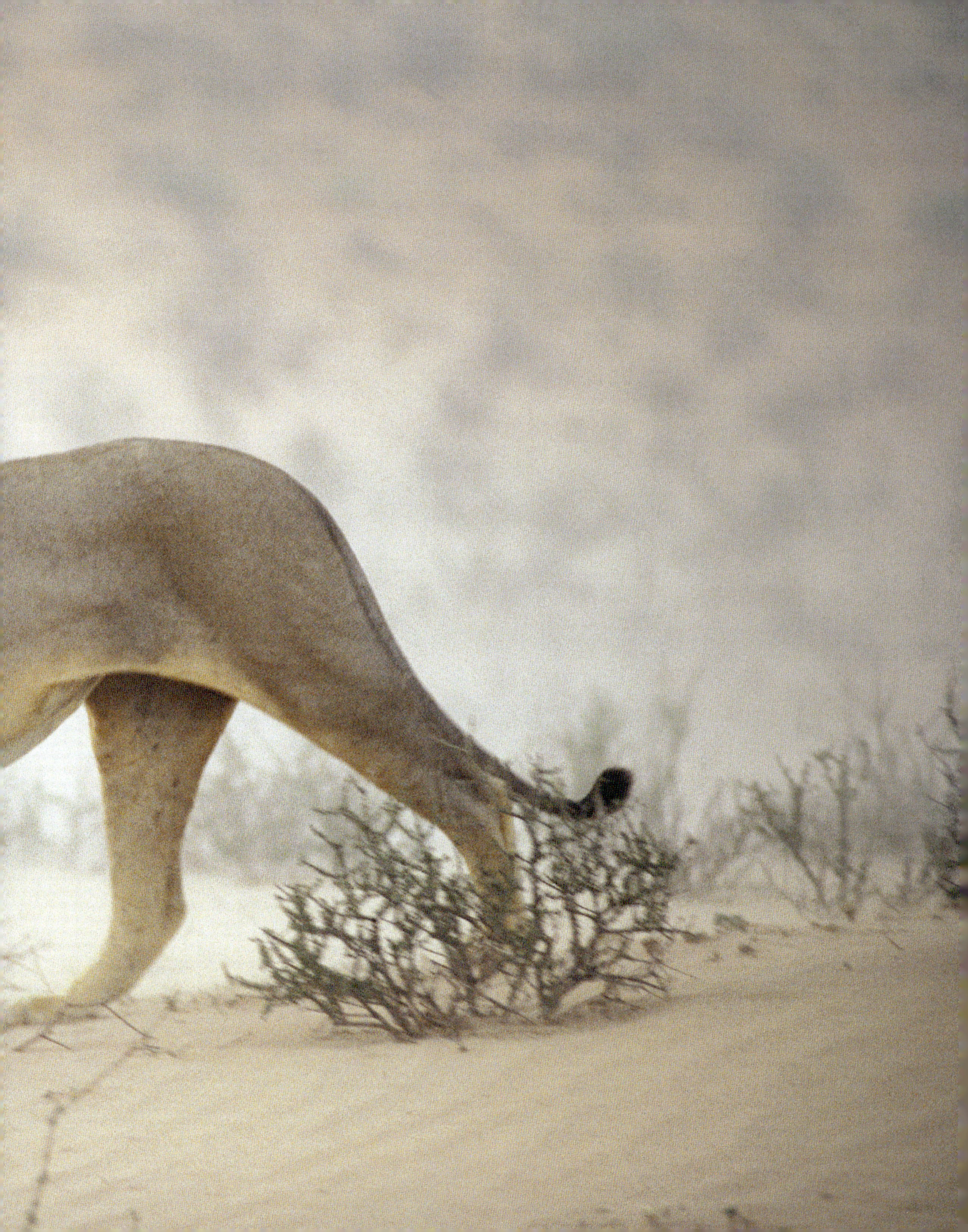

BIOGRAPHY

BRIAN SKERRY

THOUGH HE GREW UP IN A SMALL New England textile town 45 miles from the ocean, Brian Skerry fell in love with that deep blue expanse as a young boy. It was a passion that culminated in a career as a National Geographic photographer with 33 magazine stories, 13 books, and an Emmy-winning four-part television documentary based on his book *Secrets of the Whales*. In addition to being named a National Geographic Explorer in 2014 and the Rolex National Geographic Explorer of the Year in 2017, Skerry is a founding member of the International League of Conservation Photographers.

The first rule of underwater photography, he advises, is to get close to the subject; telephoto lenses don't capture images well underwater. The second rule is patience. "I get into the water for the first time, and at first all I see is chaos," he says. "Then I learn to focus and see one thing at a time. I see patterns and rhythms, and then I start to make pictures." One of the most striking of these portrays a thresher shark entangled in a gill net in the Gulf of California, documented in a story on the global crisis of overfishing. The shark had just died—its pectoral fins outstretched as if in crucifixion. Judges in the 2010 Wildlife Photographer of the Year competition called it "probably the best picture ever taken to illustrate the wastefulness of industrial fishing." Like Skerry's other work, it is a testament to the power of photography to bring light to problems that shadow the planet.

OPPOSITE TOP
BRIAN SKERRY, 2019
Naturally playful and curious, a baby beluga whale offers up a rock off Somerset Island in Nunavut, Canada.

OPPOSITE BOTTOM
BRIAN SKERRY, 2021
A gray seal surfaces in the Gulf of Maine, which is warming faster than almost any other ocean region.

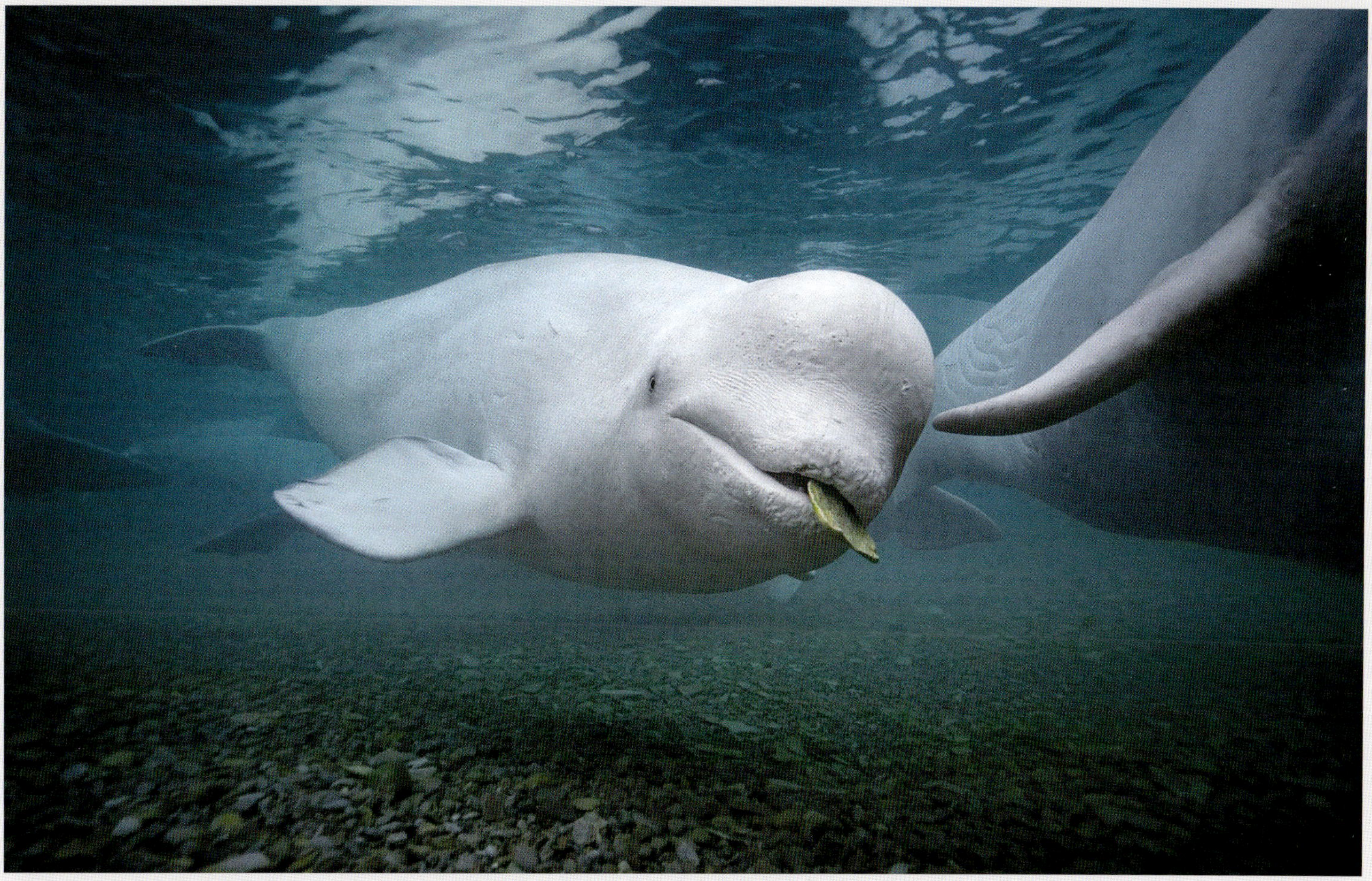

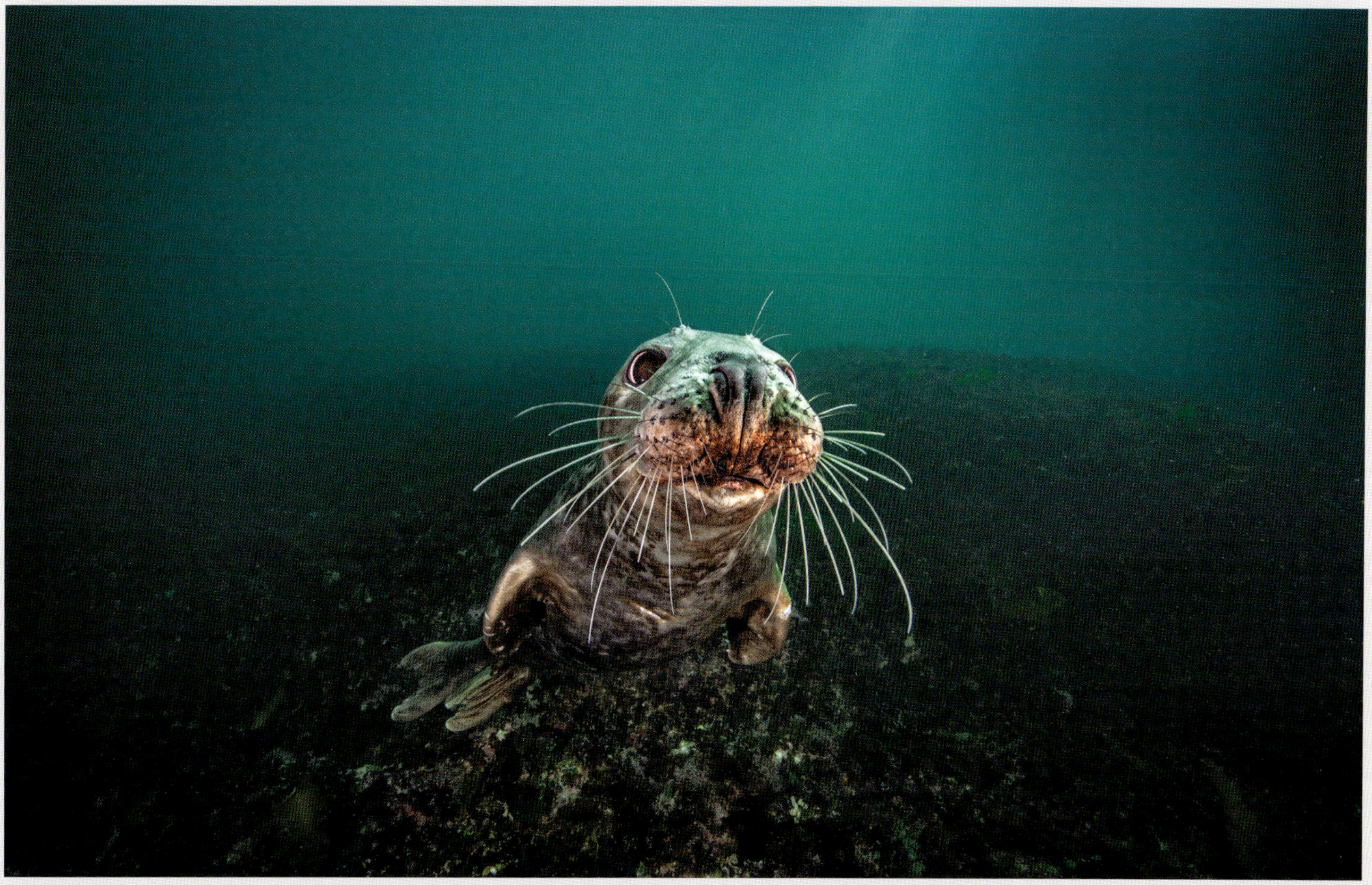

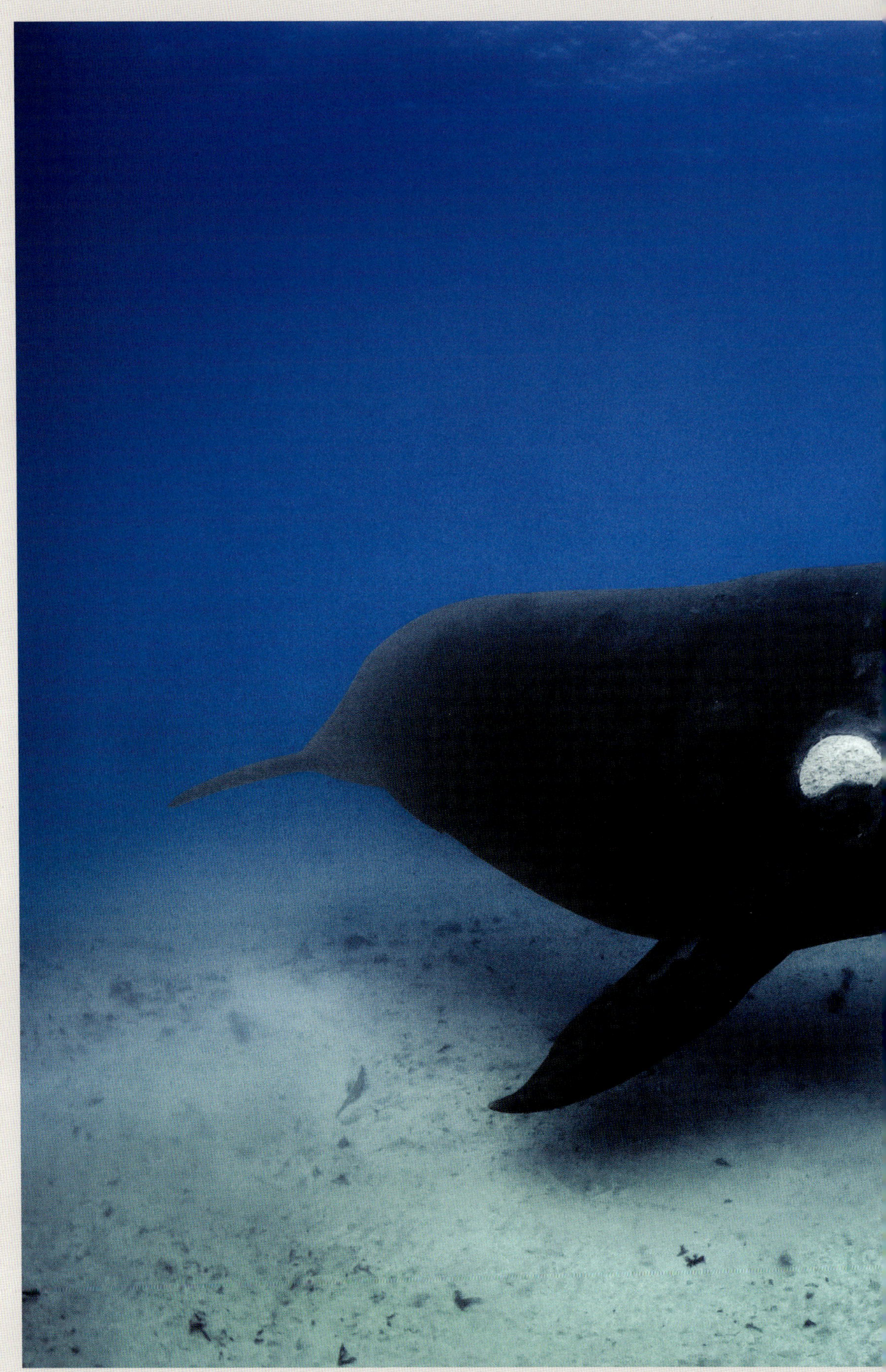

BRIAN SKERRY, 2007
A close encounter with a curious southern right whale off the Auckland Islands, 289 miles south of New Zealand

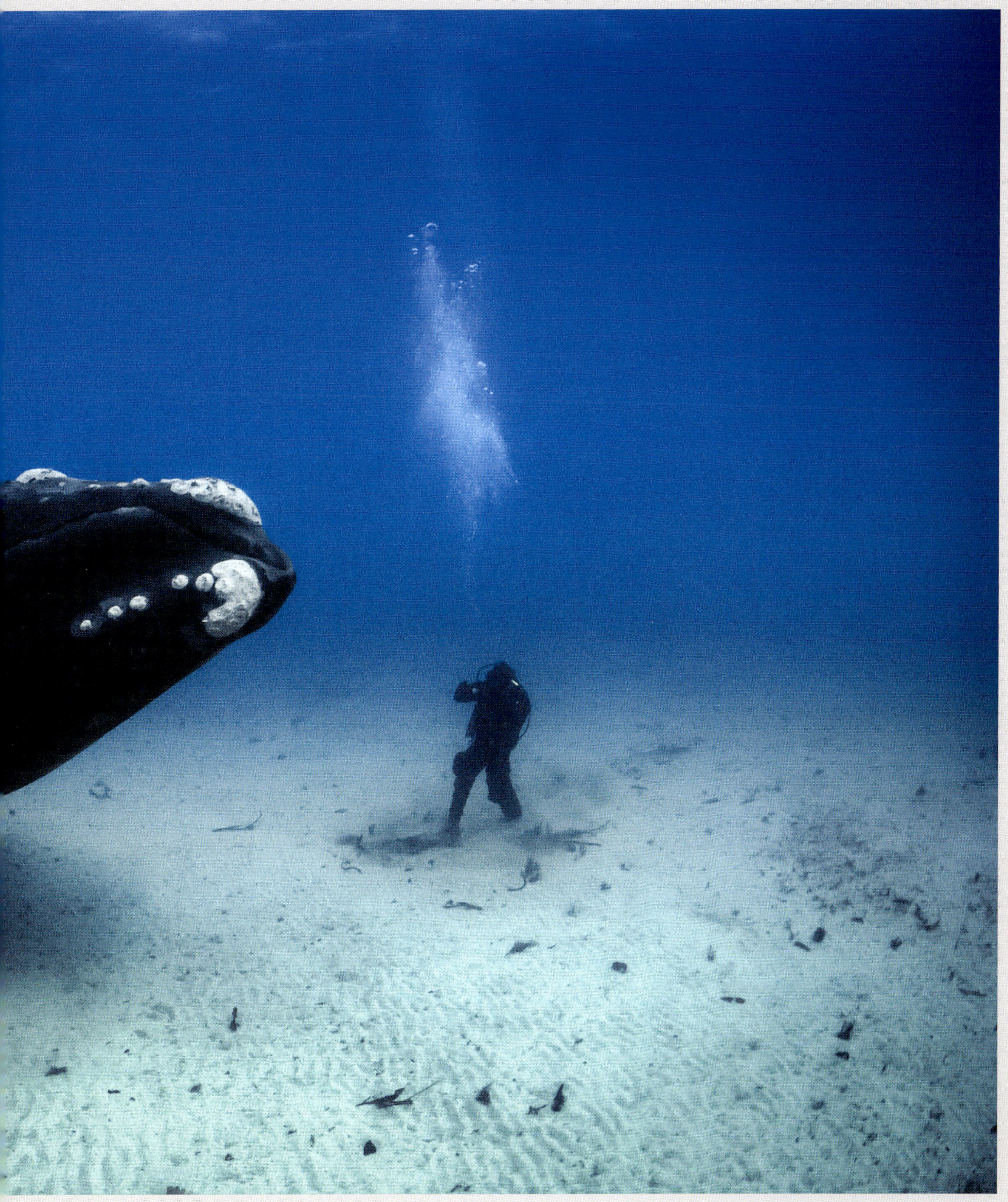

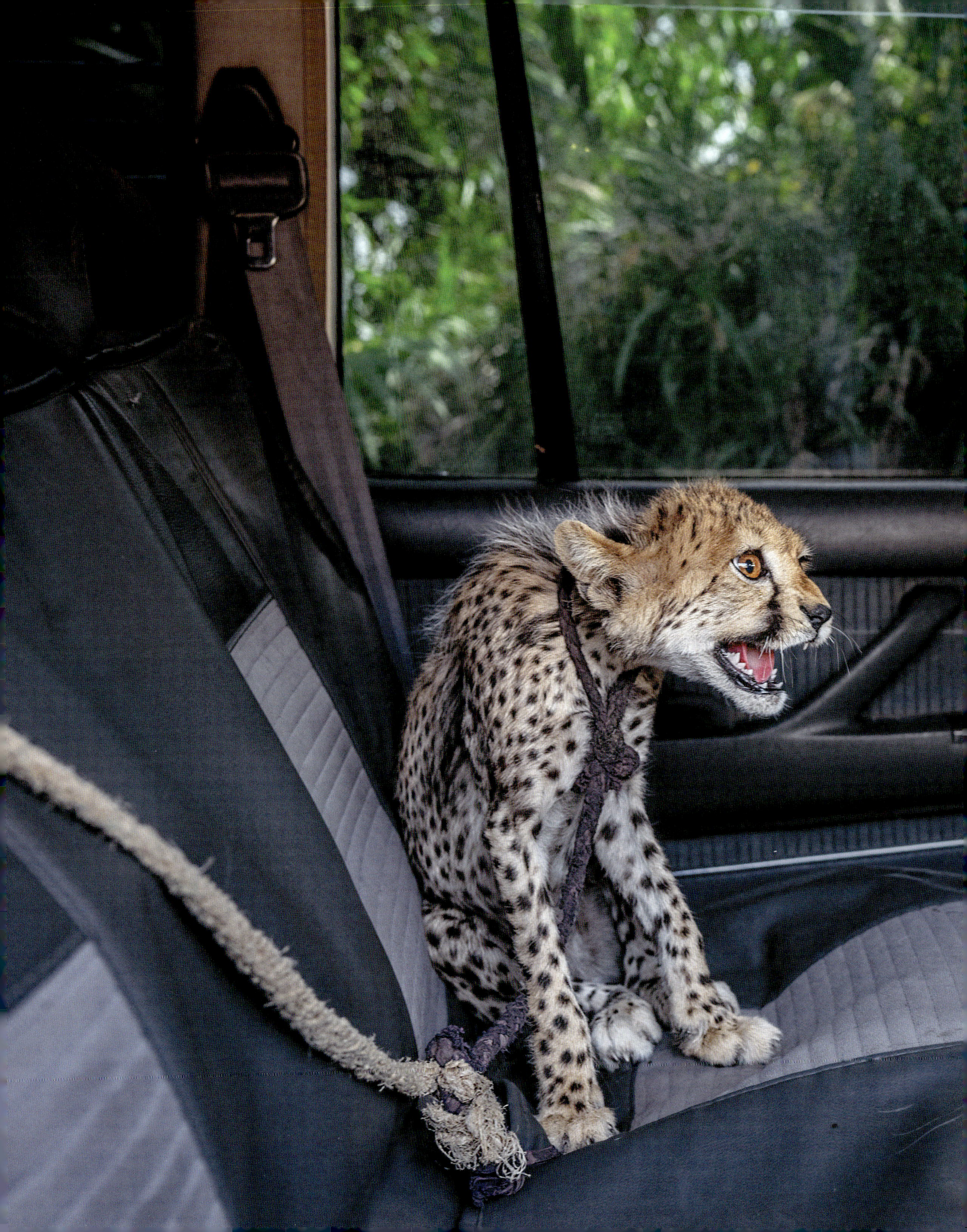

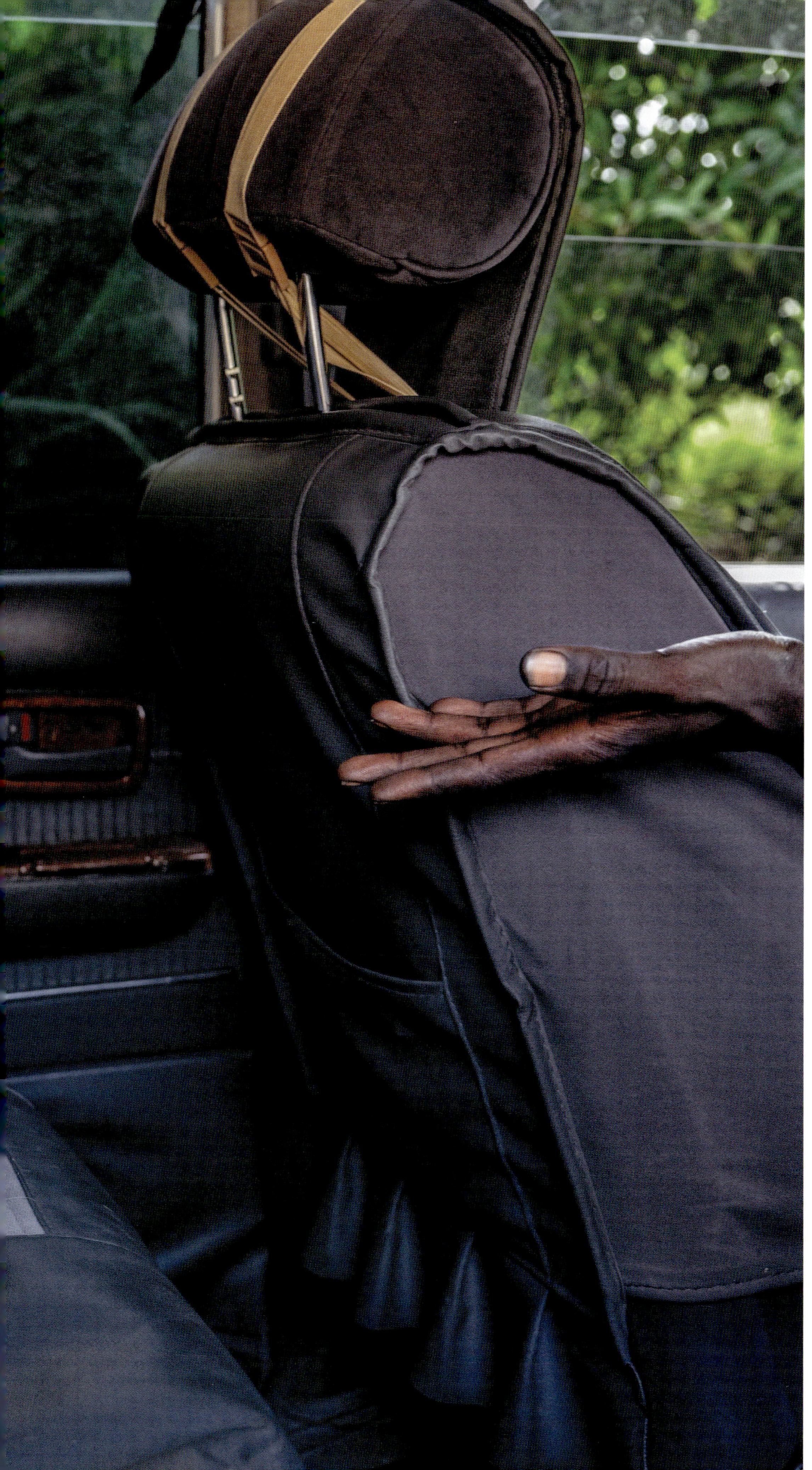

NICHOLE SOBECKI, 2020
This seven-month-old cheetah cub in Somaliland was saved from being sold by a smuggler.

FOLLOWING PAGES
BABAK TAFRESHI, 2024
Mexican free-tailed bats take flight from Texas's Frio Bat Cave, where as many as 10 million of them make their spring and summer home.

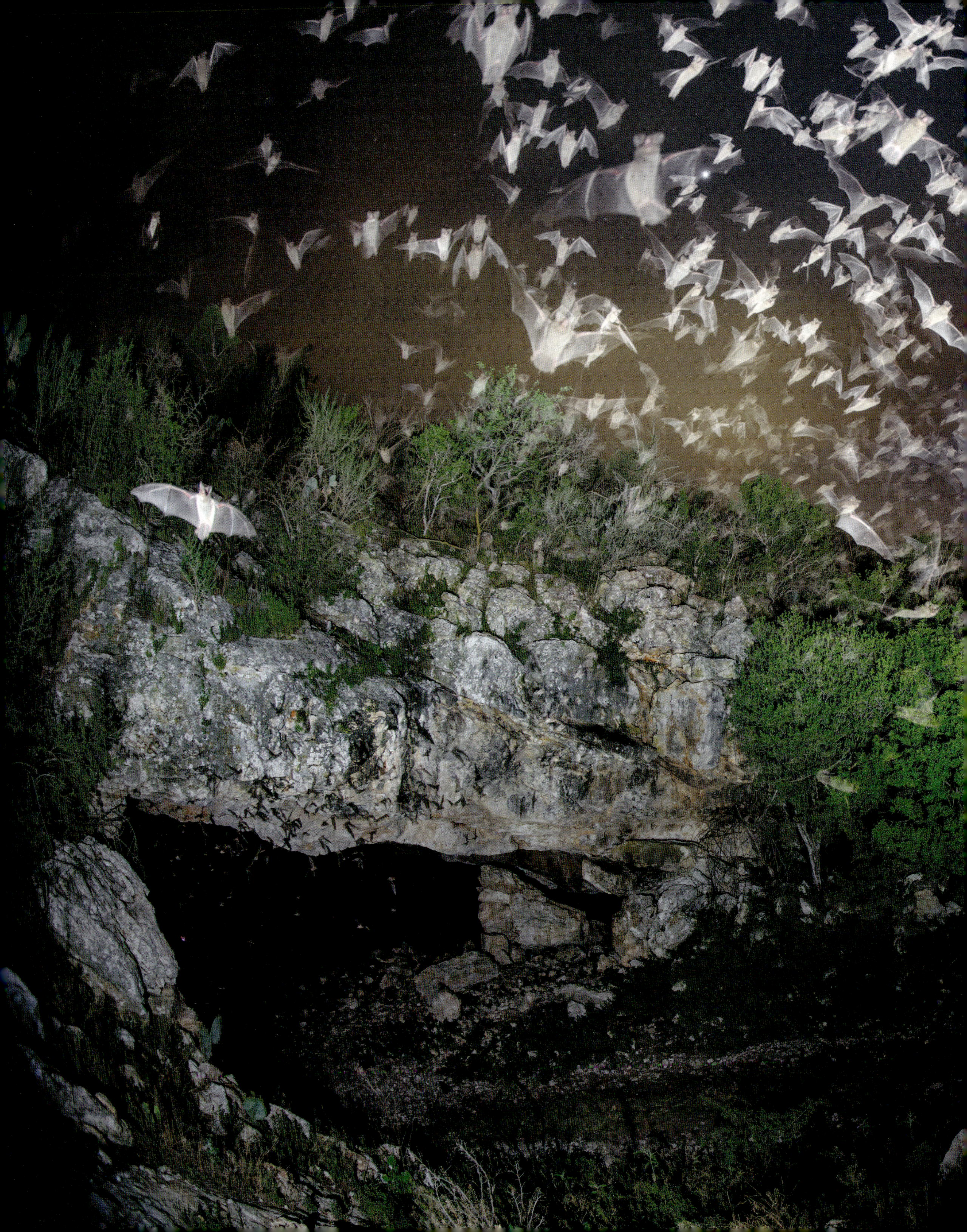

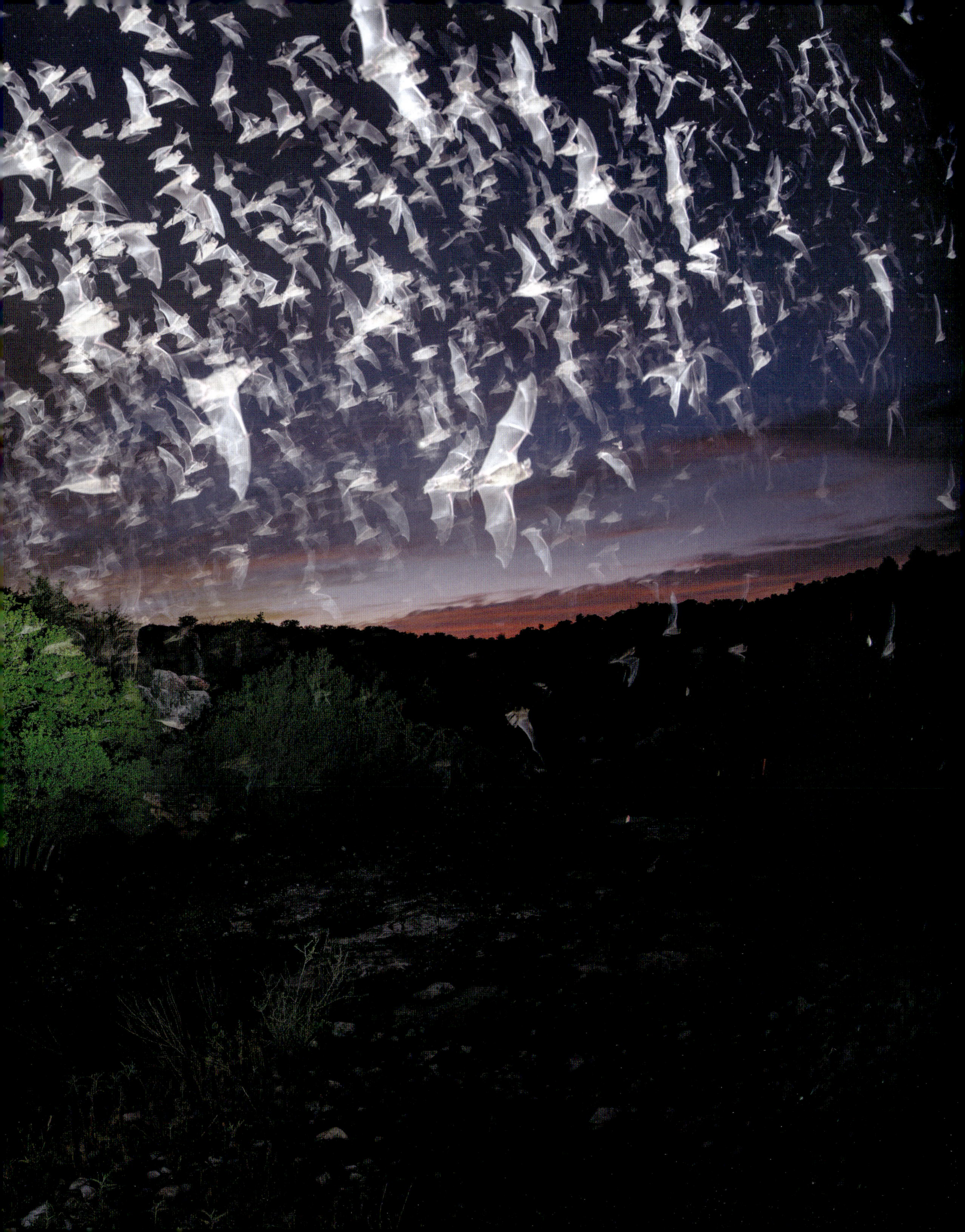

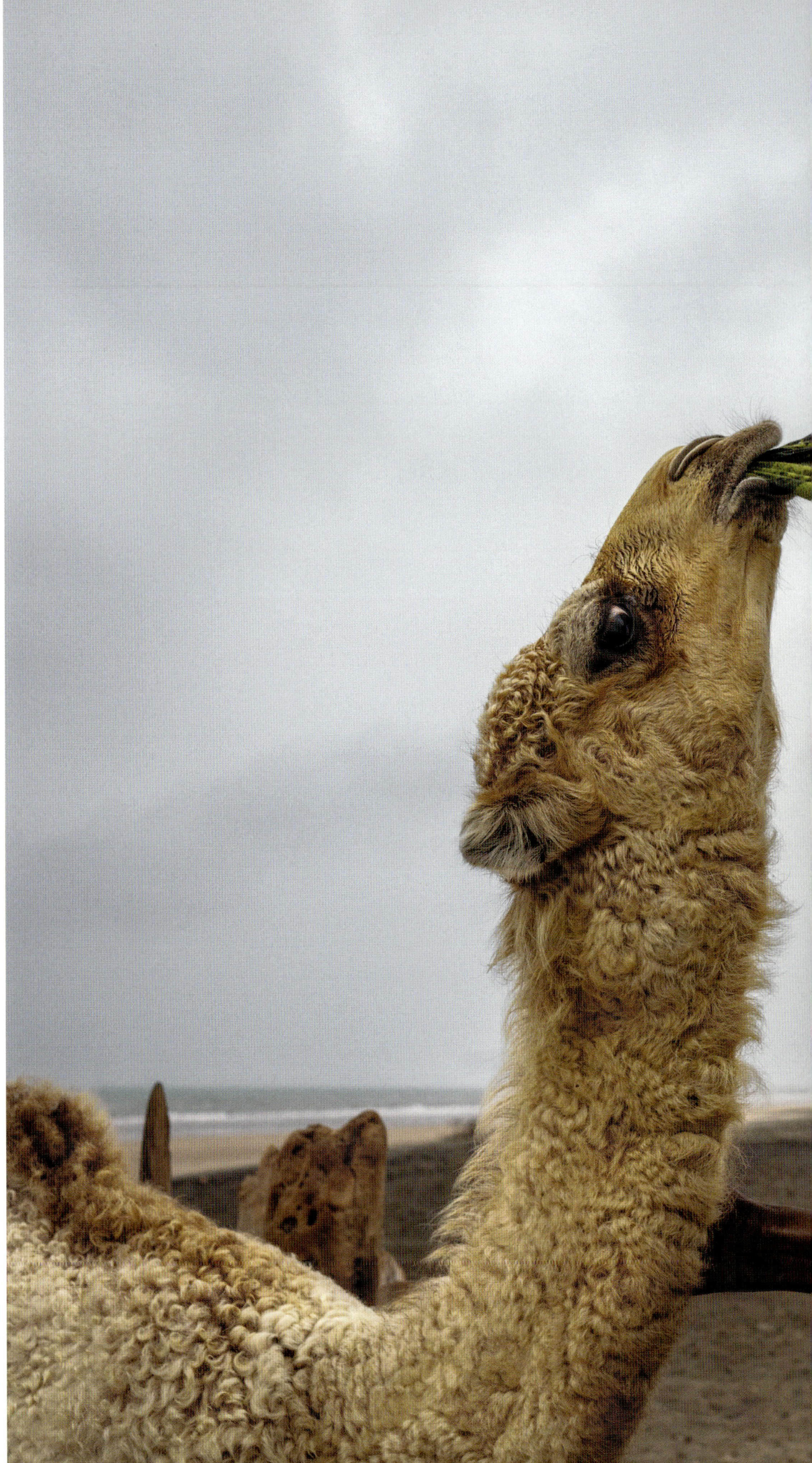

NICHOLE SOBECKI, 2020
A five-month-old camel, Baarud, tugs at a Somali woman's hijab. Its mother survived three droughts and a cyclone that killed off hundreds of other camels on Somaliland's north coast.

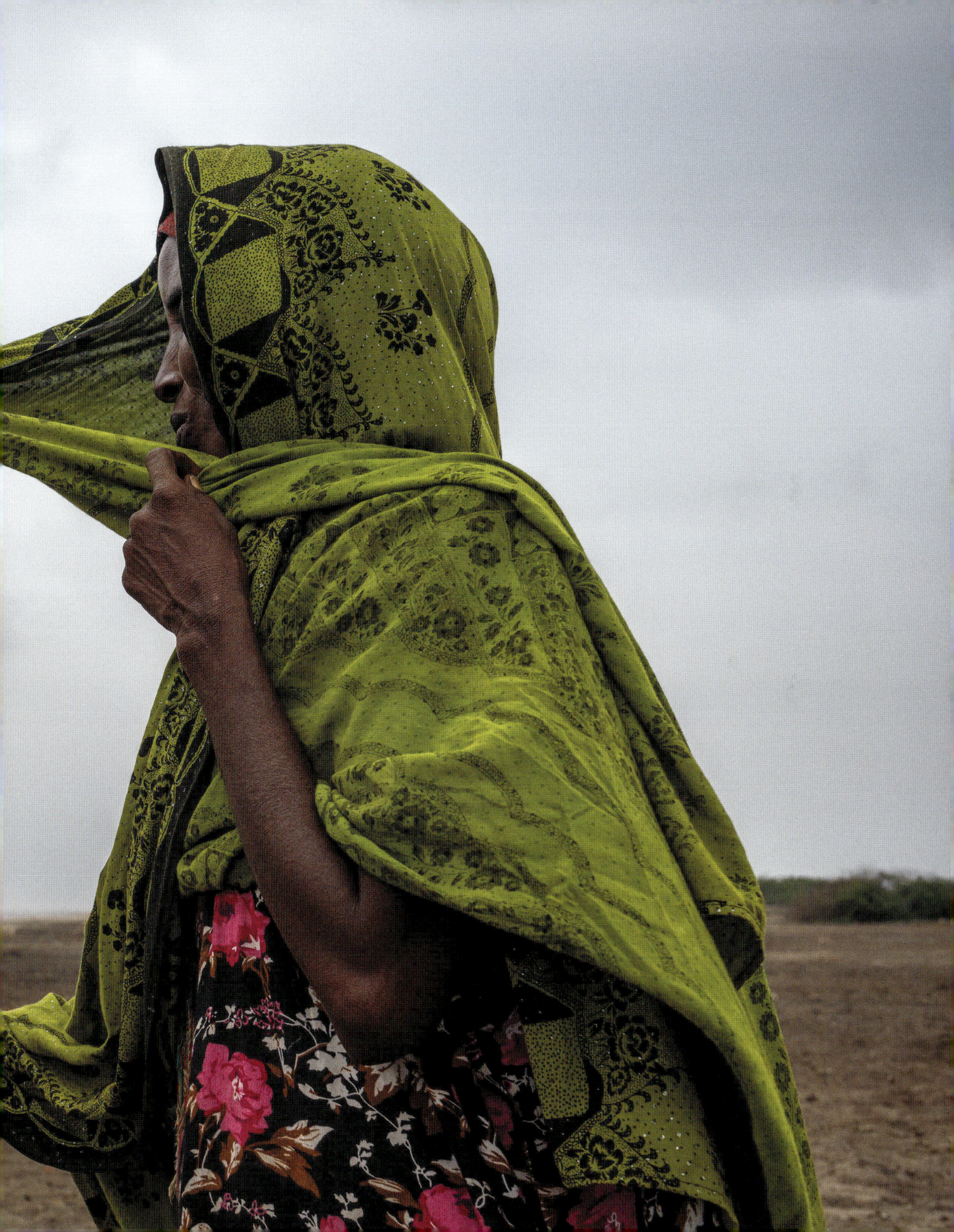

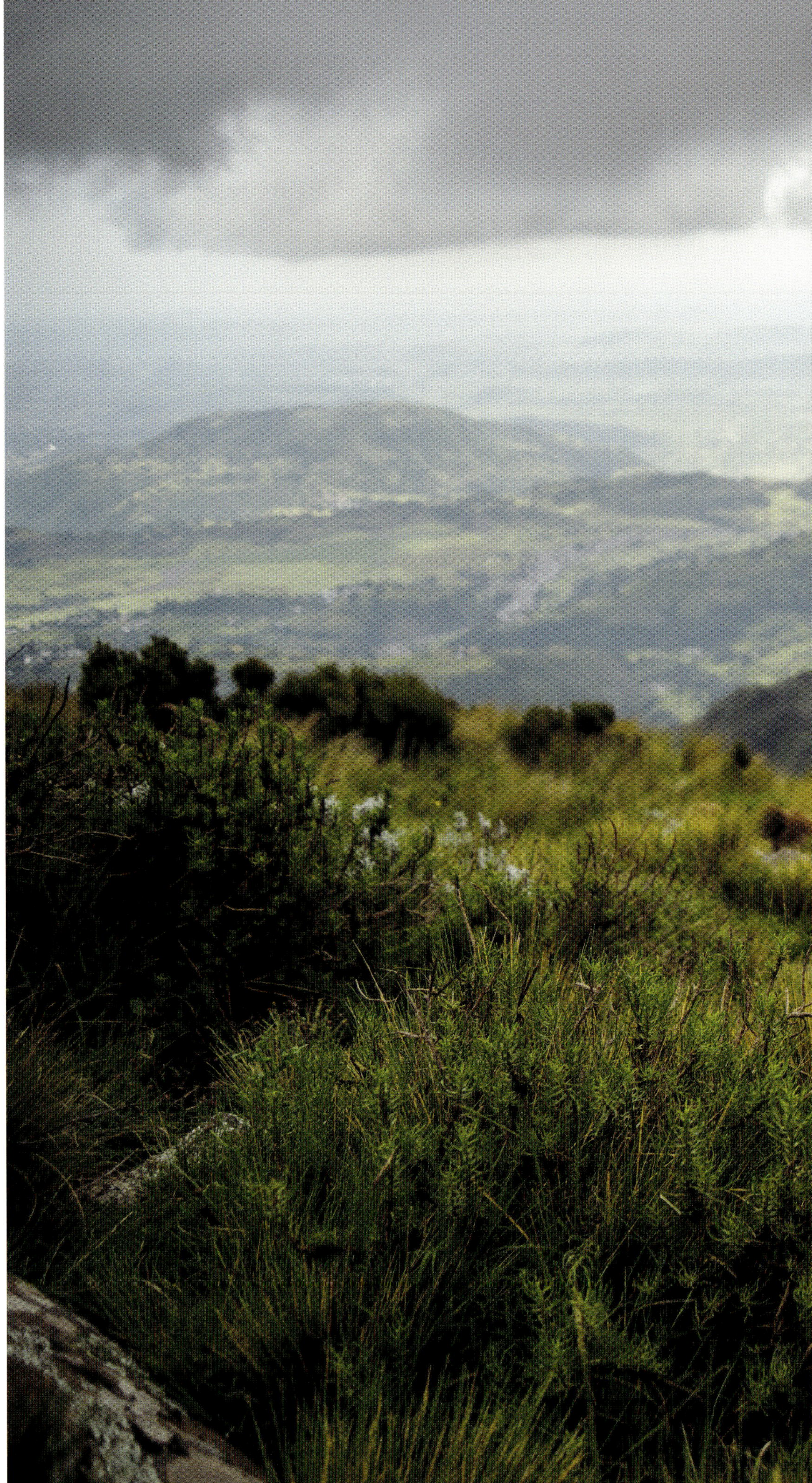

JEFFREY KERBY, 2014
A male gelada pauses amid his morning climb in Ethiopia's Great Rift Valley.

FOLLOWING PAGES
THOMAS P. PESCHAK, 2014
Blacktip reef sharks wait for the tide to refill a lagoon at Aldabra Atoll, the westernmost atoll in the Seychelles, off the east coast of Africa.

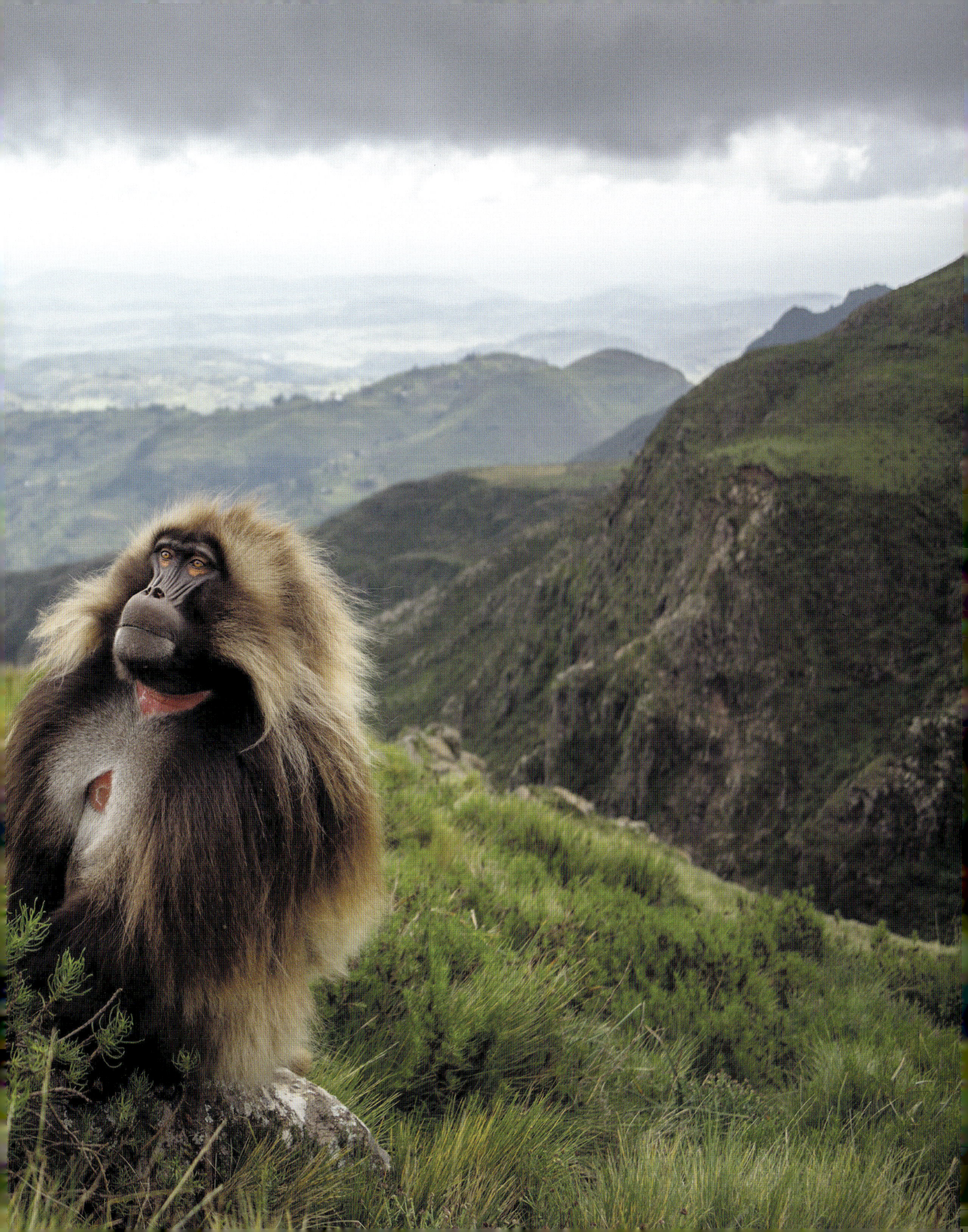

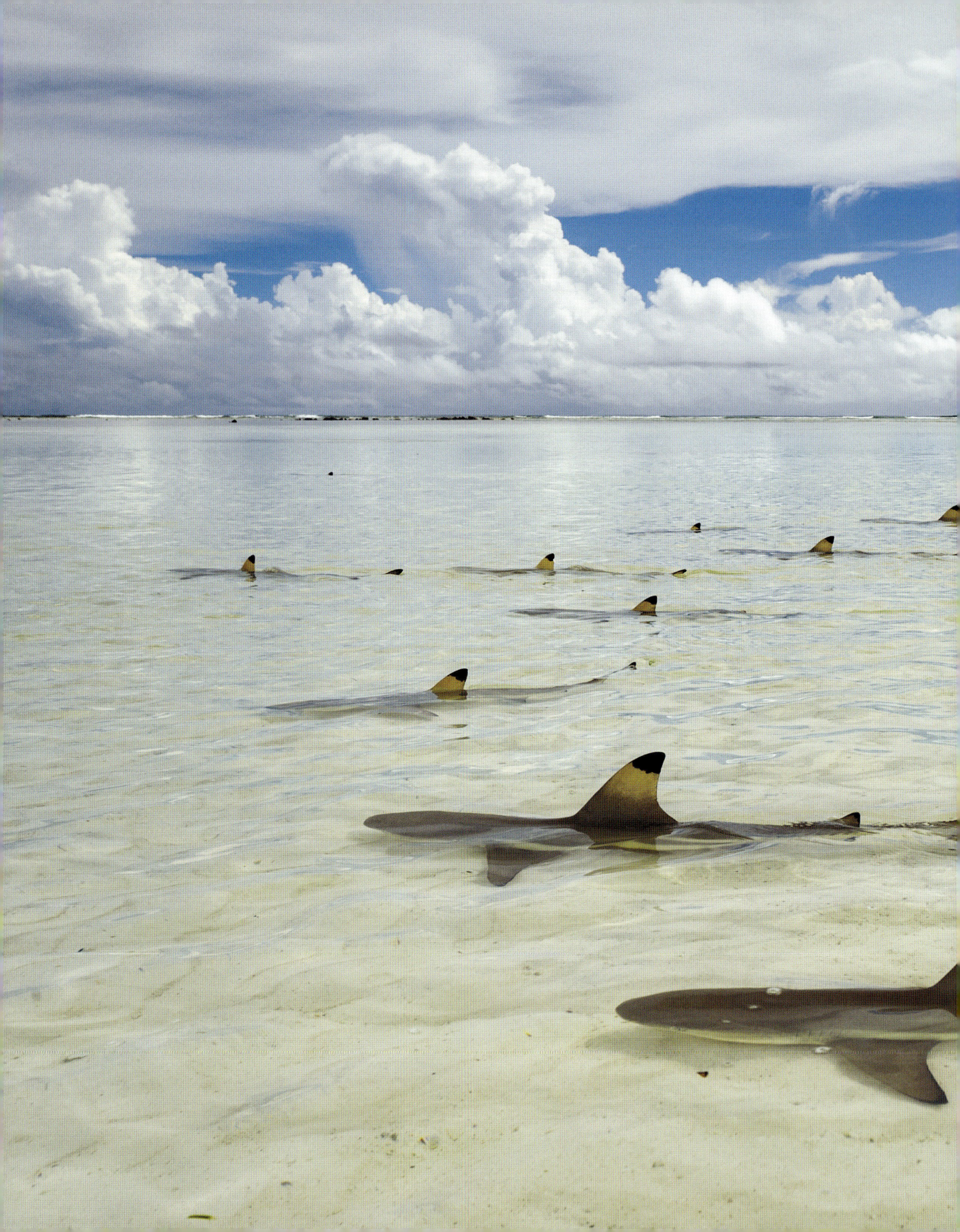

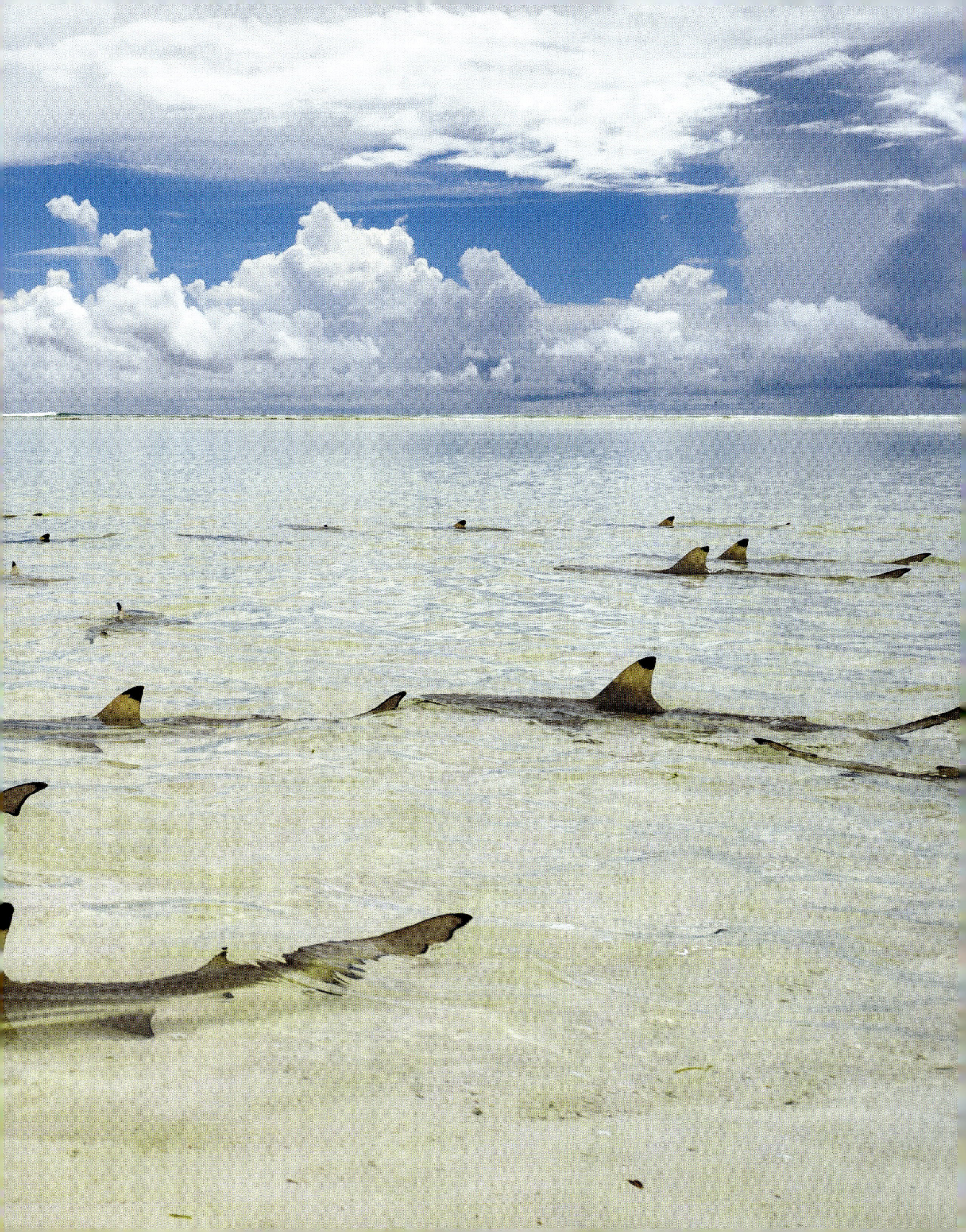

BIOGRAPHY

JOEL SARTORE

"WHEN WE TRY TO PICK OUT ANYTHING BY ITSELF, we find it hitched to everything else in the Universe," the American naturalist John Muir wrote. Joel Sartore understands those connections. He understands the link between a dam and the dwindling number of freshwater mussels; the relation between drift nets and the decline of the loggerhead sea turtle. Better yet, in his portraits of animals, he can depict these connections.

Resolutely midwestern, Sartore grew up in Omaha, Nebraska, in a house with a backyard grill and background music provided by Lawrence Welk. His interest in natural history began with weekends spent fishing and hunting with his father, who taught him about the importance of habitat, and hours reading nature books with his mother. He now lives in Lincoln, Nebraska, with his wife, Kathy, in a house filled with furniture and objects discarded by others, rescued and restored by him. "I like saving things," he says. "The rarer the better."

His fascination with endangered animals began with a picture of Martha, the last passenger pigeon, who died at the Cincinnati Zoo in 1914. Hunting had wiped out the species. He never forgot that image; it would haunt him and find expression in his project National Geographic Photo Ark, which he began in 2006. "Shooting animals as studio portraits is the great equalizer," he says. "You can make a mouse as big, as endearing, as powerful as a polar bear. I want to get people to look these animals in the eye and connect with them."

So far, he has photographed more than 16,000 species living in zoos, wildlife sanctuaries, and aquariums in his quest to create an archive of diversity and inspire people to save species while there is still time. He intends to keep going until he gets them all.

OPPOSITE TOP
JOEL SARTORE, 2011
A three-year-old cheetah at White Oak Conservation in northeastern Florida

OPPOSITE BOTTOM
JOEL SARTORE, 2012
An endangered Indian rhinoceros with her calf at Texas's Fort Worth Zoo

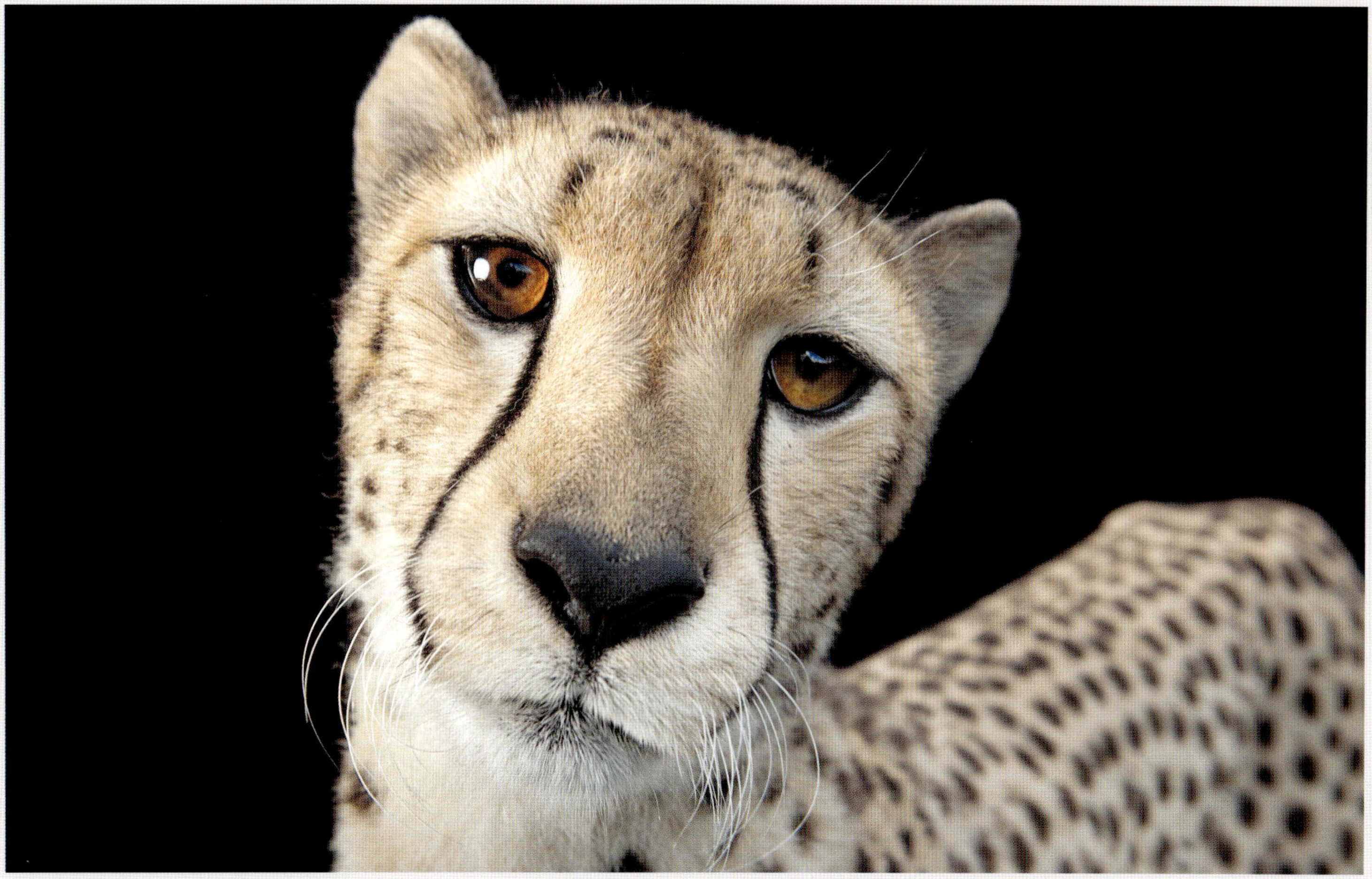

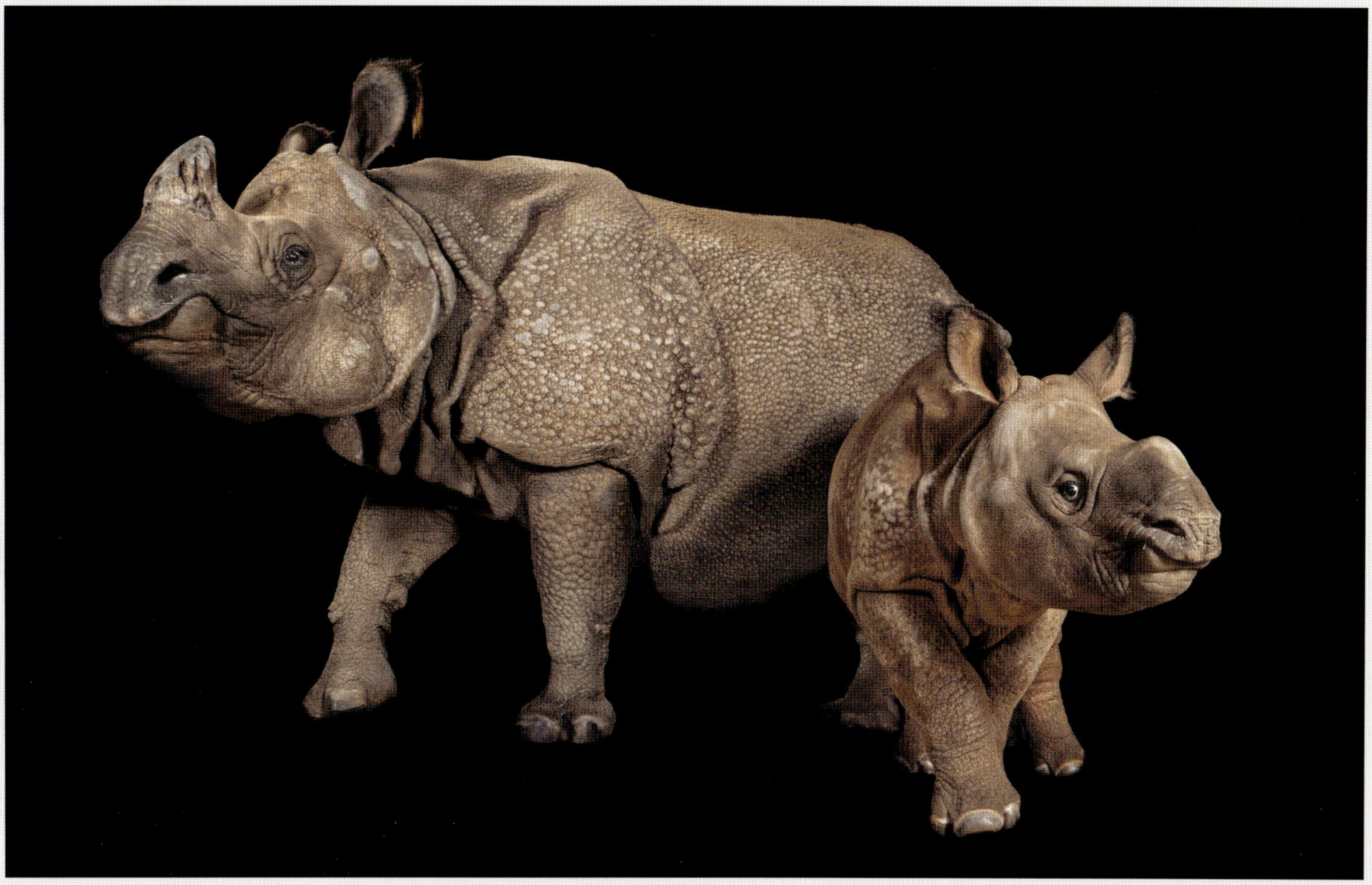

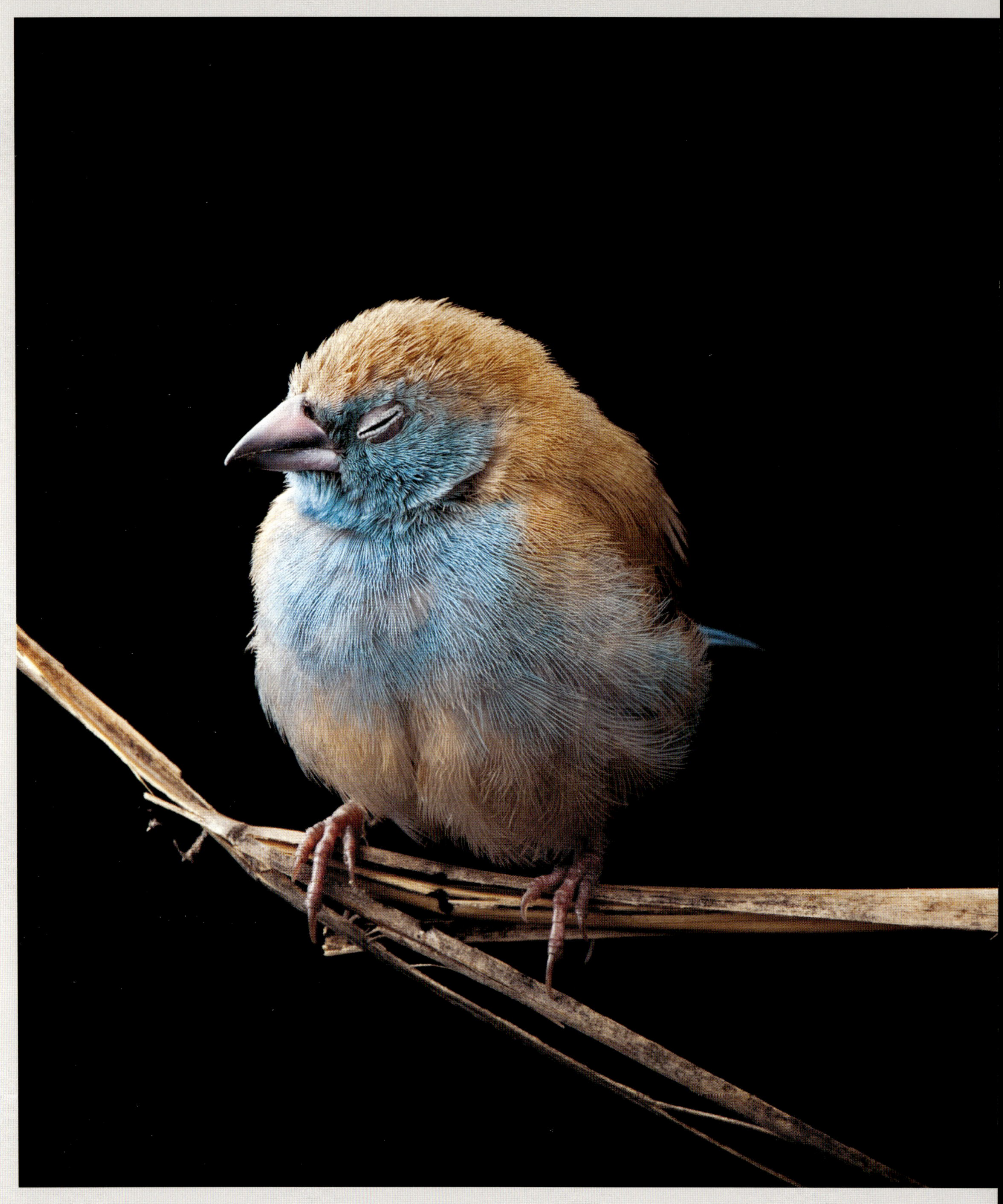

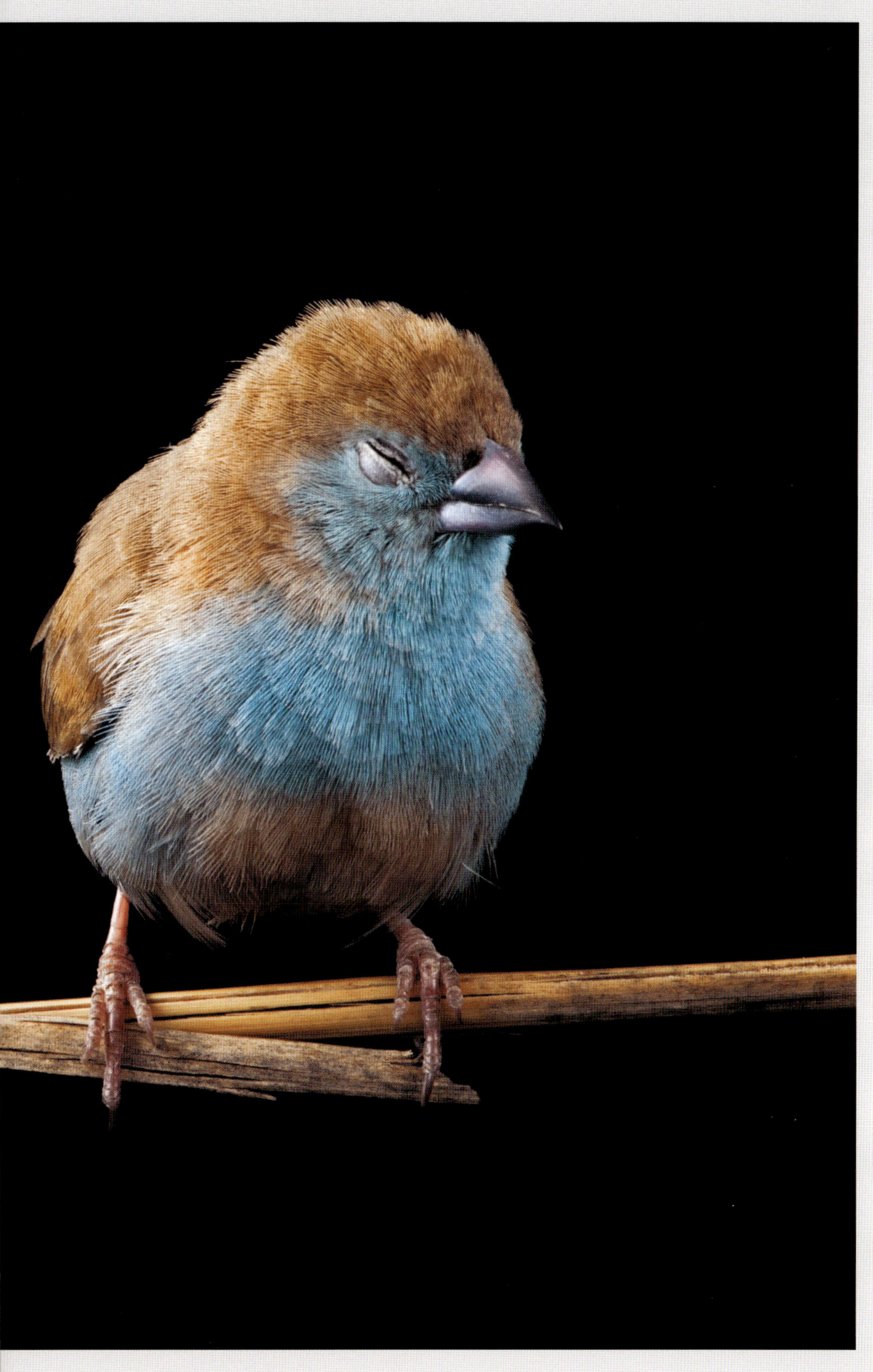

JOEL SARTORE, 2011
These blue waxbills come from Gorongosa National Park in Mozambique, where conservationists are helping native wildlife recover after the country's civil war.

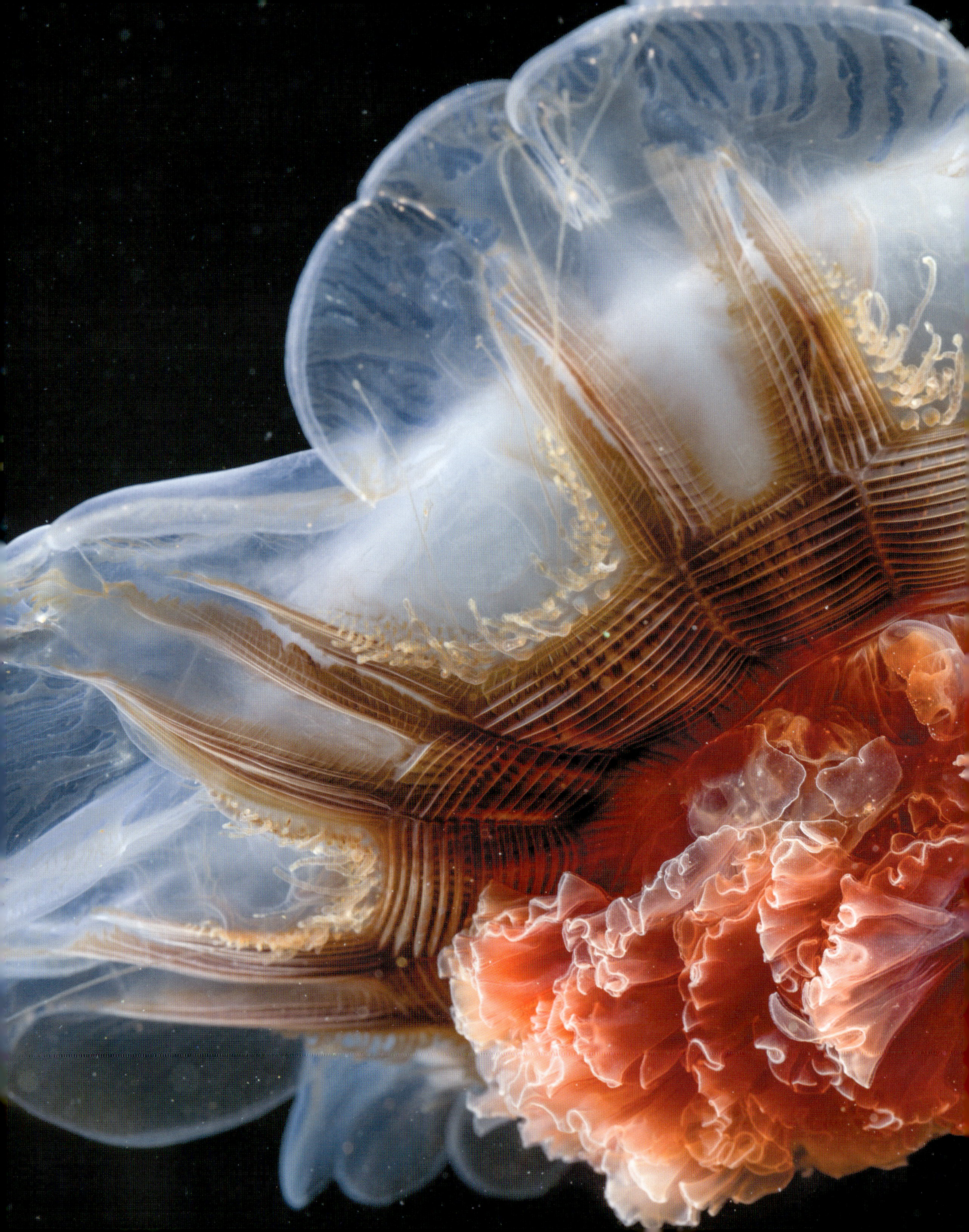

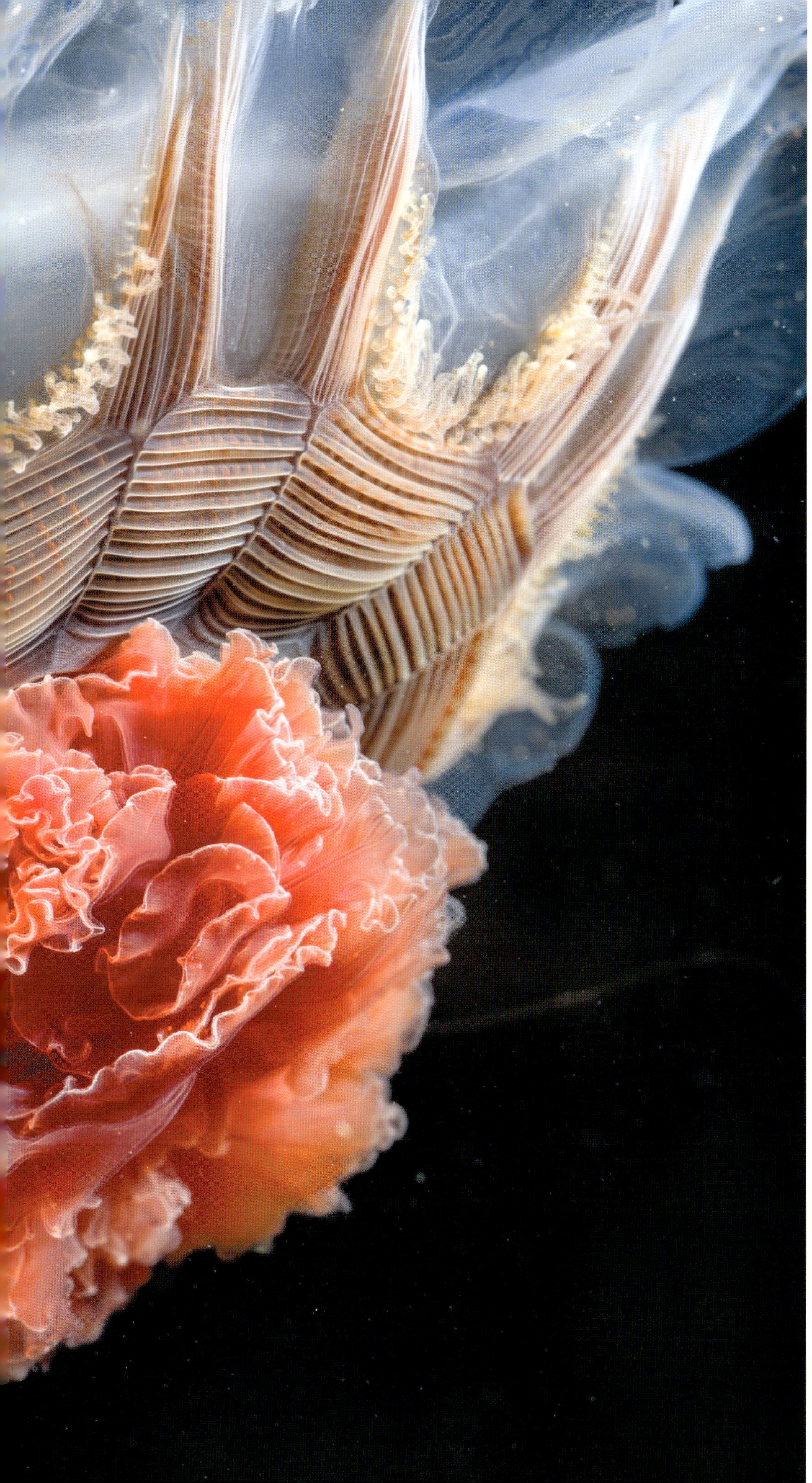

ALEXANDER SEMENOV, 2023
A lion's mane jellyfish in Russia's White Sea. Here, it has shrunk into its final stage of life: Having reproduced, it digests or sheds its hundreds of long tentacles.

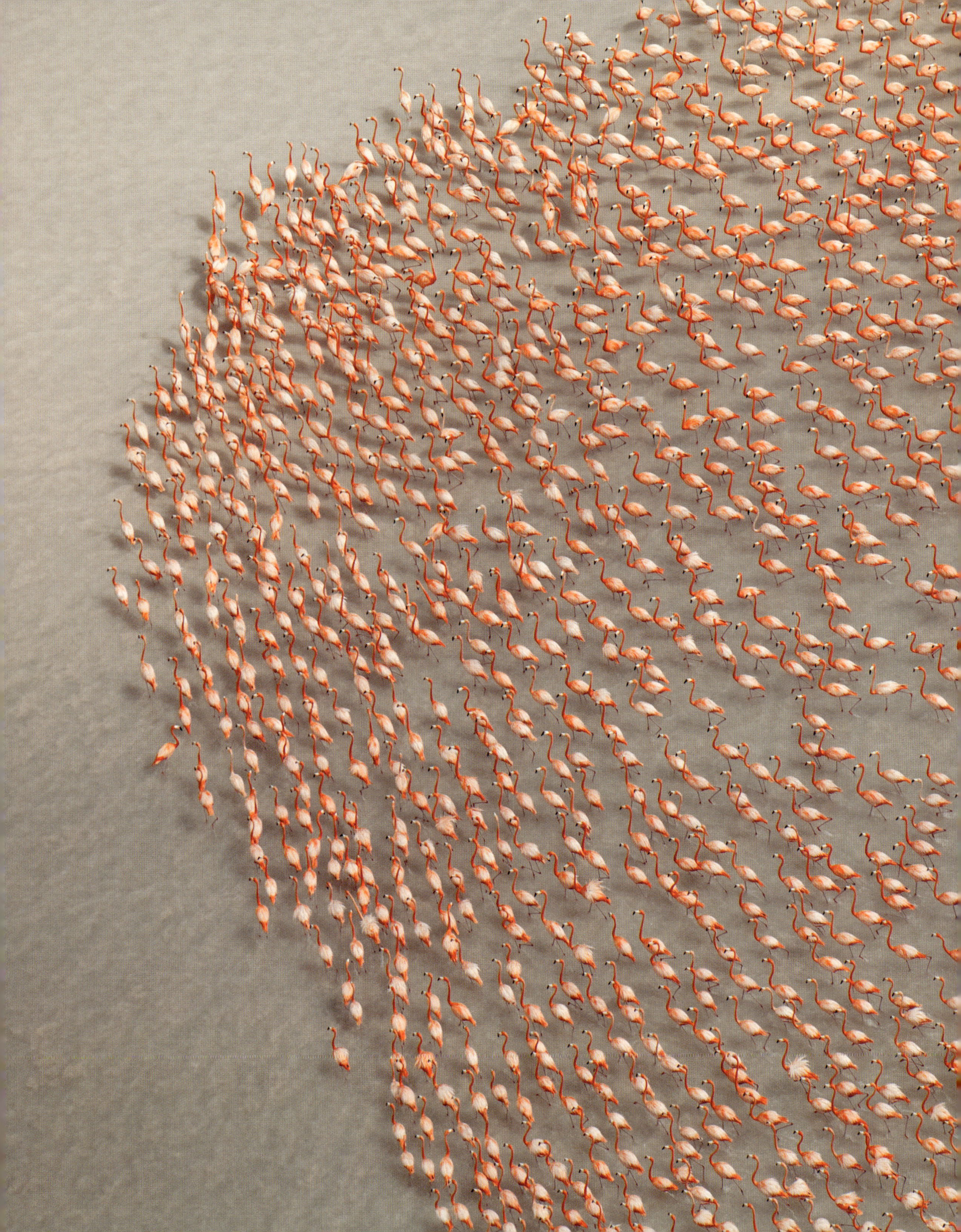

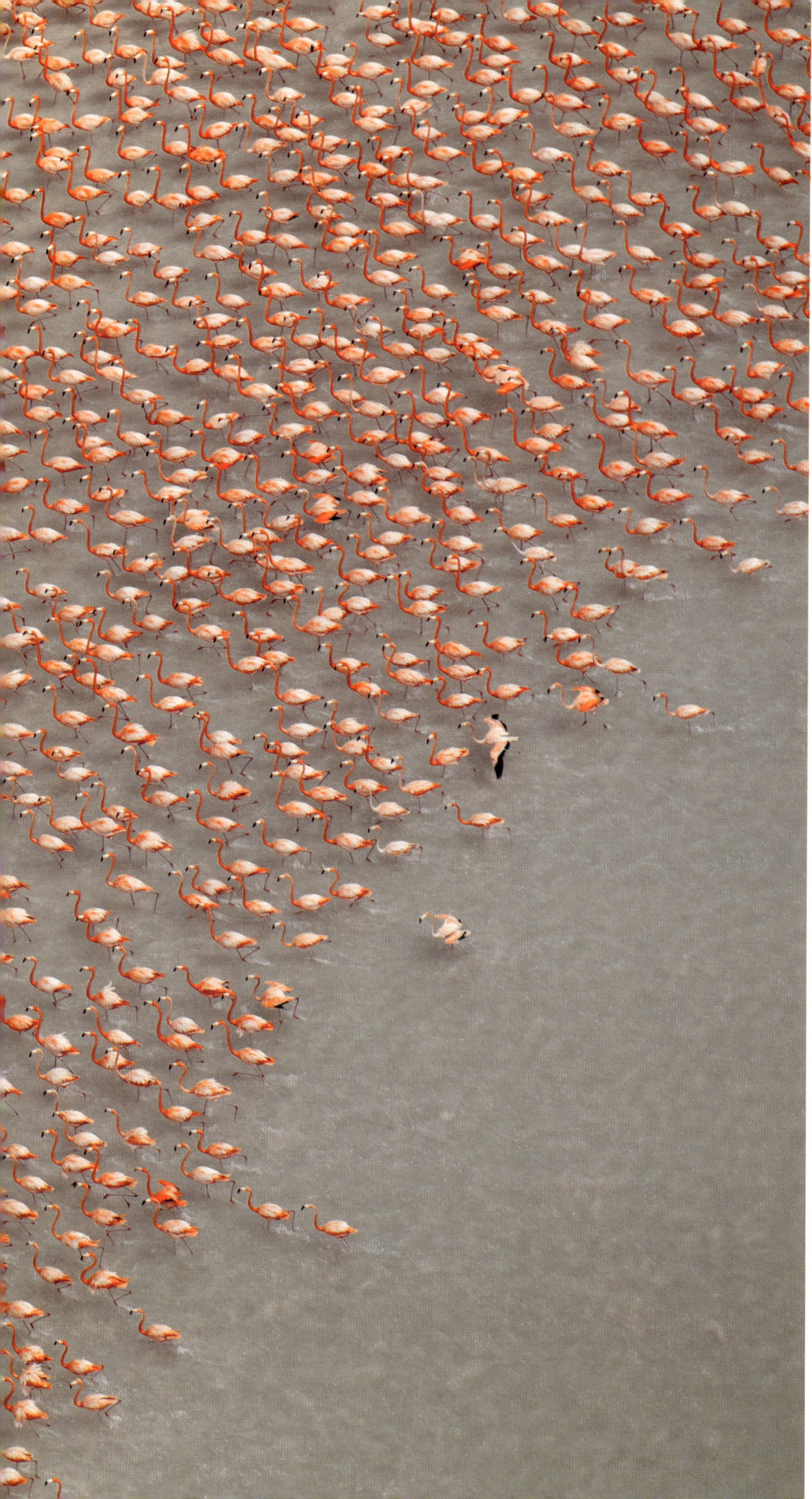

KLAUS NIGGE, 2012
As a research plane passes overhead, this flock of flamingos perceives a threat and moves in unison in Yucatán, Mexico.

GEORGI GEORGIEV, 2021
A praying mantis climbs a mushroom in the lush landscape of Bulgaria's Sredna Gora mountain range.

FOLLOWING PAGES
CRISTINA MITTERMEIER, 2021
Cardinalfish dart past a sea lion near the Galápagos Islands.

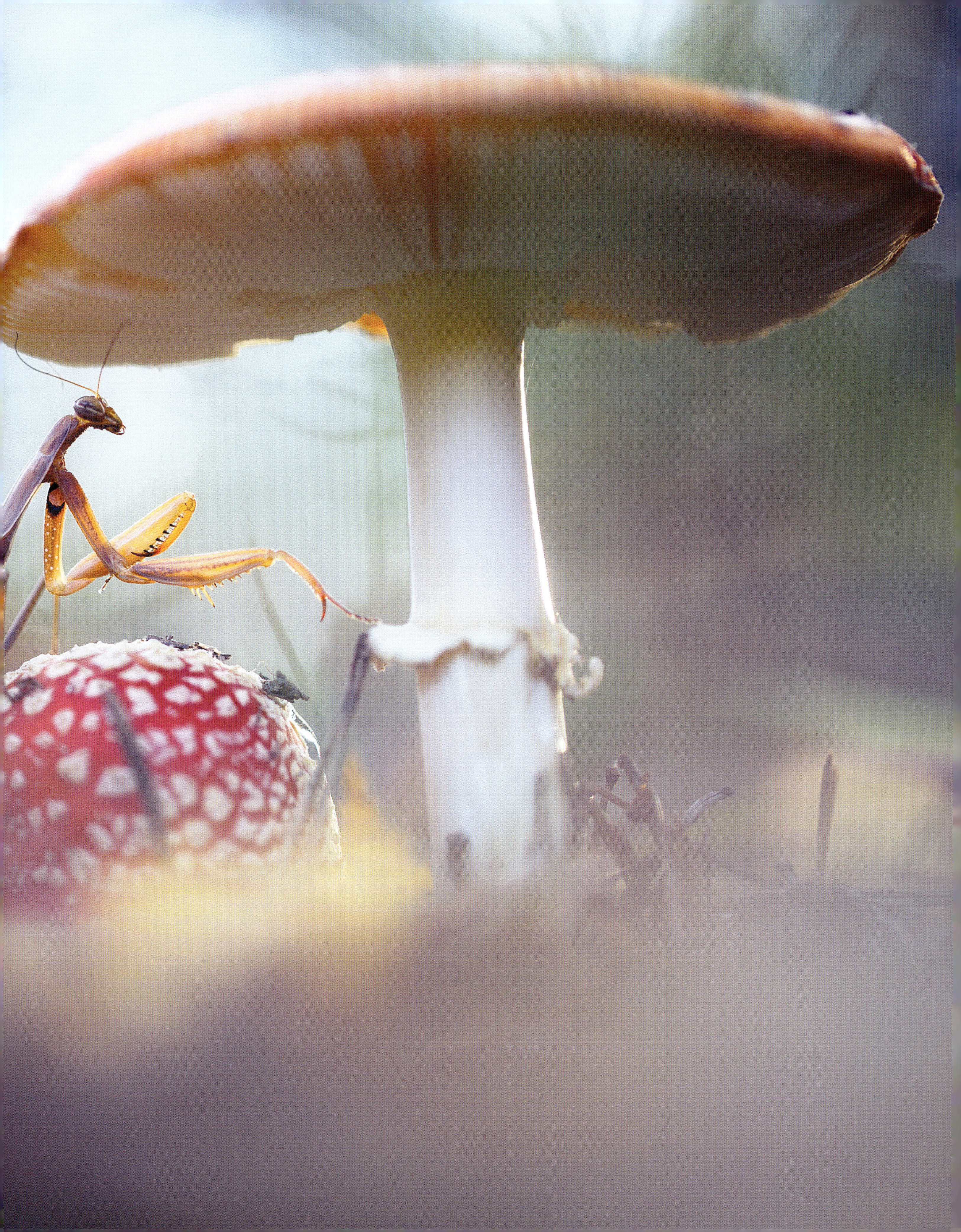

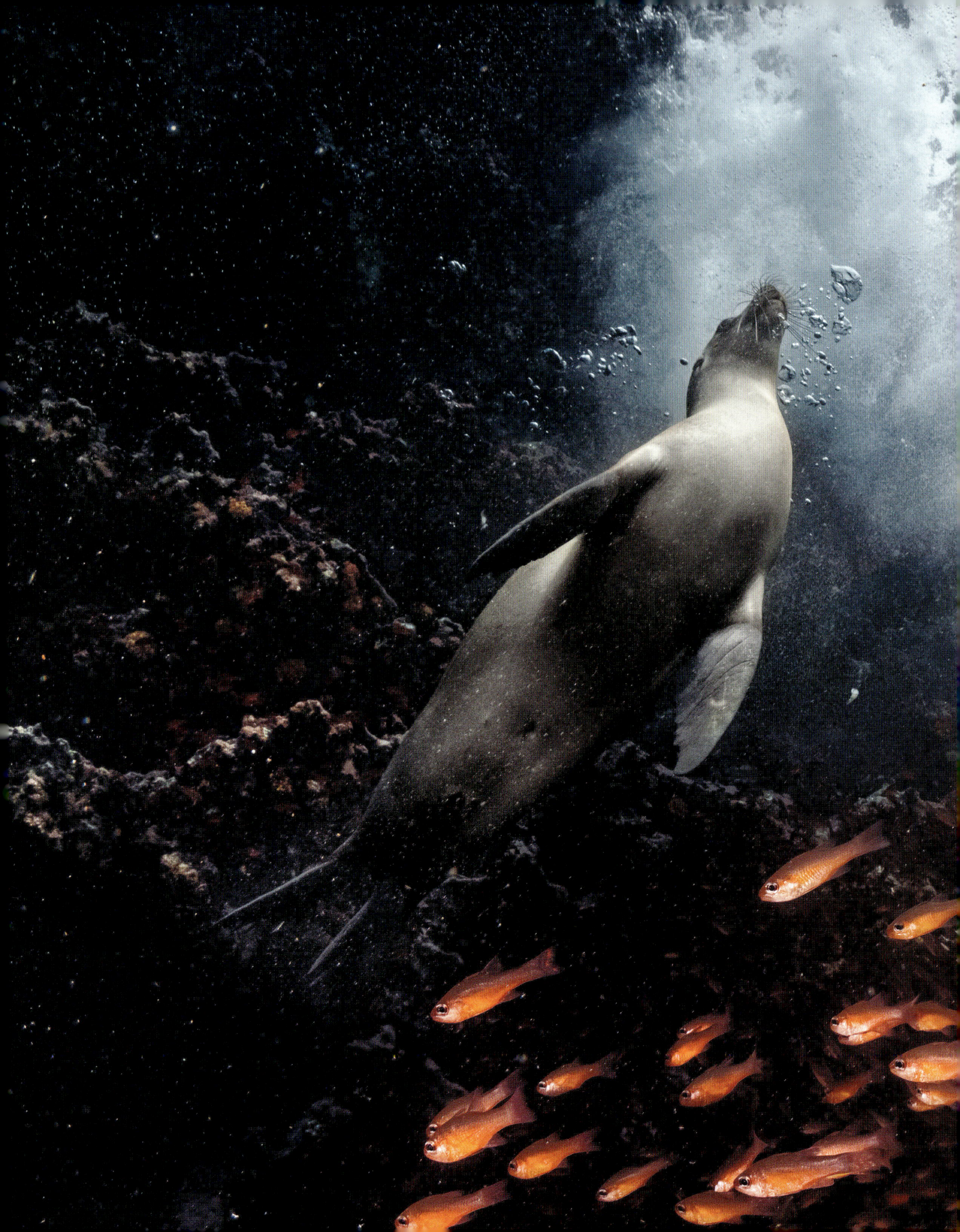

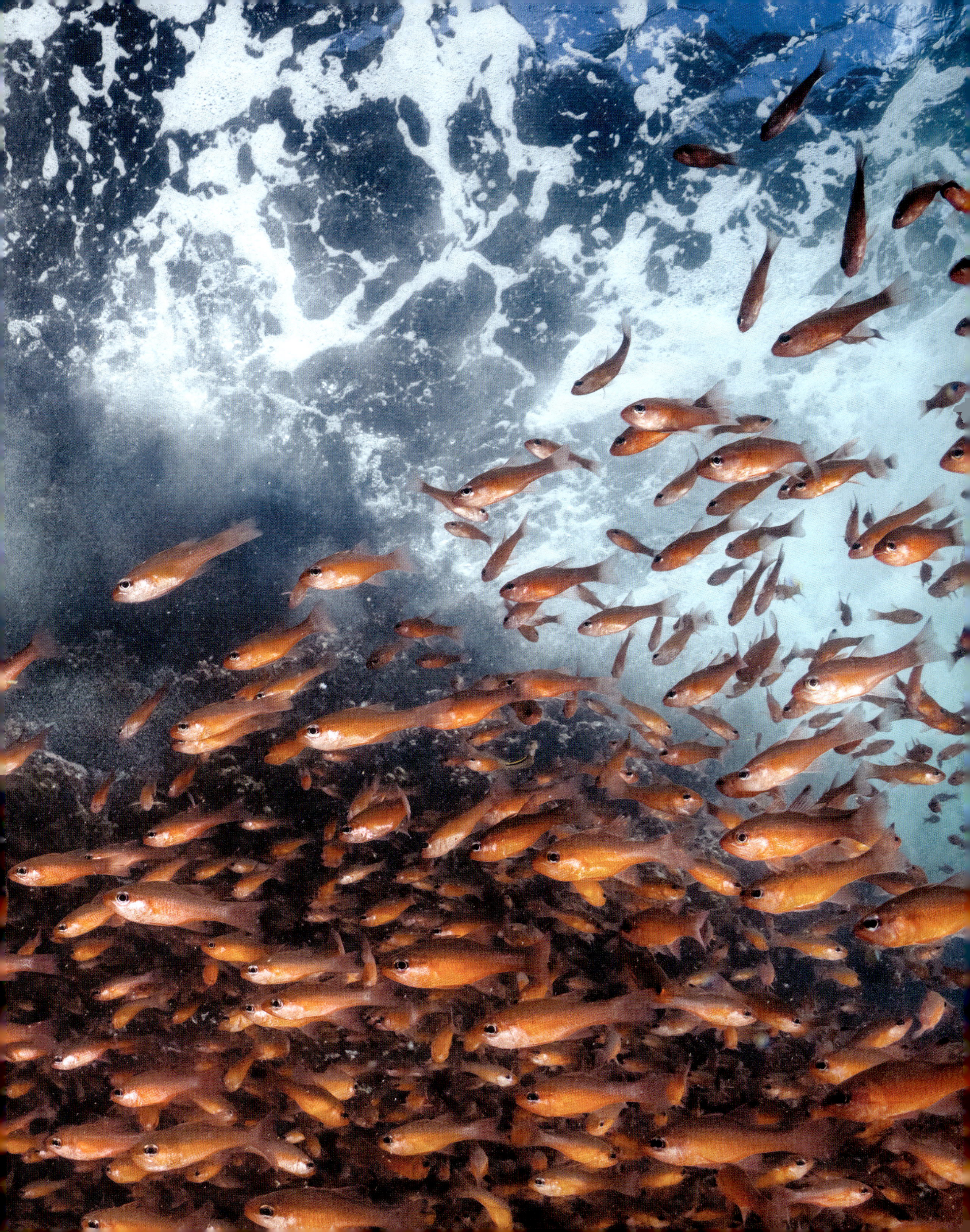

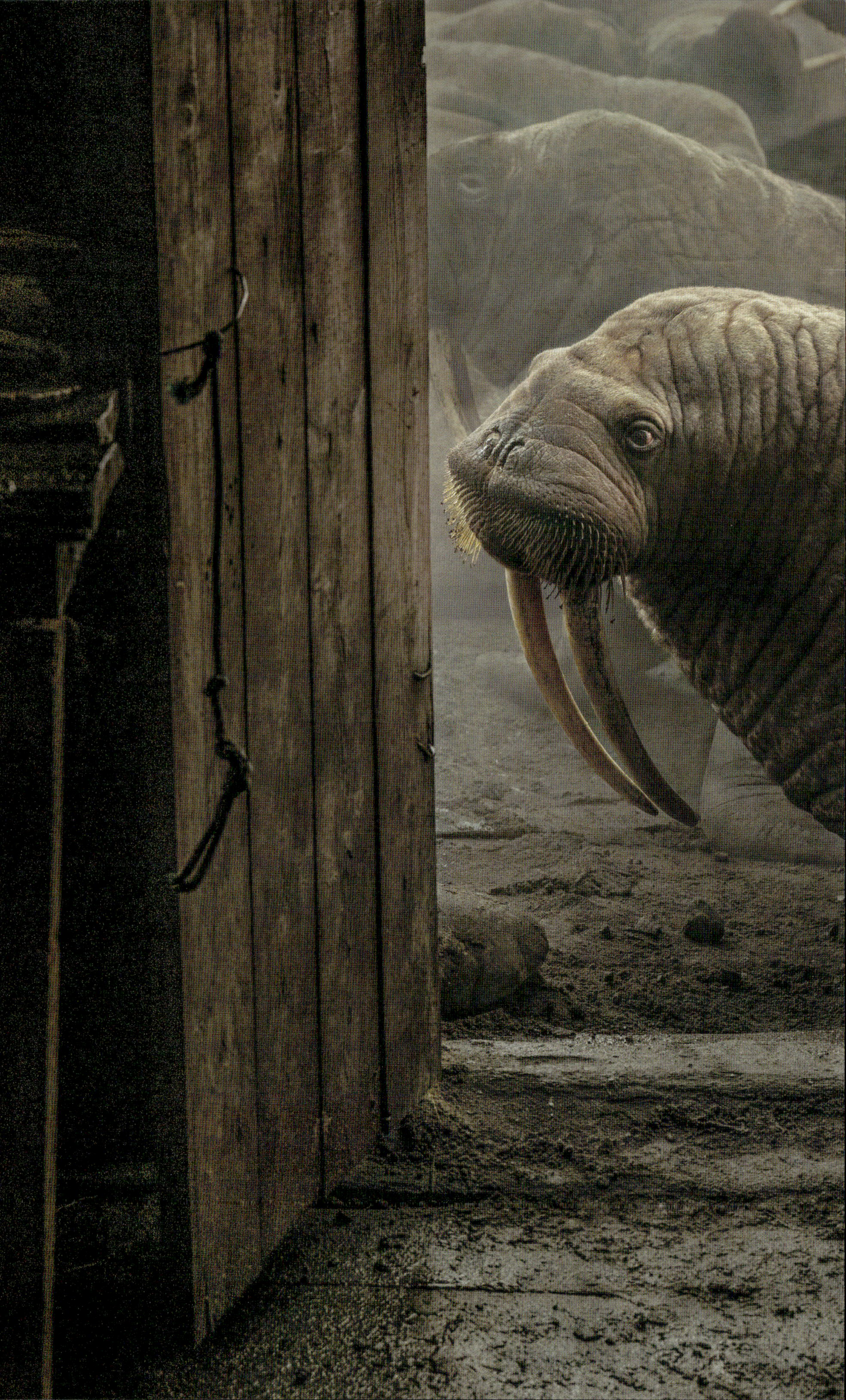

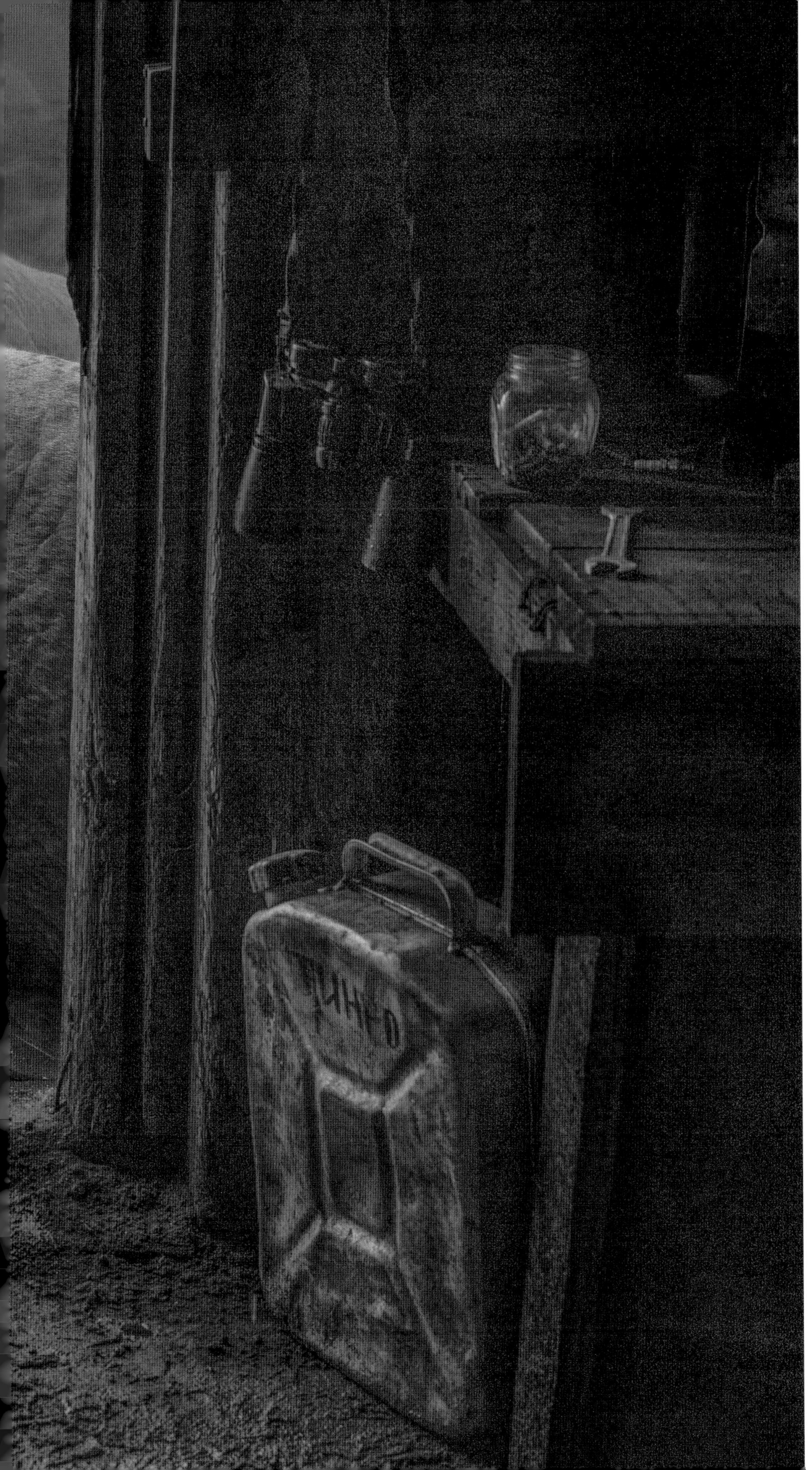

EVGENIA ARBUGAEVA, 2019
A walrus peers through the doorway of a scientist's hut in the Siberian Arctic.

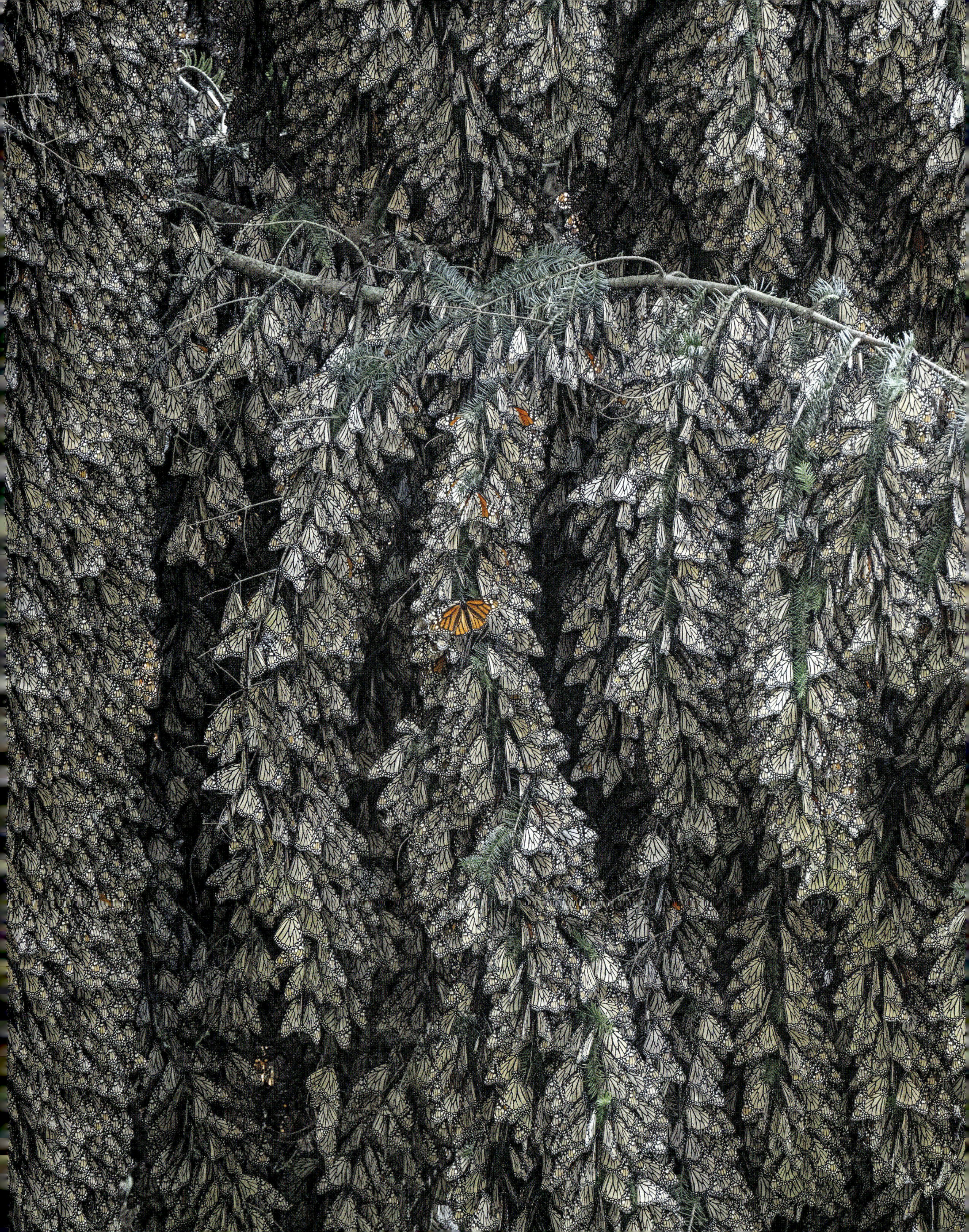

THE GREATEST STORY ON EARTH IS THE EARTH ITSELF. IT'S ALL WE HAVE. THERE IS NO PLAN B.

DAVID DOUBILET, PHOTOGRAPHER

JAIME ROJO, 2022
A single monarch butterfly opens its wings among a colony of millions in Michoacán, Mexico.

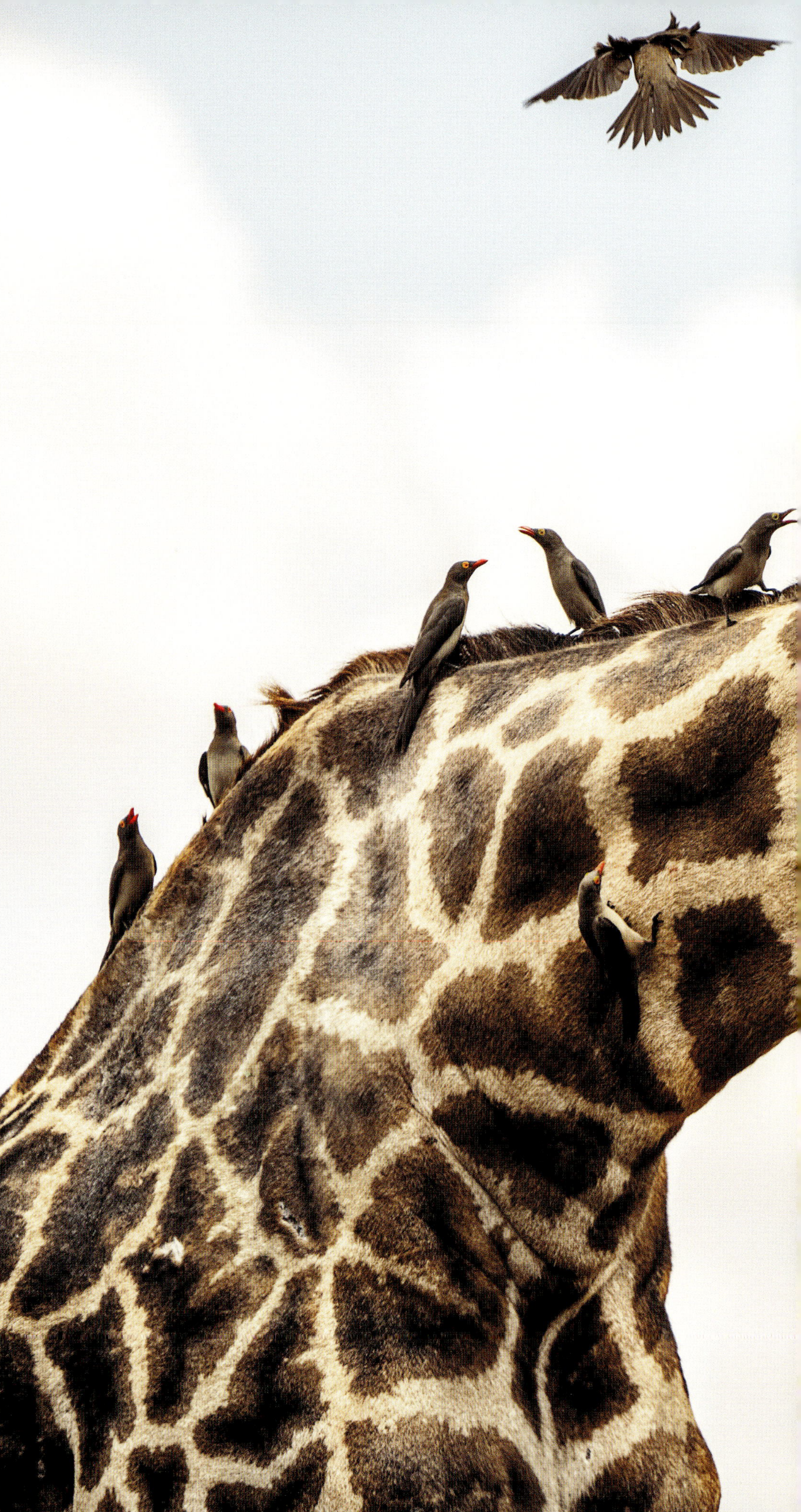

BEVERLY JOUBERT, 2023
Red-billed oxpeckers pick ticks, parasites, and loose hairs off a giraffe in southeastern Kenya.

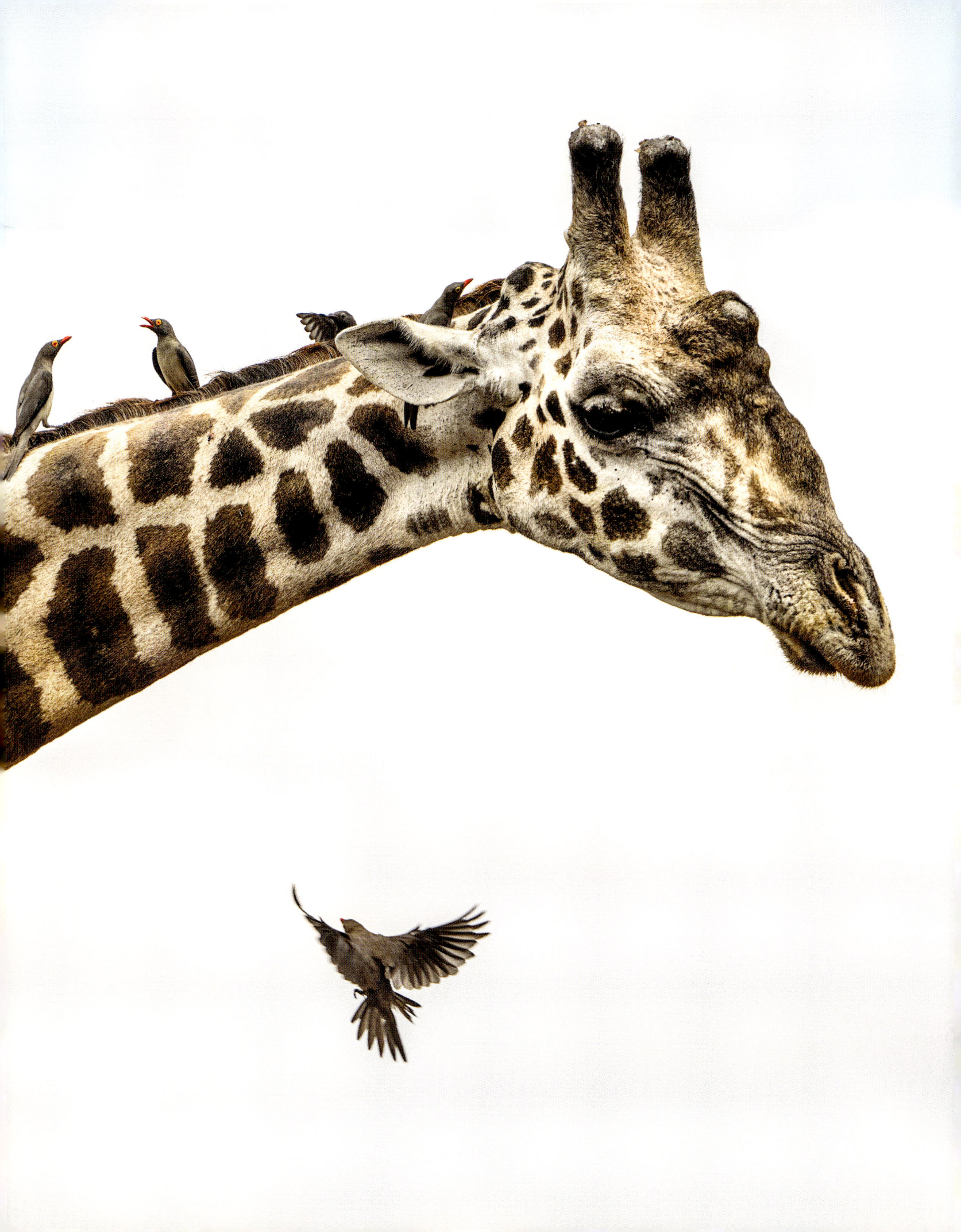

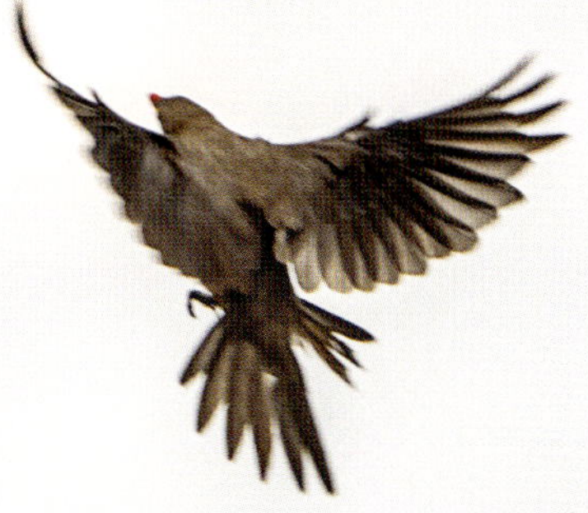

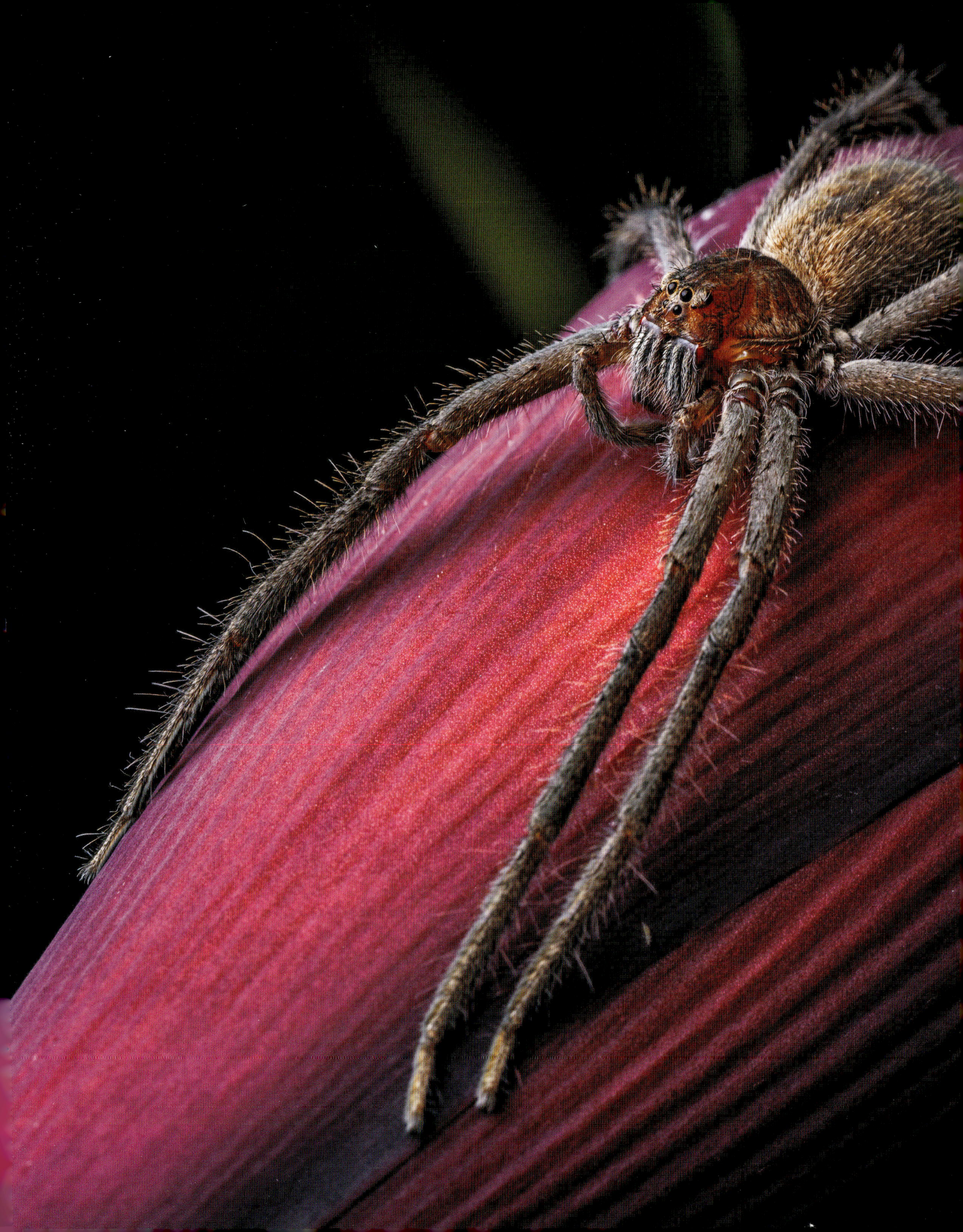

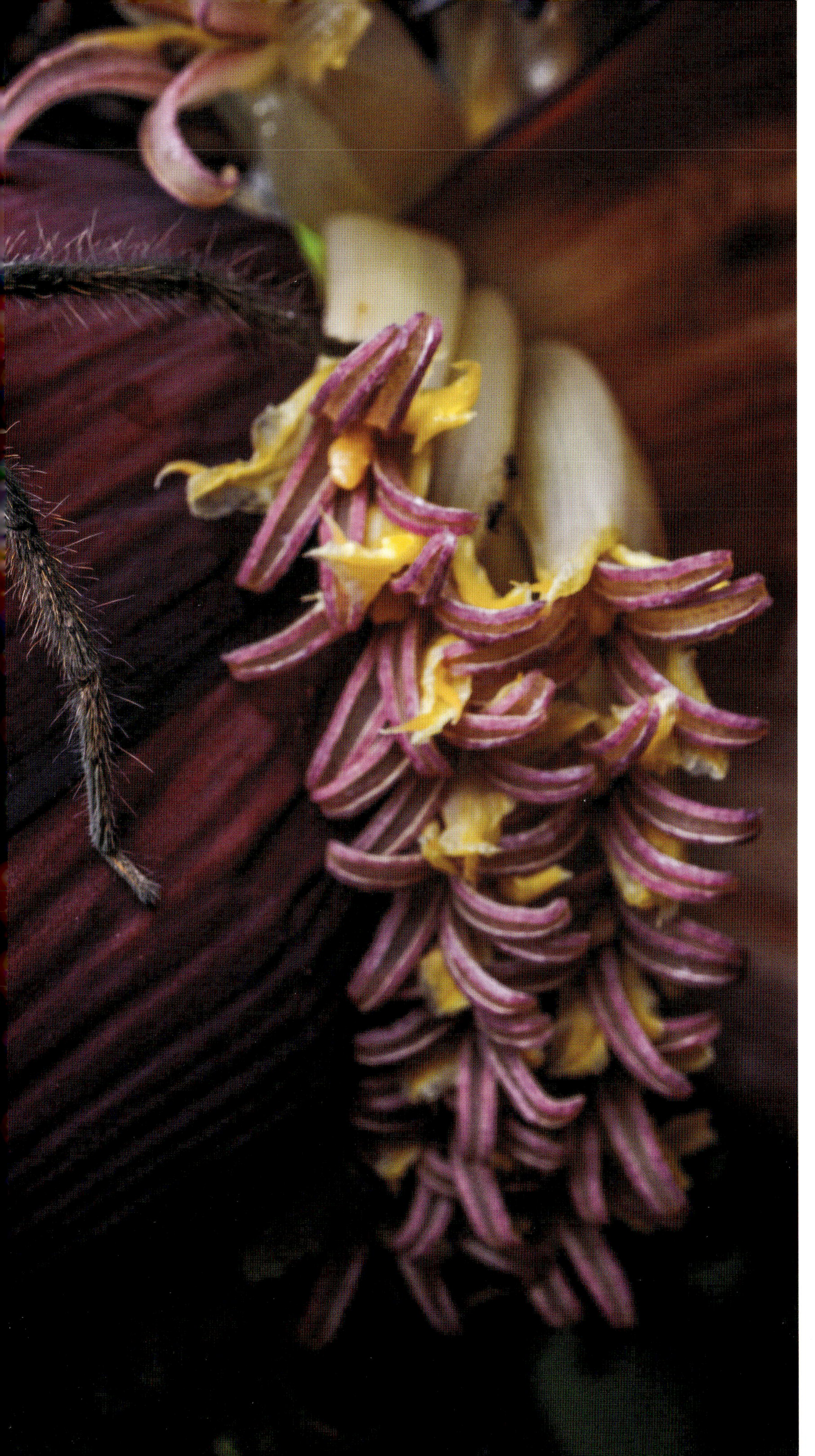

JAVIER AZNAR GONZÁLEZ DE RUEDA, 2019
A bromeliad spider sprawls across a banana flower in La Maná, Ecuador.

FOLLOWING PAGES
MICHAEL NICHOLS, 2000
A forest elephant wanders past a camera trap on a beach in Loango National Park, Gabon.

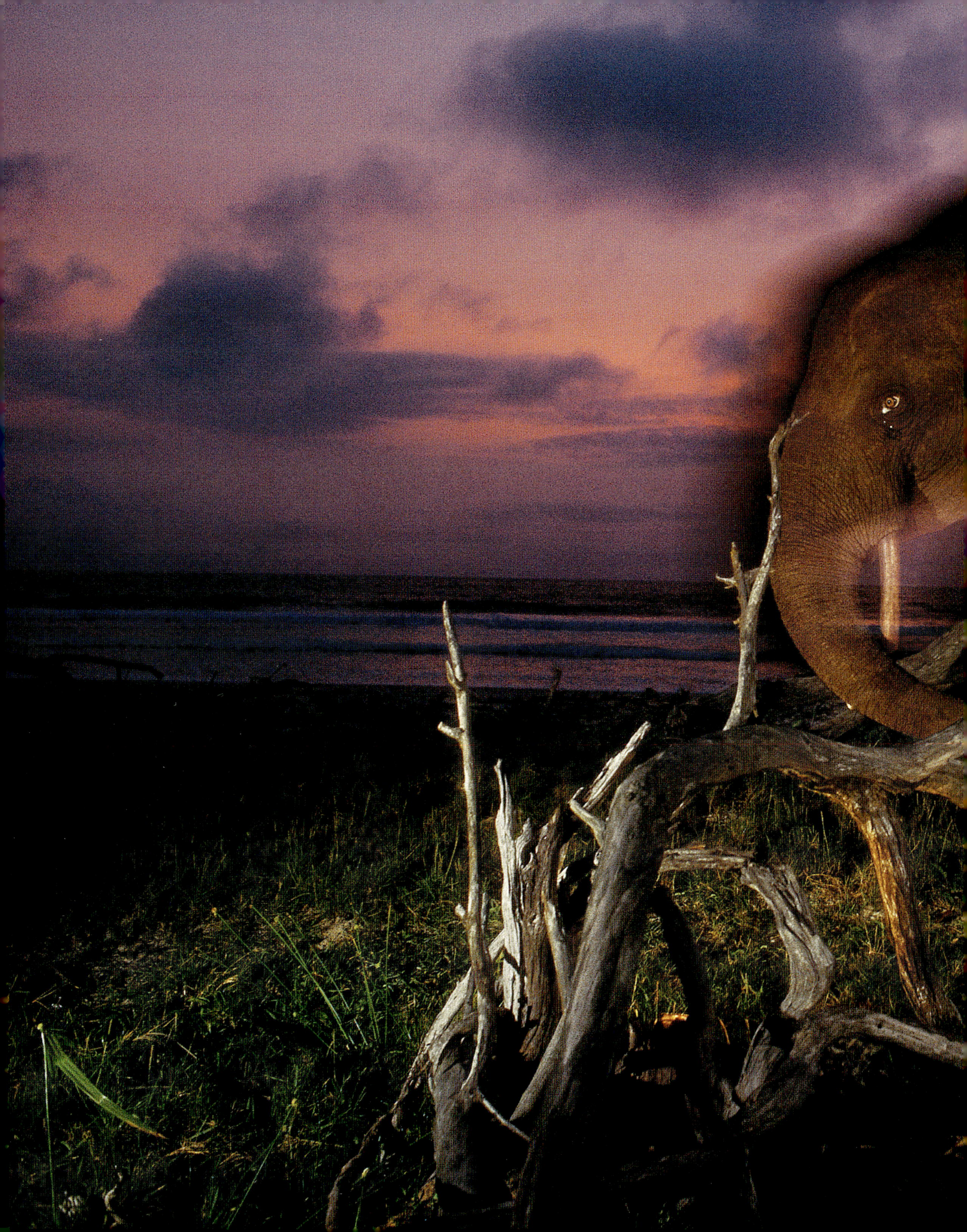

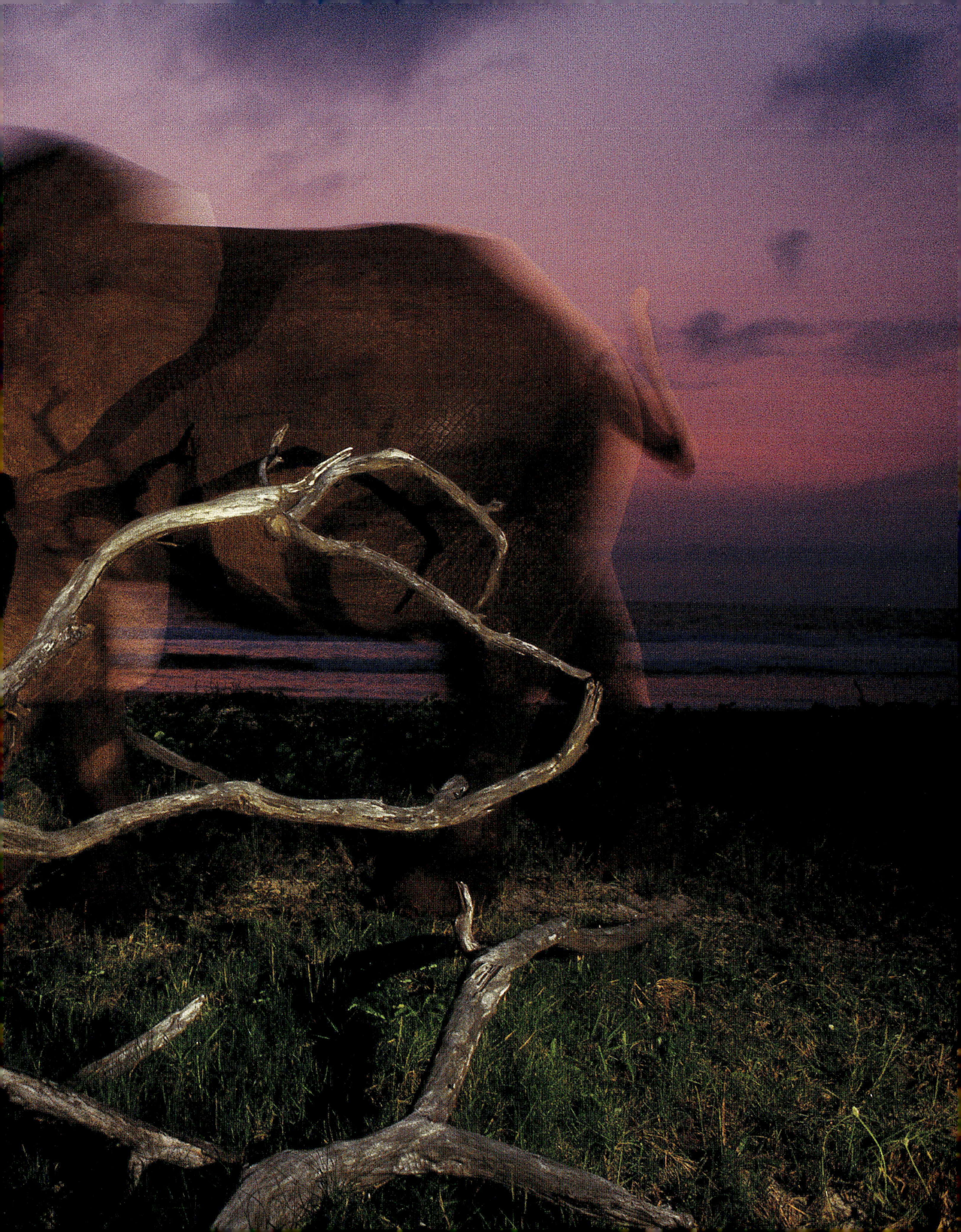

BIOGRAPHY

BEVERLY JOUBERT

"FORTY YEARS AGO, WE WENT IN SEARCH OF THE SOUL OF AFRICA," says wildlife photographer, filmmaker, conservationist, and National Geographic Explorer at Large Beverly Joubert. Forty years later, one can rightly say that she and Dereck, her husband and collaborator, both native South Africans, have helped preserve that soul and wild heart. (Theirs is a love story with each other and with Africa. When asked what they cannot travel without, both answered "each other.")

"We are in the business of changing the world," she observes. And they have—not just with her photography and their documentary films, but also with a series of initiatives that spring from an unshakable belief that an Africa without animals is unimaginable.

Media, Beverly Joubert says, is a bulwark against unawareness. "If you watch a film or read an article, you cannot claim ignorance," she explains. The couple's influence has helped stop hunting in Botswana; first to be banned was hunting lions, then hunting leopards, then, in 2014, all hunting. Great Plains, their tourism-based conservation company, created in 2006, manages and protects more than 1.5 million acres of wildlife habitat. In 2009, they founded the Big Cats Initiative to halt the decline of big cats in the wild. And Rhinos Without Borders has relocated dozens of rhinos from high-poaching zones throughout Africa.

Beverly and Dereck's articles, books, films, and conservation initiatives have earned nine Emmy Awards, a Peabody Award, a Grand Teton Award, Golden Panda Awards, a World Ecology Award, and the 2021 Explorers Club Medal, among others. They are currently at work on their memoir.

An interviewer once asked Beverly when she is the happiest. "When I am changing someone's thinking so they can be more compassionate and kind," she responded. It's a sentiment that is clearly both personal and professional.

BEVERLY JOUBERT, 2007
After she refused to share a kill with her family, this adolescent leopard, named Legadema by the photographer, was driven from her home by her mother. She later established her own territory as an adult in the forests of Botswana.

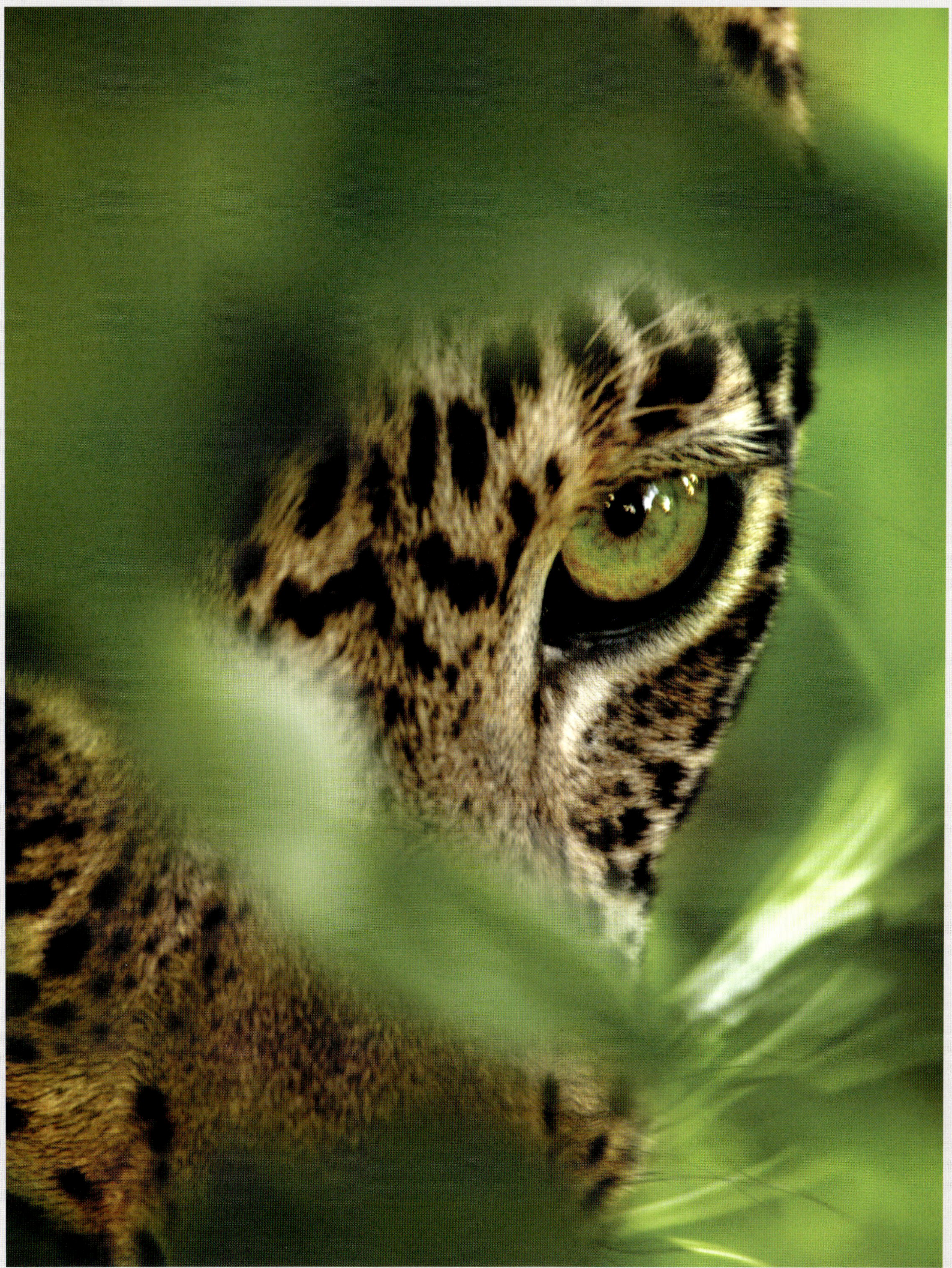

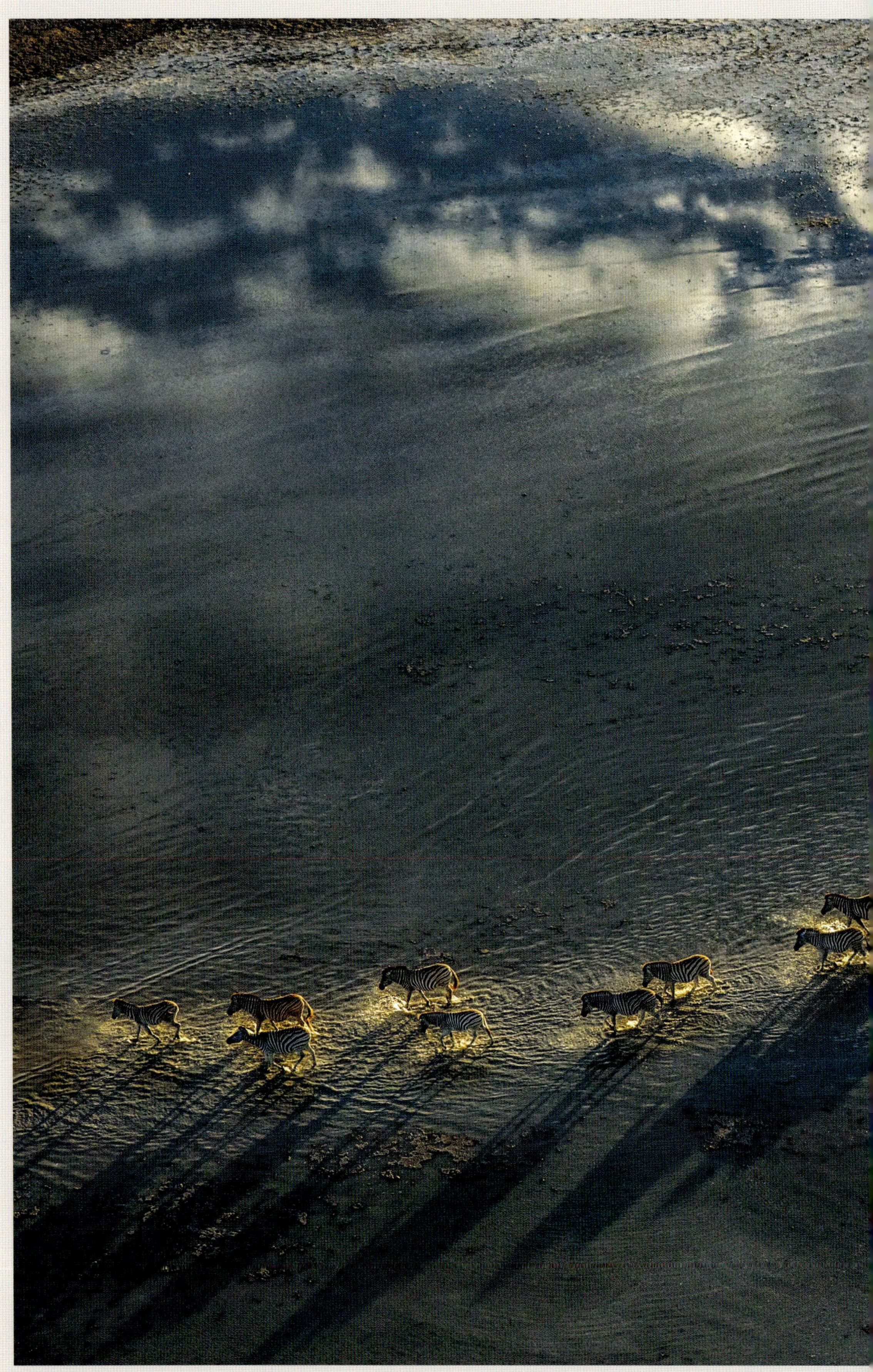

BEVERLY JOUBERT, 2018
These zebras travel as far as 500 miles to reach the Makgadikgadi salt pans in Botswana, where they give birth and soak in the mineral-rich waters for five months of each year.

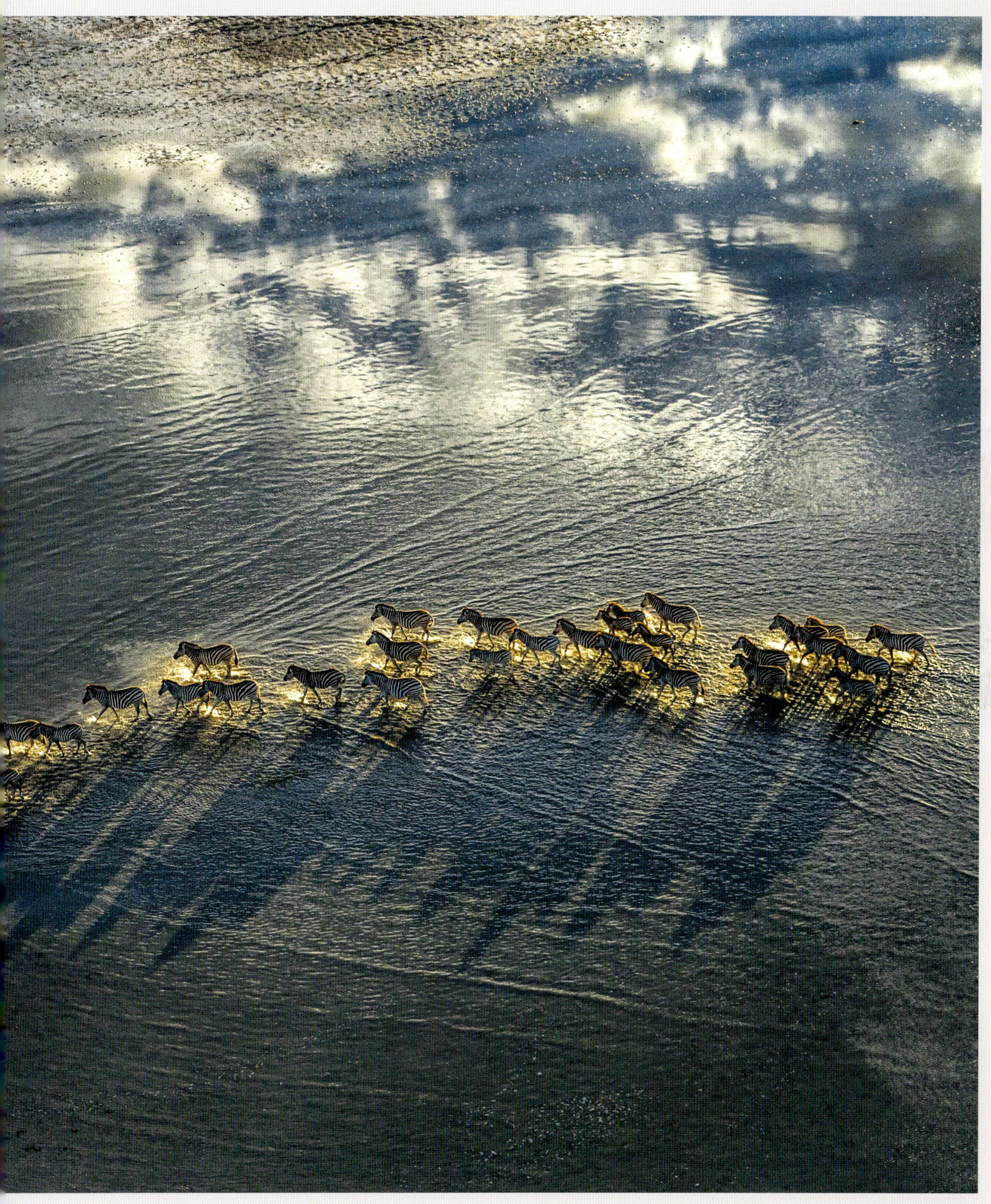

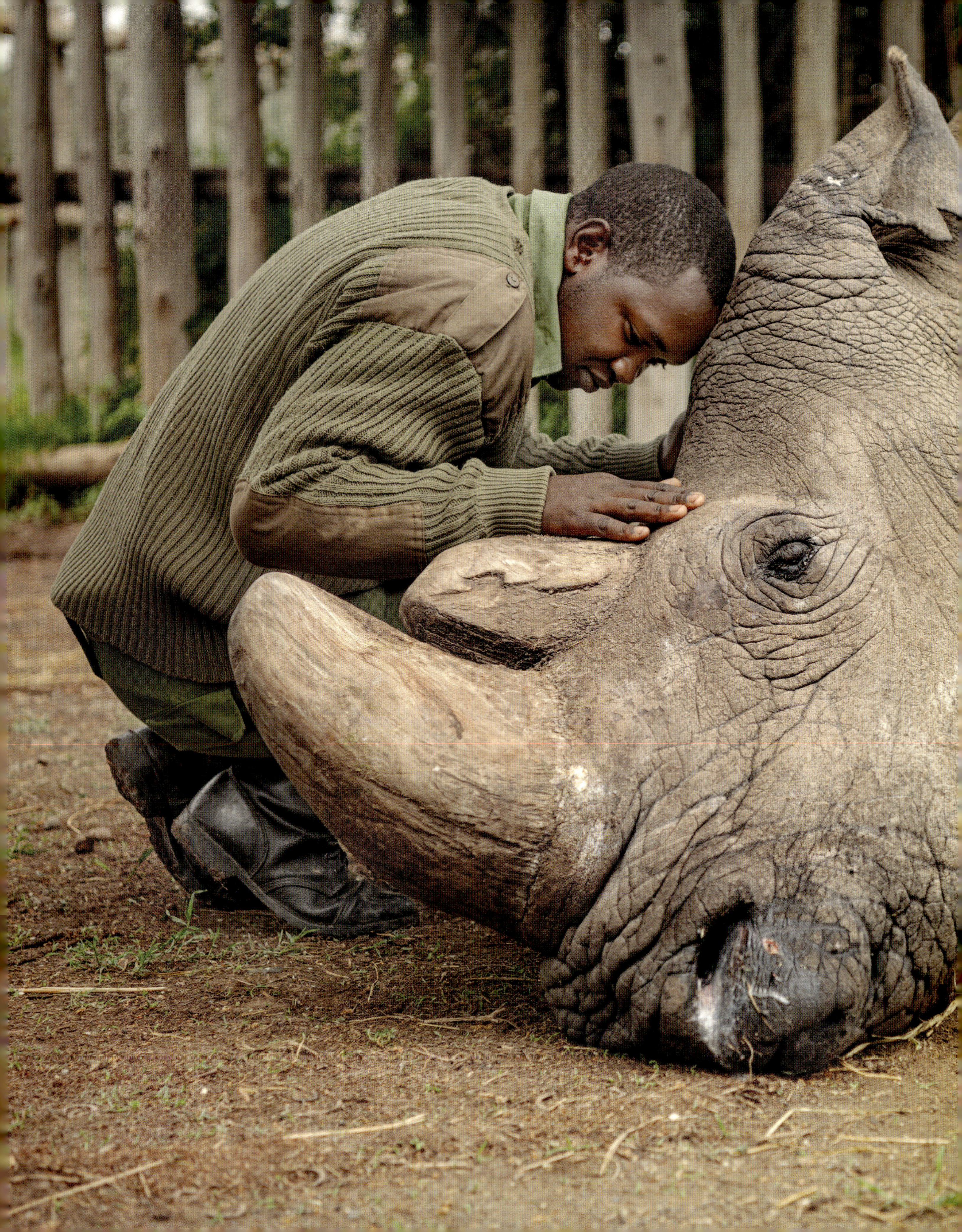

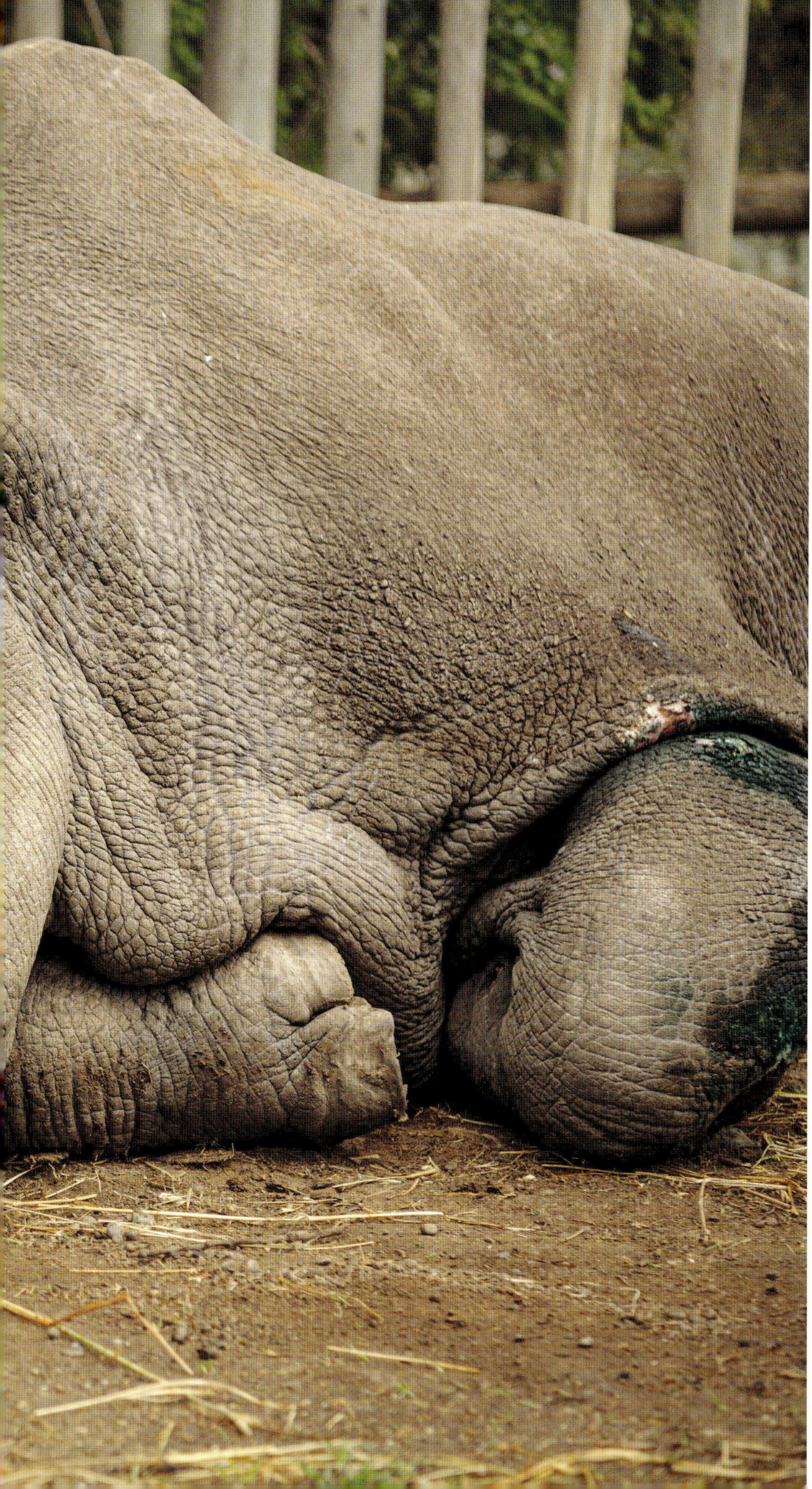

AMI VITALE, 2018
A wildlife ranger comforts Sudan, the world's last male northern white rhino, moments before the animal's death.

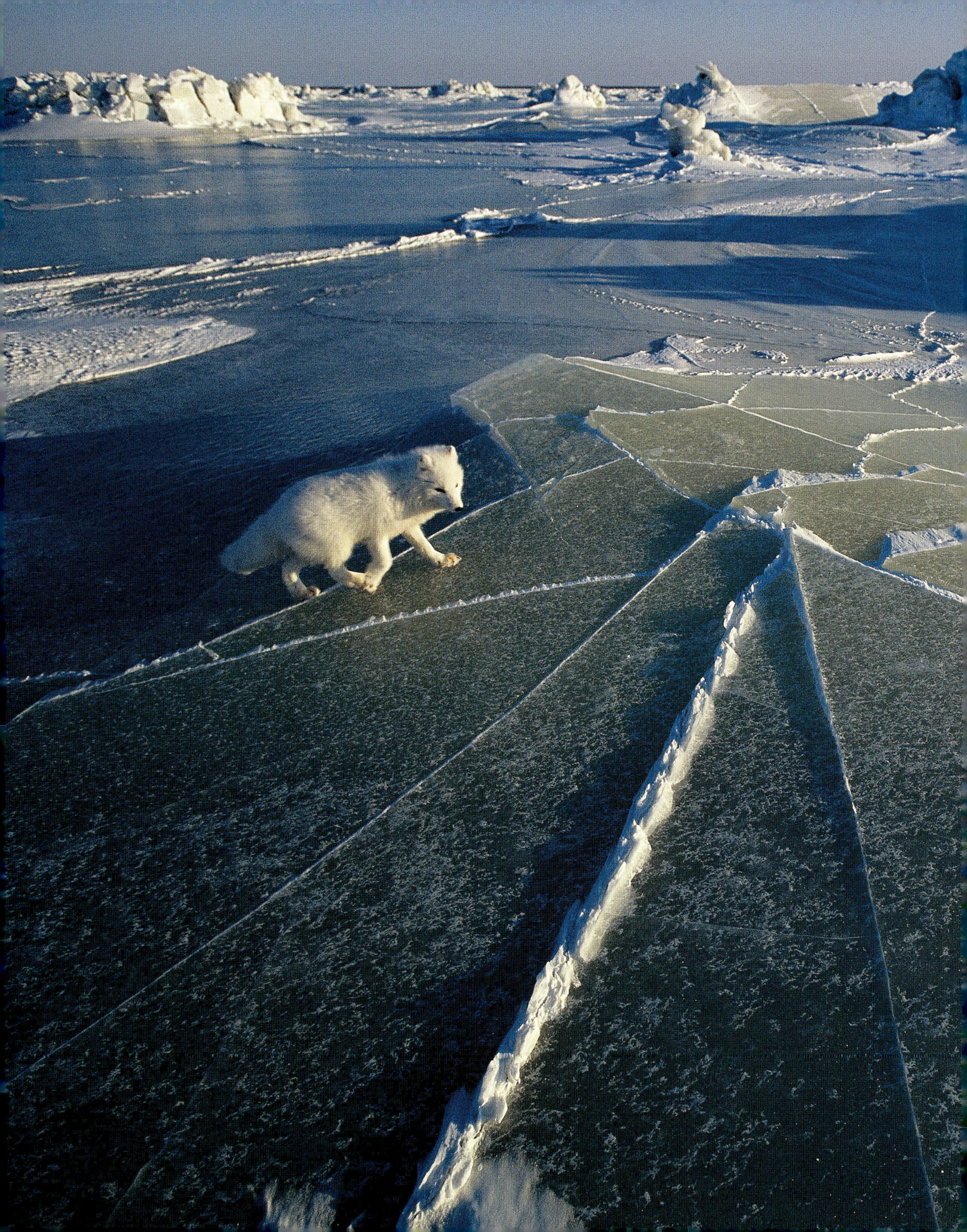

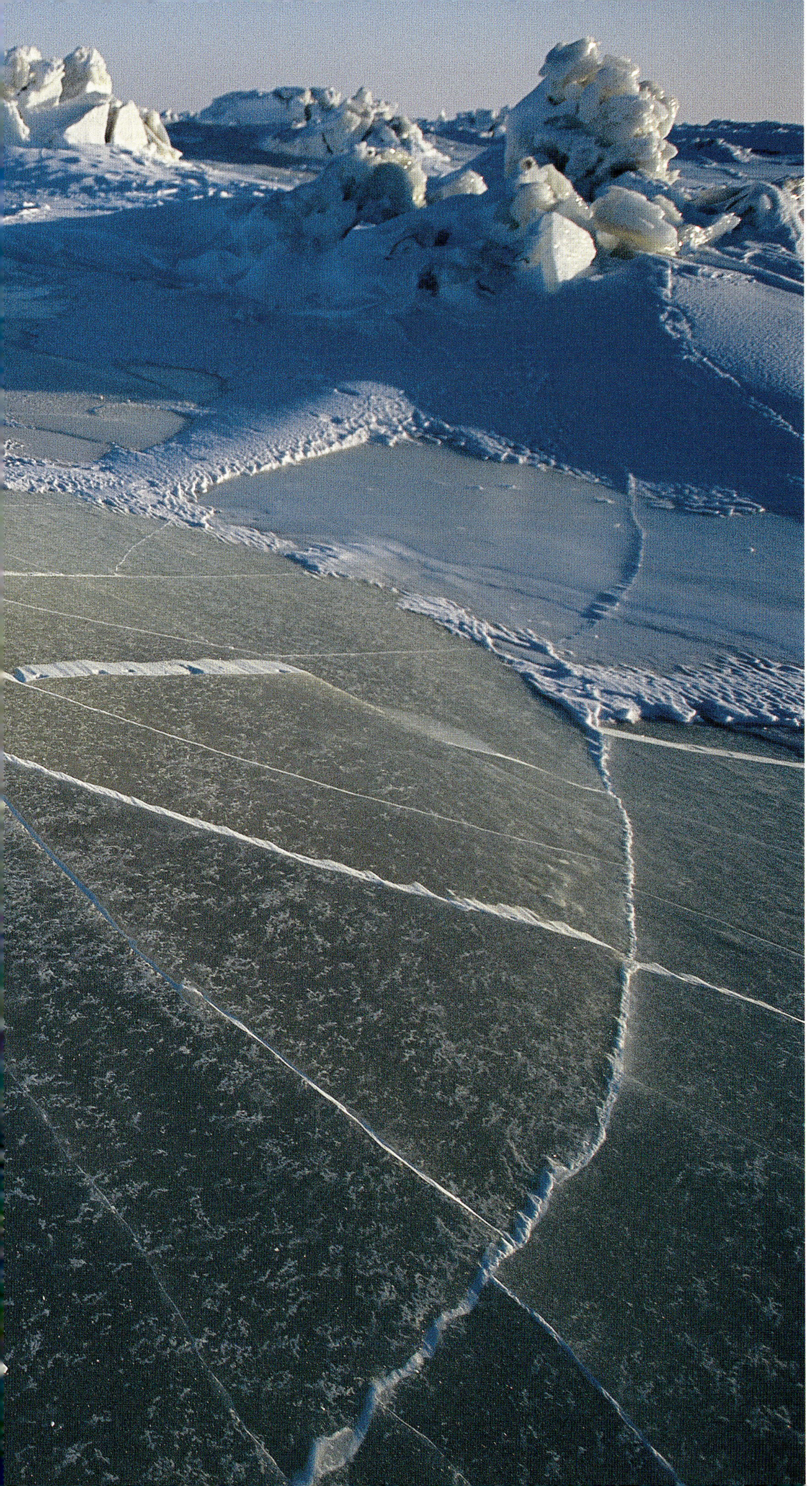

NORBERT ROSING, 2004
An arctic fox crosses the frozen tidal flats of Canada's Hudson Bay. These animals sometimes travel 600 miles over the course of a winter in search of food.

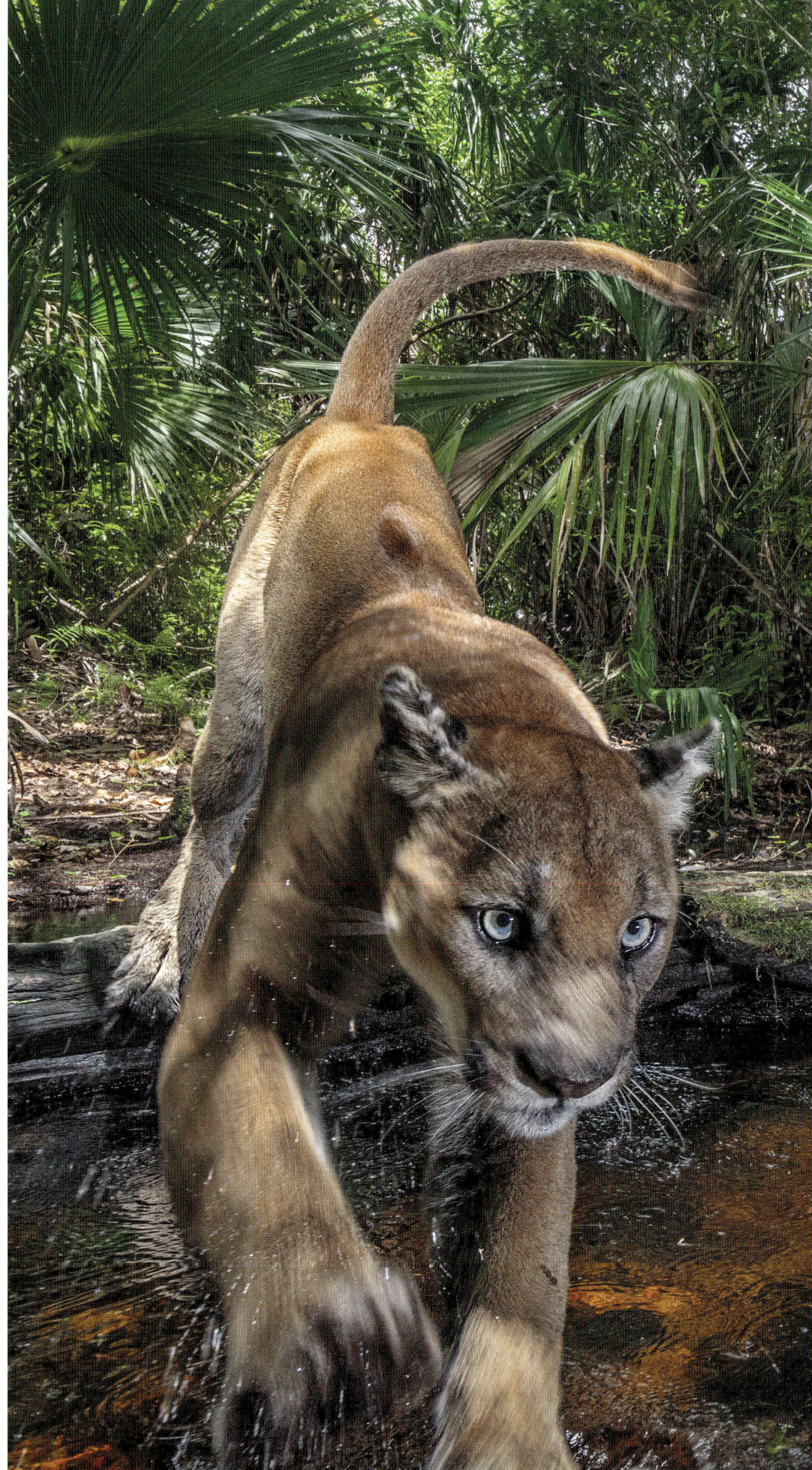

CARLTON WARD JR., 2017
A Florida panther—one of only 200 left—leaps over a creek at the Florida Panther National Wildlife Refuge in the Everglades. The Florida Wildlife Corridor project offers hope for these threatened cats.

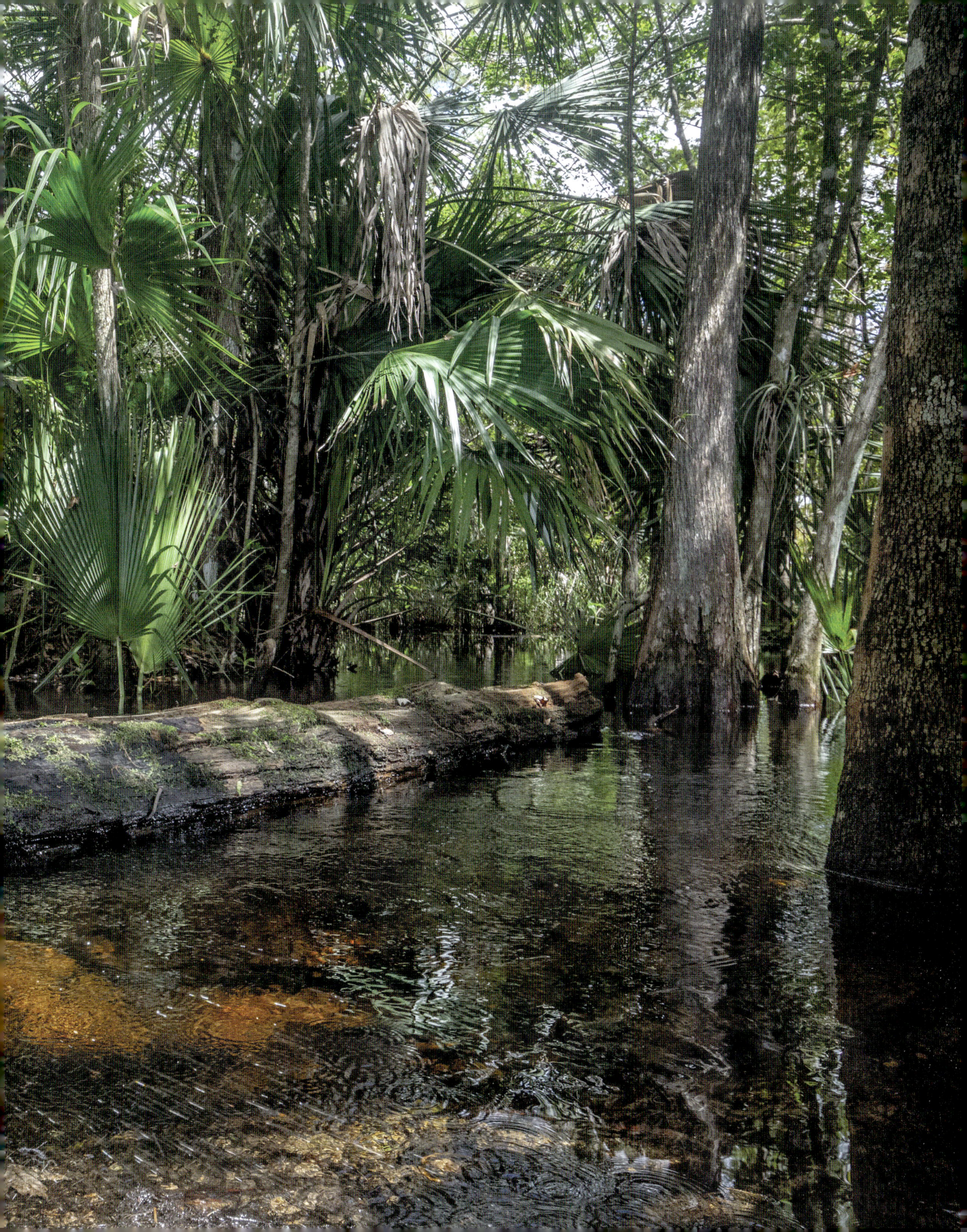

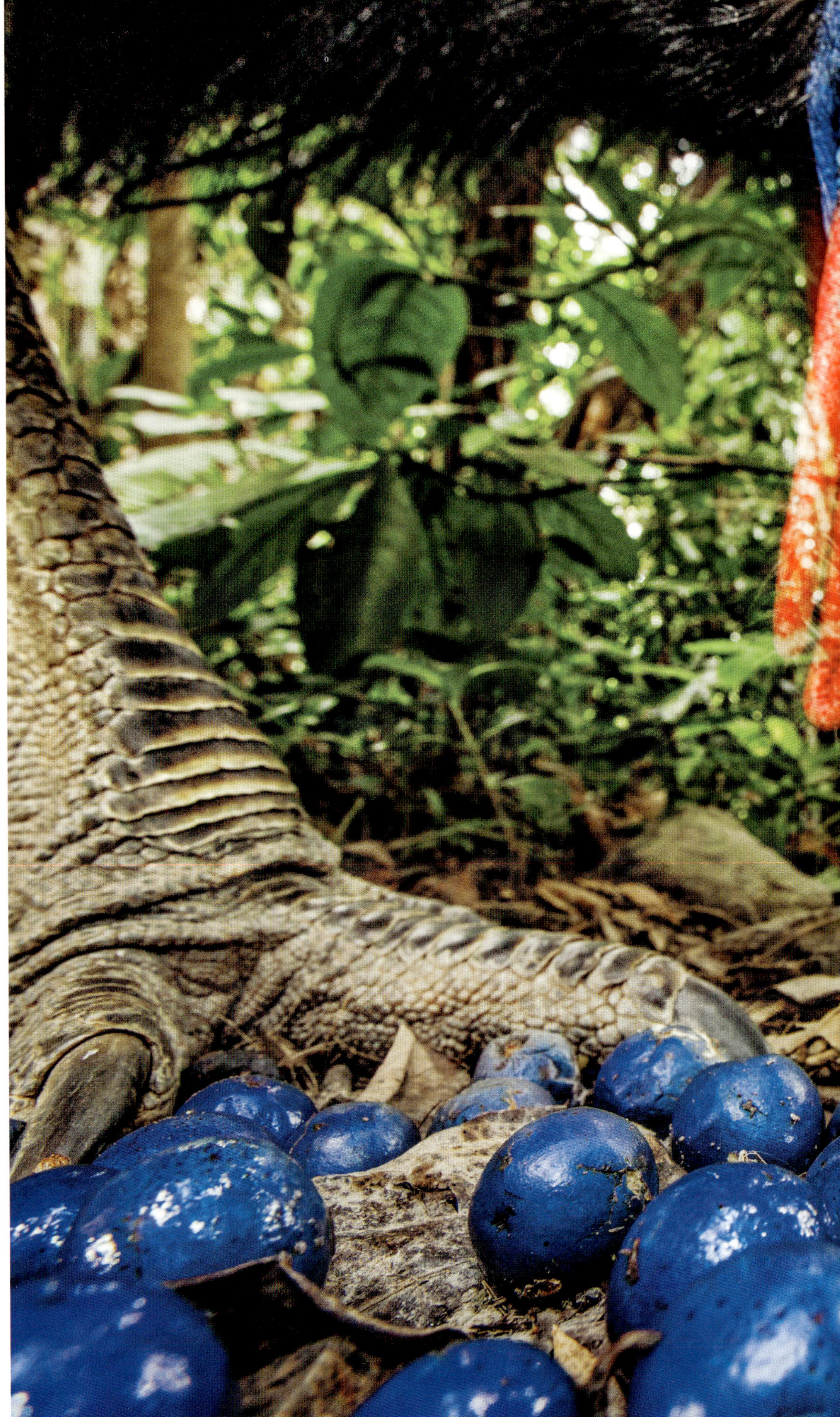

CHRISTIAN ZIEGLER, 2013
A male cassowary, a flightless bird that can weigh up to 110 pounds, feeds on quandong fruit in the Wet Tropics rainforest, a World Heritage area in Queensland, Australia.

FOLLOWING PAGES
BRIAN SKERRY, 2006
A blue cod swims among the sea pens in New Zealand's Te Tapuwae o Hua (Long Sound) Marine Reserve.

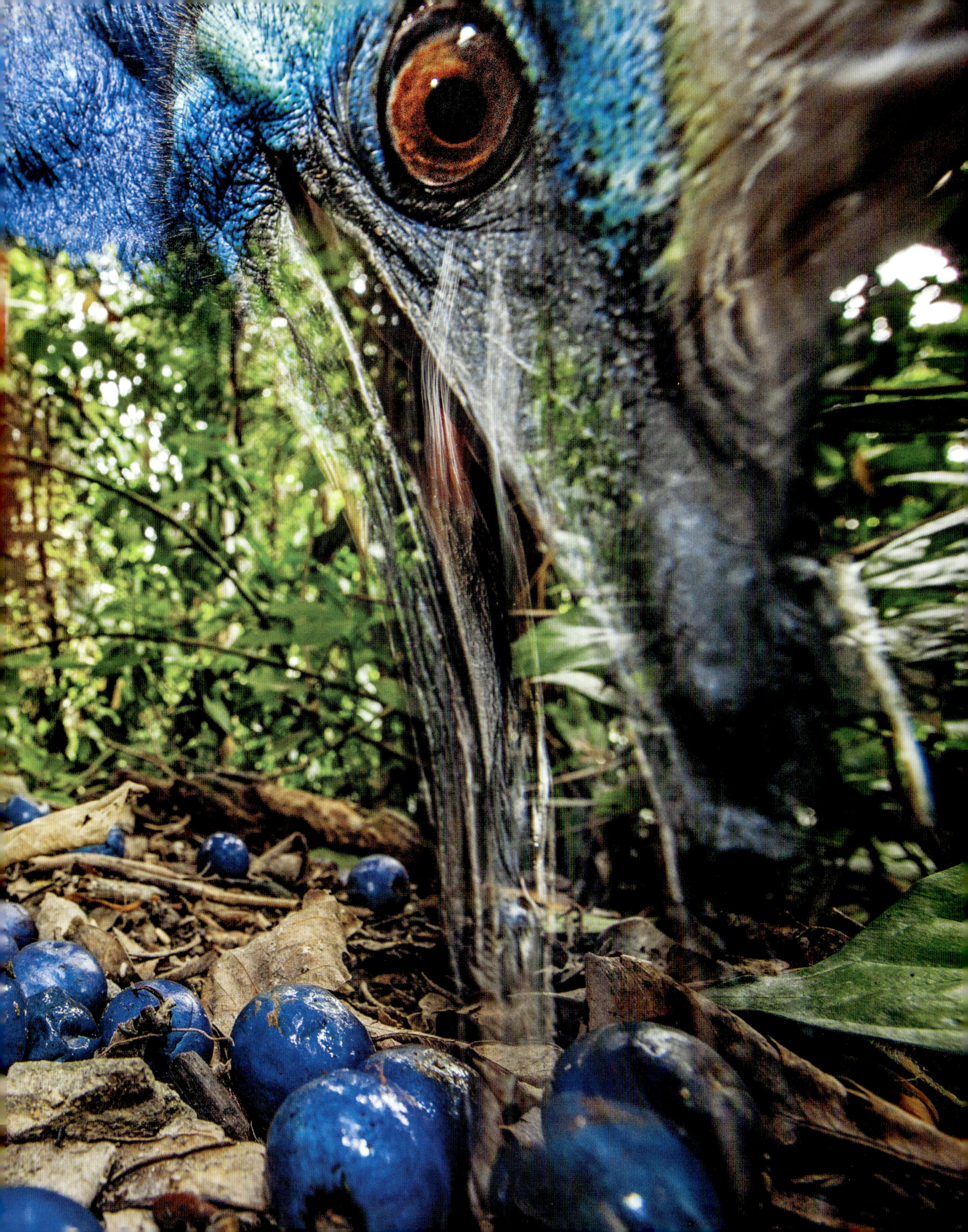

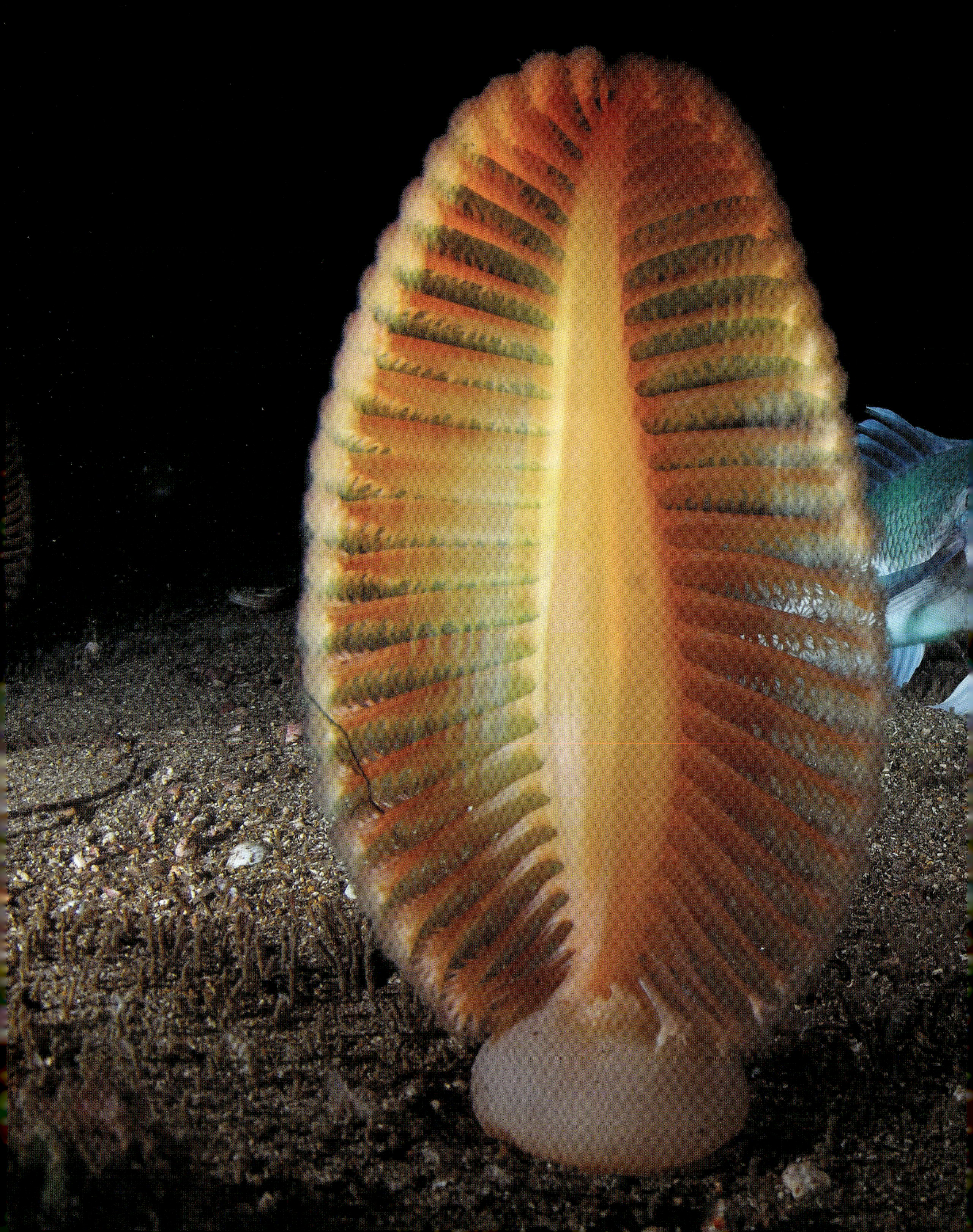

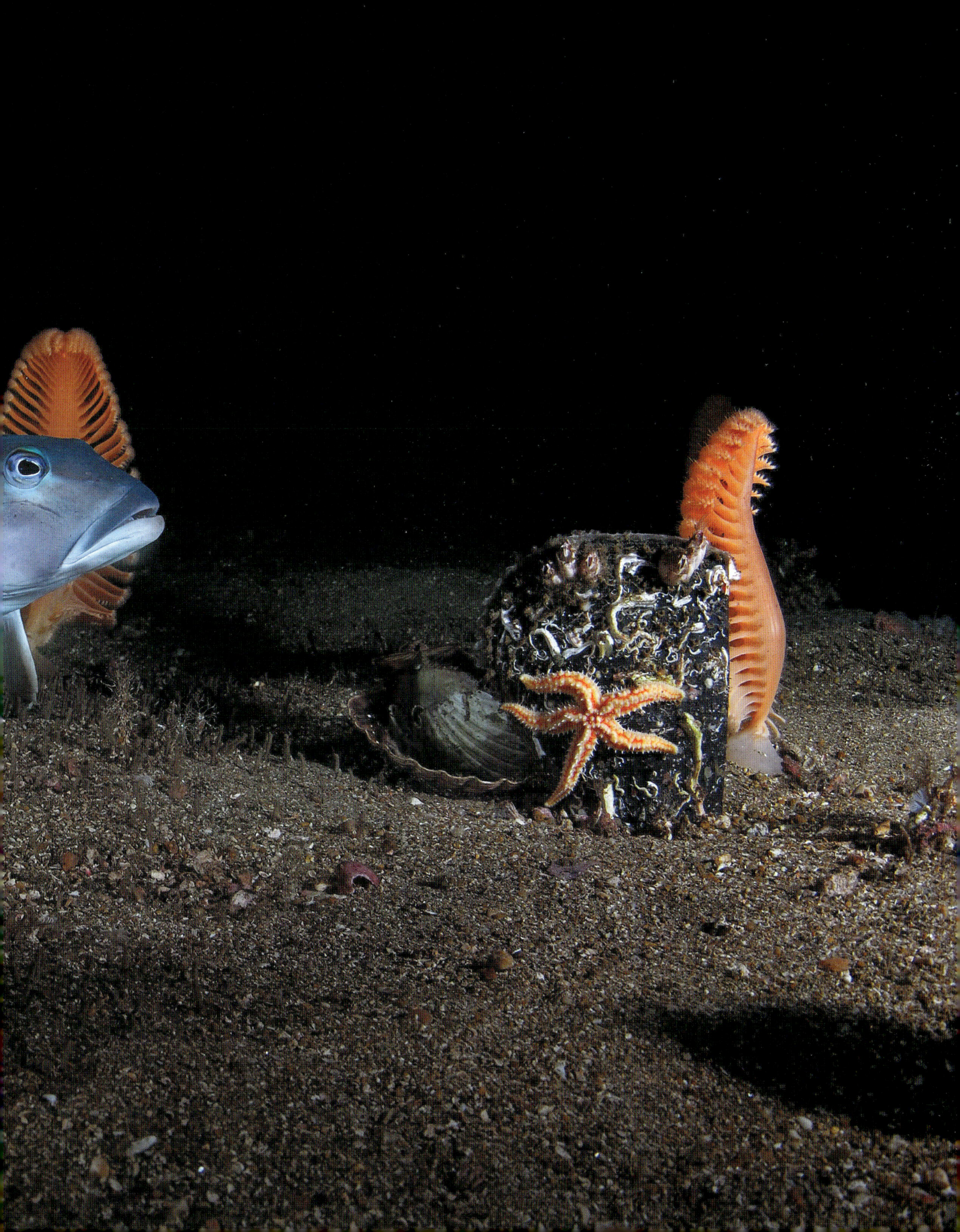

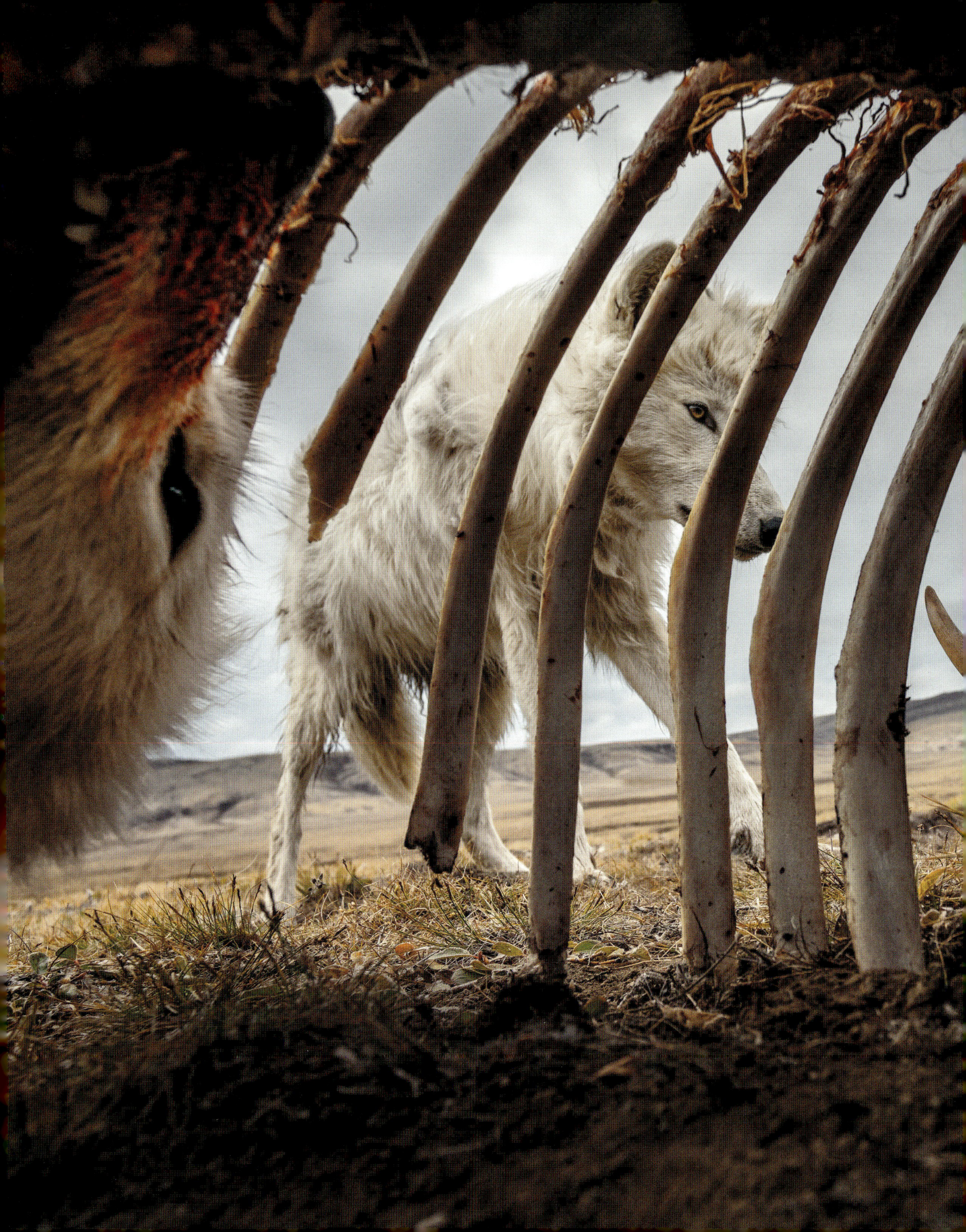

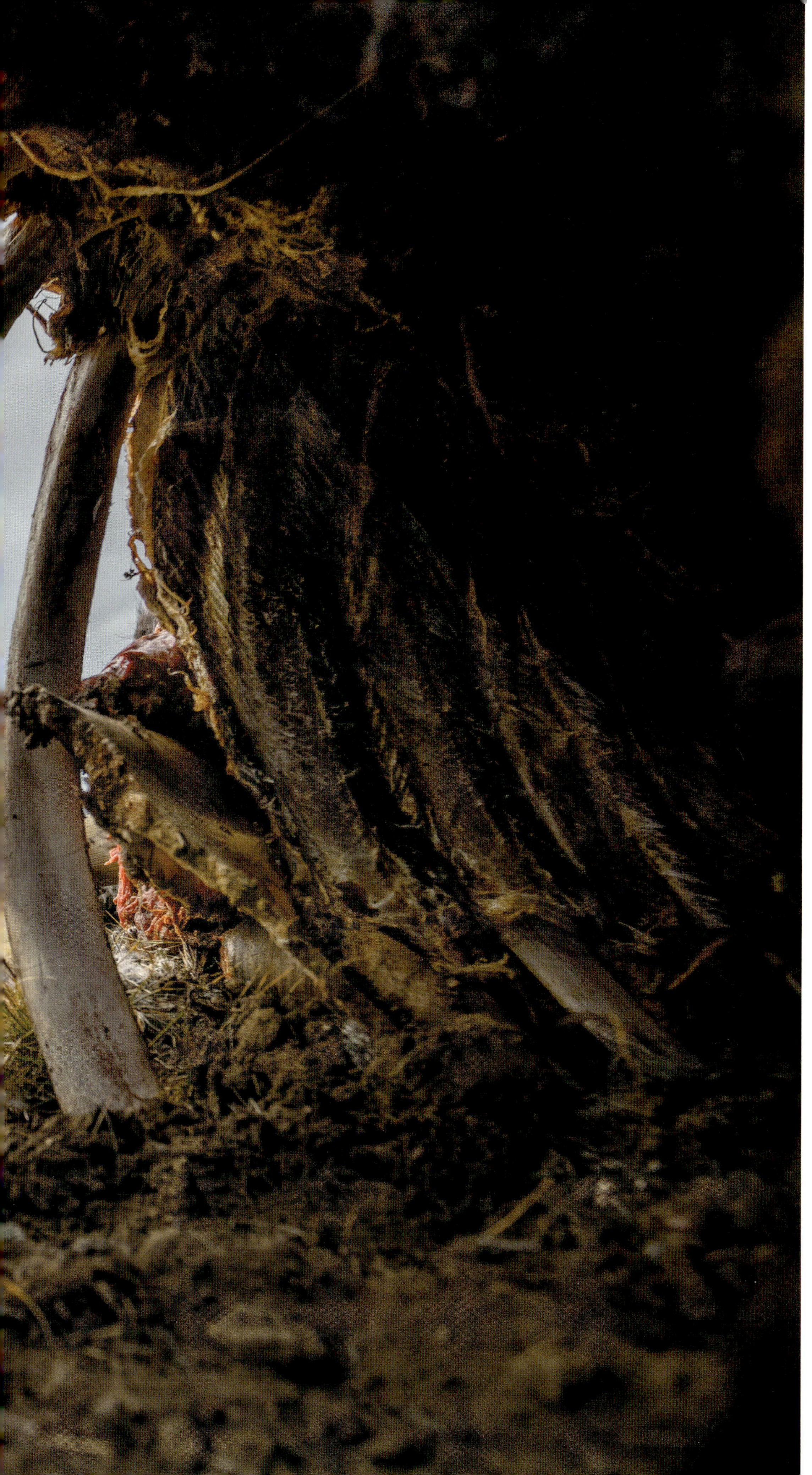

RONAN DONOVAN, 2018
Arctic wolves, photographed via camera trap, scavenge a musk ox carcass on Ellesmere Island in Nunavut, Canada.

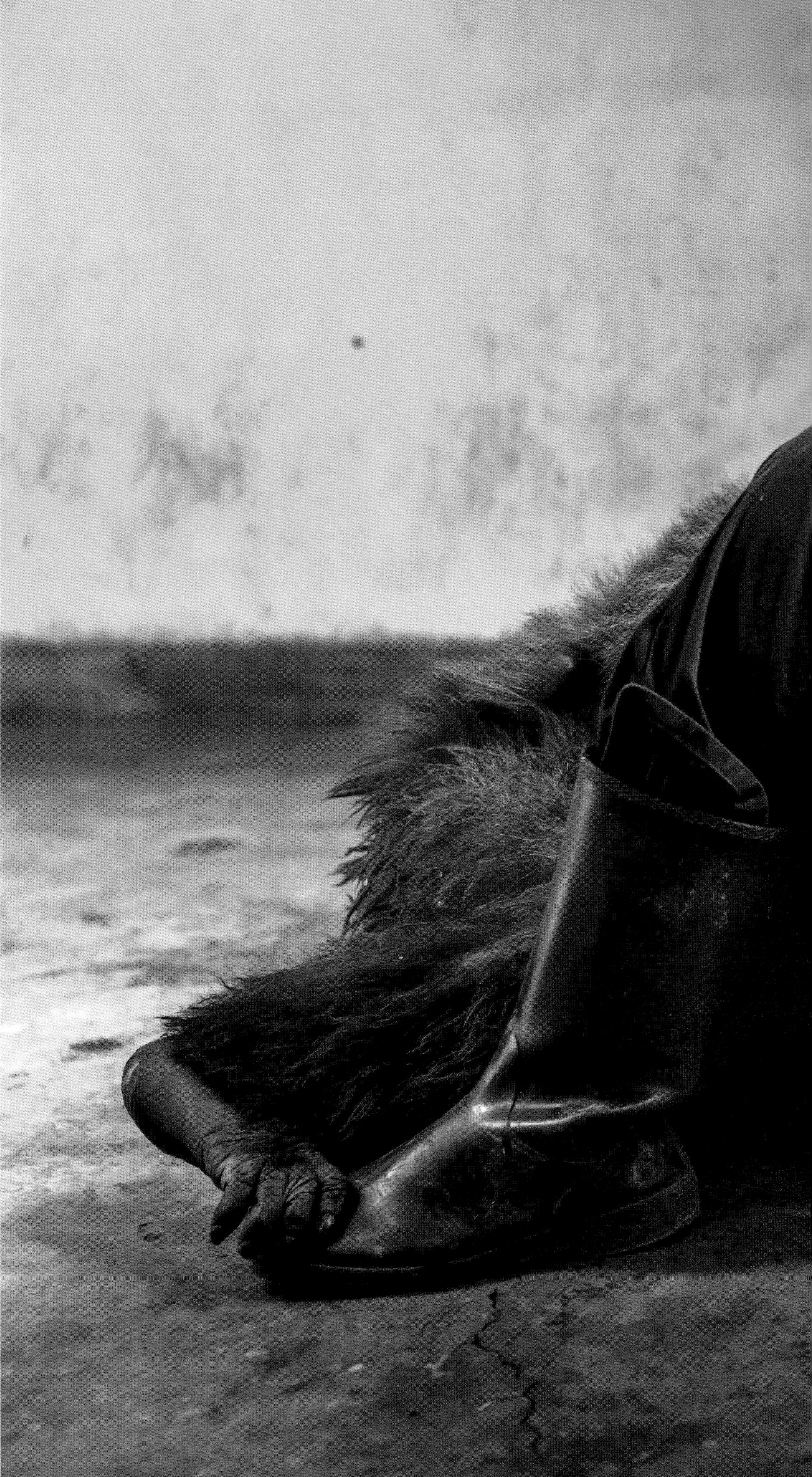

BRENT STIRTON, 2022
Andre Bauma, a ranger at the Democratic Republic of the Congo's Virunga National Park, has been caring for Ndakasi, an orphaned mountain gorilla, since the animal was an infant. Dying of an undiagnosed illness, she seeks comfort in Bauma's arms.

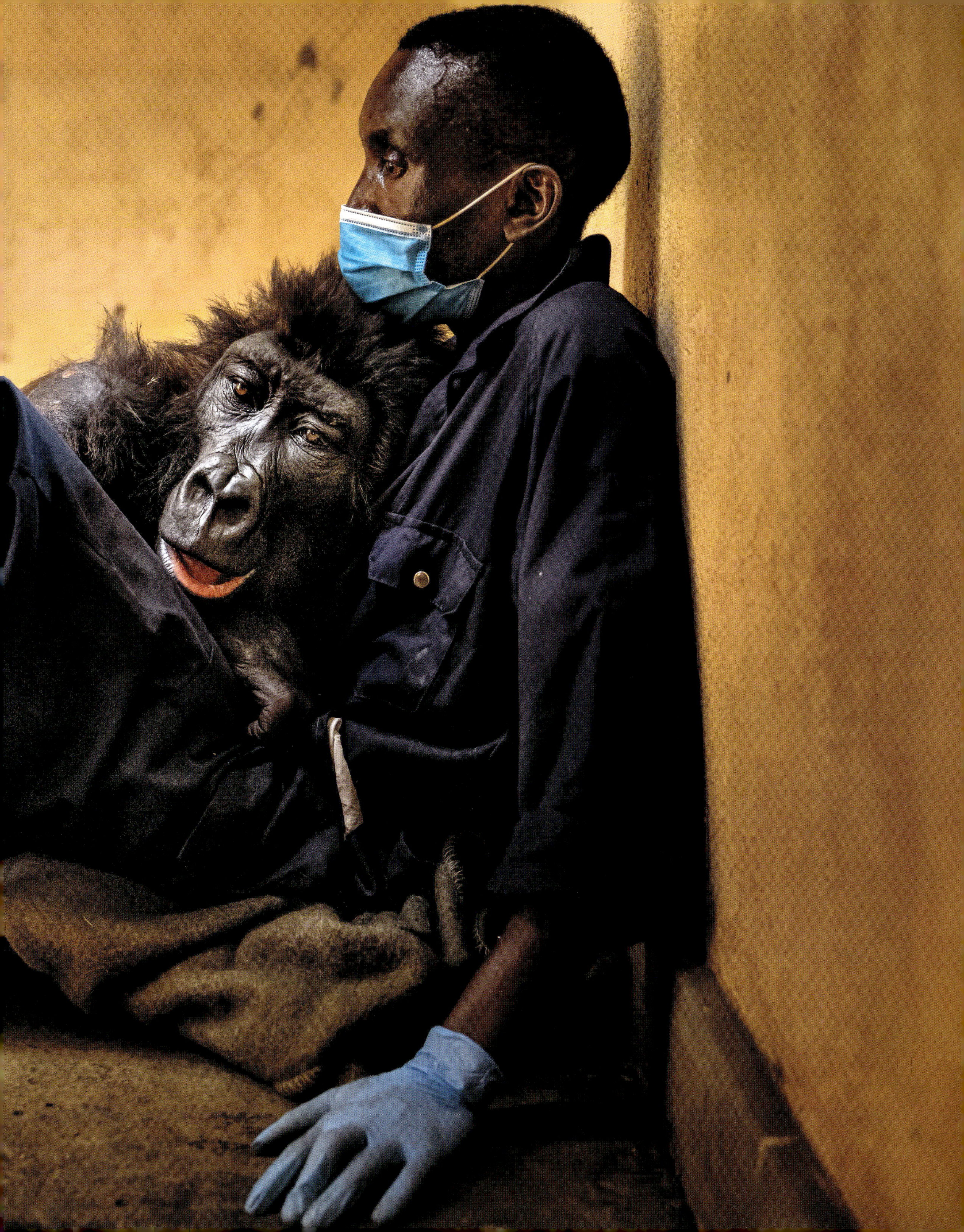

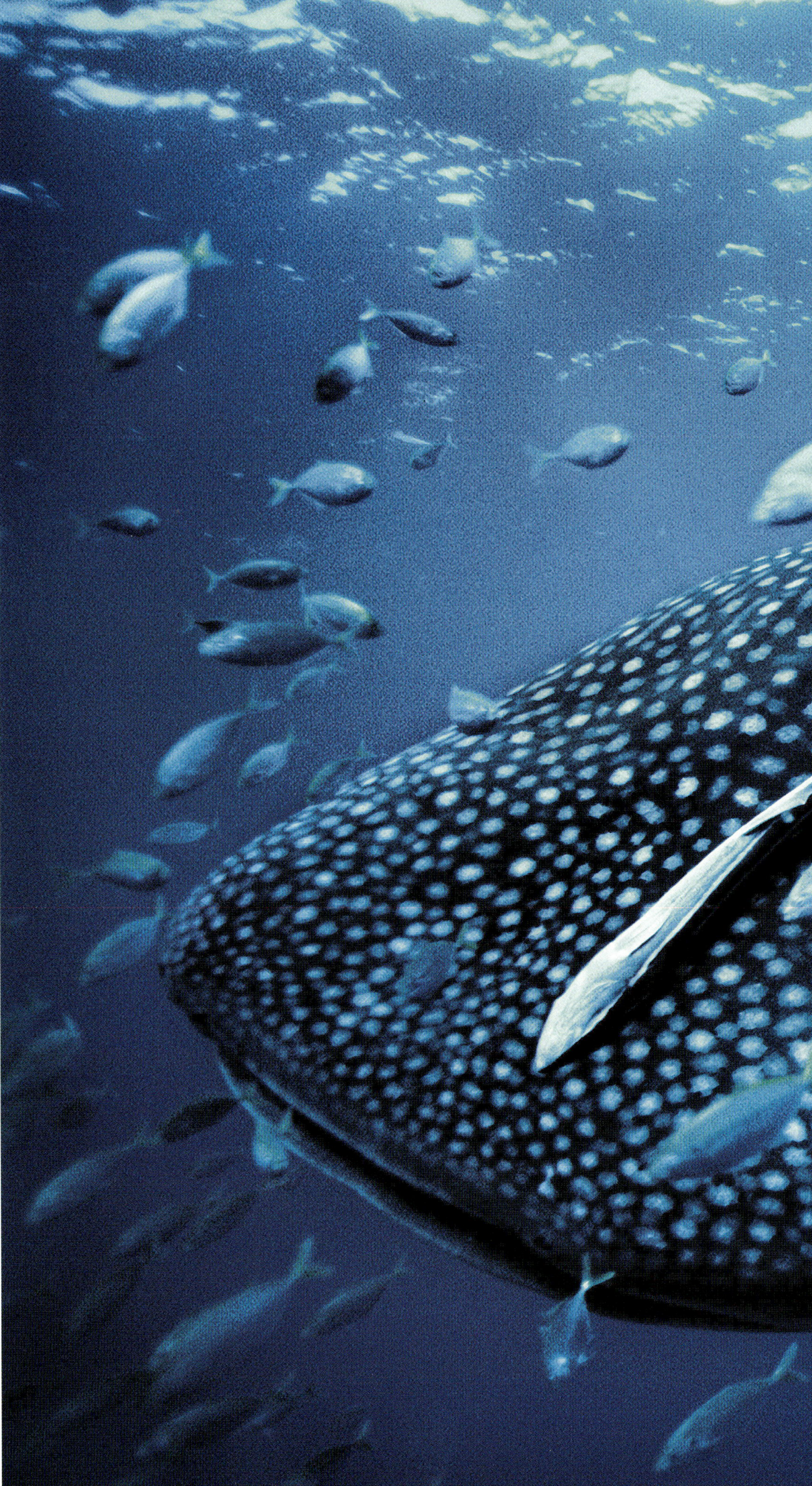

BRIAN SKERRY, 2007
A whale shark's polka-dot skin offers helpful camouflage to small fish off the western coast of Australia.

FOLLOWING PAGES
RENAN OZTURK, 2020
Tinkling bells herald the arrival of yaks carrying propane and other supplies to Advanced Base Camp on Mount Everest.

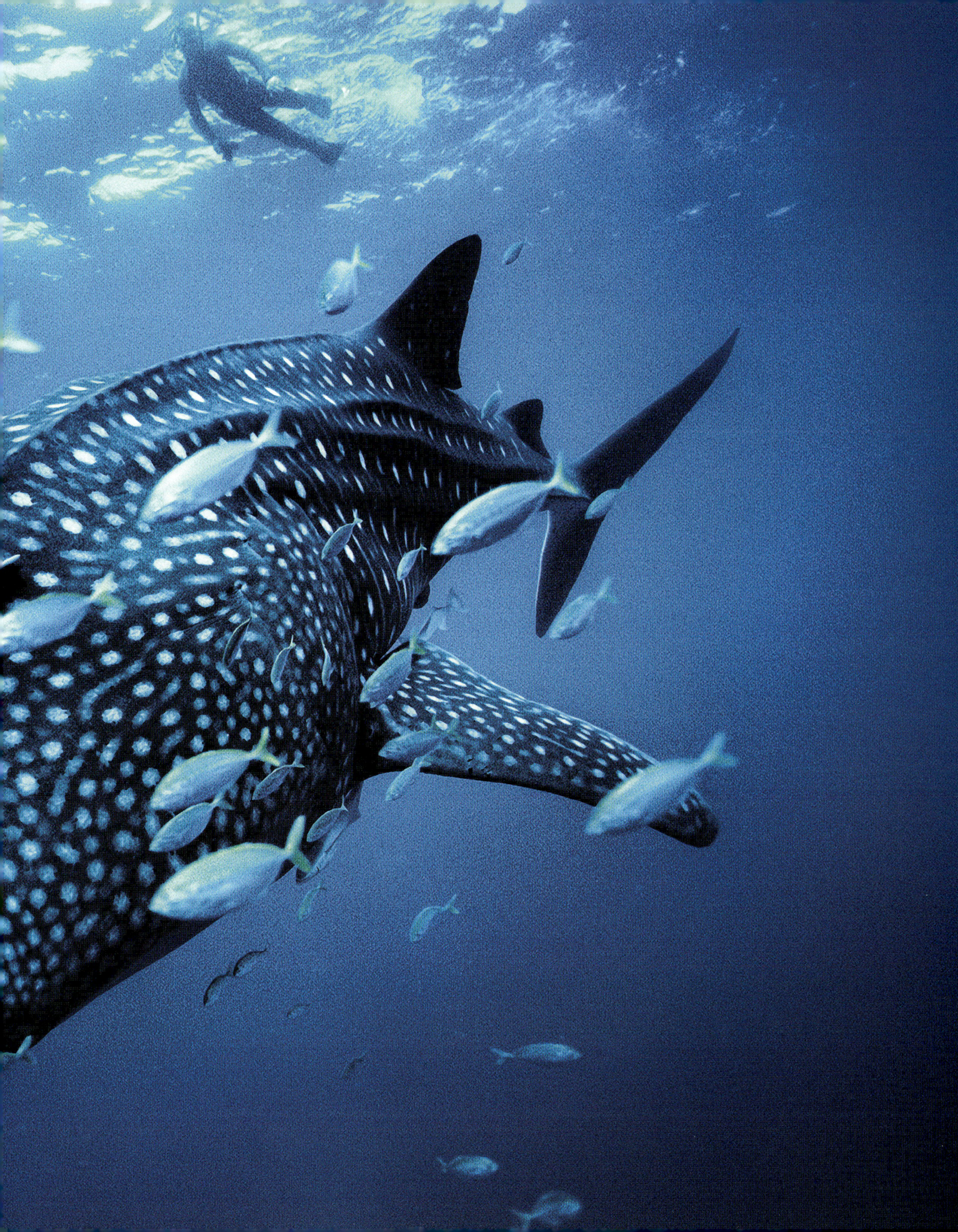

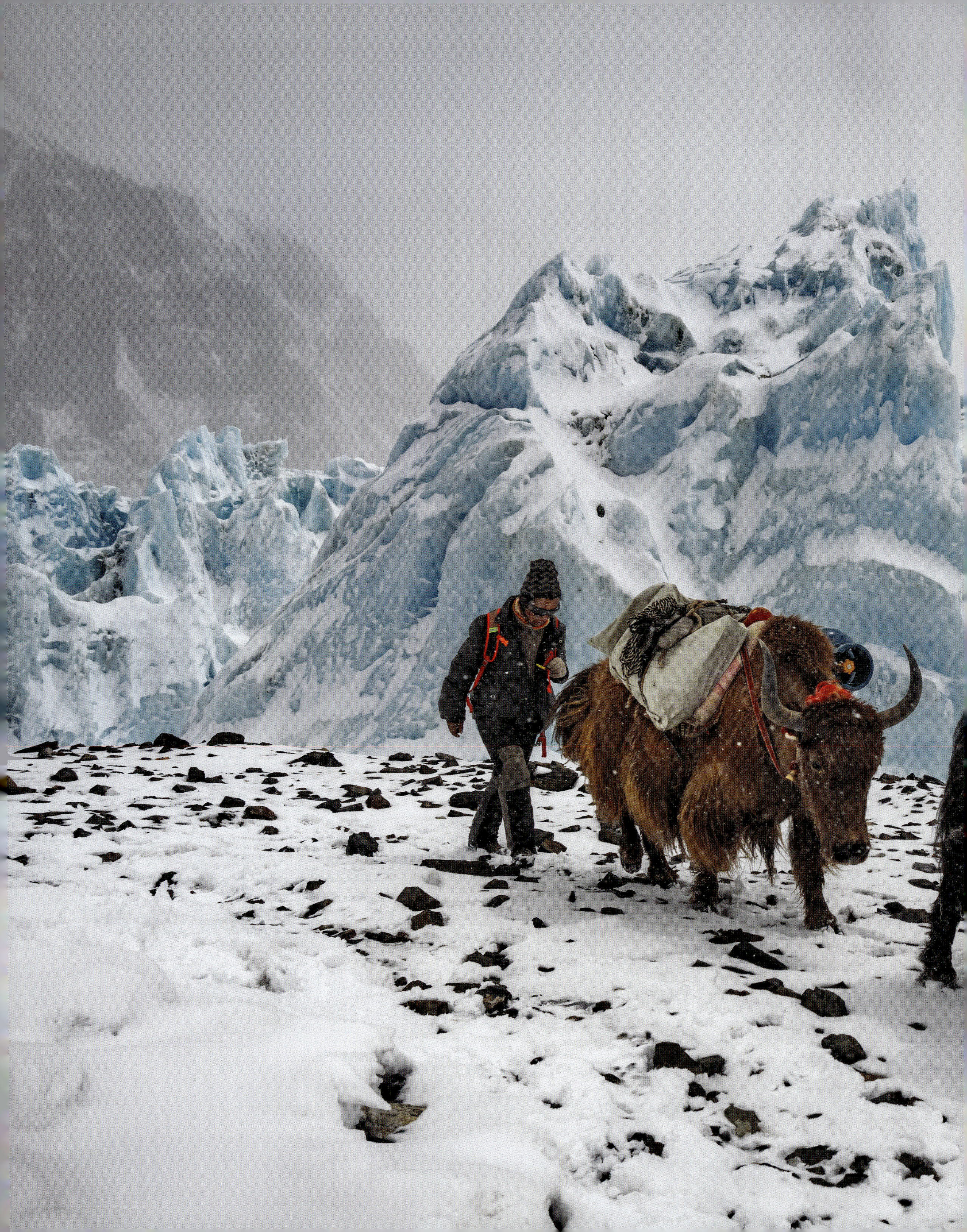

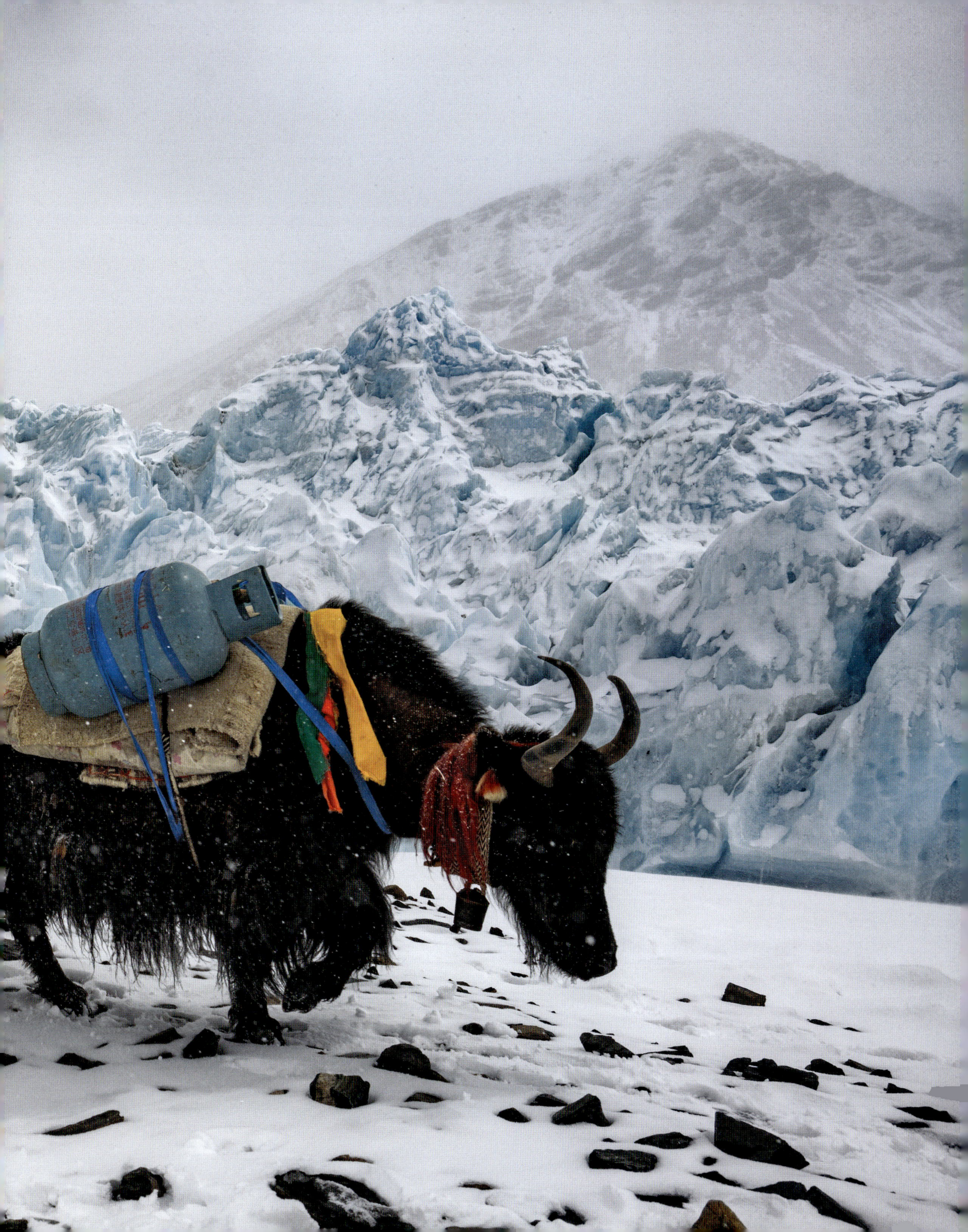

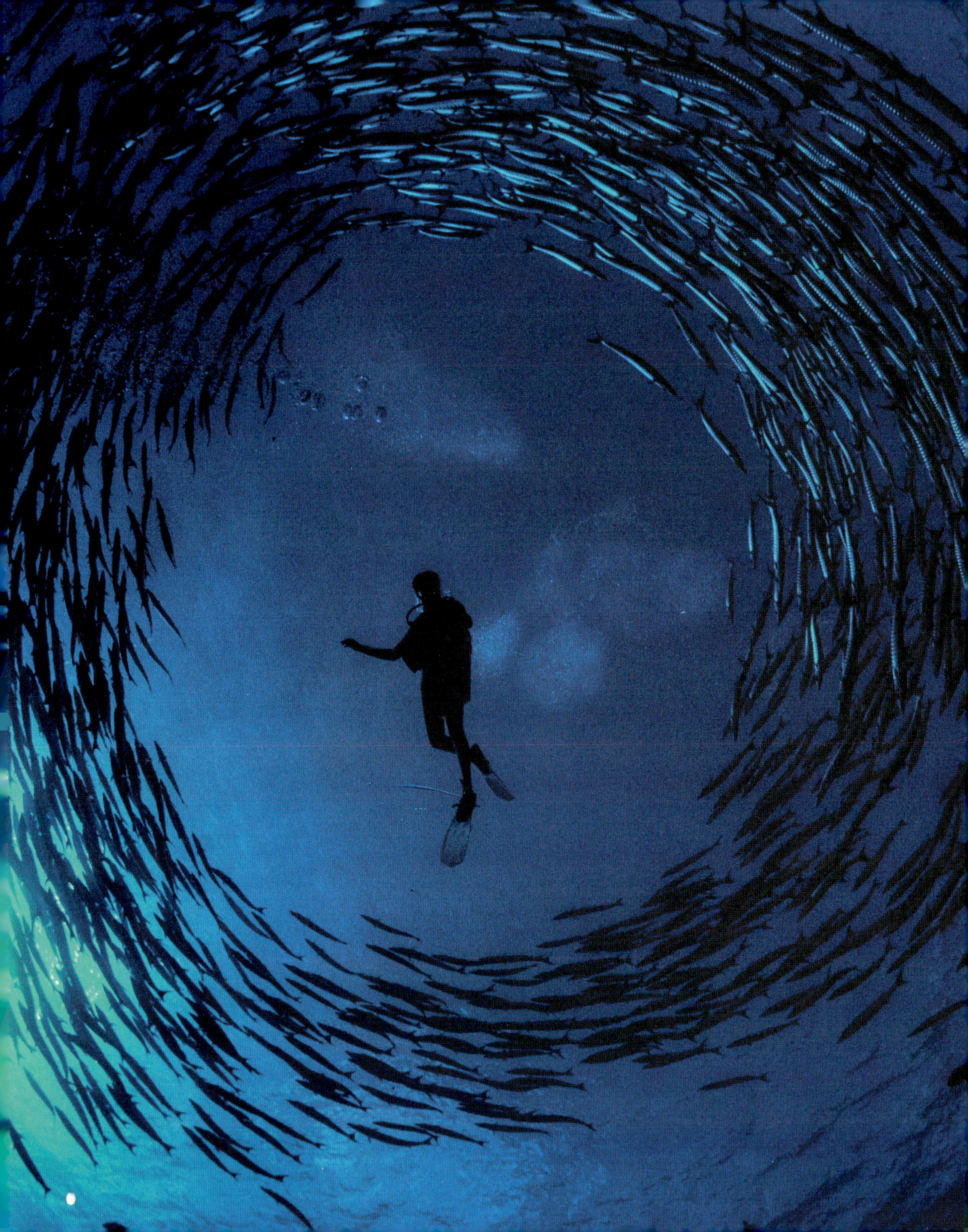

IN CONVERSATION WITH

DAVID DOUBILET

David Doubilet by the numbers is an impressive tally: Over the course of his 53-year-long relationship with National Geographic, he has spent 1,104 days—three years—underwater photographing 80 stories in 83 countries. Natural history photographers, he says, are frontline reporters on the state of the planet. Doubilet has received numerous awards, including the Natural History Museum's Wildlife Photographer of the Year, and he has been a Rolex Testimonee since 1994. He lives in upstate New York within sight of the St. Lawrence River with his wife and photographic partner, aquatic biologist Jennifer Hayes.

NATIONAL GEOGRAPHIC: You've said that "planet Earth" is a misnomer. Why?

DAVID DOUBILET: Nobody really thought about Earth as a water planet until we began to see pictures of it from space. There was our planet floating in the ether, and it's blue.

When I started at Geographic, an editor said to me, "You're never going to make a career here shooting pictures underwater." But I said, "This planet is 70 percent water. You want to ignore that?" That was the crusade I was on. This is a water planet. It operates in an entirely different way than we think life operates: in a world that is weightless, a world that is fabulous, a world that is dreamlike, but a world that is very, very real. As the oceans go, so do we.

NG: What made you take a camera underwater in the first place?

DD: I grew up on the Upper East Side of New York City, and children in New York were sent to summer camp in the Adirondacks. I hated it. I had asthma, and I hated baseball and football—anything with something that flew through the air. So the junior counselors sent me down to the waterfront. They said, "Here, kid. Put on this mask and go under the dock and clear out some of the branches." They knew there was a giant water spider there, and they thought I would be frightened of it and come out of the water screaming.

But when I went under, I thought the water spider was fascinating. And then I saw the light streaming down, and the sunfish going in and out of the light under the dock, and it was heaven. That was the place I wanted to be.

NG: Your, shall we call them, landlubber colleagues talk about the importance of making a connection with the subjects they photograph. Is that irrelevant in dealing with marine life?

DD: Intimacy is the key to all imagery at National Geographic. But the hardest pictures to make underwater concern animal behaviors, like a fish doing something they wouldn't normally do with a photographer present. You have to wait. And when you want to leave, wait longer.

But there are always surprises. In fact, a recent time we were in the water, I was photographing an anemone when it opened up and began to spawn. It looks like smoke spewing out of the anemone's central disc. As it happened, a few clownfish were inside the anemone, watching the whole thing. They looked so confused, as if they were saying, "What's going on here?" I hadn't seen that in 50 years of diving.

NG: What are some of the unique challenges of underwater photography?

DD: Well, you live in a world where you can see, at best, 100 feet in any direction. You live in a world

DAVID DOUBILET, 1987
A naturalist framed by a ring of barracuda in the Bismarck Sea off New Hanover Island, Papua New Guinea

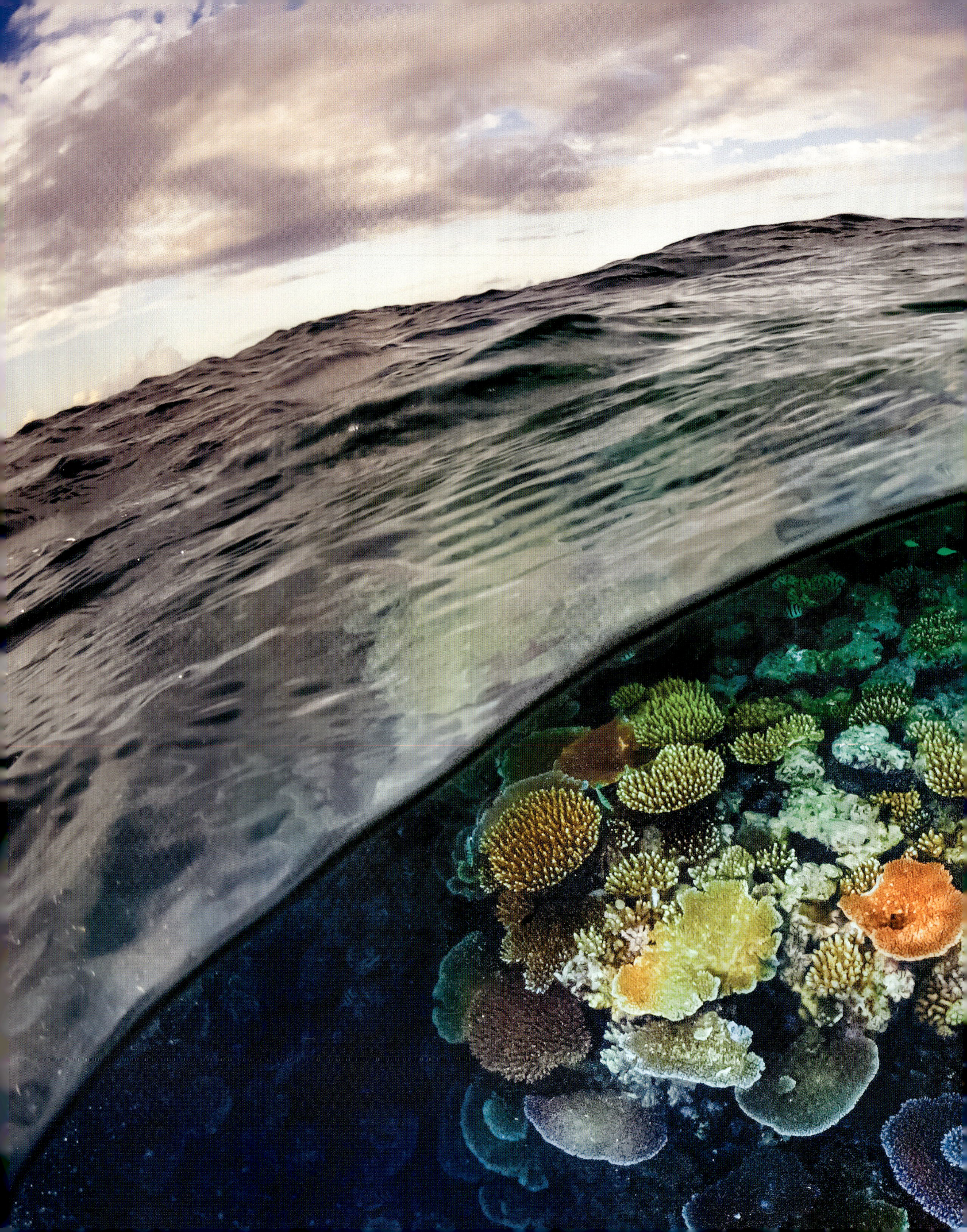

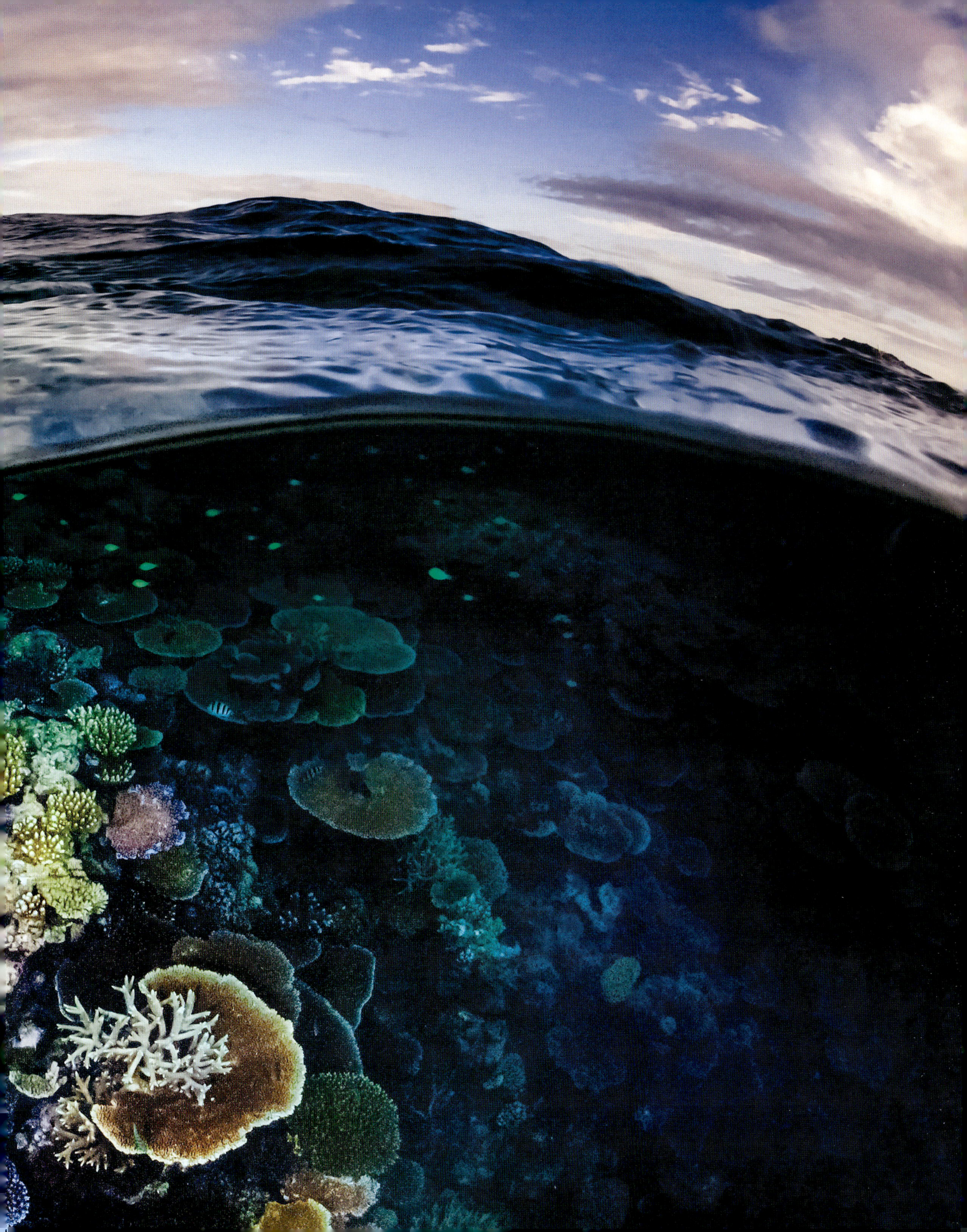

where colors disappear within the first two feet of water, and by 40 feet, brilliant red turns black. You have to restore the spectrum with artificial light. And you live in a world where everything is magnified 33 percent. So you have to correct that magnification.

NG: Tell us about the role of technology in the evolution of your work.

DD: For me, the digital revolution feels like everything I had dreamed of making is coming to fruition. Not only are the cameras able to capture all the information—the deepest shadows, the highest highlights—but we can see our work instantaneously.

I once went to shoot the full length of the Red Sea. I shot 550 rolls of film, and took six or eight camera systems. At the end of the trip, I flew out of Djibouti to Paris, then shipped the film from Paris to the office in three different shipments. I never saw those pictures for three months. I had no idea whether I'd even succeeded. But in digital, now I can see these things right away and correct them. Underwater, that's an absolute piece of genius for us.

NG: What do you aim for in making a striking underwater image?

DD: In underwater journalism, you are in an enormously difficult-to-understand place. So you have to make a picture that has an aspect of poetry to it, because if it doesn't have that, it doesn't stop people.

If you want to save something, you have to love it. And to love it, you have to know it. What photography does is bridge that gap to know it, to see it. When you do that, you go against the most impenetrable force against the protection of our planet, and that force is apathy.

NG: One of your trademark techniques is the horizontal split-screen photograph, like the over-under photograph of the Great Barrier Reef [pages 194–95].

DD: Those pictures basically say everything about how I feel, because they illustrate the largest and most important border of our planet. The surface of the water divides this air world from the water world. I make these pictures with a fish-eye lens, which curves the horizon. But in many ways it evokes the curvature of Earth too.

NG: With half a century of underwater photography under your weight belt, you've had an unprecedented opportunity to compare then with now. Let's consider the Great Barrier Reef. What changes have you witnessed?

DD: We did a Great Barrier Reef story in 2001, then another in 2009. Reefs are the glory of the planet. I always think of coral as weightless architecture—if an architect didn't have to worry about gravity.

One of the best examples from our 2009 story was Opal Reef off Port Douglas, Australia. It was dreamlike. When we went back in 2018, that section of reef was devastated—a 5,000-year-old reef dead in eight or nine years!

NG: You've photographed nearly every species of shark, from hand-size lanternsharks to great whites. Most people find them terrifying. What is their appeal to you?

DD: Sharks are ancient ghosts of the sea. They're very old, and they've survived for quite a long time. When I began diving, sharks were on almost every reef, but now they are rare or nonexistent in many places. But they can come back. We are seeing efforts to rewild sharks in Raja Ampat [an Indonesian archipelago], for example. The presence of sharks is something to celebrate. Their presence tells us the reef is healthy enough to support apex predators.

NG: Have you ever had any close calls with a shark?

DD: A few times. Once in the South Neptune Islands, I left the cage and walked into a bed of seagrass to watch a great white shark circling. I kept my foot on the cage in case I needed it, but I was so mesmerized by the shark that at one point I looked around and the cage was gone. A swell had moved it. I could just see it at the edge of visibility. I thought, It's all right. I'll just swim back to the cage. But I had no swim fins.

The shark all of a sudden became interested in me. When I started paddling backward, it charged, and I had to use the camera to bat him away. He was about an 11-foot great white. I got back to the cage, and as the door slammed behind me, the shark went *bang* against it. Another diver, Rodney Fox, and I looked at each other and said, "That was close!"

NG: Explain this image of circling barracuda [page 192]. What's the behavior all about?

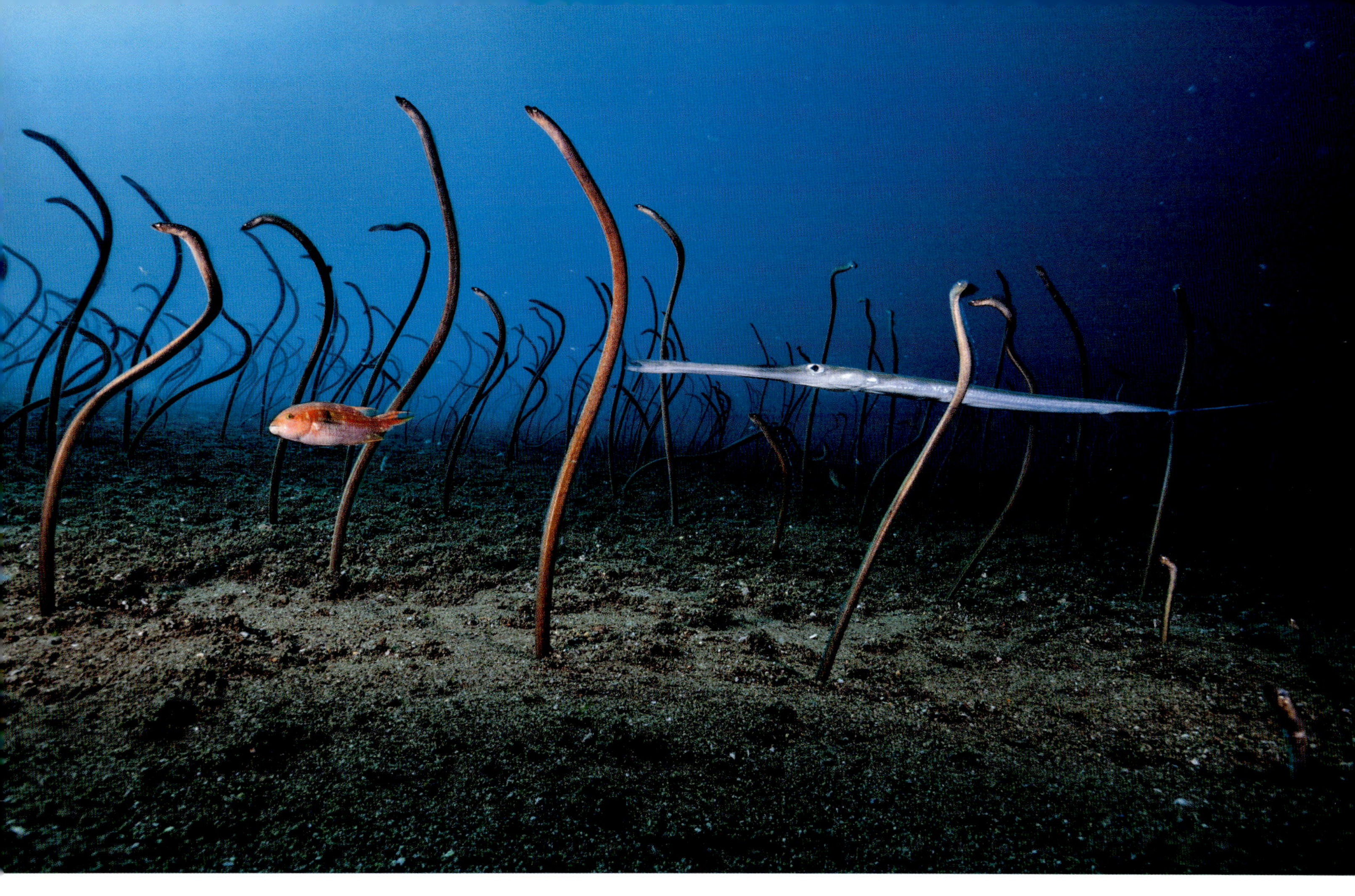

DAVID DOUBILET, 2016
A two-spot wrasse and cornetfish amid a colony of garden eels in Dauin on Negros Island, Philippines

PREVIOUS PAGES
DAVID DOUBILET, 2009
A split image offers a glimpse above and below the colorful Opal Reef, part of Australia's Great Barrier Reef.

DD: Barracuda actually form a circle as a self-protection strategy. If you're inside it, it means they think you might attack them. It's a tool of confusion.

But what it does for us is create a nearly perfect geometric pattern in a totally weightless, cornerless environment. When I swam into the school and they started to circle, I realized that I was in the middle of a photograph. I swam back to the boat and returned with a friend of mine, then swam 40 feet below the school and rolled onto my back. I shot three or four frames, but then my friend did this amazing thing where she stuck out her hand, ballet-like. For me, this picture is in that gesture.

NG: Is there an underwater creature you find especially difficult to photograph?

DD: Underwater, the bizarre is a given, and the surreal is constant. And garden eels are both of those.

When you approach a garden eel, no matter how quiet you are, they disappear in the sand, and you will never get a picture. We were able to capture a field of garden eels in the Philippines with a remote-controlled camera, strobes, and a 30-foot remote lead to a button. We set it up on the first day, and on the second day, the tide came up in the absolute right direction, and the current began to roll across the top of the seabed. It made the eels sway back and forth with a mesmerizing beat. We hid behind a shipwreck, poked our heads up, and took the picture [above].

NG: The ocean is in peril because of insults like climate change and overfishing. Are you an optimist or a pessimist about our ability to conserve it?

DD: There's always hope. What helps are the underwater photographers coming up today who are making images that are far more complete than anything we've seen yet. Every click of the shutter is a collaboration, and at National Geographic, we stand on the shoulders of those who came before. I arrived at a revolution in underwater photography, when Bates Littlehales and Gomer McNeill developed an underwater camera housing called the OceanEye. It changed everything, and it unlocked the oceans to photographers. Now those pictures have the power to open minds and hearts to the sea. That work—the work that Geographic does—makes a difference.

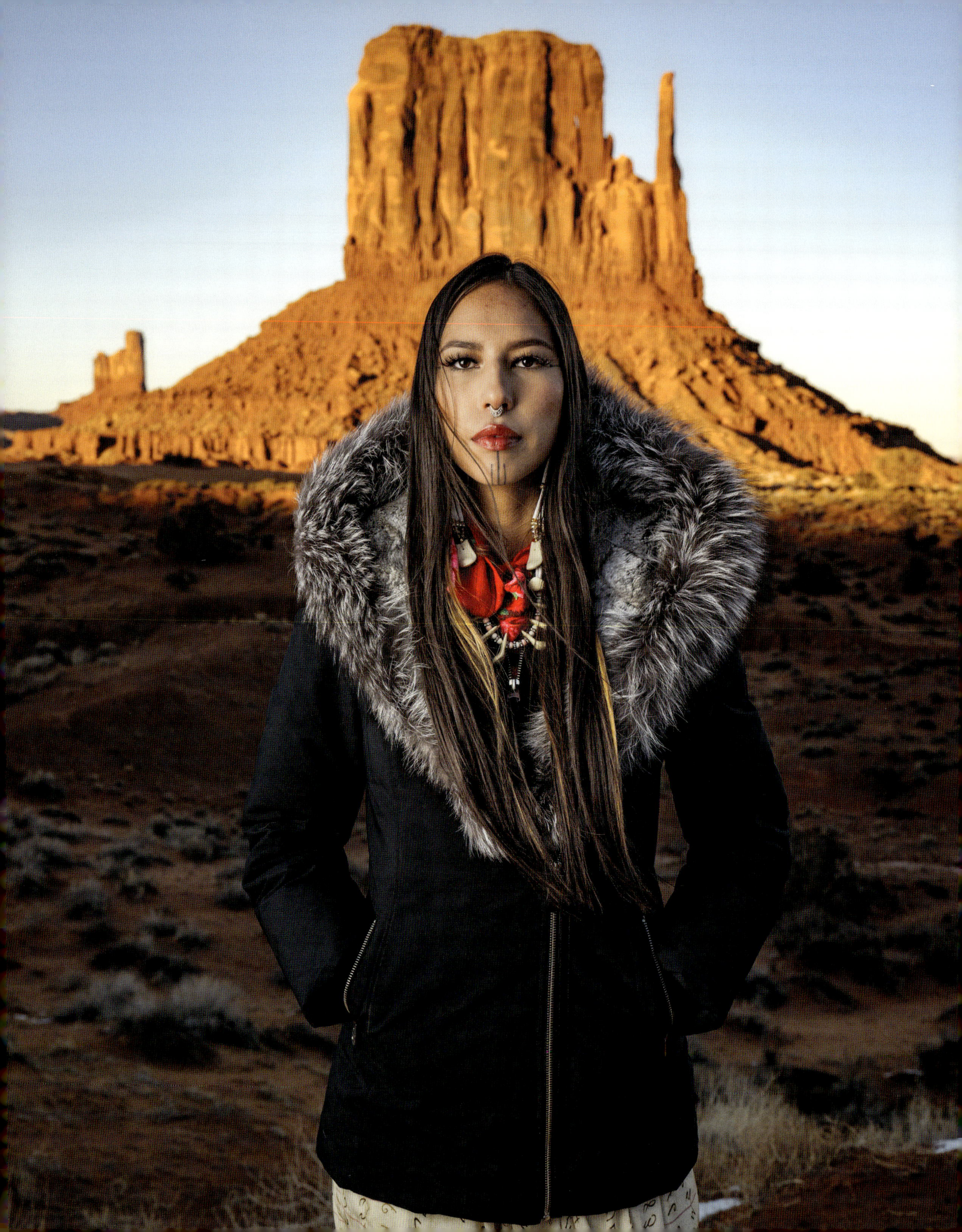

PEOPLE & CULTURE

THE POWER TO HONOR

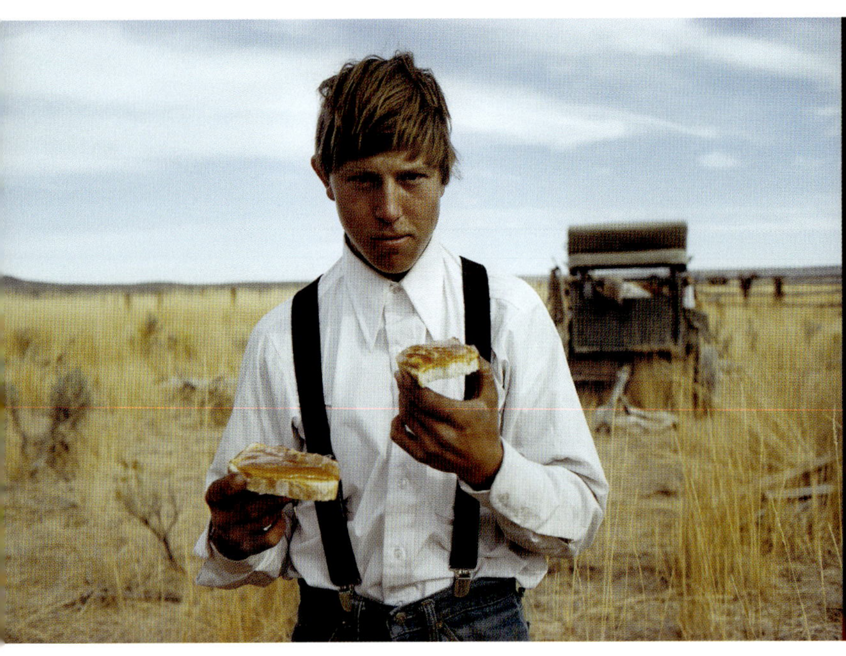

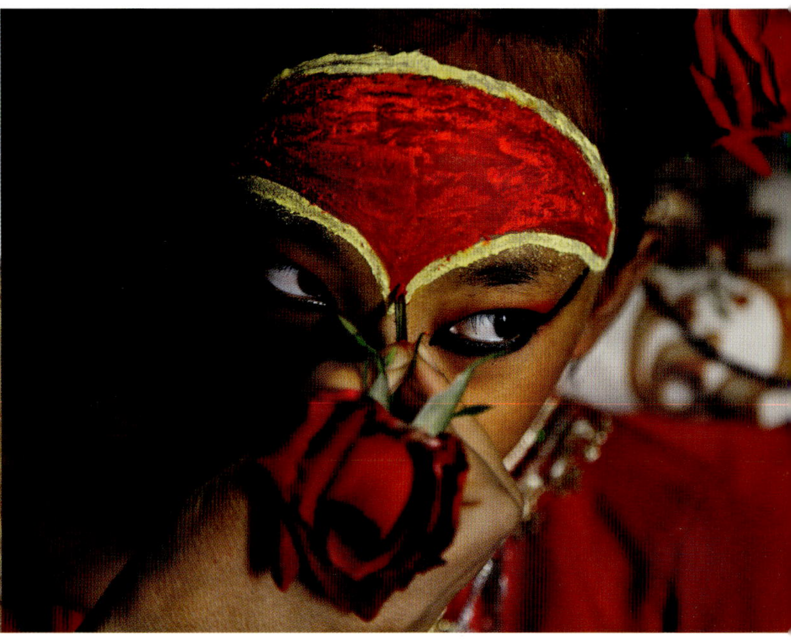

THE UNIVERSAL LANGUAGE OF THE HUMAN FACE

PAGE 198
KILIII YÜYAN, 2022
In an authentic portrayal of Native Americans infused with joy and determination, Navajo activist and model Quannah Rose ChasingHorse is framed by Monument Valley's West Mitten Butte near the Arizona-Utah border.

ABOVE LEFT
WILLIAM ALBERT ALLARD, 1979
A 17-year-old cowboy snacks on camp bread with peanut butter and syrup at IL Ranch, Nevada.

ABOVE RIGHT
STEPHANIE SINCLAIR, 2015
In Nepal's Kathmandu Valley, this nine-year-old has been worshipped as a living goddess since her infancy. For religious festivals, her forehead is painted red as a sign of creative energy.

TO PHOTOGRAPH A PERSON, family, community, or culture can sometimes mean not taking the picture. At least, not yet. There is room for silence and stillness and waiting.

"I don't drop in. I creep in," says photographer Lynn Johnson. "I do more listening. When you are young, you feel the urgency to 'get' the picture. You are all appetite. That's not how it should be. It should be thoughtful. I am here to tell a story if you will allow me and if you want me to."

Telling the story means leaving assumptions behind.

"We shouldn't come in saying, 'This is their story,'" Hannah Reyes Morales has said of her subjects. "We should always be taking our cues from them." Reyes Morales's photographs of refugees, migrants, and sex workers speak of resilience and tenderness in the face of adversity.

"It's easy to show what's wrong ... What's not easy to see is the resilience people manage under dire circumstances," says Sarah Leen, the magazine's director of photography from 2013 to 2019. And, she adds, it is presumptuous to walk into someone's life and assume they will give you what you need. Telling a story sometimes means being pulled up short by the person you are photographing.

"When I took this portrait," Anastasia Taylor-Lind wrote of a mother and daughter she photographed while they waited out Russian attacks in a Kyiv, Ukraine, bomb shelter, "the mother looked at me and joked, 'Do you want me to look like a refugee right now?'" The joke was serious. It was a powerful reminder, Taylor-Lind continued, "of the harmful stereotypes photographers perpetuate when people lose their homes."

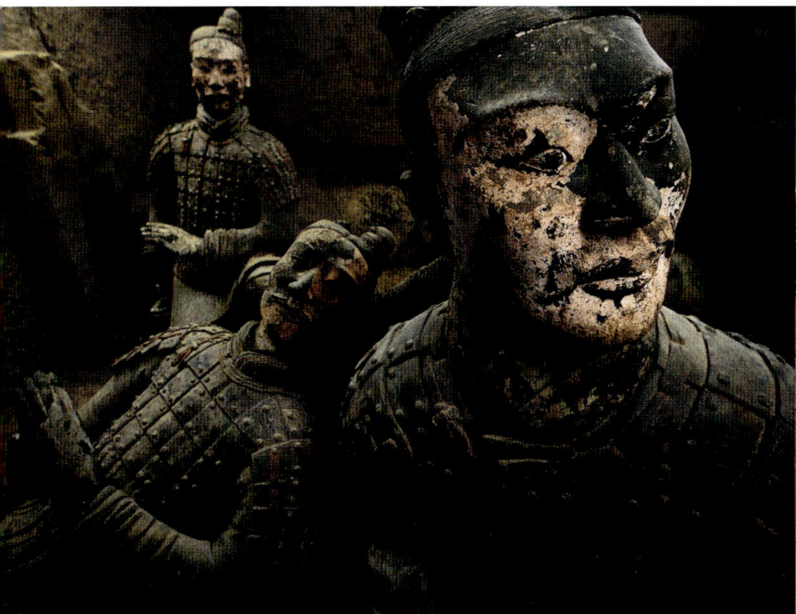

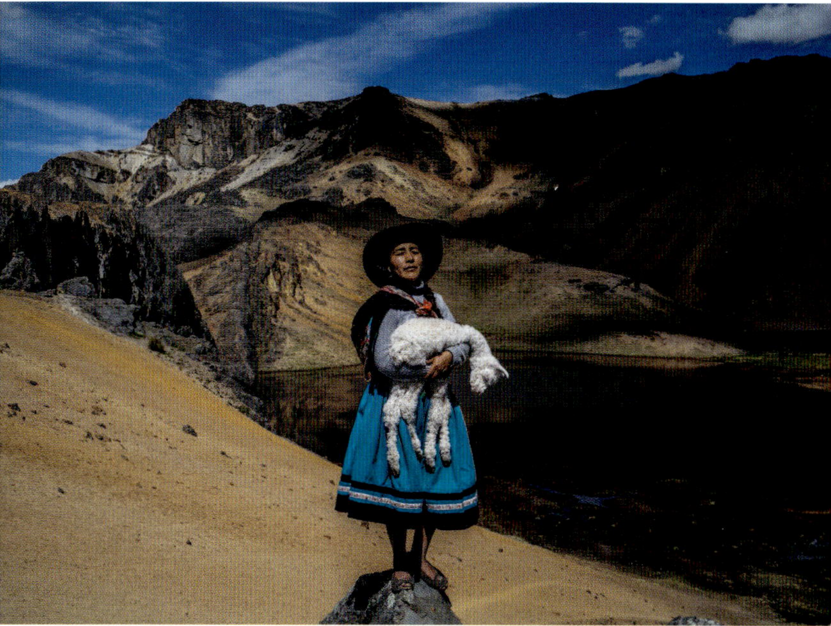

In photography there is room for humility, for knowing what you don't know, for not barging in but waiting for the moment, which may be long in coming. Or may never come. According to Lynn Johnson, the best photographs are the ones you have no control over; you simply respond. "Something happens and you say, 'My God, this is why I do this,'" she explains.

For Lynsey Addario, whose assignments habitually take her into spaces of conflict and humanitarian crisis, the work unveils "a world that most people don't see, showing people what they don't necessarily want to see."

For Jodi Cobb, good photography is about "being in the human heart." But gaining entrance demands generosity and empathy from the photographer as well.

Photo editor Todd James agrees. Making a portrait as good as the ones created by Wayne Lawrence, a Brooklyn- and Detroit-based photographer, he observes, requires that "you care about the person you are photographing as much as you care about the photograph." Lawrence assents. "I think I'm somehow changed by everything and everyone I photograph," he says.

How could it be otherwise? Spend time with Lawrence's portrait of Elaine Fields (page 268), whose husband of 45 years, Eddie, died of complications from Covid-19. The contagion prevented her from being with him at the end, so the mourning, she says, was "stunted." In the photograph, she stands tall, resolute, stricken by grief, a rivulet of tears etched on her right cheek.

The human spirit is perhaps photography's greatest subject. As American documentary photographer Dorothea Lange said, "The human face is the universal language."

ABOVE LEFT
O. LOUIS MAZZATENTA, 1995
Colored pigments still enhance the faces of these 2,200-year-old terra-cotta soldiers, buried near Xi'an, Shaanxi, to accompany China's first emperor, Qin Shi Huang Di, in the afterlife.

ABOVE RIGHT
ALESSANDRO CINQUE, 2022
In the Andes of southern Peru, a third-generation *alpaquera* (alpaca farmer) cradles a baby alpaca on her way to the pastures where her family's herd will graze in summer.

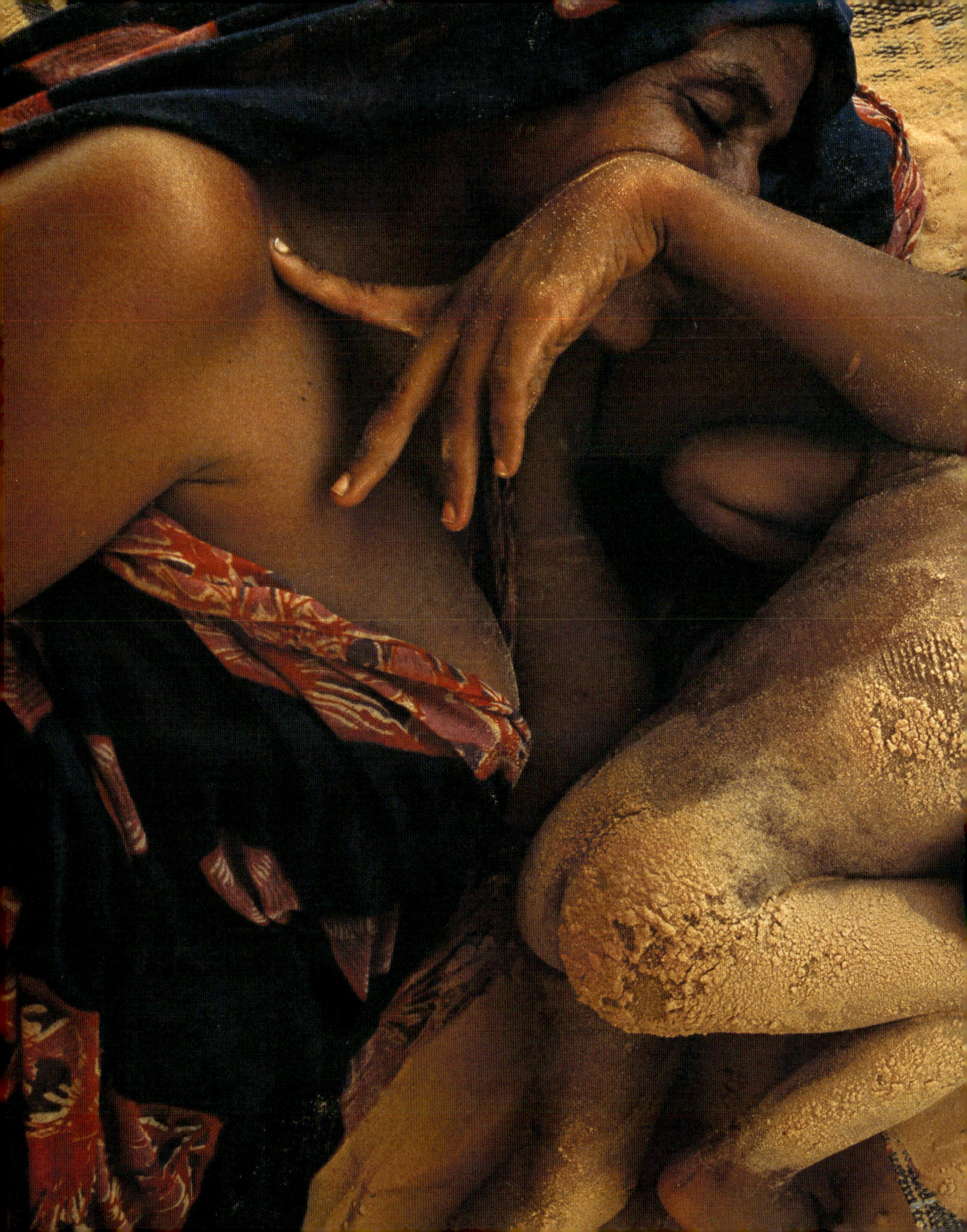

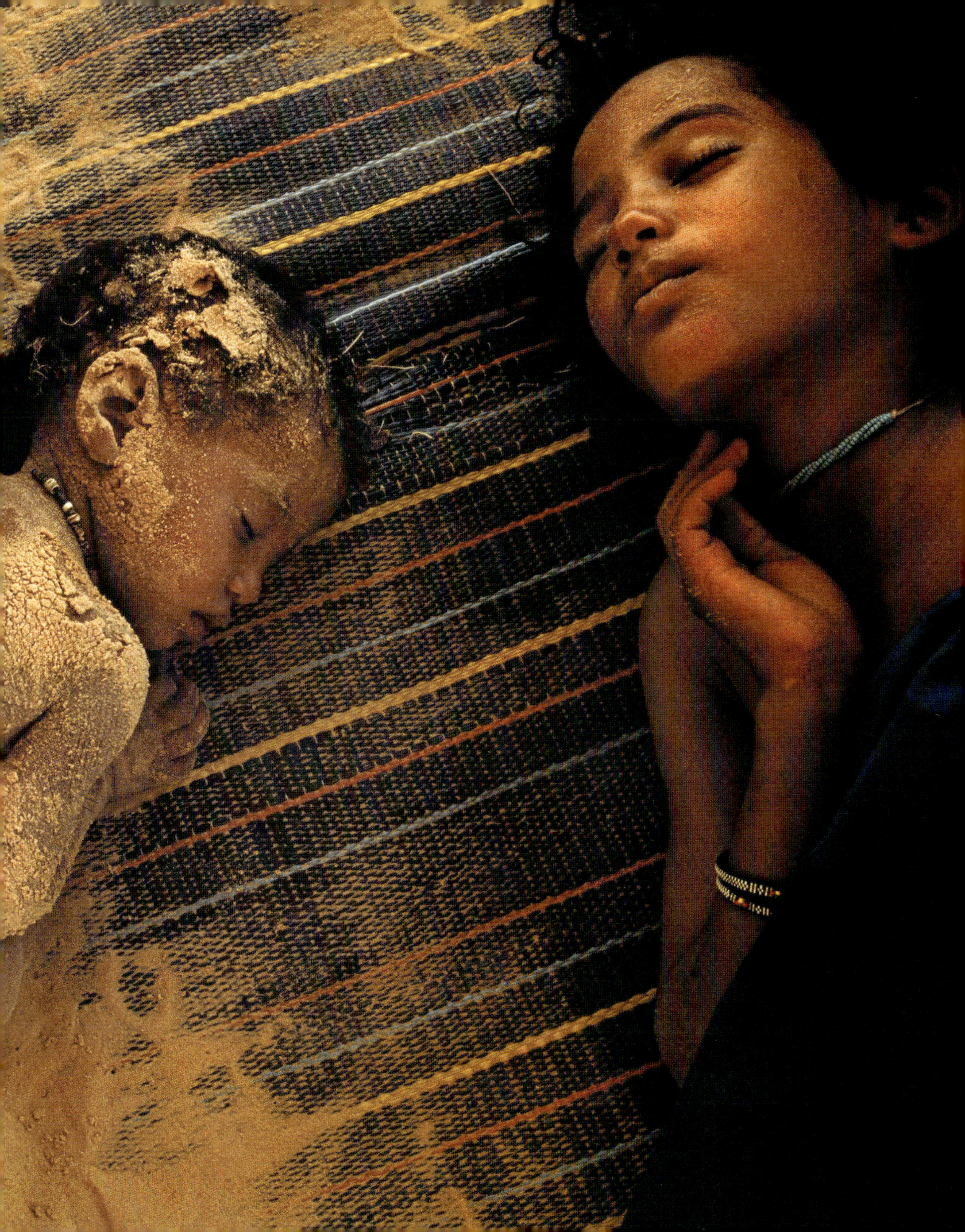

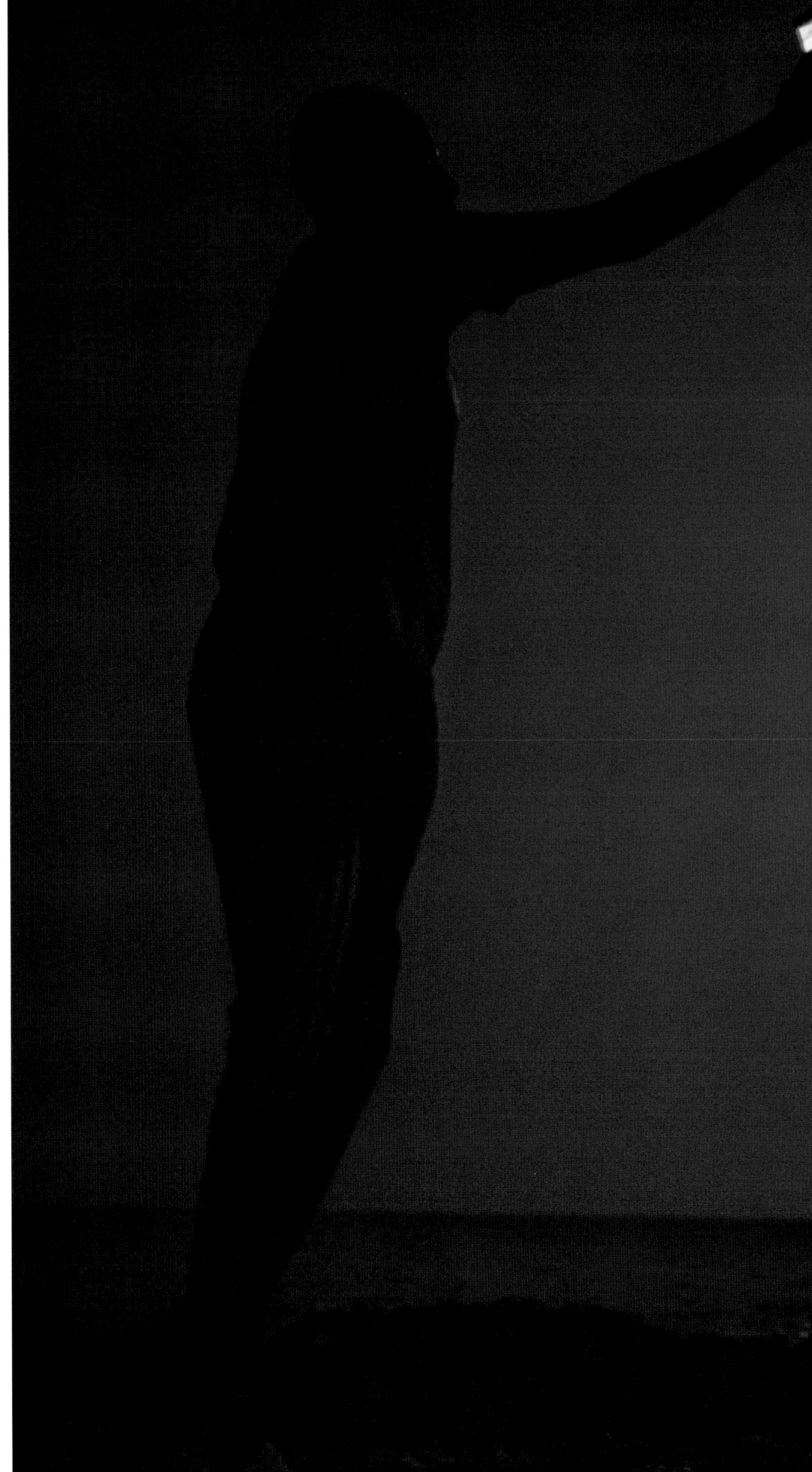

JOHN STANMEYER, 2013
On the shores of Djibouti city, African migrants try to capture a cell signal from neighboring Somalia.

PREVIOUS PAGES
JOANNA B. PINNEO, 1997
A woman and two children—members of the seminomadic Tuareg people—escape the midday heat in the shade of a tent near Timbuktu, Mali.

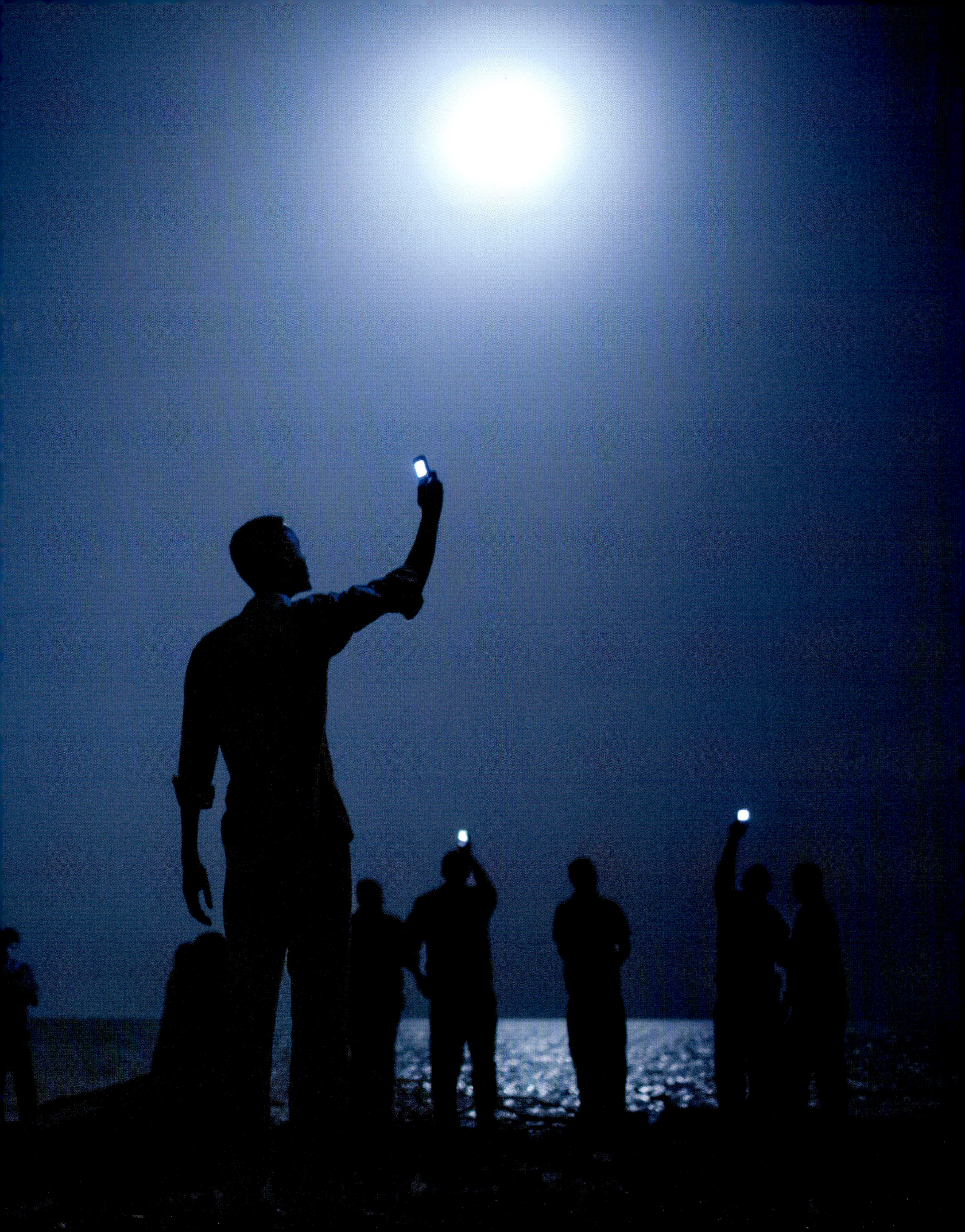

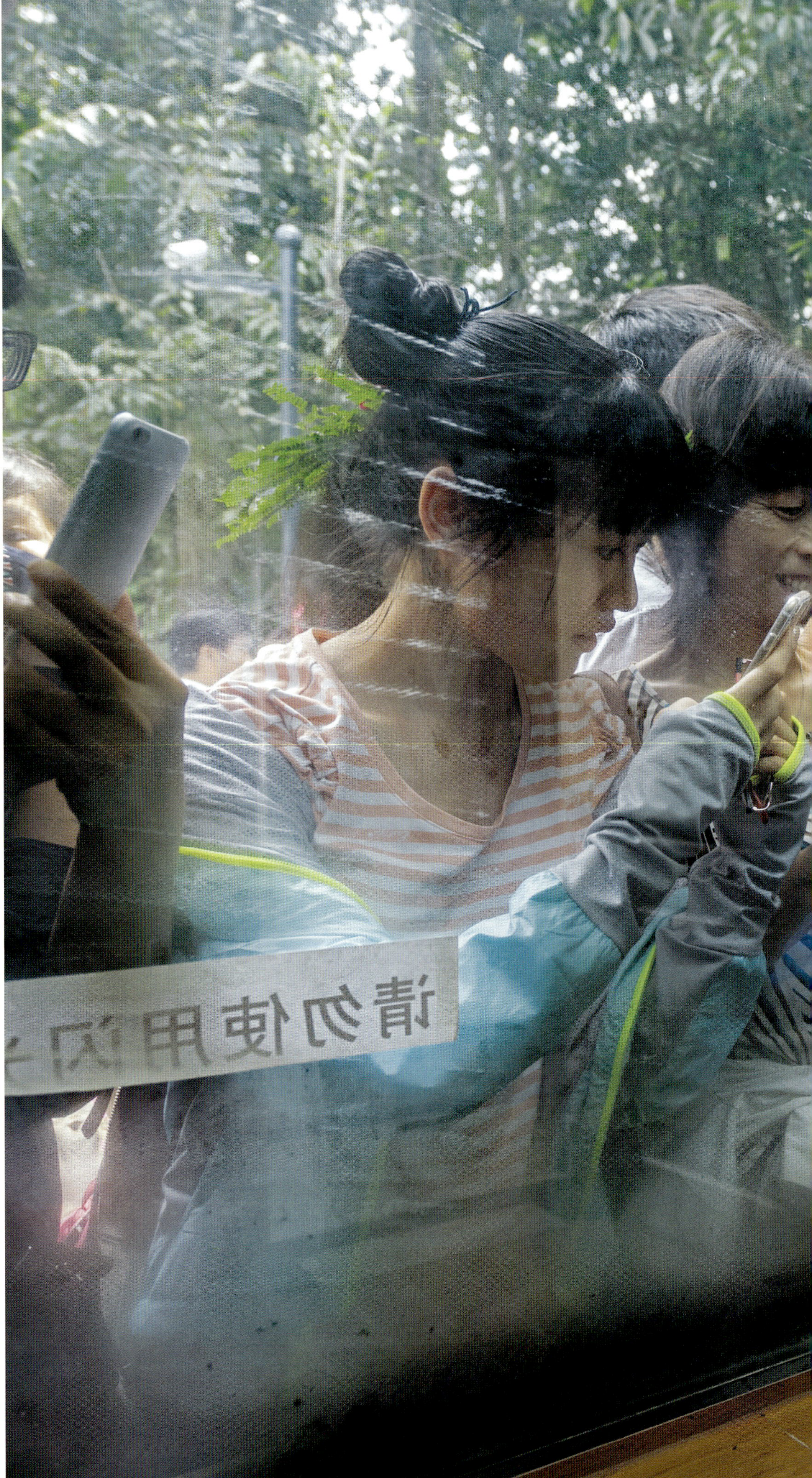

AMI VITALE, 2015
The nursery is the most popular stop on tours of Bifengxia Panda Base in China's Sichuan Province.

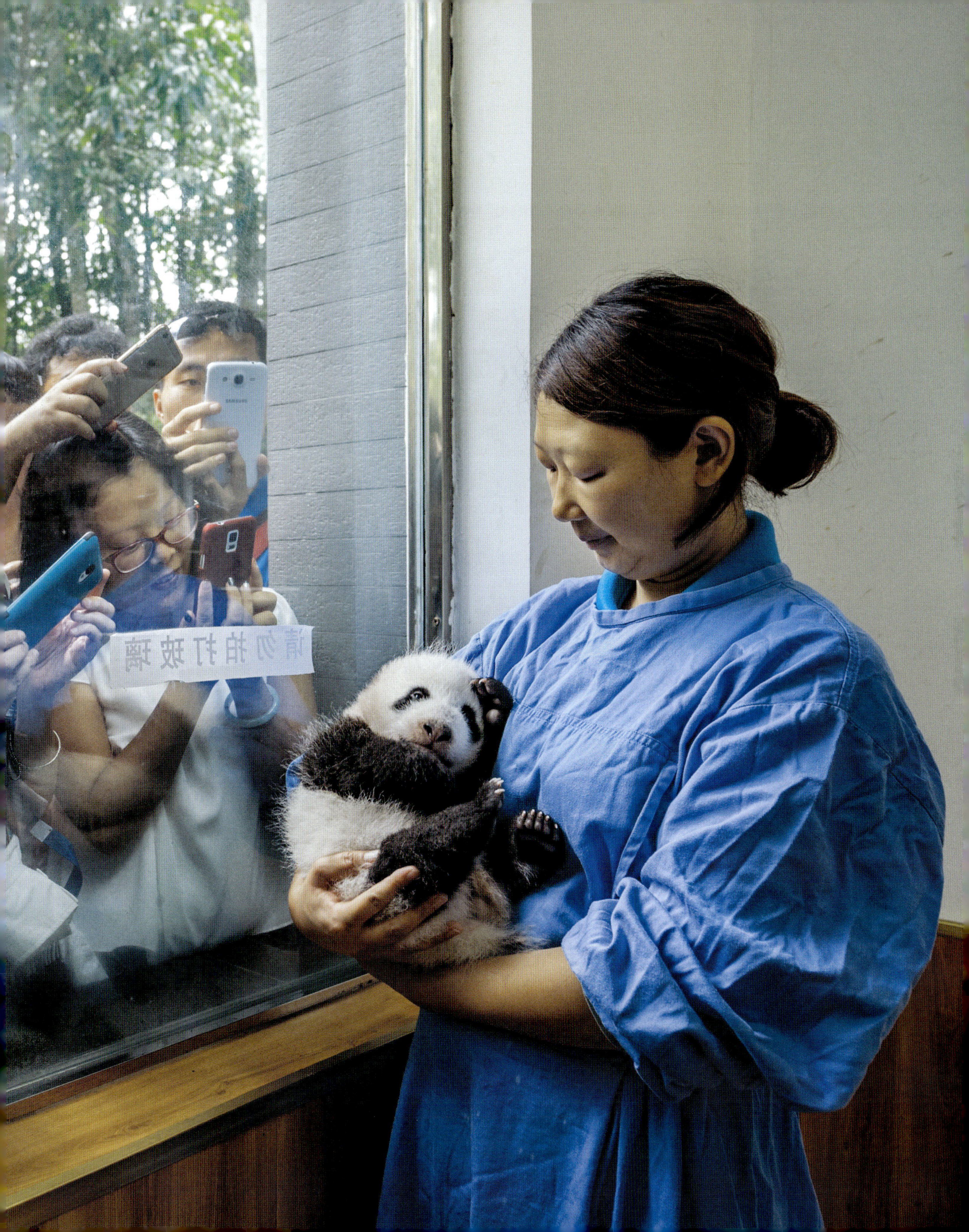
请勿拍打玻璃

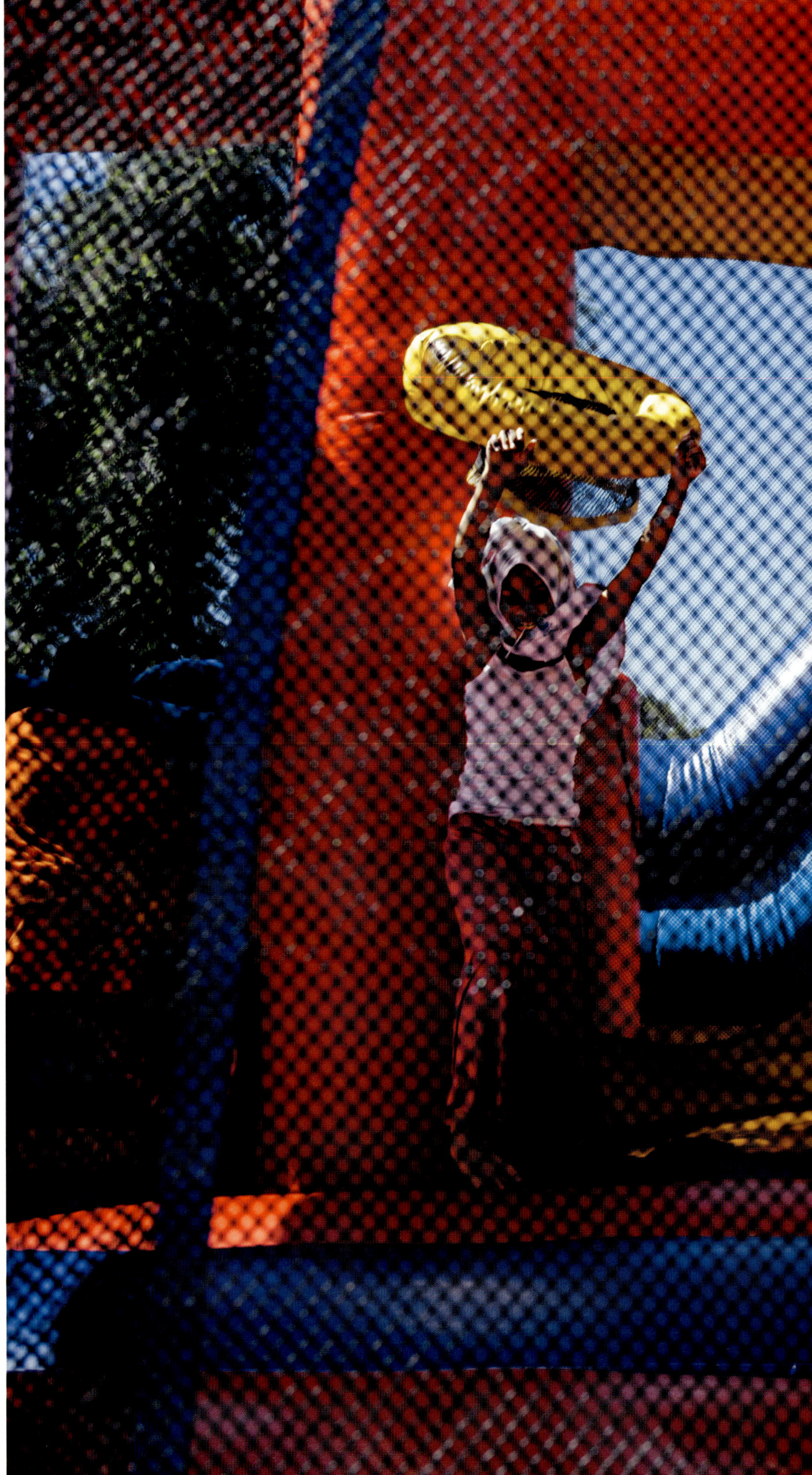

LYNSEY ADDARIO, 2017
Children celebrate Eid al-Fitr, the end of Ramadan, in South Los Angeles.

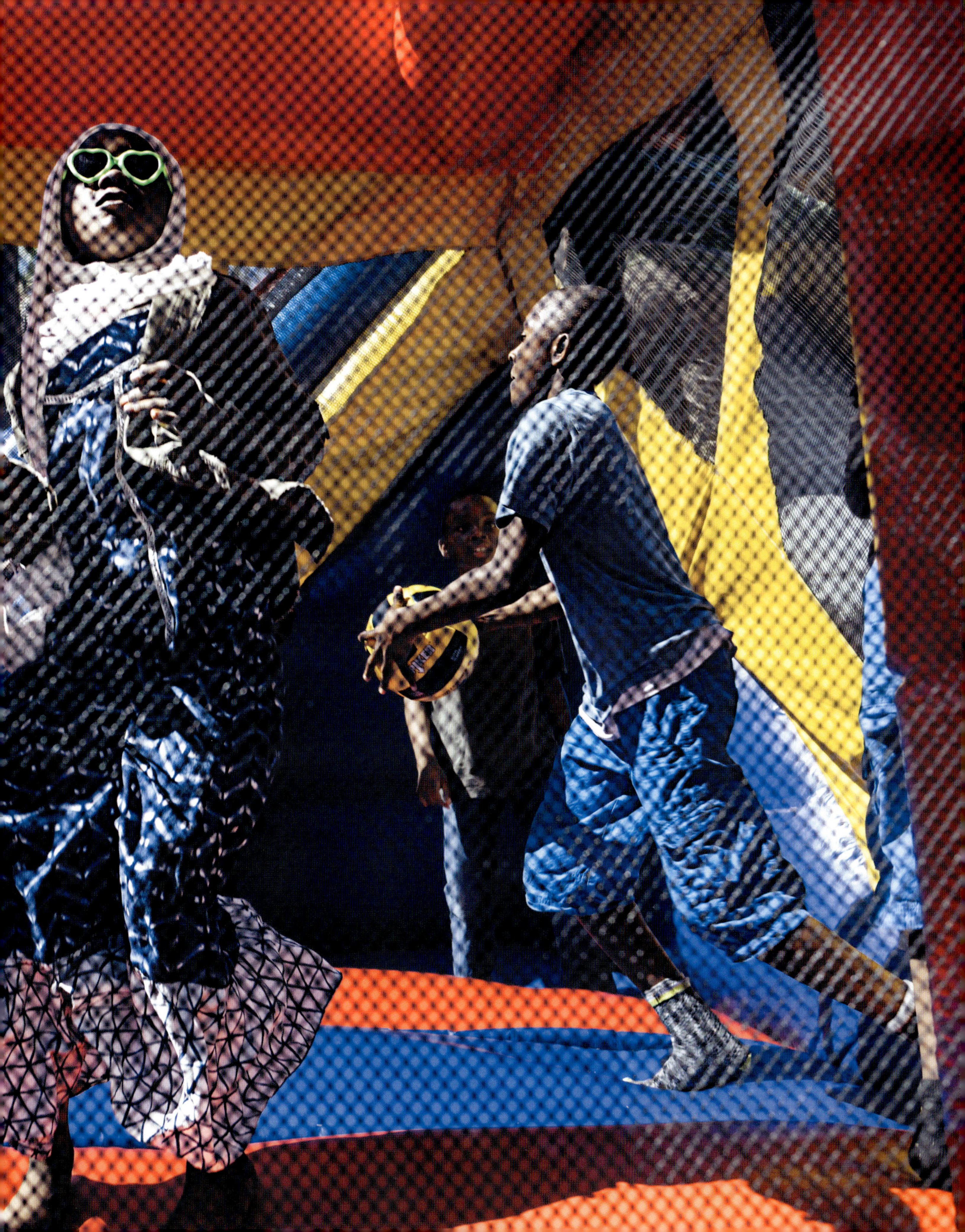

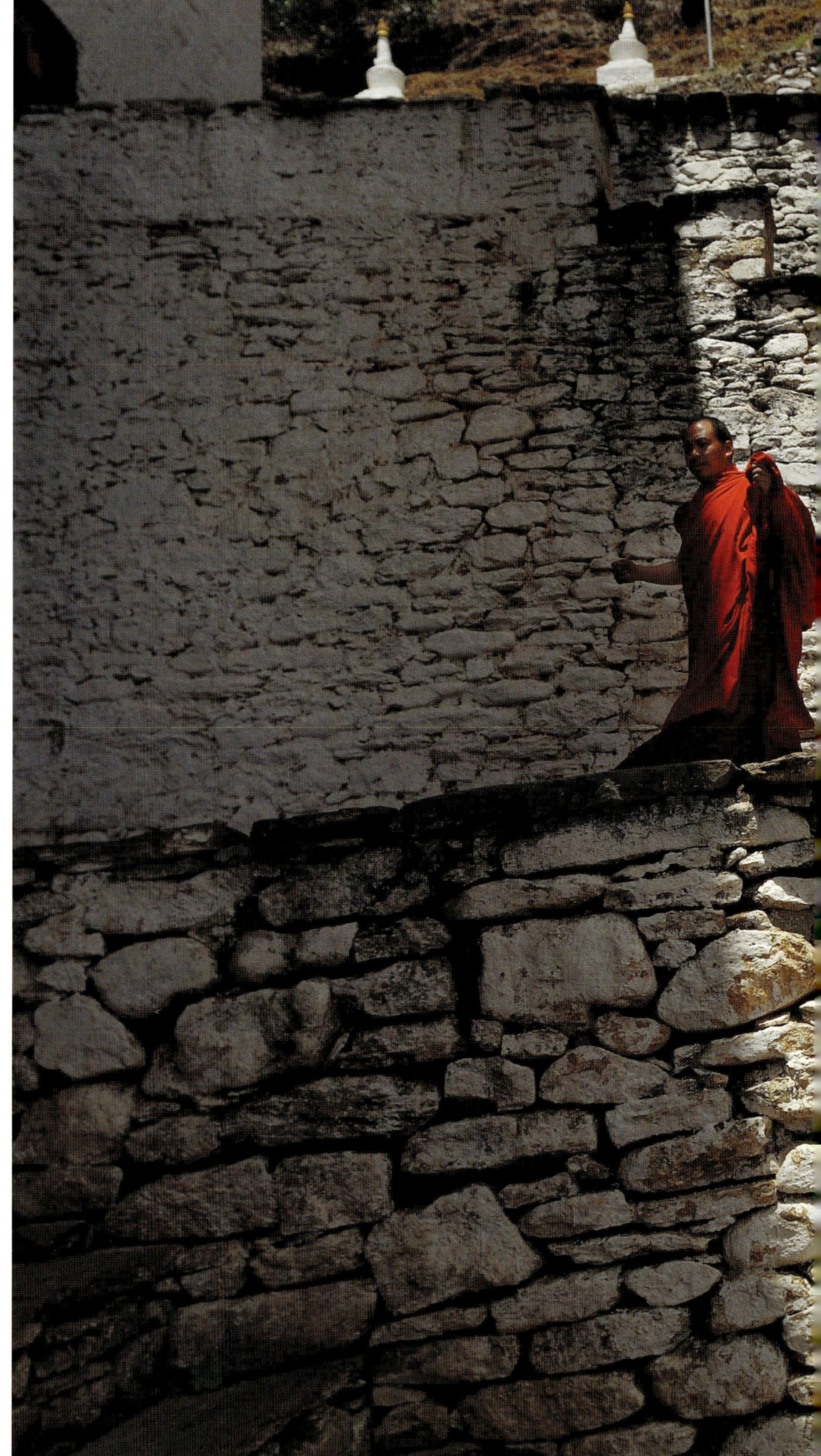

LYNSEY ADDARIO, 2007
Monks at Bhutan's Kurjey Lhakhang monastery, the final resting place of the country's first three kings

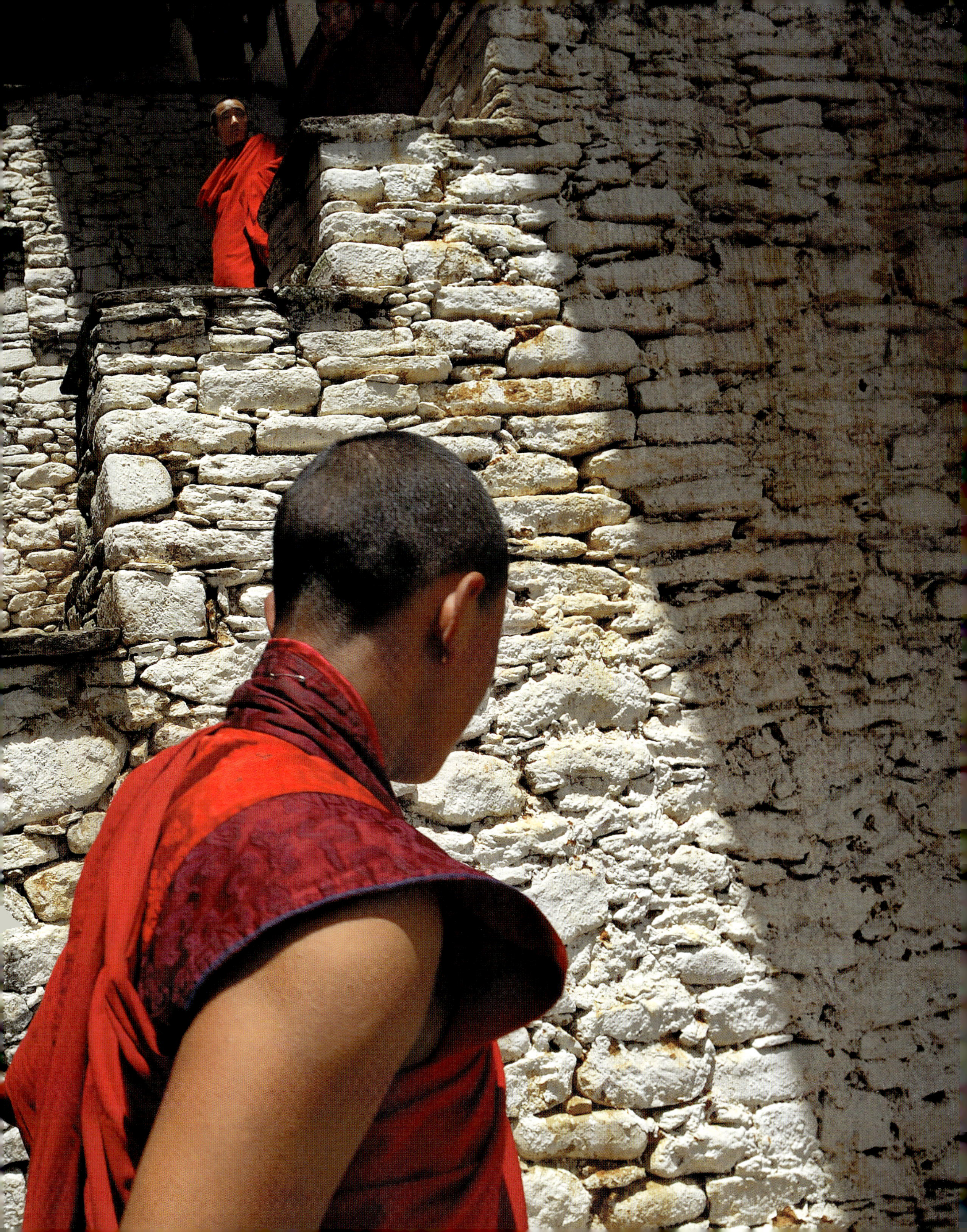

ACCORDING TO PHOTOGRAPHER LYNN JOHNSON, THE BEST PHOTOGRAPHS ARE THE ONES YOU HAVE NO CONTROL OVER; YOU SIMPLY RESPOND.

THOMAS J. ABERCROMBIE, 1968
A woman carries caged goldfinches atop her head from a market in Kabul, Afghanistan. When this photograph was published, her red chador was no longer required under Afghan law. Today, the ruling Taliban has again ordered Afghan women to cover their faces in public.

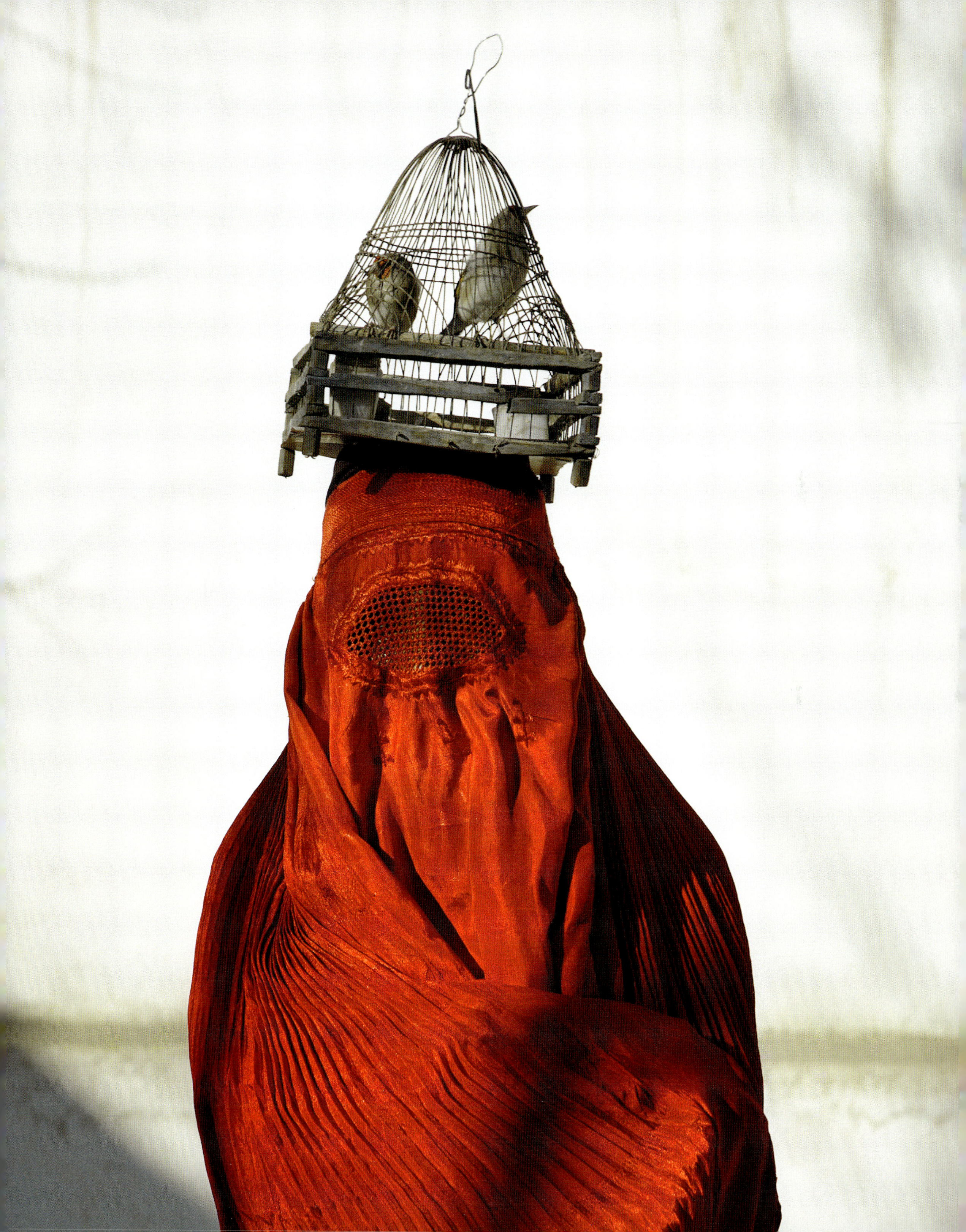

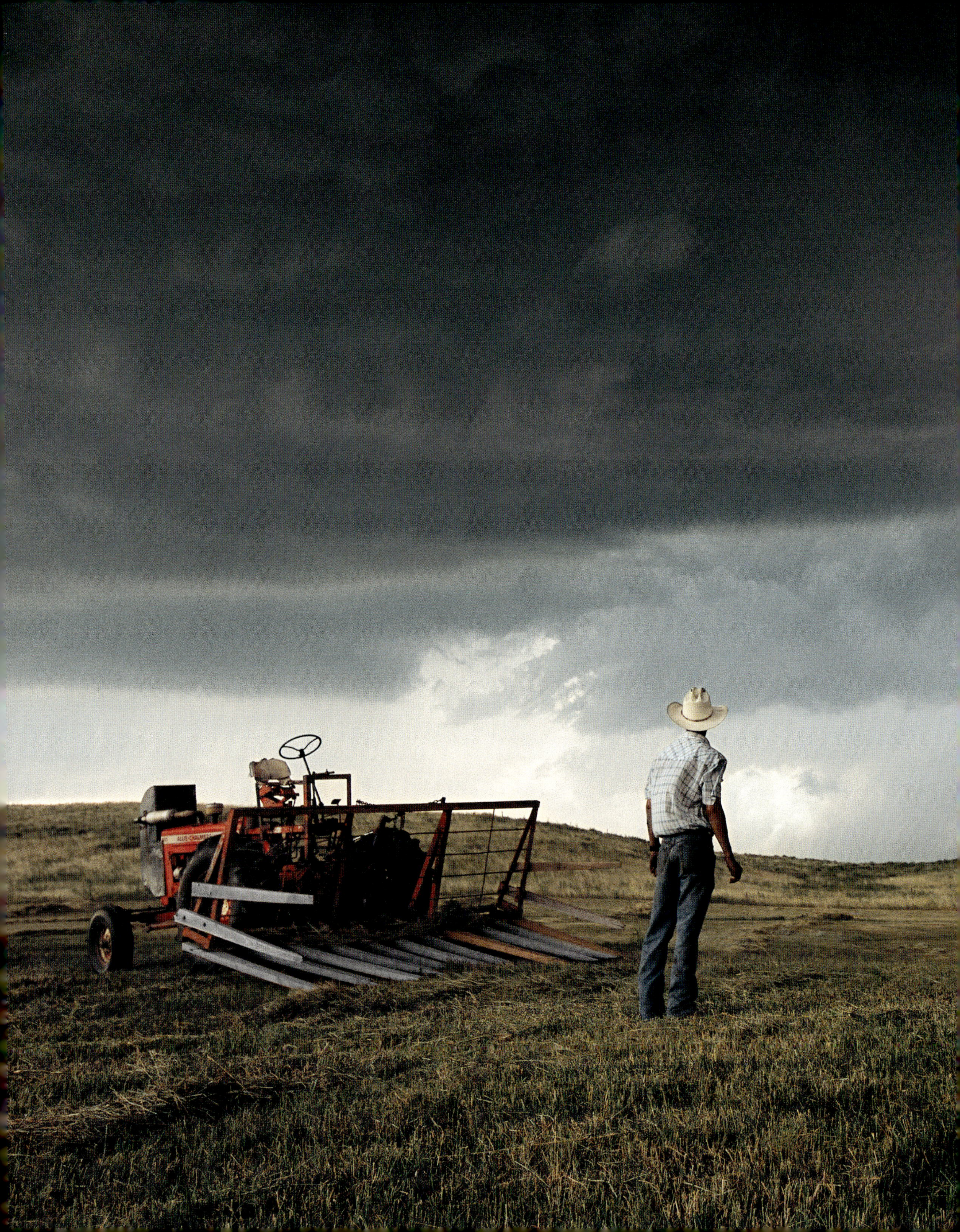

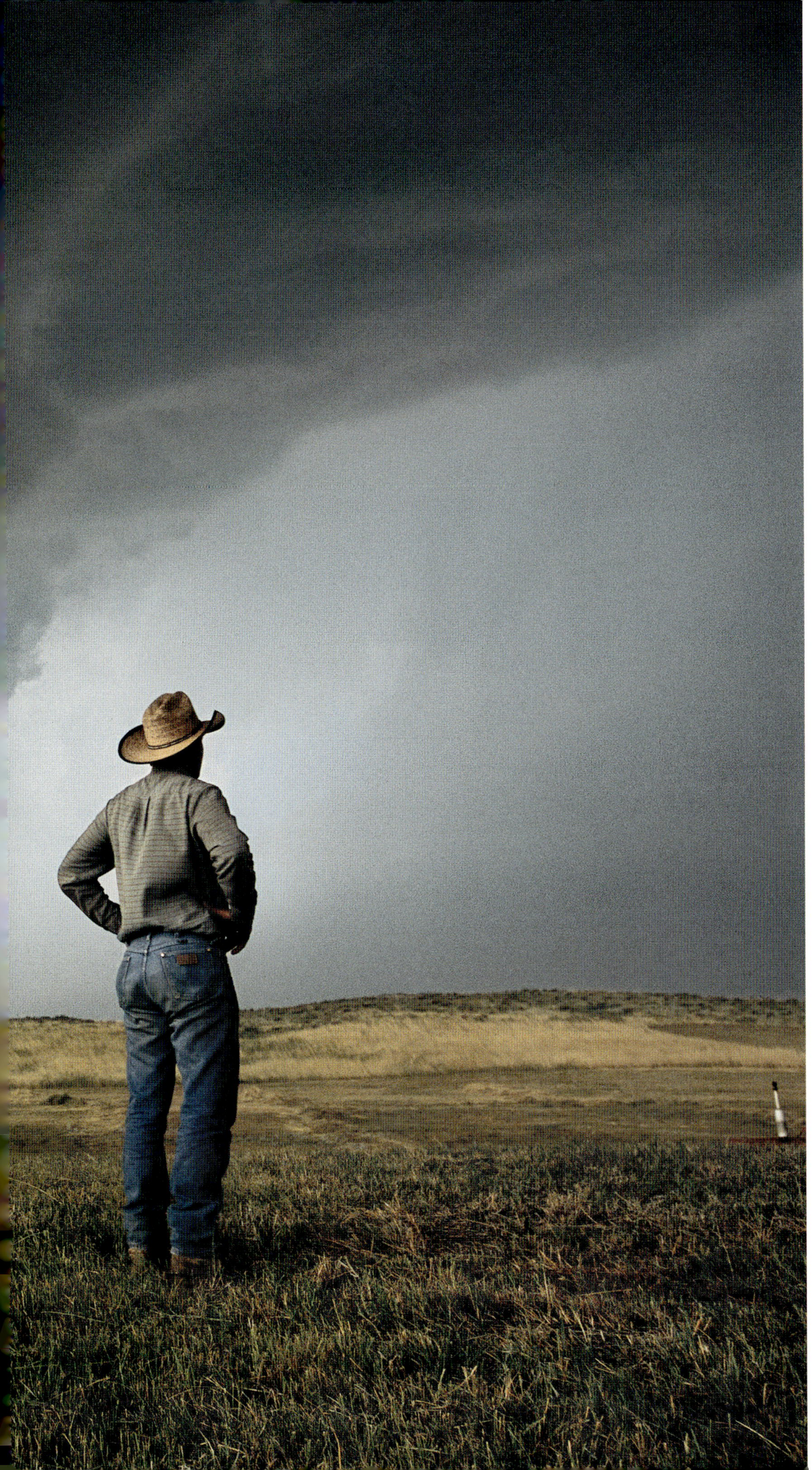

JIM RICHARDSON, 2004
A thunderstorm halts haying in Nebraska's Sandhills region. At the time, the area held five of the 10 poorest counties in the United States.

FOLLOWING PAGES
JONAS BENDIKSEN, 2006
A child finds joy in the red lights hung for a wedding in the Dharavi slum in Mumbai, India.

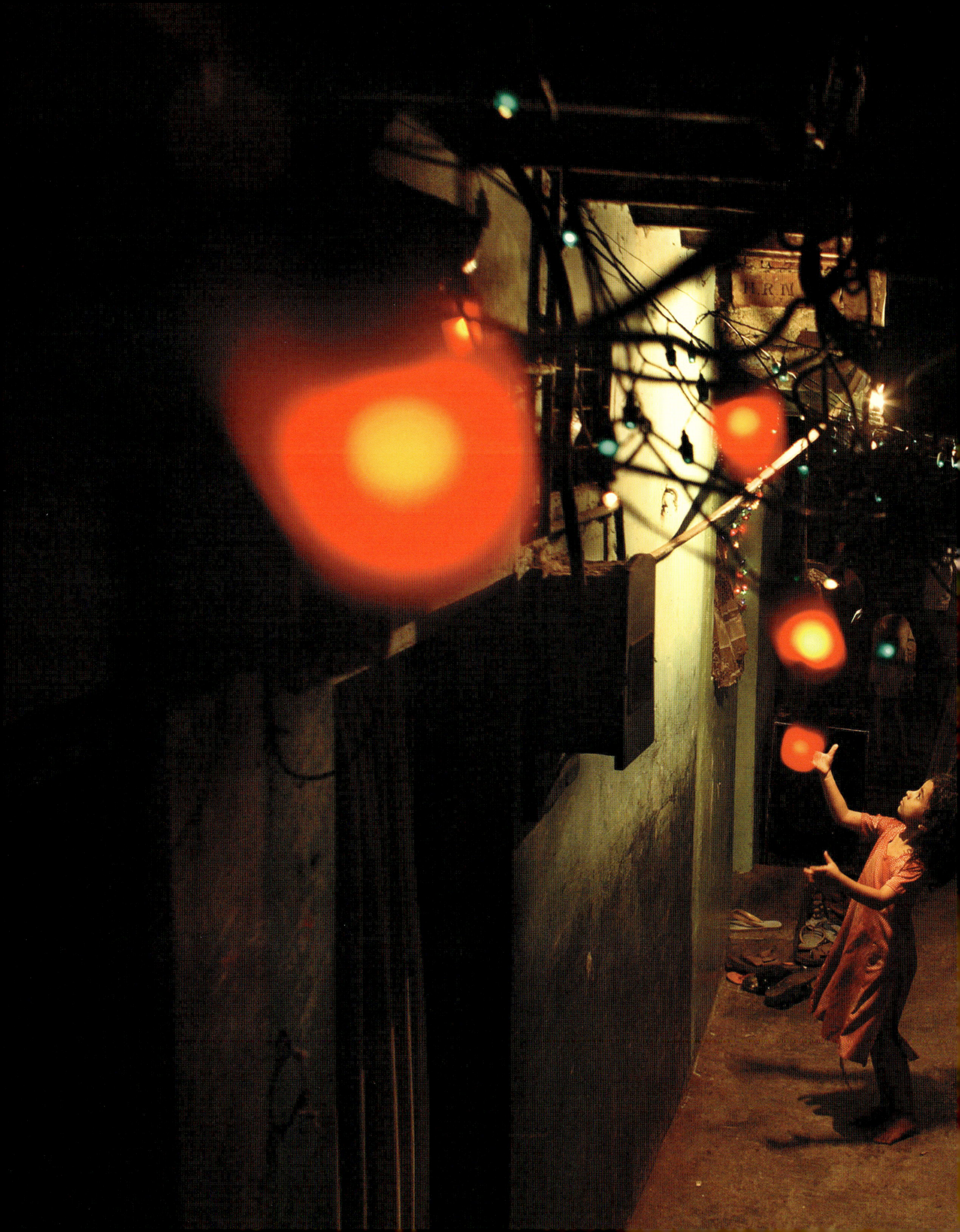

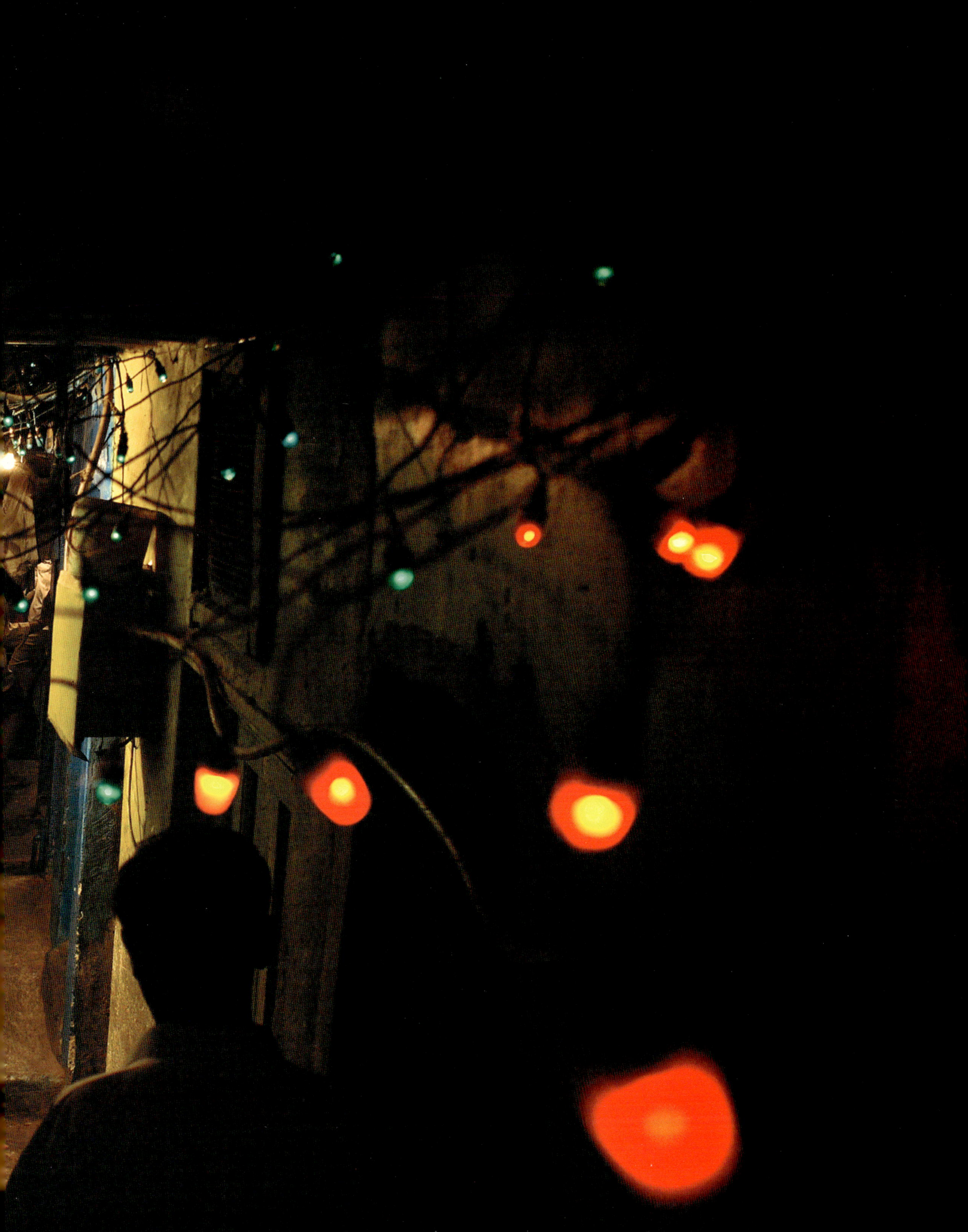

BIOGRAPHY

HANNAH REYES MORALES

OPPOSITE TOP

HANNAH REYES MORALES, 2020

In Ulaanbaatar, Mongolia—a city with some of the world's worst air pollution—a kindergartner naps at a day care center equipped with air purifiers not available at her home.

OPPOSITE BOTTOM

HANNAH REYES MORALES, 2019

Halima Aden, a barrier-breaking model who graced the cover of *British Vogue* in a hijab, has her makeup retouched during Istanbul's Modest Fashion Week.

HANNAH REYES MORALES is a Filipina photojournalist and National Geographic Explorer whose work has depicted individuals mired in complex situations created by inequality and poverty. Her current focus is on how historical memory informs the present and shapes daily life.

In 2013, a grant from the National Geographic Society allowed Reyes Morales to document Indigenous cultures in her home country. She grew up in Manila, and initially, she says, "I wanted to use photography as a tool and as a passport to leave this country. But as I went deeper into my practice, I realized that it was really important for me to understand home."

Reyes Morales's ongoing project *Living Lullabies* was featured in the December 2020 issue of *National Geographic.* It explores how caregivers create safer spaces in challenging environments for their children through nighttime songs and stories. "Lullabies revealed to me that our fears can be used to forge our reassurance," she says.

Reyes Morales is a co-founder of Emerging Islands, a grassroots program that connects artists with scientists to tell stories through art. In addition to *National Geographic,* her work has also appeared in the *New York Times* and the *Washington Post,* among other outlets.

The recipient of a 2023 Pictures of the Year International award, Reyes Morales has received a 2023 World Press Photo Award, the Tim Hetherington Trust Visionary Award, and the International Center of Photography's Infinity Award for Documentary Practice and Visual Journalism. In 2024, she was a finalist for the Pulitzer Prize in Feature Photography.

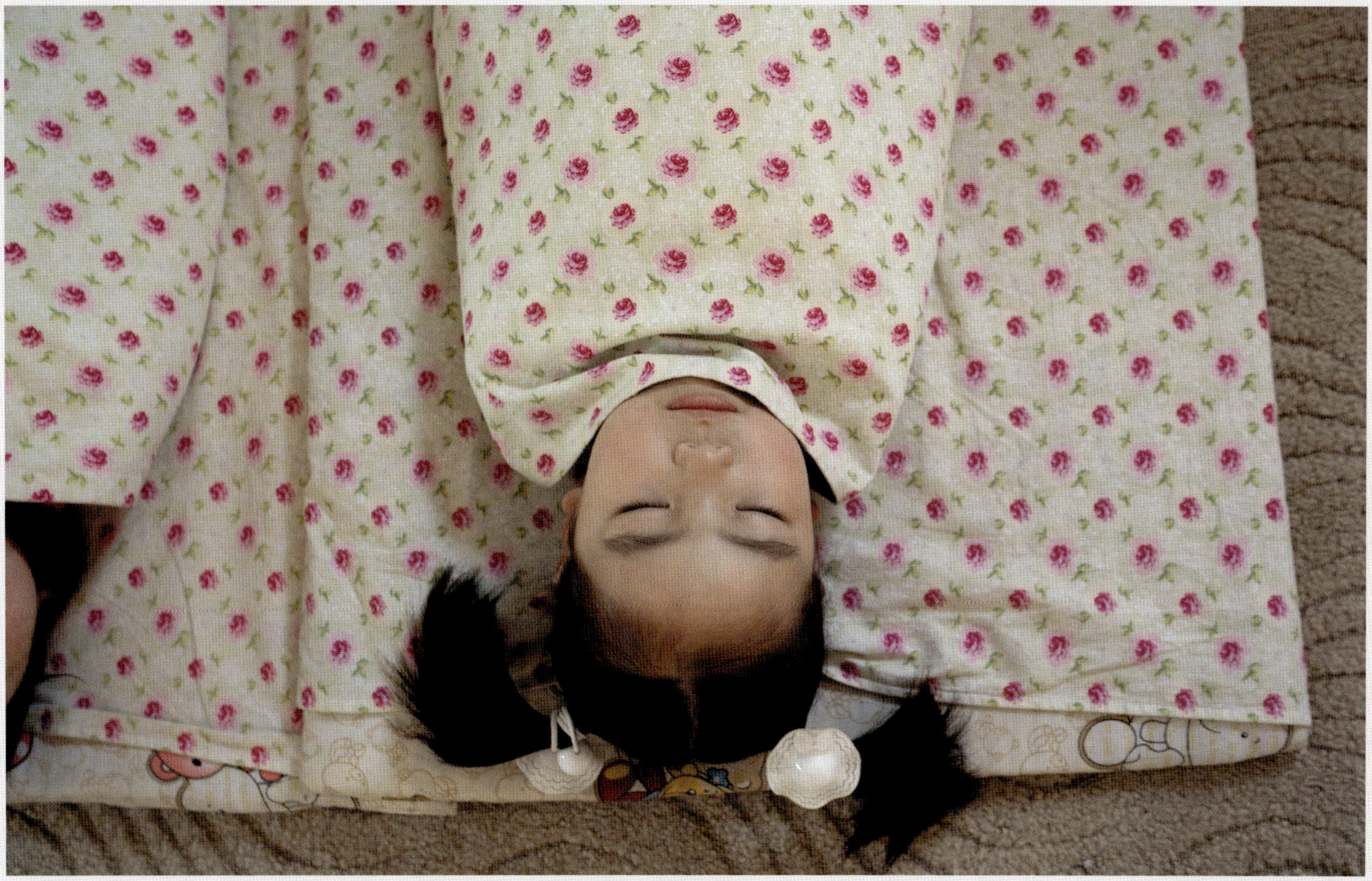

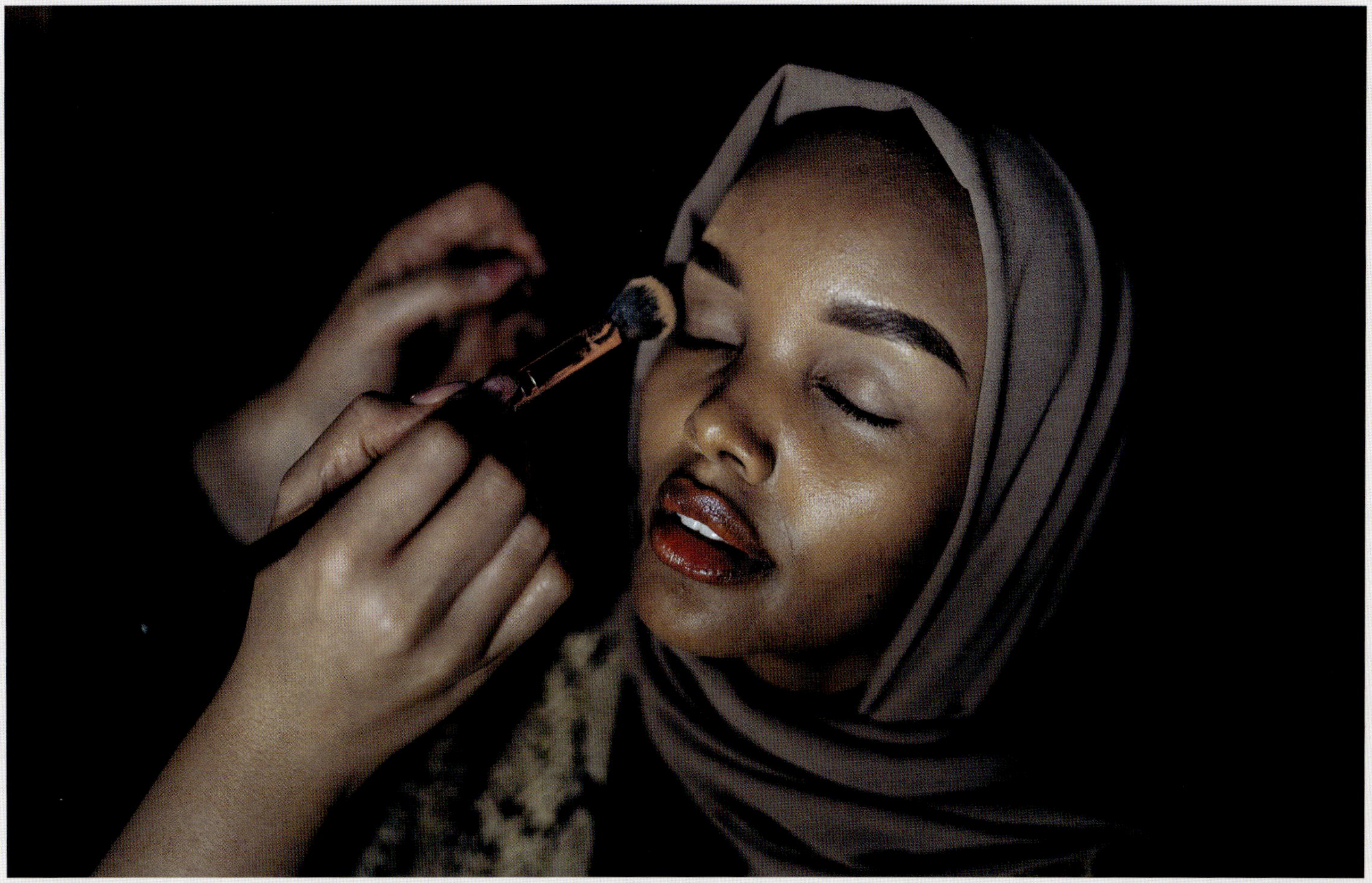

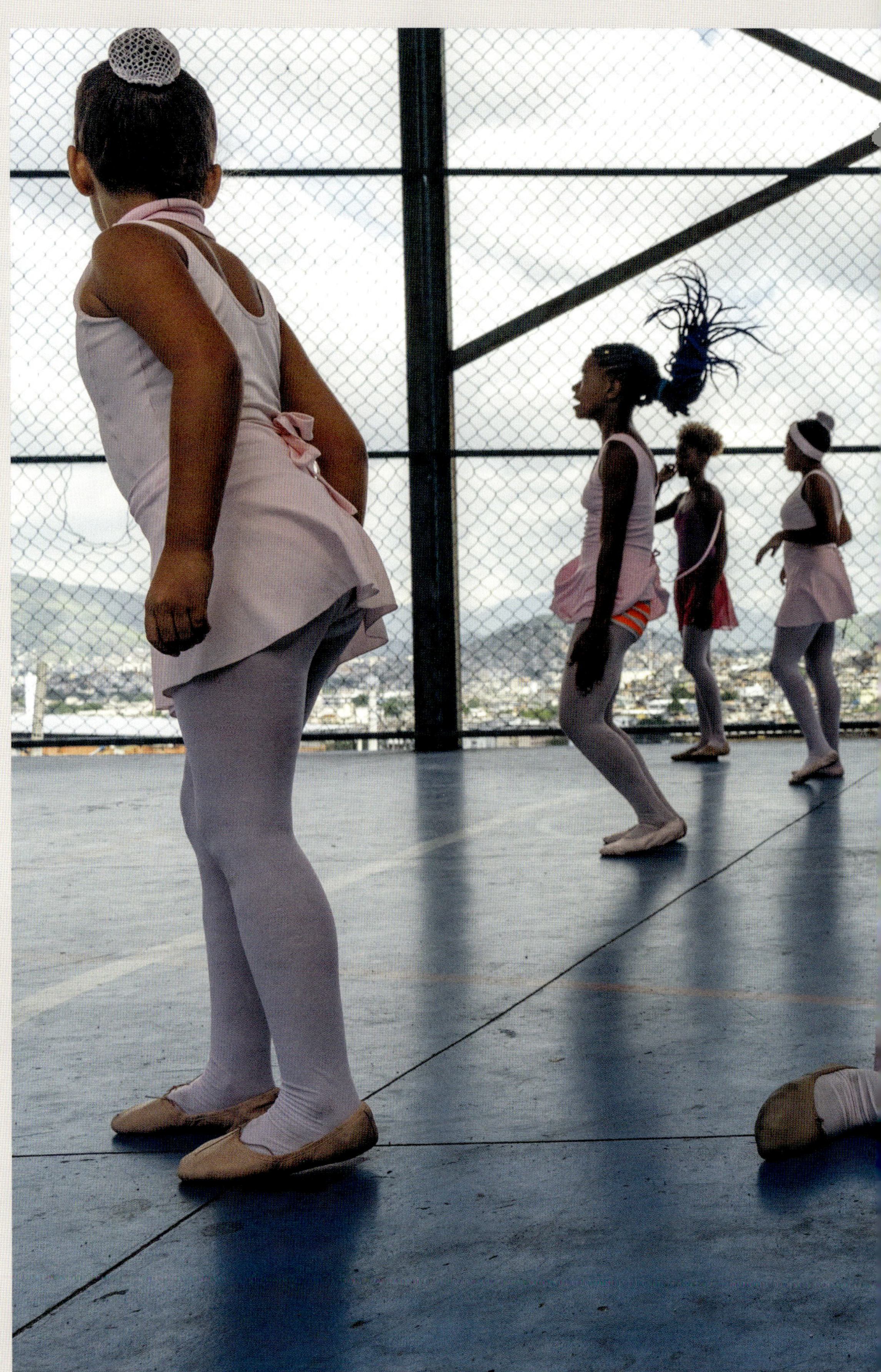

HANNAH REYES MORALES, 2019
Girls from Rio de Janeiro's favelas, or shantytowns, take lessons at a ballet initiative founded by Tuany Nascimento, who also grew up there.

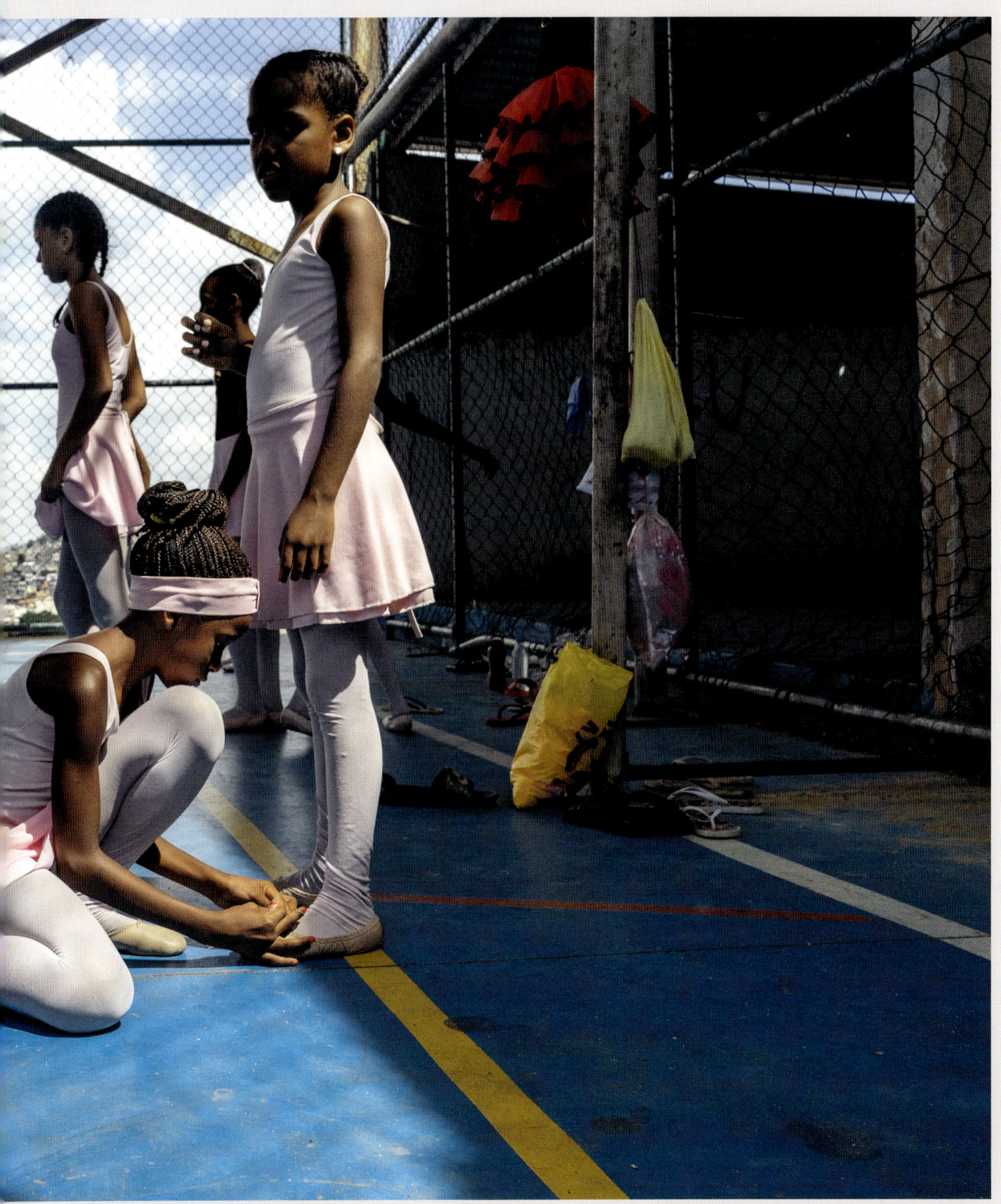

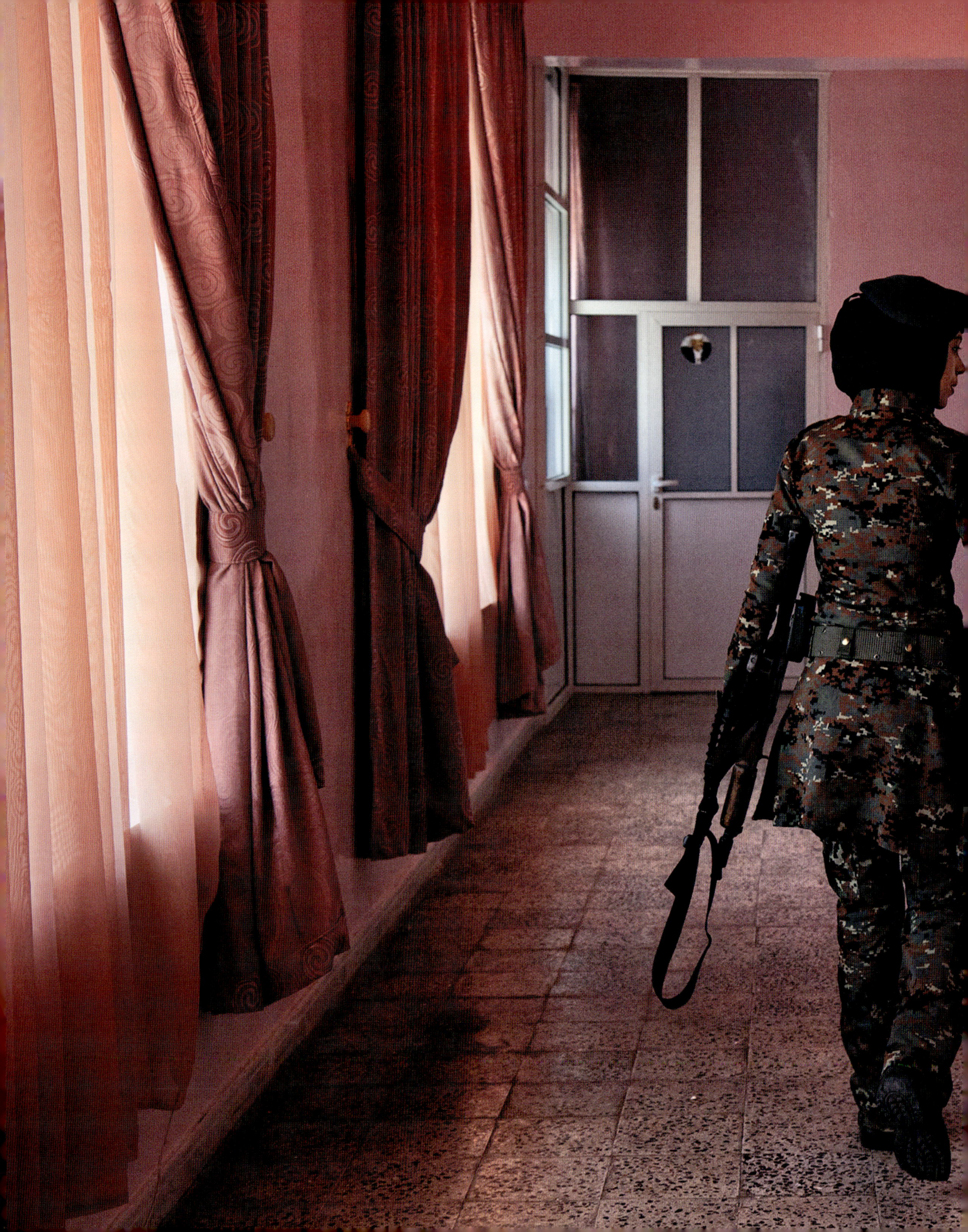

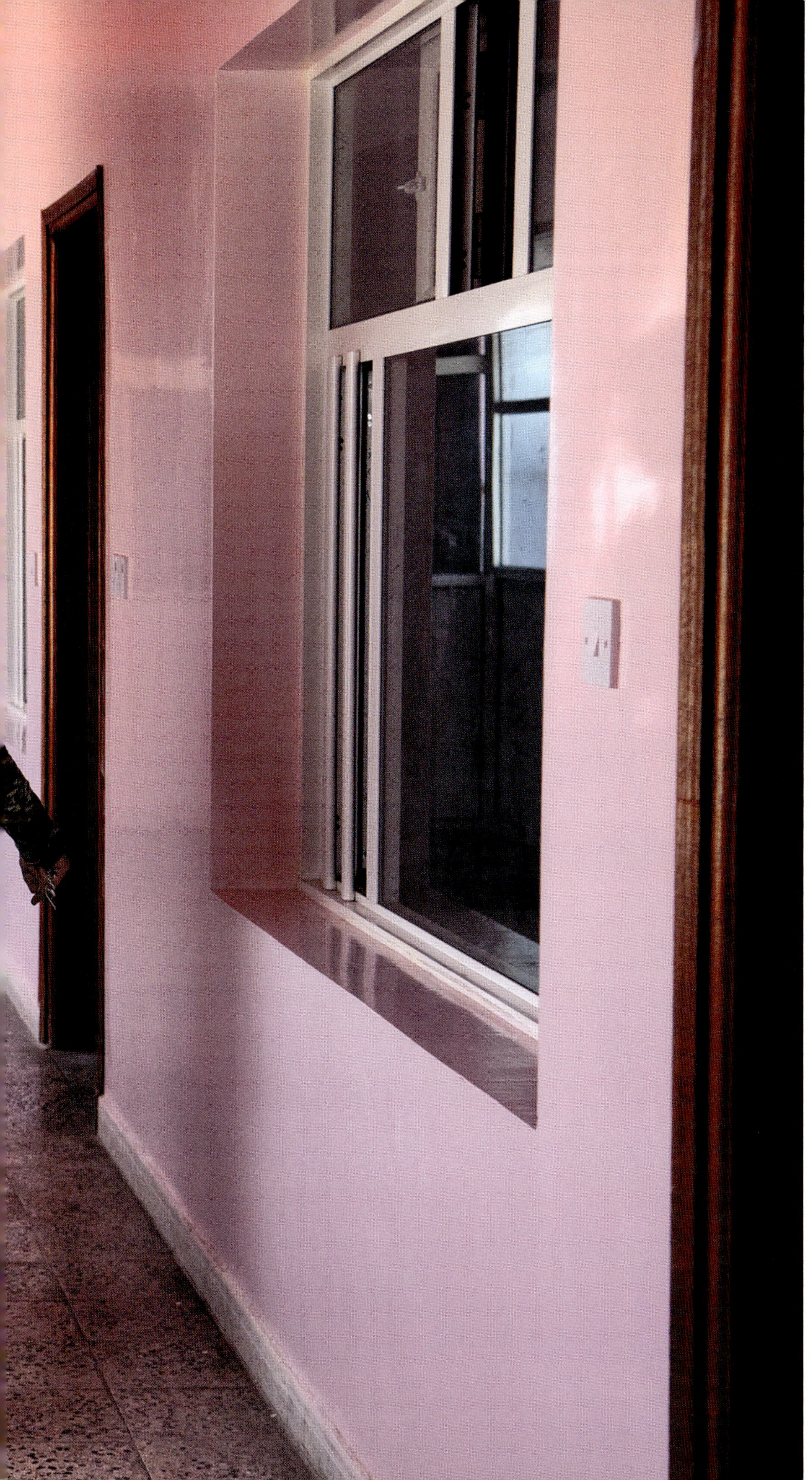

STEPHANIE SINCLAIR, 2012
A lieutenant patrols the barracks of Yemen's female counterterrorism unit in Sanaa.

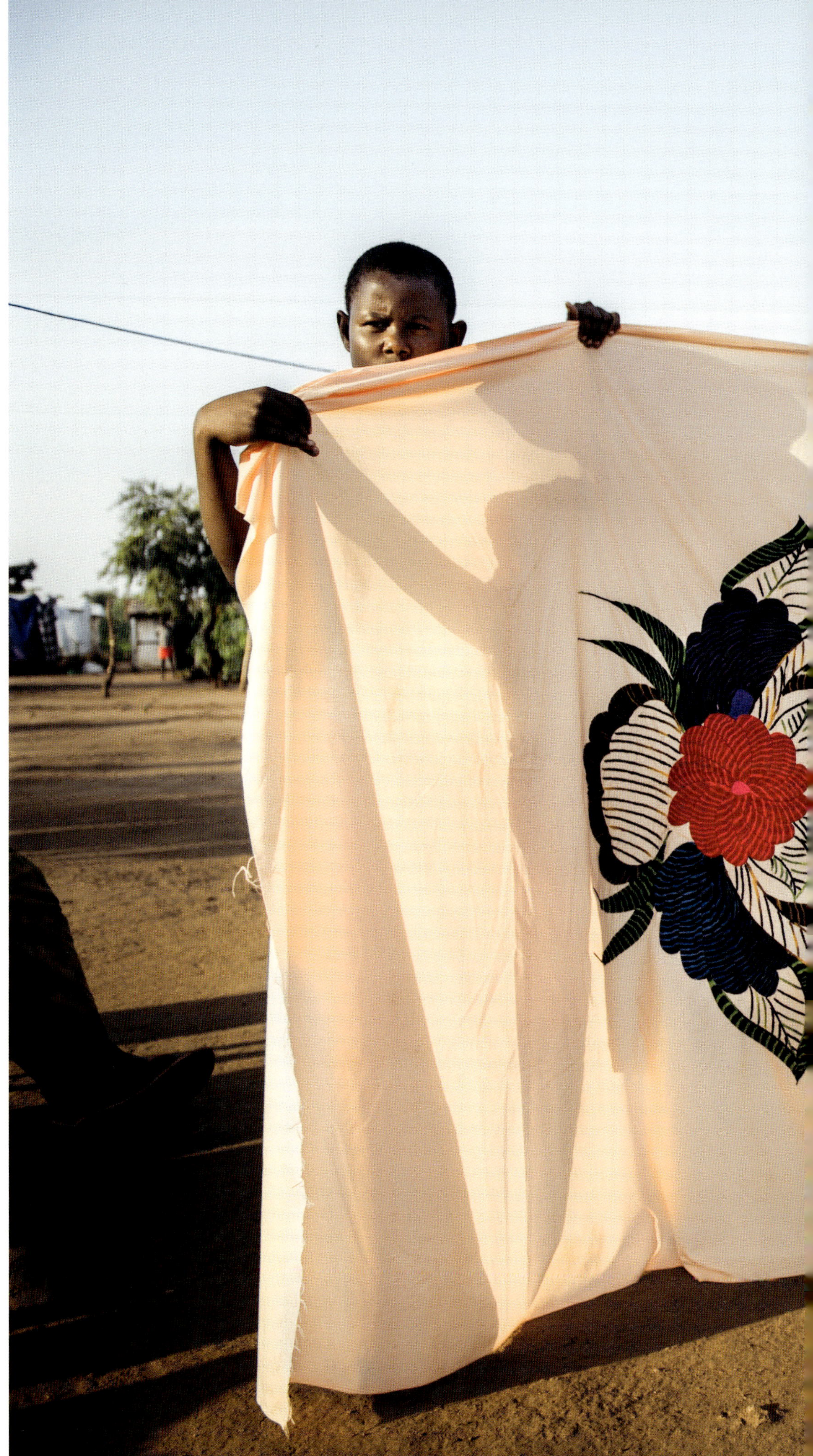

NORA LOREK, 2017
Hundreds of thousands of people fled the war in South Sudan to the Bidibidi refugee settlement in Yumbe, Uganda, their belongings packed in treasured bedsheets.

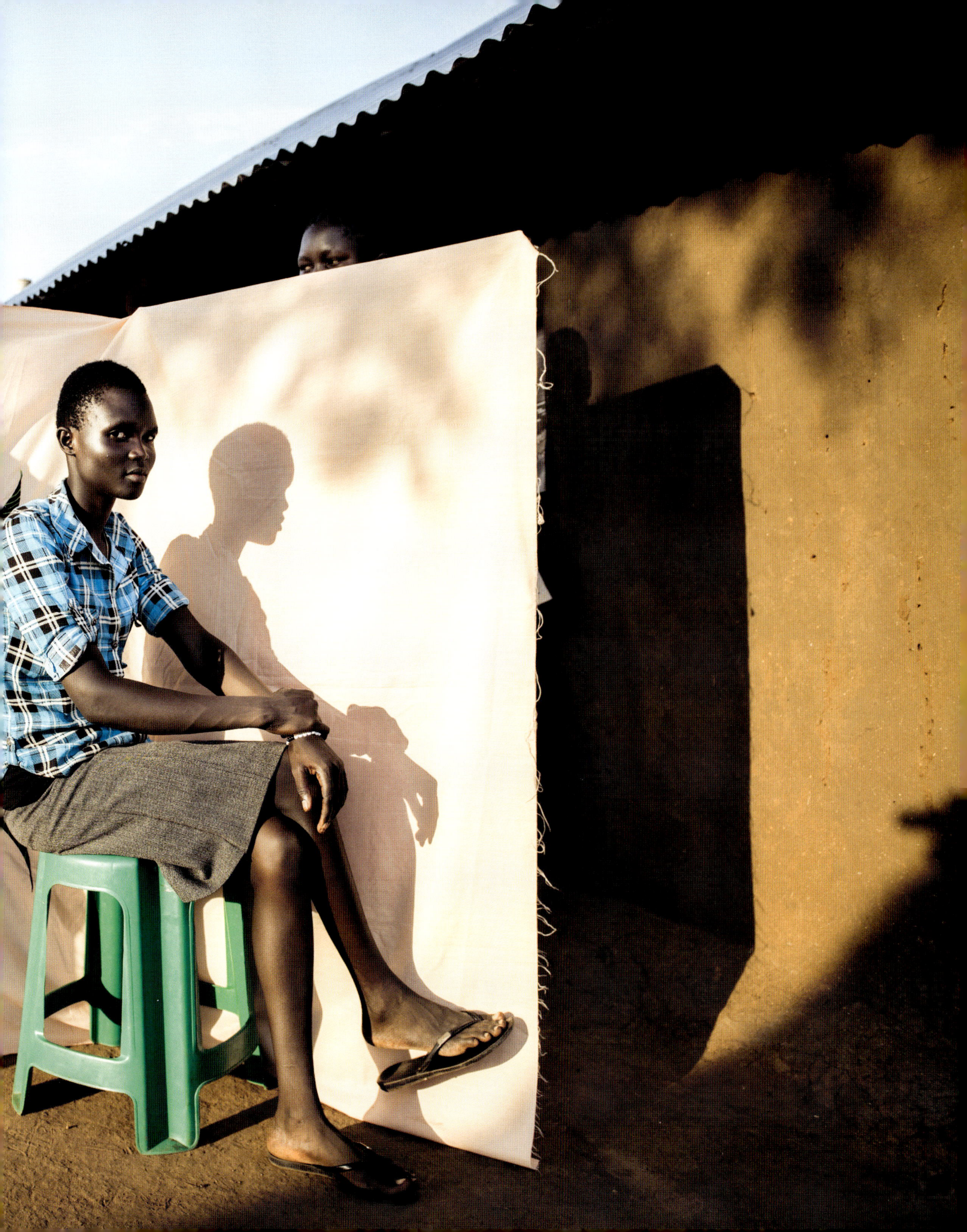

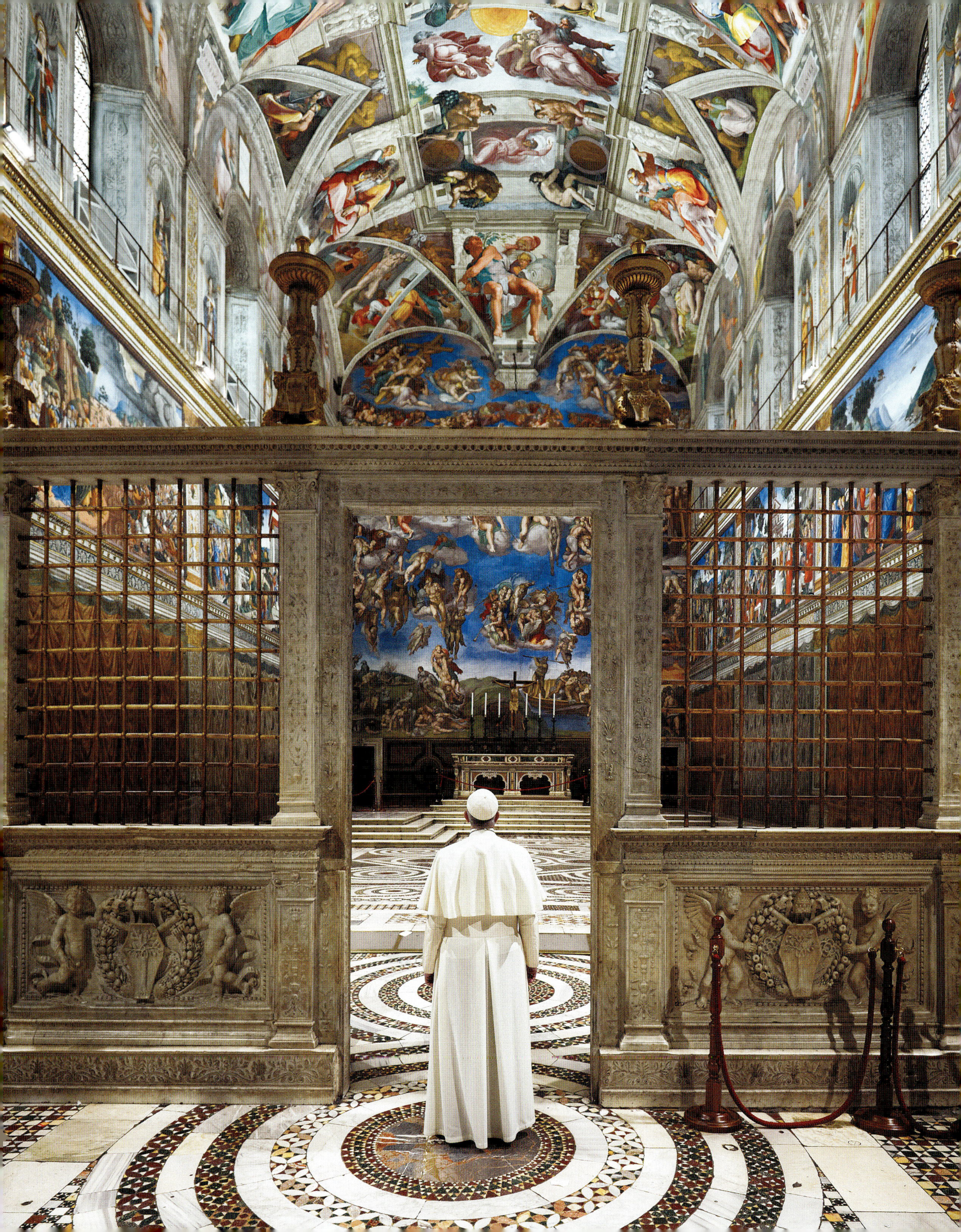

IN PHOTOGRAPHY THERE IS ROOM FOR HUMILITY, FOR KNOWING WHAT YOU DON'T KNOW.

DAVE YODER, 2014
After delivering his papal address on Christmas Day, Pope Francis makes an unscheduled visit to the Sistine Chapel in Vatican City.

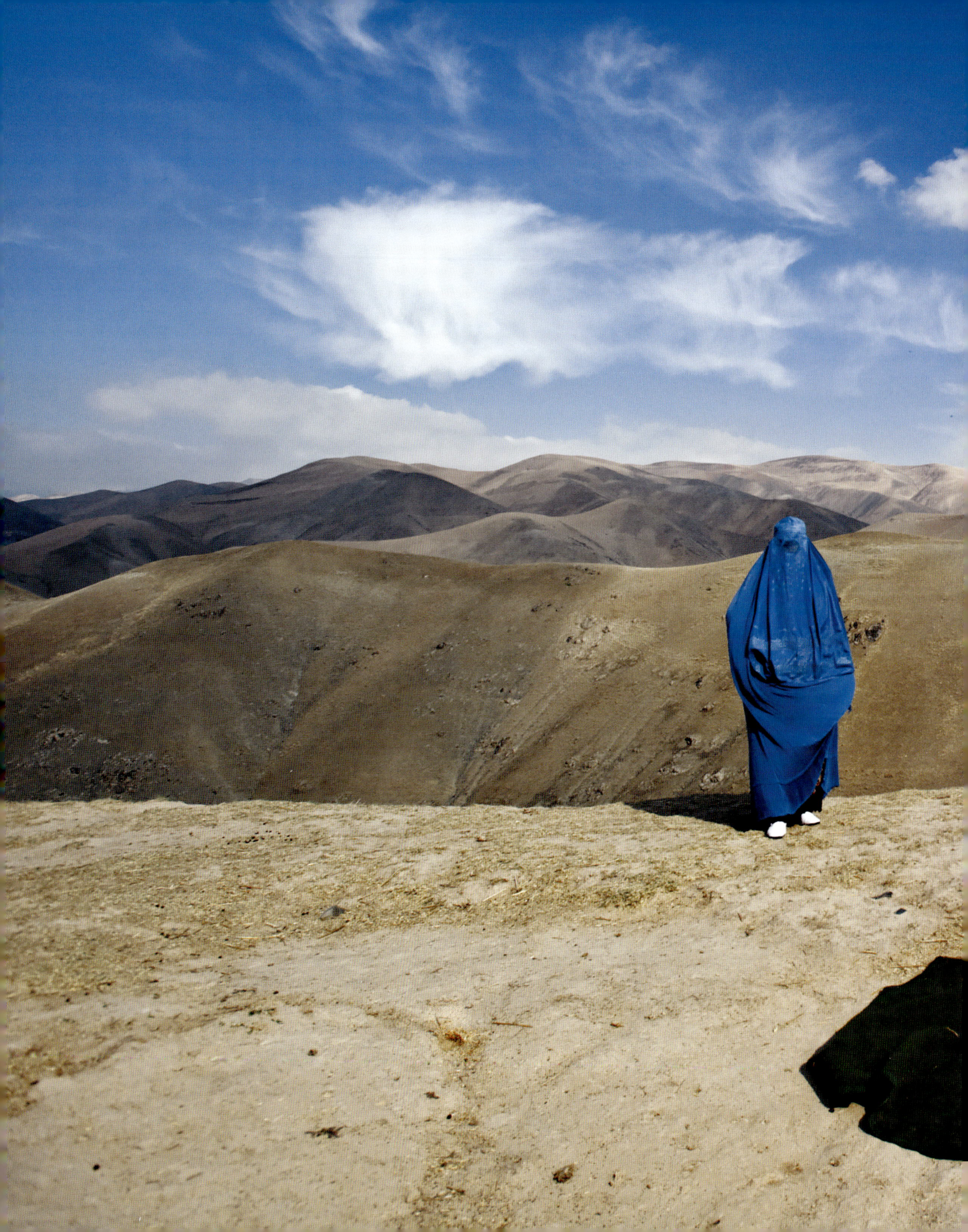

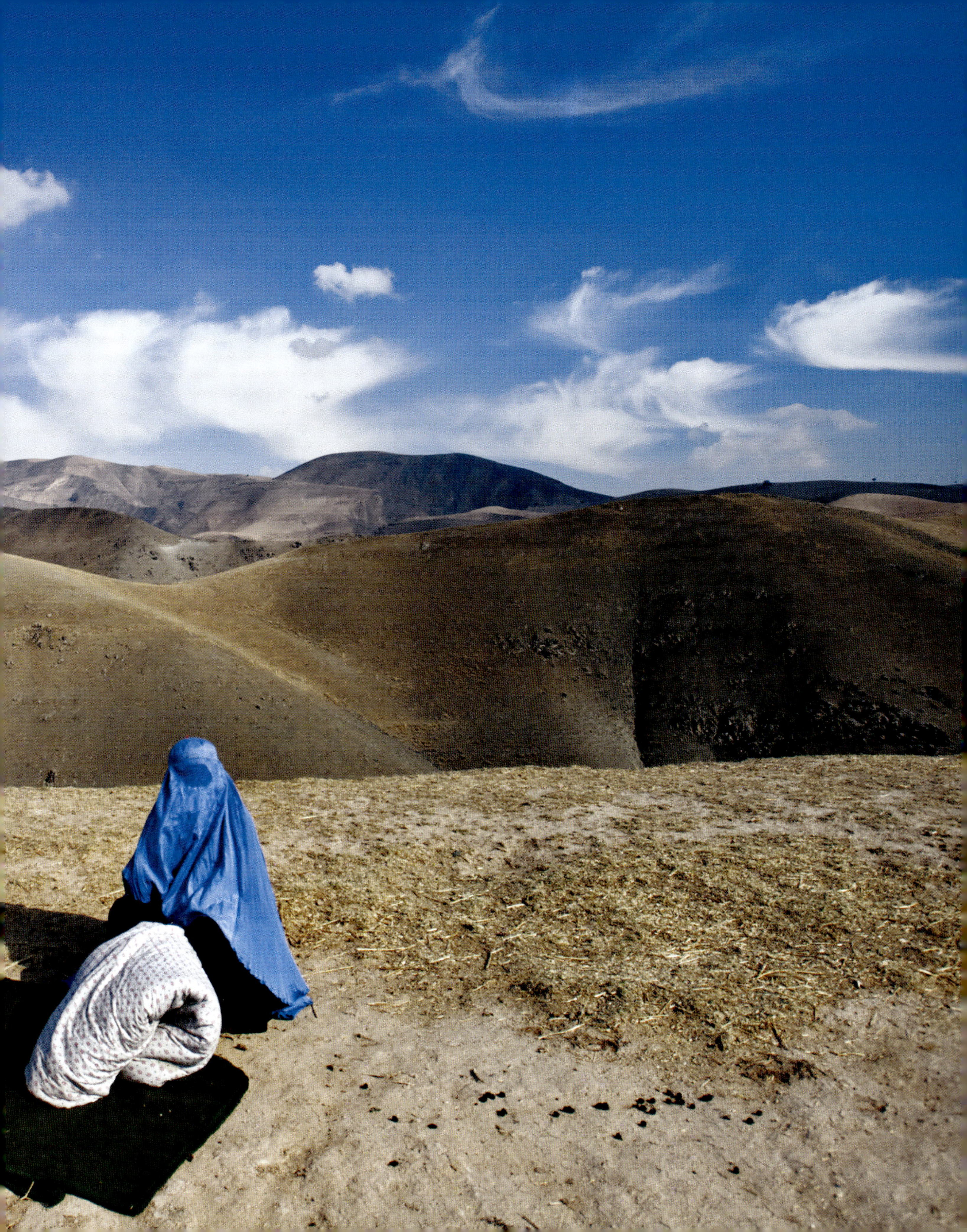

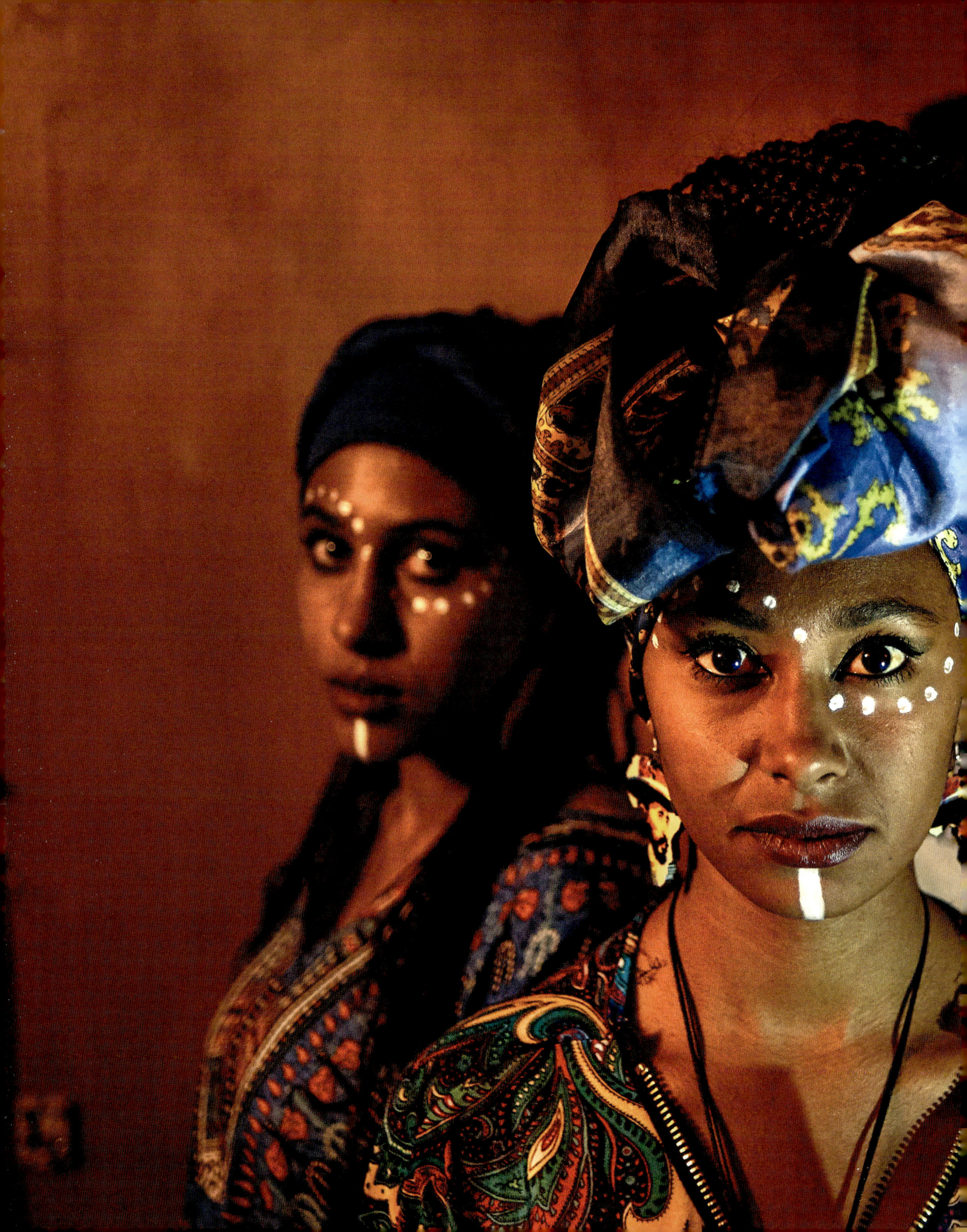

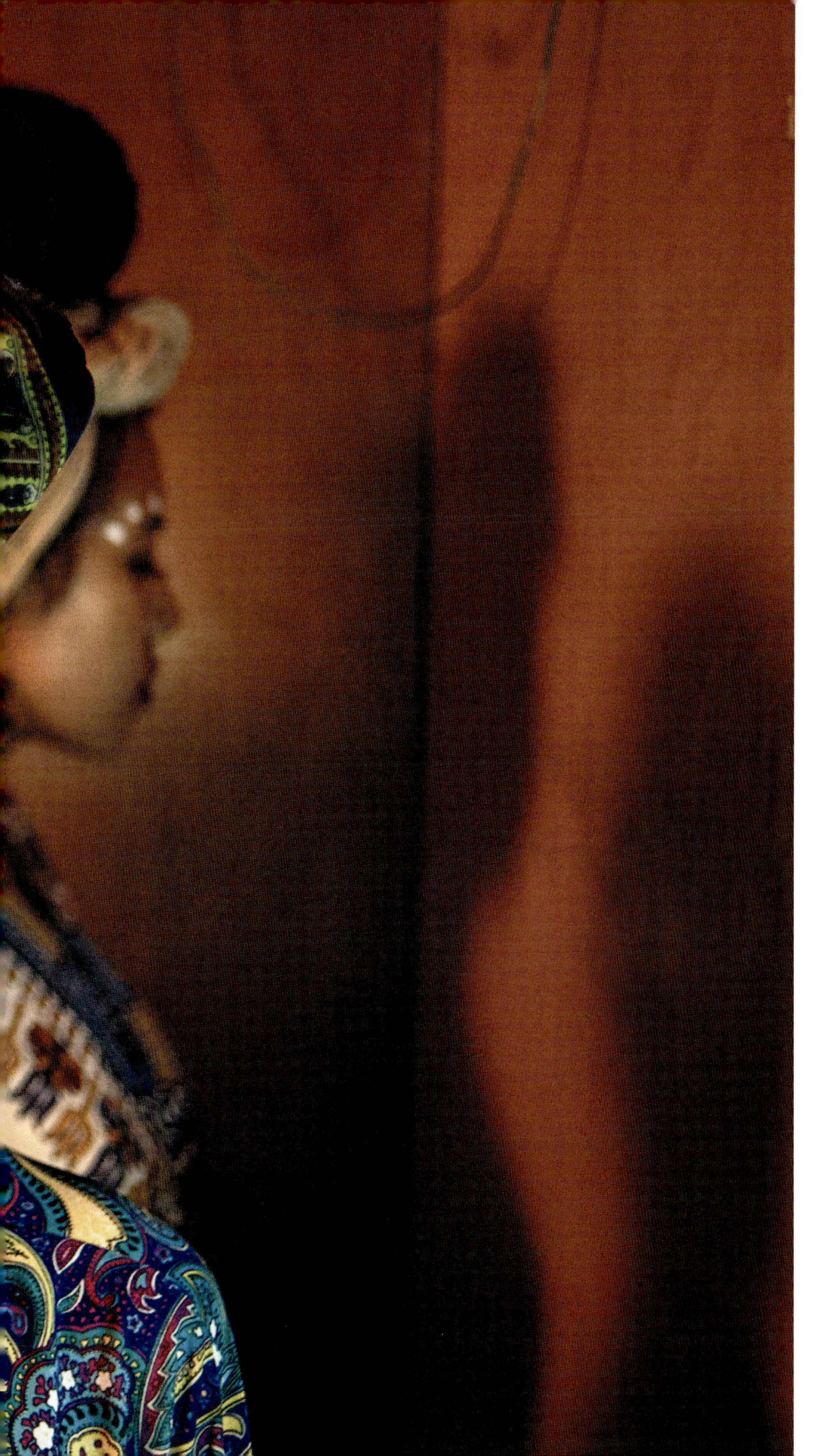

JOHANNA ALARCÓN, 2018
Members of the Ecuadorian Pan-African activist group Addis Ababa pose for a portrait, their turbans and ancestral crowns symbolizing their African heritage. Afro-Ecuadorian communities are descended from enslaved people brought to Ecuador.

PREVIOUS PAGES
LYNSEY ADDARIO, 2009
After her water breaks, a pregnant woman (right) and her mother search for a ride in Badakhshan Province, Afghanistan.

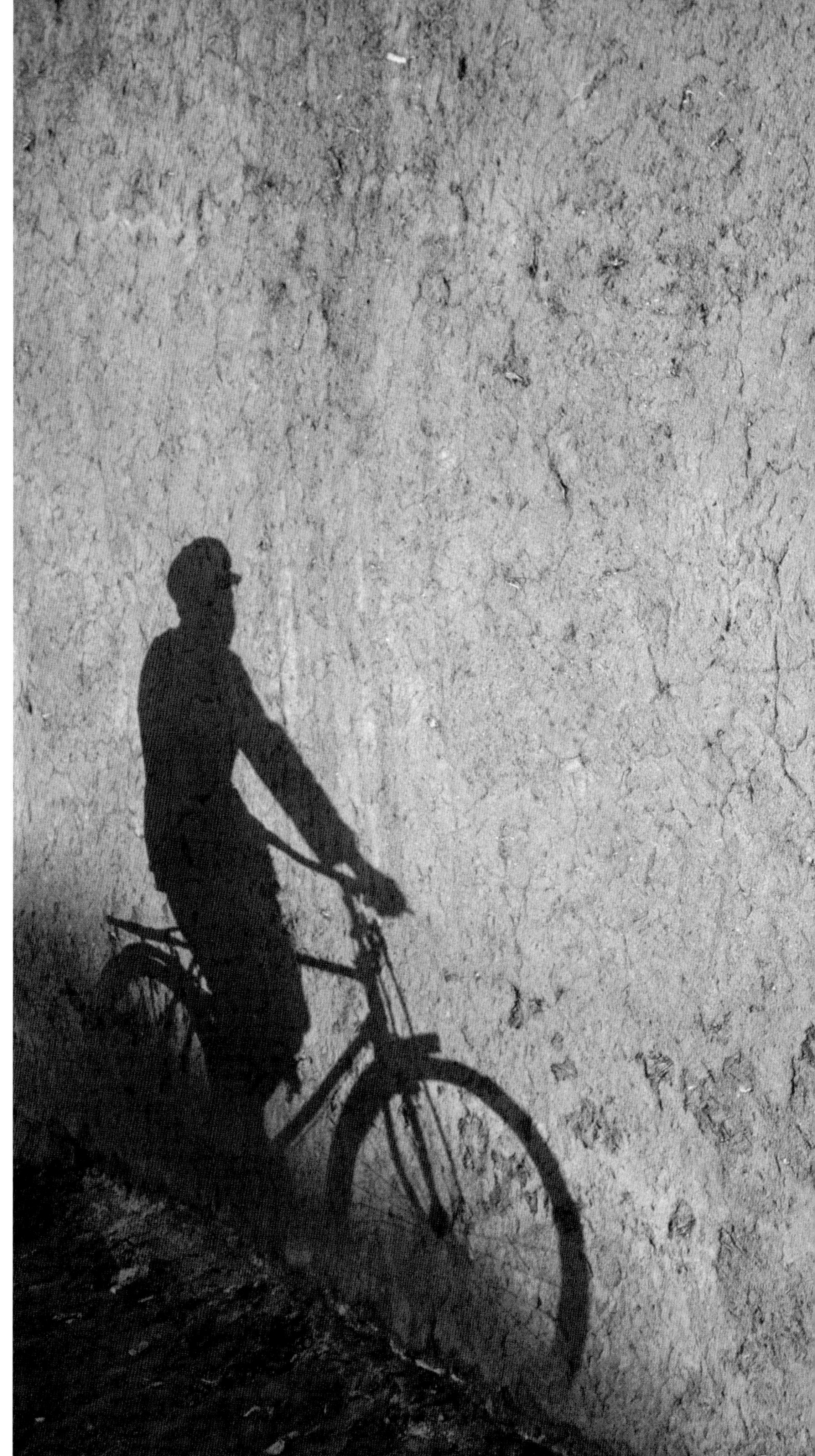

JAMES L. STANFIELD, 1980
In the autonomous region of Inner Mongolia, which lies within Chinese territory, villagers live among abandoned garrisons built for Chinese soldiers dating to the Ming dynasty.

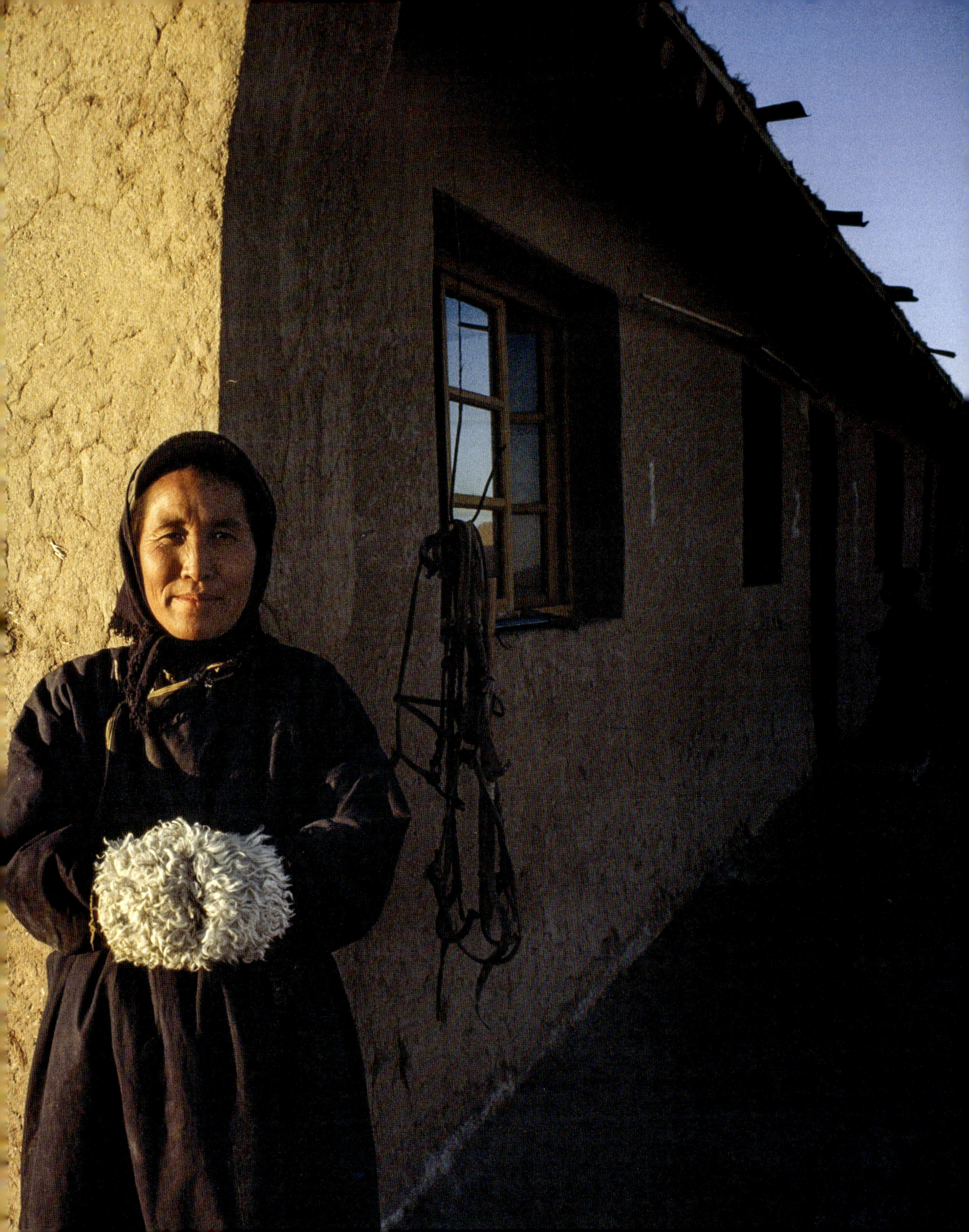

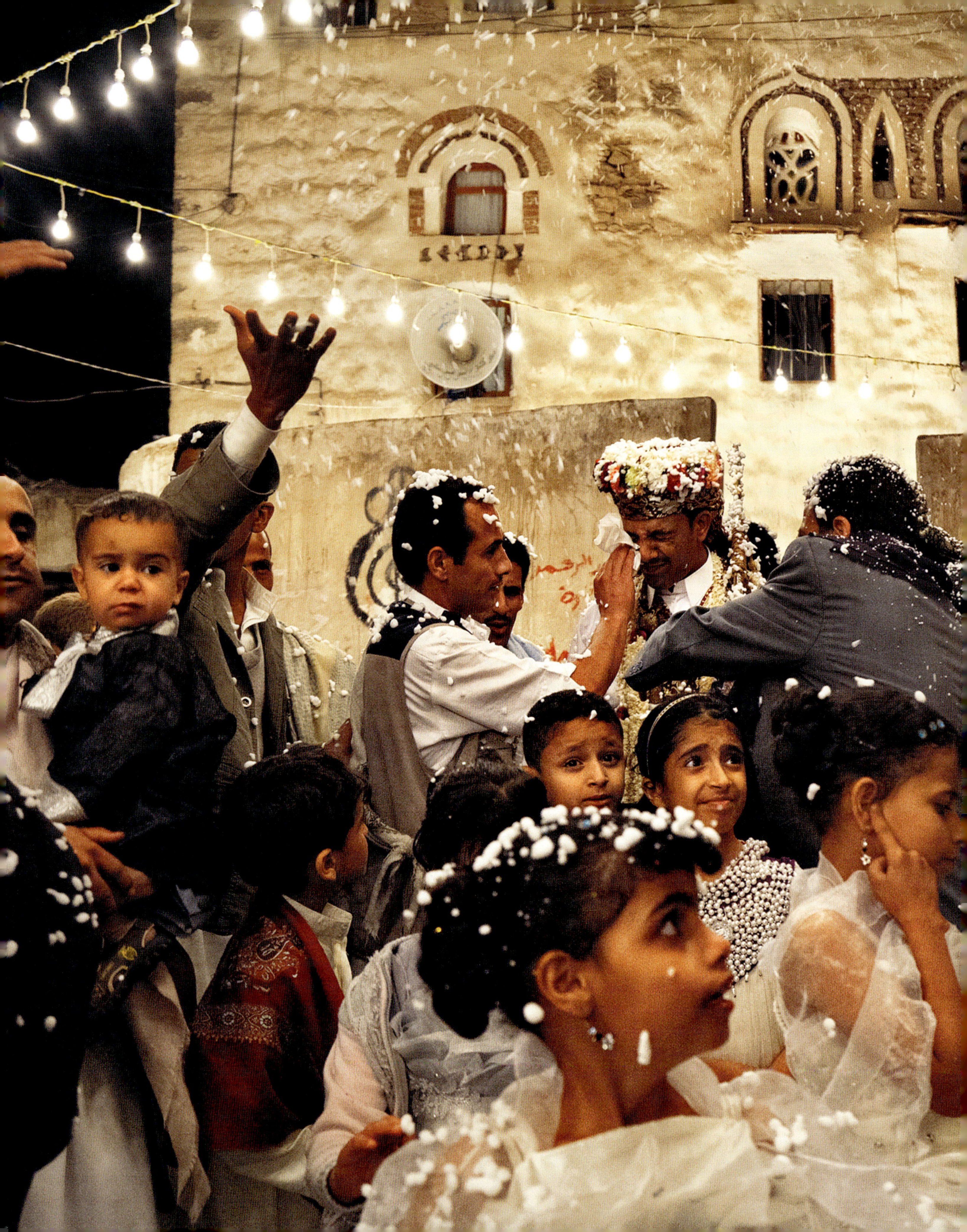

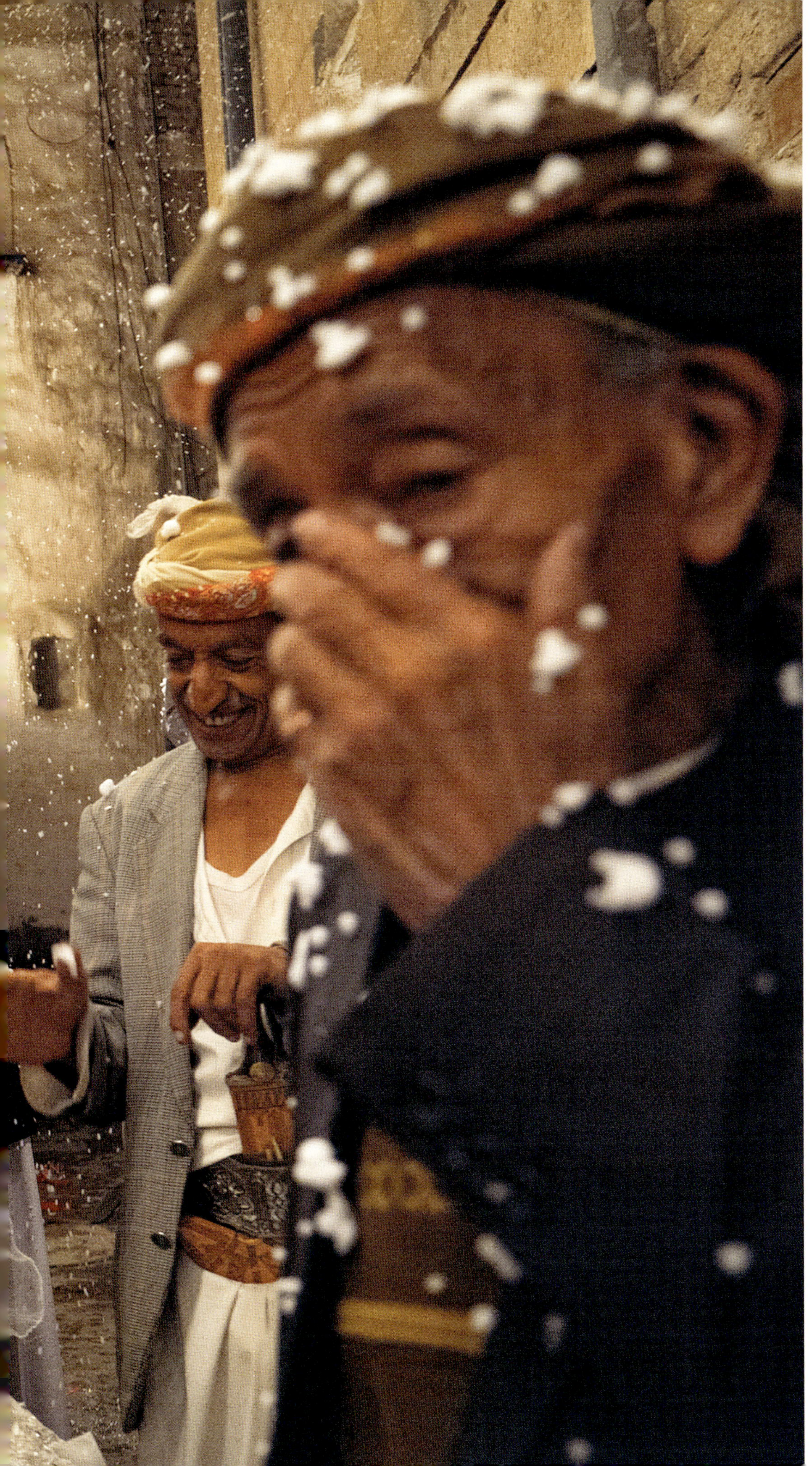

STEPHANIE SINCLAIR, 2012
A wedding celebration in the Old City of Sanaa, Yemen

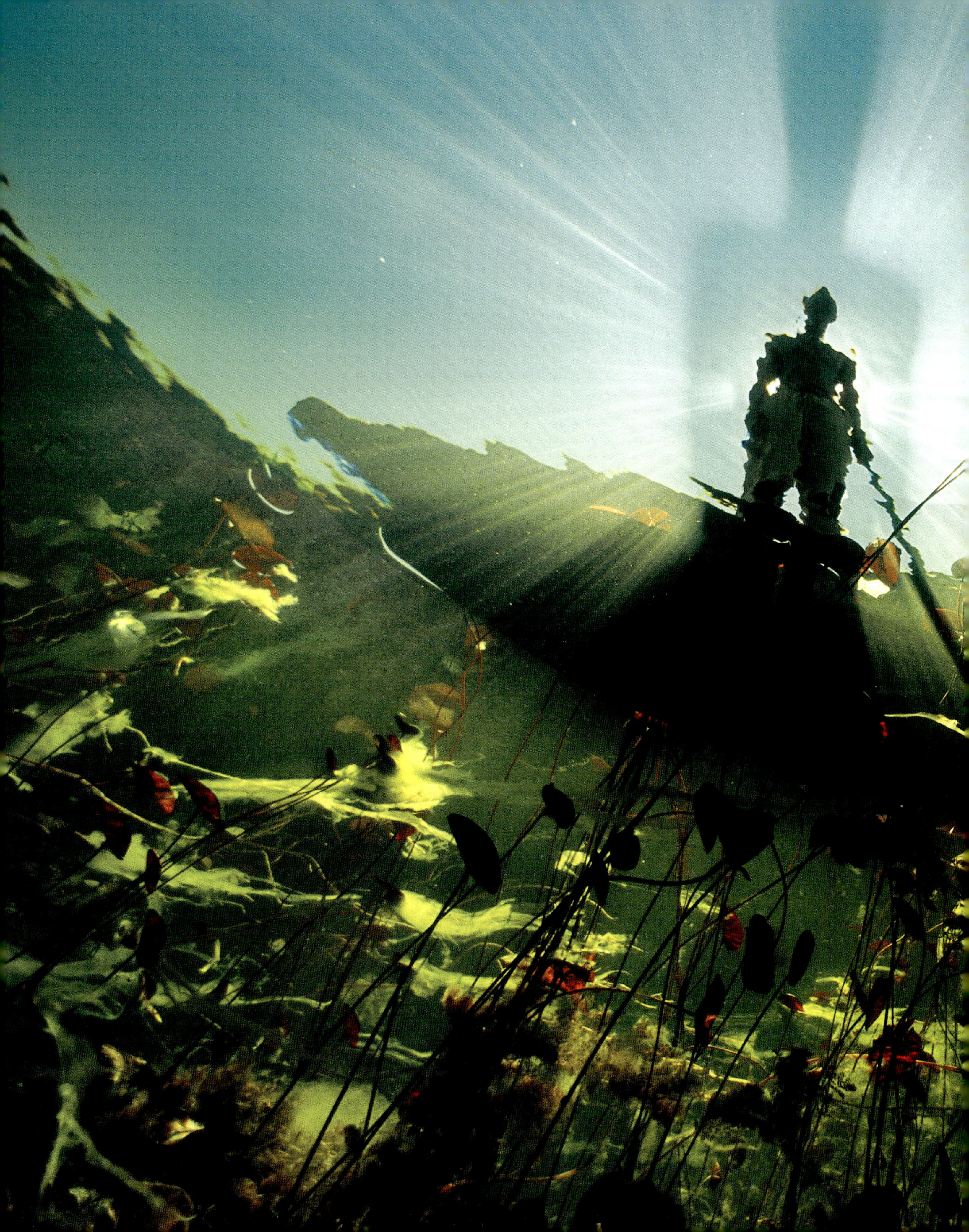

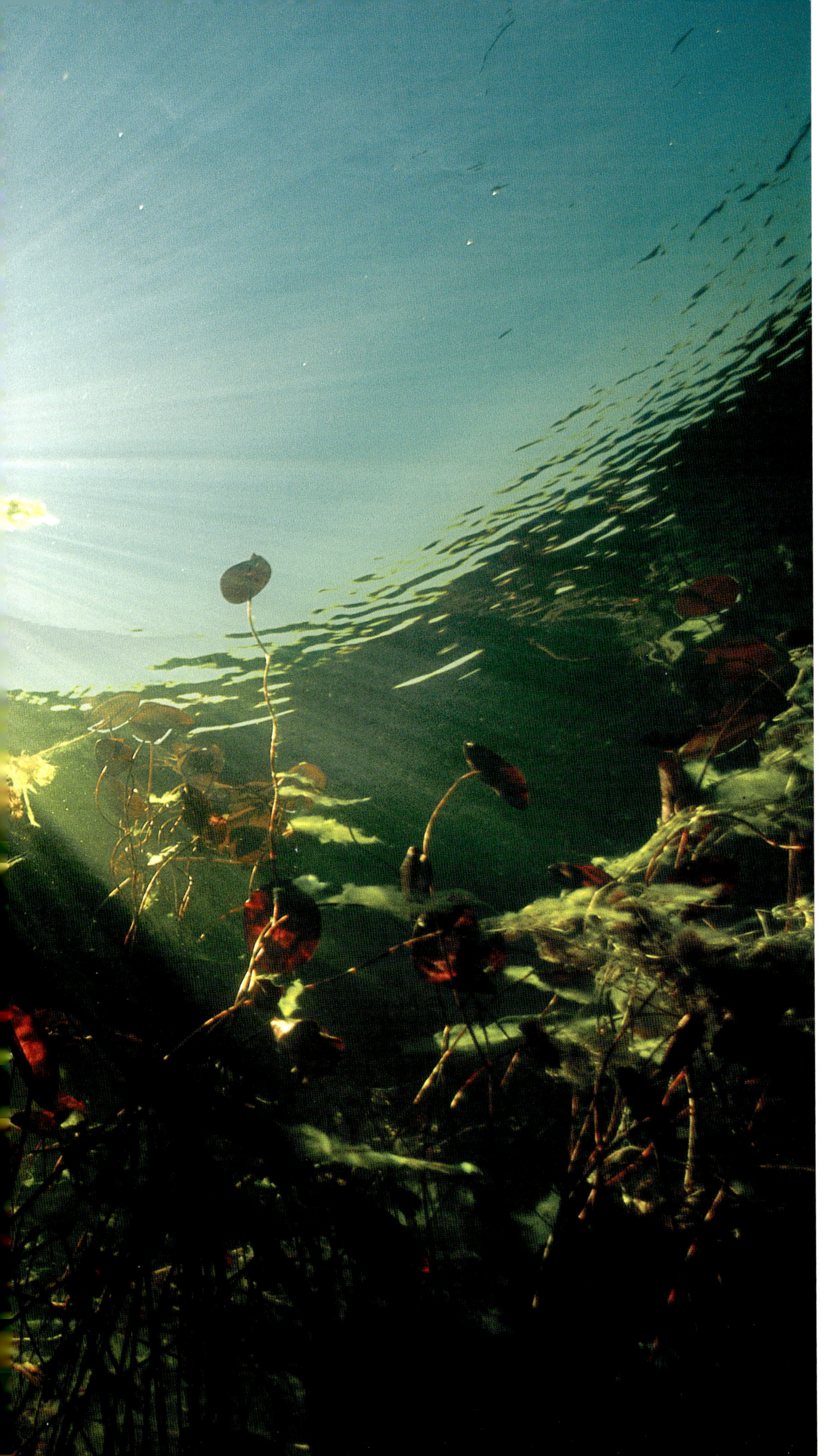

DAVID DOUBILET, 2004
A Bushman in a canoe peers down into floodwaters of the Okavango River in Botswana. The lesser known waterway sustains one of the world's largest wetlands and one of the most biodiverse regions in Africa.

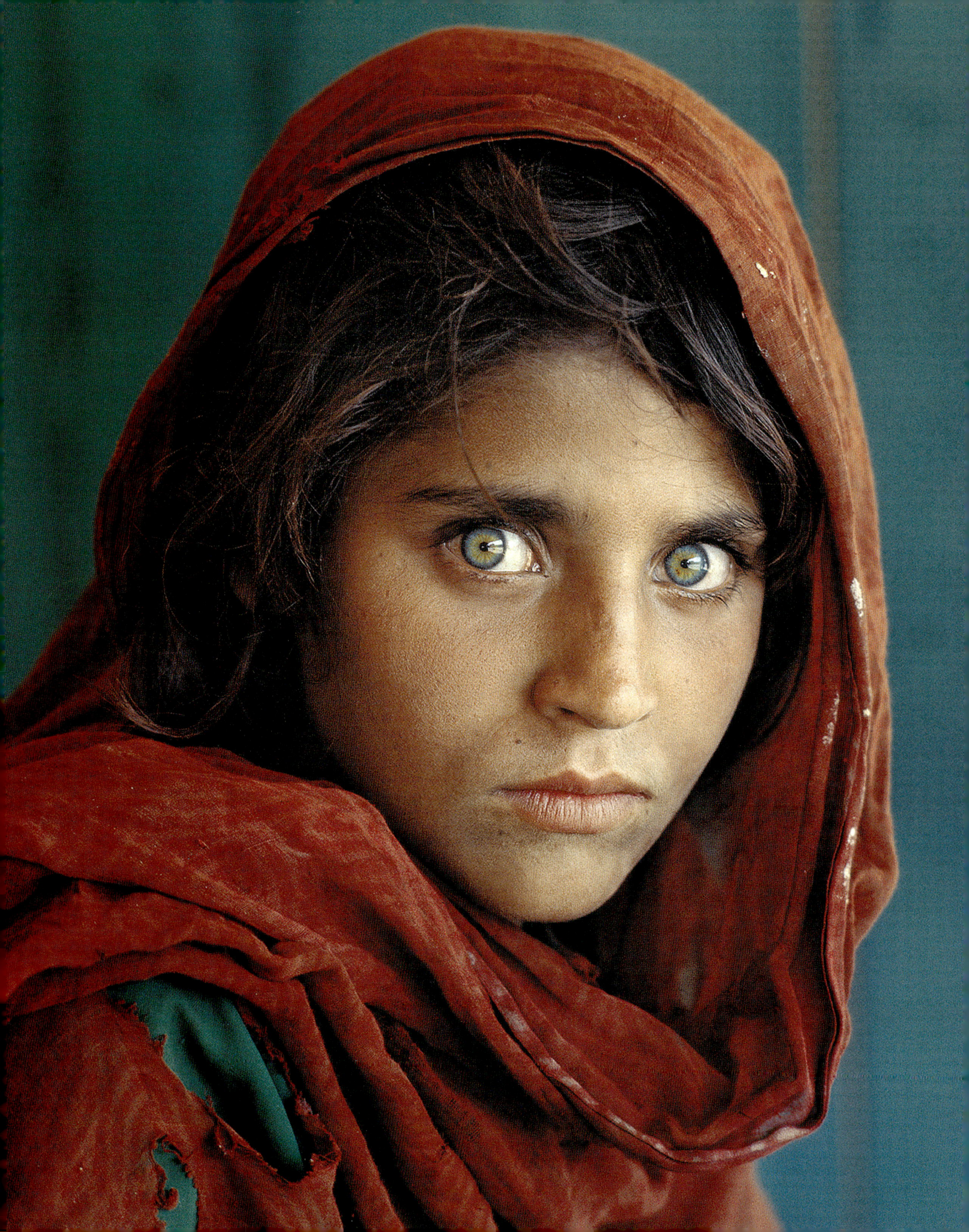

THE HUMAN SPIRIT IS PERHAPS PHOTOGRAPHY'S GREATEST SUBJECT.

STEVE MCCURRY, 1984
Sharbat Gula, a refugee of the Soviet invasion of Afghanistan, graced the iconic cover of the June 1985 issue of *National Geographic*. It was later revealed that she was photographed without her permission.

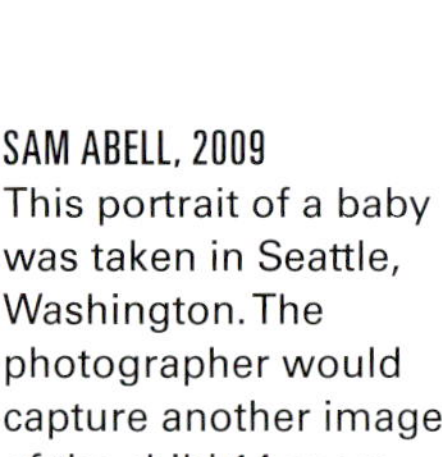

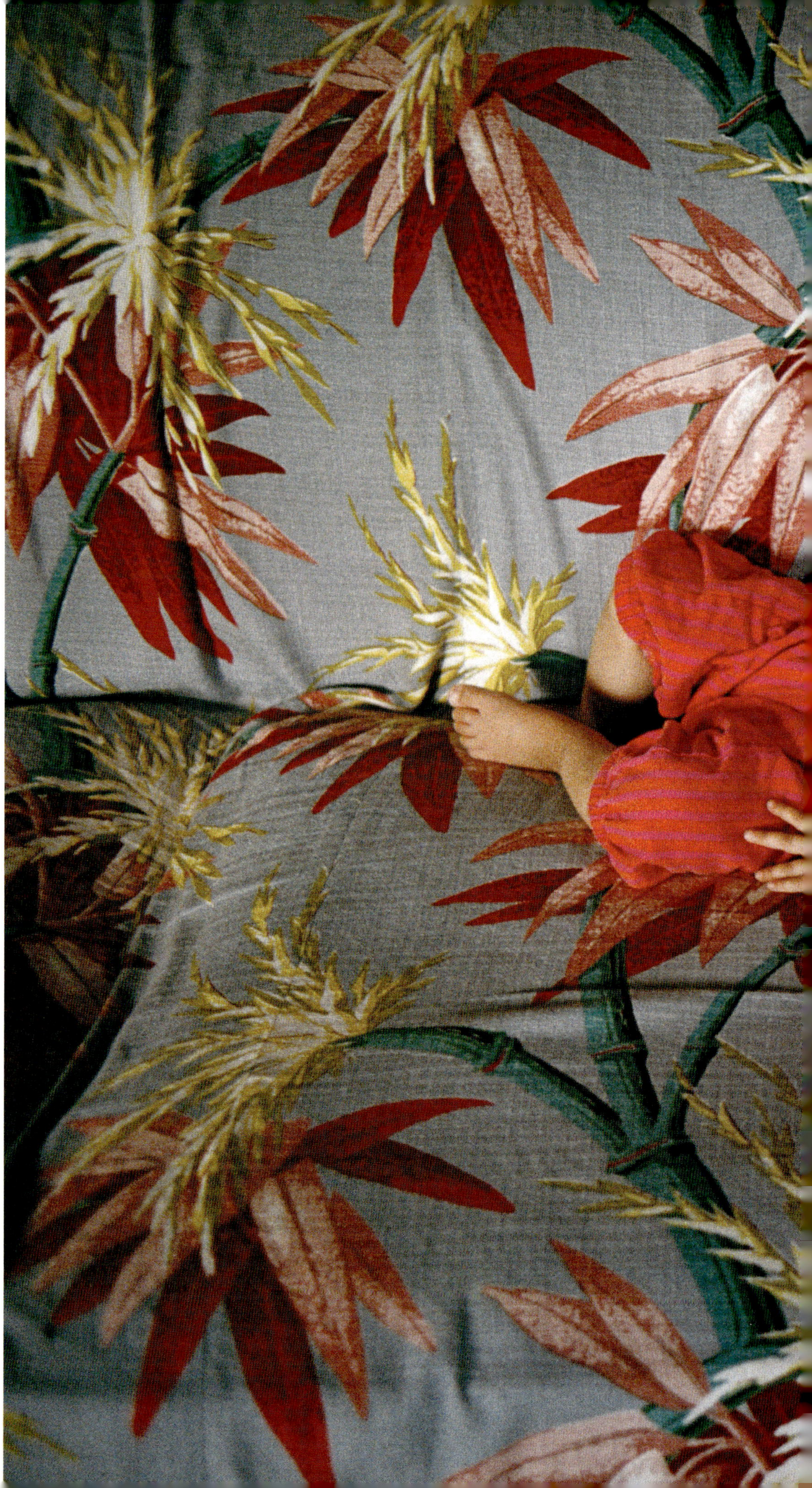

SAM ABELL, 2009
This portrait of a baby was taken in Seattle, Washington. The photographer would capture another image of the child 14 years later.

FOLLOWING PAGES
RIVER CLAURE, 2019
In a modern photographic reimagining of Antoine de Saint-Exupéry's *The Little Prince,* a Bolivian boy walks through a metaphorical rose garden, where buds blossom from the braids of Indigenous women known as *cholitas.*

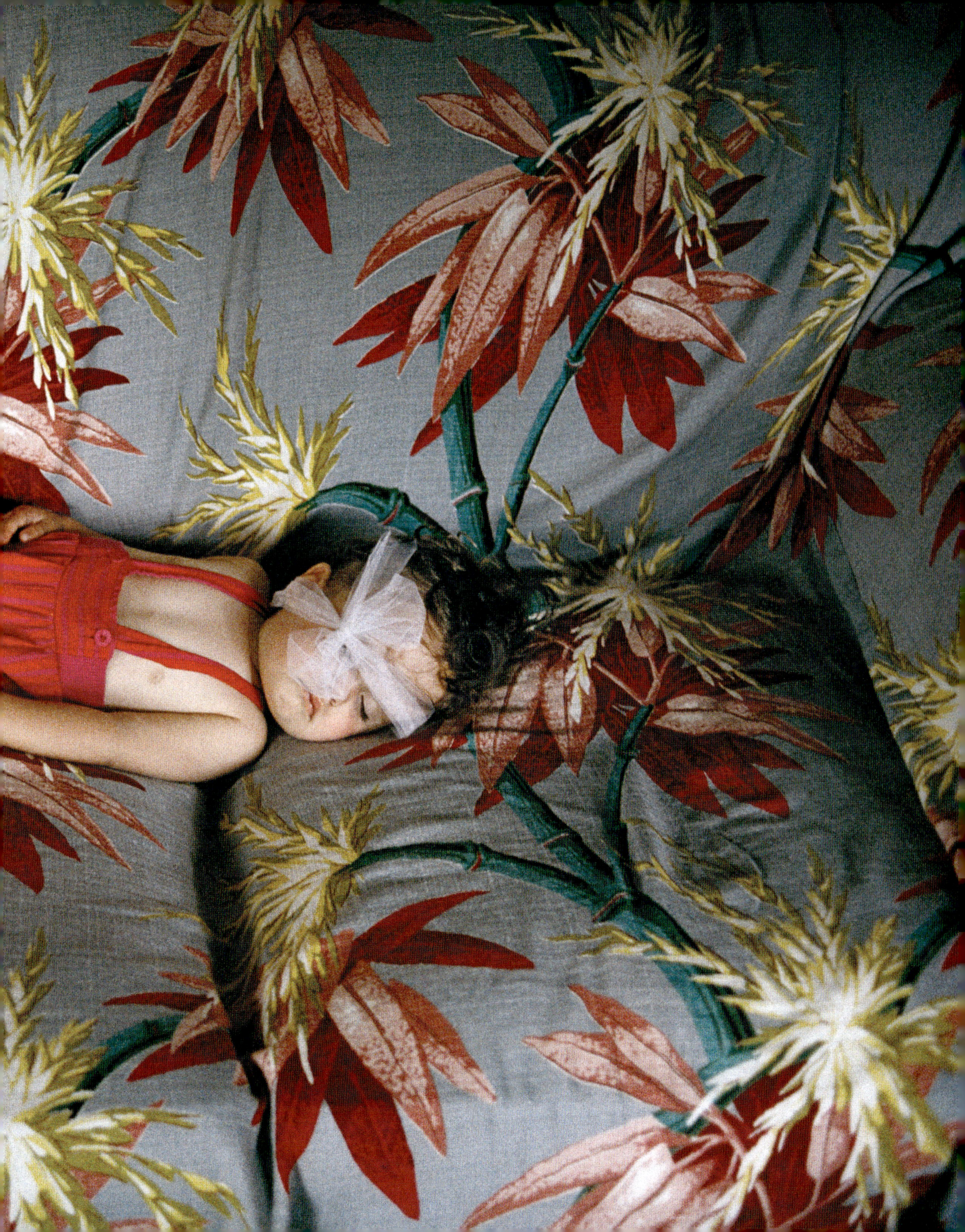

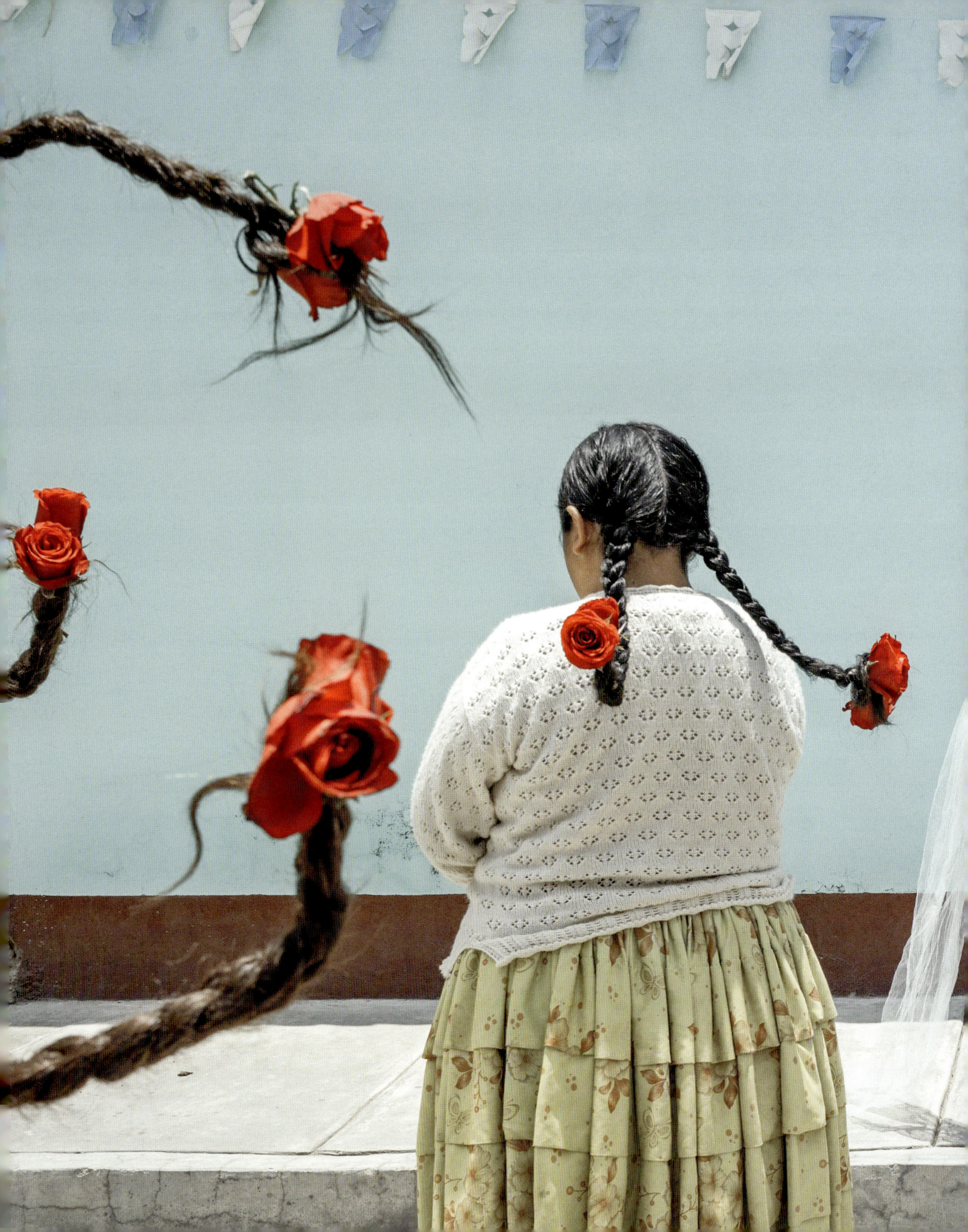

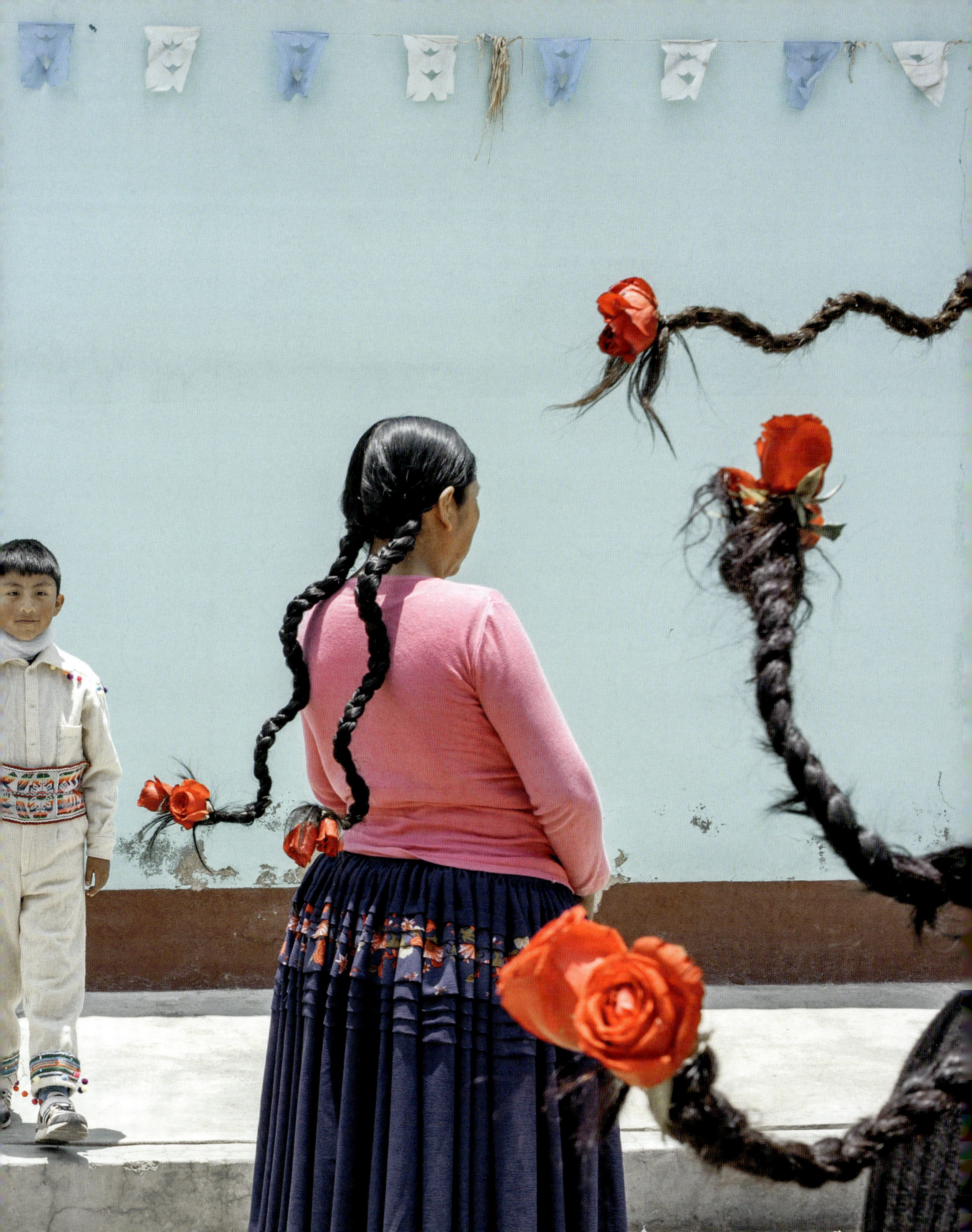

BIOGRAPHY

JODI COBB

THE INDELIBLE IMAGES OF JODI COBB have the power to twist the heart and haunt the mind. But the singular trailblazing path she carved at *National Geographic* as the pioneer woman on the photographic staff was not a foregone conclusion.

First, the magazine itself had to evolve, and Cobb's groundbreaking stories were part of that evolution. She has traveled through 100 countries in pursuit of stories in some of the world's most impenetrable environments. Her career is a litany of firsts: She was one of the first photographers to cross China when it reopened to the outside world, the first woman named White House Photographer of the Year, the first photographer given permission by the king of Saudi Arabia to photograph the women of that country for a story, and one of the first photographers to be welcomed inside the secret world of Japan's geisha. "I like intimate stories that show a closed world," Cobb says. Her story on Saudi women was a near miracle, since photographing women is a taboo in that culture. "I didn't think I was going to pull it off," she says. But she did.

In her searing story "21st-Century Slaves," published in the September 2003 issue, she exposed the brutal reality of global human trafficking. "You know, I've not recovered from it—from having to seek out evil every day and finding it," she says. "You can never recover. It's just a complete destruction of your faith in human nature."

Cobb has photographed royalty, rock stars, and terrorists, and was claimed as a wife by a desert Bedouin. Named a "Nikon Legend," she has won many World Press and National Press Photographers Association Pictures of the Year awards, and has received Lifetime Achievement Awards from both the American Society of Media Photographers and National Geographic's Photo Society, an independent group of photographers who have contributed their work to the organization. Her photographs have been exhibited worldwide and are in the collection of the National Gallery of Art.

OPPOSITE TOP
JODI COBB, 1998
At the Miss Universe contest, Wendy Fitzwilliam of Trinidad and Tobago adjusts her costume. She would go on to win the competition.

OPPOSITE BOTTOM
JODI COBB, 2010
Twin sisters on the set of a comedy-horror film in Indianapolis, Indiana

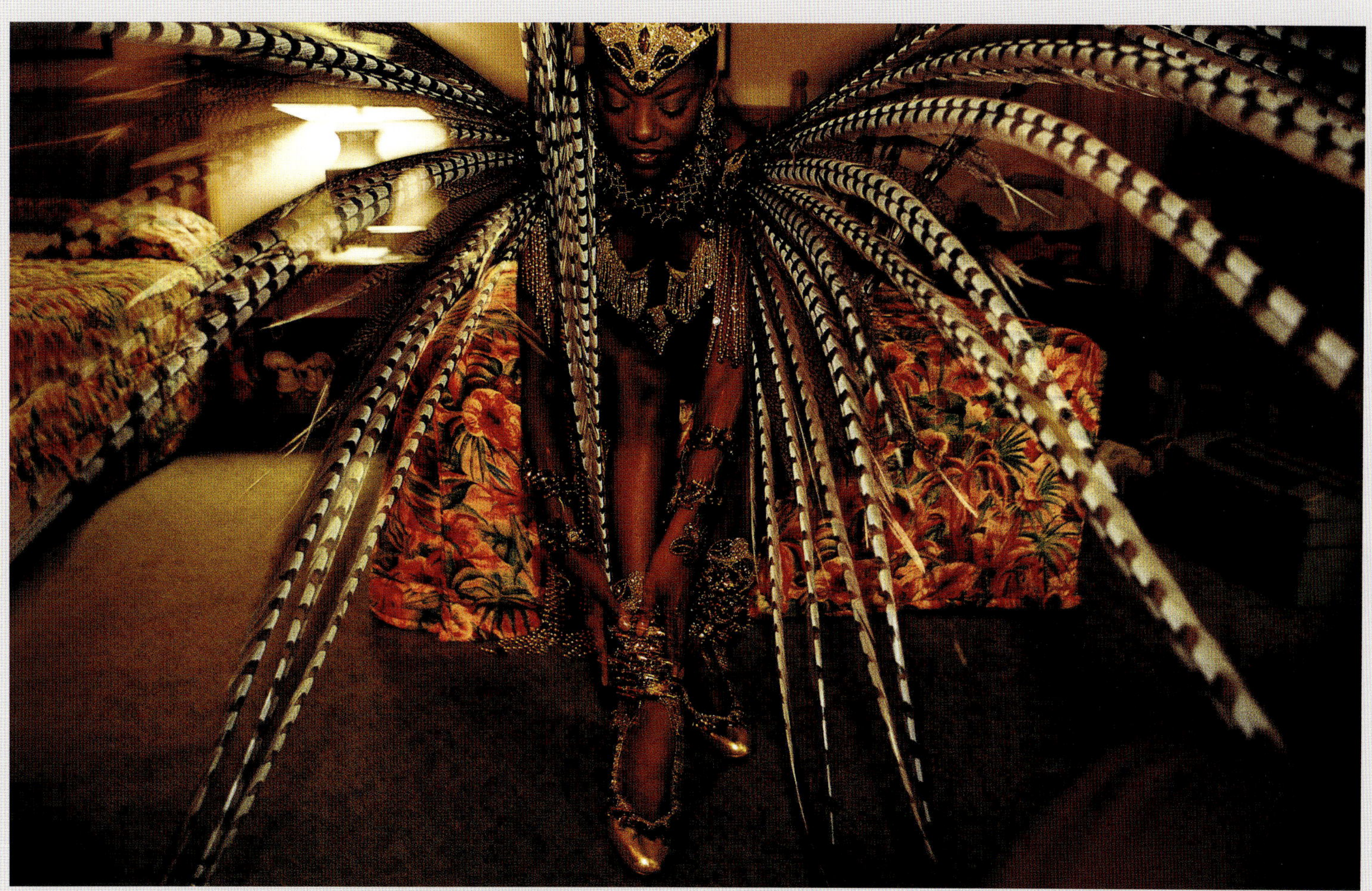

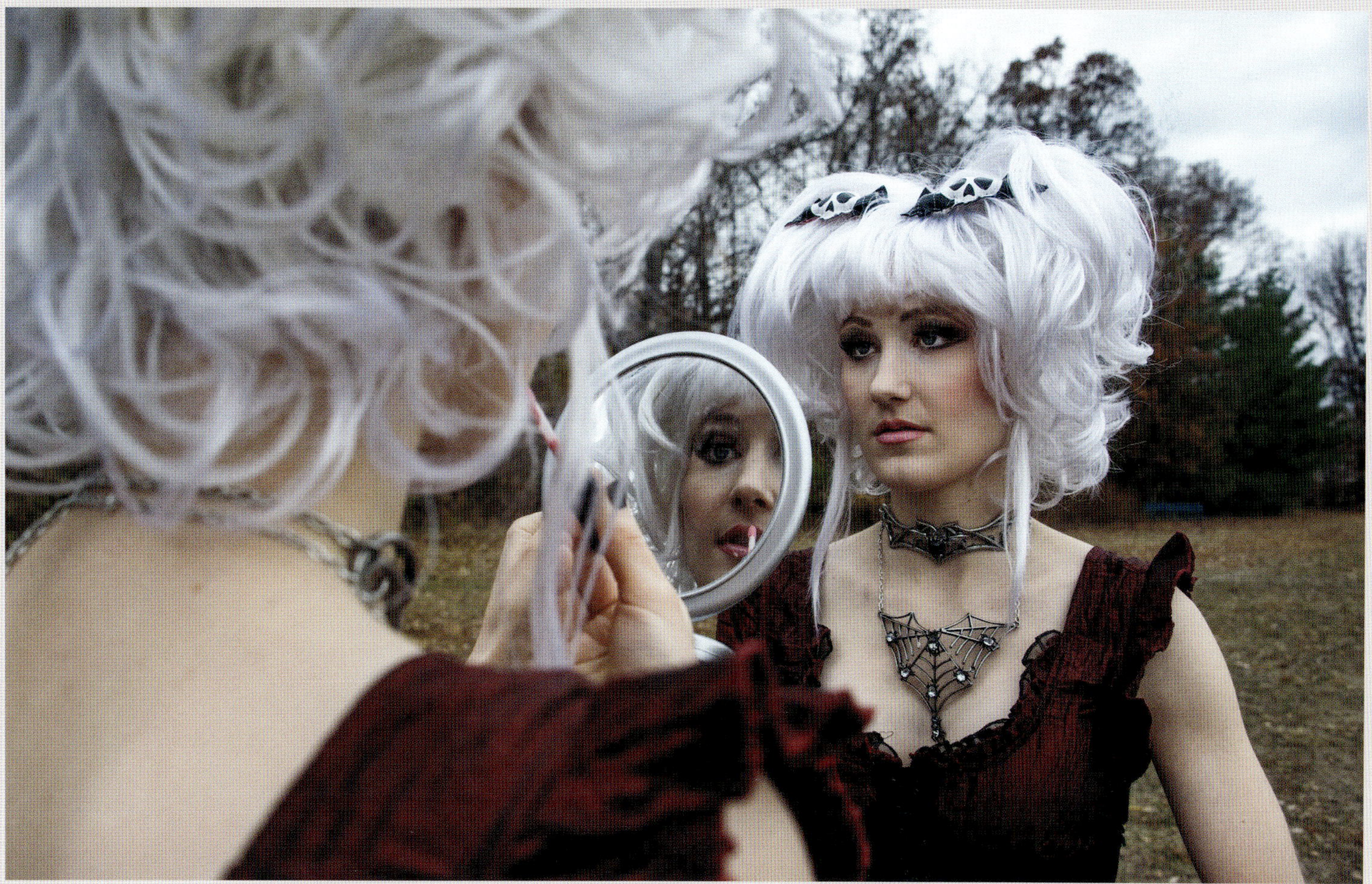

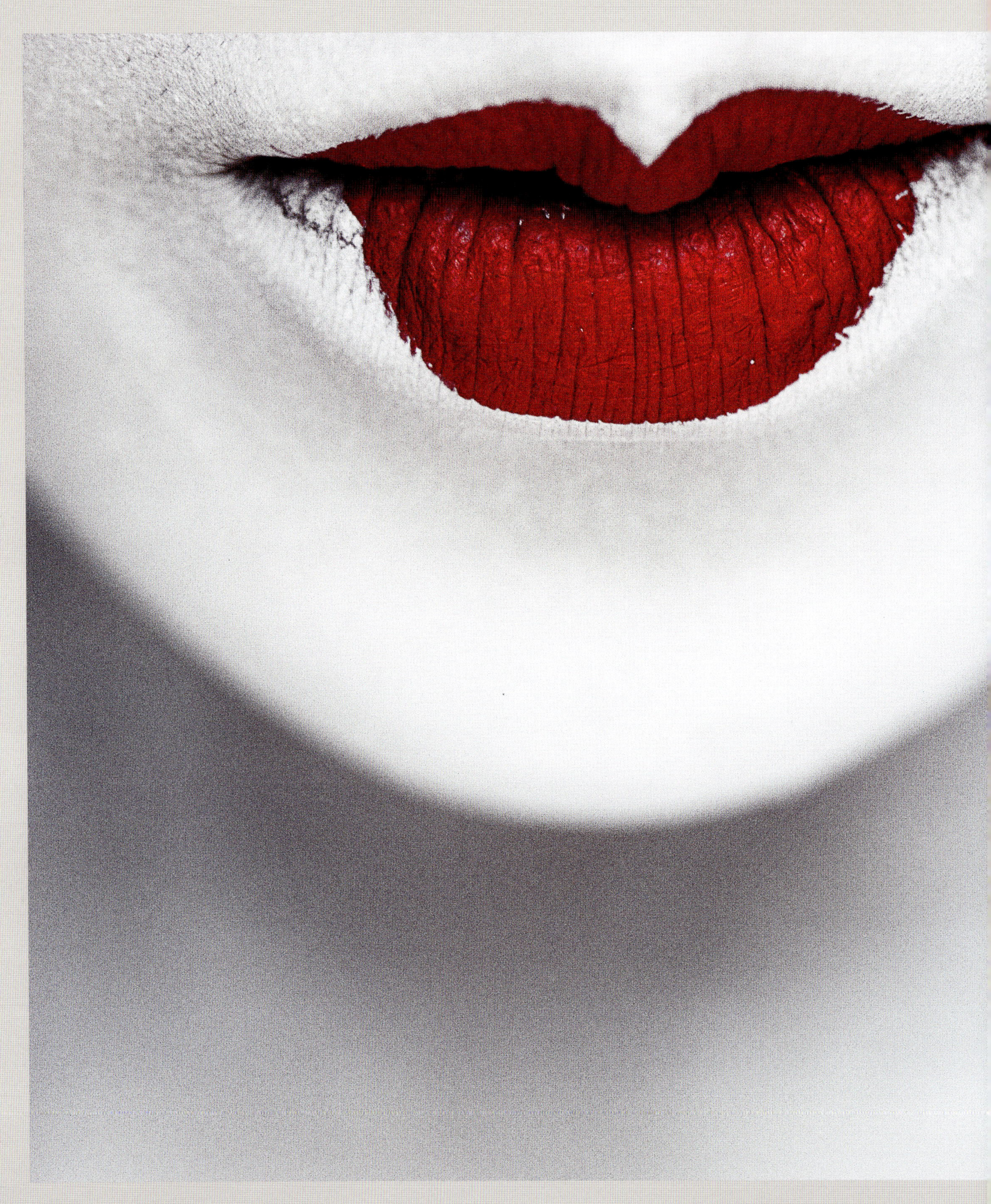

JODI COBB, 2008
The sealed lips of a geisha speak to a code of discretion and honor kept by these icons of Japanese culture. Cobb was one of the first photographers welcomed into an otherwise secret world.

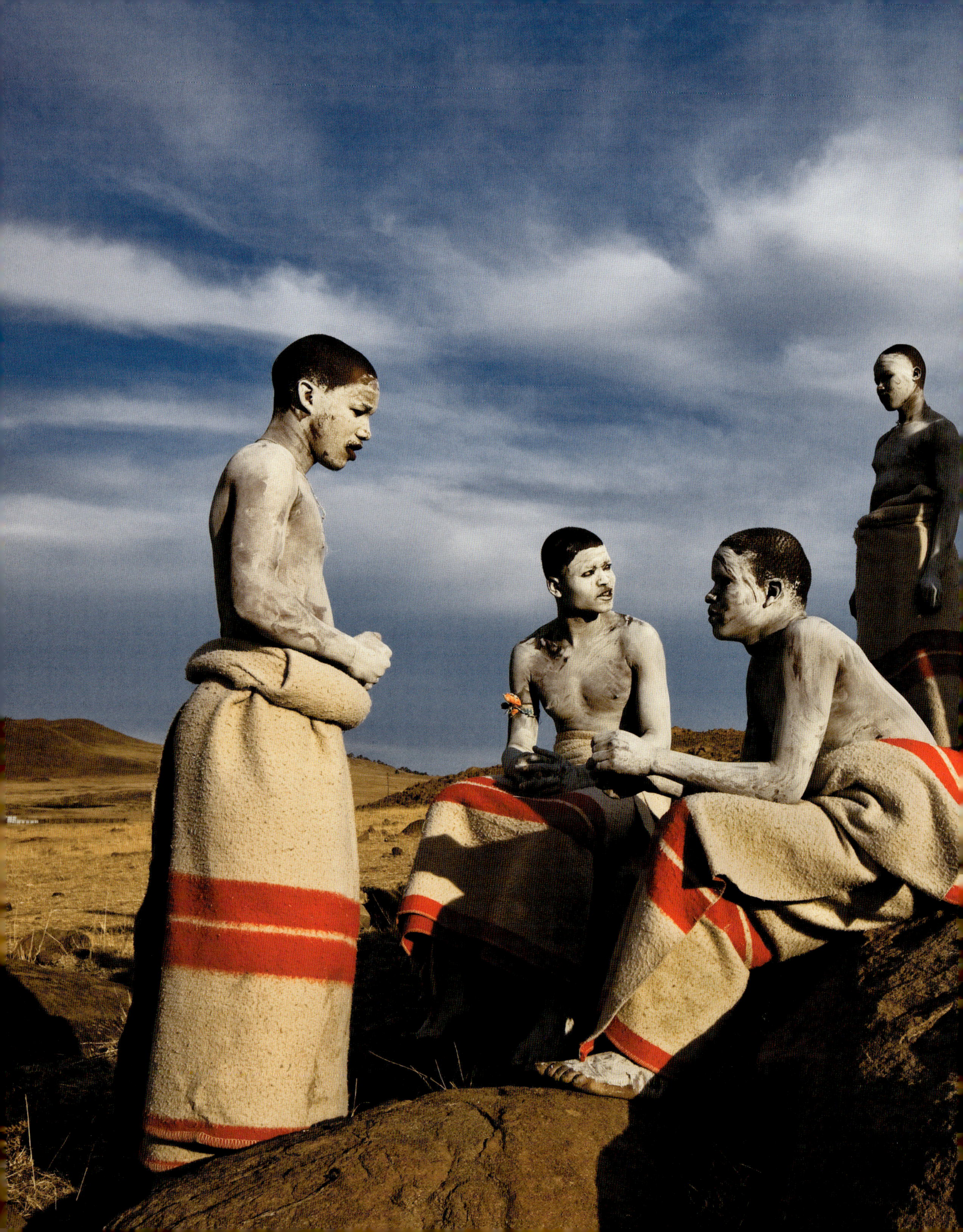

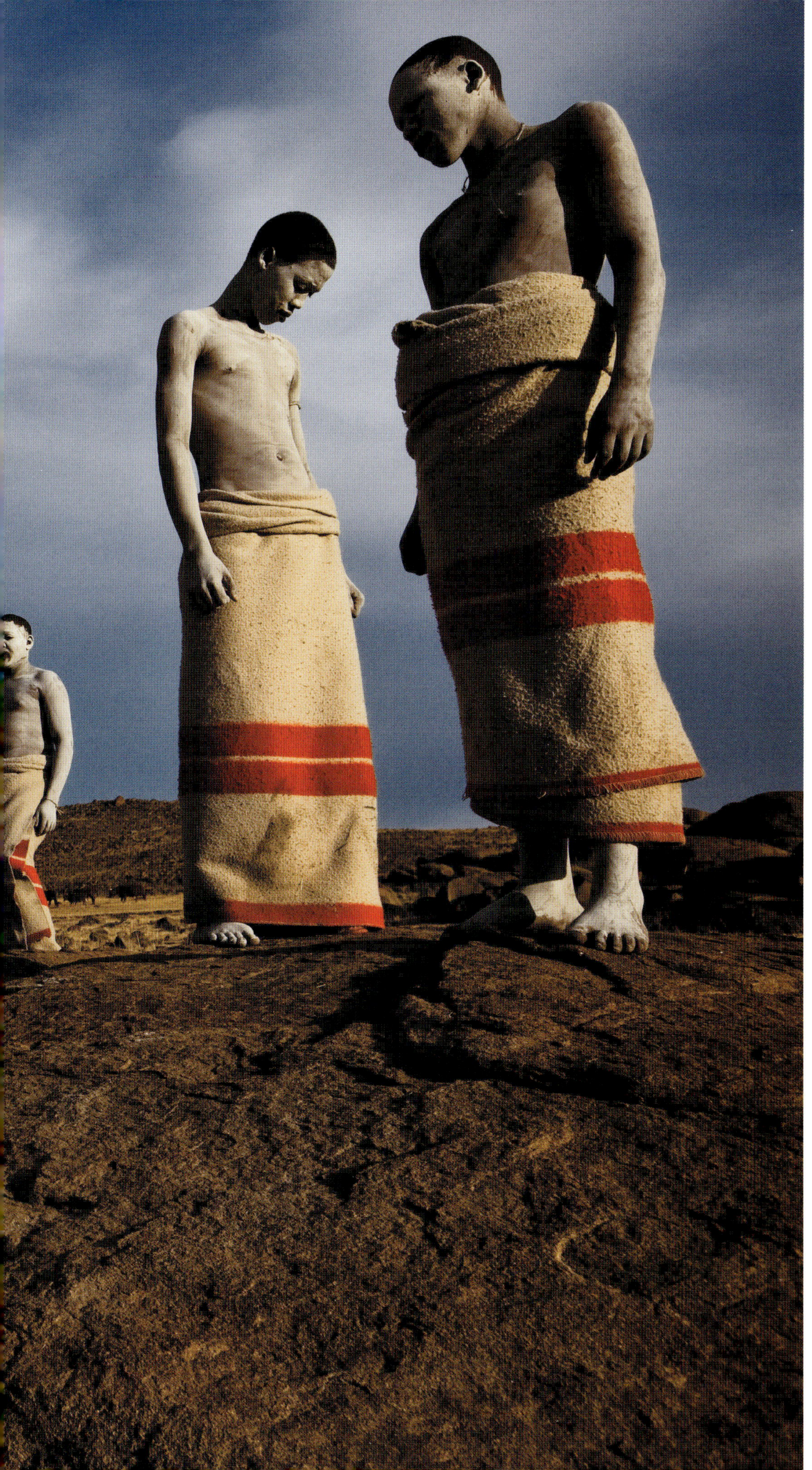

JAMES NACHTWEY, 2009
Xhosa teenagers, wrapped in blankets and painted white for purification, await a circumcision ritual outside their Eastern Cape village in South Africa.

FOLLOWING PAGES
EVGENIA ARBUGAEVA, 2016
In her family's camp near the Kara Sea, a girl from the Indigenous Nenets tribe dons a curtain and cardboard crown to become a "tundra princess" near Western Siberia.

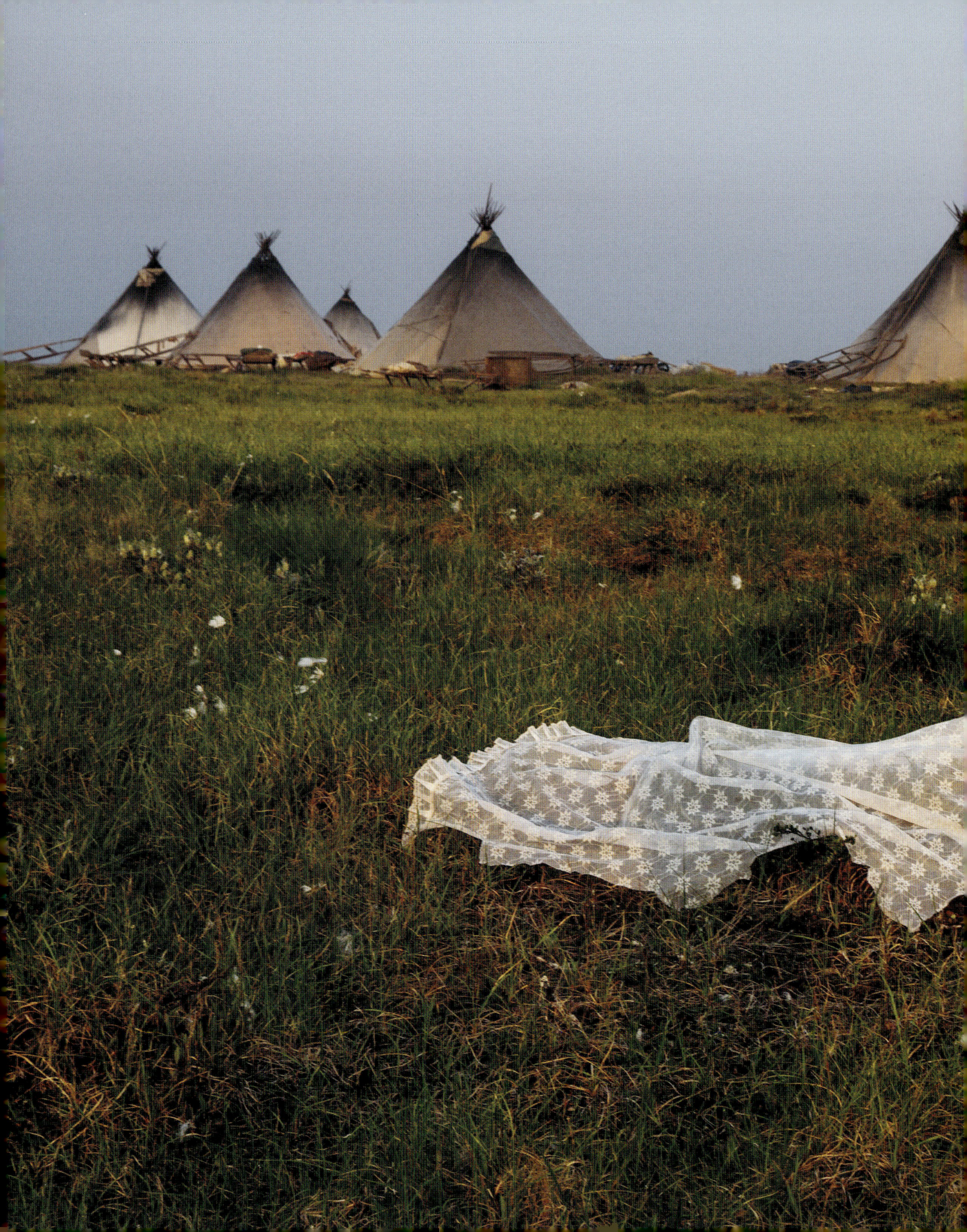

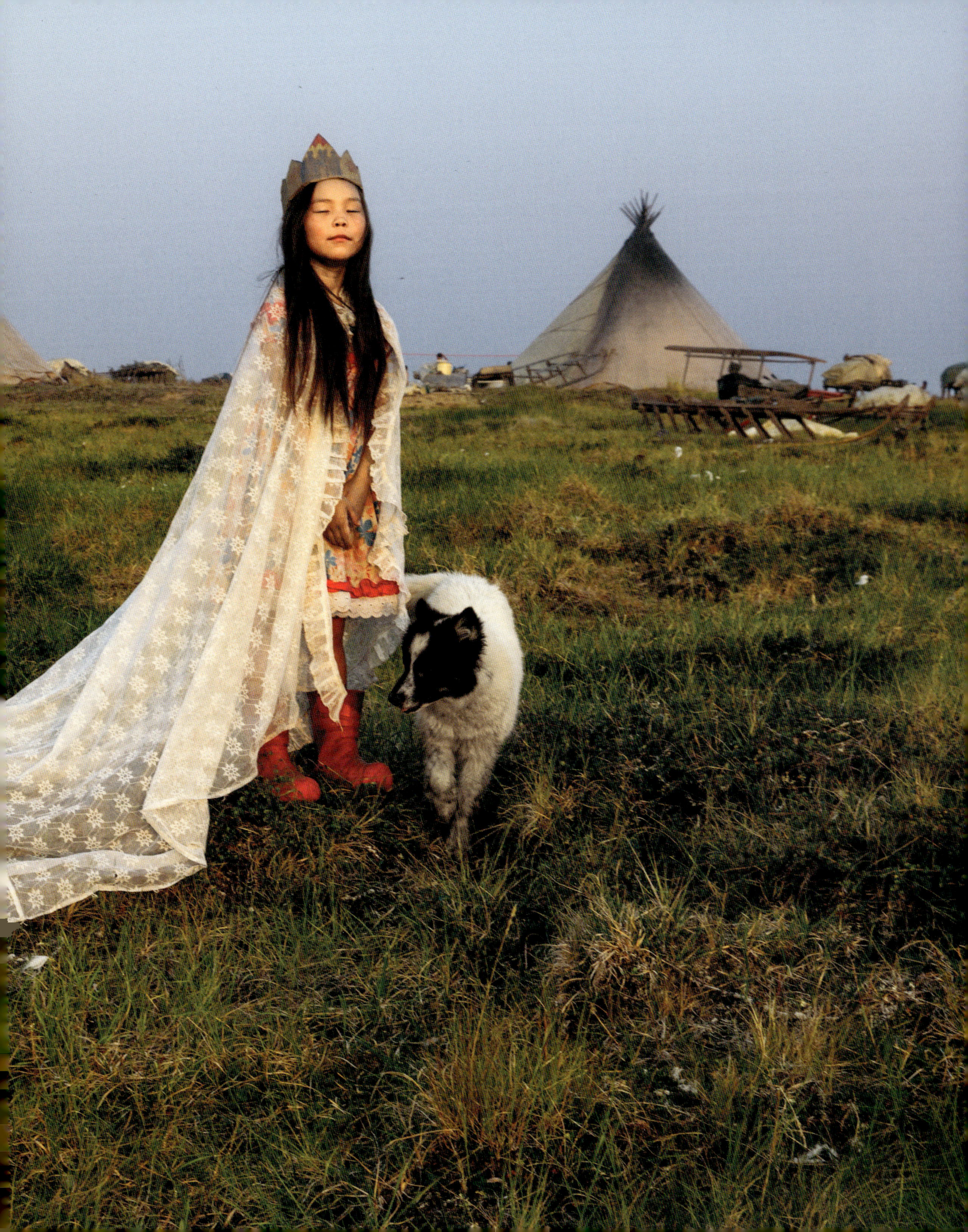

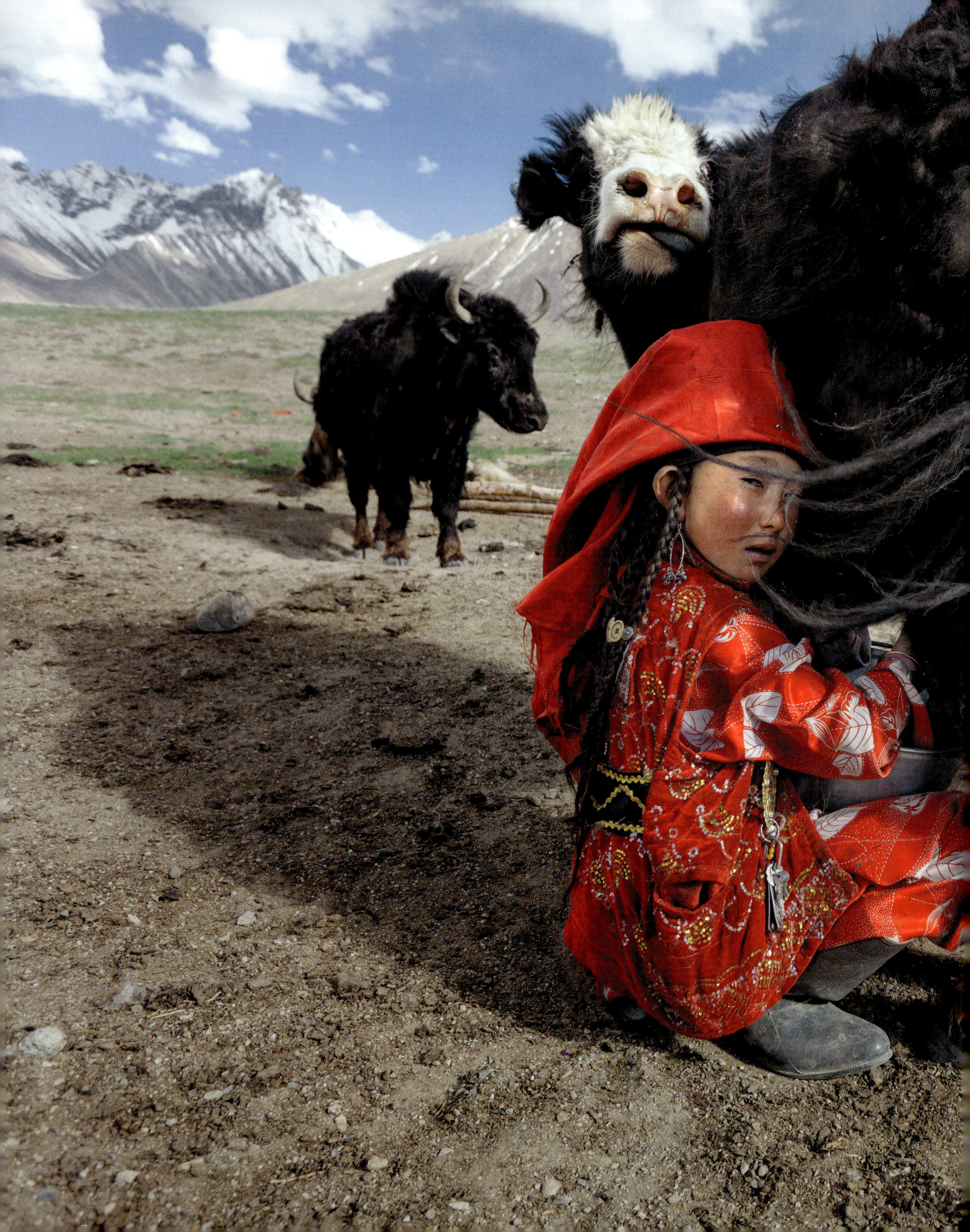

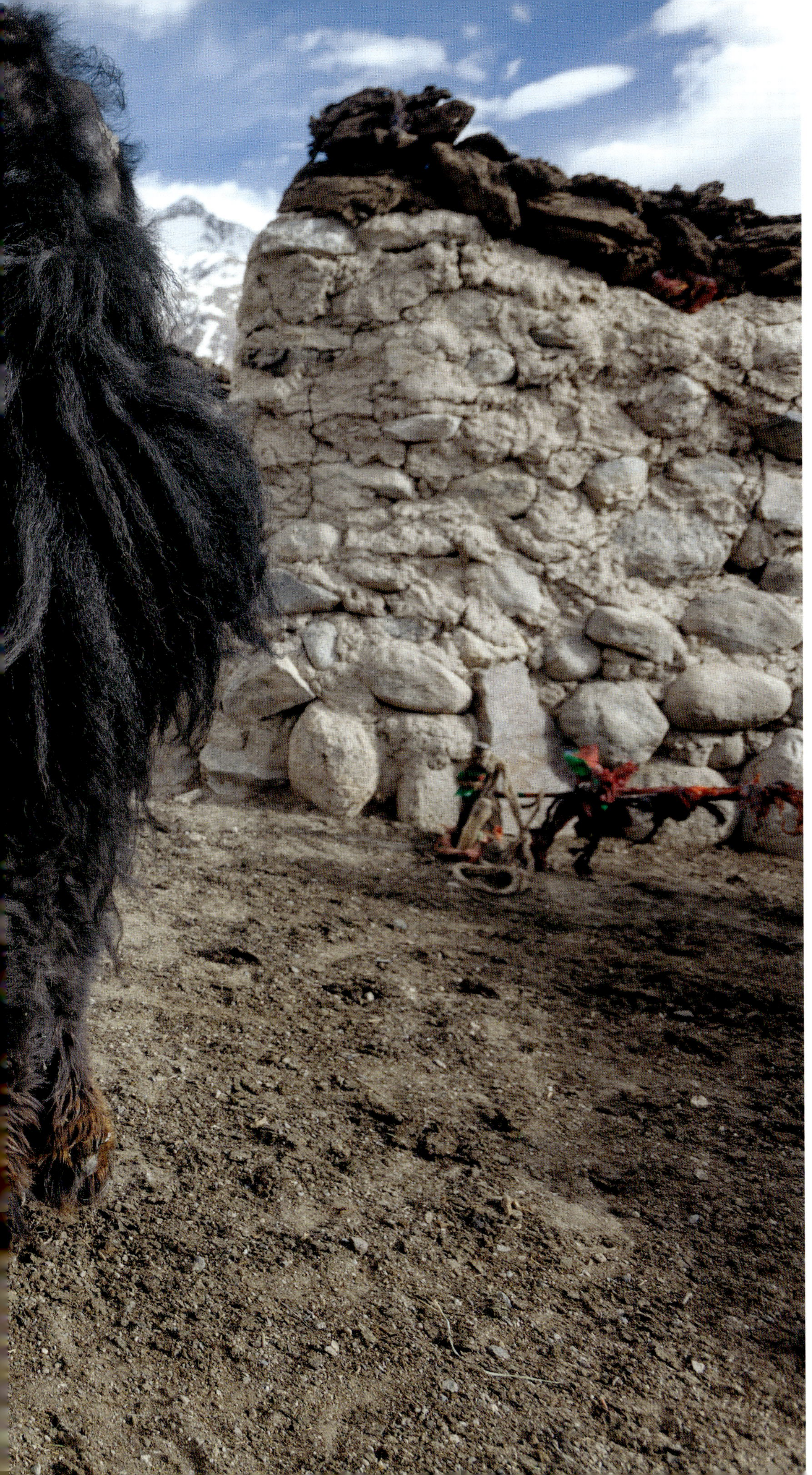

MATTHIEU PALEY, 2014
A girl in the remote Wakhan region of Afghanistan milks the family yak. A member of the nomadic Kyrgyz tribe, she and her family rely on these animals to carry their belongings and produce dung for fuel.

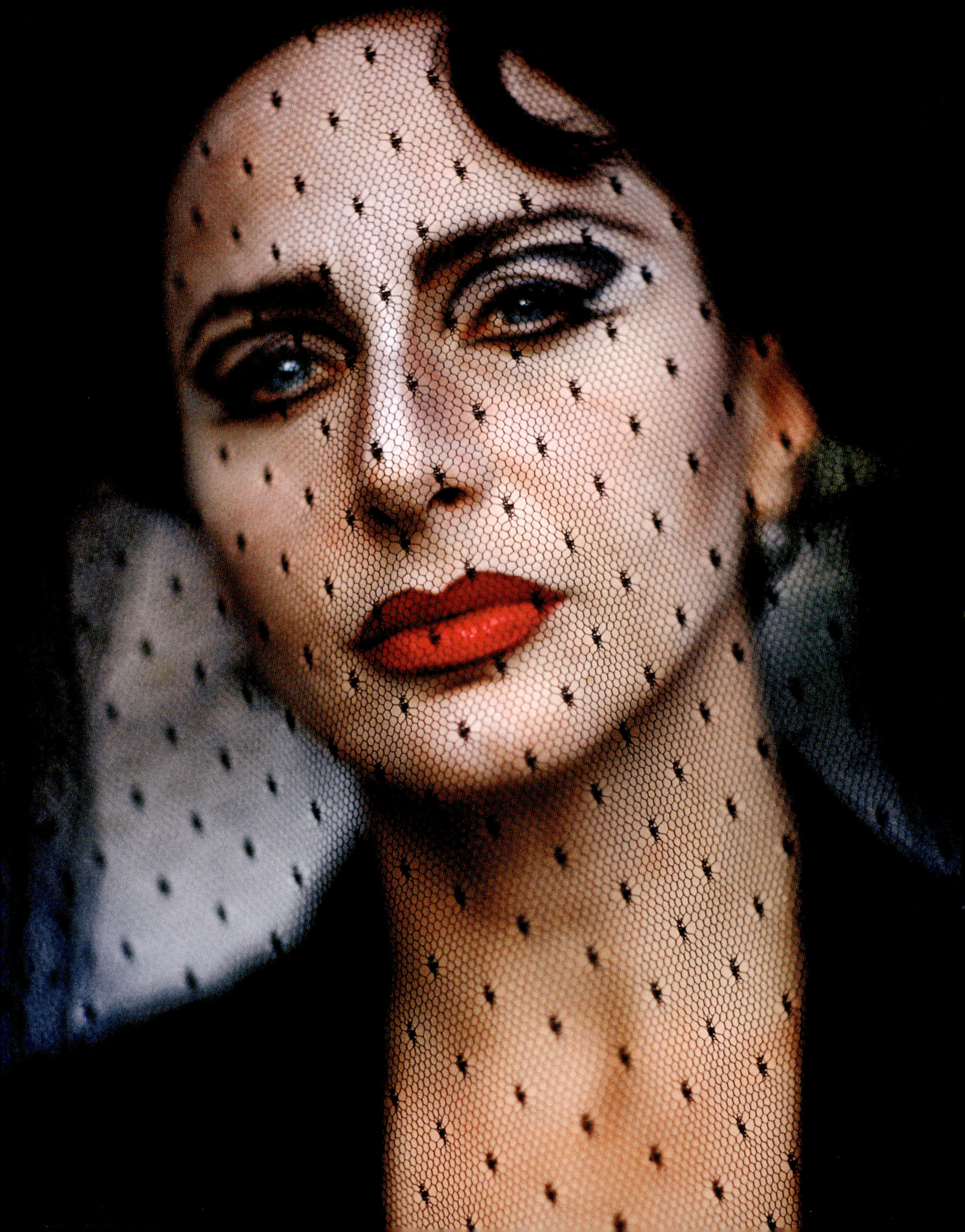

THE EXCELLENCE OF THE IMAGE IS THE HALLMARK OF NATIONAL GEOGRAPHIC.

WILLIAM ALBERT ALLARD, 1994
Italian actress Benedetta Buccellato prepares to take the stage in Syracuse, Sicily.

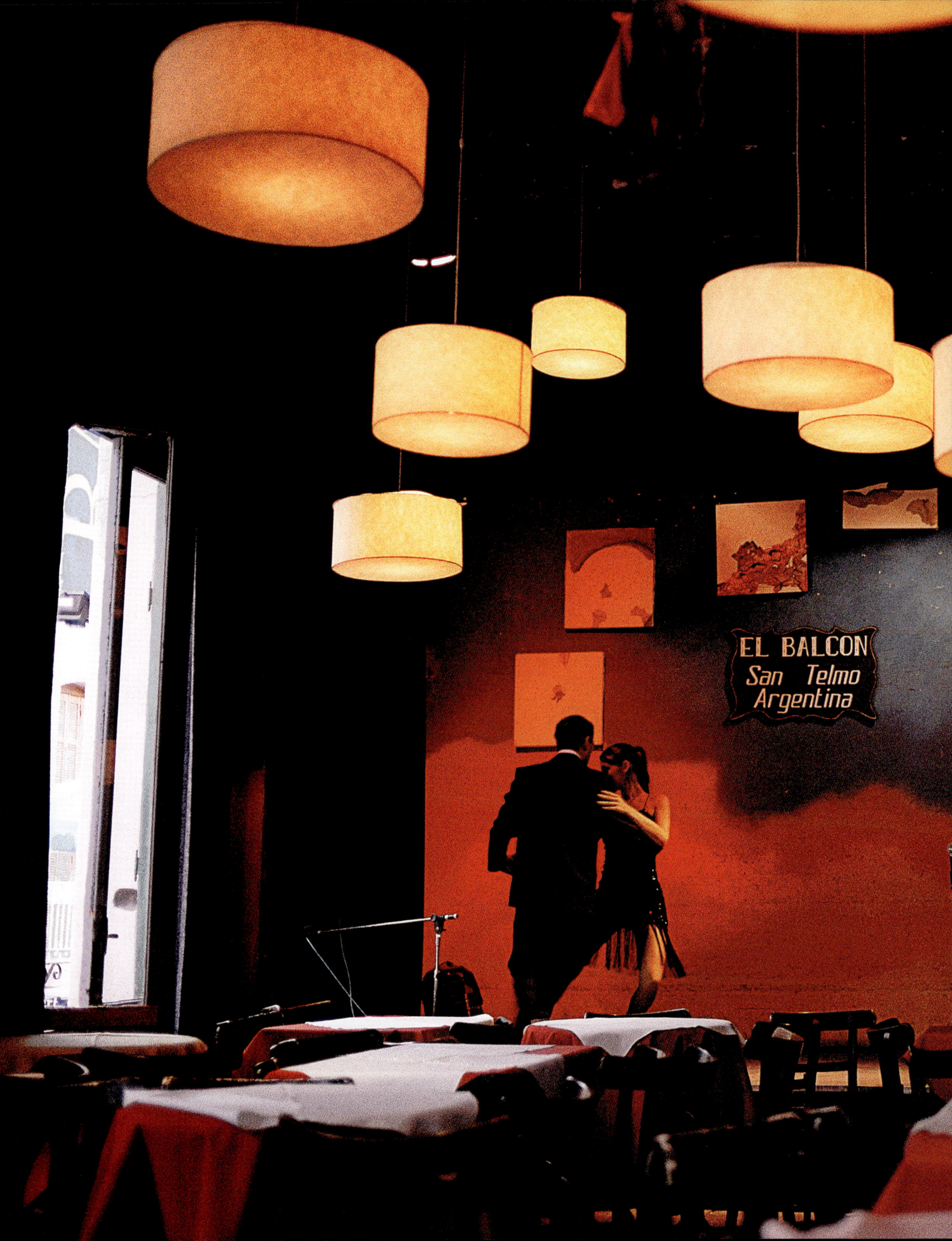
EL BALCON
San Telmo
Argentina

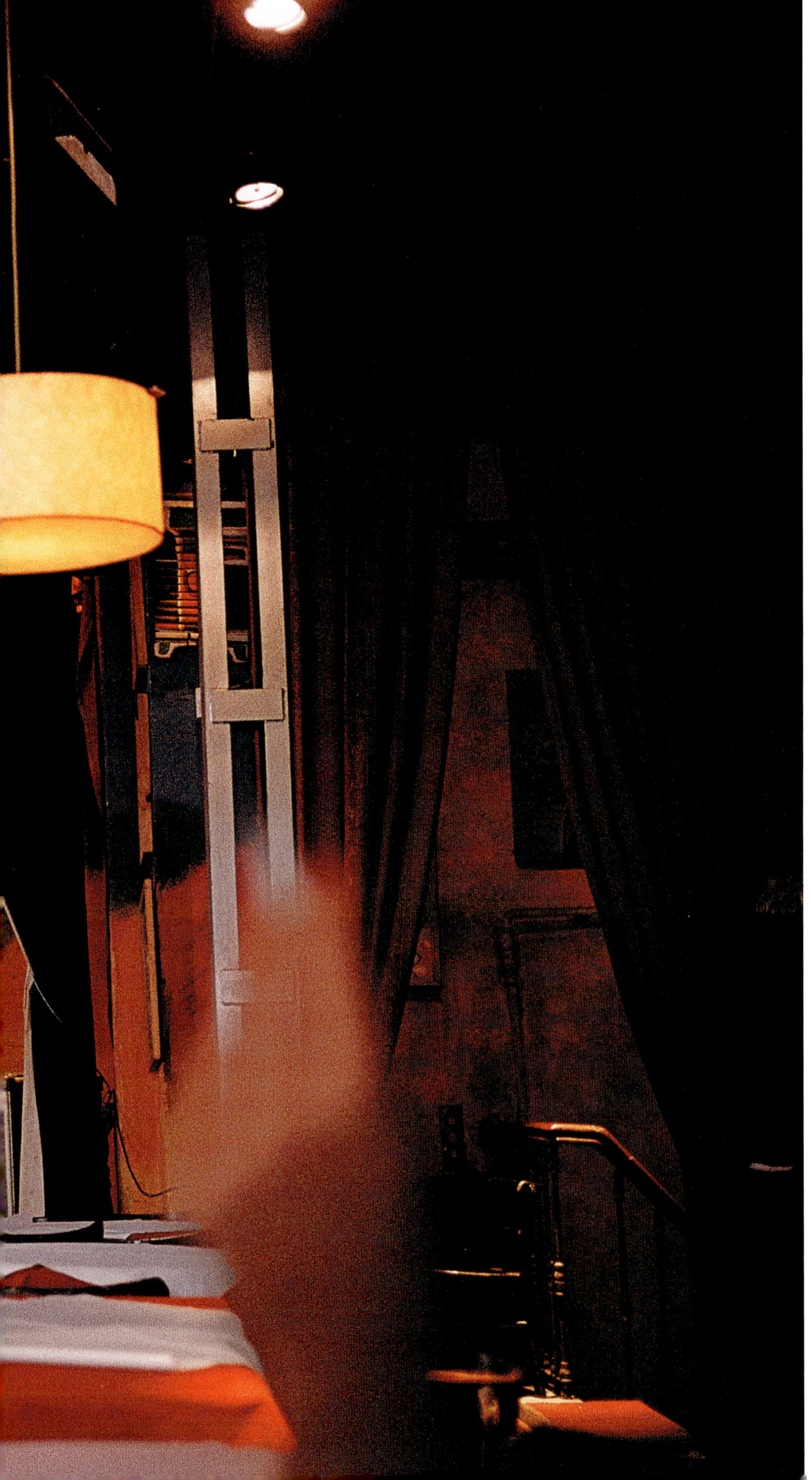

PABLO CORRAL VEGA, 2003
A couple dances the tango at a club in San Telmo, one of the oldest districts in Buenos Aires, Argentina.

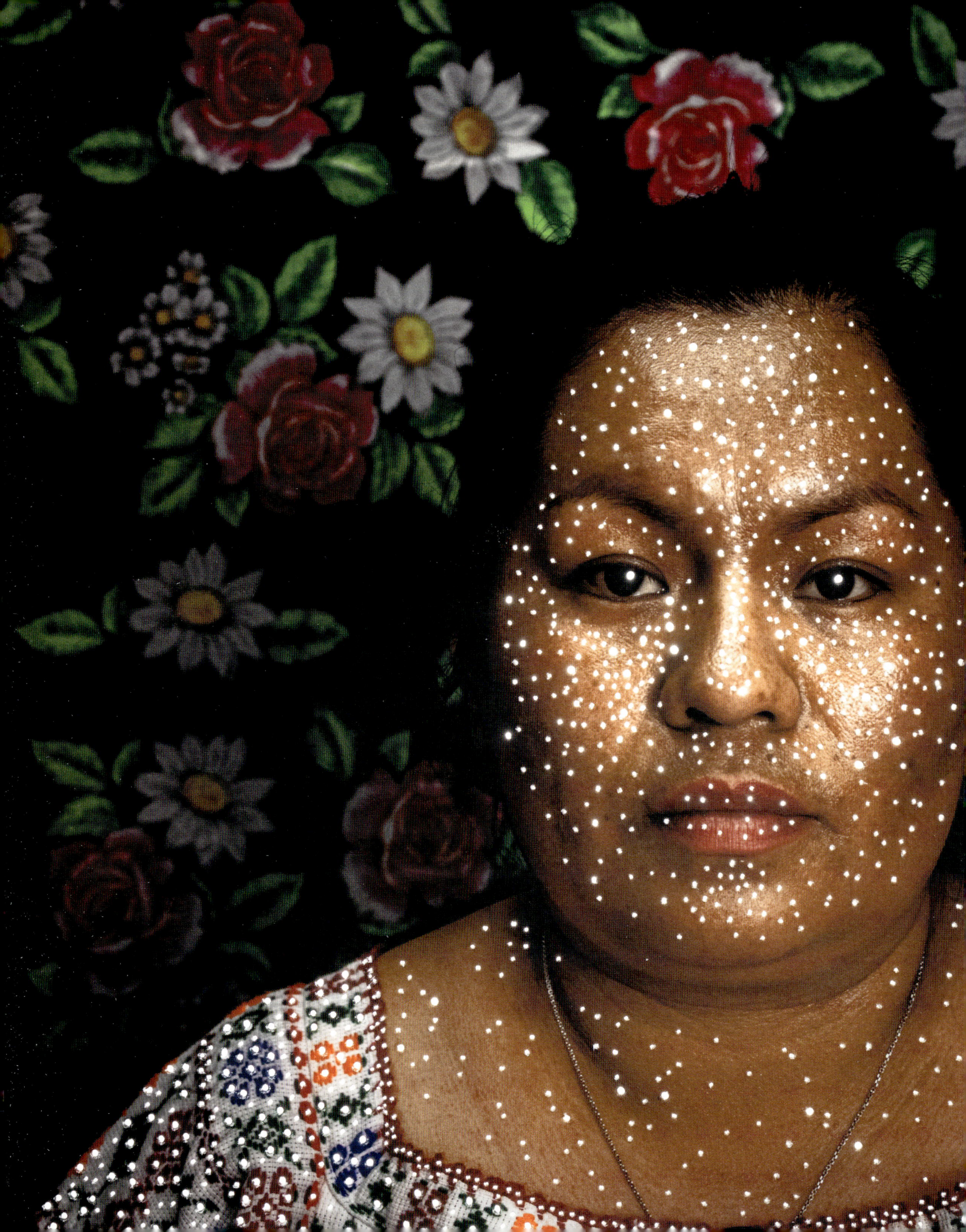

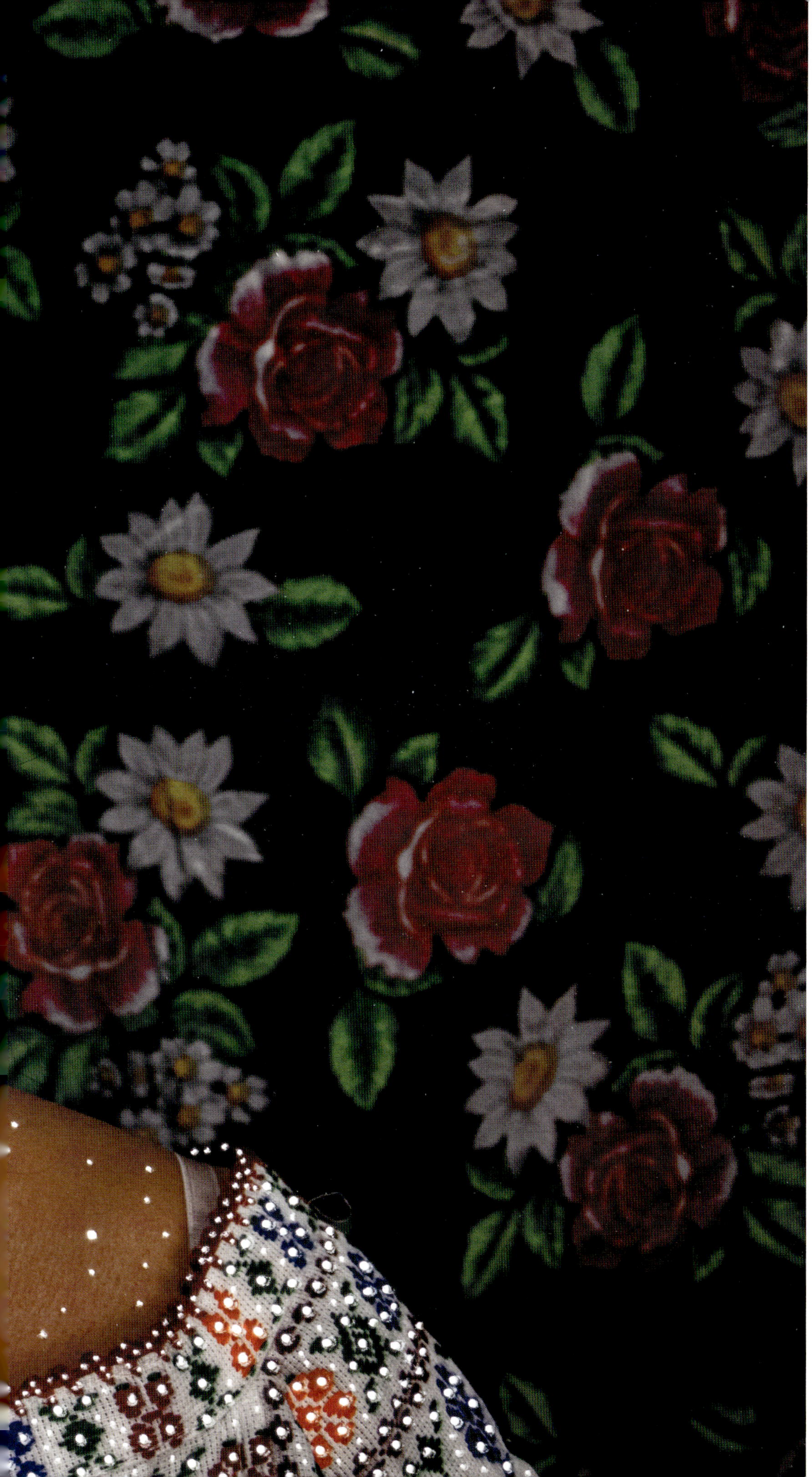

YAEL MARTÍNEZ, 2021
Joséfina Prudente Castañeda, an immigrant from the Mexican state of Guerrero living in Brooklyn, New York, has Indigenous Mixtec ancestry. The light in this image was created with pinpricks representing the violence her people have suffered.

FOLLOWING PAGES
SAMANTHA APPLETON, 2011
First Lady Michelle Obama meets with former South African president Nelson Mandela at Mandela's home in Houghton, South Africa.

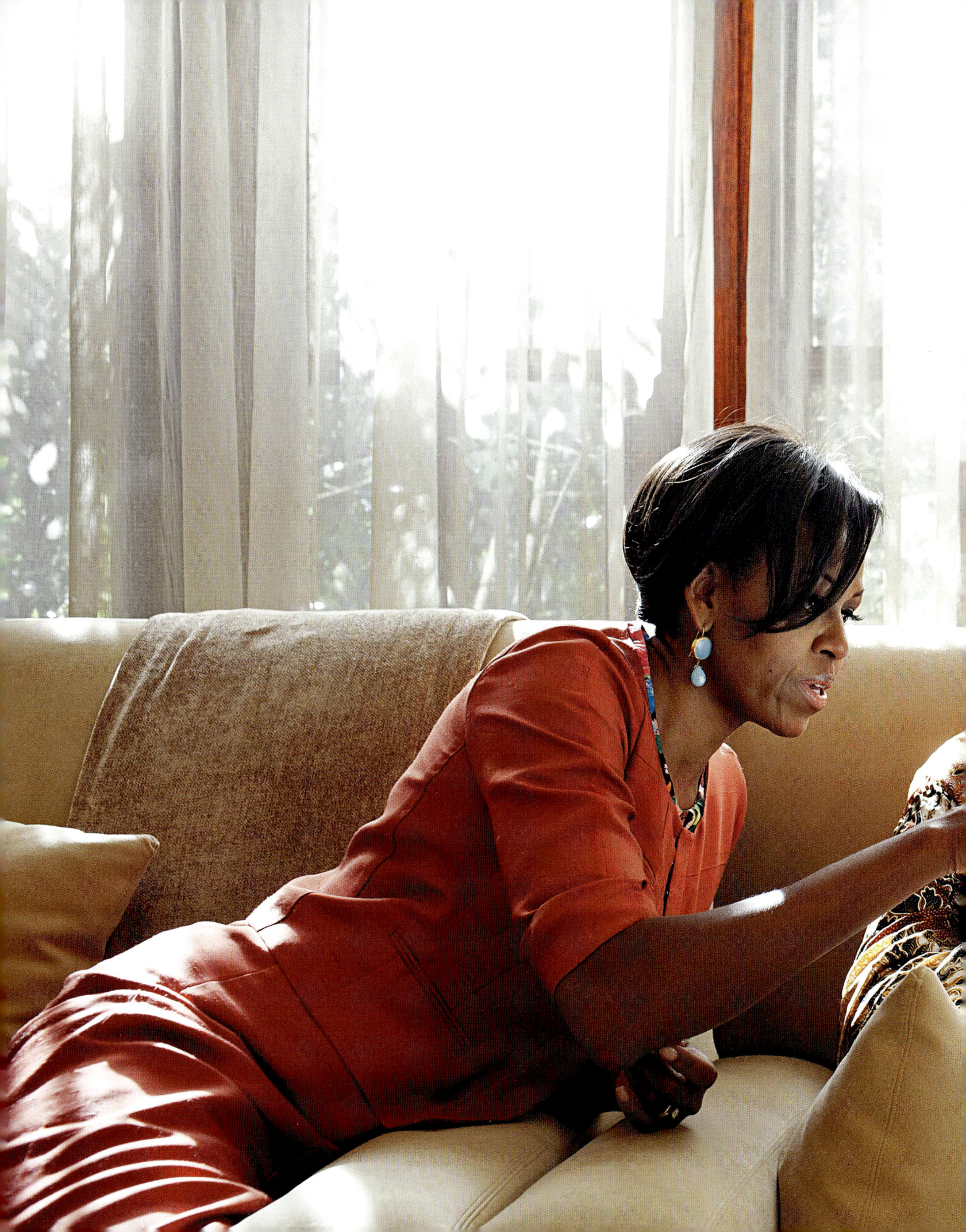

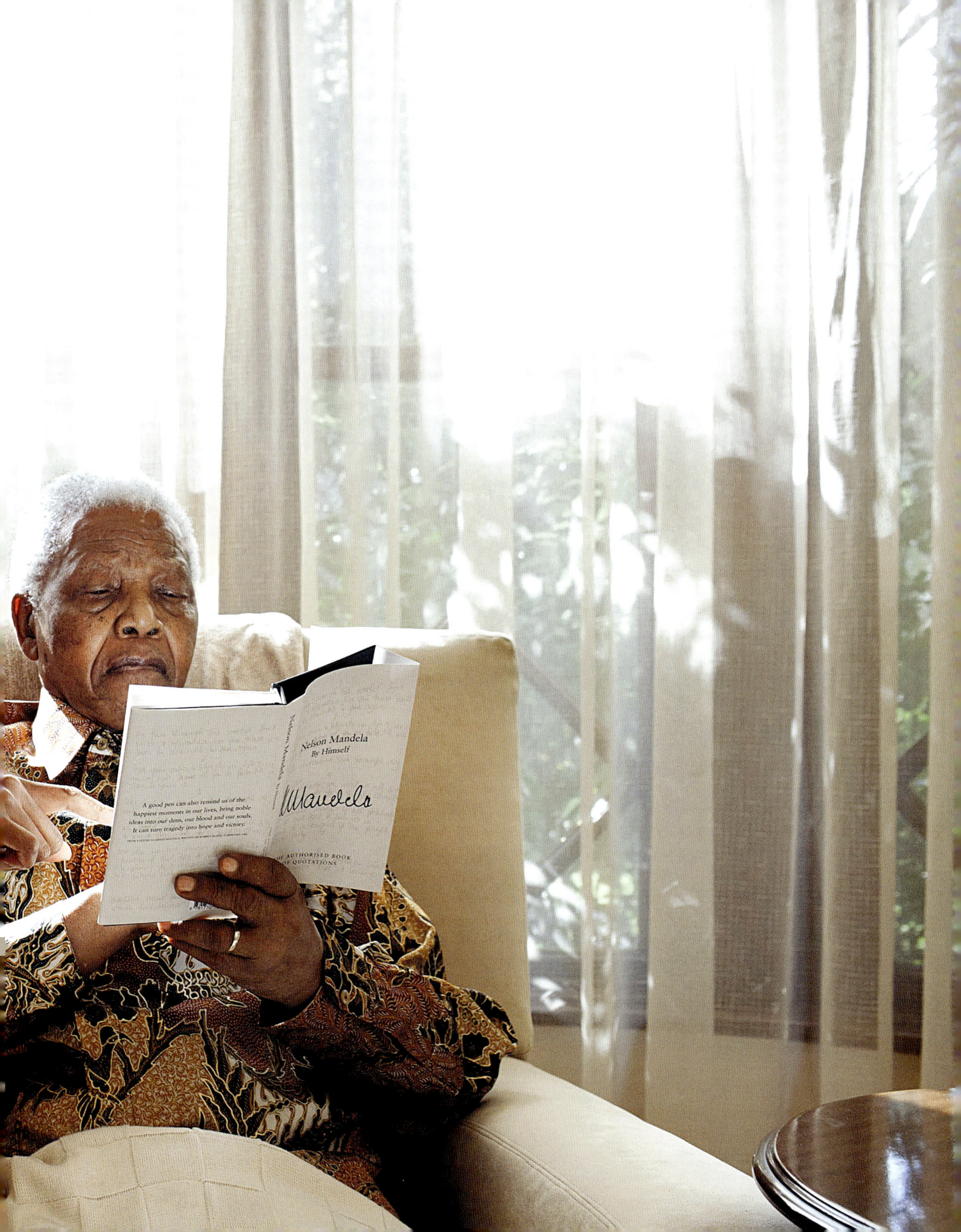
Nelson Mandela
By Himself
A good pen can also remind us of the happiest moments in our lives, bring noble ideas into our dens, our blood and our souls. It can turn tragedy into hope and victory.
AUTHORISED BOOK
QUOTATIONS

BIOGRAPHY

LYNN JOHNSON

LYNN JOHNSON OFTEN TURNS HER LENS on the shadowlands of the human condition: the struggles of ordinary people coping with extraordinary challenges, including adults with autism, children with life-threatening illnesses, and village health workers.

A photograph, she believes, is more than form, color, and composition. Photography needs—no, demands—a mission. "I think we're supposed to improve the world," she observes. She often shoots in black-and-white, which sends the message that her work is serious: Pay attention. Color, she says, can distract.

In "Hate Kills," her master's thesis project as a Knight Fellow at Ohio University, Johnson chronicled the toll of hate crimes on American society. Through the years, she has also worked with National Geographic Photo Camp, using the power of the image to help at-risk youths around the world find and share their own voices.

Johnson studied photography at the Rochester Institute of Technology, where a teacher dismissively told her to "forget it." The advice drove her harder. Among her many awards are the Robert F. Kennedy Journalism Award, World Press Photo Awards, and a Pictures of the Year International award. She was twice a finalist for a Pulitzer Prize and has been recognized by her peers at the National Geographic Photo Society.

Despite all the accolades, Johnson prefers to remain out of the frame. "The story is hopefully never about me," she says. "It's hopefully about [my subjects] and what they have to teach the world."

LYNN JOHNSON, 2015
Marine Cpl. Chris McNair (Ret.) sits on his parents' porch in Virginia. He wears a mask he made during an art therapy session to treat the brain trauma he received from blast force during the U.S. campaign in Afghanistan.

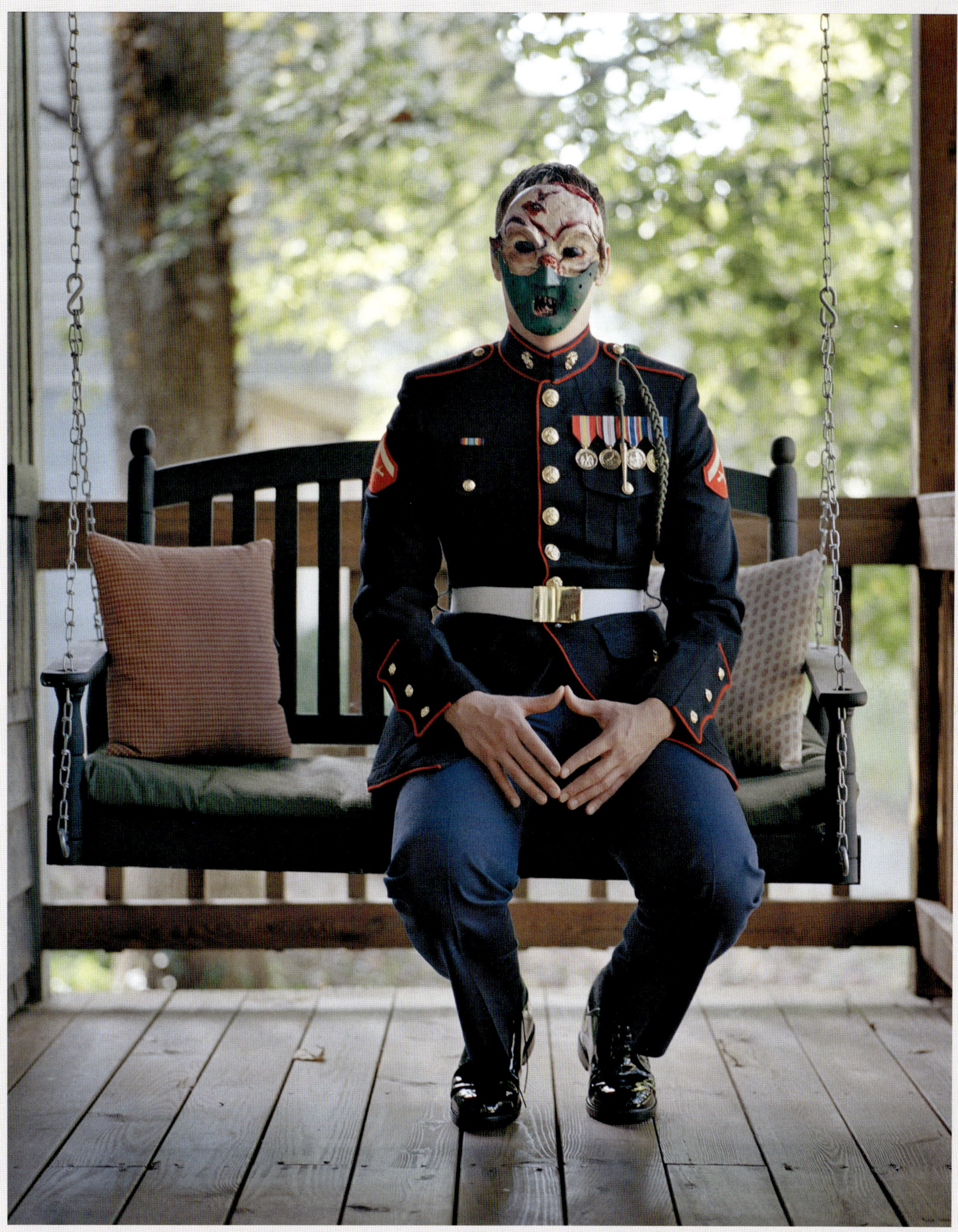

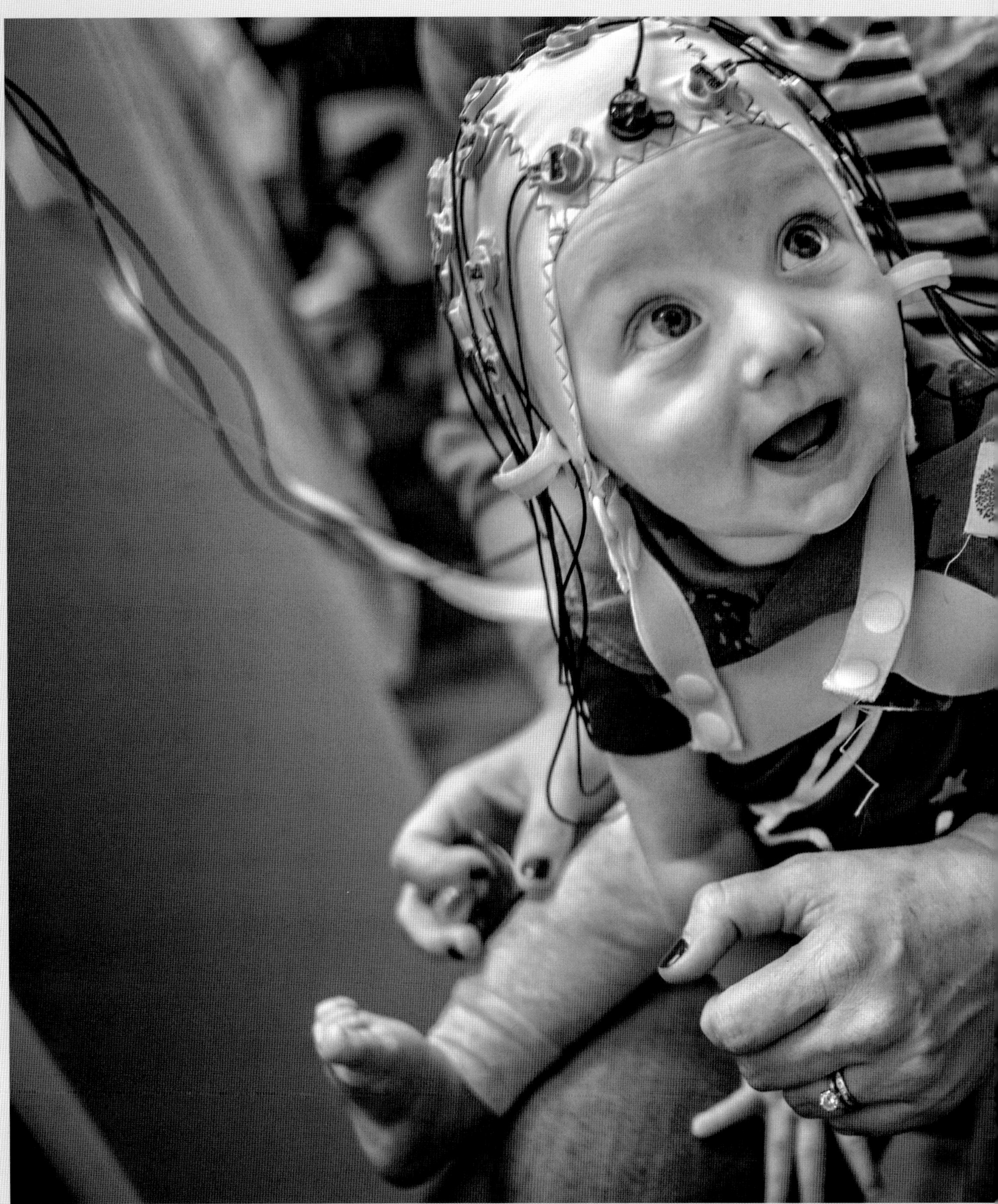

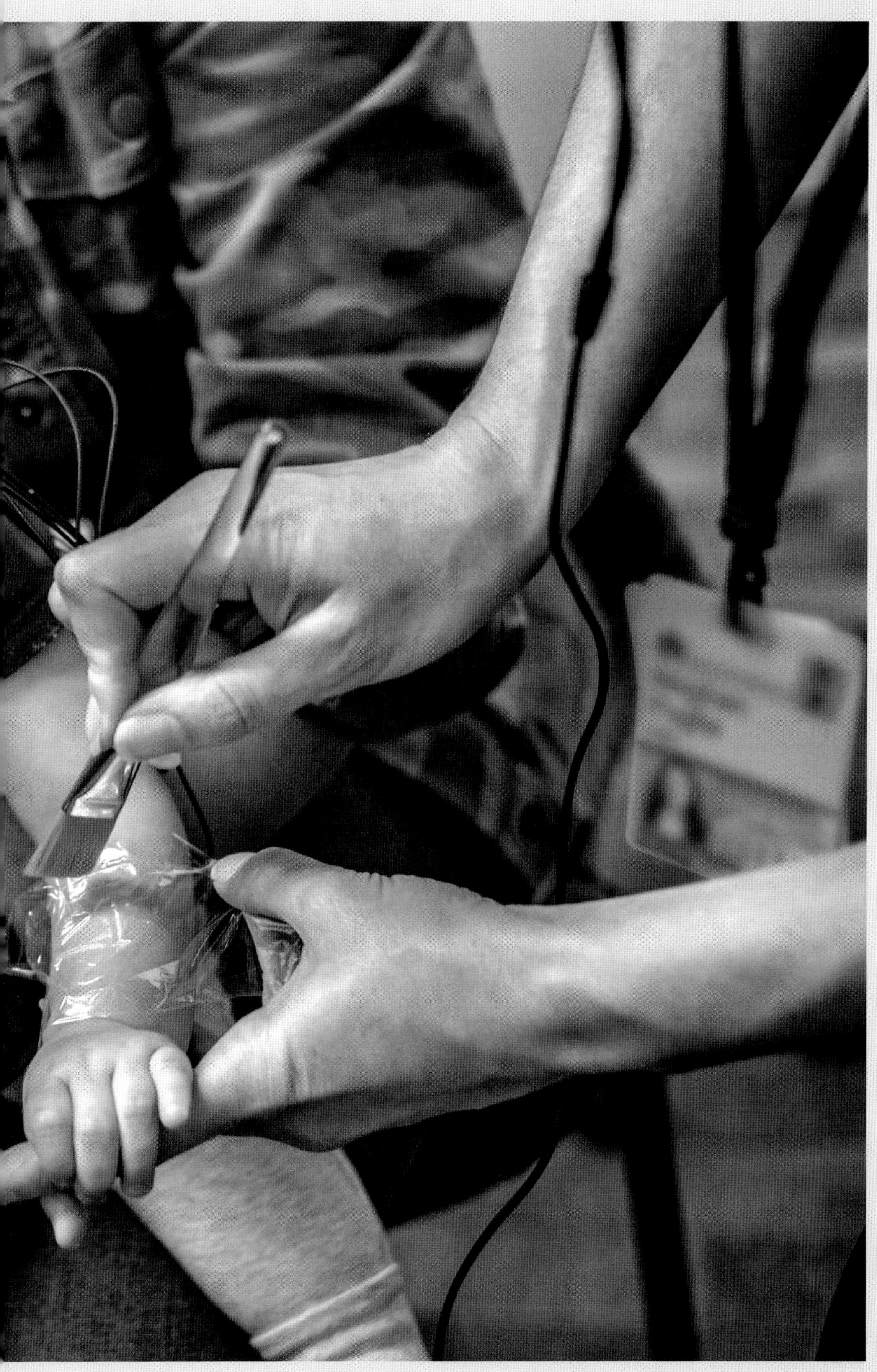

LYNN JOHNSON, 2021
Researchers at the University of Virginia brush the arm of a typically developing baby to measure the response of his CT afferents—nerve fibers that can make people feel pleasant and connected to others.

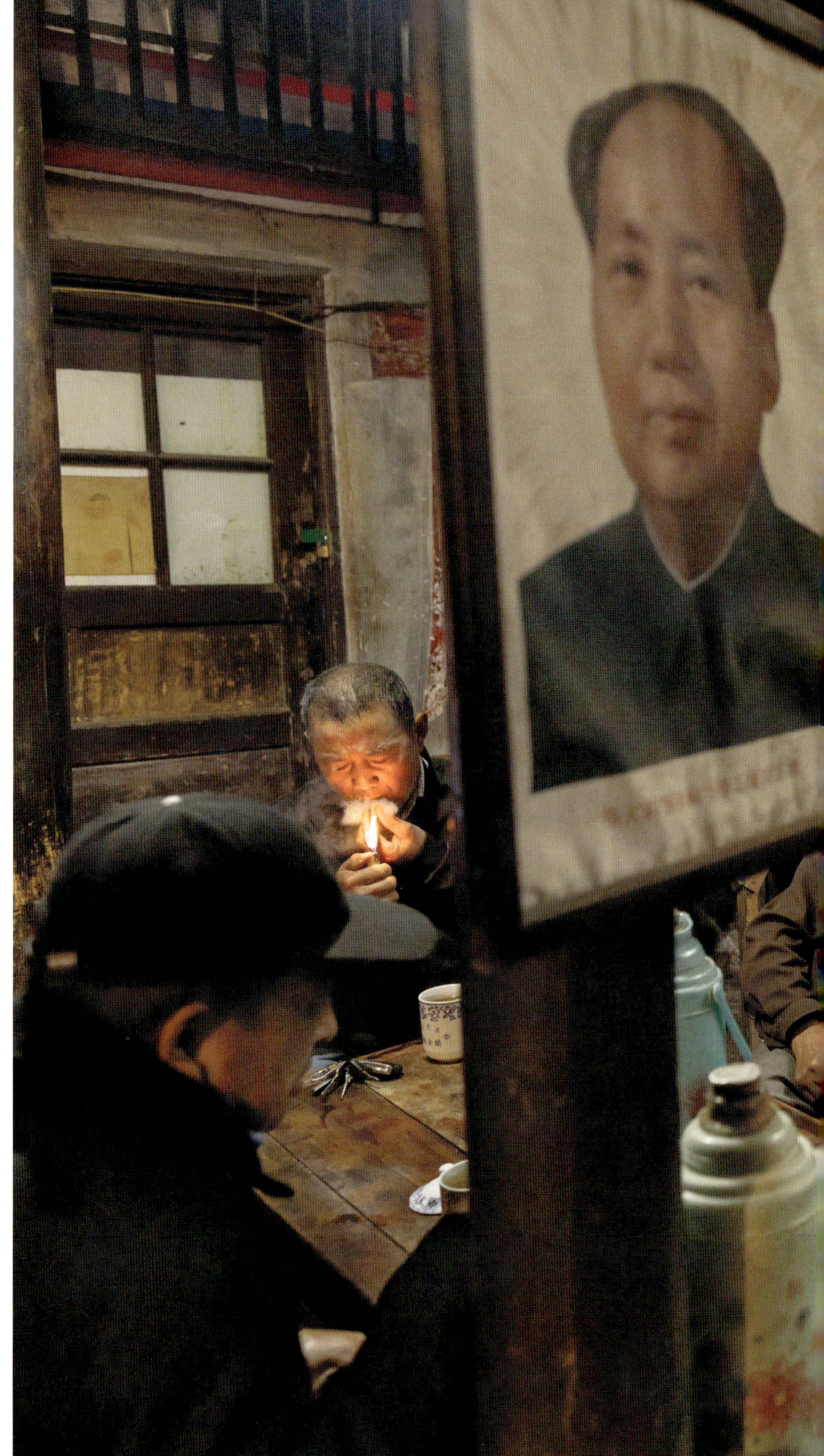

JOHN STANMEYER, 2024
Mao Zedong's portrait keeps watch over patrons at a teahouse in Pengzhen, China. This photo appears with National Geographic's Out of Eden Walk initiative, in which writer Paul Salopek retraces the footsteps of the first humans to migrate out of Africa. Salopek's journey took him along the path traveled by the Chinese Red Army during the Long March of 1934–35.

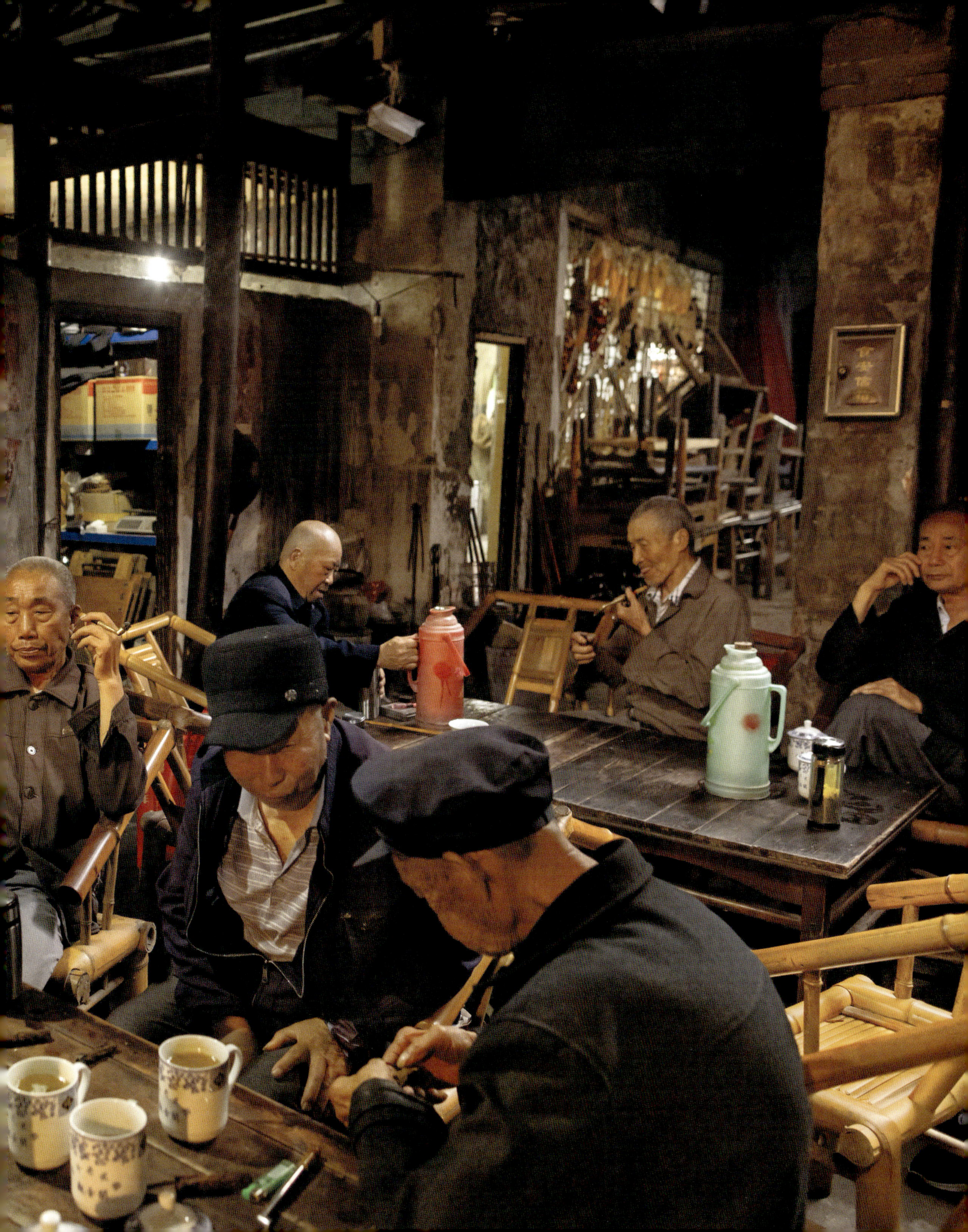

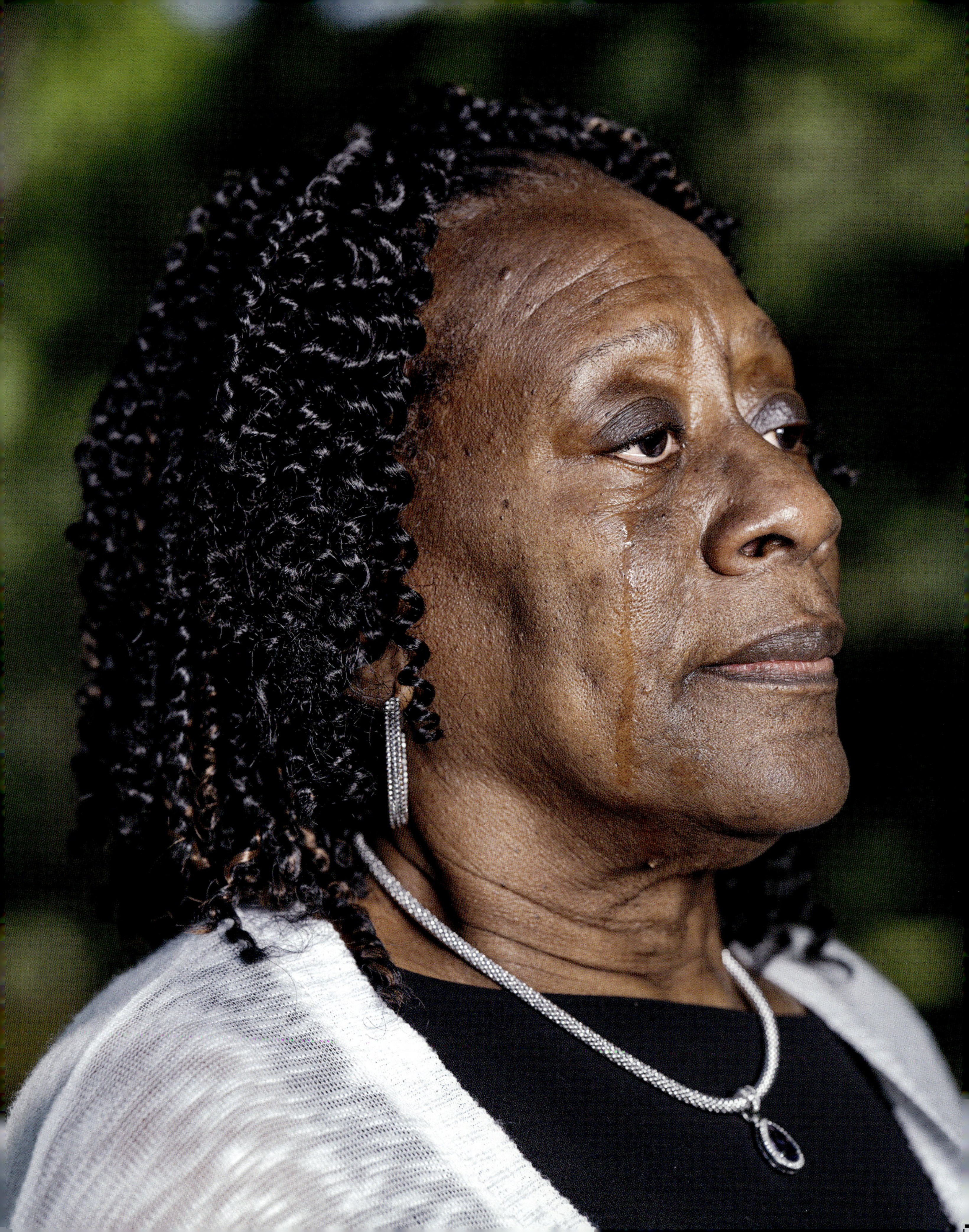

THE HUMAN FACE IS THE UNIVERSAL LANGUAGE.

DOROTHEA LANGE, PHOTOJOURNALIST

WAYNE LAWRENCE, 2021
In April 2021, Elaine Fields of Detroit, Michigan, stands by her husband's grave. Fields lost her husband, Eddie, and her mother-in-law, Leona, to complications from Covid-19.

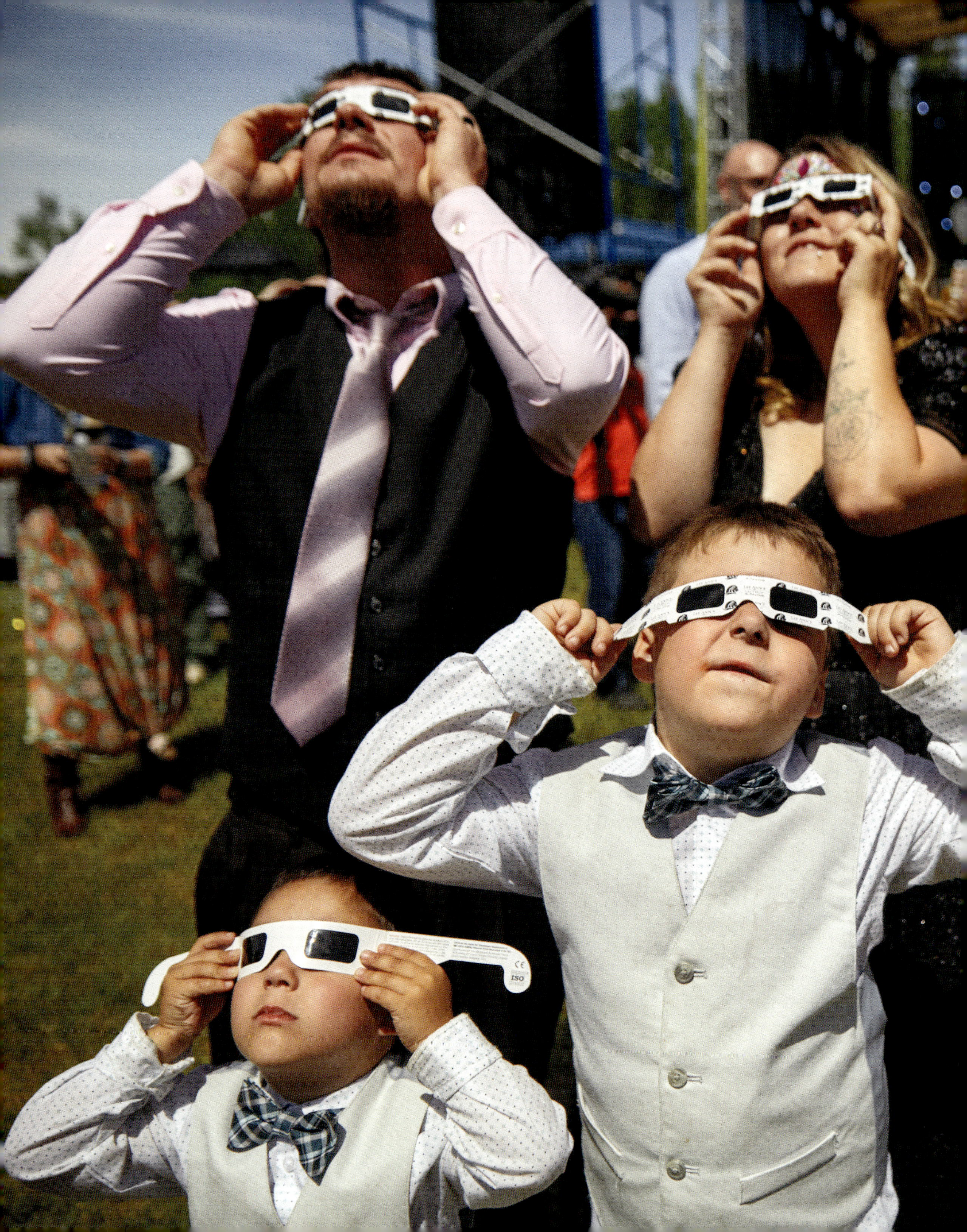
CE
ISO

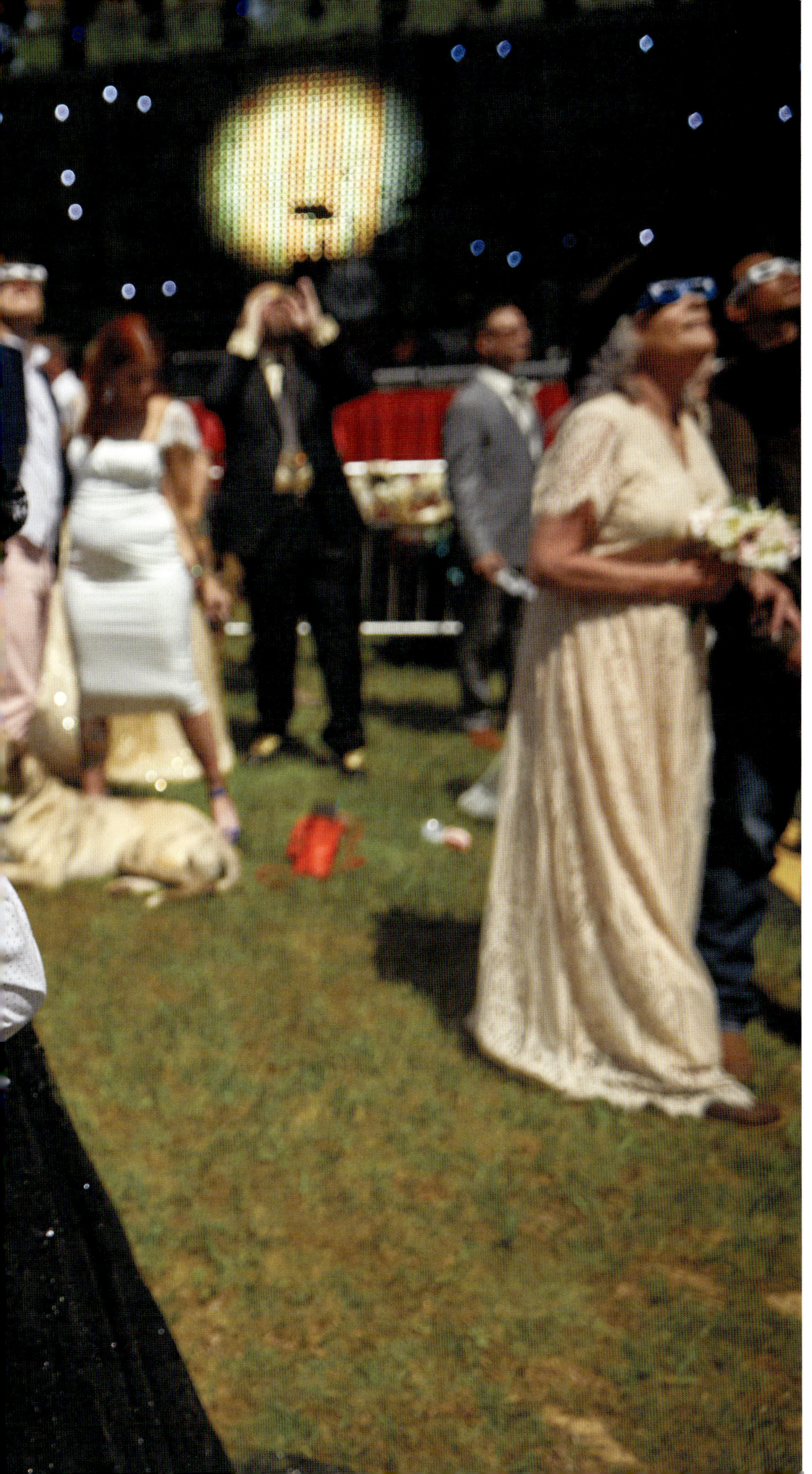

AARON HUEY, 2024
A family gazes upward while attending the mass wedding celebration Elope at the Eclipse in Russellville, Arkansas.

FOLLOWING PAGES
AARON HUEY, 2011
A Lakota *heyoka* (sacred clown) burns sage to ritually purify his surroundings in South Dakota.

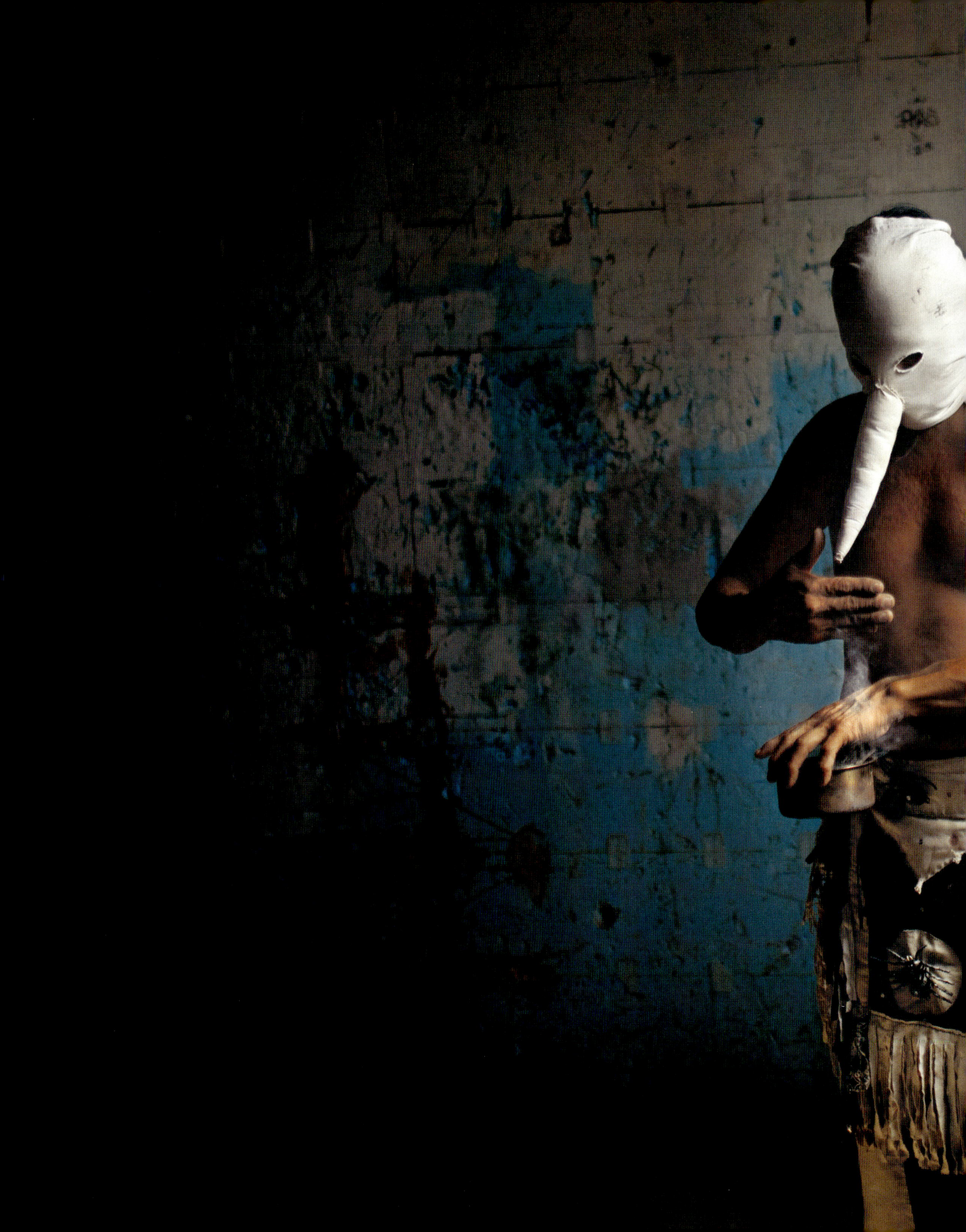

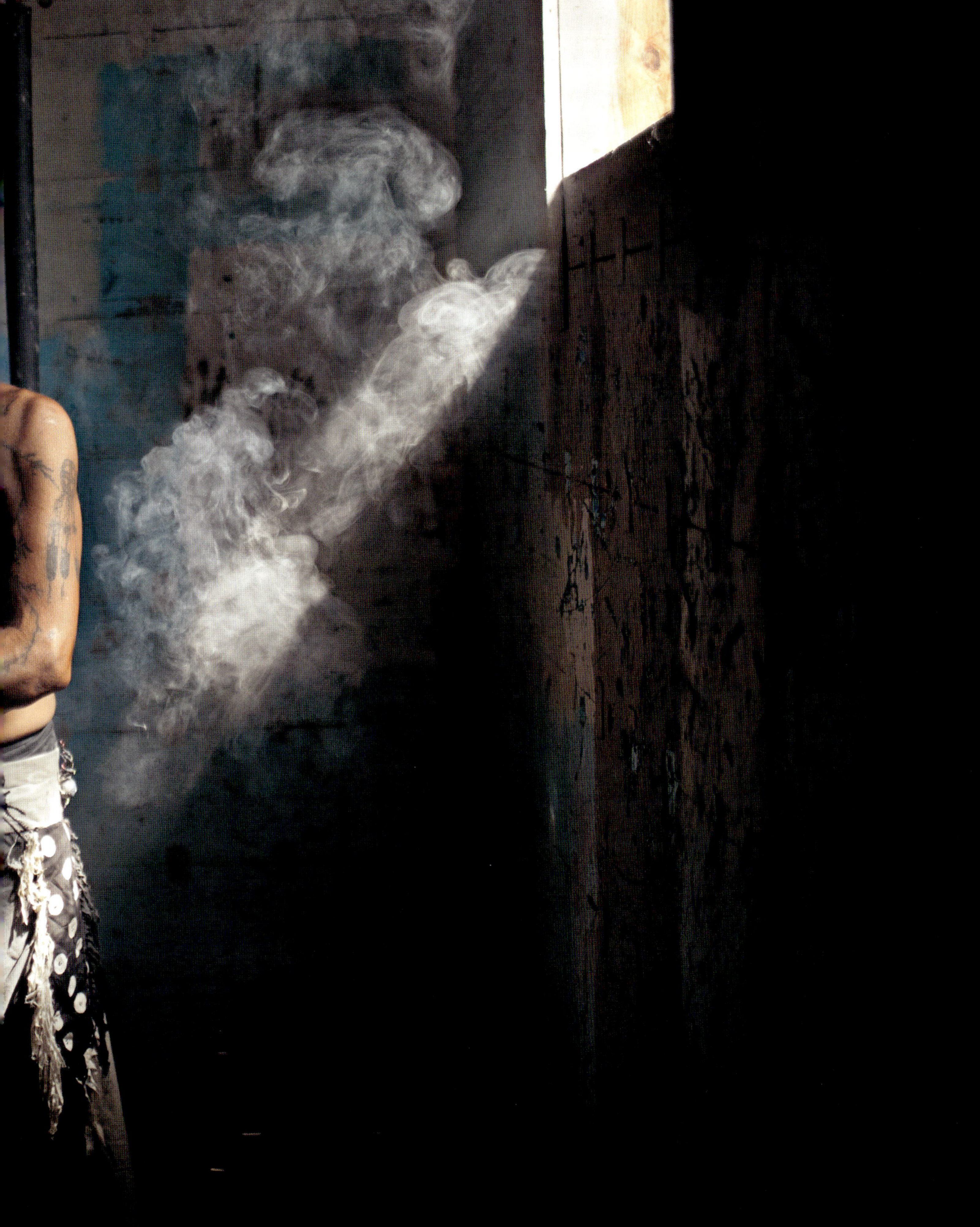

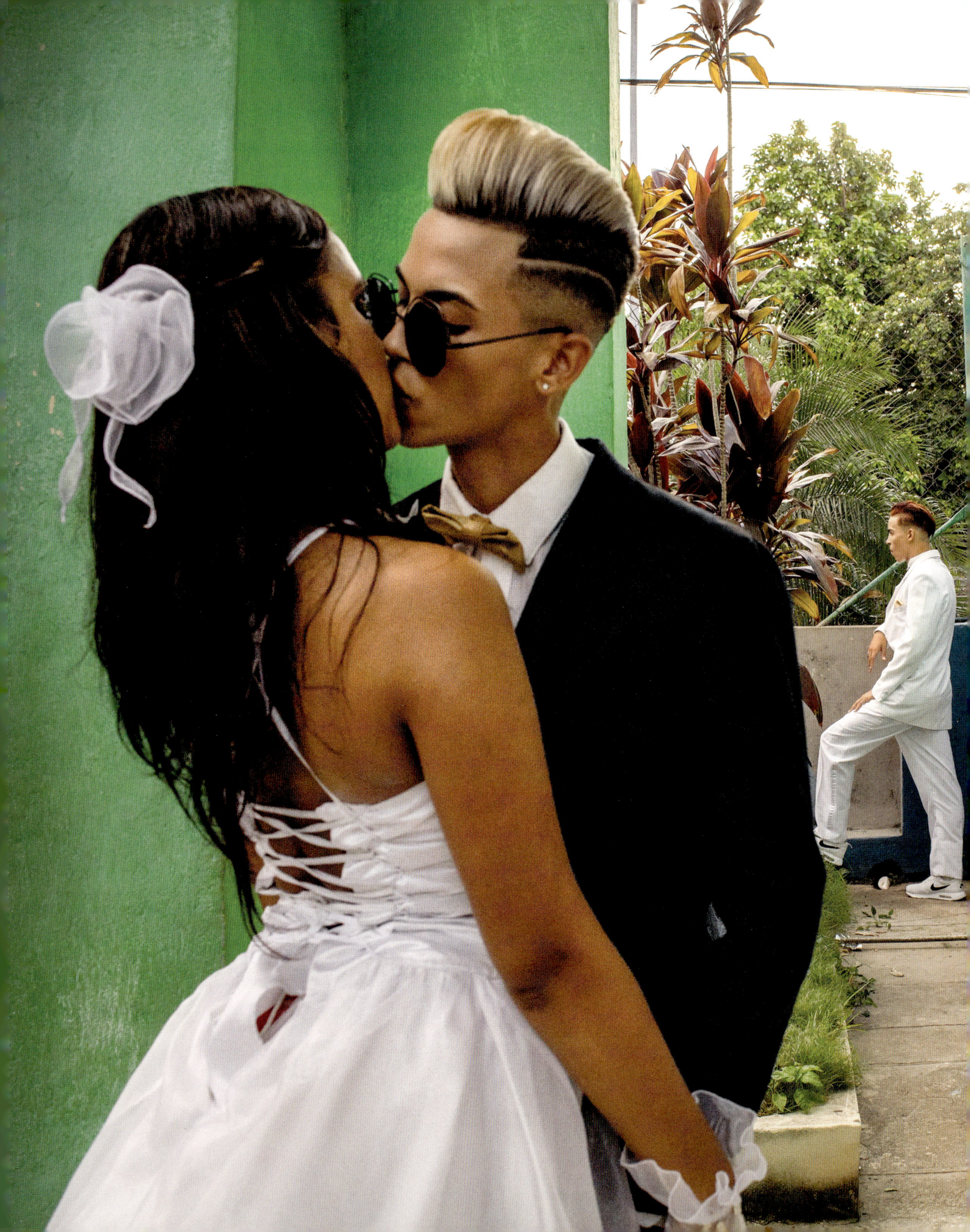

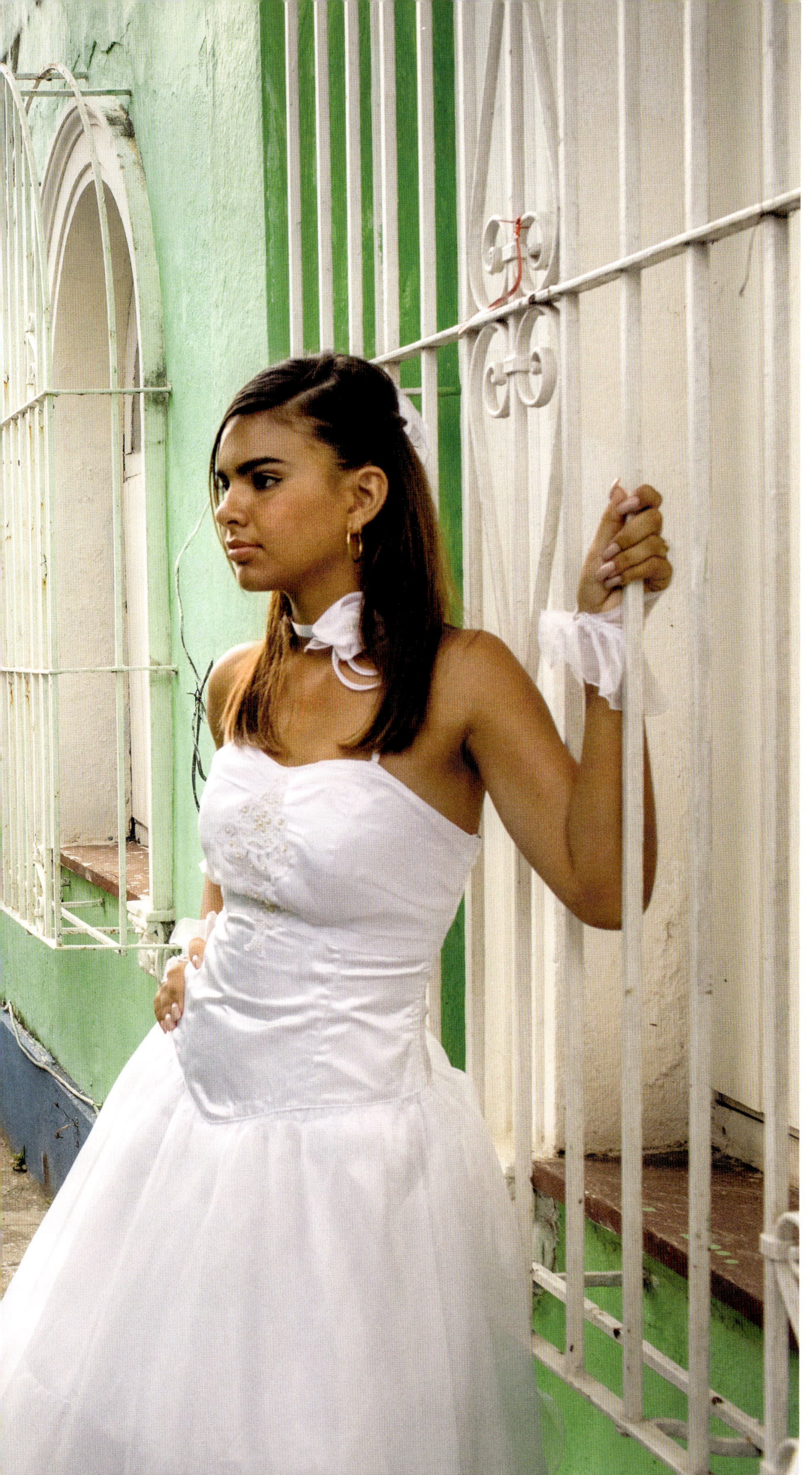

DIANA MARKOSIAN, 2023
Teenagers await the beginning of their friend's quinceañera in Havana, Cuba. This rite of passage, celebrated on a girl's 15th birthday, is common in many Latin American cultures.

FOLLOWING PAGES
CAROLYN DRAKE, 2010
A novice shaman makes an offering of milk to the spirits at her initiation outside Ulaanbaatar, Mongolia.

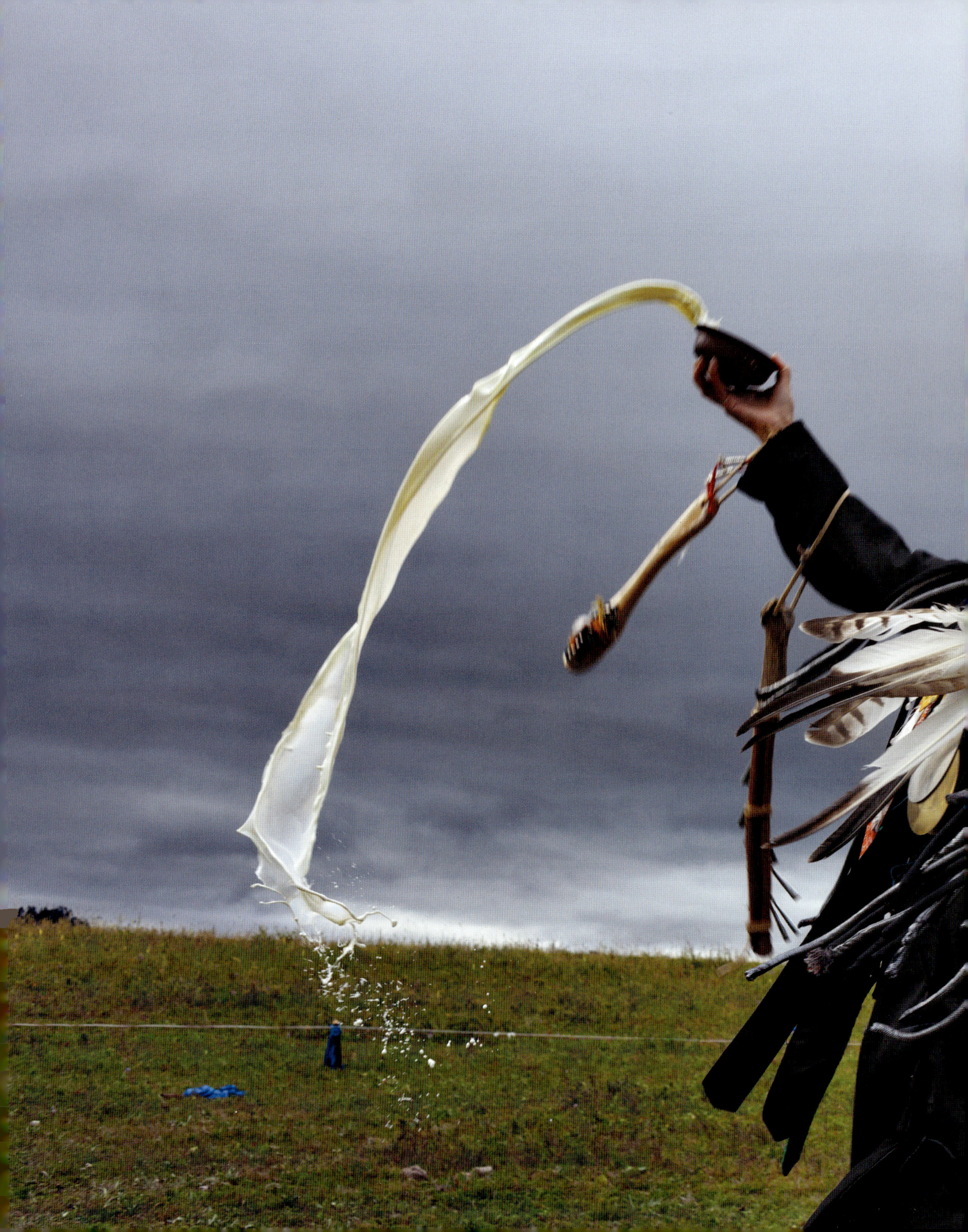

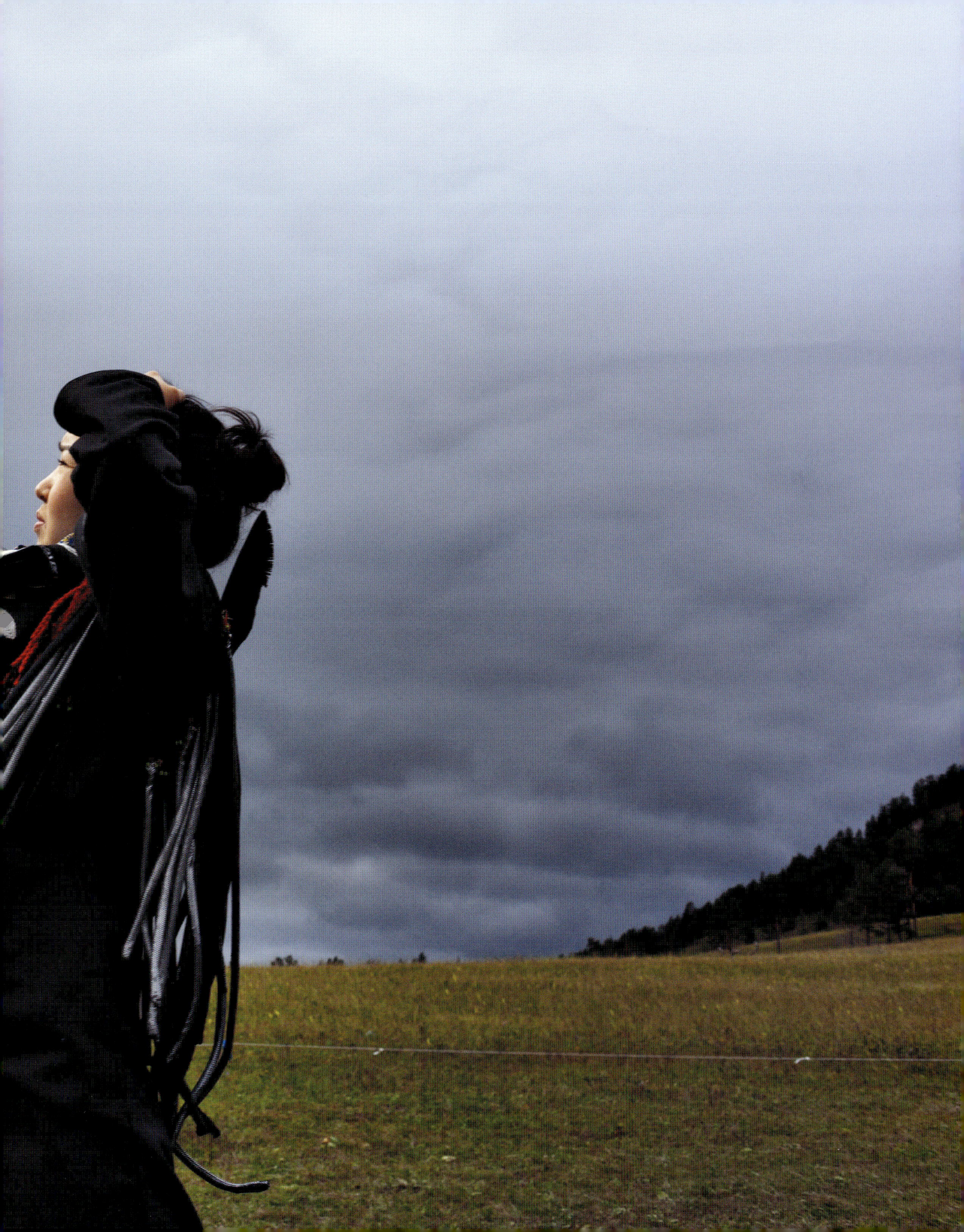

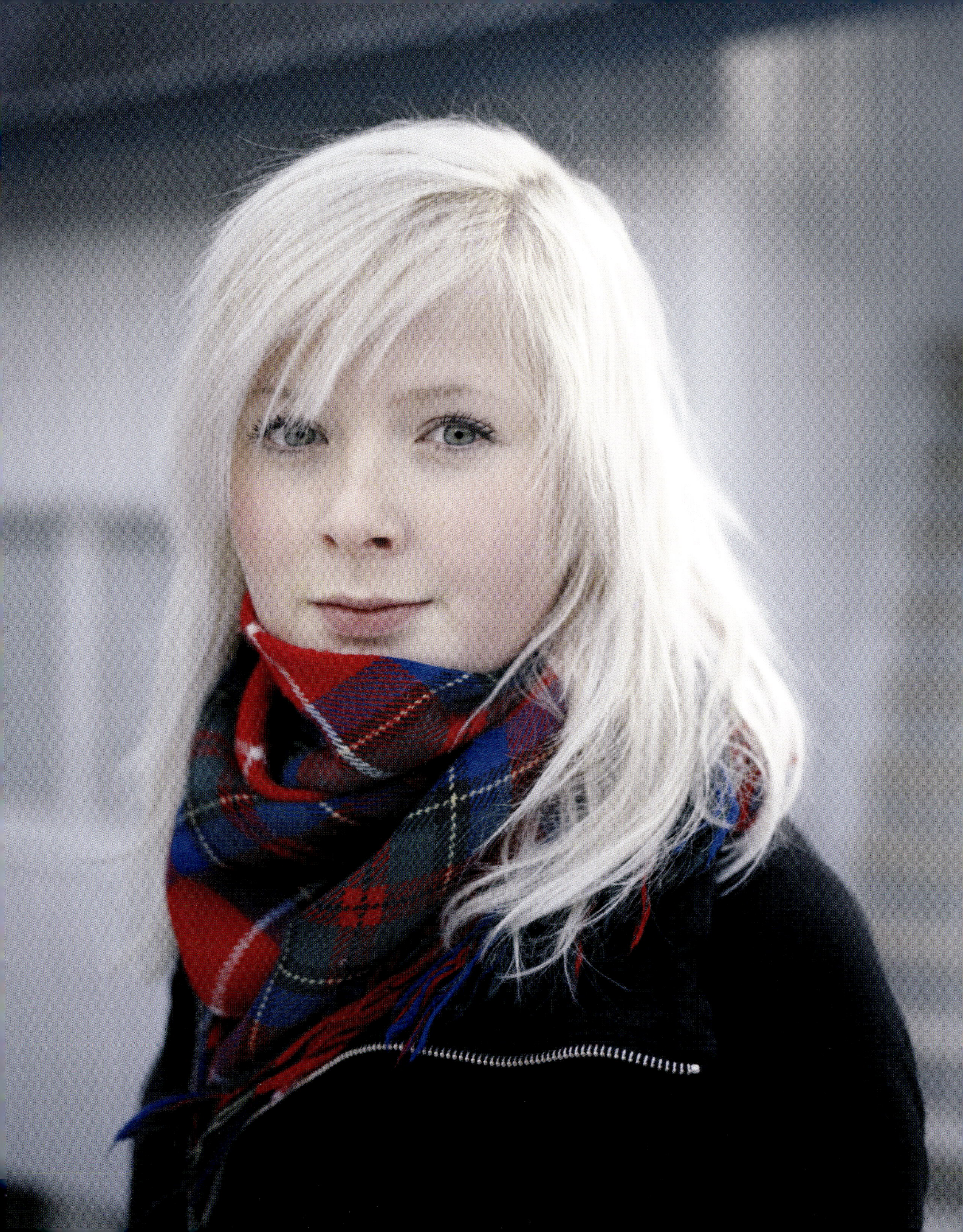

IN CONVERSATION WITH

ERIKA LARSEN

Erika Larsen is known for photographing cultures that maintain close ties with nature. For years-long projects like following Sami reindeer herders across the Scandinavian Arctic and exploring the significance of the horse in Native American culture, Larsen immerses herself in the languages, beliefs, and rituals of other peoples to gain a deeper sensitivity into our unique ways of being. She sees storytelling as a shared exchange, opening her life in the process, building intimate relationships, and forging transcendent connections through time and space. Larsen has been a Fulbright Fellow and is currently a National Geographic Explorer.

NATIONAL GEOGRAPHIC: What kind of stories do you gravitate to and why?

ERIKA LARSEN: I've always been interested in the way that we relate to the natural world and what it means to be human. That, in turn, relates a lot to consciousness: What it means to be connected to everything that we think and feel, how we process information, and how we deal with the unknown. This word is hard to define, but I think I'm really attracted to magic—our ability to control and also to not control.

From a really young age, I looked at the natural world around me. I was driven by nature, the cosmos, by the stars. We are nature, but if you take a step back, nature can teach you a lot about the cycles of being human.

NG: How do you think of the camera in the context of those kinds of stories?

EL: I remember when I was very young, my dad, who worked on the Hubble Space Telescope, brought home some of the early pictures. I held Saturn in my hands on Kodak paper. And I thought to myself, Wow, how is this even possible? The photograph brings something so far away so close.

The camera's changed as I've changed; it's an extension of how I interact with the stories or in the world. That is now very different than 25 years ago. But after all these years, I still think to myself, This is magic. The camera's magic. How is that moment in time on a literal piece of paper or in the digital realm?

NG: Do you remember when you first held a camera?

EL: In middle school, the photography class was in a small section of the metalworking shop. We made pinhole cameras there from oatmeal boxes or something like that. I remember flipping myself upside down to take a picture of someone else in the class, which is interesting because for the majority of my career, I've used a large-format camera where everything's upside down because there's no mirror inside.

NG: How does shooting in a large format affect your process?

EL: I take very few photographs. I generally use a 4 × 5 camera, so in a given situation, I'll often take two frames and that's about it. It's very slow. And with that kind of photography, when you're deciding that you're going to be a part of a story, it takes a deep listening. That allows you to connect, and the story becomes alive. You can smell the past, you can hear the future, you can feel a space. I love it.

NG: You spend a long time on your stories. You

ERIKA LARSEN, 2008
Ella-Li Spik of Jokkmokk, Sweden, is a member of the Indigenous Sami tribe, which makes its home across Scandinavia and Russia. She grew up herding reindeer.

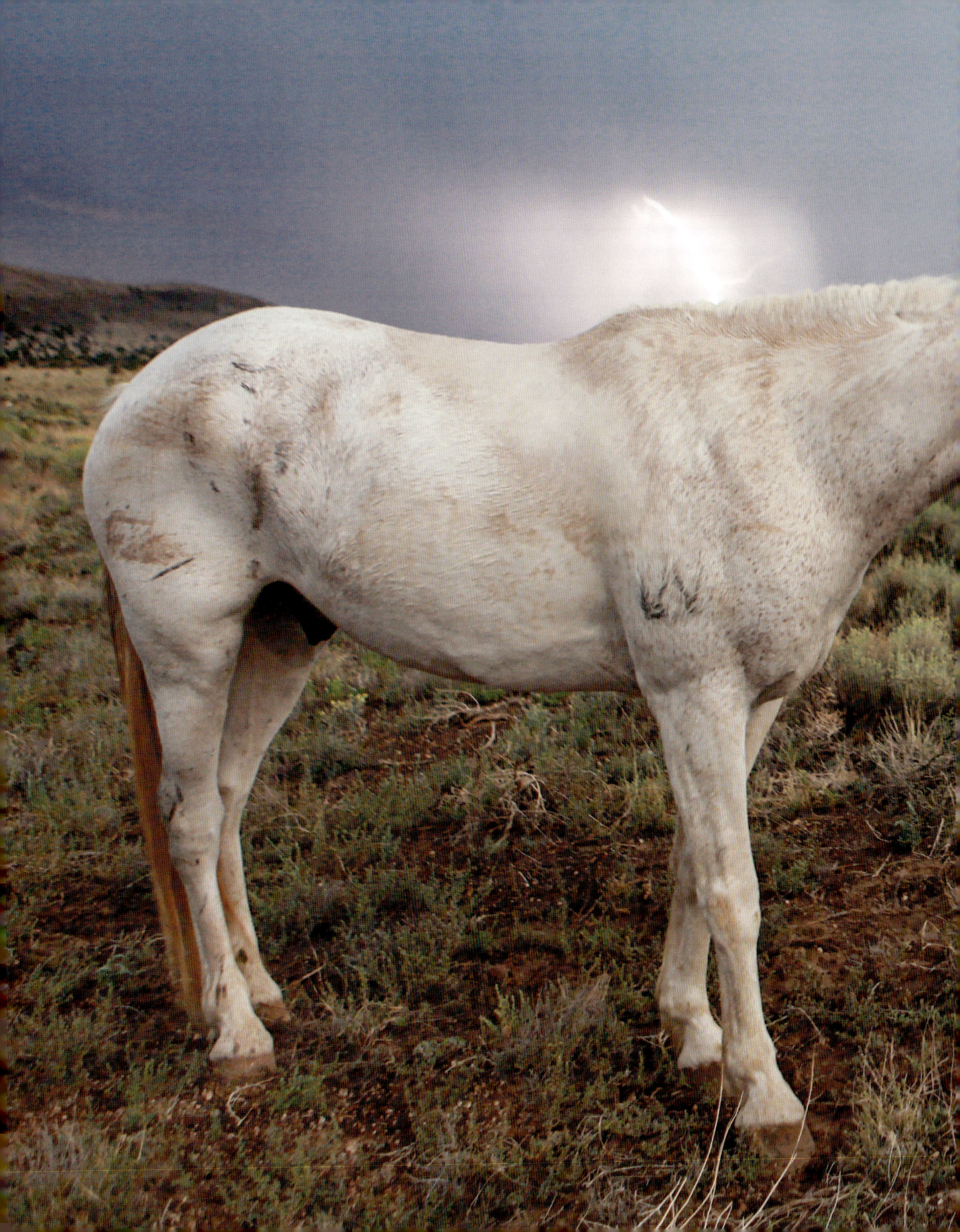

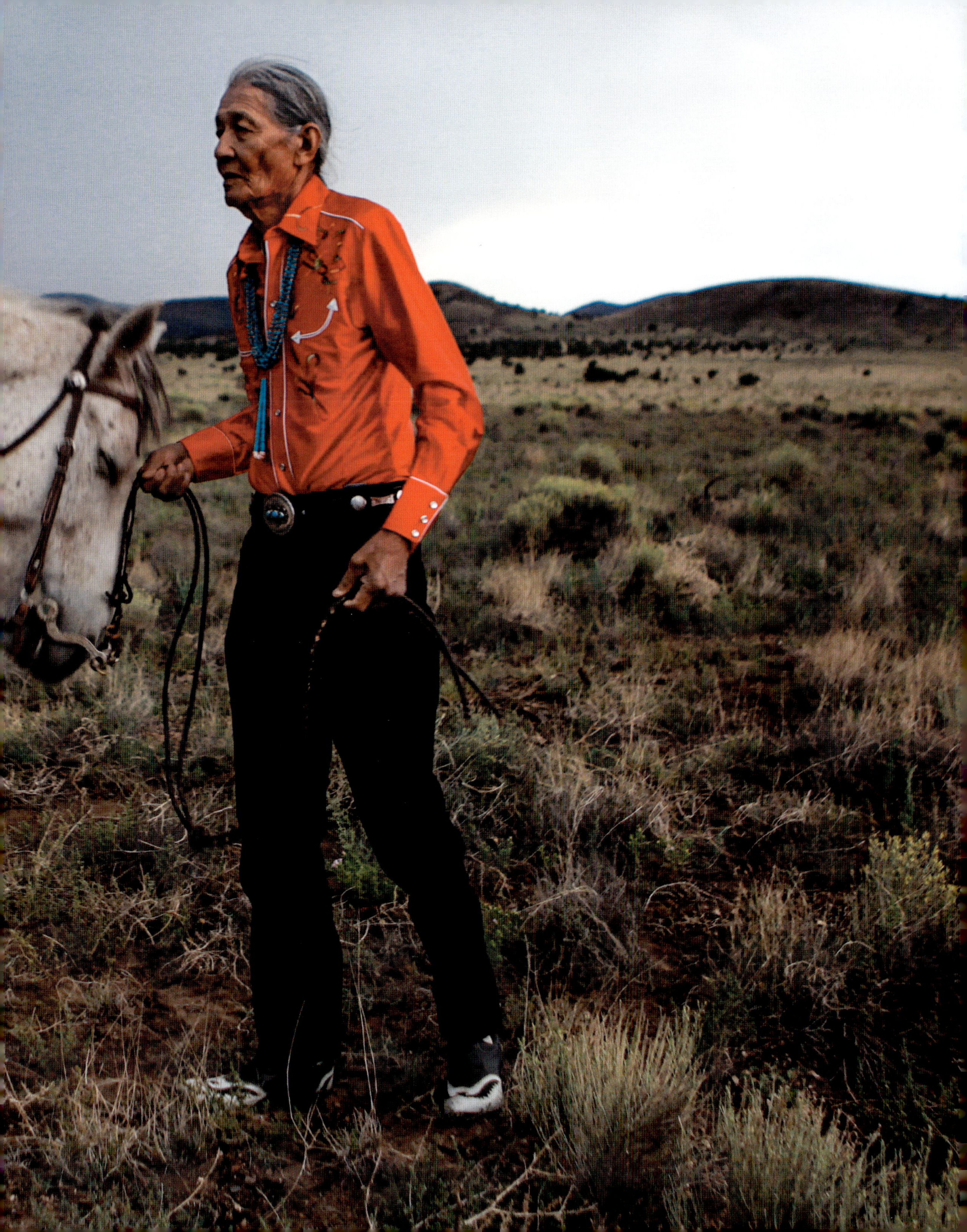

reported your story about the North Sami people for four years, for example, and you reported "People of the Horse" for two years. Why?

EL: When I studied, they taught that you're the photographer and you're telling the story. But that's not what's happening. You're co-creating. You can't ever wholly tell something about somebody else, but you can learn and contribute to the conversation that's happening.

Each of my stories leads to the next one. In fact, I feel like I couldn't go on to the next story had I not been in the one before. So I think of the people in the story as guides who can offer insights that reveal the next layer of the onion of life.

NG: "Onion of life!" That's fabulous. It sounds like you have to live your stories, in a way. When you photographed the Sami people, you learned their language and spent time with them as a housekeeper. Why did you make that choice?

EL: Storytelling is created by the act of seeking out and asking questions. With the Sami specifically, I had so many questions to ask and so many things that I wanted to learn about who they were, so I approached it quite genuinely.

I always say the photograph's given, not taken. And in terms of my career, I've never asked for anything I wasn't willing to give of myself. If I'm going to go live with someone for a year, I promise you they will come live with me for a year. And that has happened!

NG: For "People of the Horse," you spent two years traveling through the American West interviewing Indigenous communities about the significance of the horse to their culture, land, and history. You wrote of their relationships, "Once they find him, they find themselves." Do your pictures help you find yourself?

EL: I don't know about a finding of myself, because I don't quite believe we ever discover definitive answers when searching for who we are. But you do have to be able to give of yourself to be able to get anything in return.

NG: You were the primary photographer for the book *Women: The National Geographic Image Collection,* for which you photographed many influential women, including Jane Goodall and Oprah. Tell us about that experience.

EL: In that project, everybody wanted to give something of themselves. They spoke of such intimate things about beauty, about loss, about pain, about strength, about power. When do you get that kind of opportunity?

Oprah gave us a lot of time. She walked in, she said hello to everybody, and she recognized everybody in the room. I felt like her team also went out of their way to make my job easy.

NG: What about Jane Goodall?

EL: I photographed her in her backyard in London. But you don't need to be in the middle of Africa to photograph Jane Goodall, because Africa is already with her. This goes back to what I said earlier about each story bringing me to the next one: We become the sum of these things. Why would I think that Jane needed to be photographed in Africa when she's the sum of everything in this London backyard?

NG: Was there any particular conversation you had around your image of the Sami girl in the scarf?

EL: Normally, I don't talk much when I'm creating images, but I told Ella-Li that I was struck by how much she blended into the light. She said the Sami have the light people and the dark people. Which you are depends on the time of year you are born, the winter months or the summer months. There are also light reindeer and dark reindeer, and the light seasons and the dark seasons. That story has agency in this image.

NG: A lot of portraiture is set up beforehand. But what about your portrait of the Sami reindeer herder? Surely that couldn't have been planned ahead of time.

EL: This is where I go back to the fact that I'm not creating this image. I can't make these reindeer do that, right? But I can become a part of the conversation happening around the image. This herder wants to show me what it means to be a *boazovázzi,* or reindeer walker, and therefore I'm listening and these images can be created.

NG: Did this philosophy guide you through your work on "People of the Horse"?

EL: I knew I couldn't frame those pictures or make them happen; people have to want to give

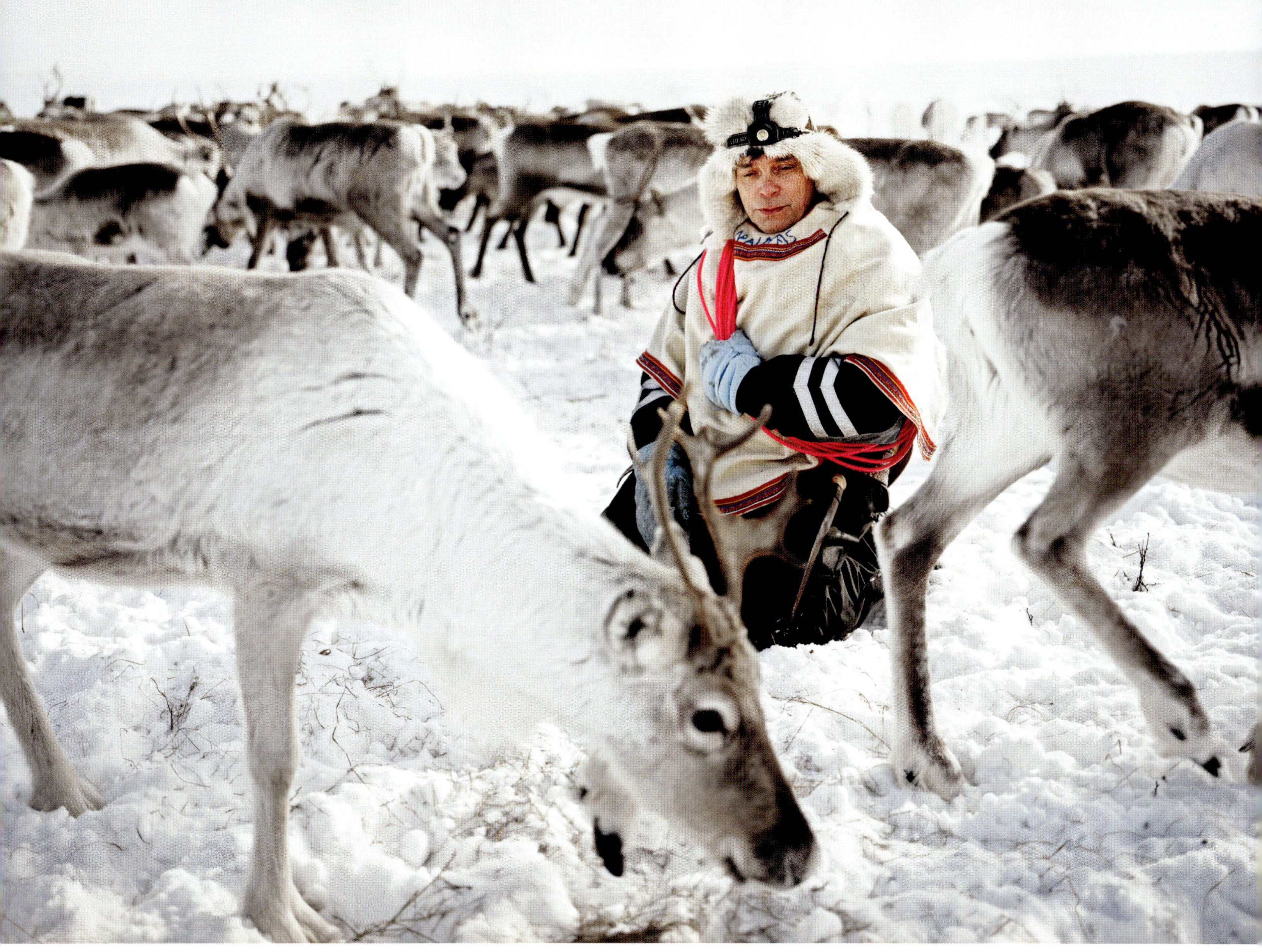

ERIKA LARSEN, 2011
Nils Peder, a Sami herder, kneels and sings to his reindeer to prevent them from spooking.

PREVIOUS PAGES
ERIKA LARSEN, 2011
Jones Benally stands with his horse, Moonwalker, in Arizona. The respected Navajo elder received the horse in return for his services as a medicine man.

the picture to you. When I went to photograph a man named Jones Benally with his horse Moonwalker, he started telling me about the Navajo beliefs in lightning and about their creation stories. I have a philosophy where if someone tells me an ontological belief like that, I choose to believe it. I think that's really important.

For a situation where a person and I are clearly going out to create a portrait, there are elements that we orchestrate together. We're looking for the right spot, the right space that has meaning. And that's often something I'll ask so people can lead me to where they want the image to be created.

NG: How did the animals affect your connection to the story you were telling?

EL: Often, people in the tribal communities I worked with shared their relationship with the horse. I came to realize that the horse has its own story to tell, beyond what is conveyed through the people. In general, when you're creating a story, you're working between realms because of that translation.

Photography's a beautiful tool for telling stories of time because it has a way to remind us that time isn't linear. In "People of the Horse," the camera allowed the animals to move through a story that was being told over hundreds of years. That's the magic of storytelling.

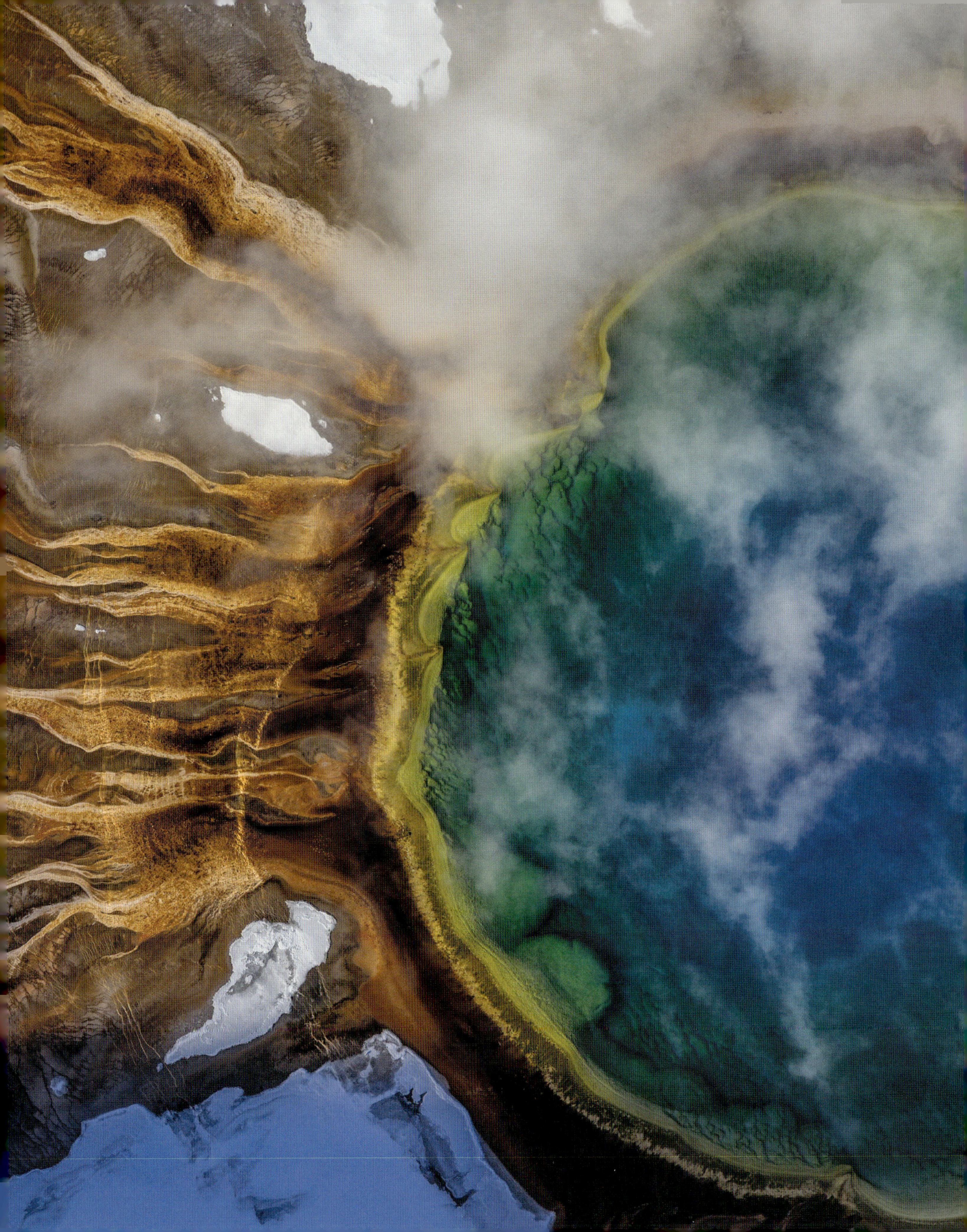

LANDSCAPE & ENVIRONMENT

THE POWER TO

CHERISH

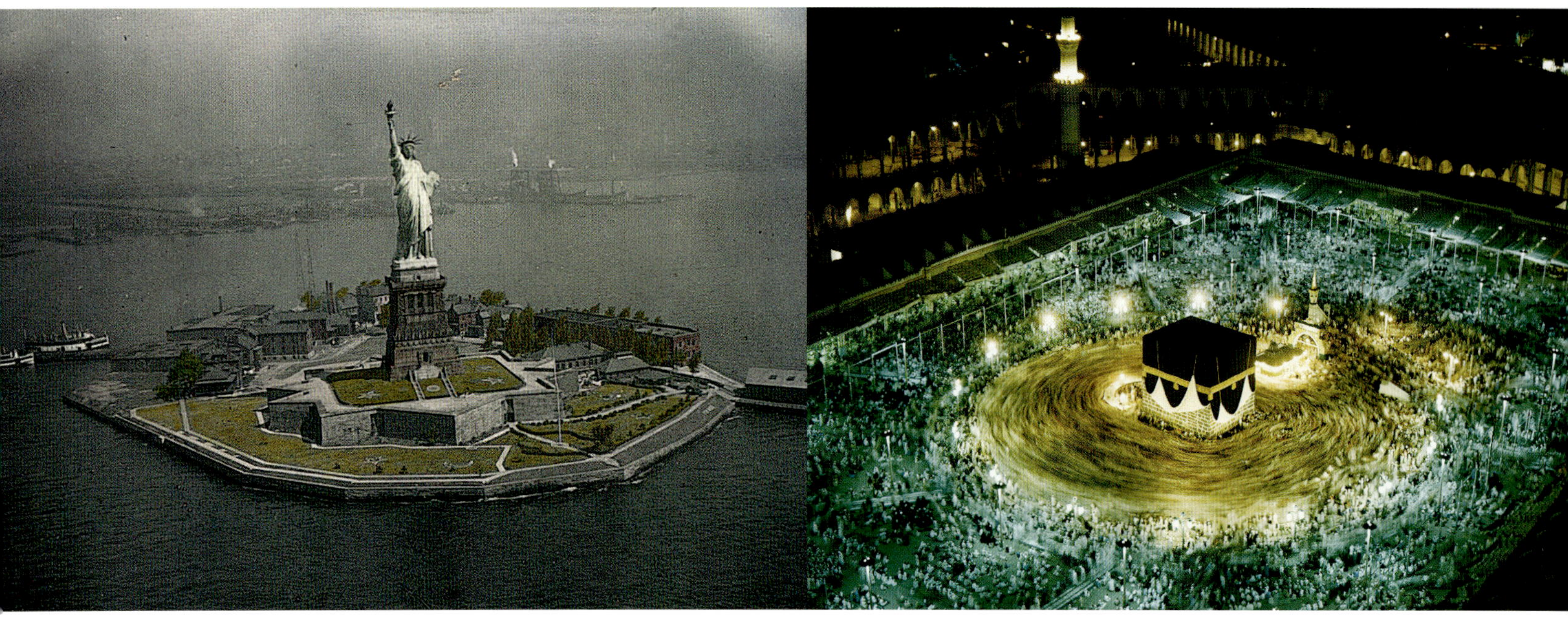

PORTRAIT OF A PLANET

PAGE 284
MICHAEL NICHOLS, 2014
A dazzling aerial view of Grand Prismatic Spring in Yellowstone National Park

ABOVE LEFT
MELVILLE BELL GROSVENOR, 1930
In the very first successful aerial color photograph, taken by National Geographic's third president and editor in chief, the Statue of Liberty stands proud on Liberty Island, New York.

ABOVE RIGHT
THOMAS J. ABERCROMBIE, 1965
Thousands of pilgrims circle the Kaaba at the center of the Masjid al-Haram mosque in Mecca, Saudi Arabia.

LANDSCAPE IS THE HISTORY OF THE PHYSICAL WORLD written by wind, water, fire, and ice—and starting in the Anthropocene, how it's been changed by humanity.

Scenery can be many things. It's Mac Stone's portrait of a Florida swamp marked by the overhead arc of a rocket launch. It's Guy Davies's lily pad of a salt island in the opalescent stillness of the Dead Sea. And it's George Steinmetz's long horizon of the bare-bones terrain of the Sahara. "A desert," says Steinmetz, who has a particular passion for that landscape, "is the earth with its skin pulled away."

The first photograph published in the pages of *National Geographic* was a landscape: an image of Herald Island, a whalelike hump of rock against the backdrop of a pewter sky in the Arctic Sea, which appeared in 1890. The black-and-white picture had no pretense of being anything but dry, factual documentation: the antithesis of the breath-arresting landscapes emblematic of the magazine in later decades.

It looks easy. It isn't. "Landscape photography is the supreme test of the photographer—and often the supreme disappointment," said one of the supreme practitioners of that art, Ansel Adams.

"There's a fine line between a picture postcard and an editorial image," explains former photo editor Kurt Mutchler, who worked at National Geographic for 30 years. "The trick is finding the drama. It's like making a portrait of a person; you have to wait and listen to the landscape so you can understand its character and what makes it tick."

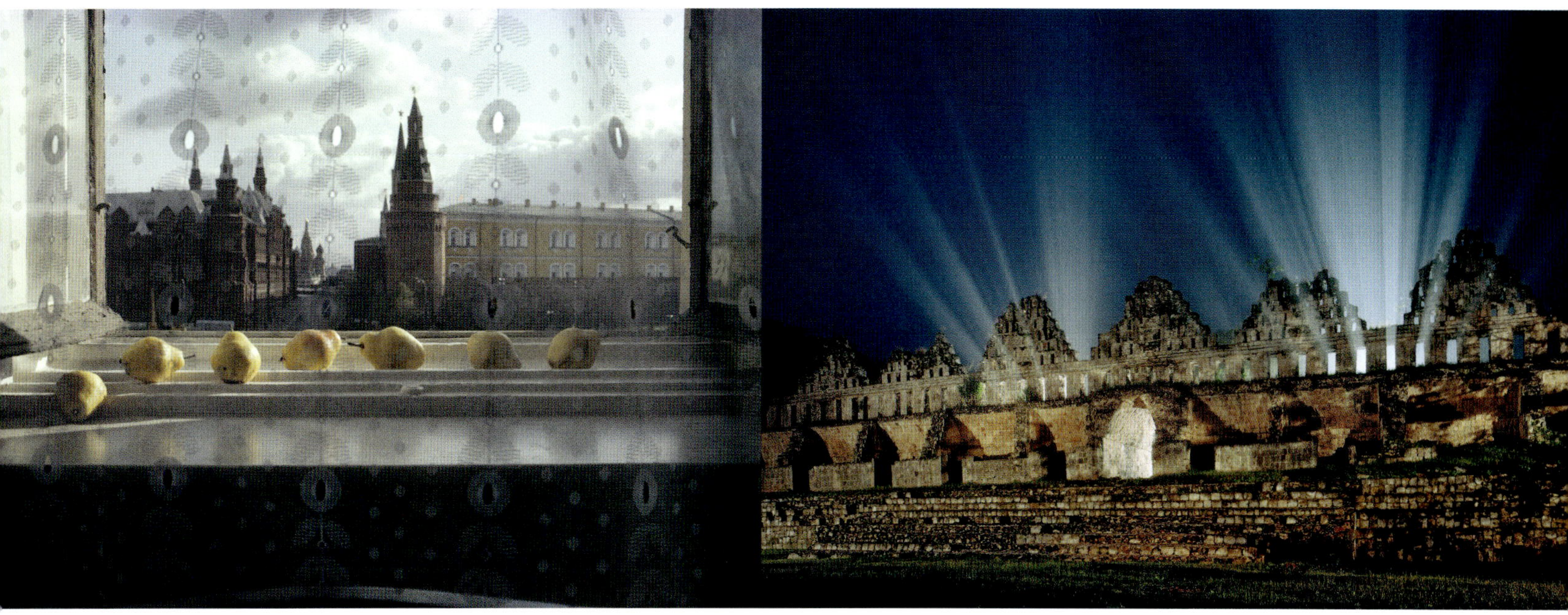

Landscapes seem ageless. Mountains "live in deep time," says Robert Macfarlane, a British writer who collects the language of landscape.

And yet the shadow of ephemerality lingers in images like Edward Burtynsky's 2010 aerial of the dry, dusty bed of Owens Lake, California, its water diverted by an aqueduct to serve the faucets of Los Angeles. "I look for massive examples of what I call 'human taking'—the removal from the Earth of the materials used to make our stuff," he has written of his special interest: the human-altered landscape.

There are more gentle manifestations of the human hand as well. They are known as cultural landscapes and are defined by UNESCO as the "combined works of nature and man." The rice terraces in the Philippines, pilgrimage trails in Japan, and Persian gardens in Iran, for example, are places reflective of an intimate relationship between humans and environment that speak to imagination, social development, and spirituality.

In its portrayal of landscapes, *National Geographic* magazine has documented beauty and desecration alike: Forests stripped for wood. Hills hollowed for ore. And dams, which drown landscapes both physical and cultural, like the Aswan High Dam in Egypt and the Three Gorges Dam in China. Also, natural disasters that reshape a landscape: floods, hurricanes, tsunamis, earthquakes, and wildfires, many of which are traceable to human-made climate change.

Photographs that show us Earth in all its freshness—a long horizon of prairie, the thin lacquer of ice on a field after a freeze, a lush tangle of jungle—remind us how much we have to gain by its preservation, and how much we lose by its destruction.

ABOVE LEFT
SAM ABELL, 1983
In a tableau meant to evoke the life of writer Leo Tolstoy, the Kremlin is framed by lace curtains and ripening pears in Moscow, Russia.

ABOVE RIGHT
SIMON NORFOLK, 2007
The House of the Doves—once a series of vaulted rooms, now collapsed—in the ancient city of Uxmal, Yucatán, Mexico

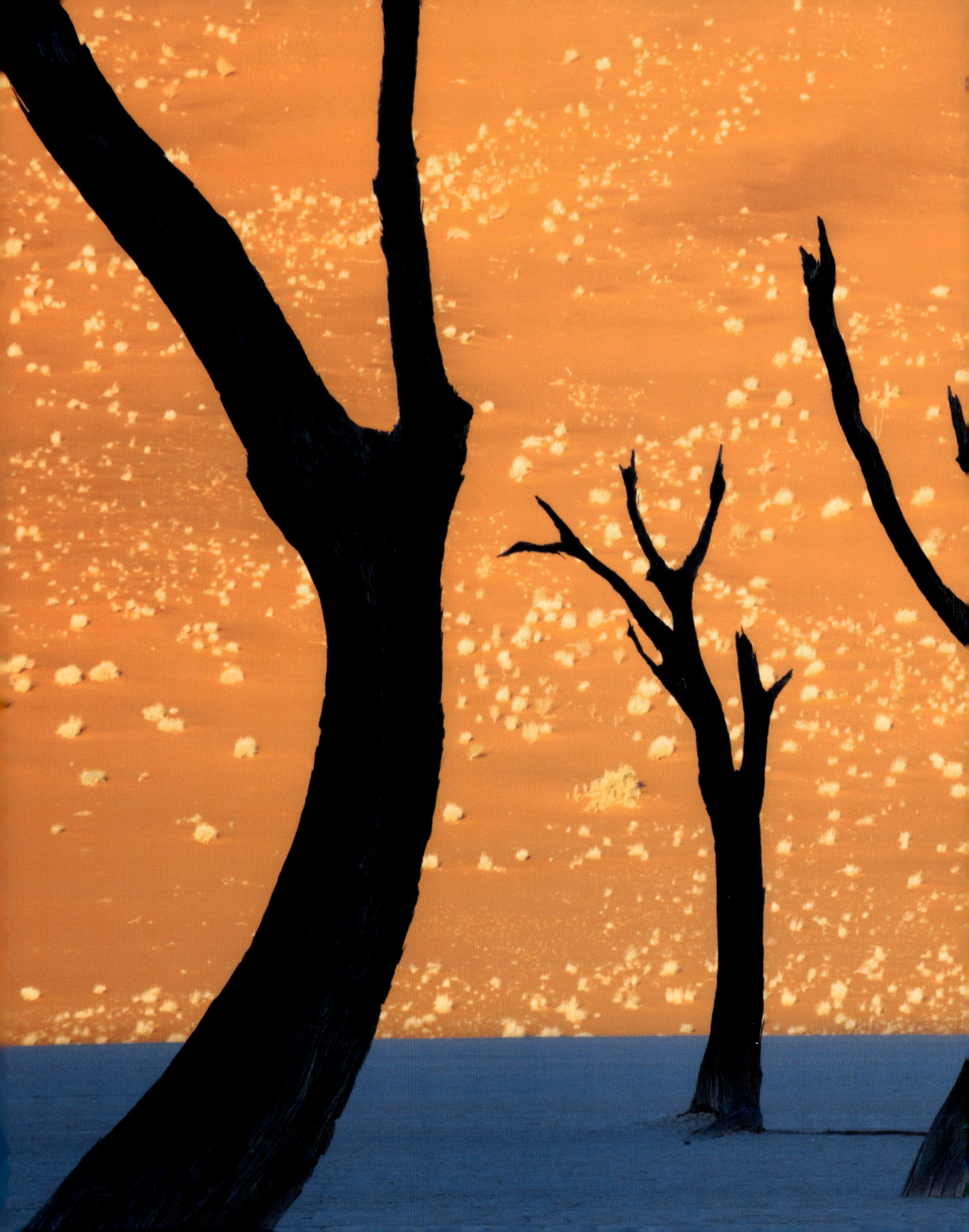

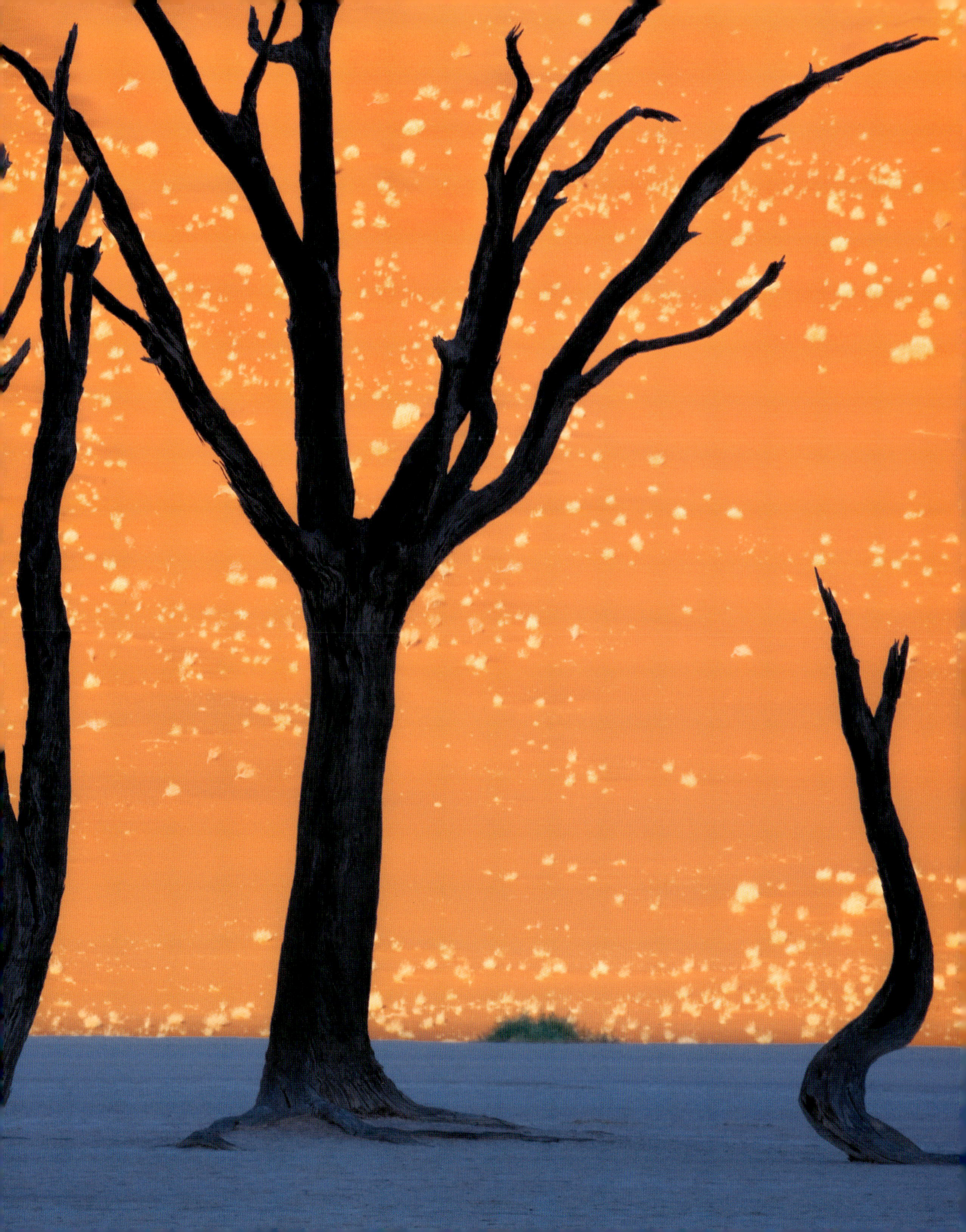

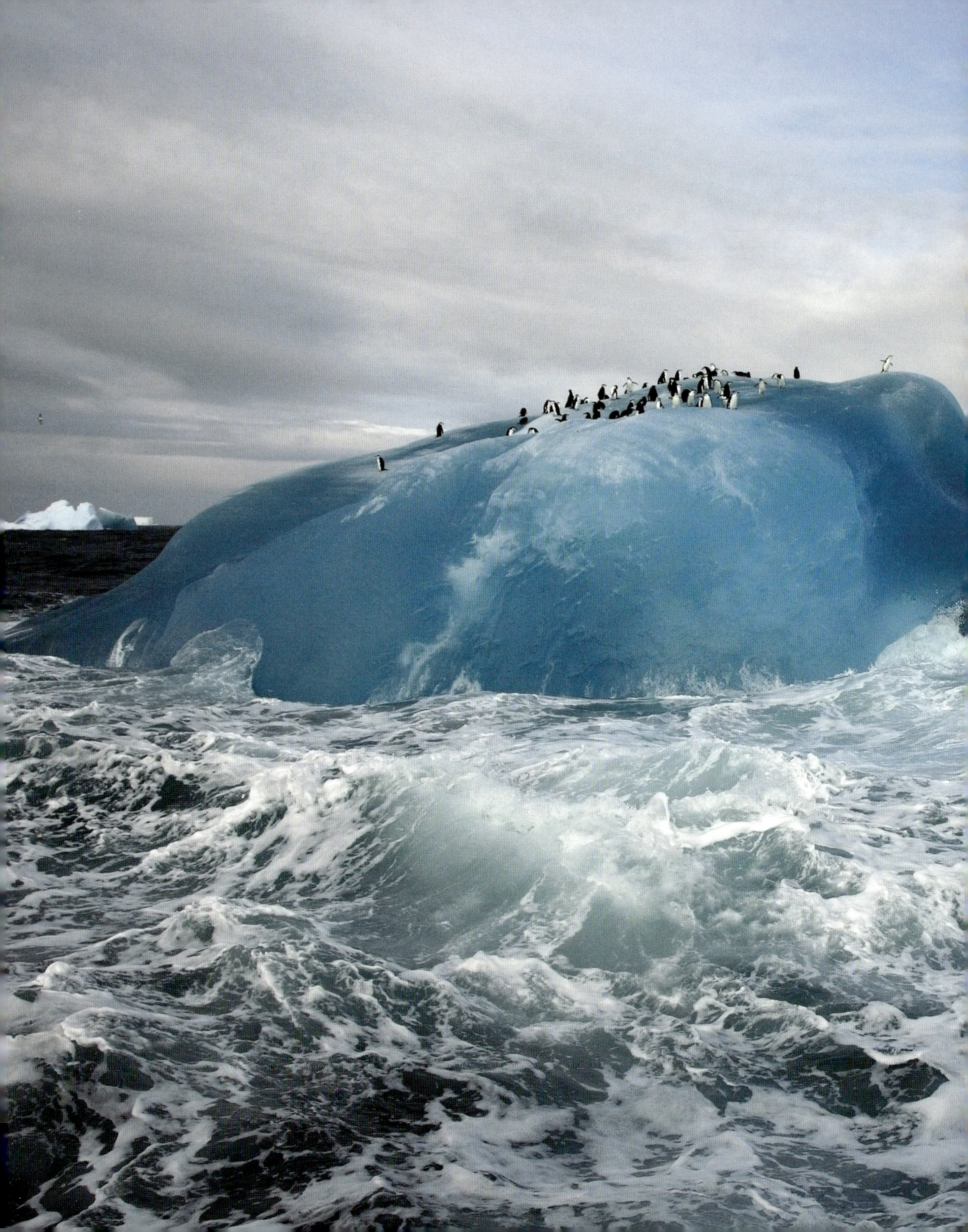

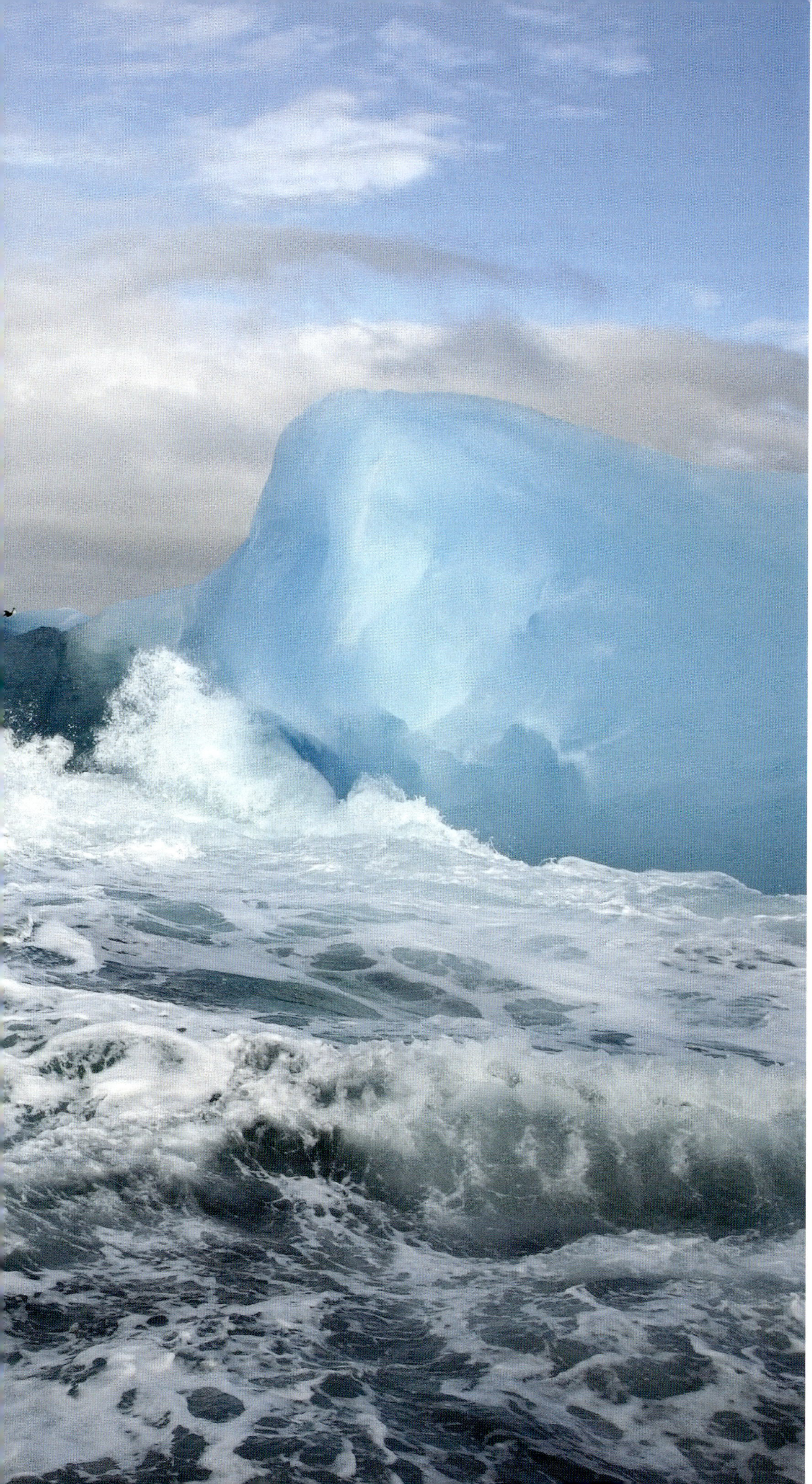

MARIA STENZEL, 2006
Chinstrap penguins convene on an iceberg near volcanic Candlemas Island in the South Atlantic Ocean.

PREVIOUS PAGES
FRANS LANTING, 2009
Tinted orange by the morning sun, a soaring dune is the backdrop for the hulks of camel thorn trees in Namibia's Namib-Naukluft National Park.

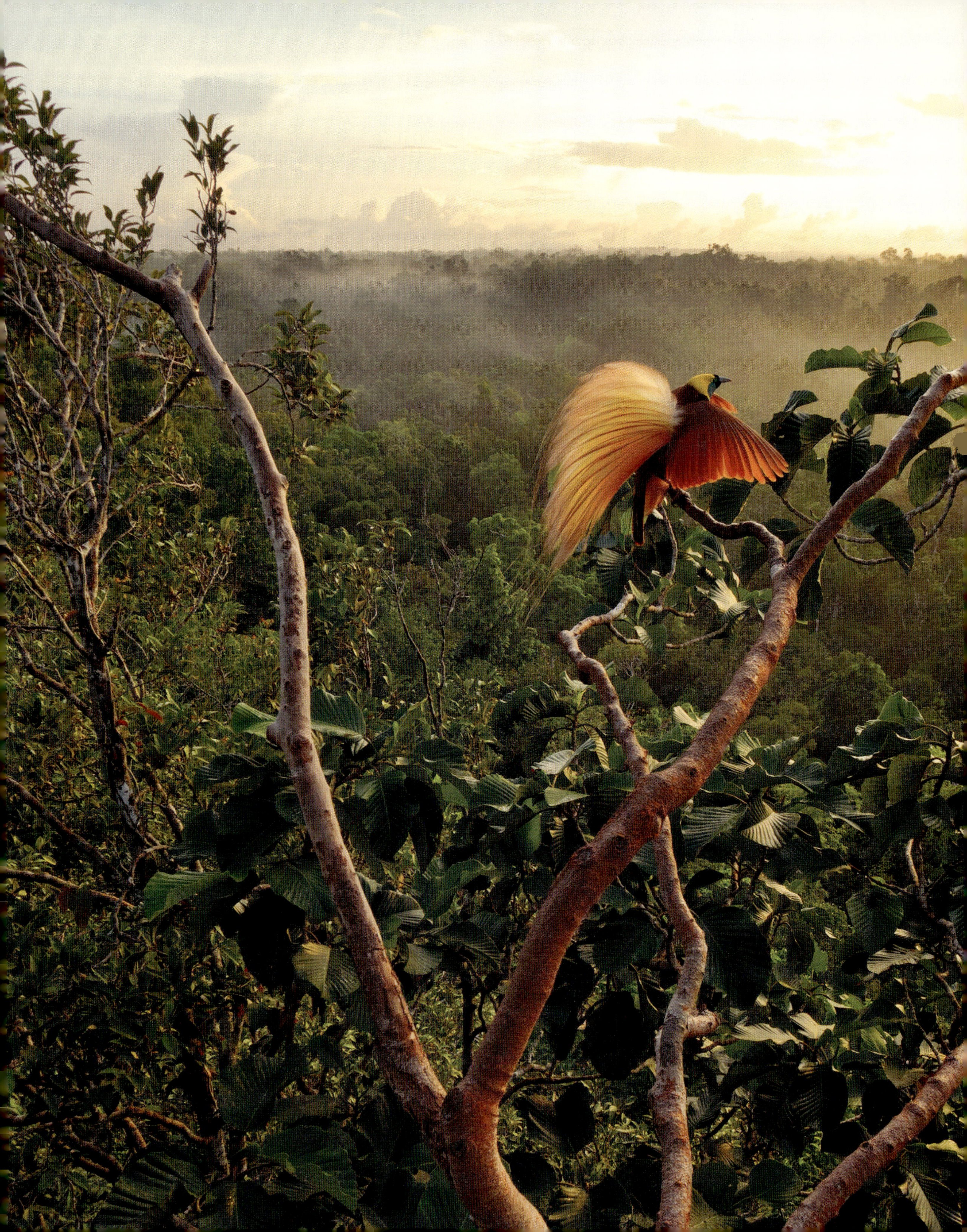

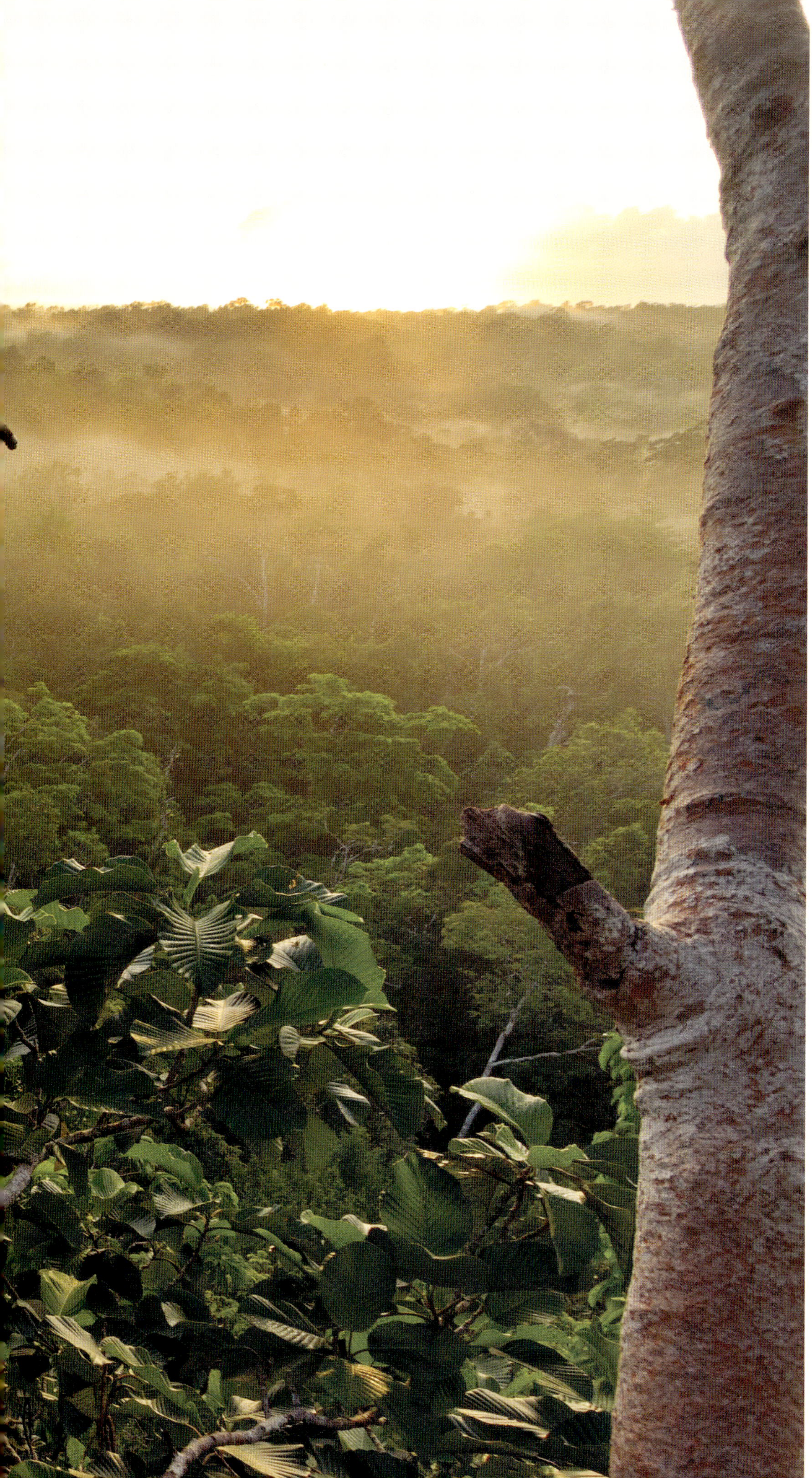

TIM LAMAN, 2010
The courtship display of a greater bird-of-paradise in Indonesia's Aru Islands

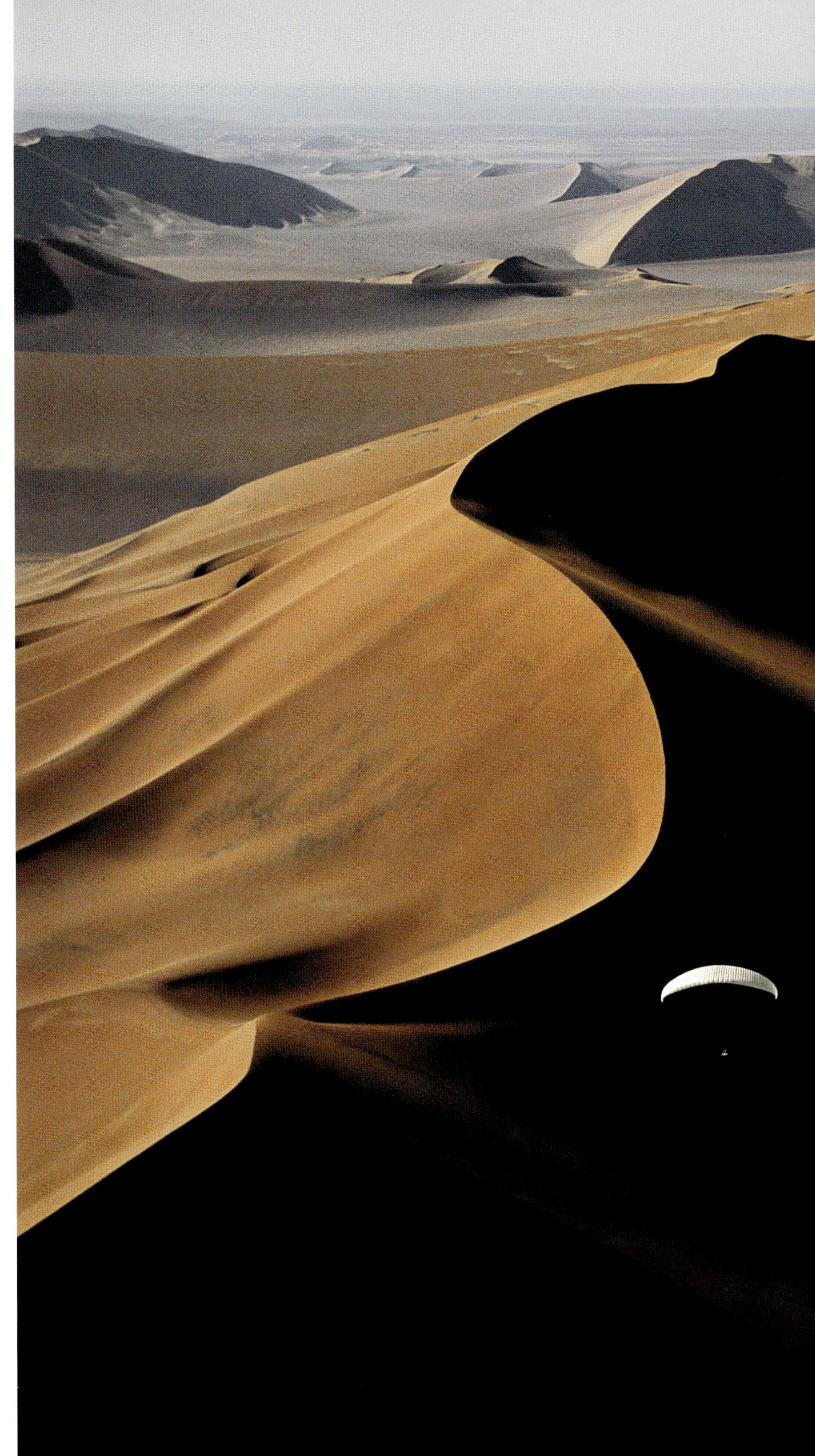

GEORGE STEINMETZ, 2013
Champion paraglider Alain Arnoux flies over a dune in Iran's Dasht-e-Lūt desert.

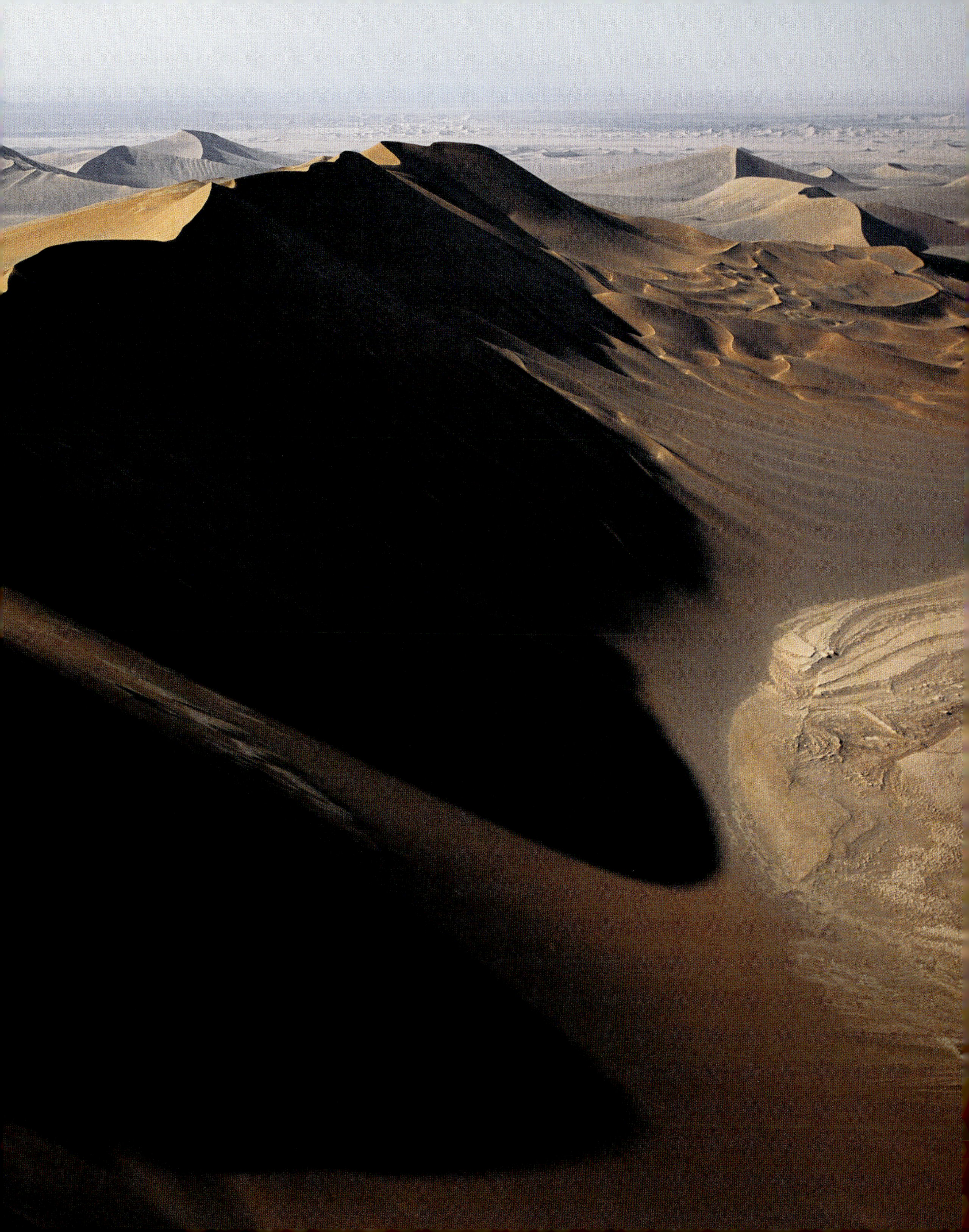

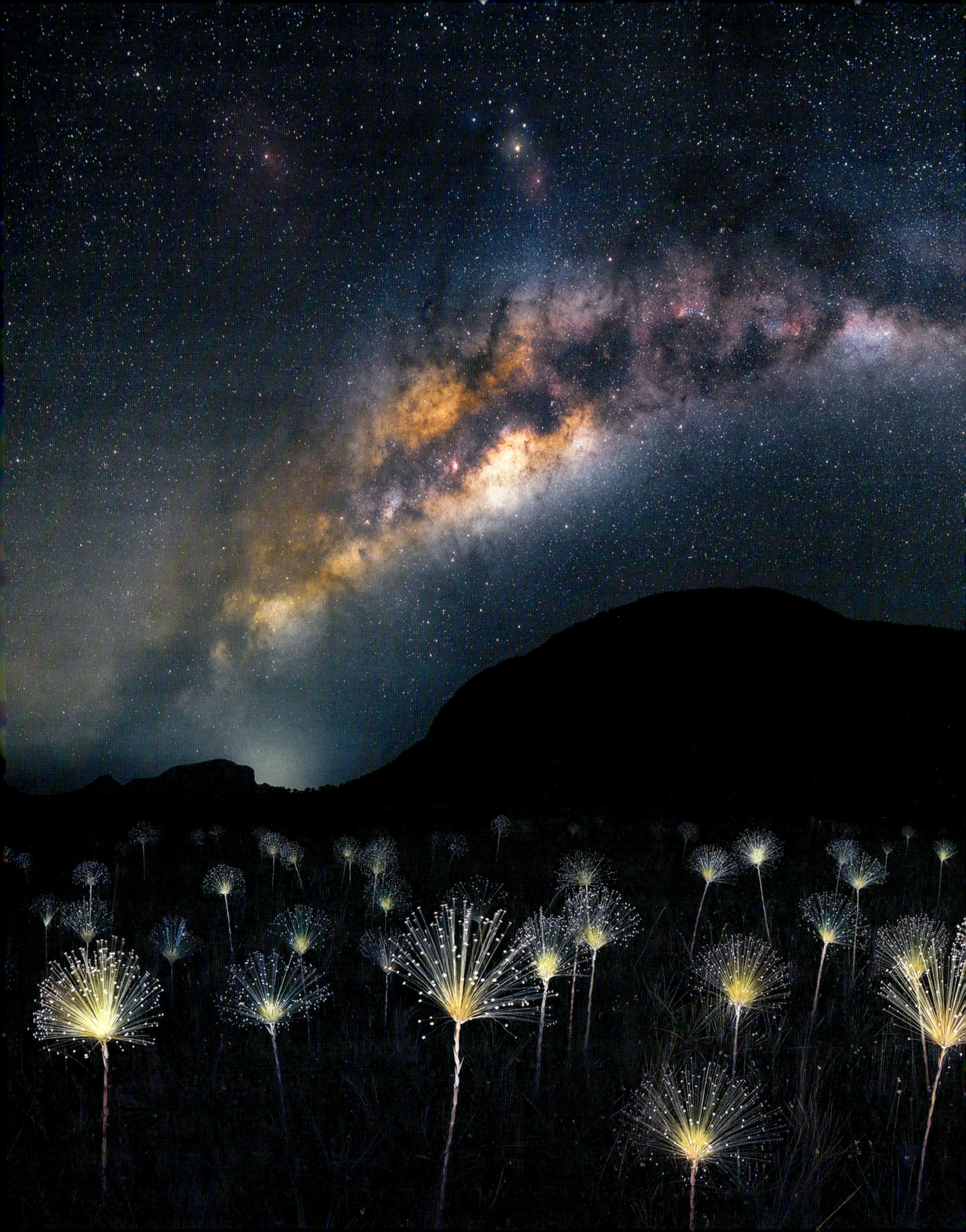

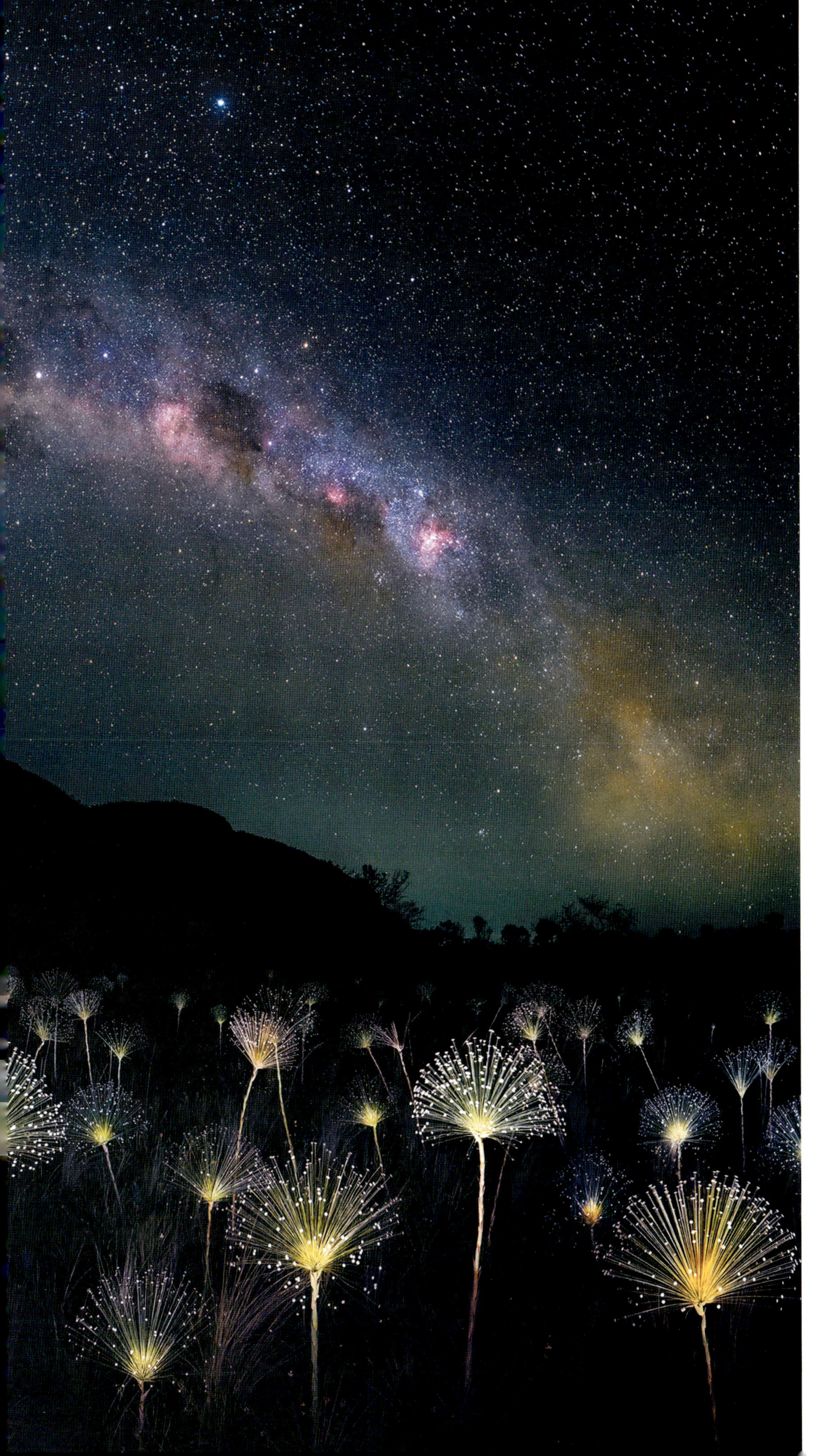

MARCIO ESTEVES CABRAL, 2023
In this panoramic image stitched from nine exposures, the Milky Way shimmers above a field of *Paepalanthus* wildflowers in Brazil's Cerrado region.

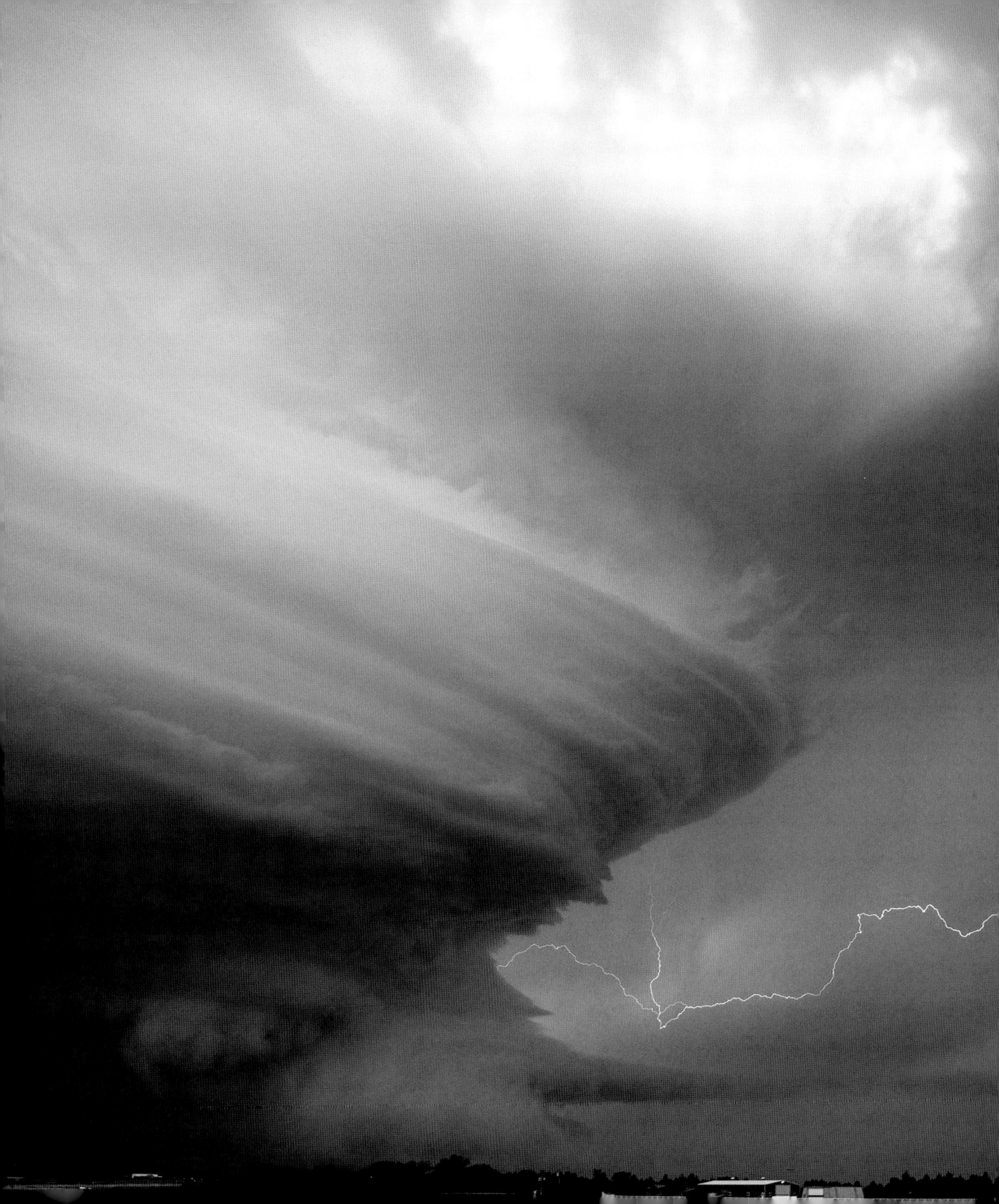

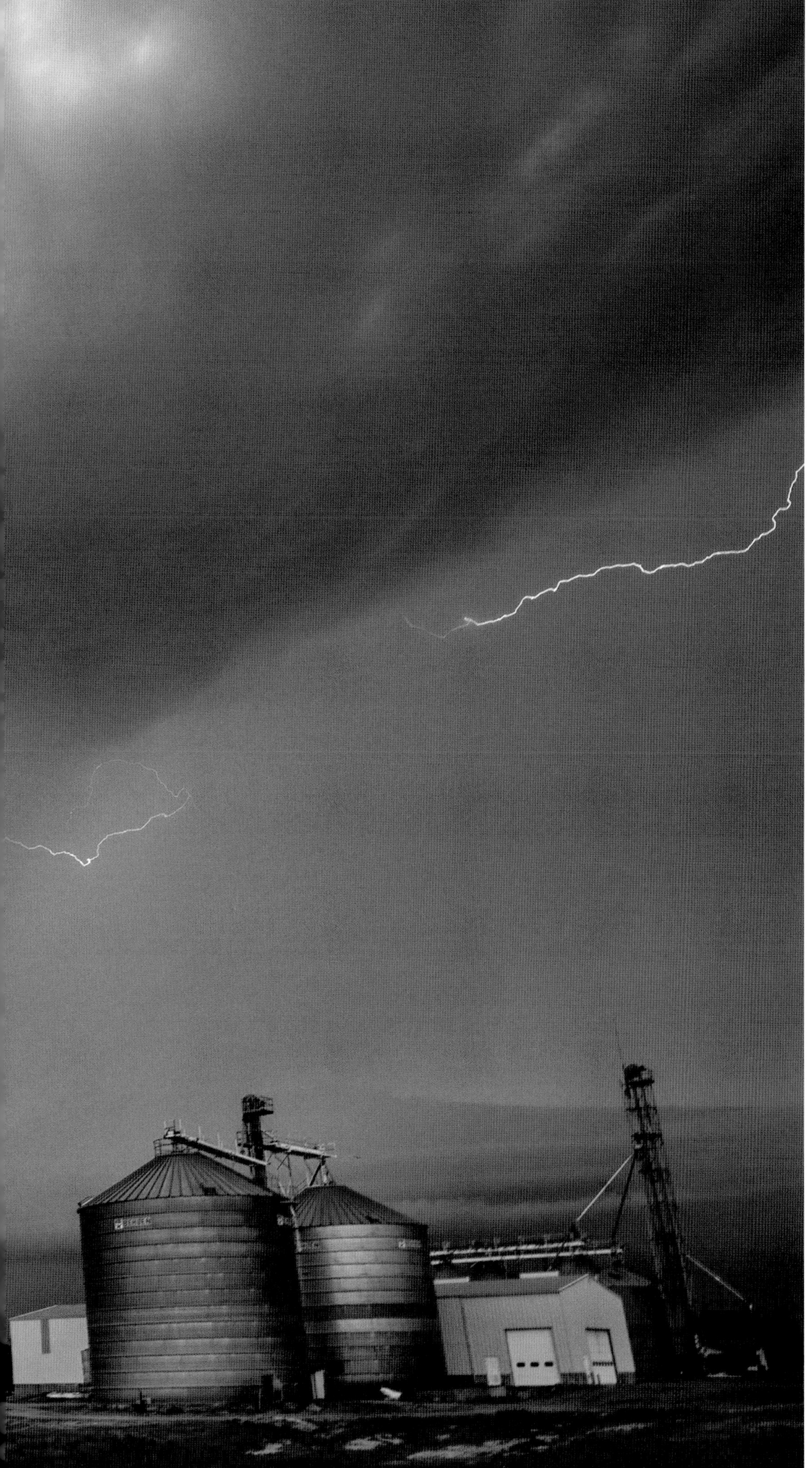

KRYSTLE WRIGHT, 2019
A dramatic supercell storm, known for its deep, rotating updraft, approaches a farm in Imperial, Nebraska.

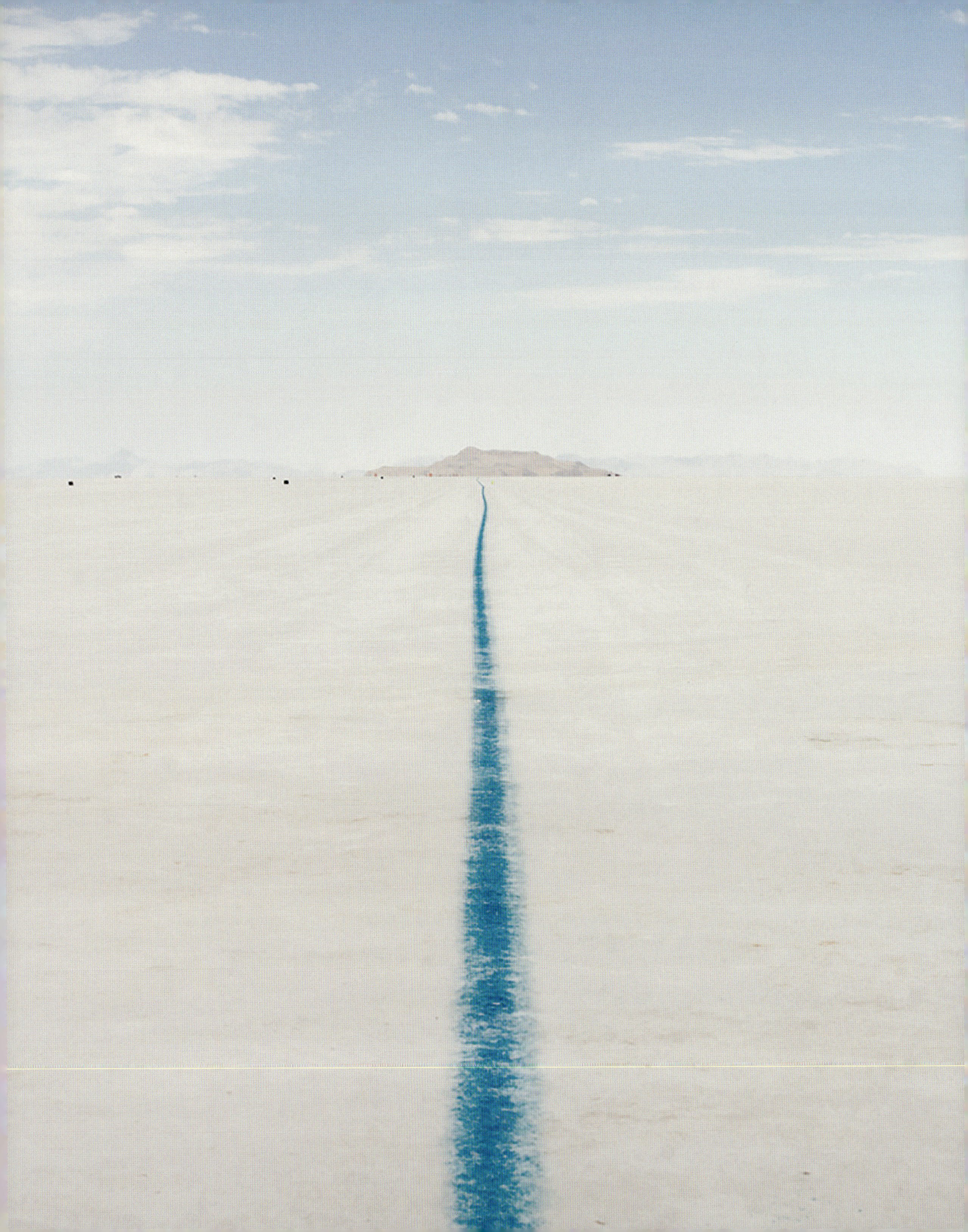

IF YOU WANT TO SAVE SOMETHING, YOU HAVE TO LOVE IT. AND TO LOVE IT, YOU HAVE TO KNOW IT. WHAT PHOTOGRAPHY DOES IS BRIDGE THAT GAP.

DAVID DOUBILET, PHOTOGRAPHER

CAROLYN DRAKE, 2016
The Bonneville Salt Flats in Tooele County, Utah. According to the U.S. Geological Survey, the flats have thinned by more than 18 inches since 1960, but the cause remains mysterious.

NICOLAS RUEL, 2013
A double exposure of the canals by Amsterdam's red-light district

FOLLOWING PAGES
MICHAEL NICHOLS, 2012
Scientists measure a giant sequoia, which can grow as tall as 250 feet, in California's Sequoia National Park.

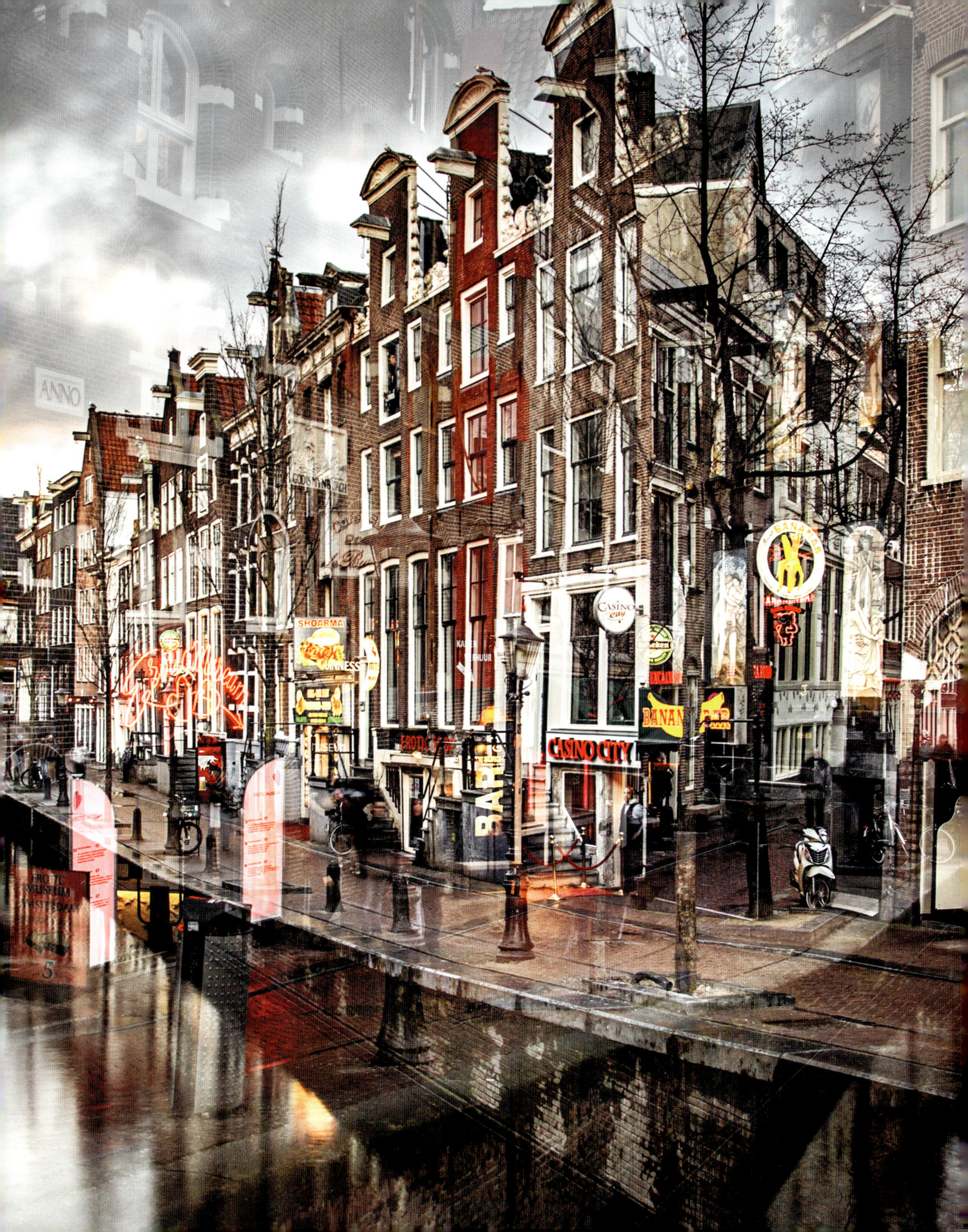
ANNO
SHOARMA
GUINNESS
CASINO CITY
BAR

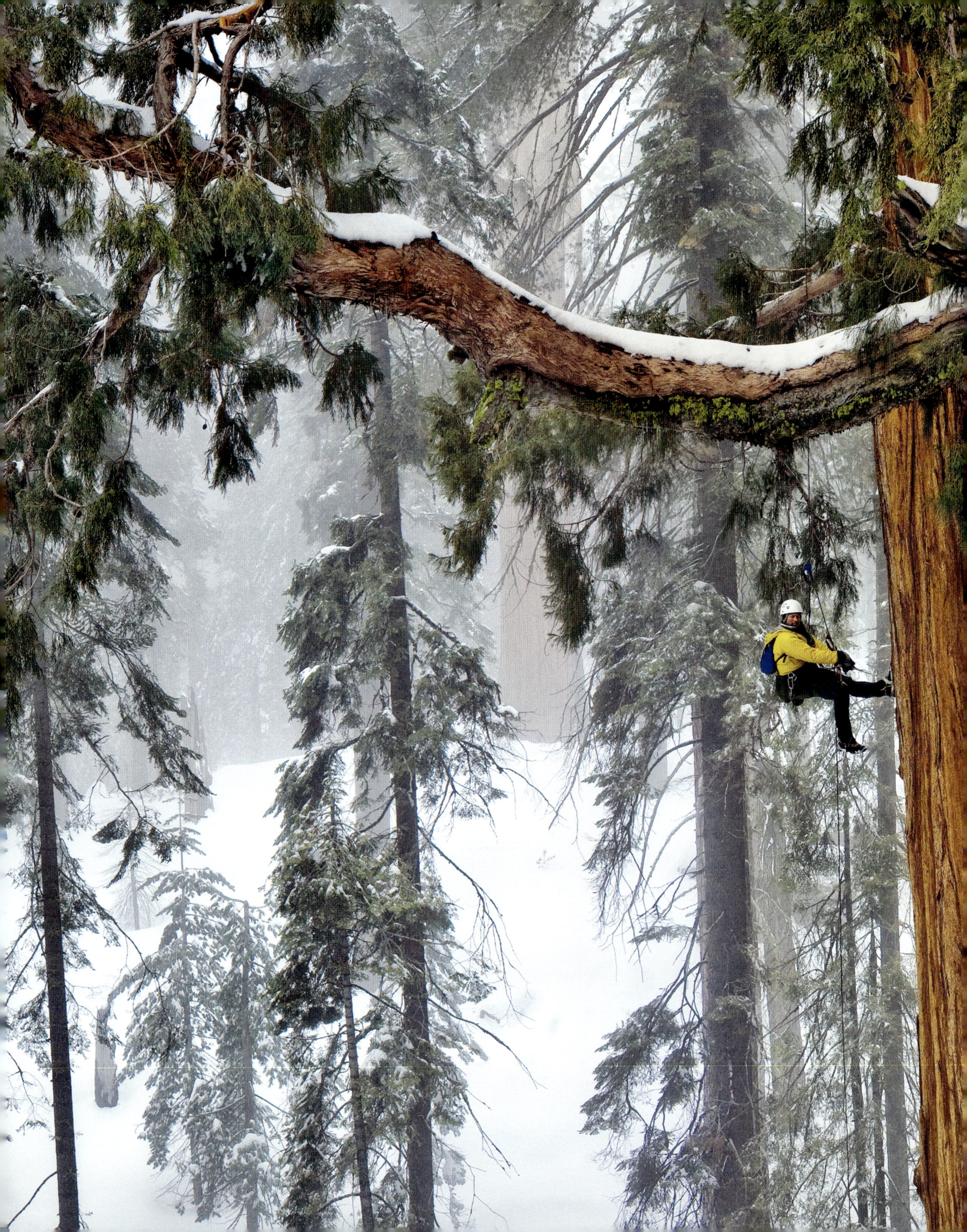

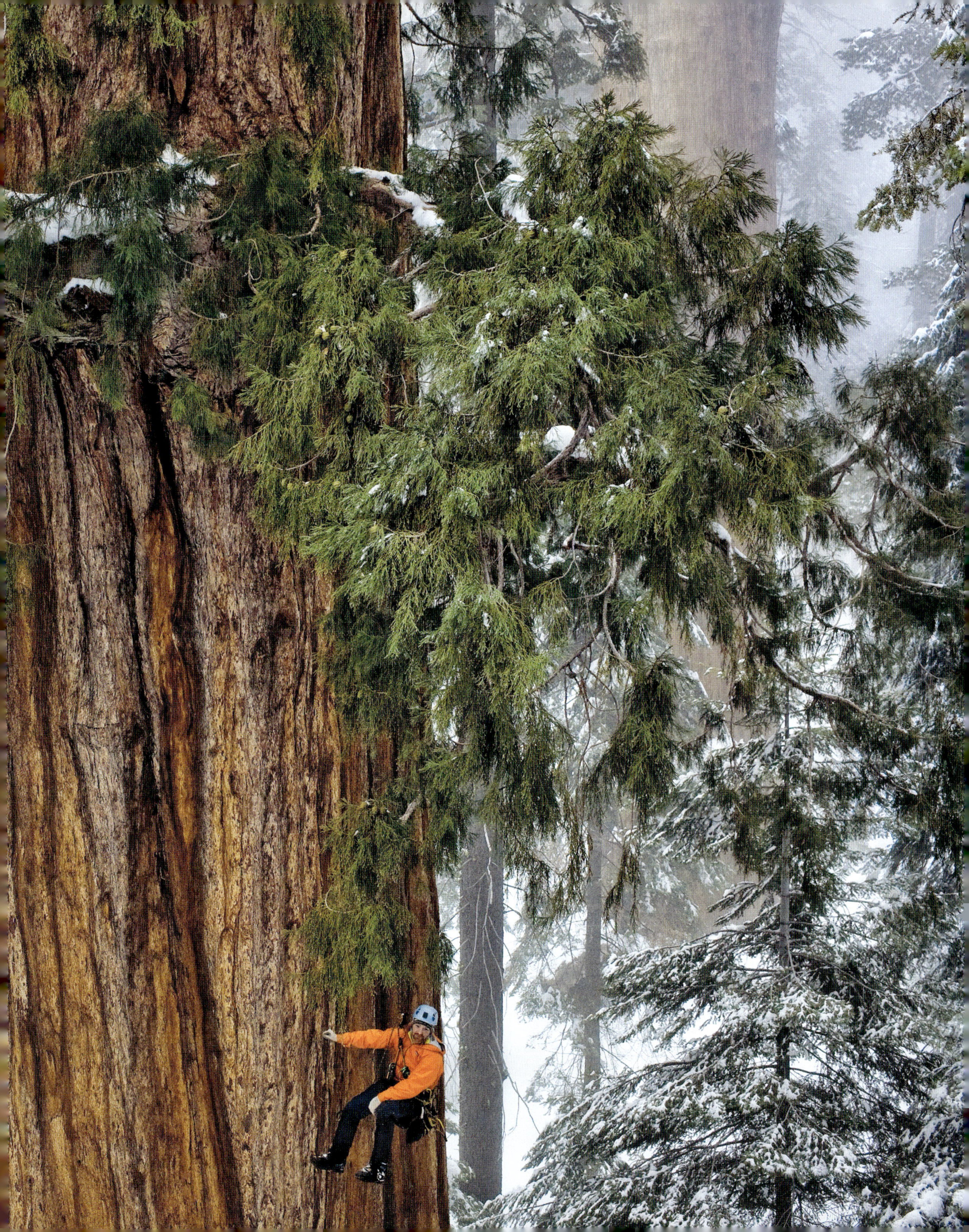

BIOGRAPHY

SOFÍA JARAMILLO

FOR COLOMBIAN AMERICAN PHOTOGRAPHER, filmmaker, and National Geographic Explorer Sofía Jaramillo, it all started with a photo of a lighthouse. She was 15, on a road trip with her father along the California coast to visit colleges, and took a snap of one with his point-and-shoot camera. She looked at the back of the camera to check out the image she'd made and thought: This is it. This is what I am going to do for the rest of my life.

With a father from Colombia and a mother from Idaho, Jaramillo felt suspended between two worlds, "in the middle, not knowing where to land." This was particularly true of the ski community of Ketchum, Idaho, a place where she grew up and where there weren't any other people like her. That experience, as well as her move to Jackson Hole, Wyoming, to become an adventure photographer, inspired her to change the narrative and to tell stories of Black, Indigenous, and other people of color in outdoor spaces, as in her piece for *High Country News* featuring a Latina woman who works for the National Park Service.

In addition to her work for National Geographic, Jaramillo has been published by the *New York Times, The Guardian, Outside* magazine, the Associated Press, and the *Wall Street Journal*. In 2023, she was awarded a National Geographic Society grant to produce "El Corazón de los Andes." The photography project documents the paramo ecosystem in Colombia, a freshwater source for millions of people threatened by climate change, agriculture, mining, and wildfires.

SOFÍA JARAMILLO, 2023
Sunset burnishes the spires and buttes of South Dakota's Badlands National Park.

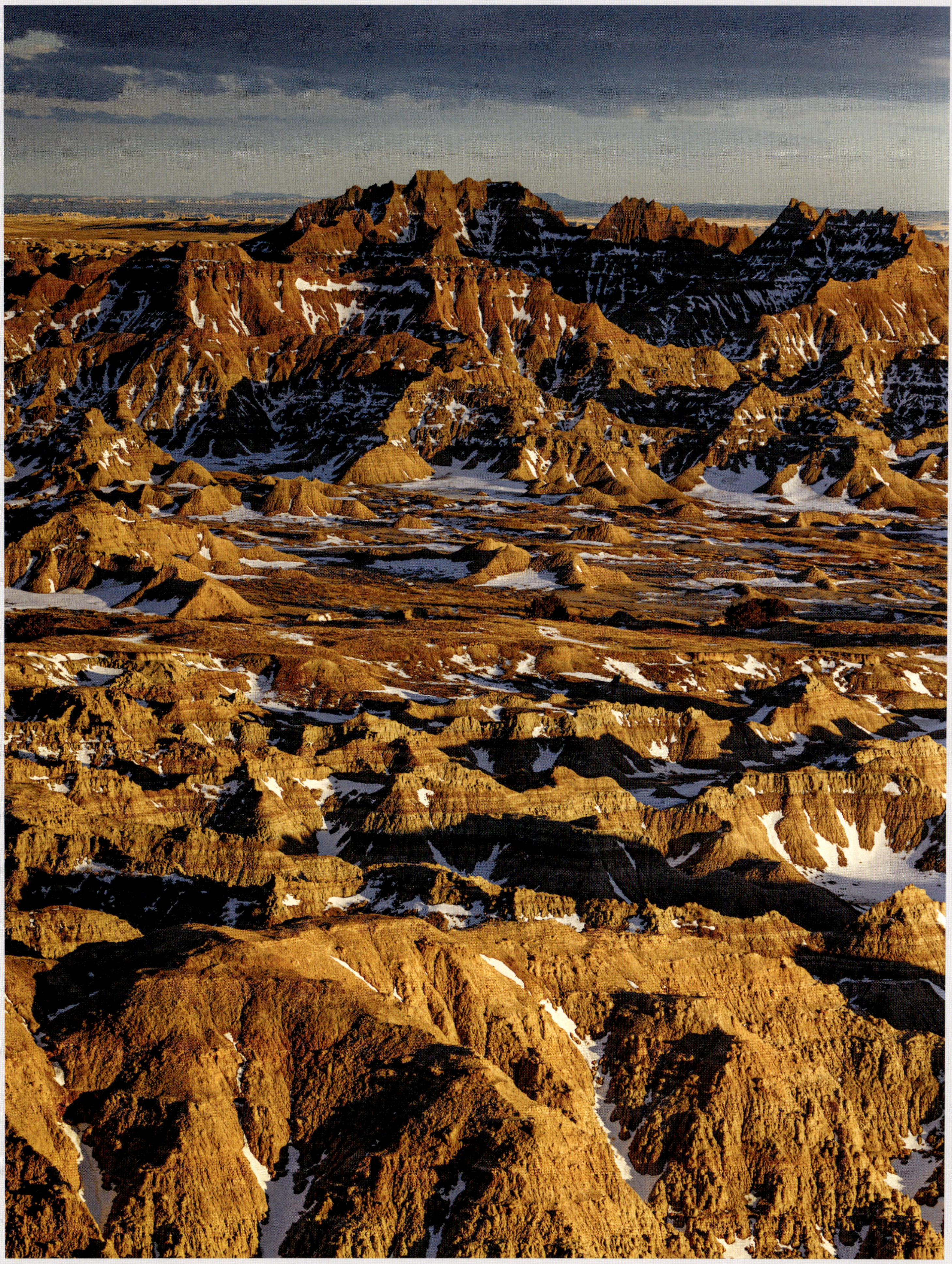

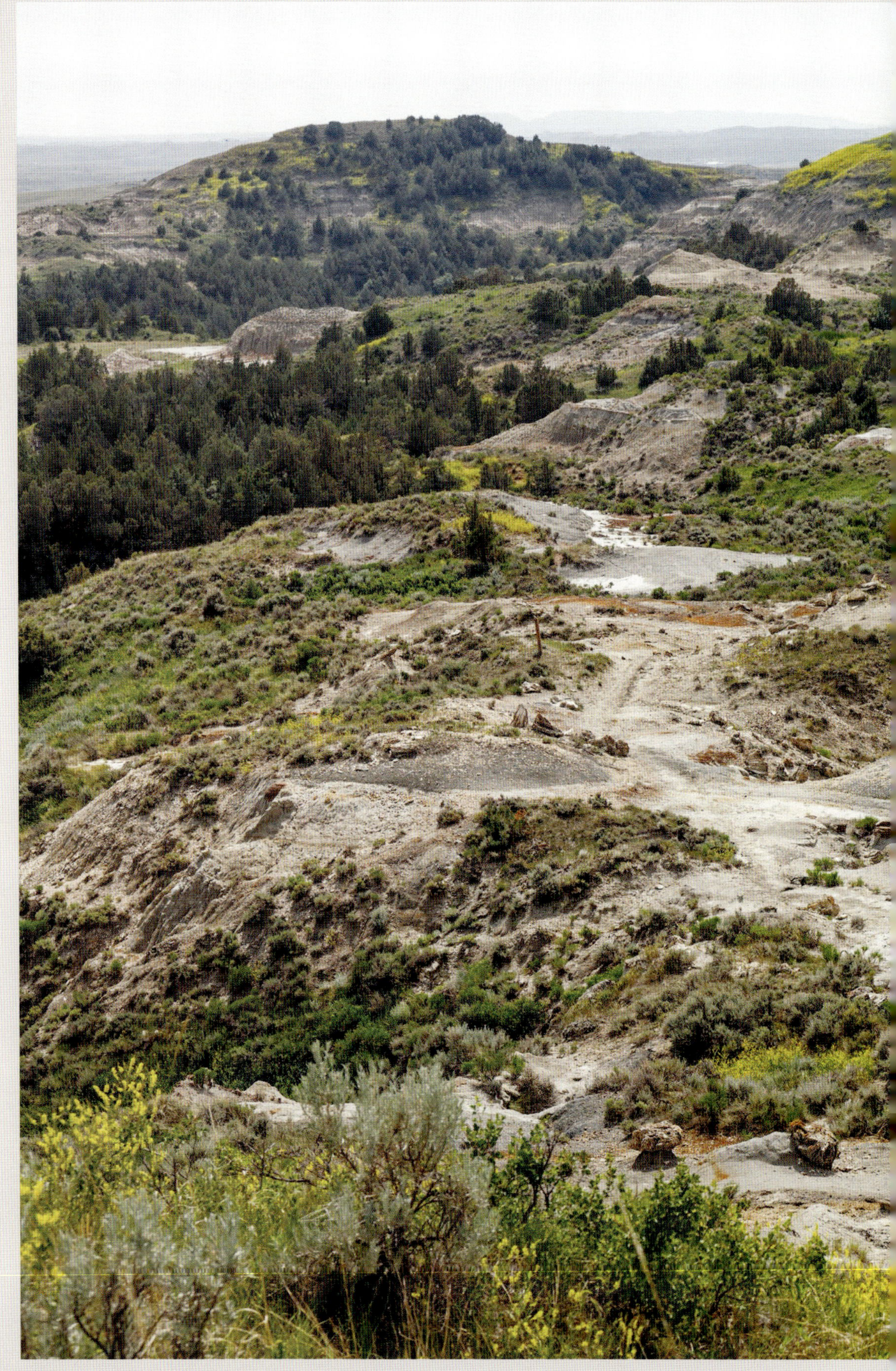

SOFÍA JARAMILLO, 2023
Riders explore the Petrified Forest Trail in Theodore Roosevelt National Park.

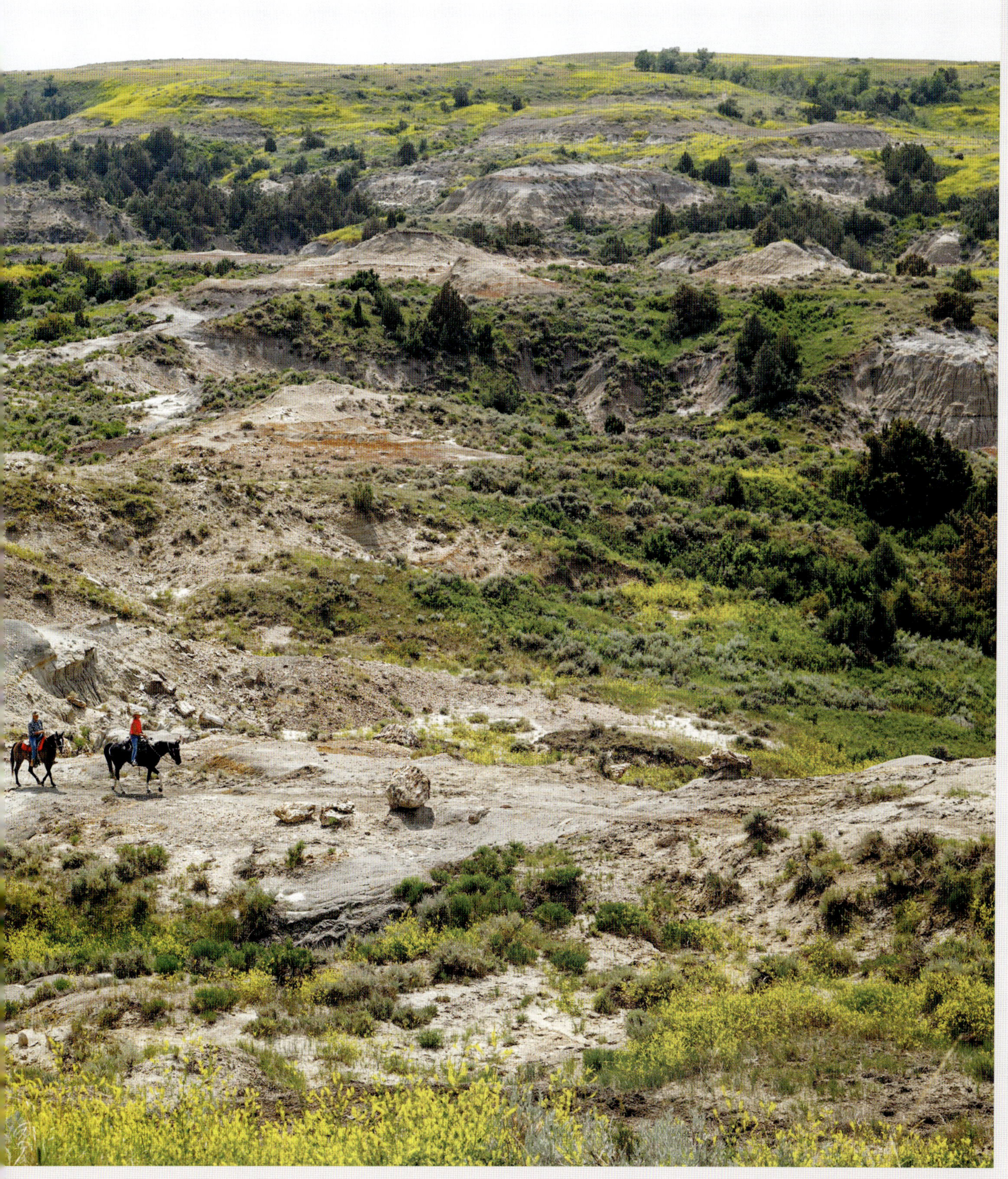

LANDSCAPE IS THE HISTORY OF THE PHYSICAL WORLD WRITTEN BY WIND, WATER, FIRE, AND ICE.

CARSTEN PETER, 2010
A rock formation beneath a skylight in Hang Son Doong—perhaps the largest underground passage on Earth—in Phong Nha-Ke Bang National Park, Vietnam

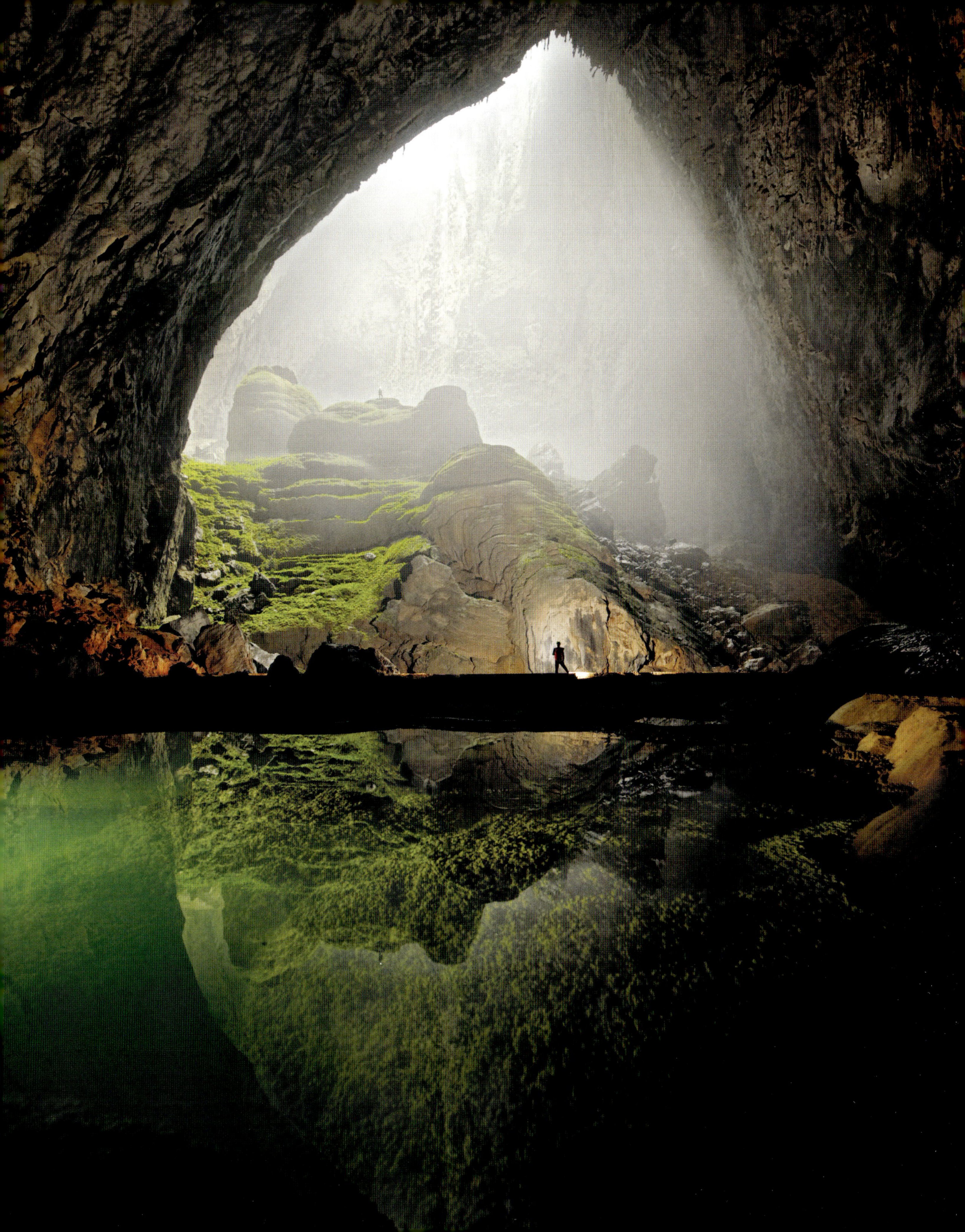

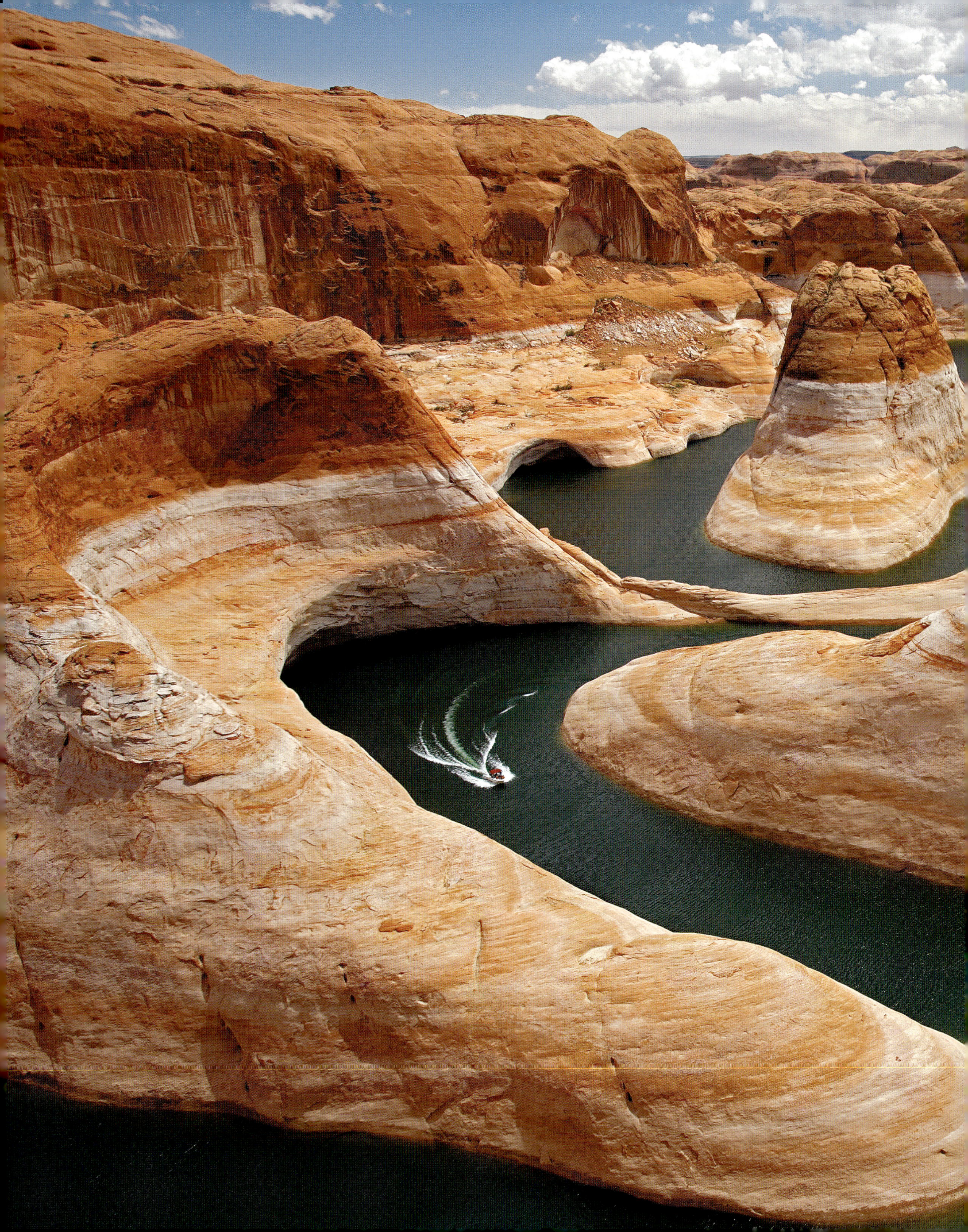

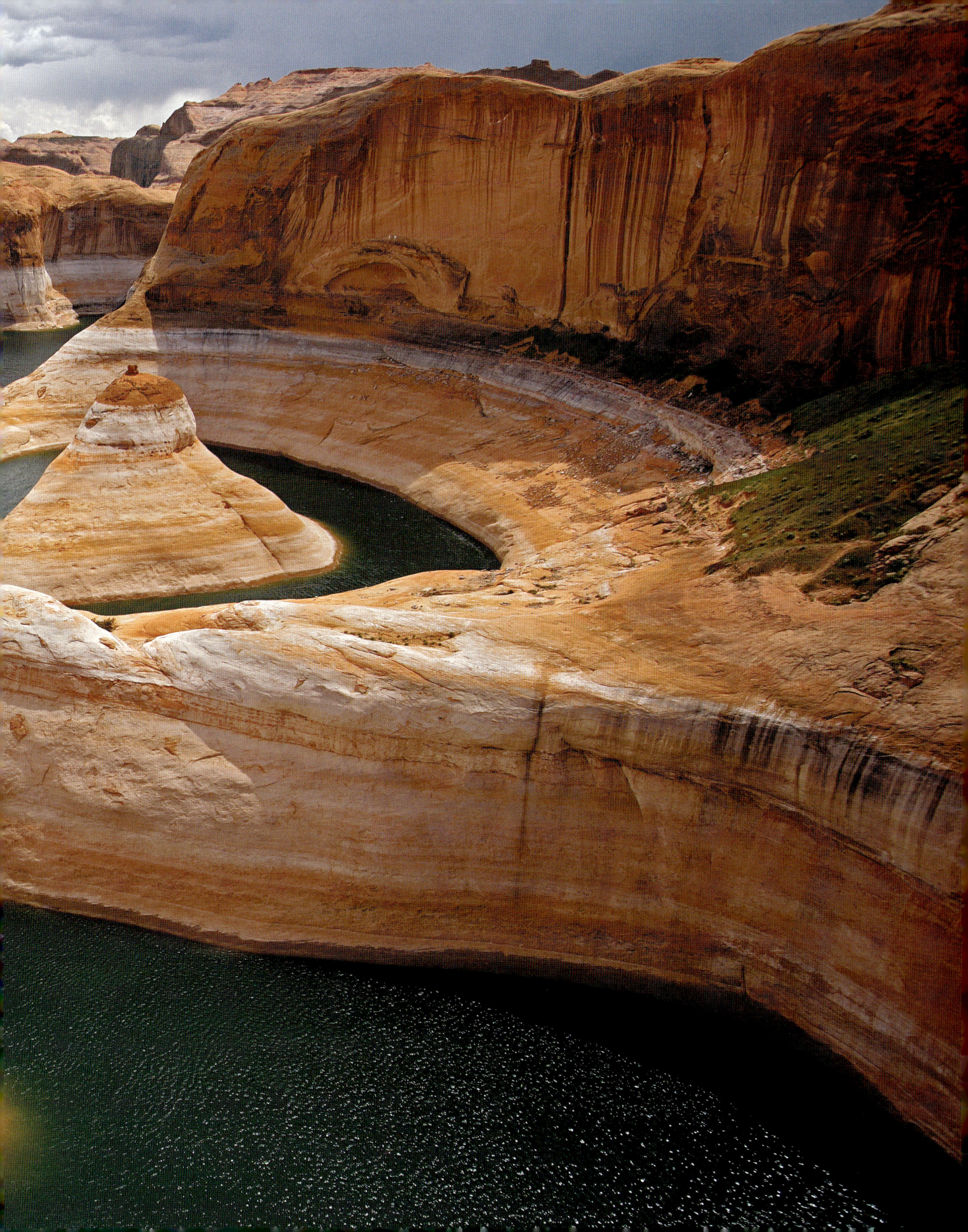

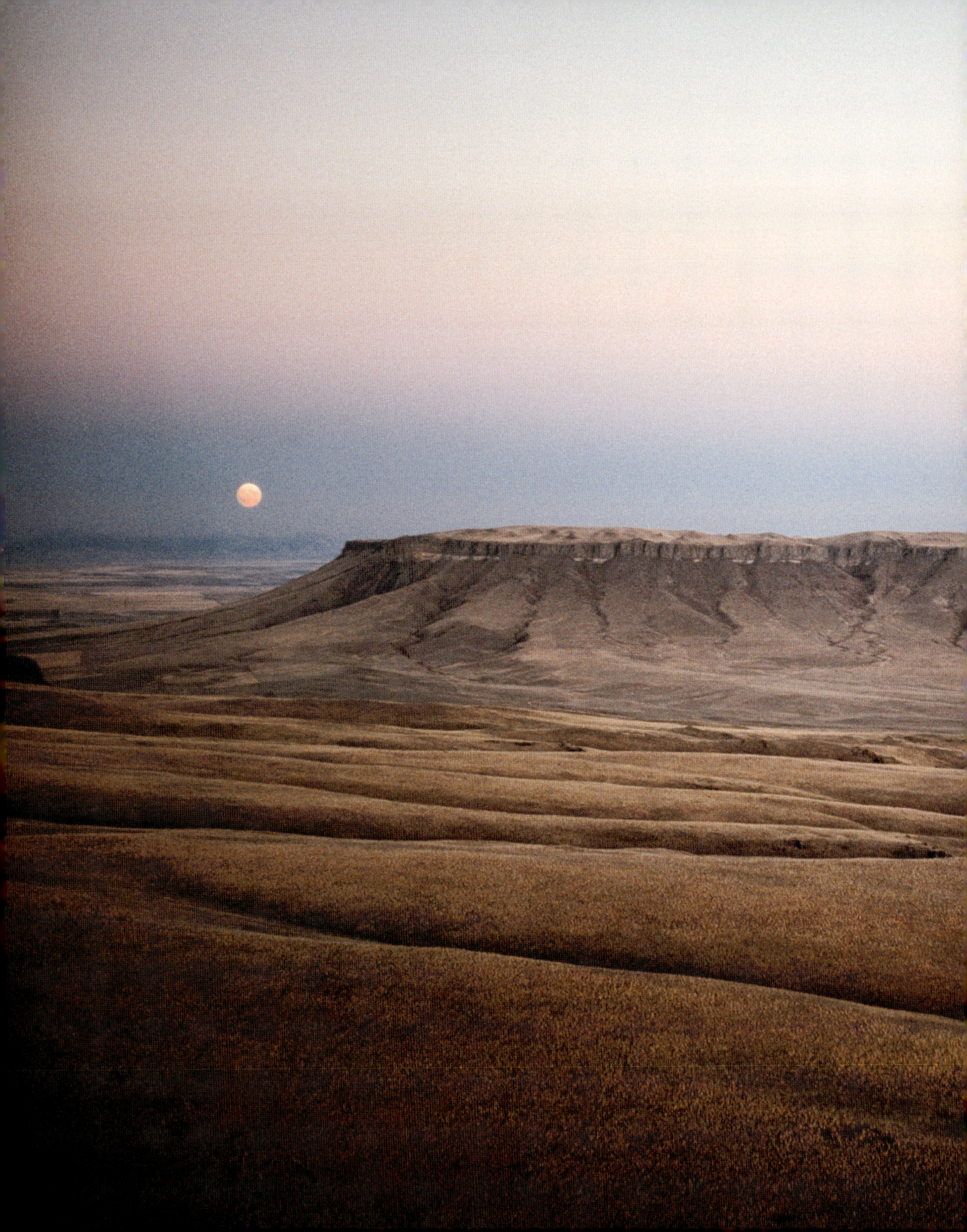

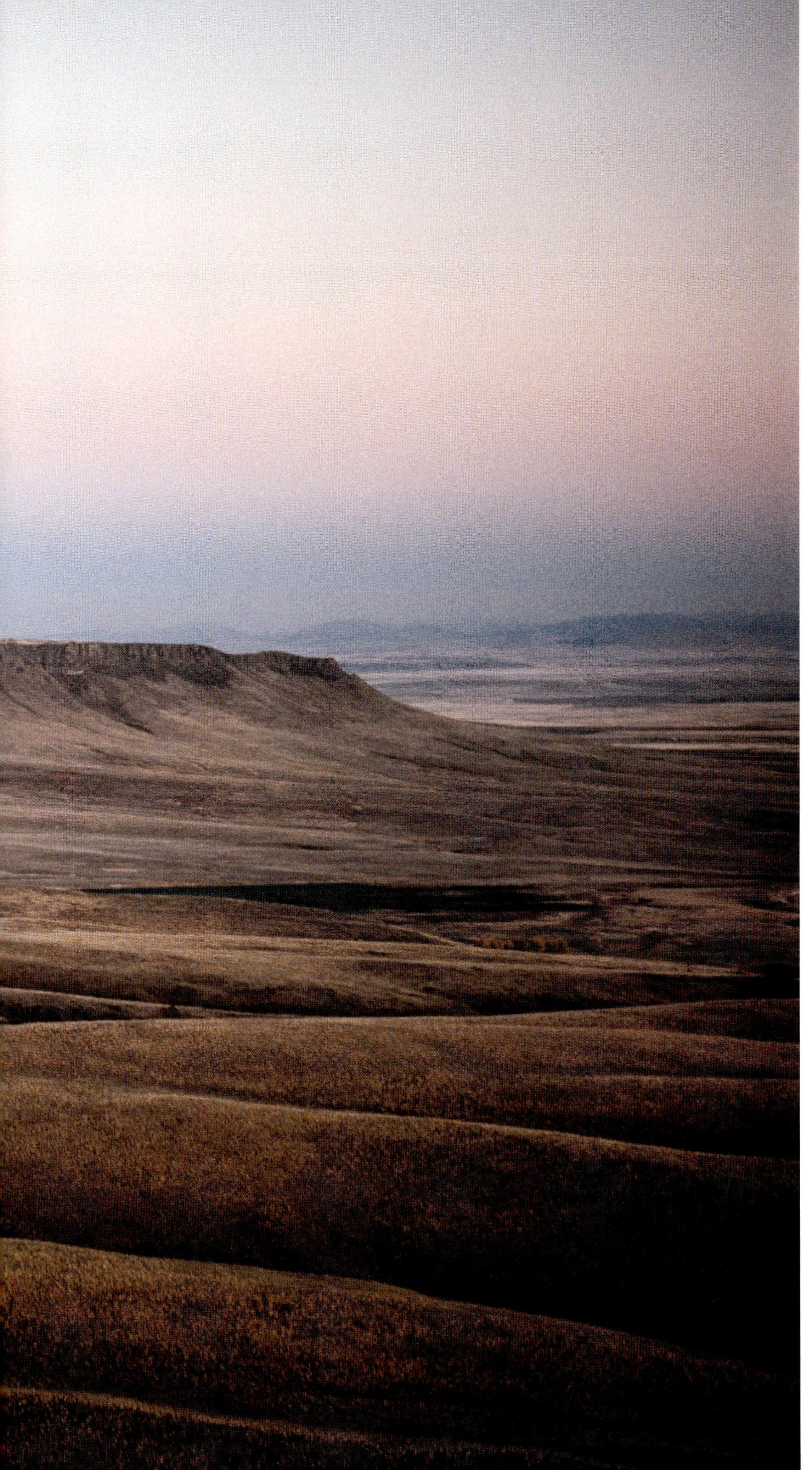

SAM ABELL, 1983
Montana's Square Butte, located near the northern Rocky Mountains, at twilight. In 1806, explorer Meriwether Lewis described it as "Fort Mountain."

PREVIOUS PAGES
MICHAEL MELFORD, 2006
A boat traces the curves of Reflection Canyon in southern Utah.

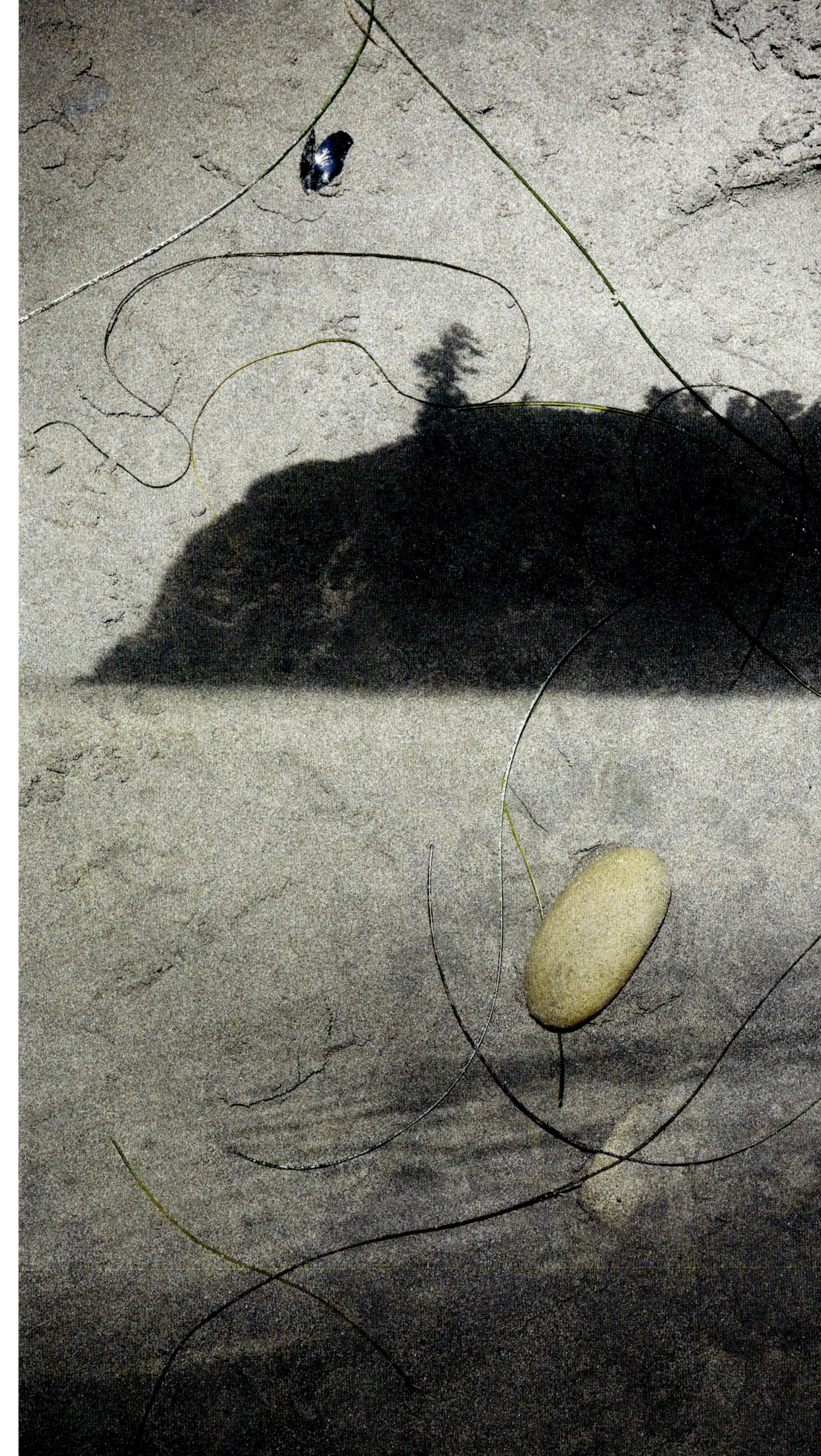

ABELARDO MORELL, 2013
A periscope lens renders Ruby Beach, in Washington's Olympic National Park, as a camera obscura image.

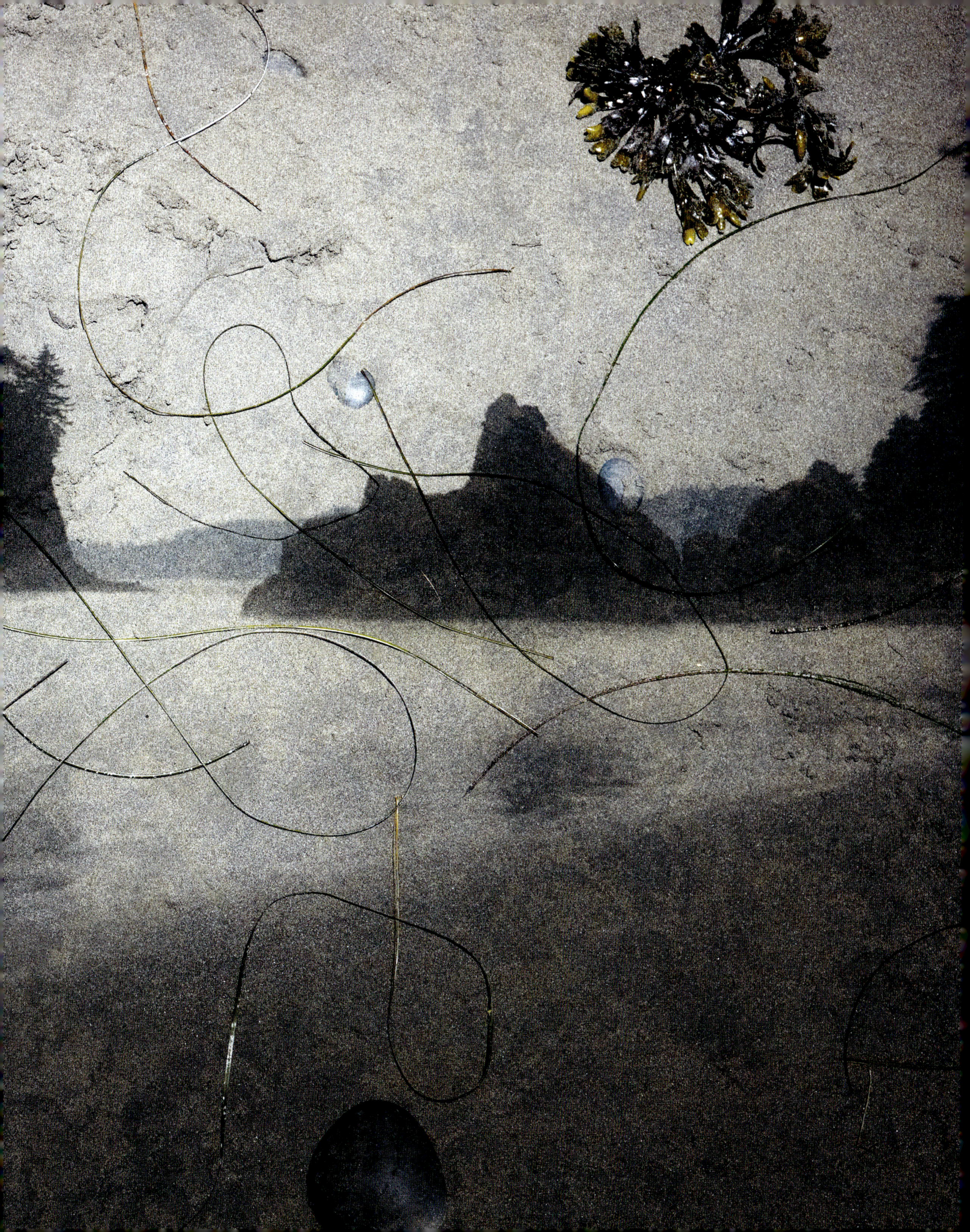

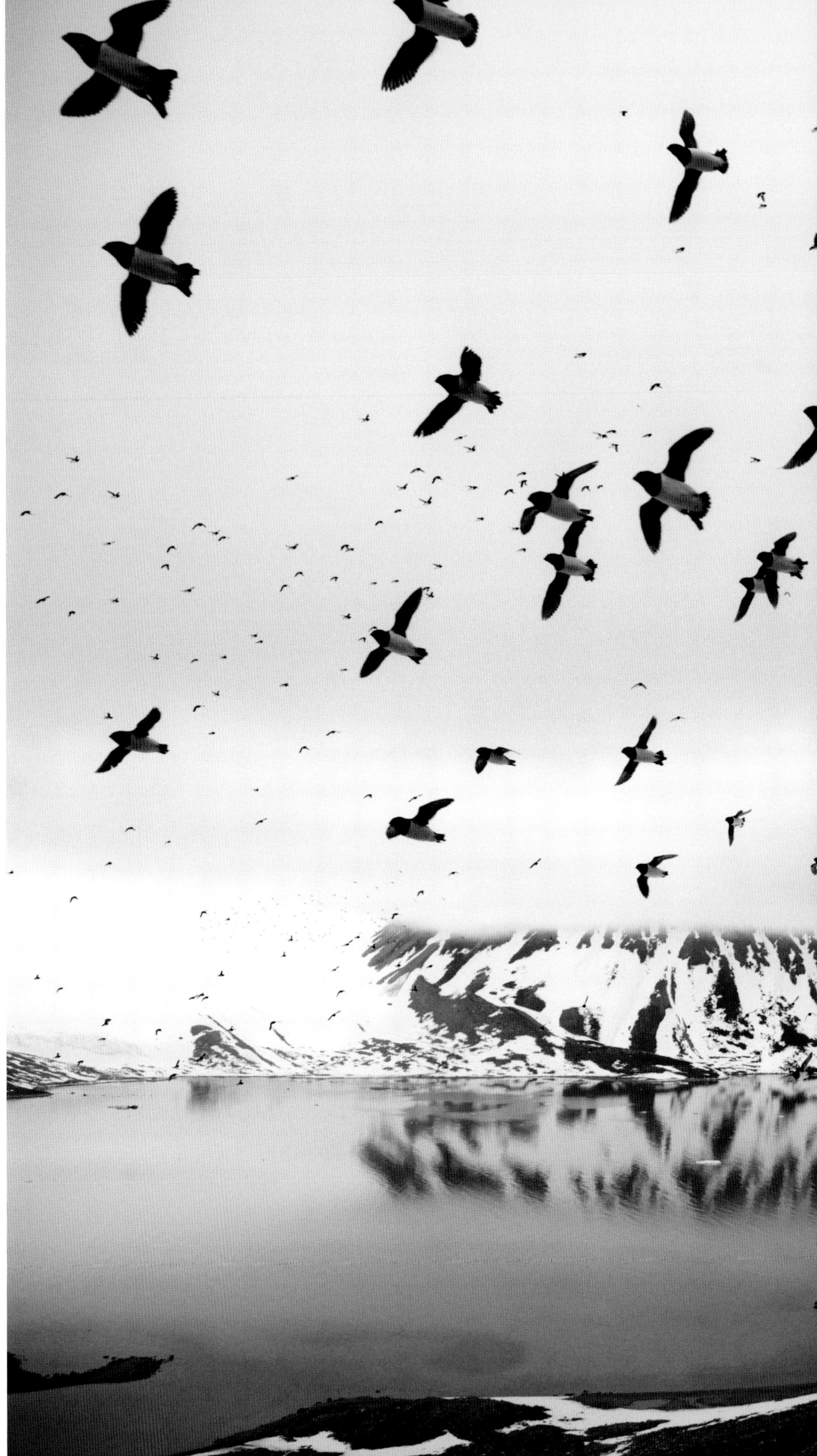

PAUL NICKLEN, 2008
Small auks called dovekies dive for crustaceans, known as copepods, and nest on the shores of Svalbard, Norway.

FOLLOWING PAGES
DIANE COOK AND LEN JENSHEL, 2014
Sixth graders line up in front of a Montezuma cypress known as the Árbol del Tule (Tree of Tule) in Oaxaca, Mexico.

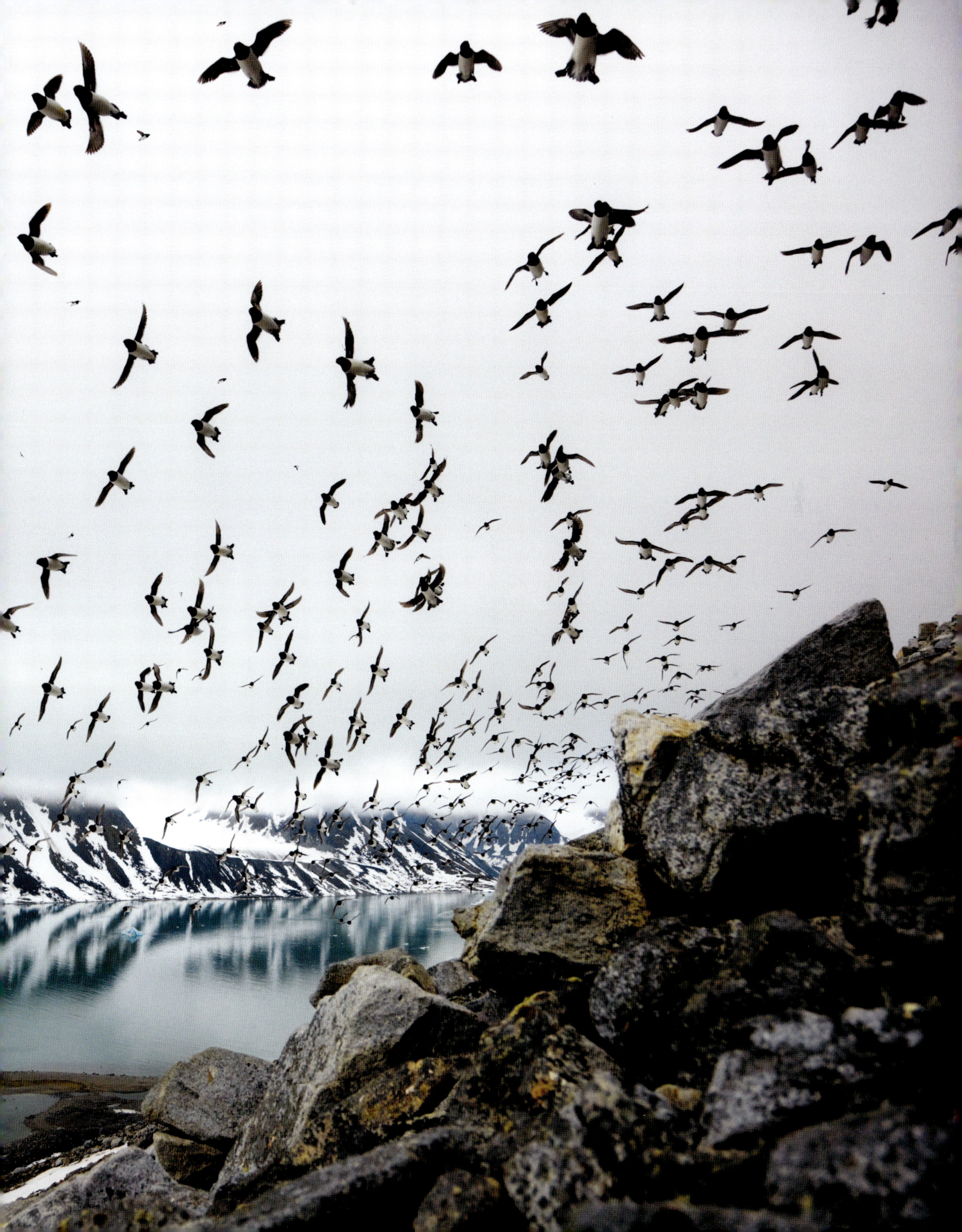

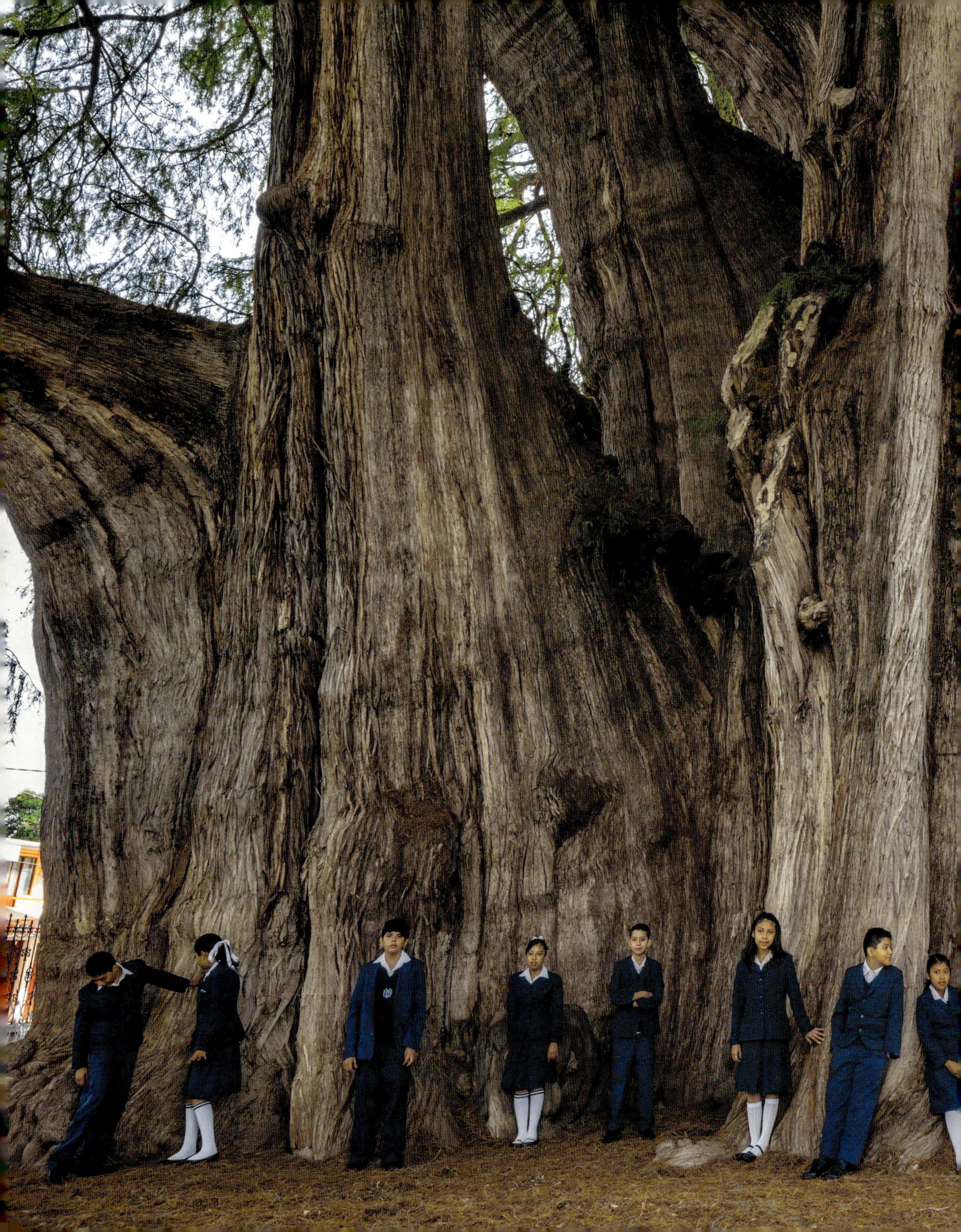

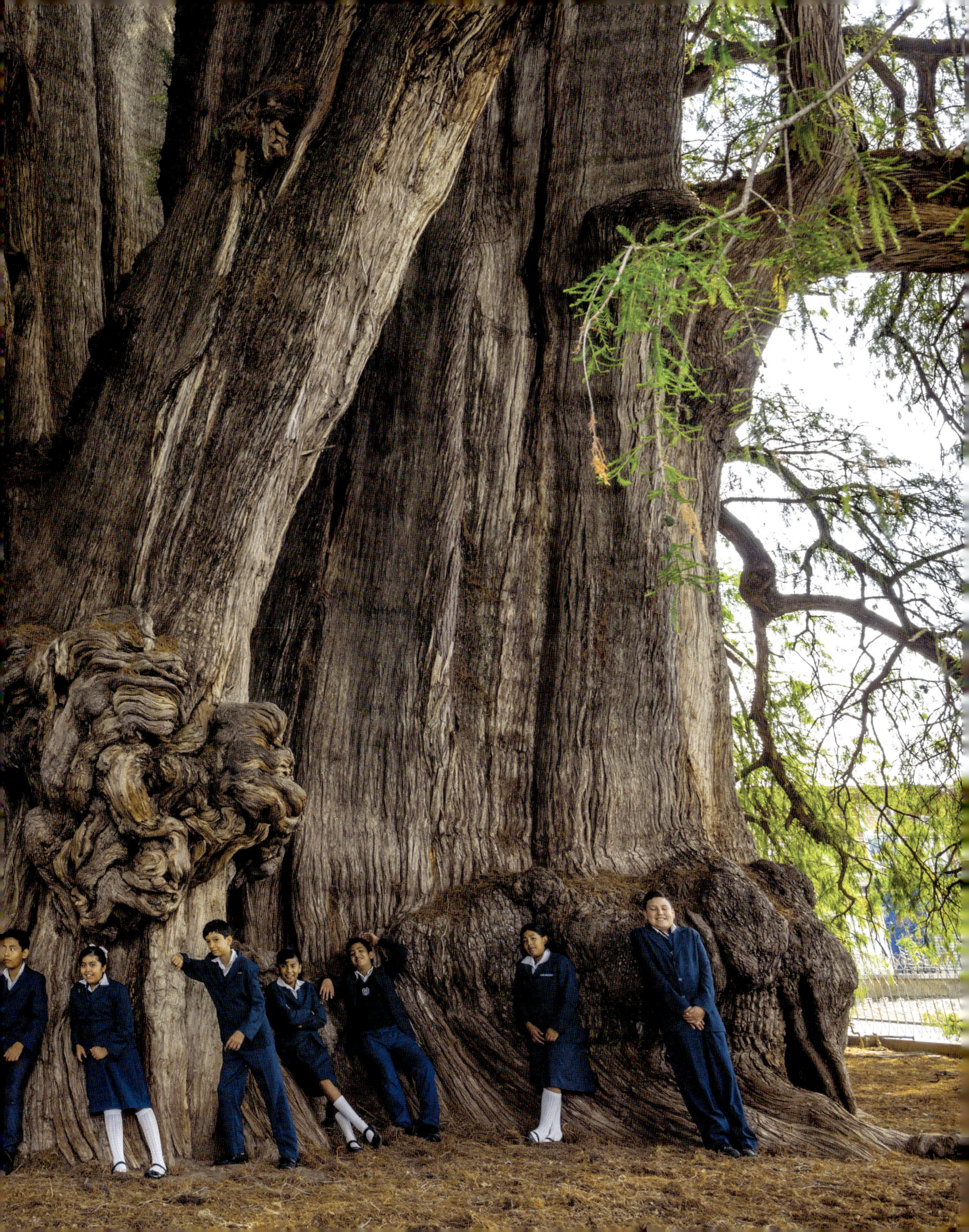

BIOGRAPHY

FRANS LANTING

FOR MORE THAN THREE DECADES, Frans Lanting has documented the globe from the Amazon to Antarctica to promote understanding about our planet through image making. "I use my work to express wonder about the natural world and concern about the perils it faces," he says.

Born in Rotterdam, the Netherlands, he earned a master's degree in economics before moving to the United States to study environmental planning. Soon after, he began photographing the natural world—and never turned back. Assignments have ranged from the bonobos of the Democratic Republic of the Congo to a circumnavigation by sailboat of South Georgia Island in the subantarctic. In the Amazon Basin, he spent weeks on platform towers for rare tree-canopy views of wild macaws. He has lived with seabirds on Pacific island atolls, followed lions through the African night, and camped among giant tortoises inside a Galápagos volcano. "Photography was once an excuse for me to seek out animals on their own ground—I sought a personal connection," he says. "But now there is an equally important social component to what I do. I believe that photography is a global language which can connect people everywhere."

Lanting has photographed more than 30 stories for *National Geographic* and has published many books about the world of nature, including *Bay of Life: From Wind to Whales, Into Africa, Life: A Journey Through Time,* and *Okavango: Africa's Last Eden.* He is an ambassador for the World Wildlife Fund, serves on the Leadership Council of Conservation International, co-founded the North American Nature Photography Association, and is a fellow of the International League of Conservation Photographers.

In 2018, the Wildlife Photographer of the Year competition awarded him its first Lifetime Achievement Award. He has been inducted as a Knight in the Royal Order of the Golden Ark, the Netherlands' highest conservation honor.

"I hope my experiences can be a bridge between the animal world and the millions of people who will never crouch before an elephant or hunt with lions in the African night," Lanting observes. "My life's work is my tribute to them, and to preserving the unity of life on Earth."

OPPOSITE TOP
FRANS LANTING, 2009
Sandgrouse at a water hole in Namibia's NamibRand Nature Reserve

OPPOSITE BOTTOM
FRANS LANTING, 2009
Desert-dwelling elephants follow the contours of Namibia's ancient Huab River Valley.

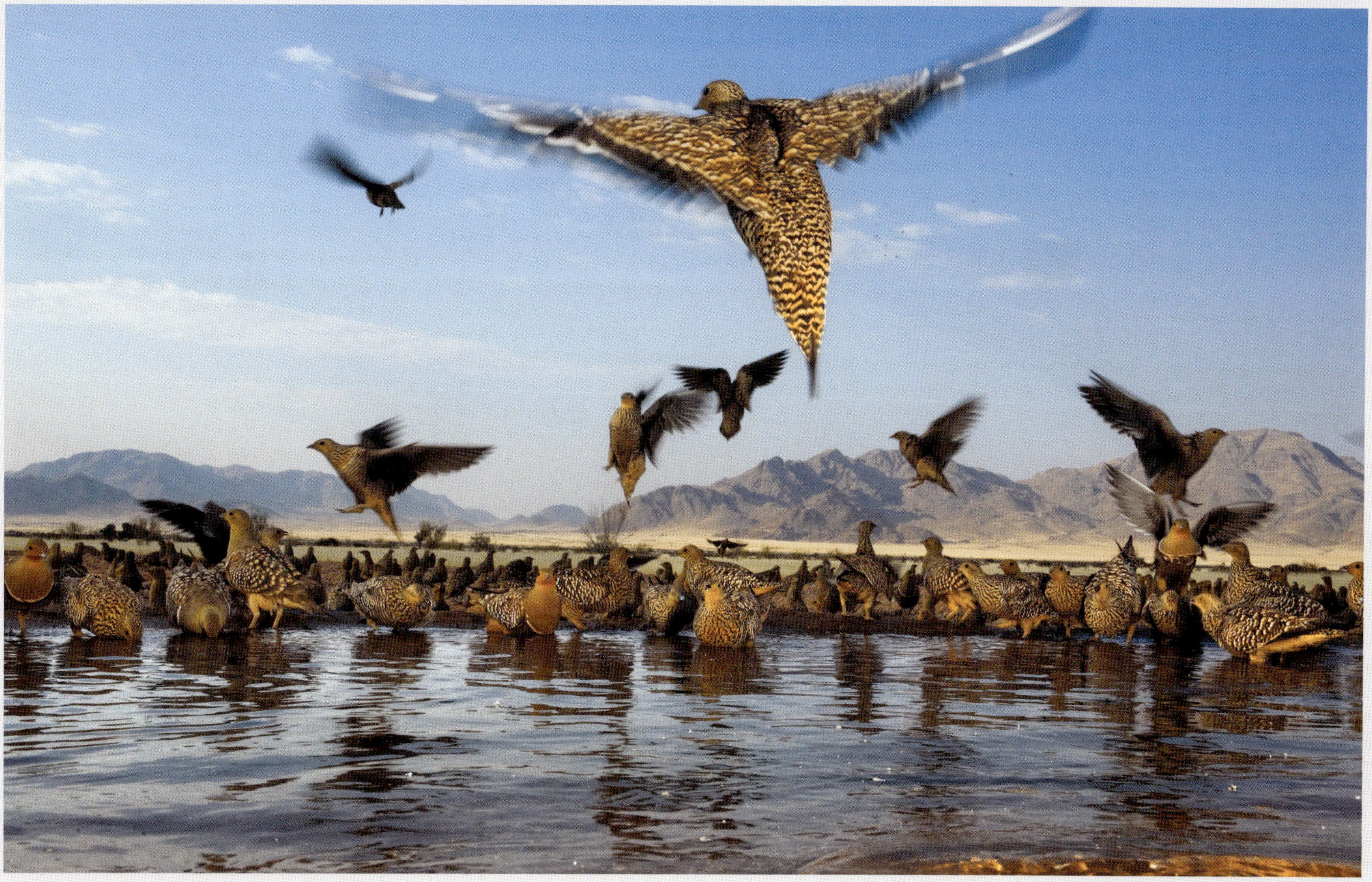

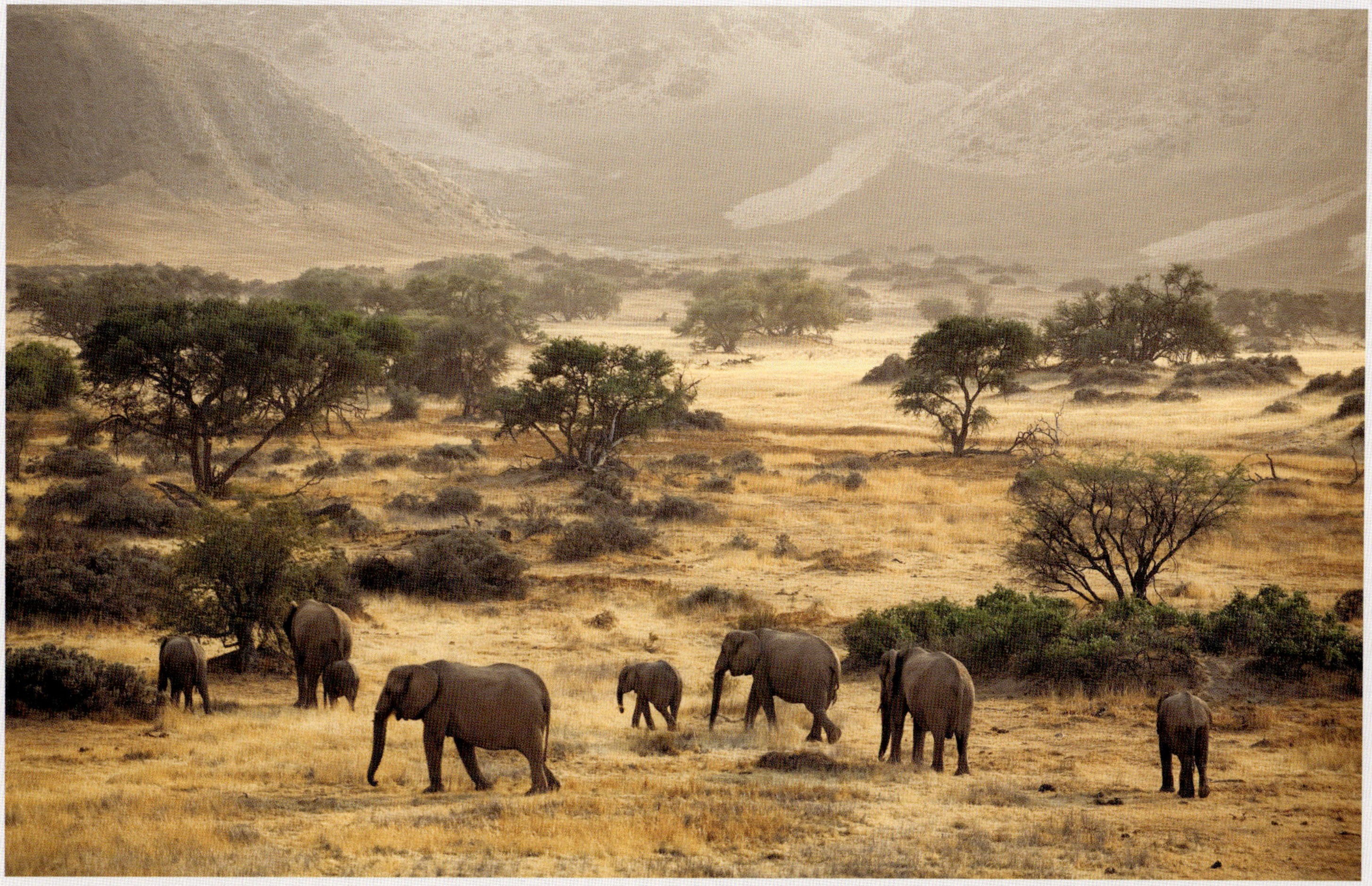

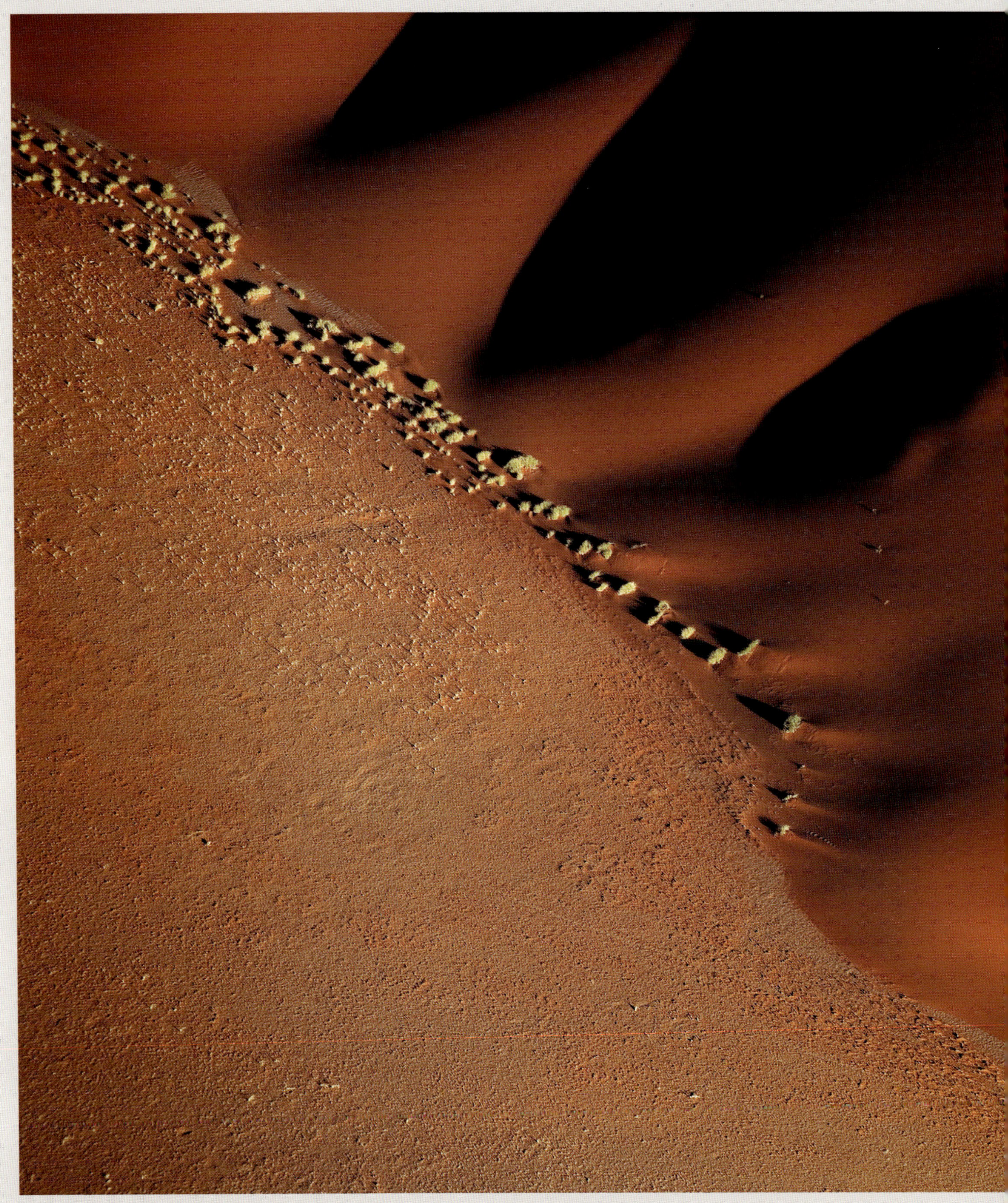

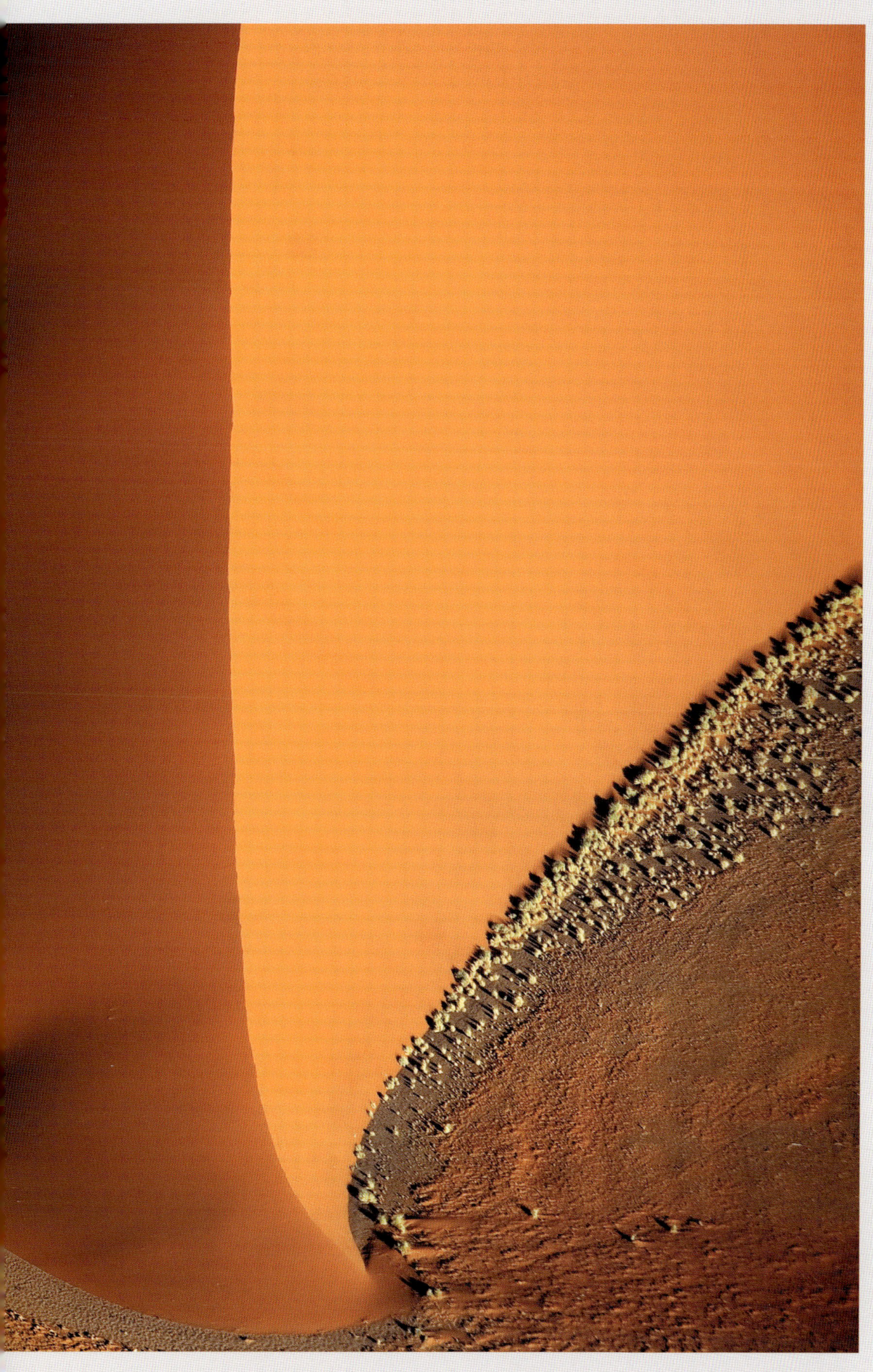

FRANS LANTING, 2009
Some of the world's tallest sand dunes, colored red by iron oxide, loom in Africa's Namib Desert.

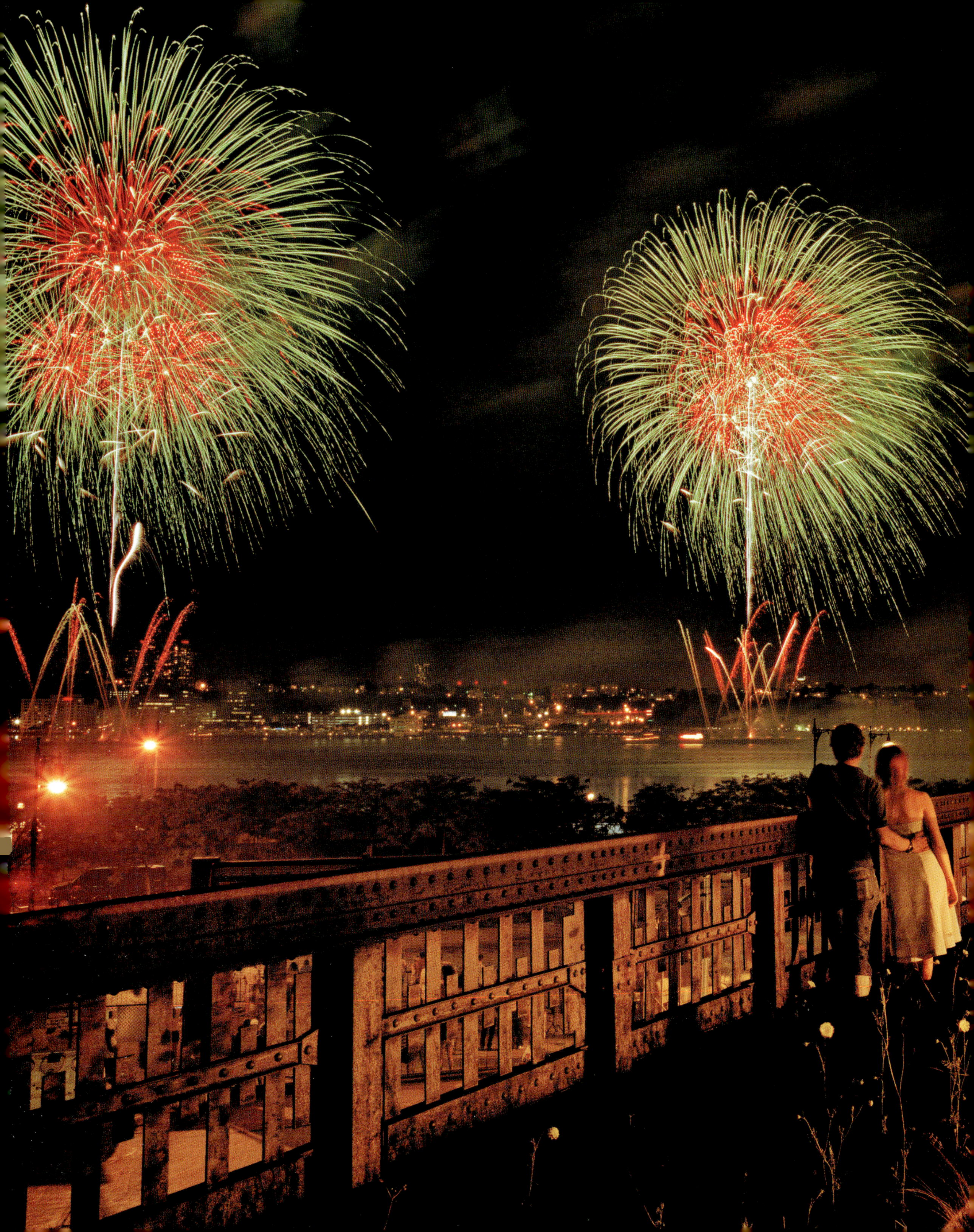

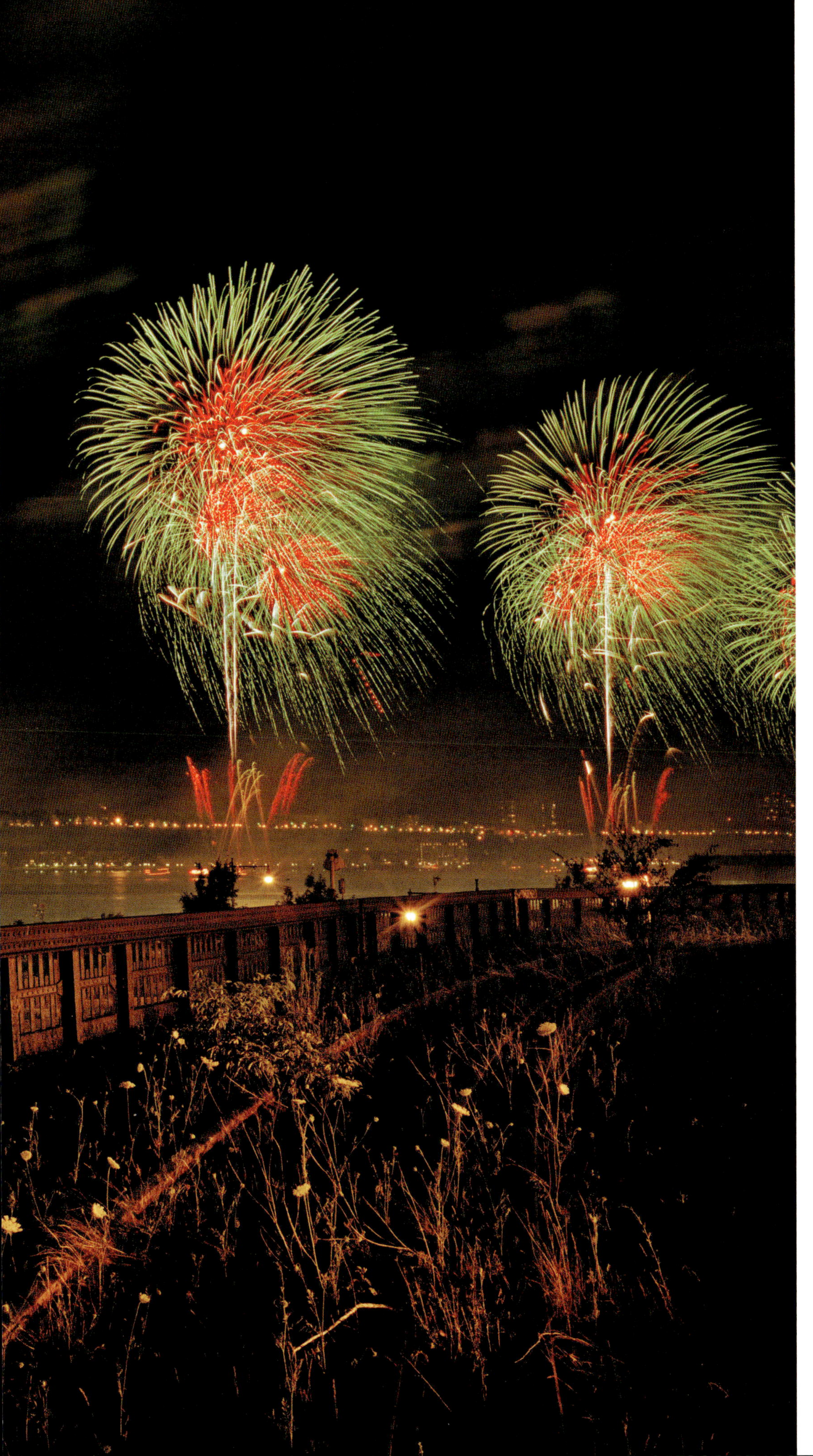

DIANE COOK AND LEN JENSHEL, 2010
Fourth of July fireworks light up the High Line and Hudson River, New York City.

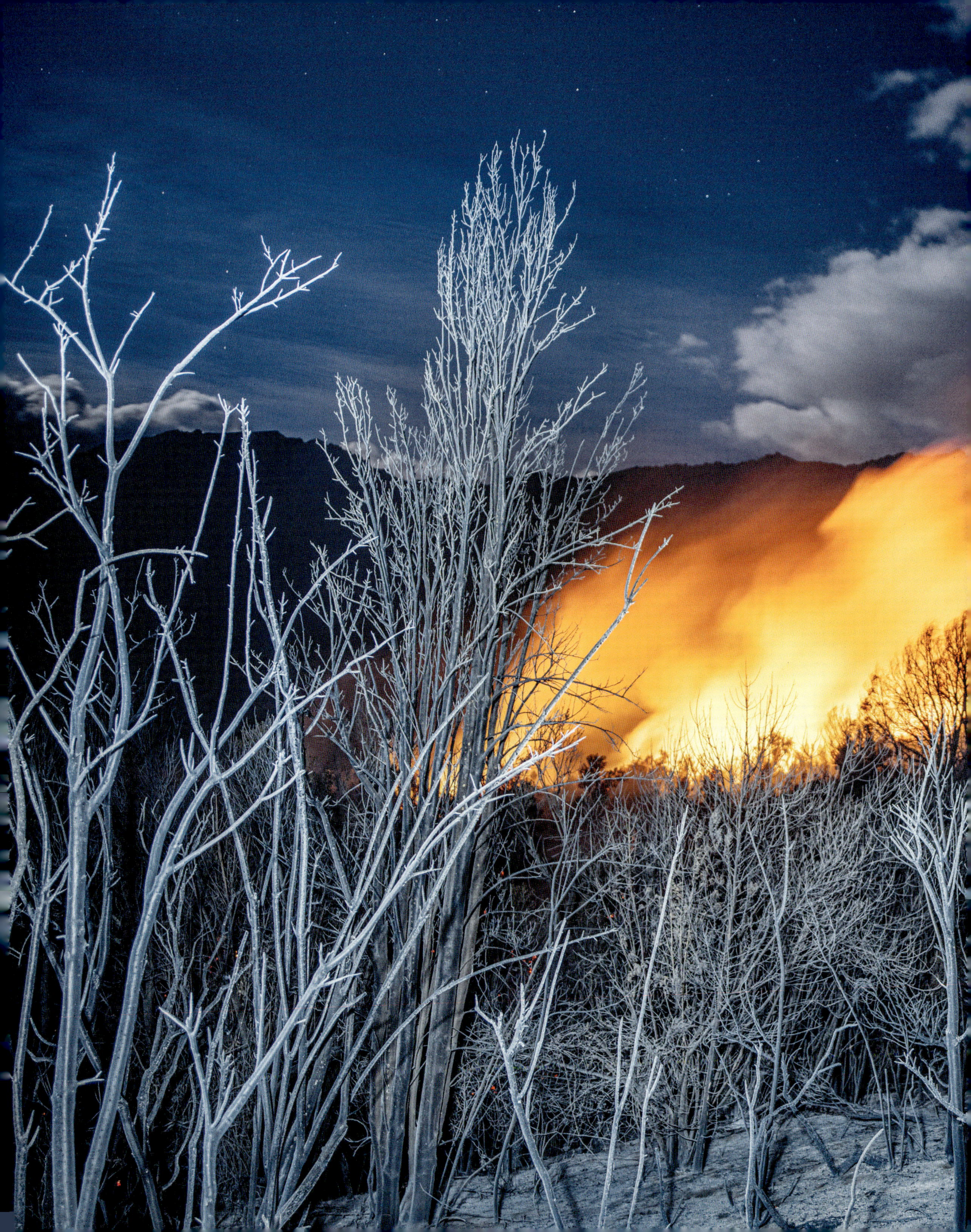

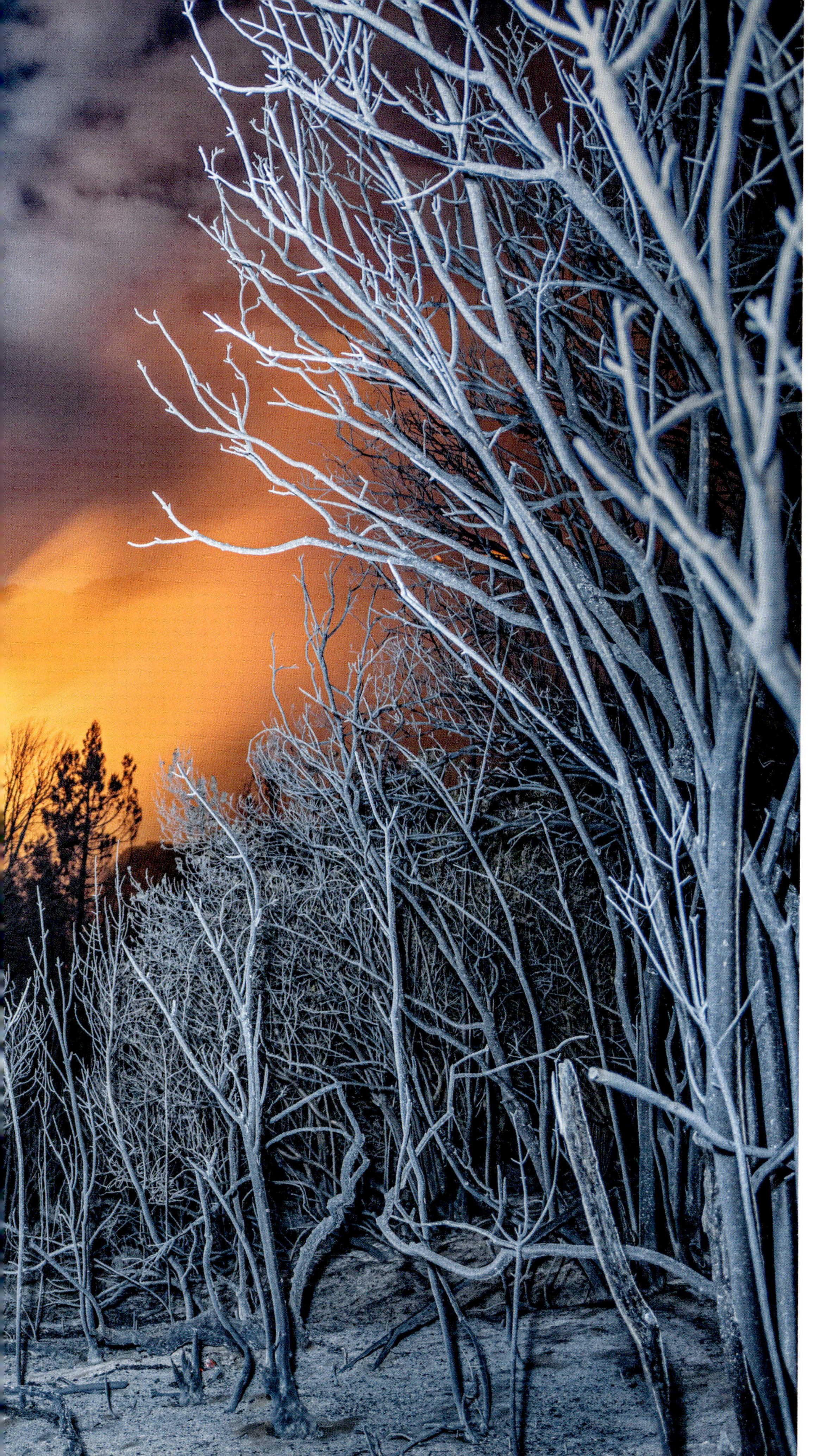

ALEJANDRO CHASKIELBERG, 2021
A blaze started by a campfire engulfs the forest near El Bolsón, Argentina. Fires are becoming more commonplace in Patagonia due to climate change and increased population in wildlands, according to researchers. This fire consumed 54,000 acres in a few days.

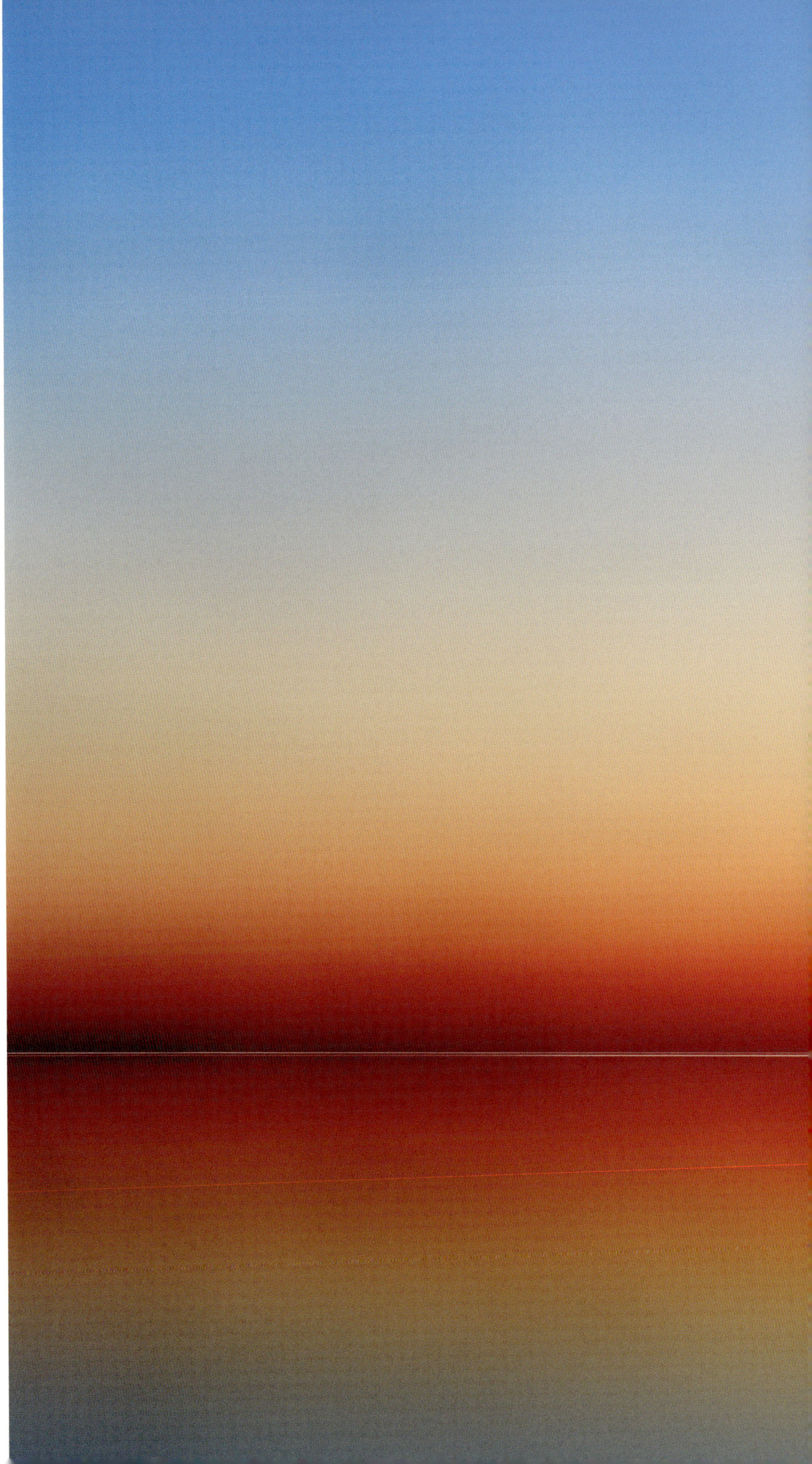

MURRAY FREDERICKS, 2011
Predawn colors reflect on a rare rain puddle at Australia's highly saline Lake Eyre. The lake covers 3,700 featureless square miles.

FOLLOWING PAGES
JOHN STANMEYER, 2008
Mount Bromo (left) and Mount Semeru (background) are sacred in Indonesia. During the Kasada festival on the island of Java, locals make sacrifices and pray for prosperity from inside Bromo's crater.

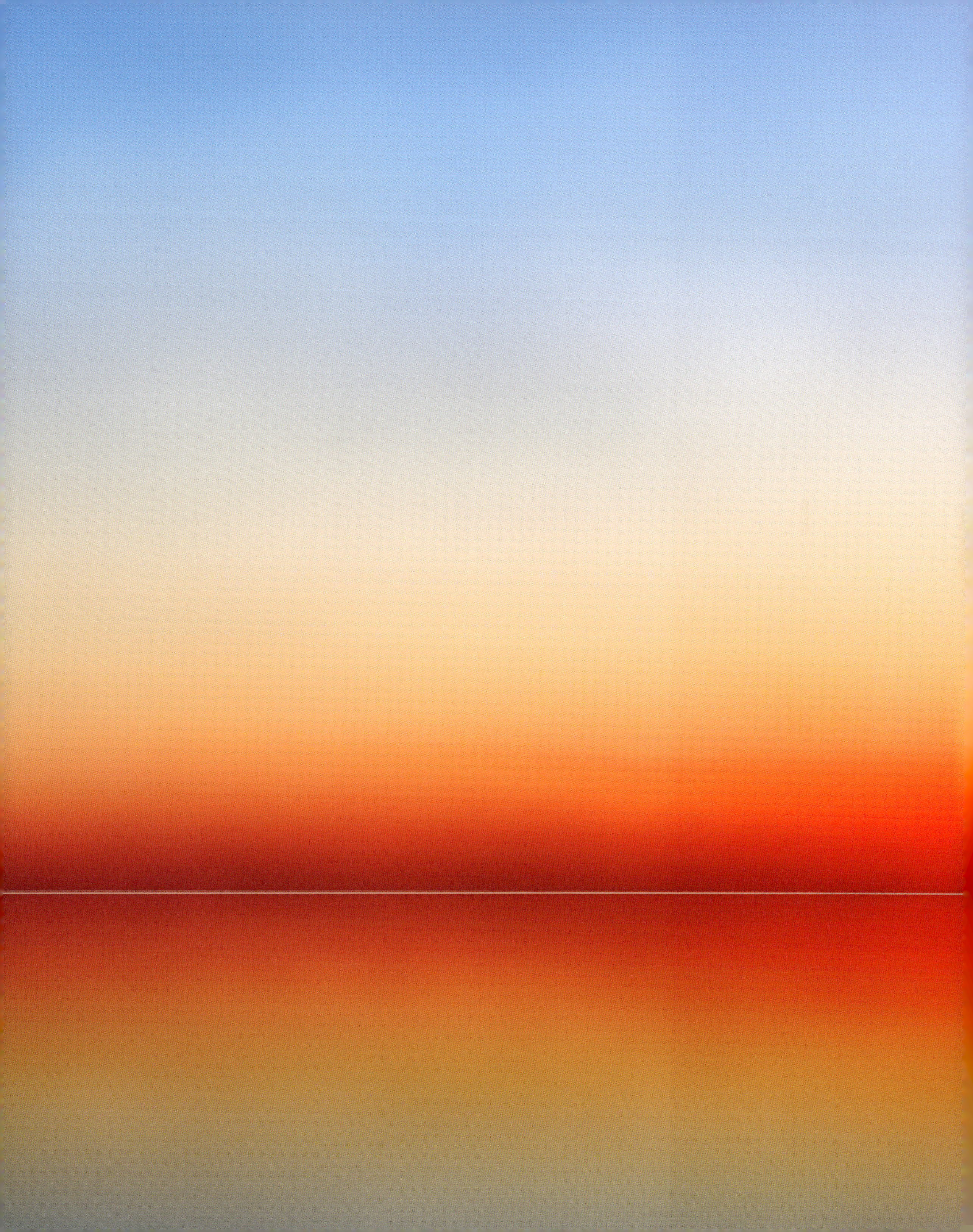

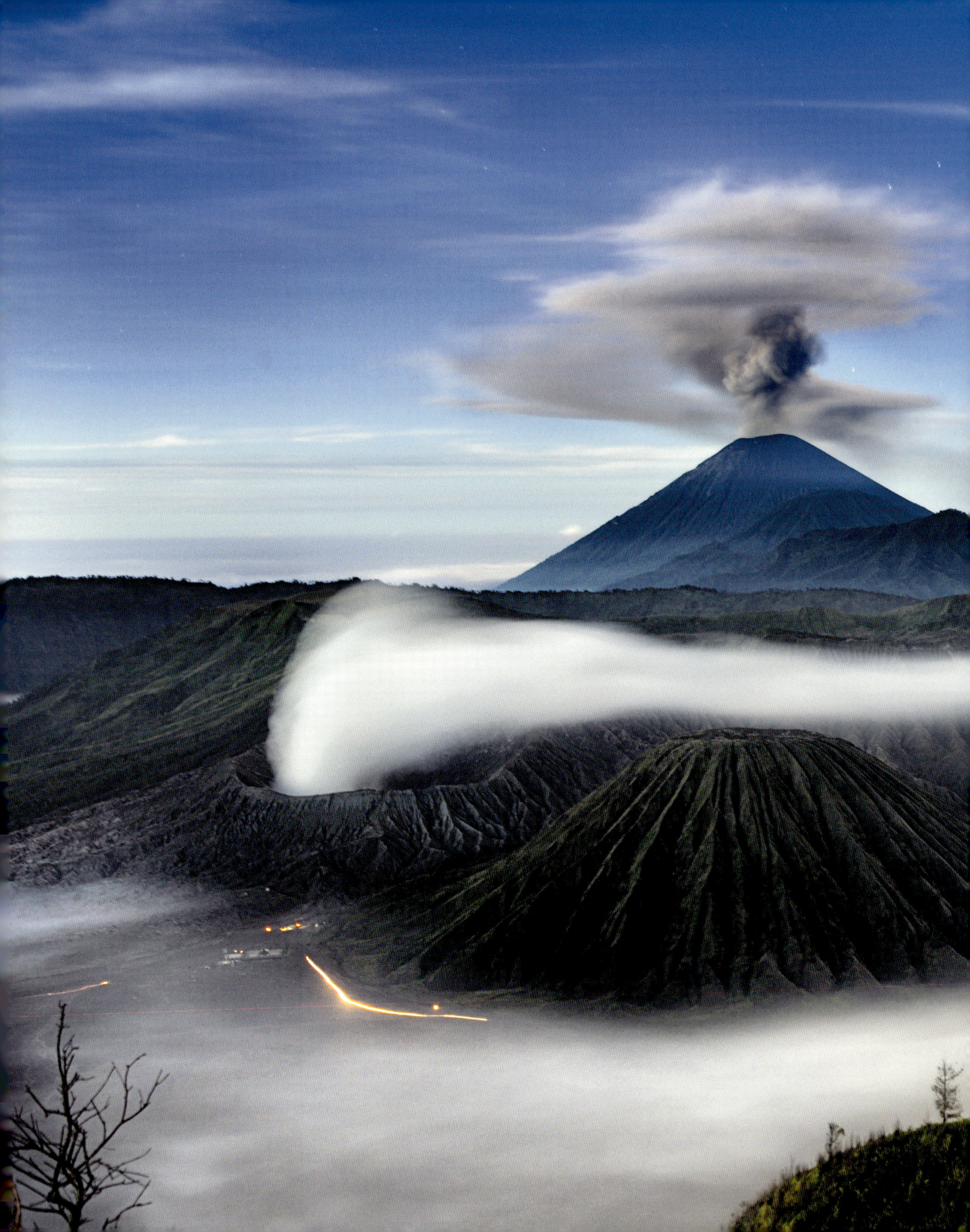

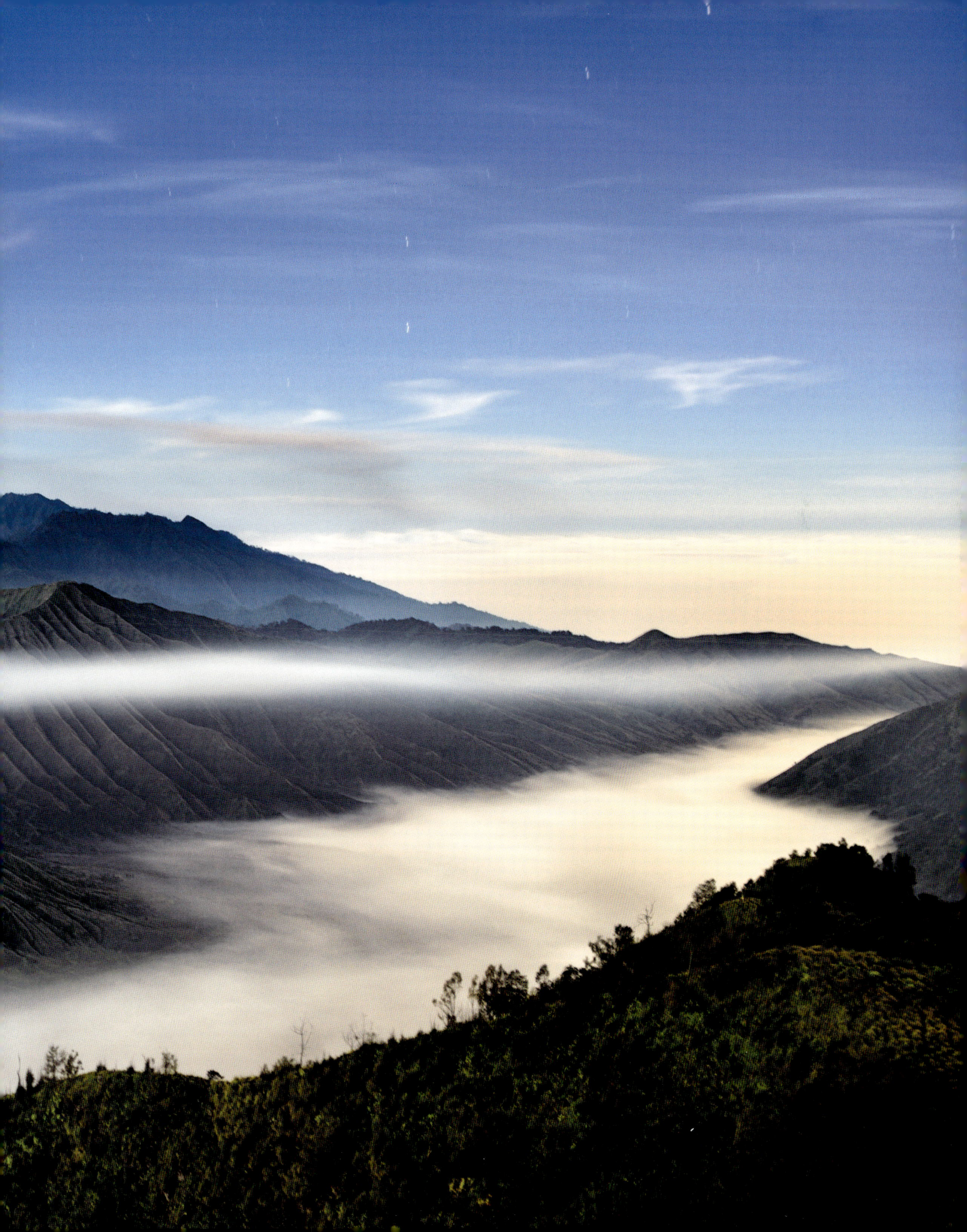

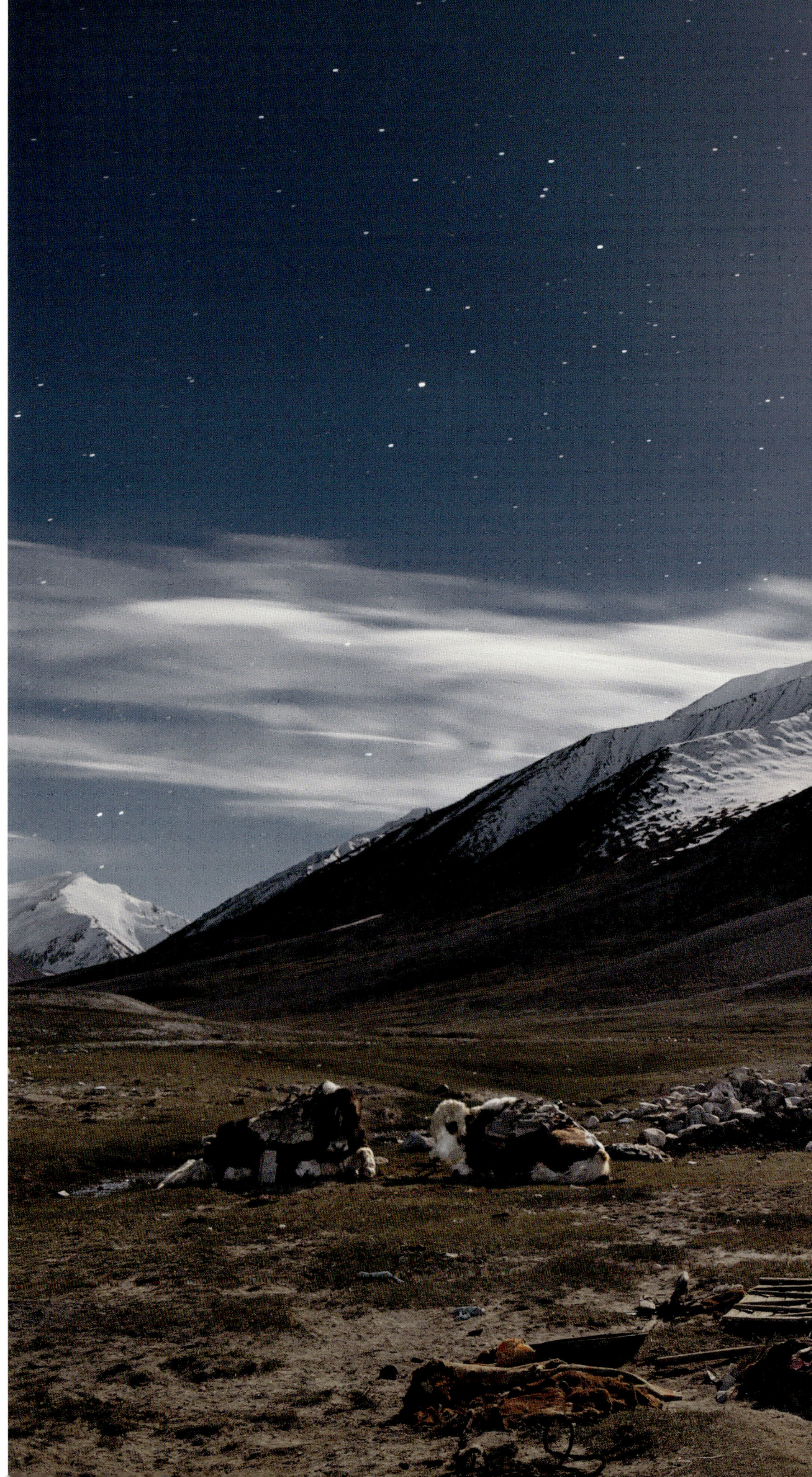

MATTHIEU PALEY, 2013
Blanket-draped yaks hunker down outside a Kyrgyz yurt in remote Afghanistan. The Kyrgyz people maintain a nomadic way of life amid a treeless landscape.

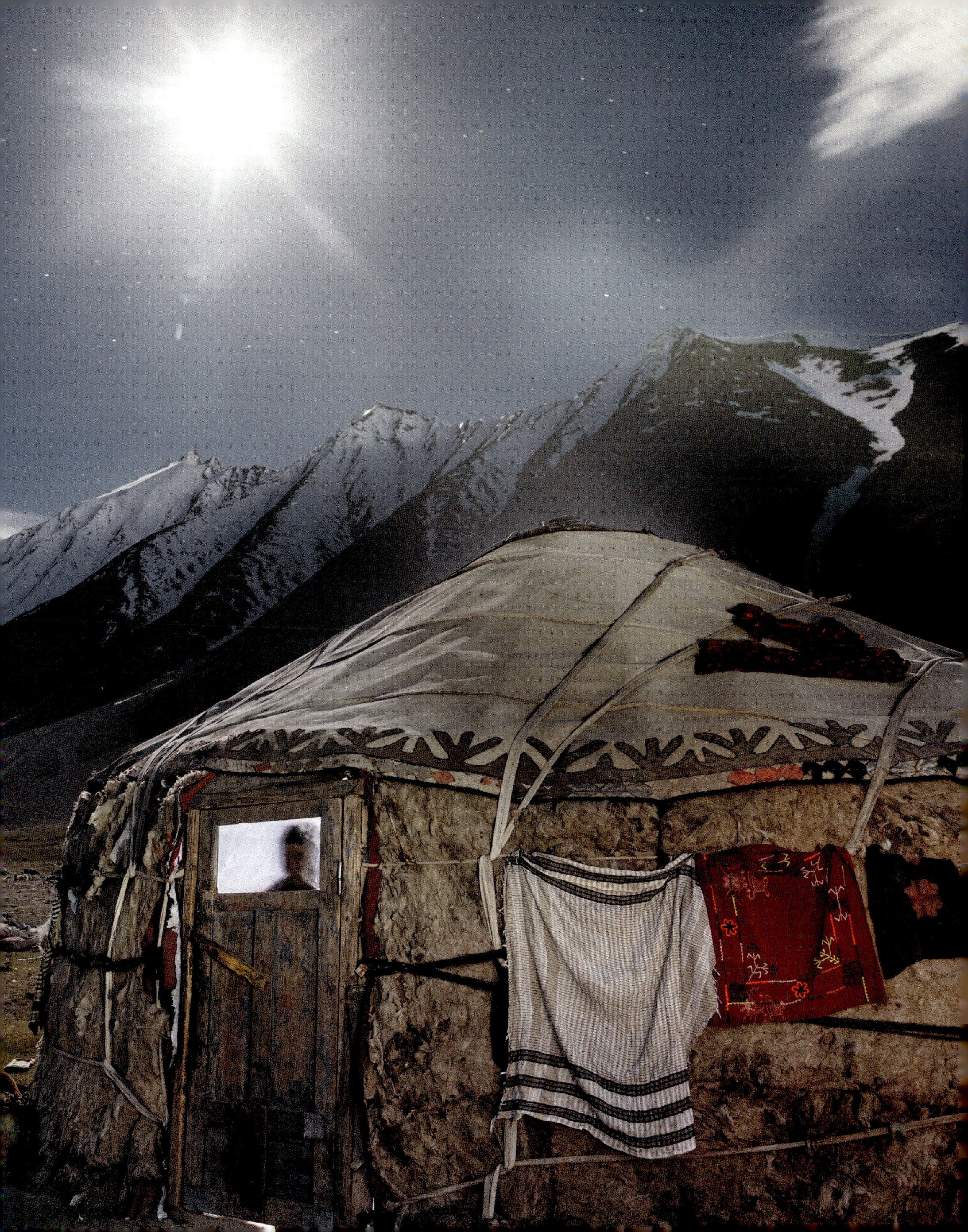

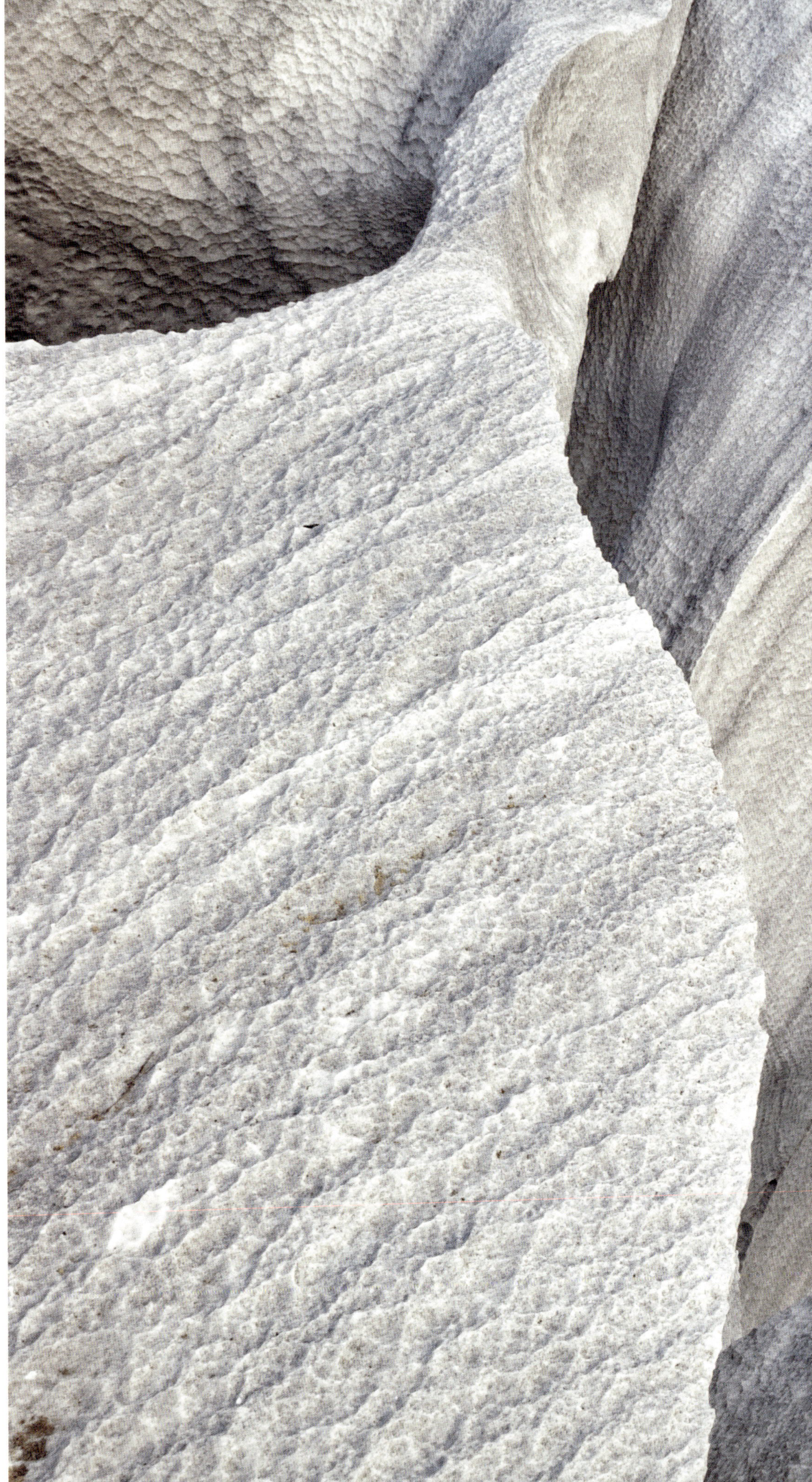

ORSOLYA HAARBERG, 2013
The Marmorslottet formation, also called the Marble Castle, was carved over millennia by the Glomåga River in northern Norway.

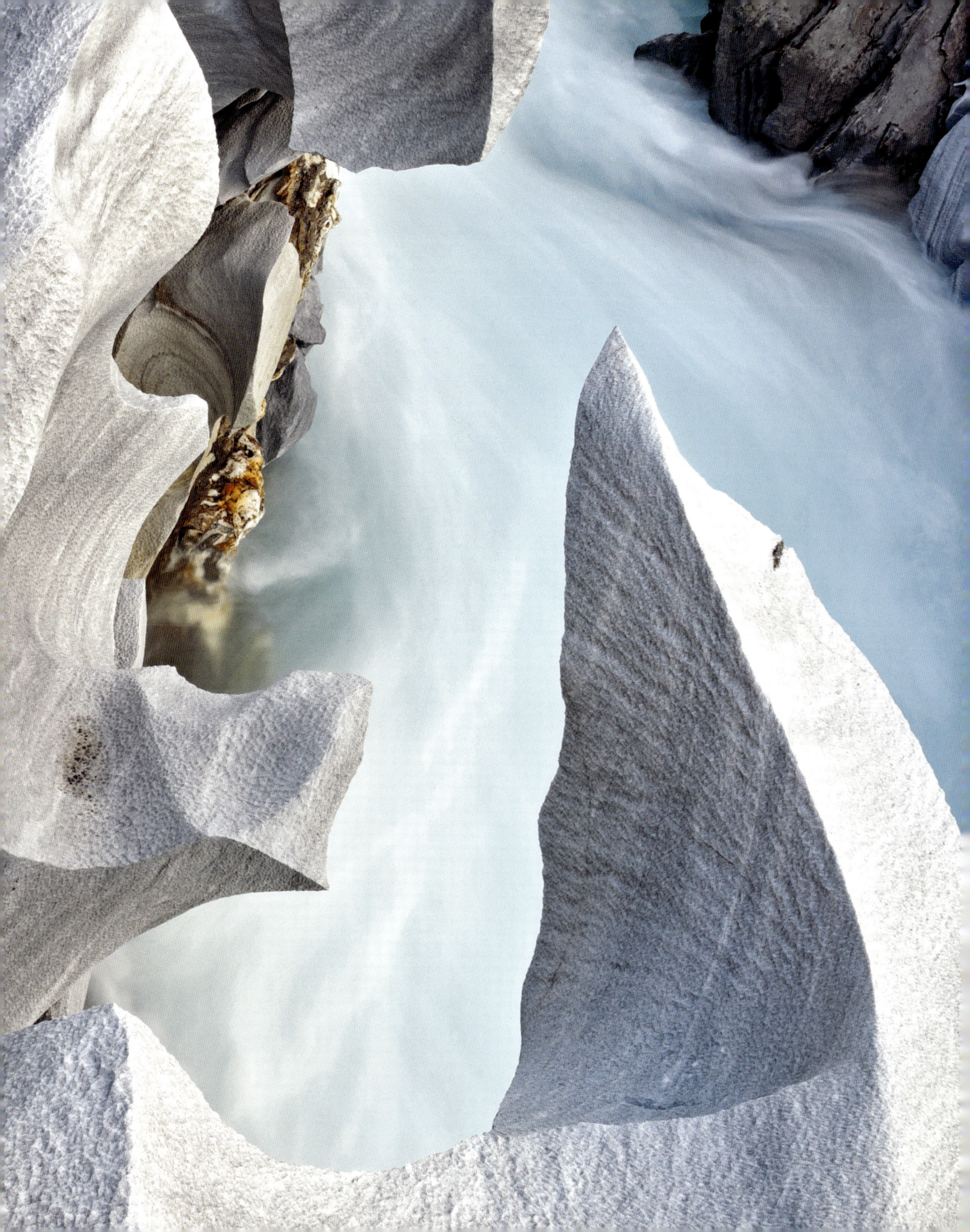

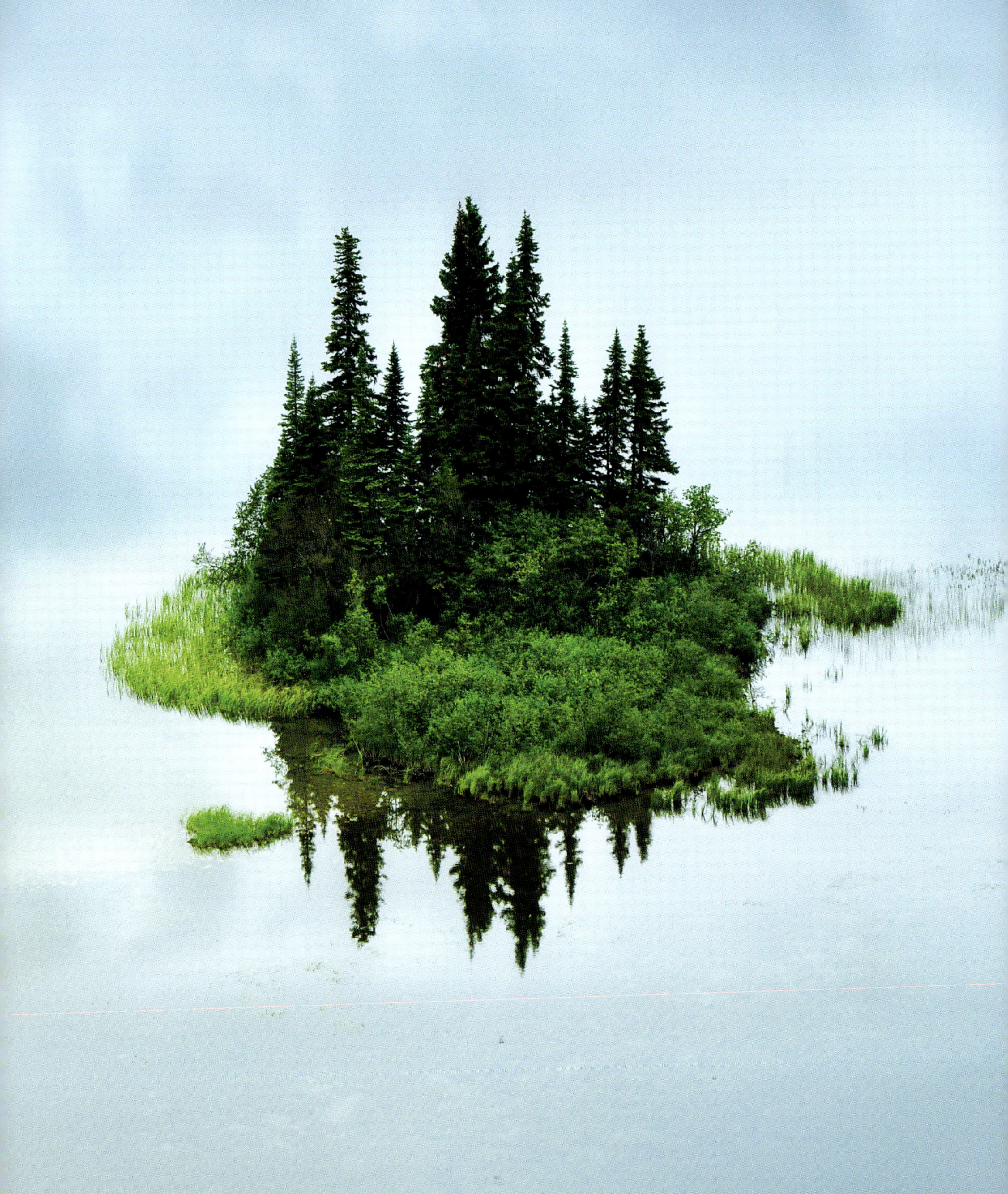

LANDSCAPE PHOTOGRAPHY IS THE SUPREME TEST OF THE PHOTOGRAPHER.

ANSEL ADAMS, PHOTOGRAPHER

SHANE KALYN, 2014
As the surrounding waters reflect the clouds, an island in the middle of British Columbia's Tumuch Lake appears to be floating.

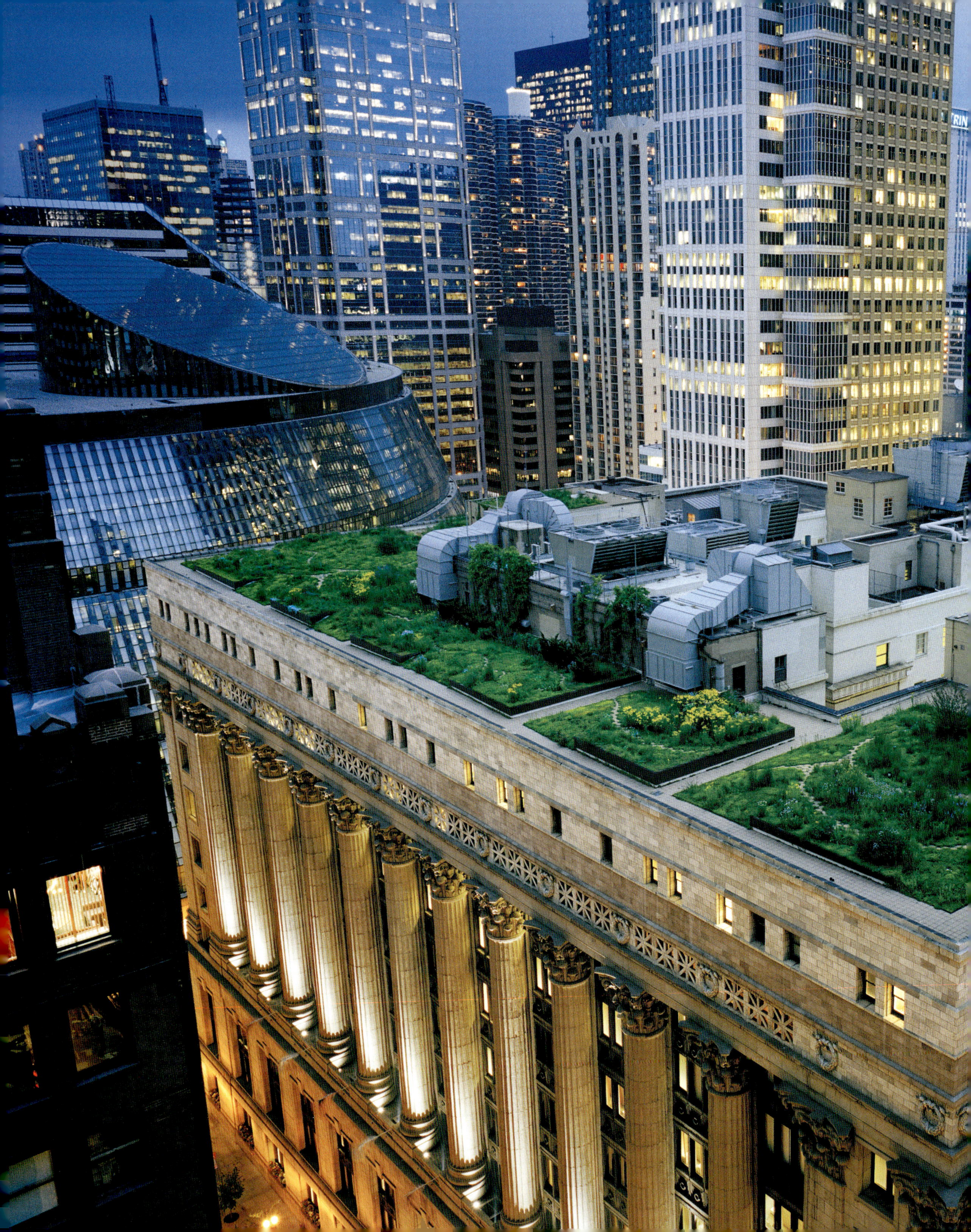

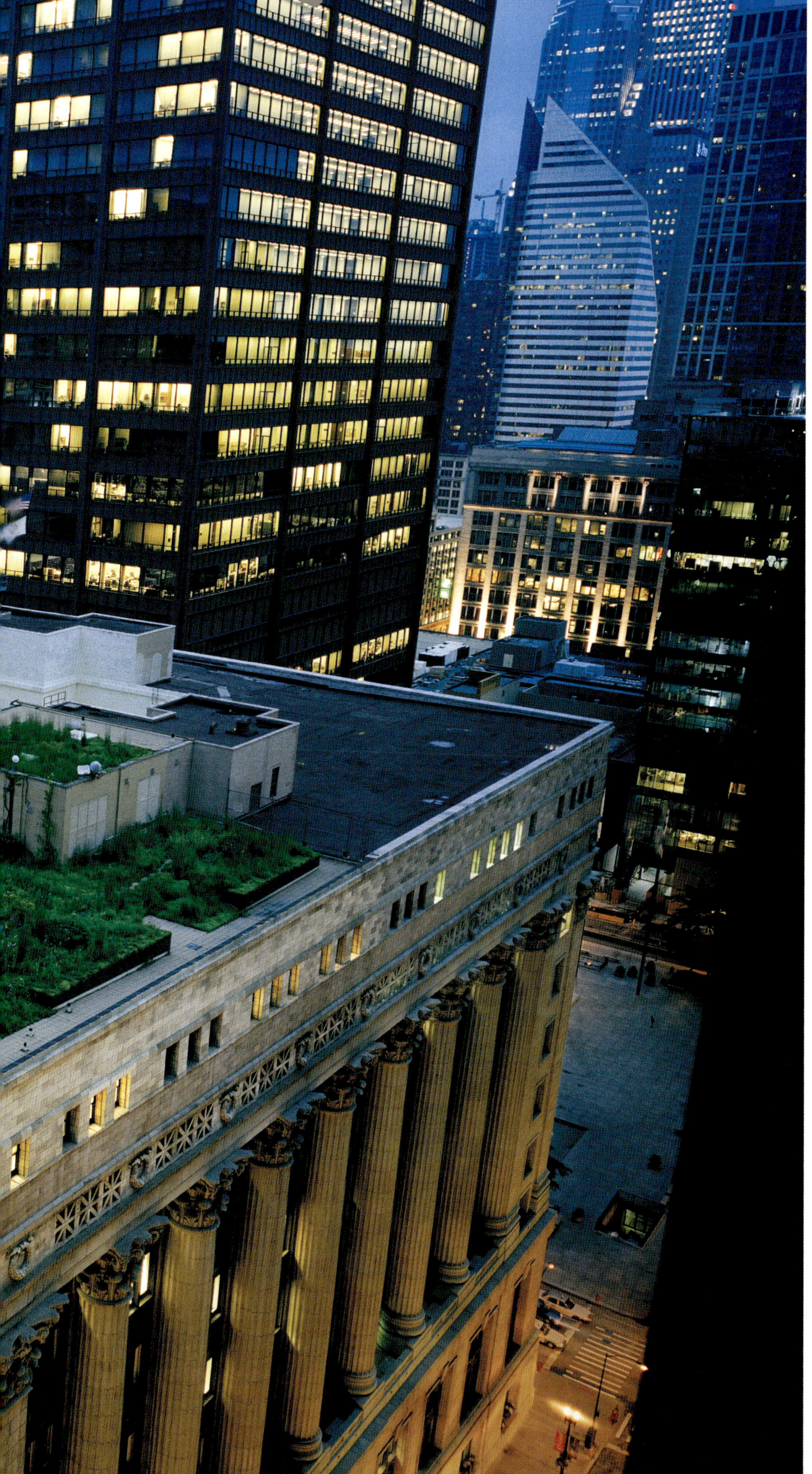

DIANE COOK AND LEN JENSHEL, 2008
"Green roofs" improve air quality, lower summer temperatures, and bring colors to urban landscapes. This one sits atop Chicago's iconic city hall.

FOLLOWING PAGES
JODY MACDONALD, 2010
An Asian elephant walks among the giant trees of India's Havelock Island (Swaraj Dweep).

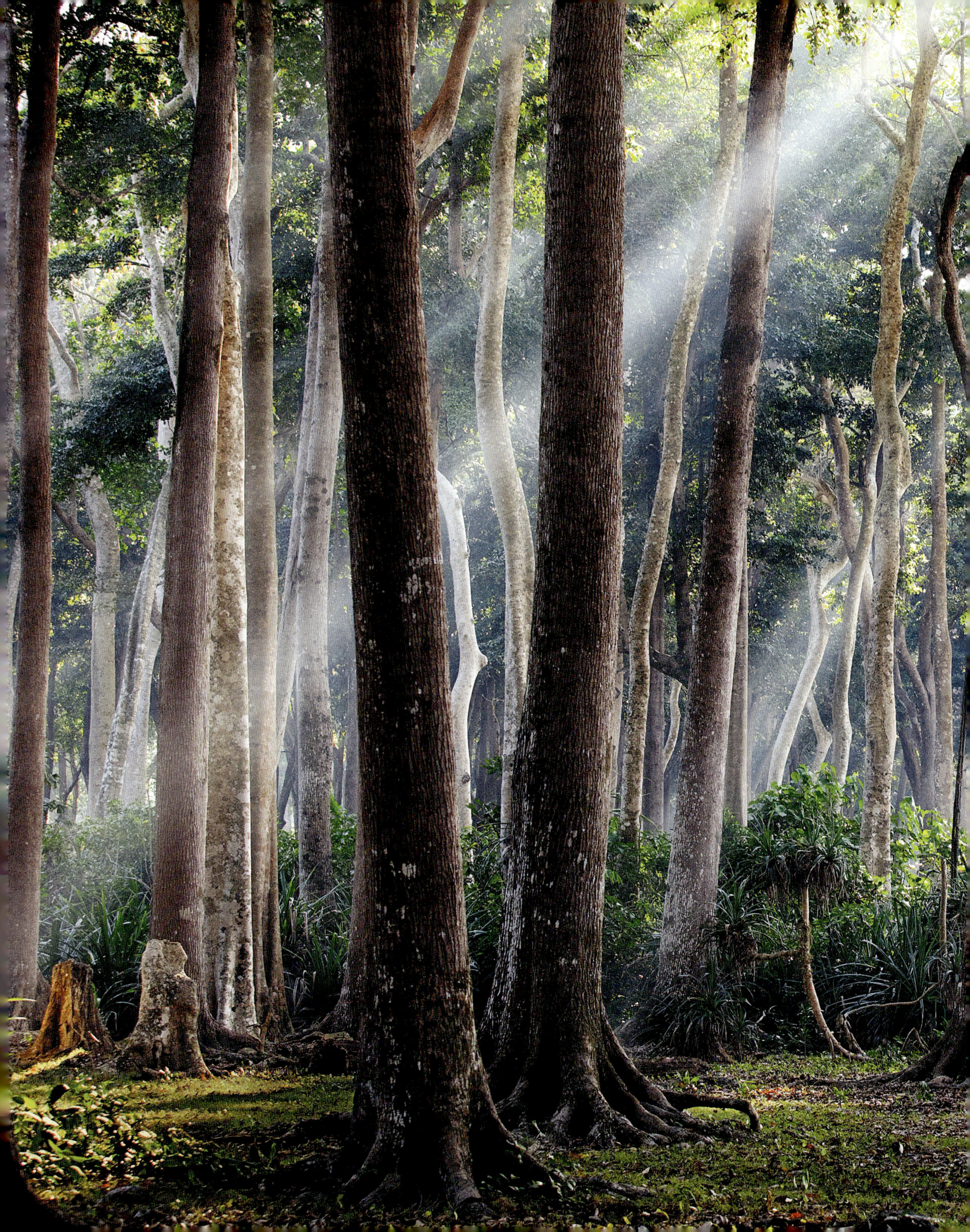

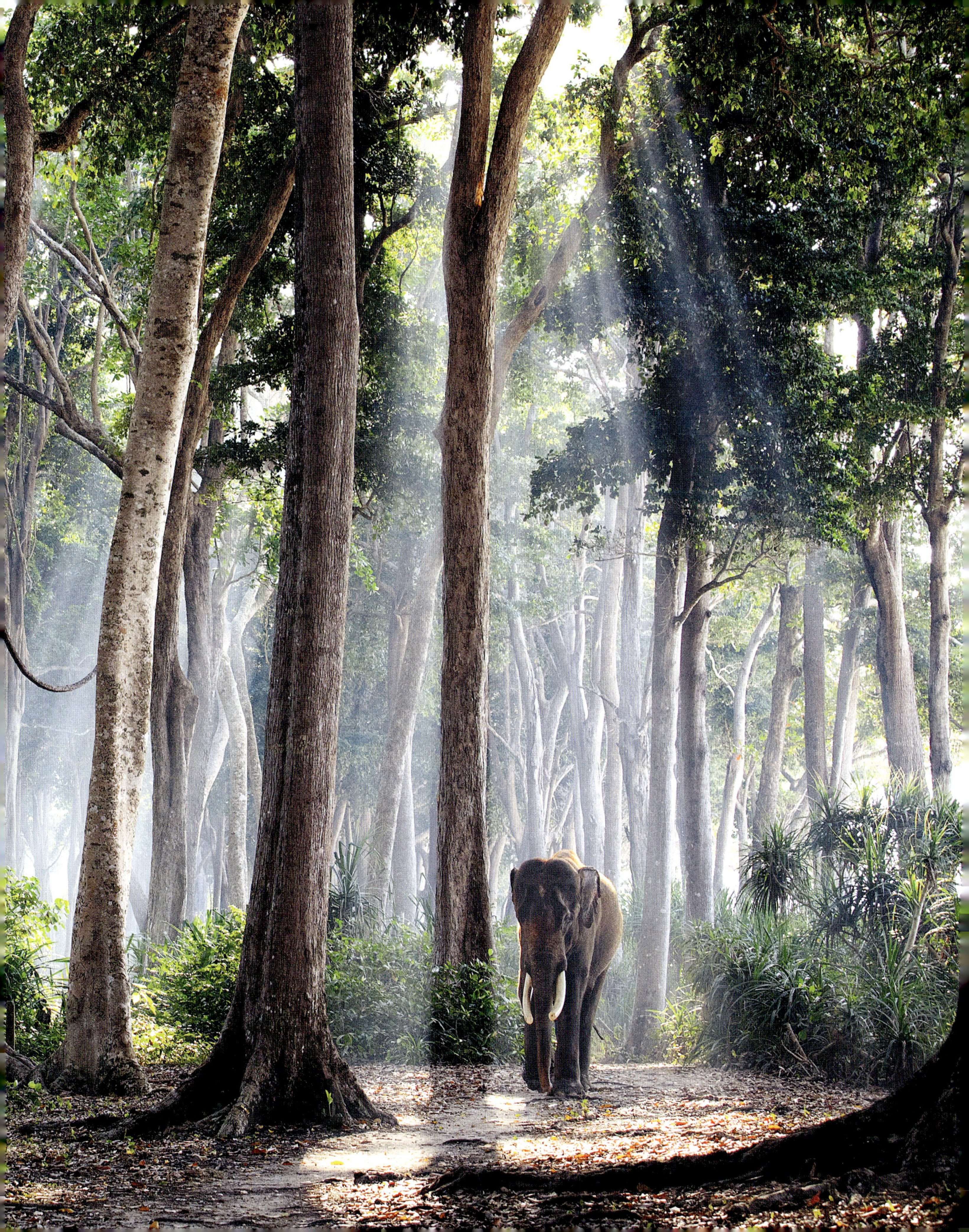

BIOGRAPHY

AARON HUEY

IN JANUARY 2002, Aaron Huey took a 3,349-mile, 154-day solo walk across the United States with his dog Cosmo, a Leica camera, and one lens. The journey from Encino, California, to New York City marked the start of his photographic career and helped define how he made pictures. It's about living with the people in your images, he says. "It's about surrender and simplicity and curiosity and letting your heart get cracked open. No tricks, special gear, or shortcuts. Just eye and heart and time."

Huey's first assignment for *National Geographic*, "In the Shadow of Wounded Knee," explored the lives of the Oglala Lakota people on South Dakota's Pine Ridge Reservation. The seven-year project set the template for his engagement with subjects in magazine stories to follow—from the family in Georgia's remote Caucasus region that he kept returning to visit, to the Sherpas in the Himalaya who help "the churning machine of tourists" summit Mount Everest, to the trapper on the edge of Yellowstone National Park whose beliefs were different from and challenged his own.

Huey has photographed some 30 stories for *National Geographic* magazine and affiliated publications, was a Stanford Knight Fellow in 2012, and, more recently, was a Stanford Starling Lab Fellow working on data integrity for visual journalism. He has been honored multiple times by Pictures of the Year International and World Press Photo and is now honing different approaches to storytelling, including the use of virtual and artificial reality.

AARON HUEY, 2014
Climbers ski across Ruth Glacier in Alaska's Denali National Park and Preserve.

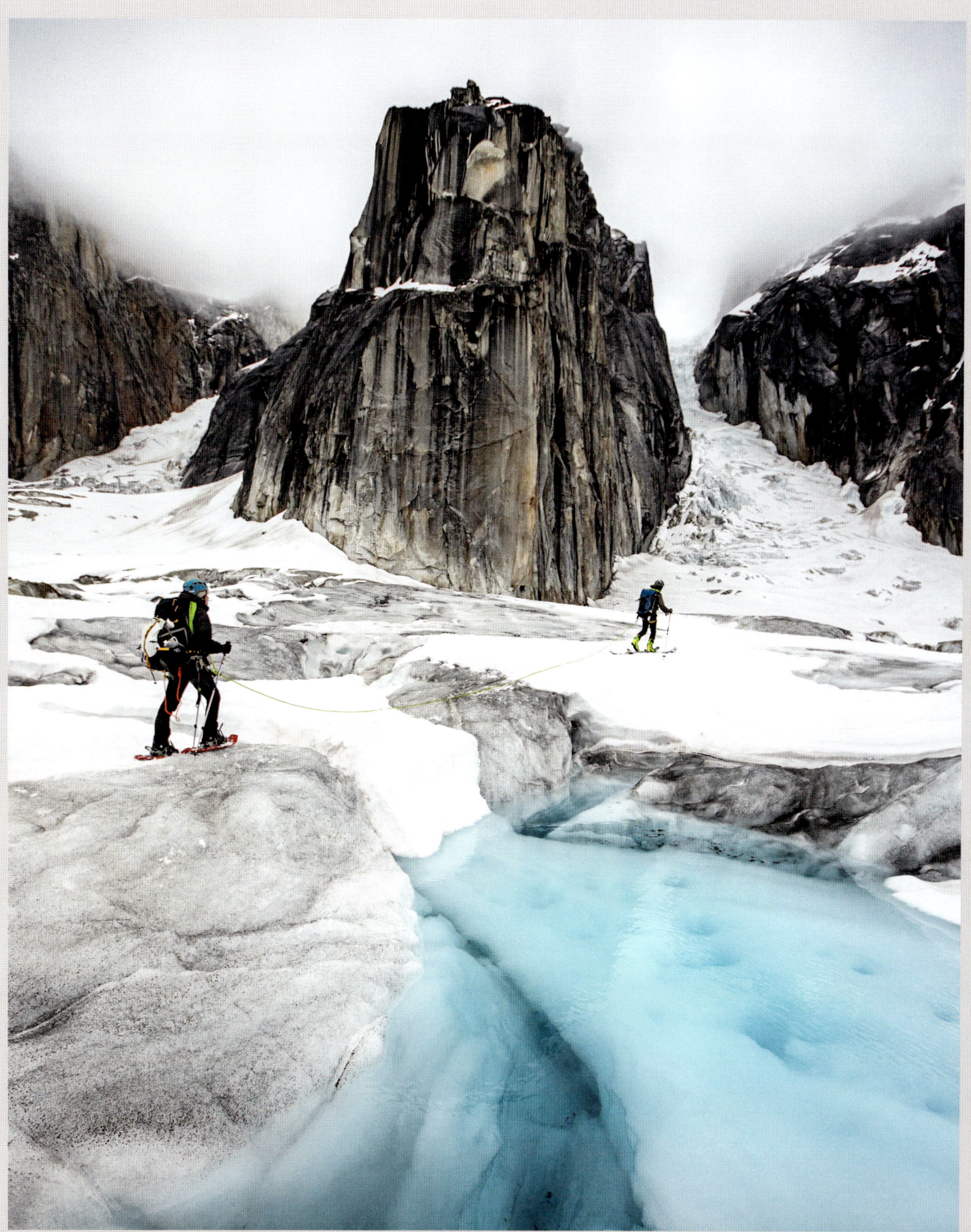

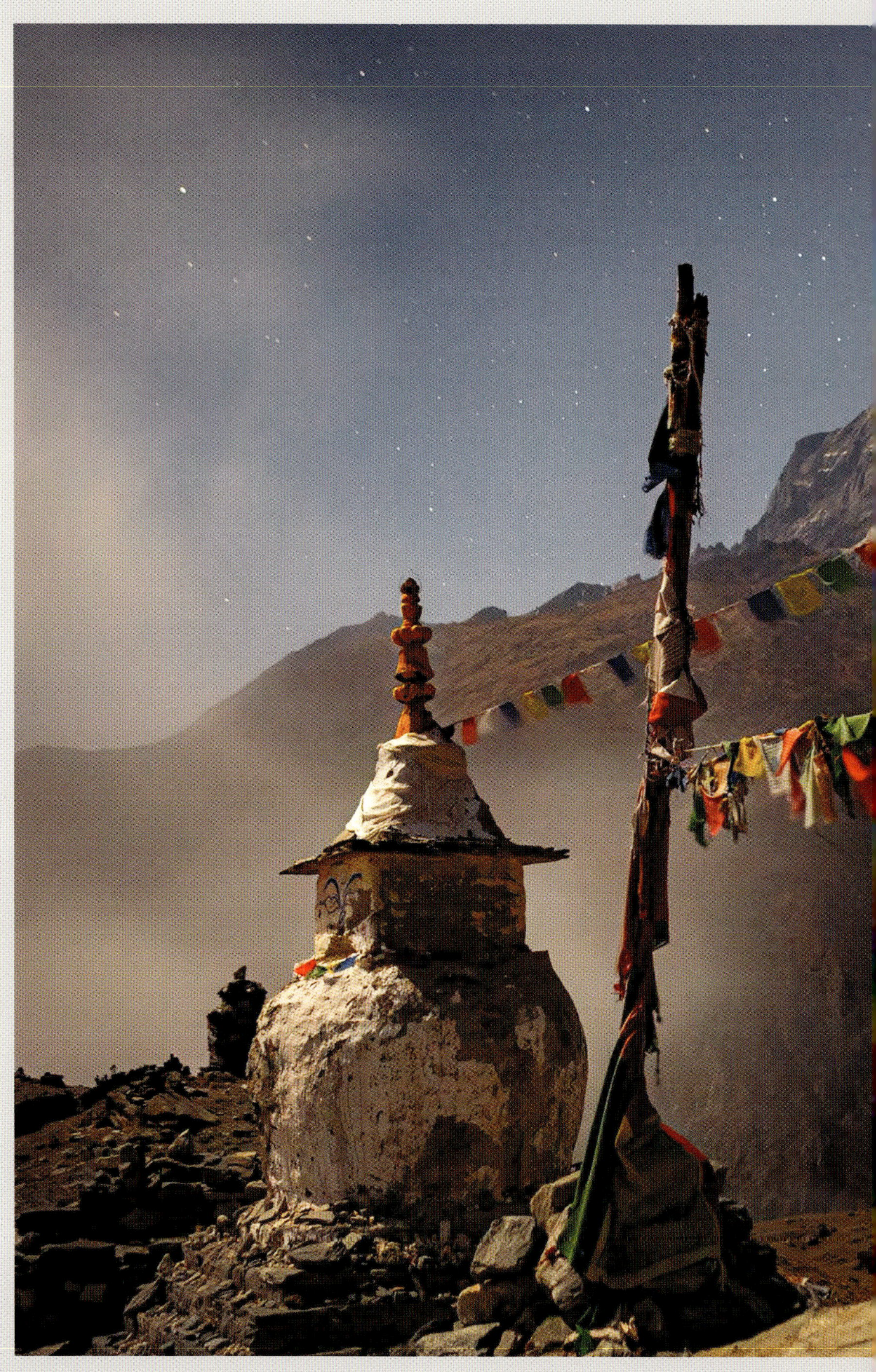

AARON HUEY, 2013
In the shadow of Mount Taboche, a stupa and prayer flags overlook the village of Dingboche, Nepal.

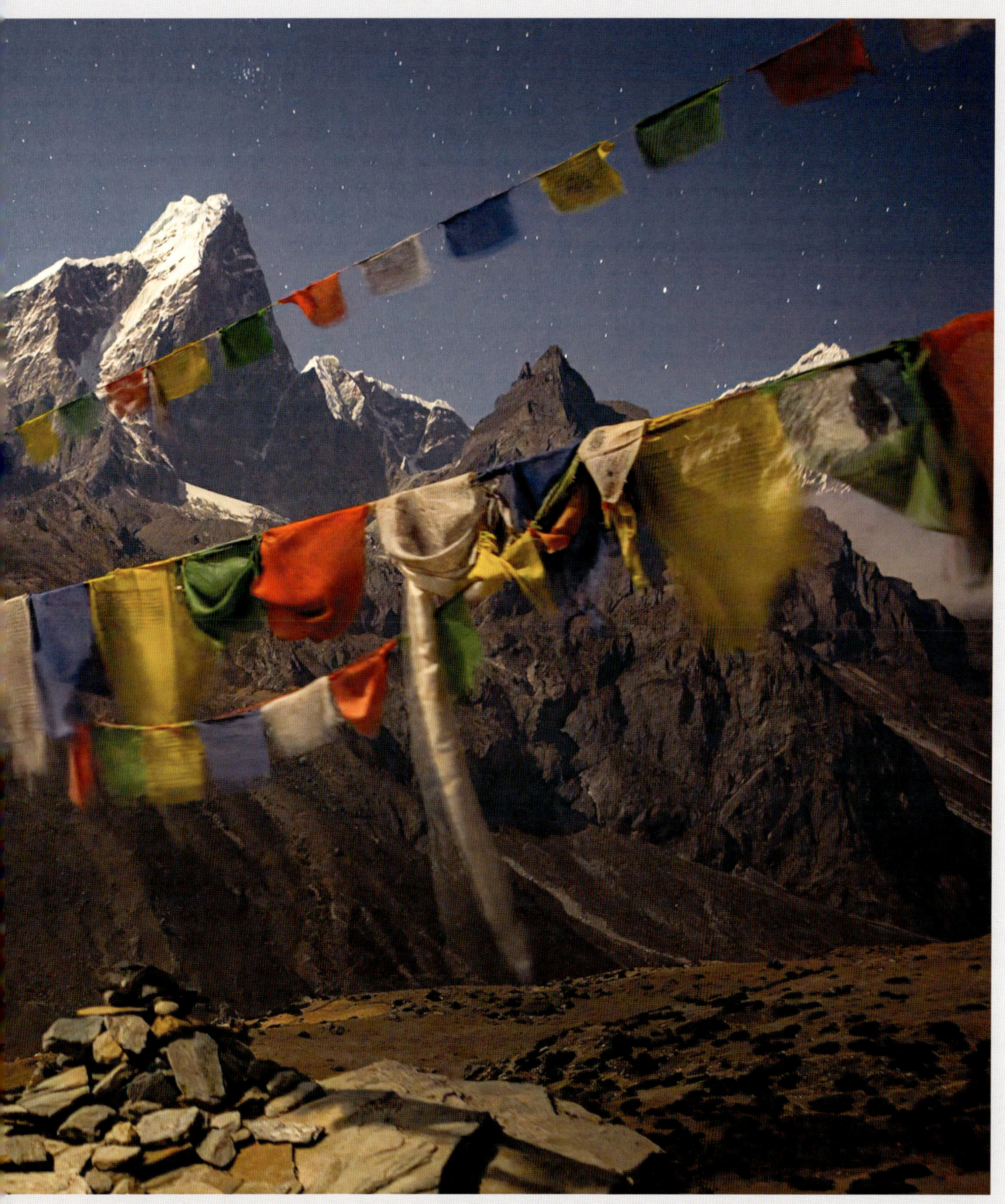

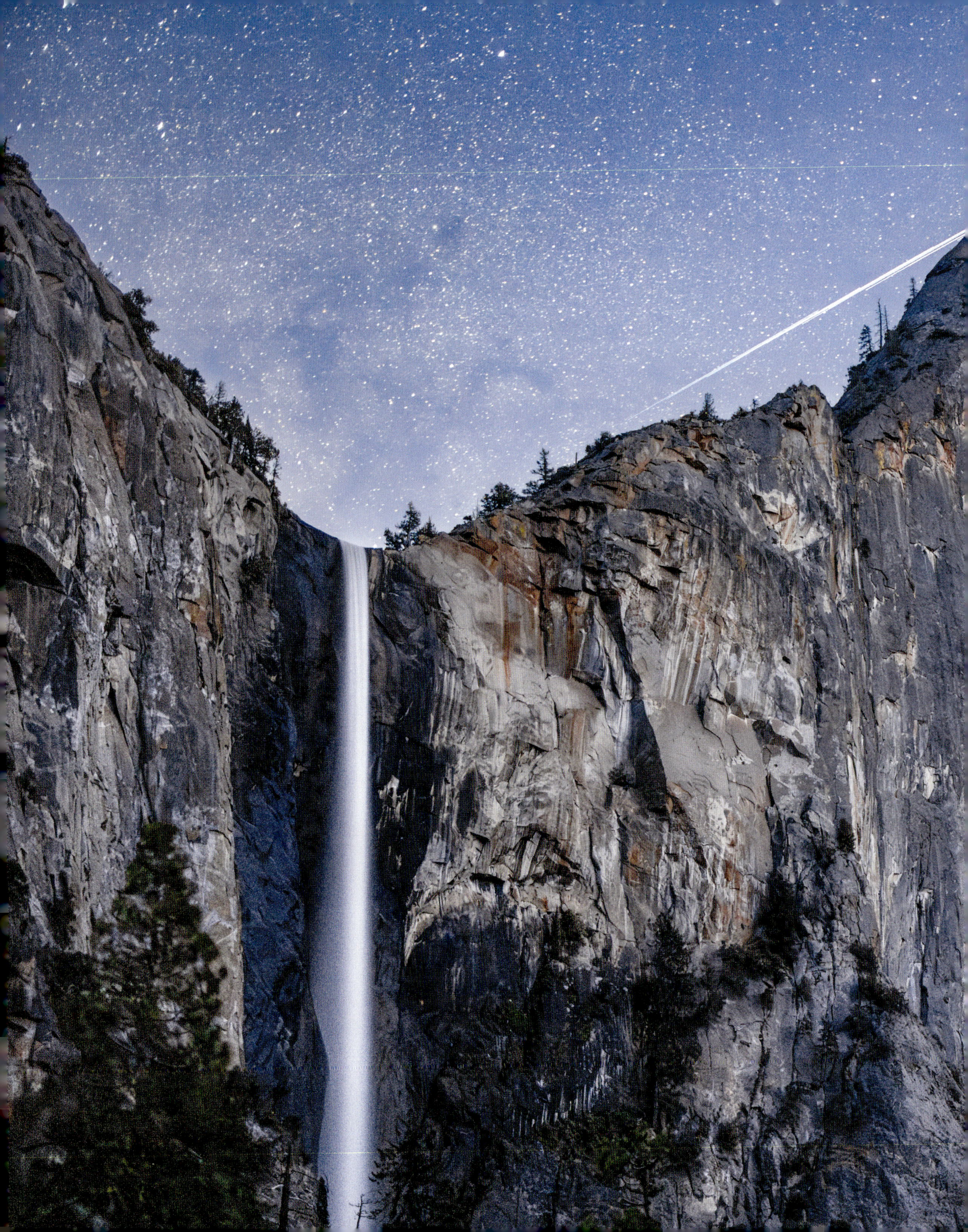

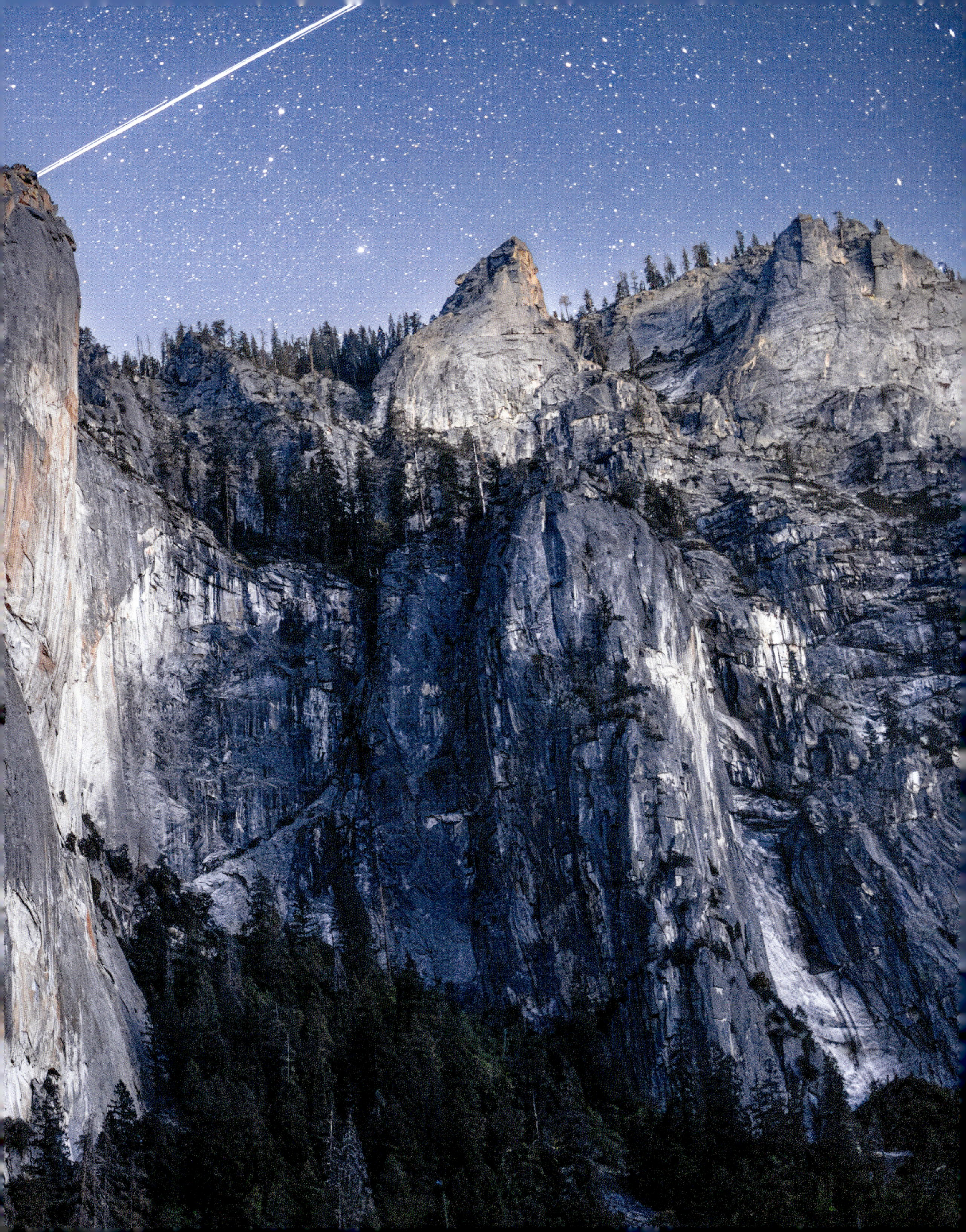

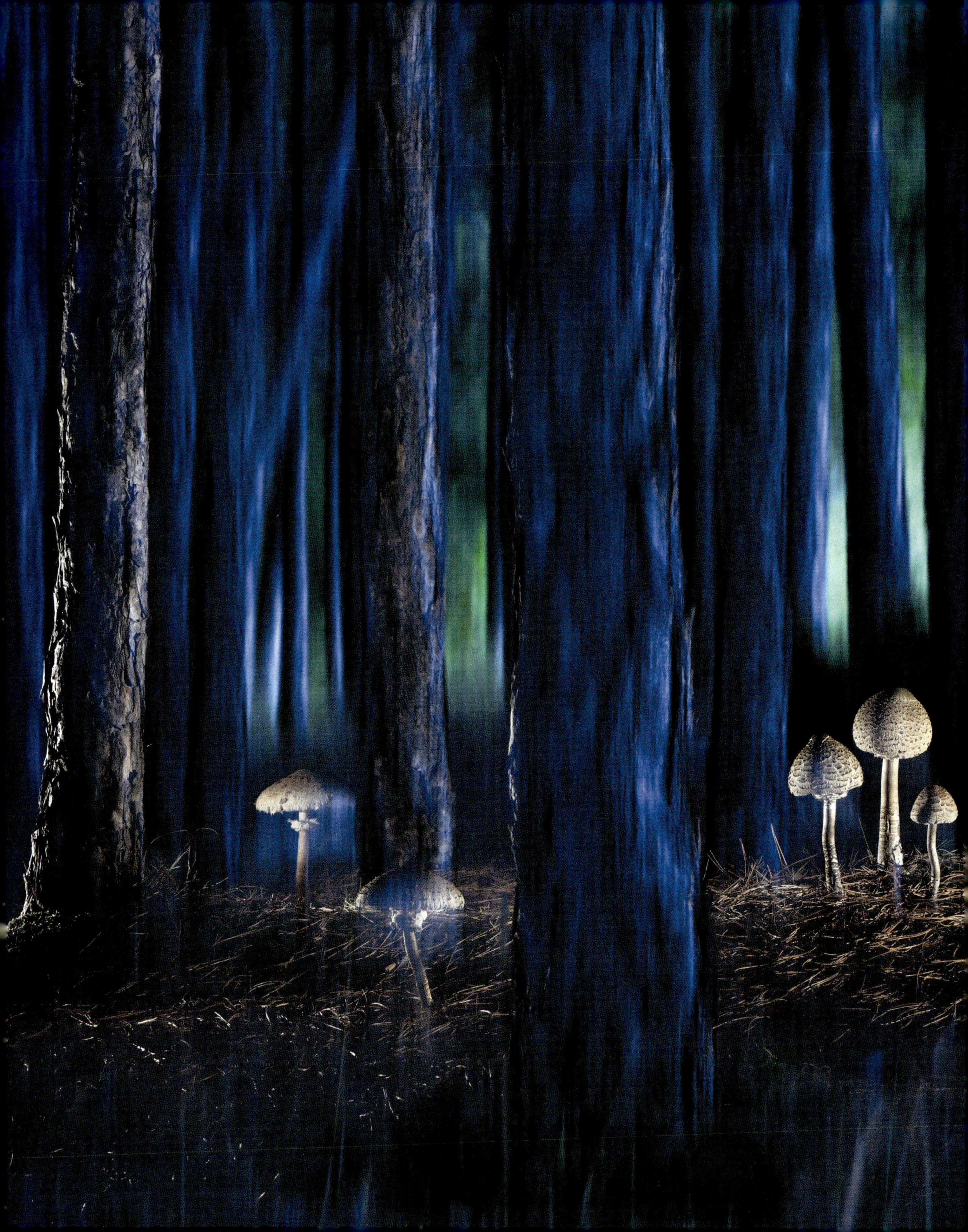

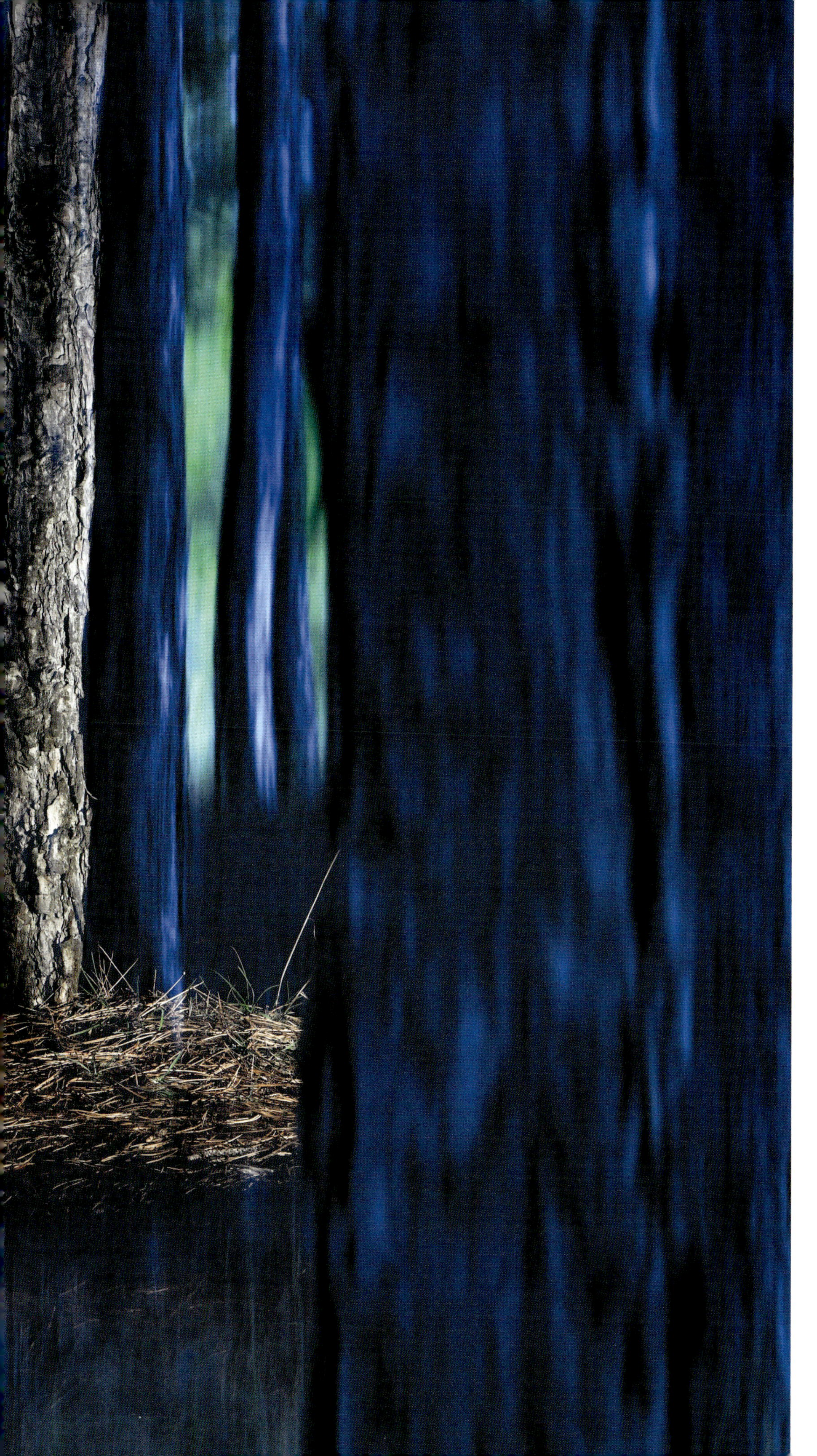

AGORASTOS PAPATSANIS, 2019
At dusk, parasol mushrooms stand among the pines in Deskati, Greece.

PREVIOUS PAGES
BABAK TAFRESHI, 2023
A long-exposure view of Starlink satellites streaking over Bridalveil Fall and Cathedral Rock in California's Yosemite National Park

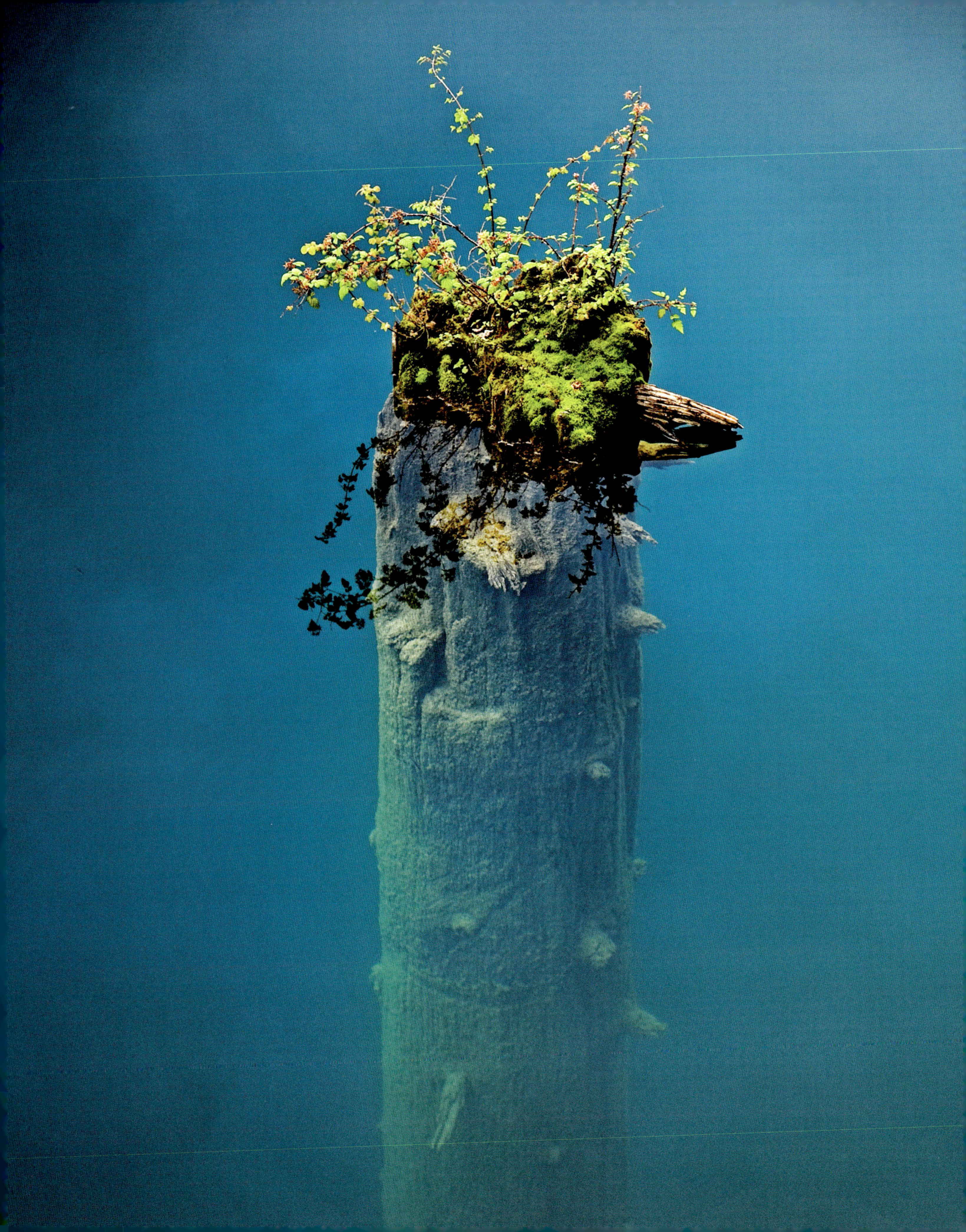

THERE'S A FINE LINE BETWEEN A PICTURE POSTCARD AND AN EDITORIAL IMAGE. THE TRICK IS FINDING THE DRAMA.

KURT MUTCHLER, *NATIONAL GEOGRAPHIC* MAGAZINE PHOTO EDITOR, 1994–2024

MICHAEL YAMASHITA, 2007
Plant life atop a dead tree submerged in China's Panda Lake

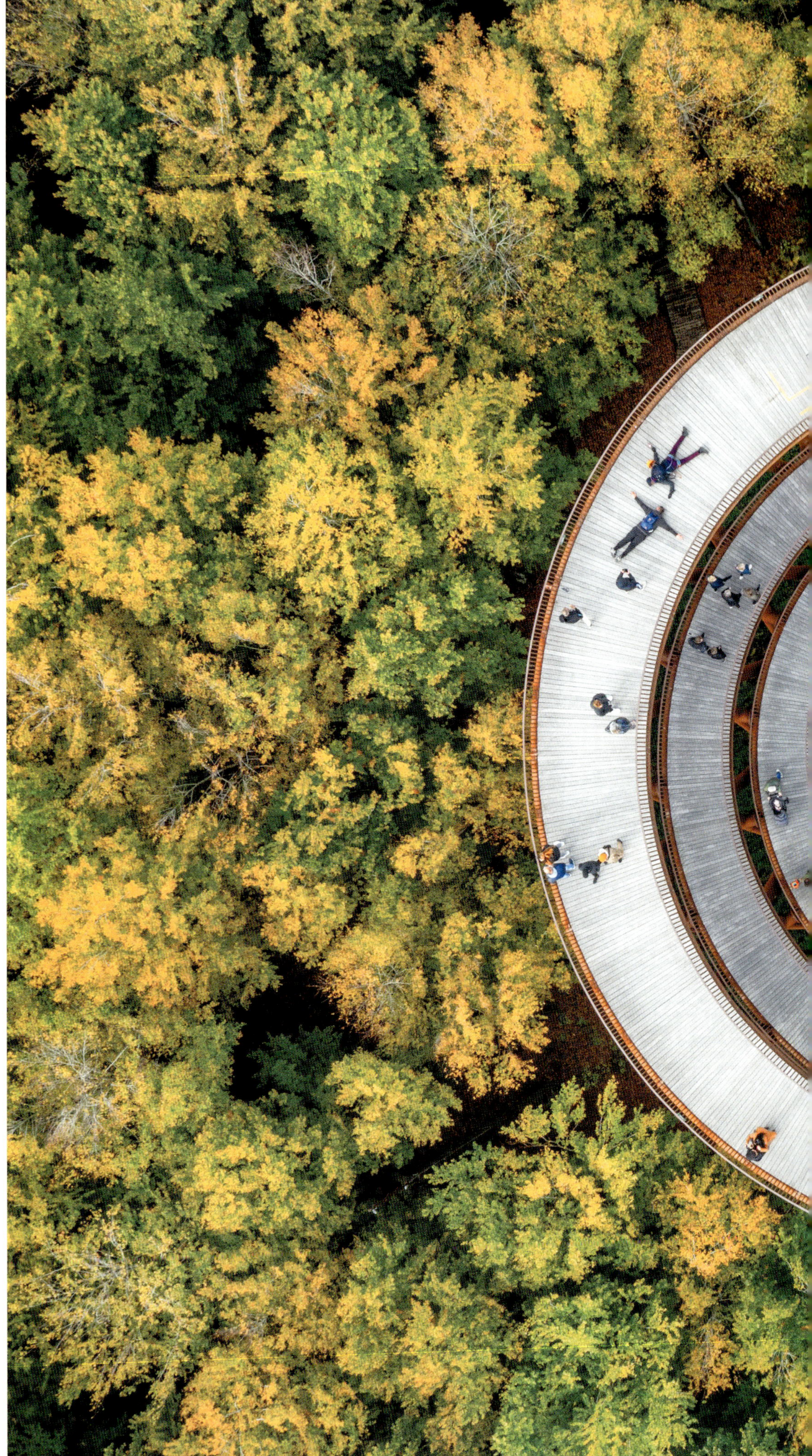

ORSOLYA HAARBERG, 2021
Visitors ascend the 150-foot-high tower Skovtårnet in the preserved forest of Gisselfeld Kloster outside Copenhagen, Denmark.

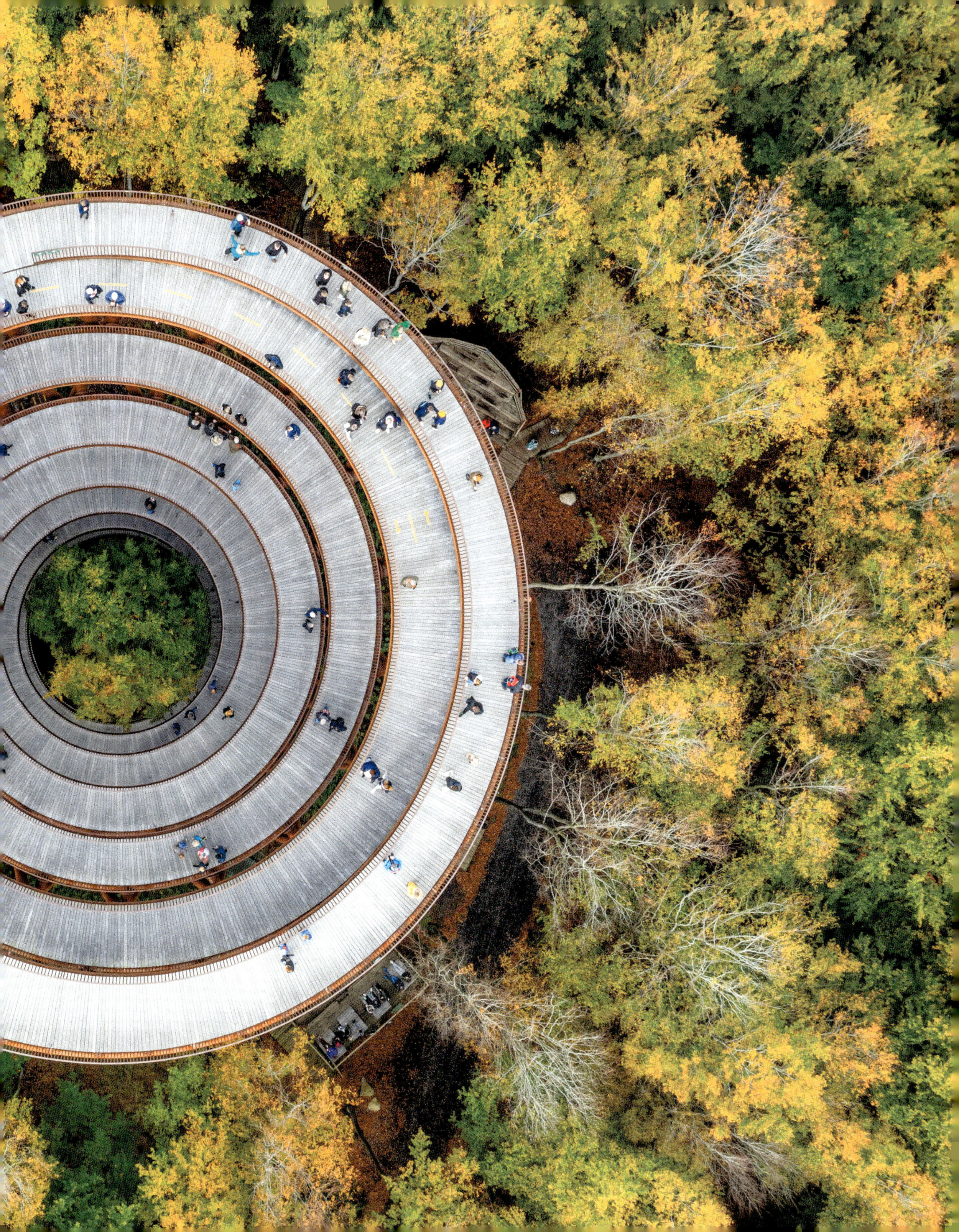

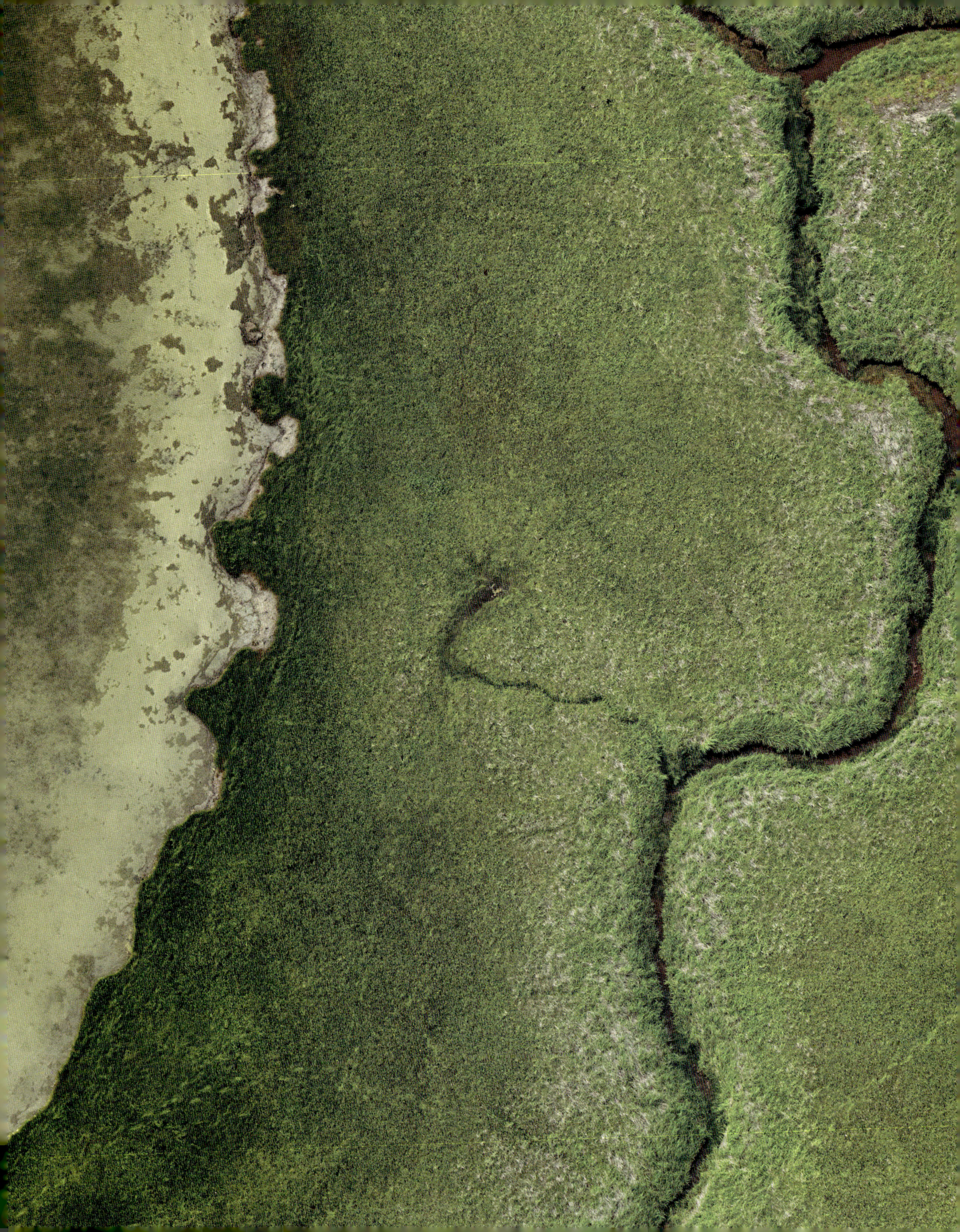

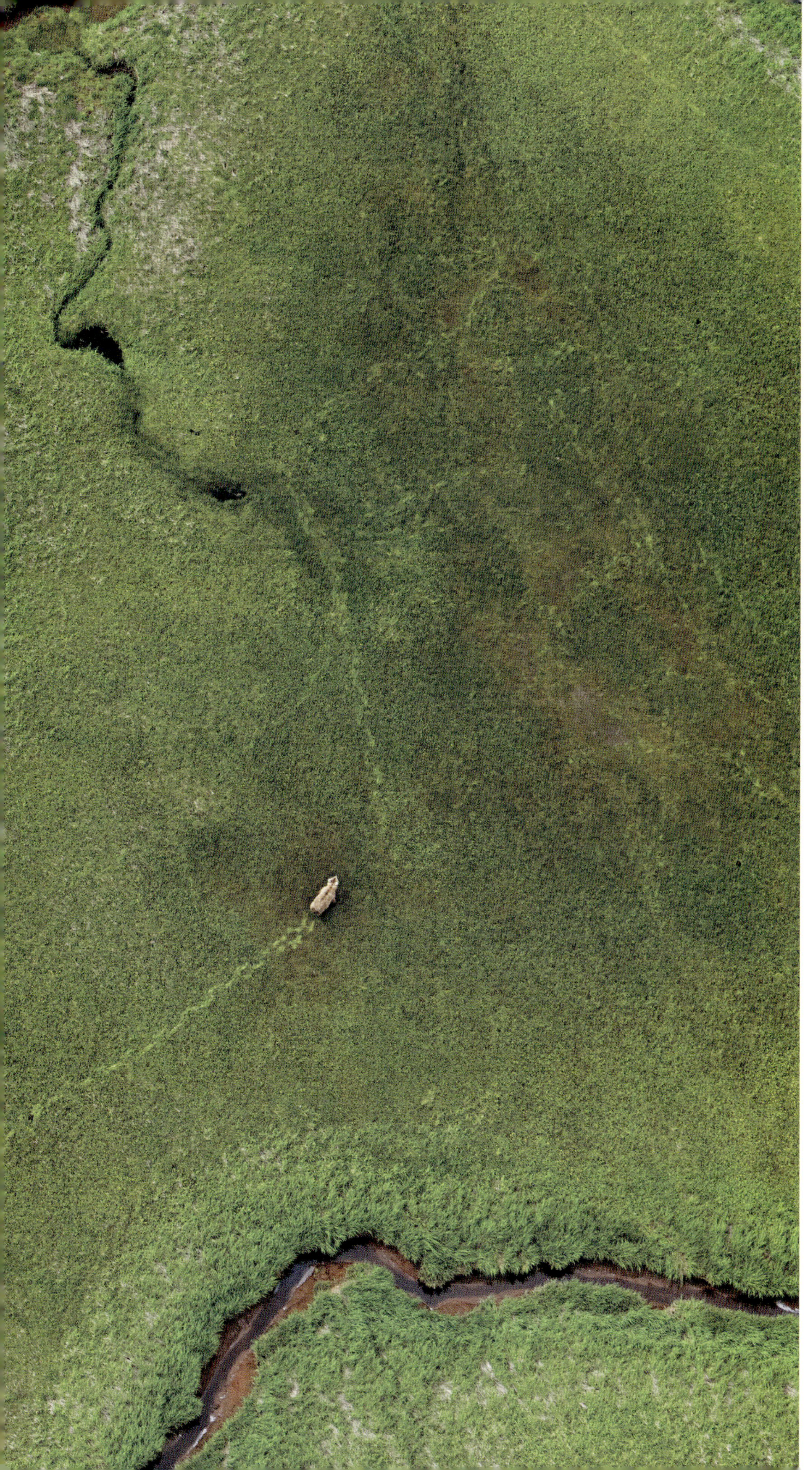

ACACIA JOHNSON, 2024
From the air, the green sedge of Alaska's Katmai coast appears etched with brown bear trails, illuminating a web of passages that have been followed by generations of wildlife.

FOLLOWING PAGES
MATTHIEU PALEY, 2017
The sun beats down on Dasht-e Lūt, a salt desert in Iran and one of the world's hottest places.

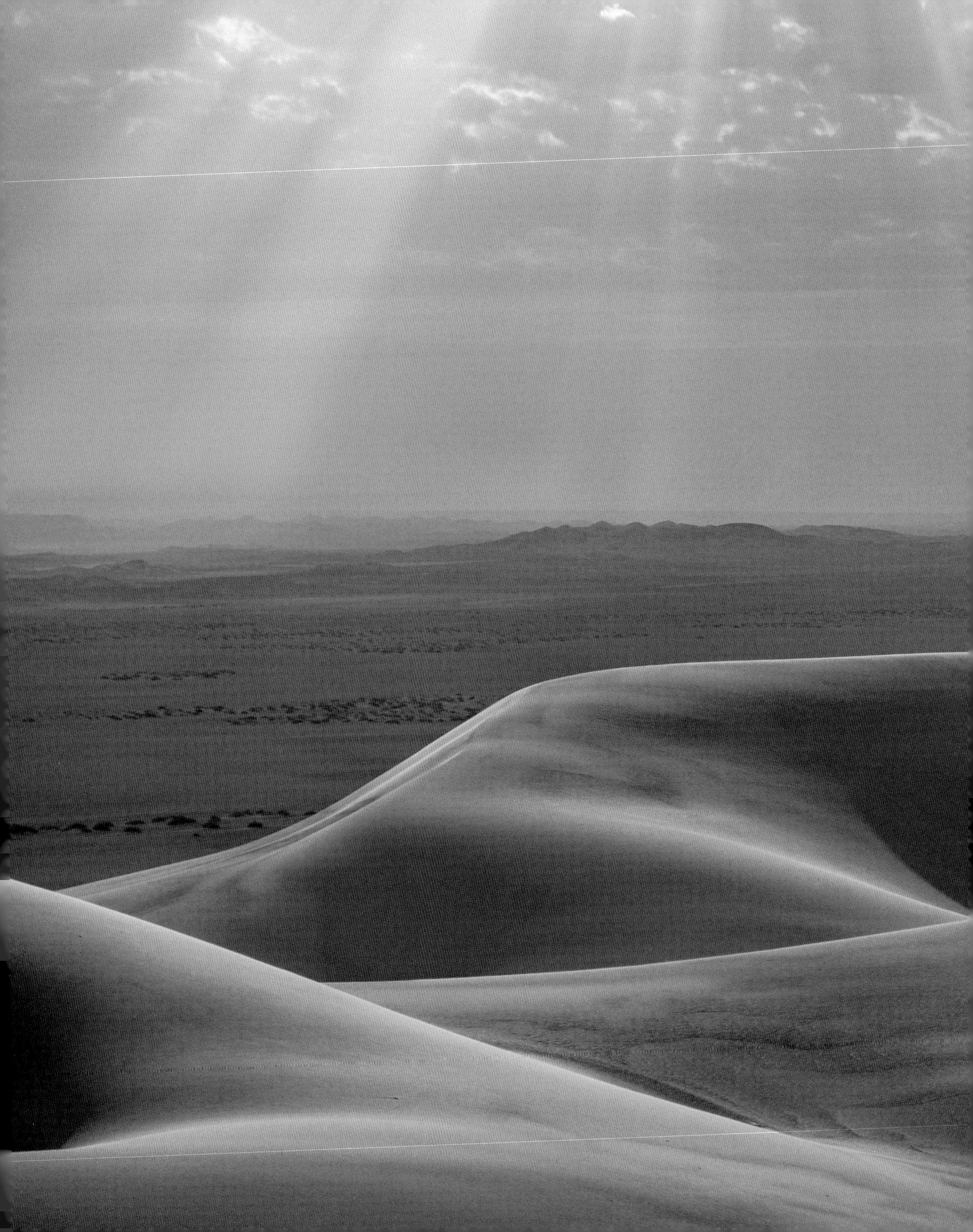

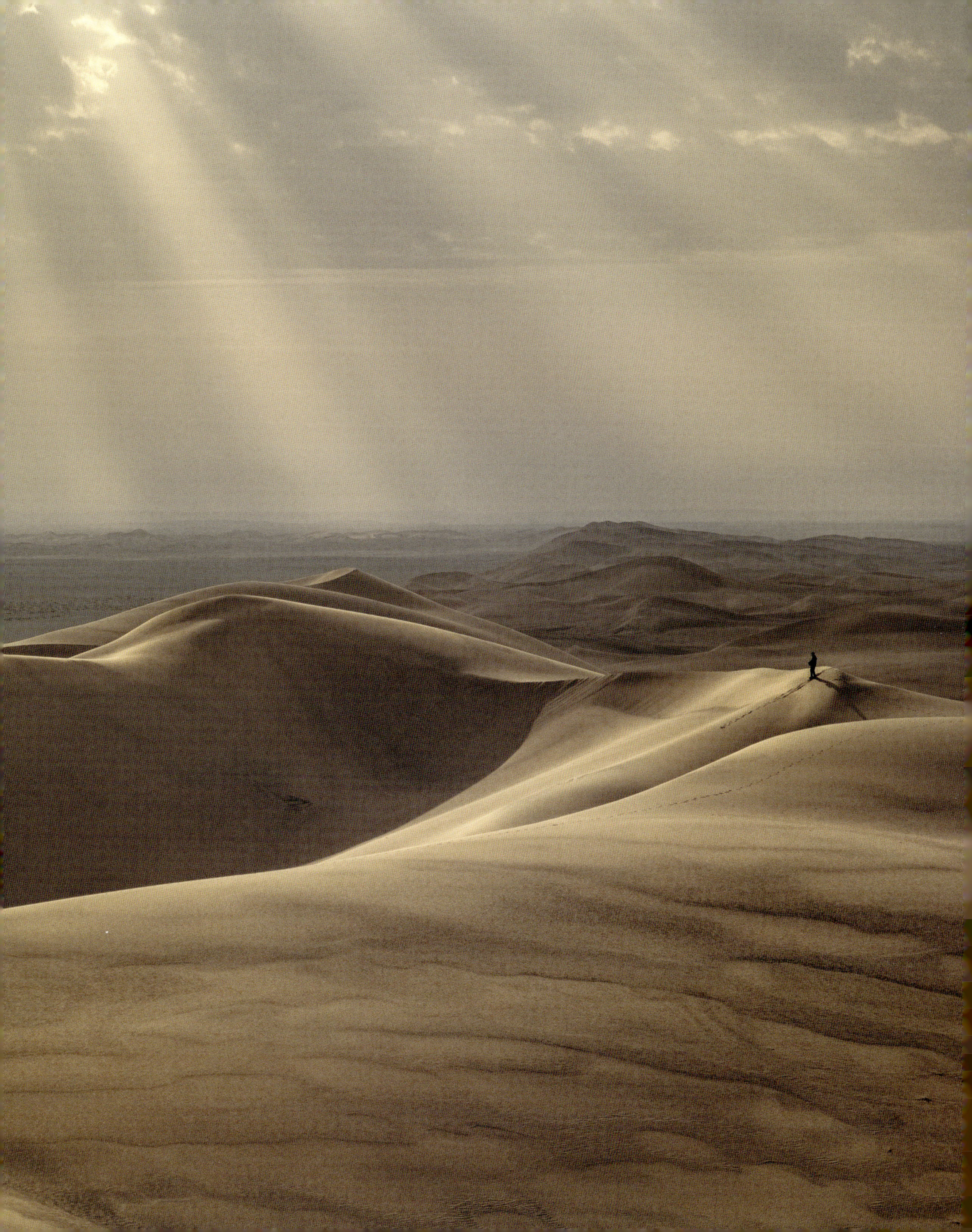

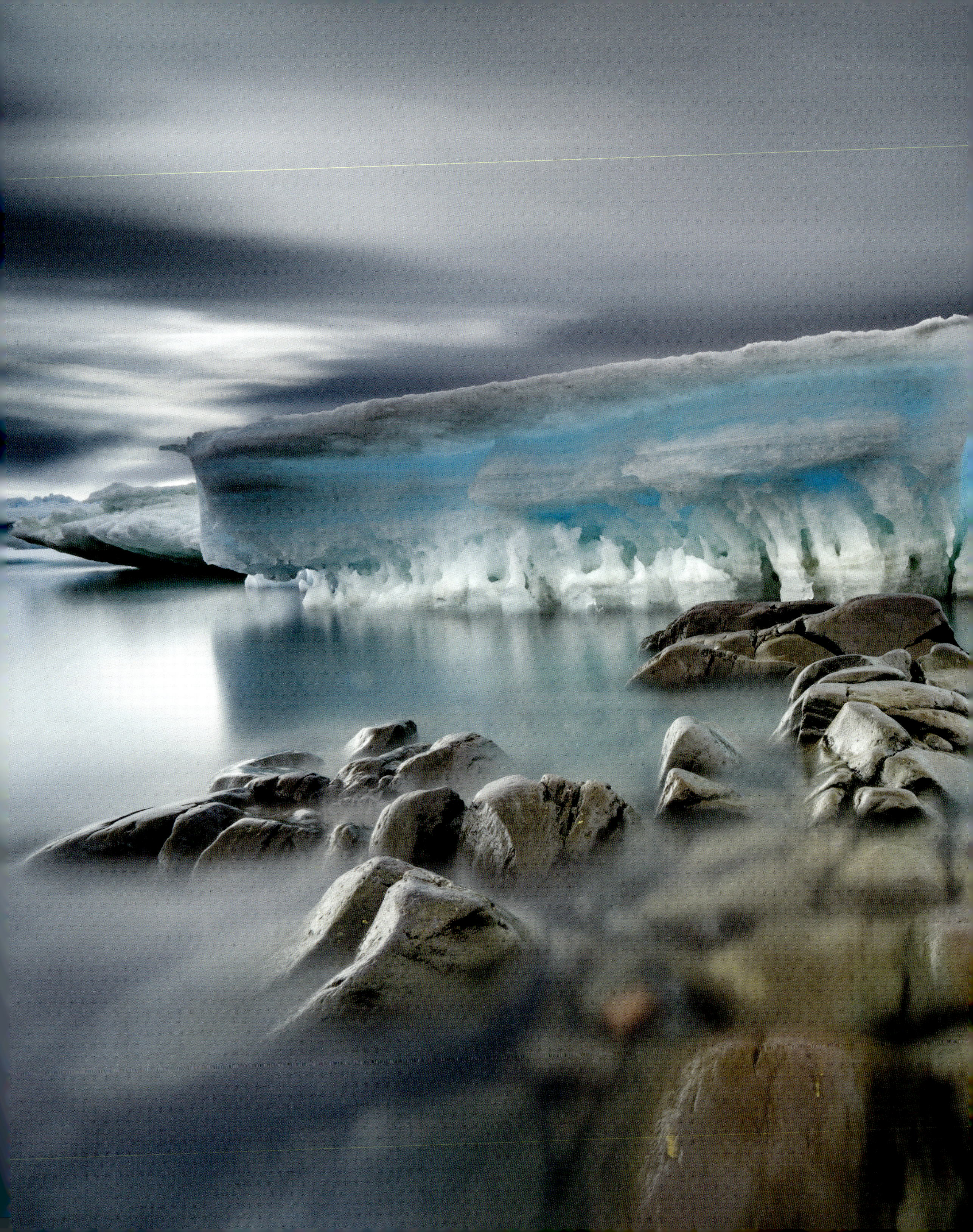

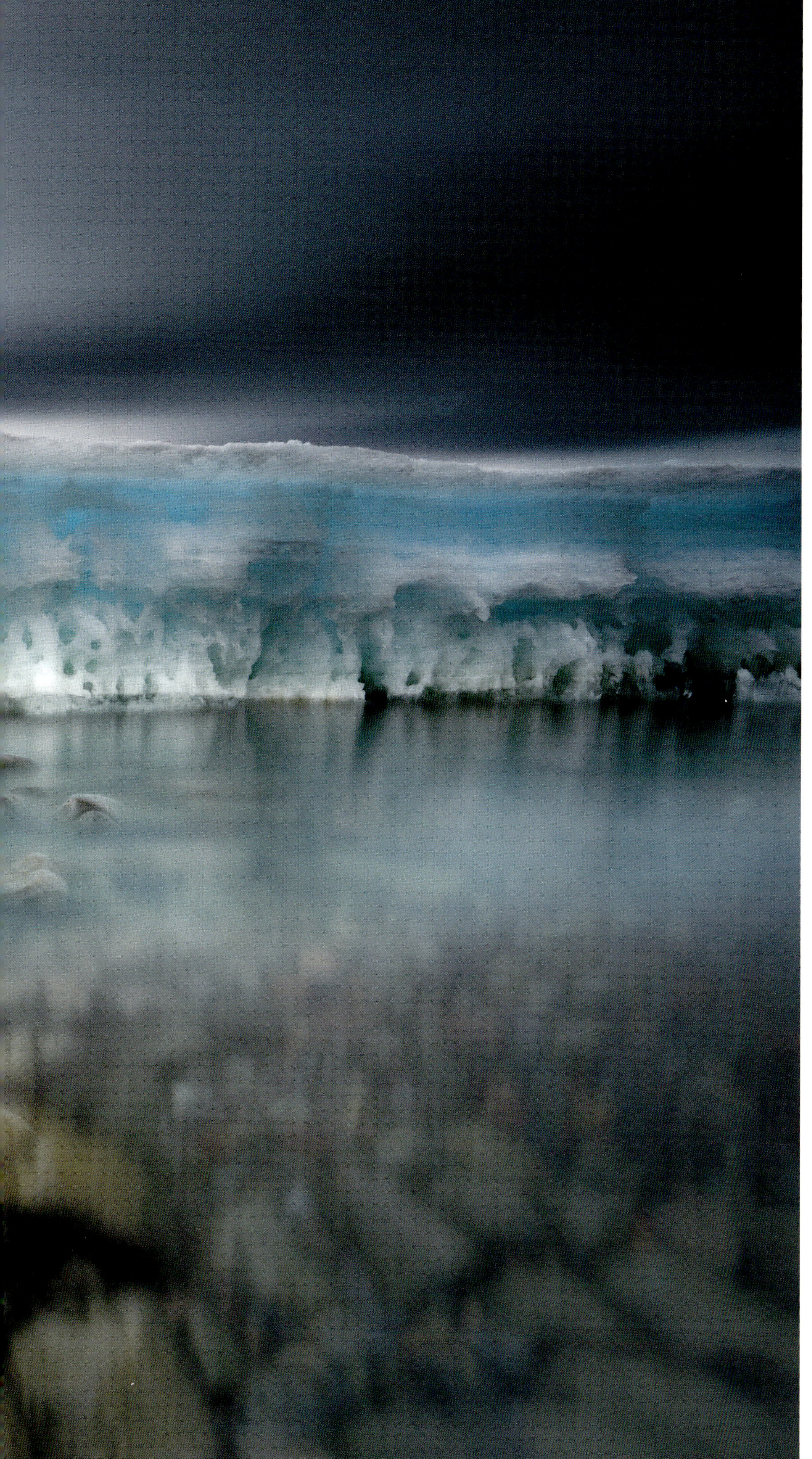

KEITH LADZINSKI, 2017
Seaworn stones form a path to beached and broken sea ice on the Antarctic Peninsula.

FOLLOWING PAGES
EVGENIA ARBUGAEVA, 2016
Windblown snow swirls past abandoned buildings in Dikson, Russia.

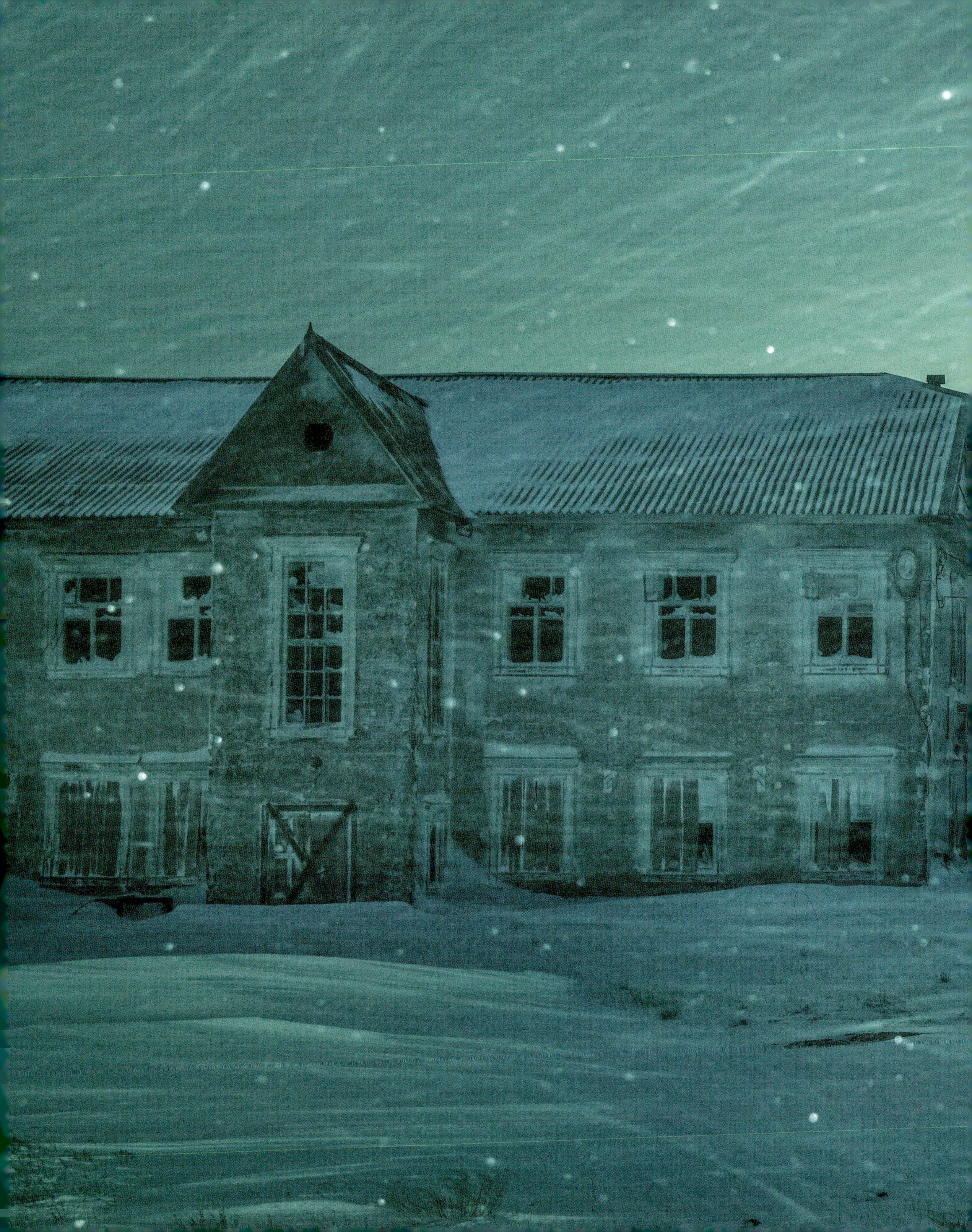

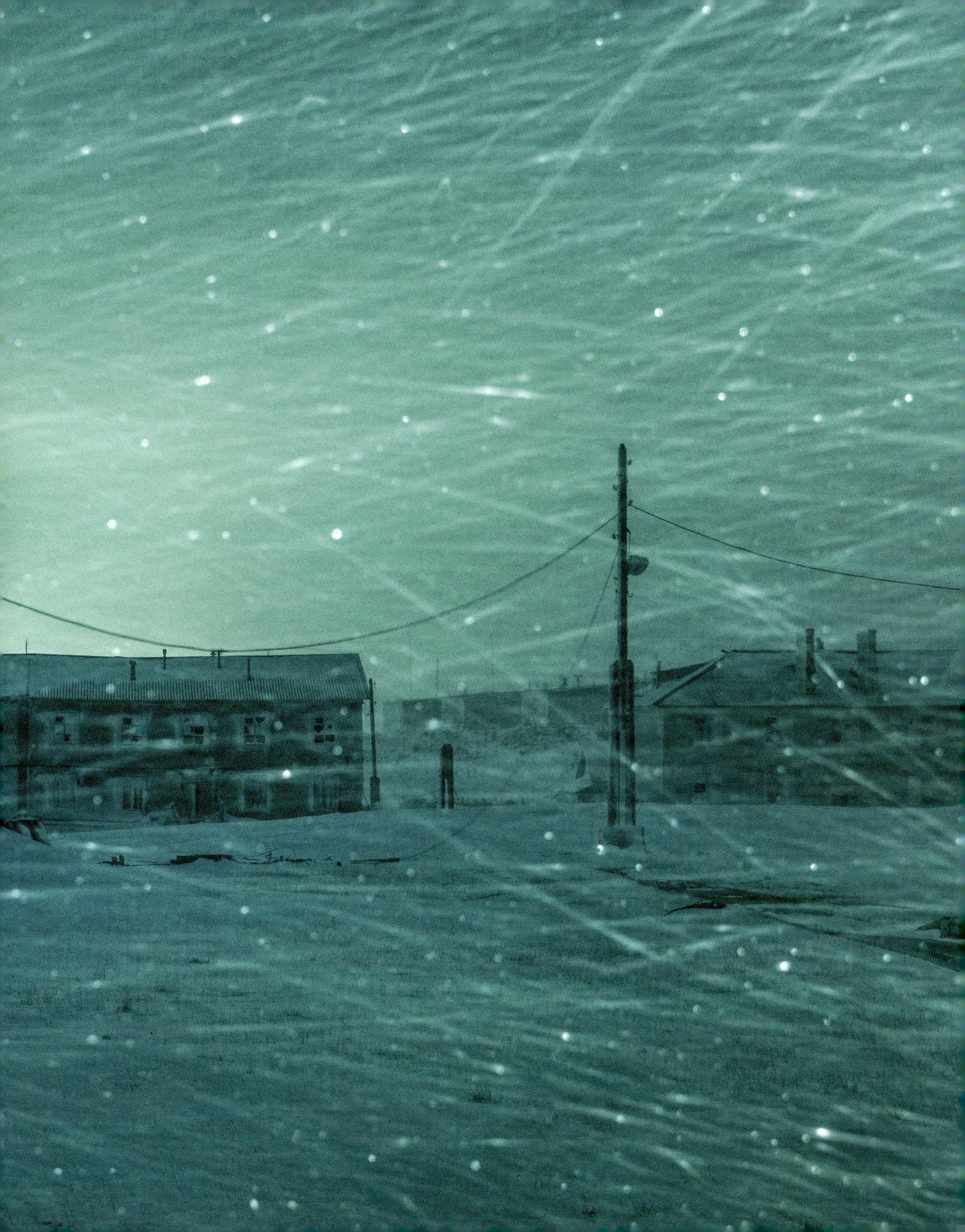

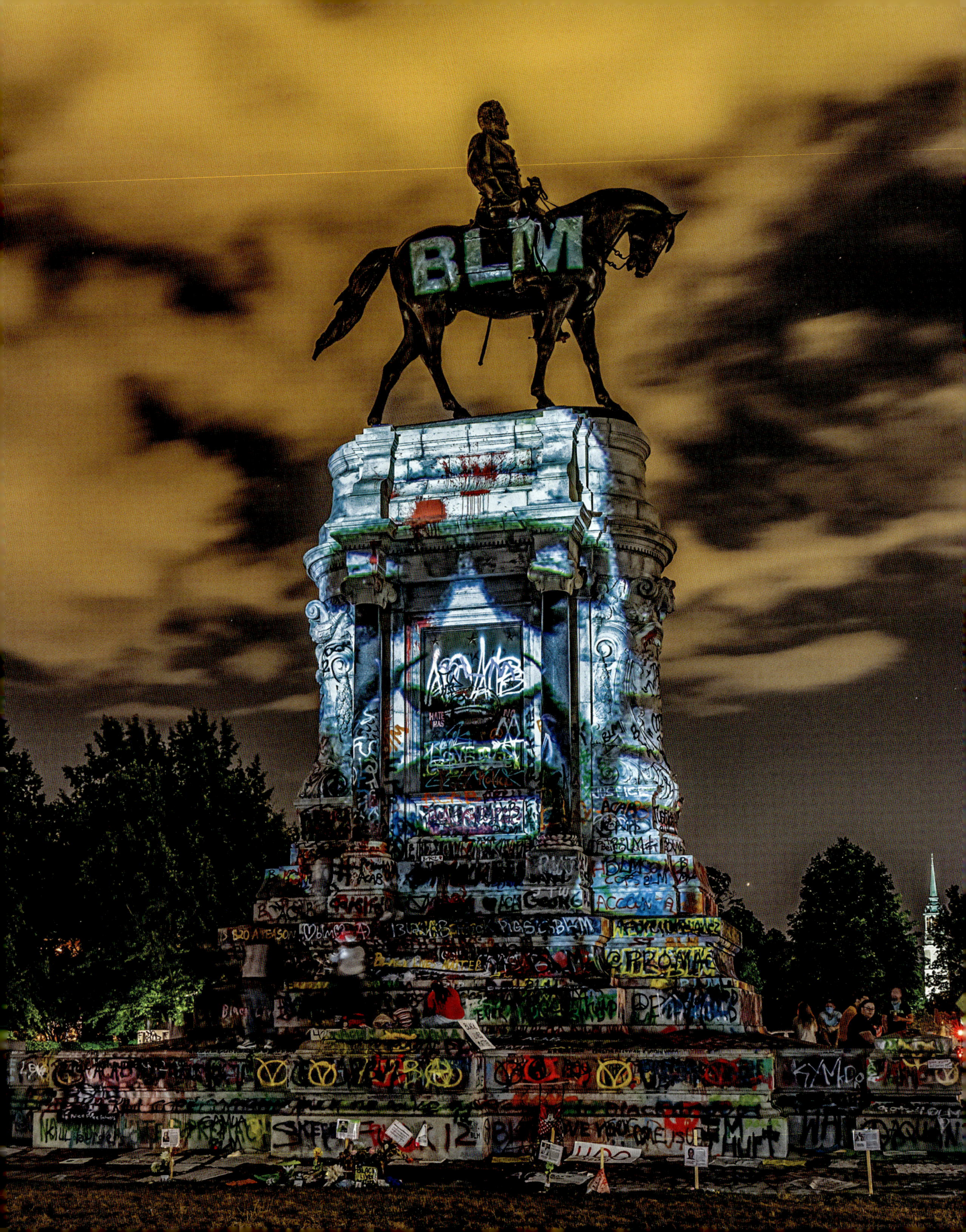
BLM

IN CONVERSATION WITH

KRIS GRAVES

Kris Graves documents the landscape of social injustice and strives to preserve our collective memory. His work blends conceptual and documentary practices to illuminate the subtleties of social issues and their impact on the environment. His landscapes are—purposefully—far from the Geographic tradition. His image of the Gen. Robert E. Lee statue in Richmond, Virginia, covered in graffiti for a *National Geographic* story documenting Confederate monuments in the American South made the cover of the magazine's 2020 "Year in Pictures."

Graves's work has been exhibited at the Museum of Modern Art and London's National Portrait Gallery, among others. He is based in New York and California and is currently working on a book about the Black history of national parks for National Geographic.

NATIONAL GEOGRAPHIC: When did you know the camera was going to be your life? Tell us that story.

KRIS GRAVES: I remember being in high school, probably around 10th grade. In school you learn these subjects that you can't really get a job in unless you're going to be a teacher. Like science, math—I didn't want to do any of that stuff. And I always liked art. I didn't know much about photography except that you can show up by yourself with a camera and maybe make enough money to survive. So I wanted that.

When I asked my parents for a camera, they said, "Not happening." But luckily, my high school had a photography teacher, and he let me use the darkroom. I could go in at seven in the morning and learn how to use it.

NG: Was that when you took your first photo?

KG: I think I photographed the superintendent of my high school for $50 cash. I made a photograph of her, went to the darkroom, made a print, and gave it to her in like three hours. That was when I was like, I could actually make a little bit of money doing this. Fifty dollars was more than I had made working six hours at McDonald's that morning.

NG: Do you think of yourself primarily as an art photographer or something else?

KG: I think I'm just a photographer. I try to straddle the line between documentary and conceptual. I don't want to give you everything in a photograph.

NG: When many people think of landscape, they think of purple mountains majesty. But you give a different twist to the idea of what a landscape is. How does that philosophy apply to your work?

KG: I've been in cities my whole life, and I never visited a national park until I was almost 30. So I've been trying to make my work in that "built landscape," photographing things that probably won't last, or things that will be transitioned gentrification-wise.

I try to visit populated places, since a lot of people can go out into the field and photograph natural landscapes. And the only thing that changes in those landscapes is the time of day. Show me an Ansel Adams picture beside one somebody made five years ago, and they'll probably look similar if they were taken at the same time of year, minus climate change. For me, that was less interesting. I wanted to photograph what immediately affected people. I believe that pure landscapes—those that are devoid of social issues—are often merely decorative.

NG: One of your interests is the idea of memory. How does that dovetail into urban landscape photography?

KRIS GRAVES, 2020
In tribute to the Black Lives Matter movement, graffiti and the projected image of George Floyd cover a statue of Robert E. Lee in Richmond, Virginia.

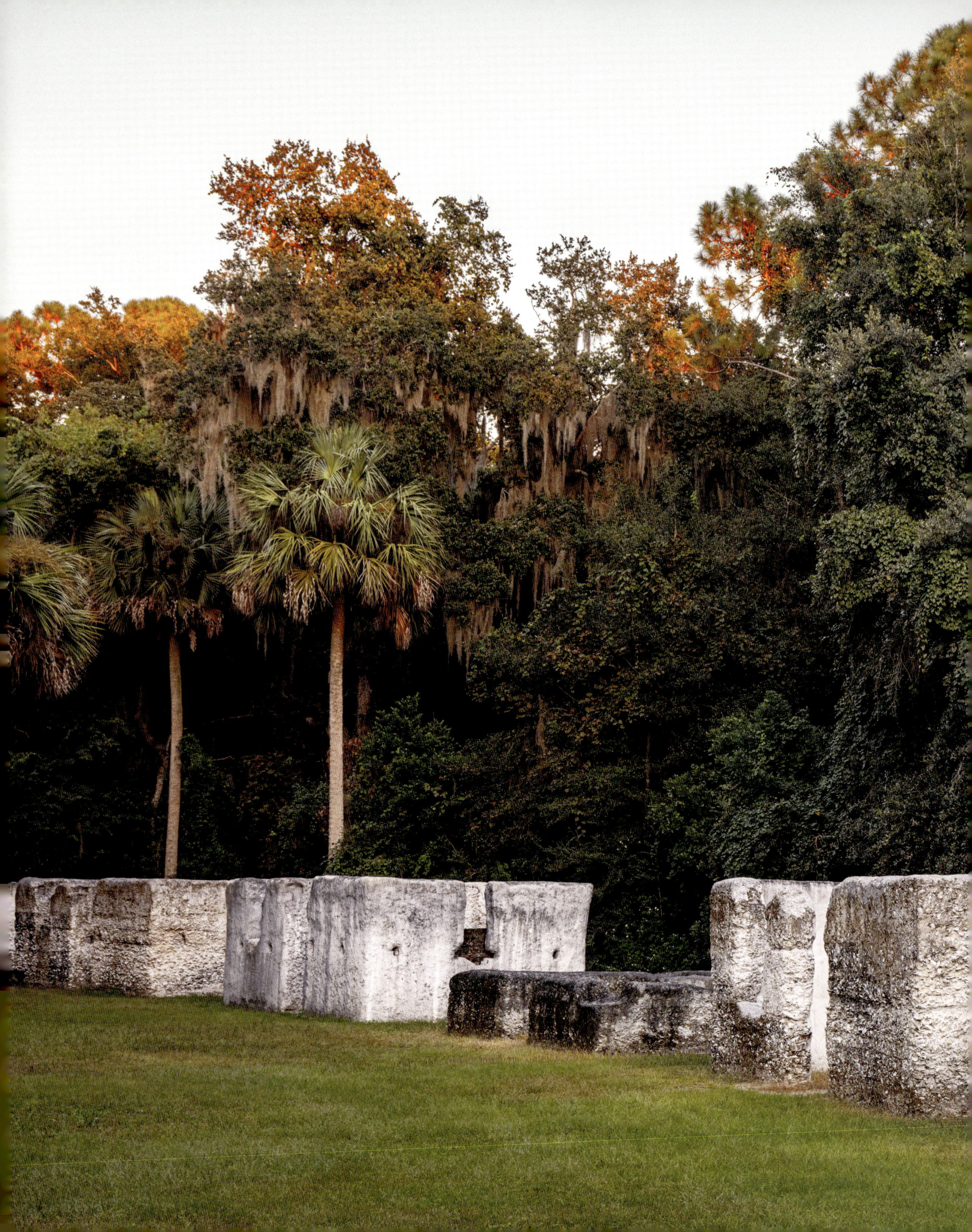

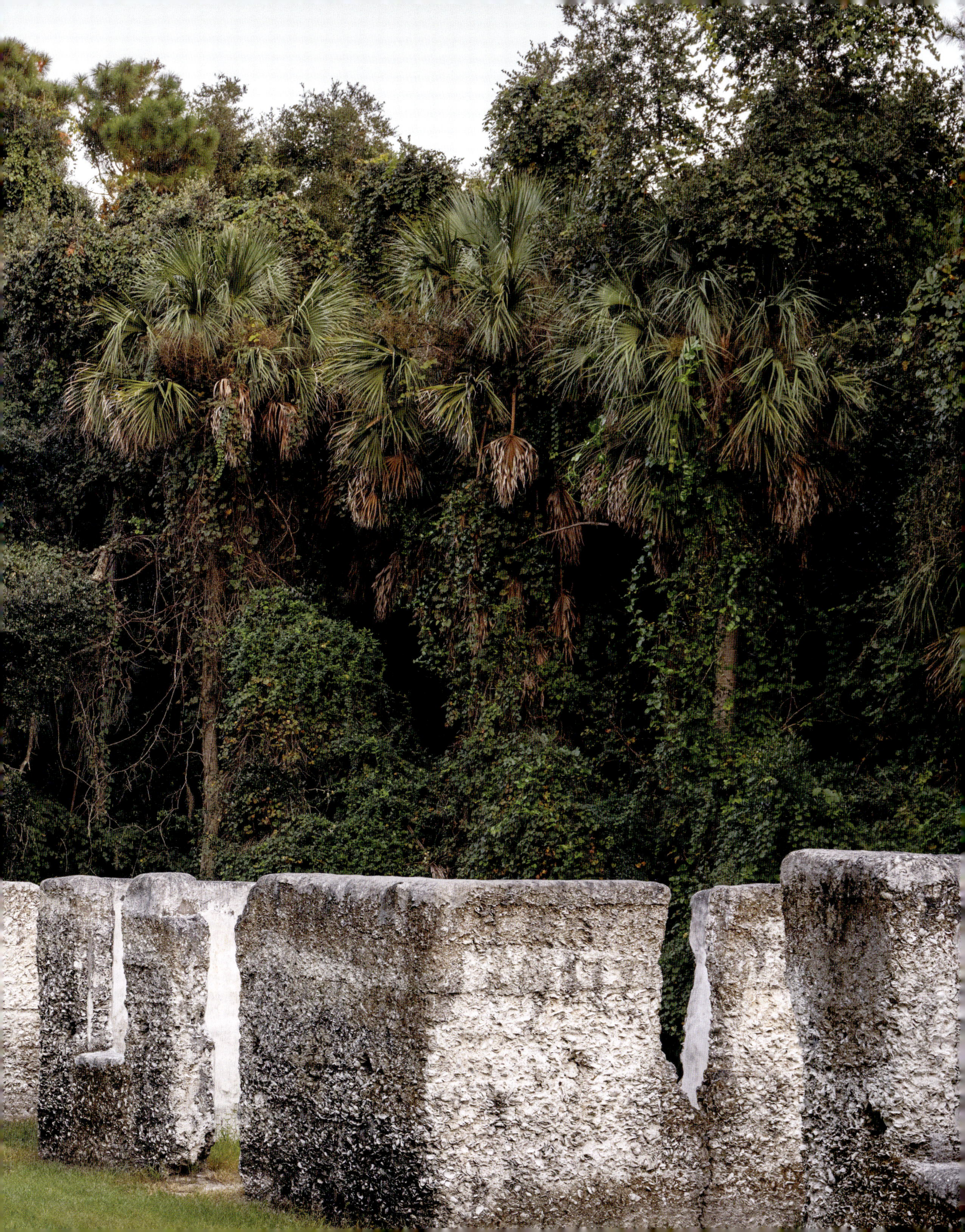

KG: That may be more personal to me, but I think I can see how pictures made by the photographers who used to shoot New York City in the fifties, sixties, and seventies have become history, because everything's so different now. The way things look here has changed so much. I think there's history built into photographing cities.

And at this point of making pictures for over 20 years, the photographs actually help me guide myself in time to see when I was somewhere. That preserves memory for me, as well as for the people in those photographs.

NG: How does your photograph of the Tuskegee Confederate Monument relate to that idea of preservation?

KG: My father and his entire side of the family are from Alabama, not far from downtown Tuskegee. When I drove throughout the southern states in search of Confederate relics, I came across only two covered statues, both in Alabama. It showed me that change was on the way. Three years later, in 2023, the government was forced to redistrict Tuskegee, which changed a lot of the state from Republican to Democrat. I imagine at some point the statue will be gone entirely.

NG: Tell me the process by which you got the monument assignment.

KG: When Covid started, National Geographic photo editor Mallory Benedict asked if I'd like to go down to Richmond and make some work for eight days. I hired a friend as an assistant, and we went there in July 2020.

It was scary as hell. We didn't know what the outcome of Covid would be. We were just in a car driving around Virginia, trying to make pictures of Confederate monuments. A month later, we did another 24-day road trip photographing as many of them as we could find.

NG: What was the biggest surprise of your monument story?

KG: I was surprised by all of it. I thought I was going down to make photographs of empty landscapes with nobody around. I didn't know it was 100 percent protest mode in America. The statue of Christopher Columbus had already been thrown into a river by the time I got there, and we were in Richmond when two others came down.

I didn't know there were going to be projections on the Robert E. Lee statue. A dude named Dustin Klein had these going. That night, he was pushing these faces of people that were killed by either police officers or deadly violence, and every picture was going up for like a quarter second, superfast. So I asked him to slow it down so I can get an exposure. It was a warm, beautiful night; everyone was having fun playing basketball, soccer. And I was just there making pictures, chilling. No harassment, no trouble, no guns, no nonsense. It was fun.

NG: You once observed that you try to step away from your personal feelings. How is that possible when you're documenting these monuments?

KG: It's not so hard when you're shooting urban landscapes. You're giving the camera very strict rules. If I'm photographing the Edmund Pettus Bridge, for better or worse, it's just a picture of a bridge, right? It's not like you can hate it or love it, and it's not racist because it's a picture of a bridge. I let people put themselves into the photographs.

NG: So you don't see yourself as the interpreter of the photo, merely the presenter of it?

KG: You show people what you want them to see. You're already giving them a bias because you're there photographing this certain thing. But that bias can go either way. For example, my book *Privileged Mediocrity* features 200 Confederate monuments and descriptions of why they exist. It's not about why they should be torn down. It's just a documentation of the place. So if you were a Confederate historian, it's useful as the opposite, you know what I mean?

NG: For your forthcoming book *Unhidden* with James Edward Mills, why did you choose to present the slave quarters at Kingsley Plantation in the way that you did [pages 366–67]?

KG: Kingsley Plantation is administered by the National Park Service. There's a lot of national parks in the South that were either plantations or battlefields, or Black towns that were leveled to make battlefields. Stupid, stupid shit. And this is not an anomaly. I've been to many of these places that have slave quarters, and they are now national parks.

I had never seen slave quarters before going to these places. I didn't know that people were living

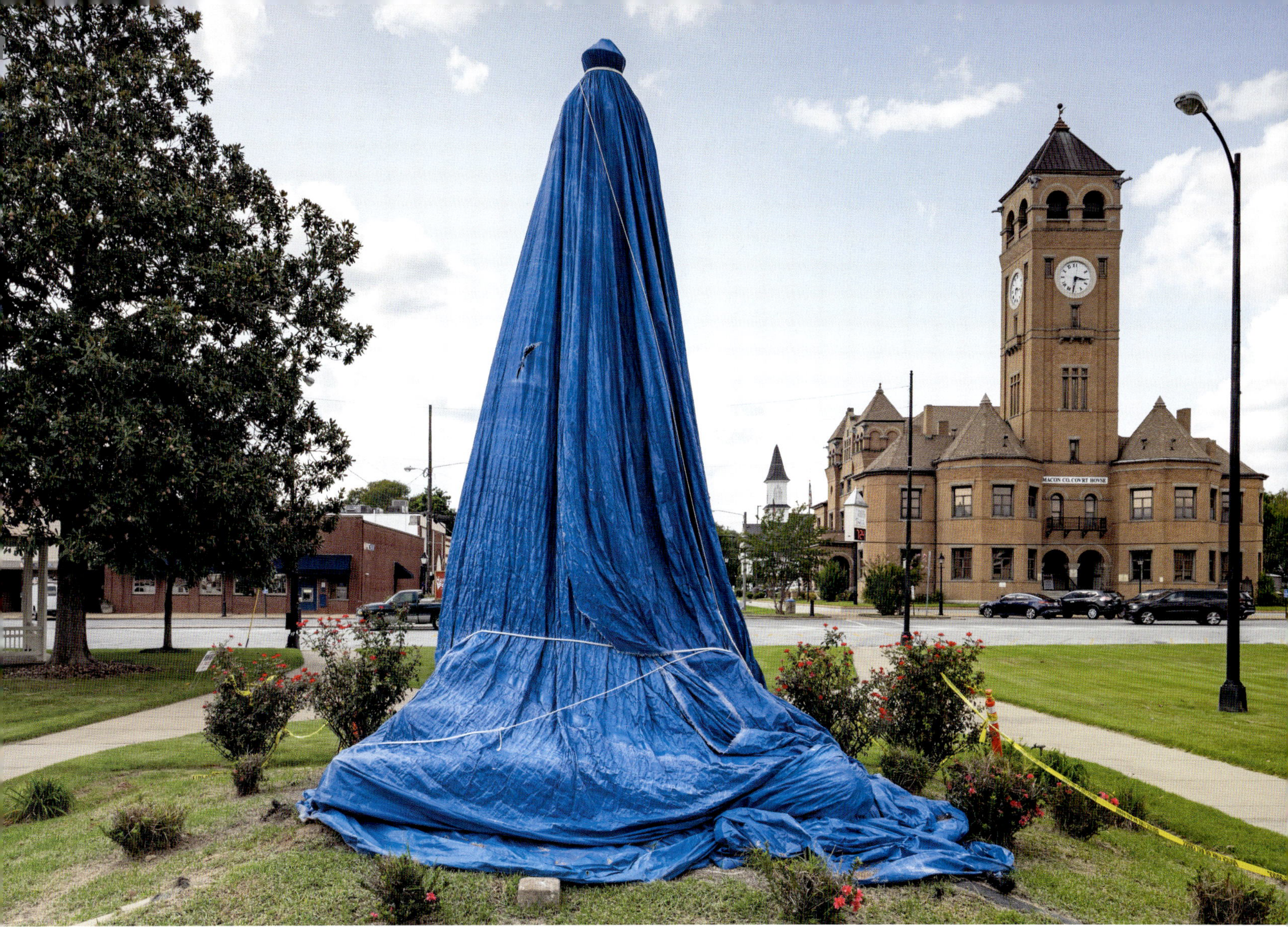

KRIS GRAVES, 2020
At the peak of the Black Lives Matter movement, a Confederate memorial is concealed by a tarpaulin in Tuskegee, Alabama.

PREVIOUS PAGES
KRIS GRAVES, 2021
Slave quarters at the Kingsley Plantation in Jacksonville, Florida's Timucuan Ecological and Historic Preserve

in these conditions, so it was kind of shocking to see how beautiful the land was.

NG: Is there a landscape we haven't discussed that is especially meaningful or evocative to you?

KG: I have to go back to the South. I haven't seen enough of Montgomery. If you look at a topographical map, you'll see this oval of land that starts in Montgomery, heads west, and then goes up into Mississippi. It's called the Black Belt prairie. It's where most cotton was produced, and where most of the Black people live. Then if you look at gerrymandering rules, you'll see that's exactly where they gerrymander Black people into neighborhoods. It's something that I want to figure out more for myself.

NG: What do you want to learn about it?

KG: Who lives there? What are the communities like? What kind of picture can represent what this place feels like? What can be memorable? That's very difficult and takes a lot of time to see, because there's not that many photographers down there, and most of their work will never be shown. So if I have a chance to go down there and be more intimate with the land, then maybe I can figure out a way that people would actually give a shit about these people.

NG: Do you find that your desire to remove your personal feelings from your work ever conflicts with your desire to make people care about what you photograph?

KG: I feel no tension, because the viewer either wants to stick with the image or not. What I personally feel about each scene is almost irrelevant, or at least it should be. My job is to create a strong image that can lead to more questioning. And I hope that my images convey a clear message about our lived environment—positive and negative.

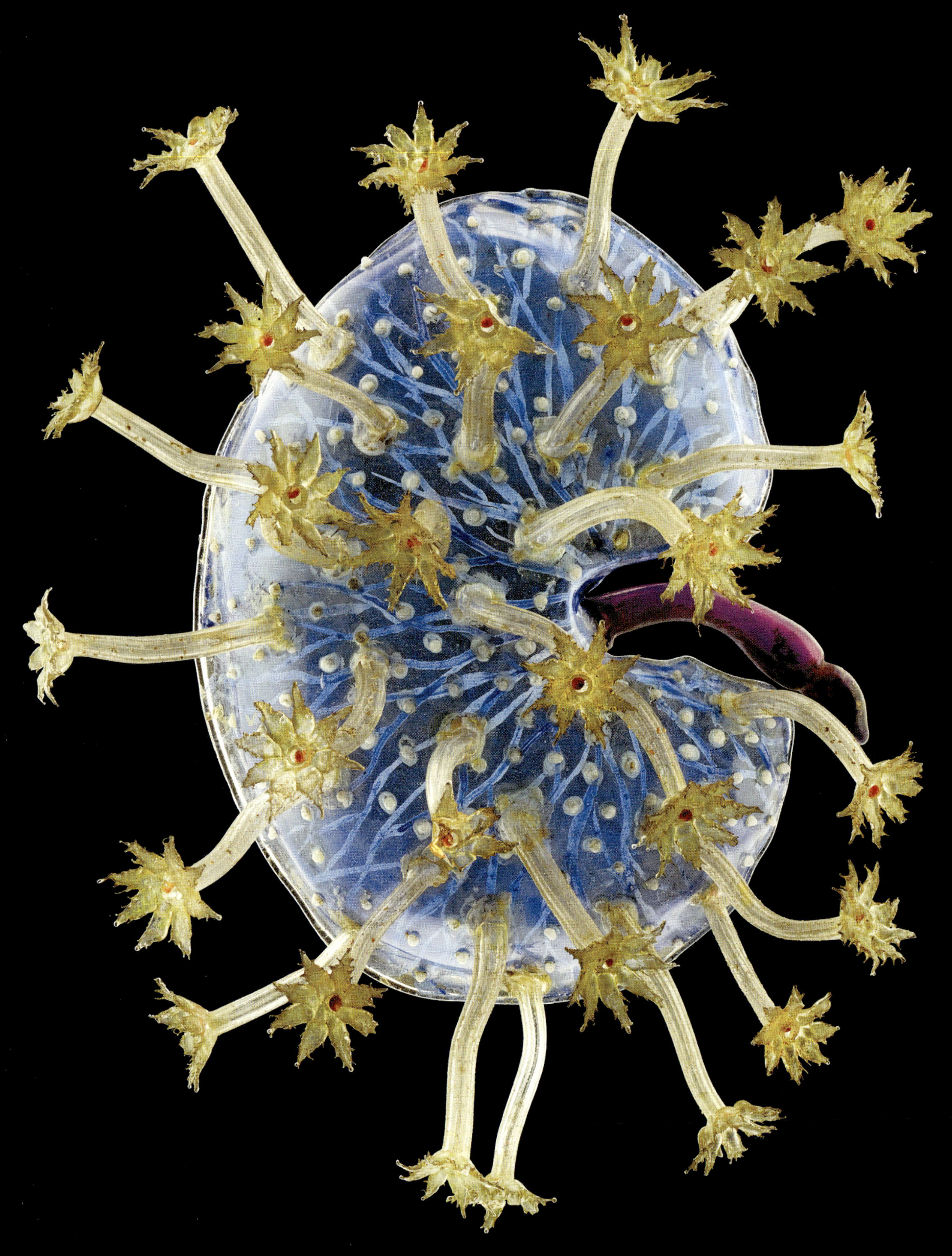

SCIENCE & TECHNOLOGY

THE POWER TO

REVEAL

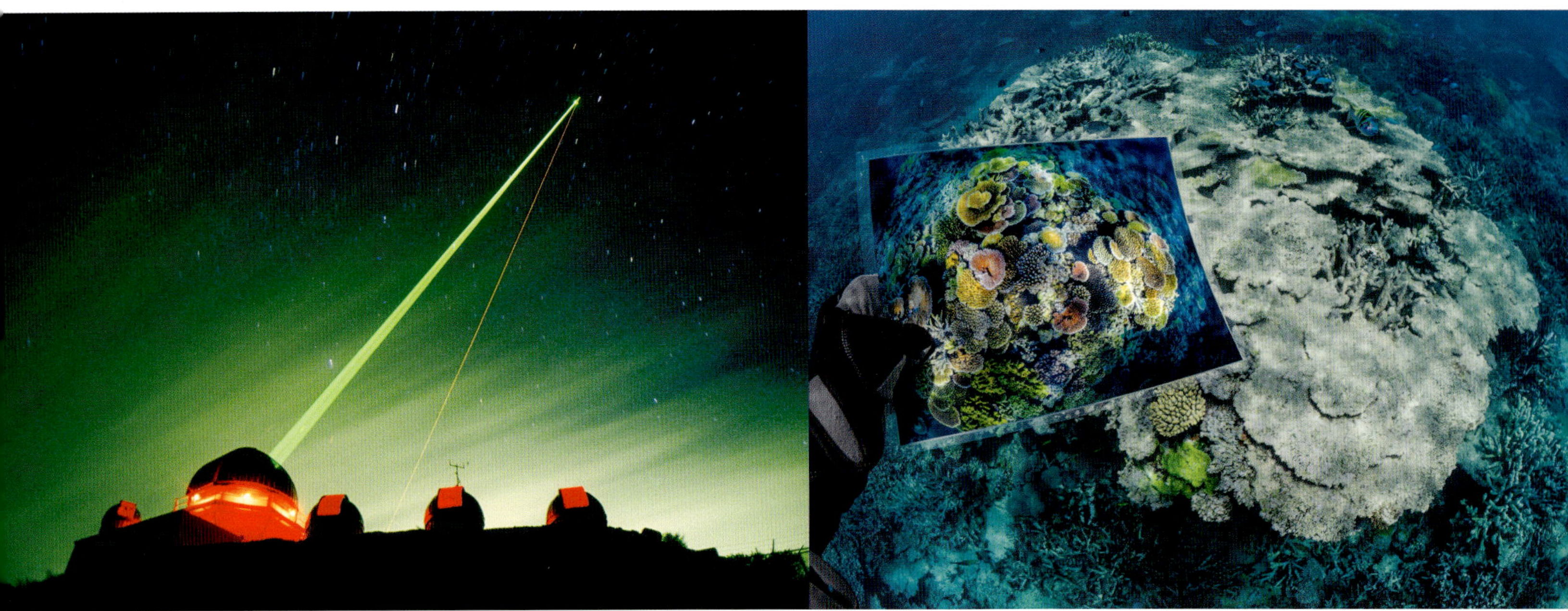

GOING TO EXTREMES

PAGE 370
GUIDO MOCAFICO, 2014
Nineteenth-century father-and-son glass artists Leopold and Rudolf Blaschka made true-to-scale models of sea invertebrates to use as classroom aids. This one—*Renilla muelleri,* a type of sea pansy—is between two and three inches tall.

ABOVE LEFT
ROGER RESSMEYER, 2013
At the Starfire Optical Range in New Mexico, telescopes beam a green copper vapor laser and an orange sodium-wavelength laser to create an artificial star.

ABOVE RIGHT
DAVID DOUBILET, 2018
A comparison image shows the damage that rising ocean temperatures inflicted on Australia's Great Barrier Reef in just nine years.

ILLUSTRATING STORIES ABOUT SCIENCE AND TECHNOLOGY is often the photography of extremes: creating images of the highest, deepest, and fastest. It takes special equipment and skill to capture the spiral of a galaxy billions of light-years away, to render the hue of a shell-pink sea cucumber drifting in the depths of the Mariana Trench, or to arrest the whir of a hummingbird's wings.

The quarry may be infinitesimally small. A solitary human cell, a spiky Covid-19 virus, a single grain of pollen. Or the camera may compress time by grace of a multiple exposure to reveal the unfurling of a flower that blooms once a year.

The subject of a science or technology feature may defy conventional documentation, like a story on pain, the mind, or sleep. "Illustrating the abstract," says Robert Clark, "is not so much about finding the moment as creating it."

He's not wrong. To portray a story about the seductive nature of sugar and its detrimental effects on health, for example, Clark created a beautifully lit portrait of a doughnut buried in a snowstorm of powdered sugar. And for a story on sleep, photographer Louie Psihoyos brought the "counting sheep" trope to life by herding a small flock of live sheep into a bedroom in which a leaping stuffed sheep was hung over a sleeping model.

Sometimes the need for a compliant collaborator adds to the list of challenges. For a story on the dog genome, photographer-artist William Wegman enlisted Penny, one of his famous Weimaraners, to pose for the magazine cover. In a carefully supervised shoot to illustrate whether the fear response is hardwired or learned as part of a story on the brain, Cary Wolinsky photographed an imperturbably calm baby nestled in the coils of an 11-foot python.

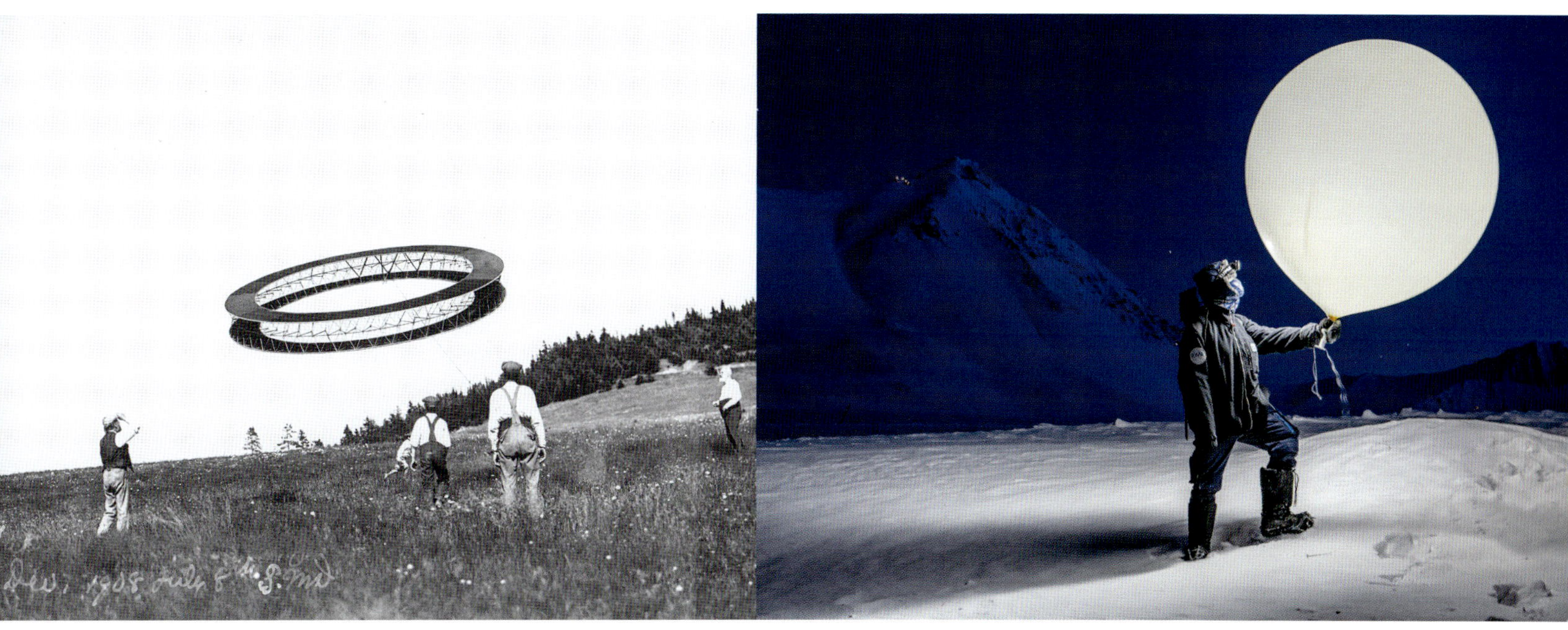

In photography, the boundary between science and art can blur. A rose frozen in liquid nitrogen, shattered with a blast of air and then photographed by Martin Klimas, presents as a piece of postmodern deconstructive art. The surface of a mosquito egg in an image by Martin Oeggerli is as delicate as Belgian lace. Dan Winters's portrait of NASA's Space Launch System rocket for Artemis I, poised at the Kennedy Space Center against a curtain of fog, is a study in cinematic drama.

Above all, the impact of science photography can be profound. "If history is any guide, every time we have built new eyes to observe the universe, our understanding of ourselves and our place in it has been forever altered," wrote the theoretical physicist Lawrence M. Krauss. After all, an image taken by physical chemist Rosalind Franklin and her student Ray Gosling, tagged photograph 51, pointed to the double-helix structure of DNA and helped lead the way to genetic research.

Consider, too, the photograph by the crew of the Apollo 17 made on December 7, 1972, known to NASA as AS17-148-22727 and to the rest of us as the "Blue Marble." The first color image of a fully illuminated Earth from space rearranged our perspective of our planet, became an emblem for the environmental movement, and appeared in multiple *National Geographic* magazine articles and books. "I'll tell you," Harrison Schmitt, one of the astronauts on the flight, said to Mission Control after the image was made, "if there ever was a fragile-appearing piece of blue in space, it's the Earth right now."

A change of perspective. Time unraveled. Time compressed. Surprise. Delight. There is a craziness to science—a wild wonder that photography reveals.

ABOVE LEFT
GILBERT H. GROSVENOR, 1908
Alexander Graham Bell watches as his latest invention—a wheel-shaped kite—flies over Nova Scotia, Canada.

ABOVE RIGHT
ESTHER HORVATH, 2021
A scientist holds a weather balloon carrying a radiosonde, an instrument that measures temperature, humidity, and pressure, in Svalbard, Norway.

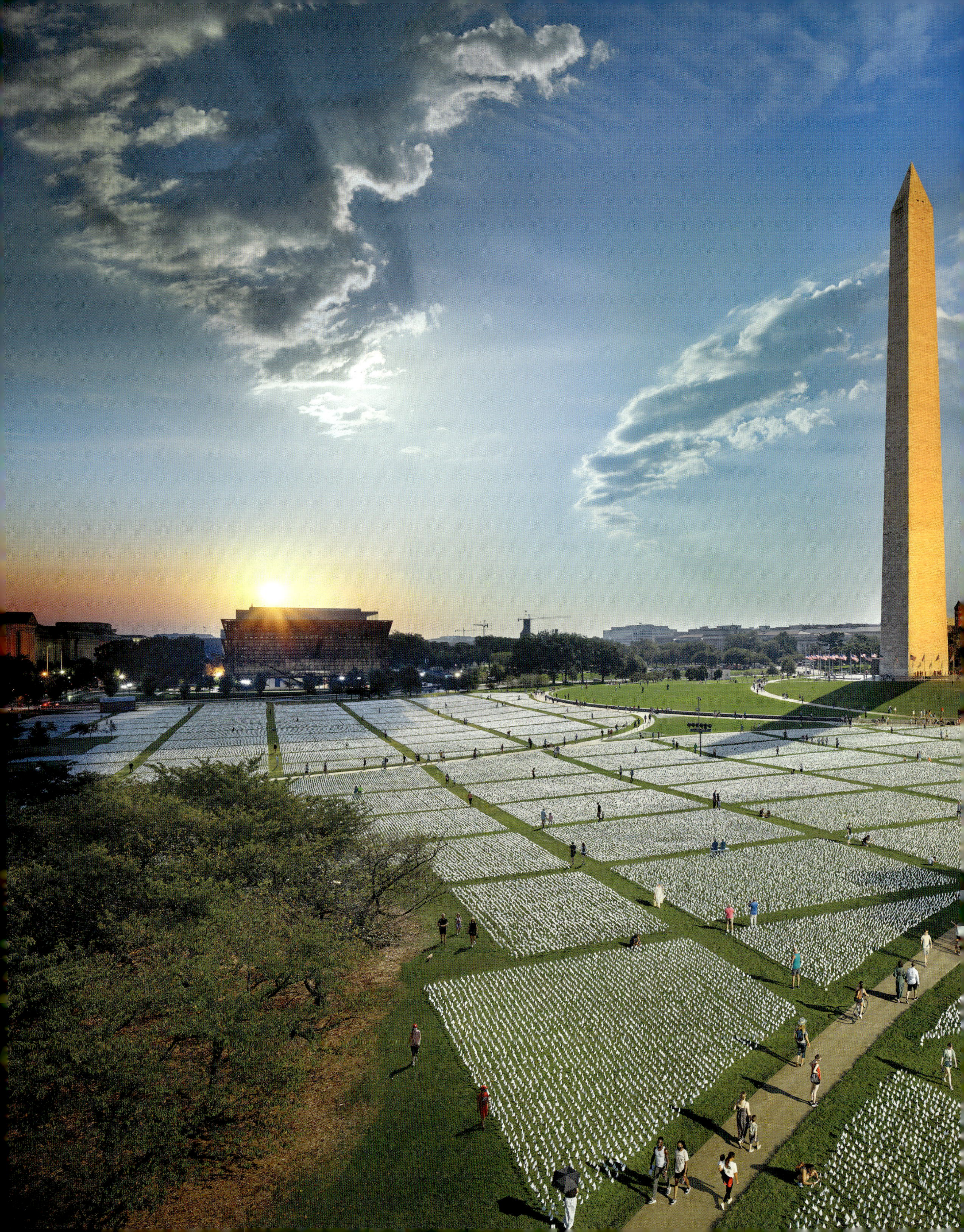

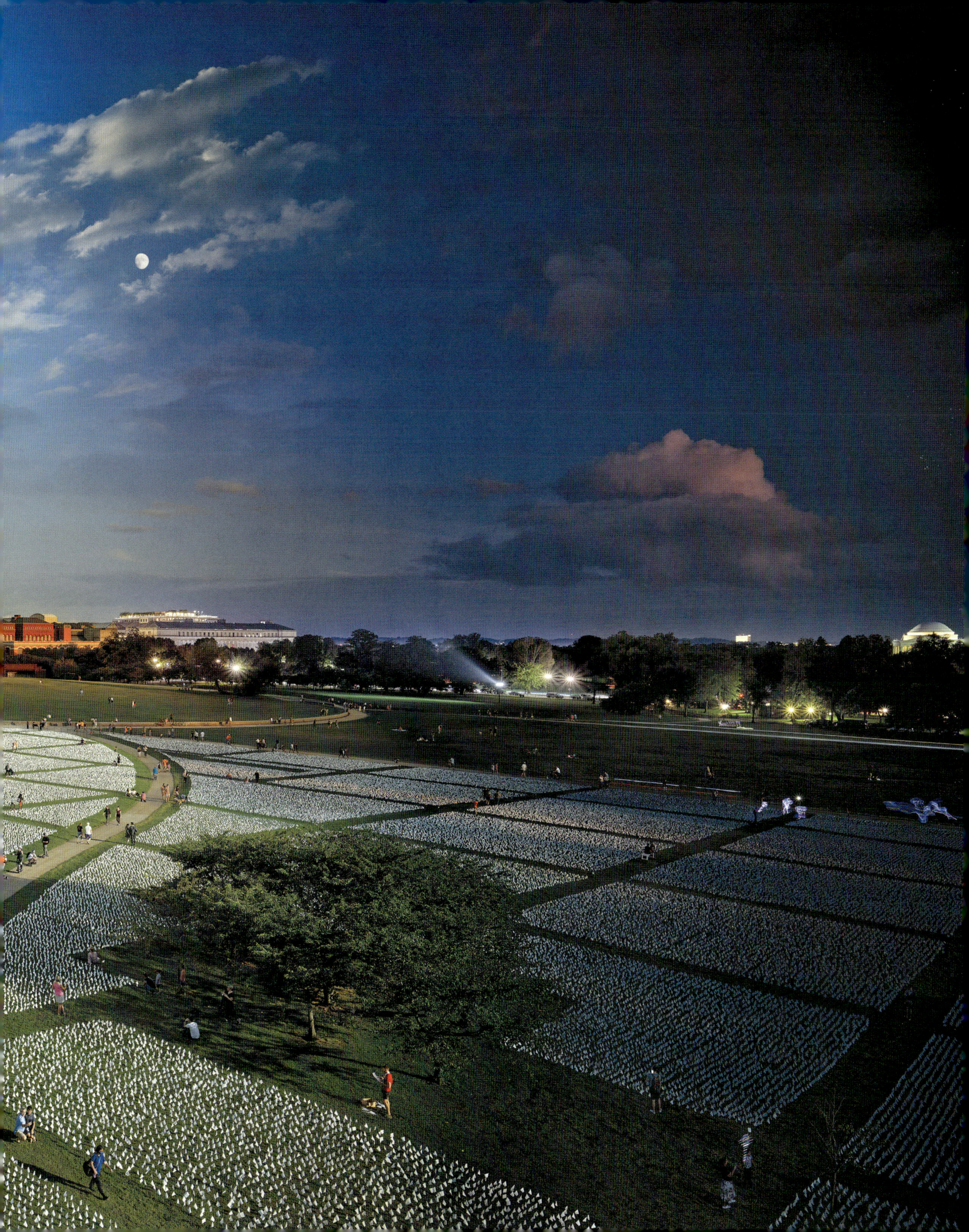

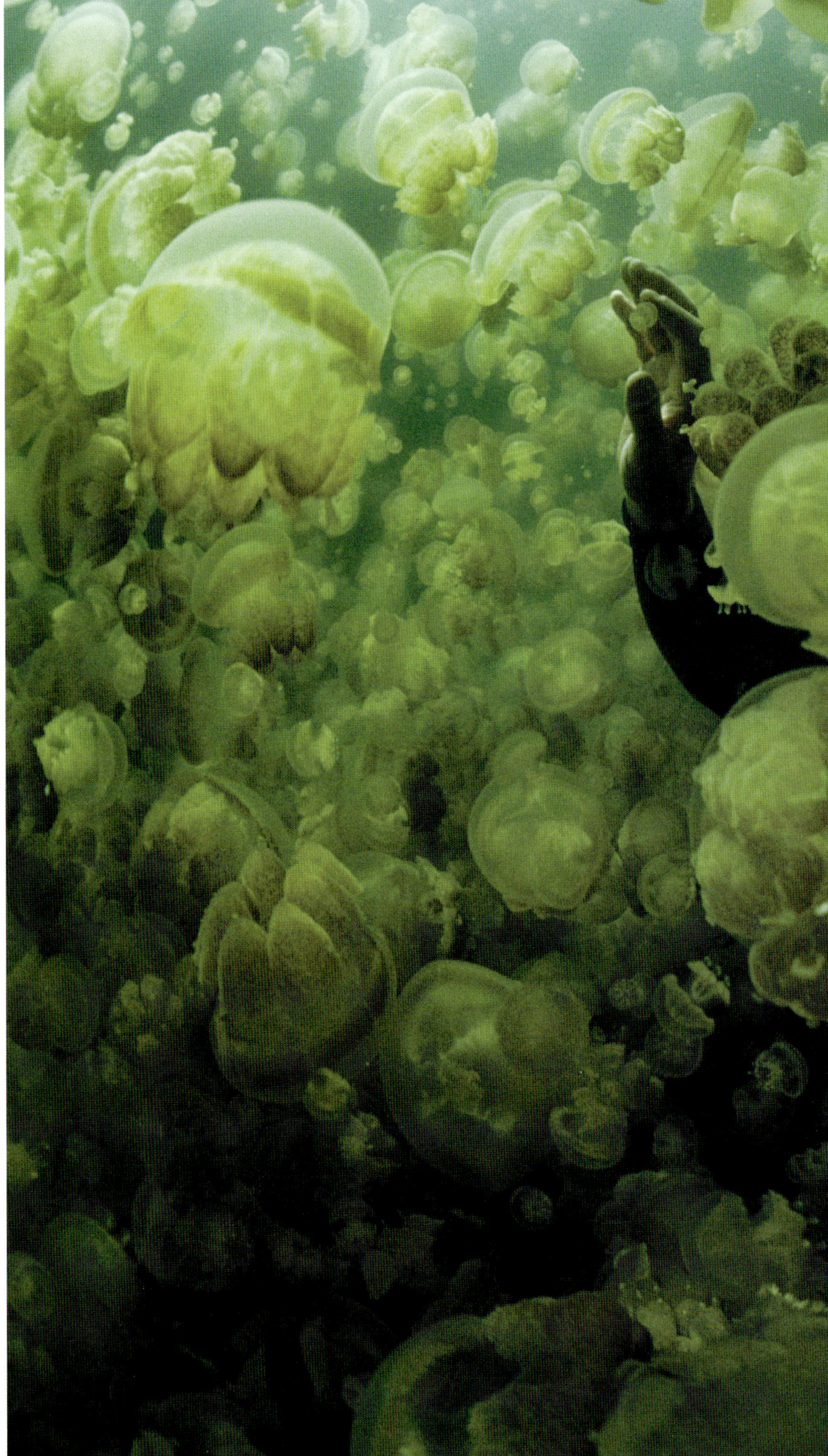

DAVID DOUBILET, 1981
A marine biologist rises through a cloud of nonstinging *Mastigias* jellyfish in Palau, Micronesia.

PREVIOUS PAGES
STEPHEN WILKES, 2021
Planted on parkland around the Washington Monument in the District of Columbia, small white flags symbolize each life lost to Covid-19 in the United States.

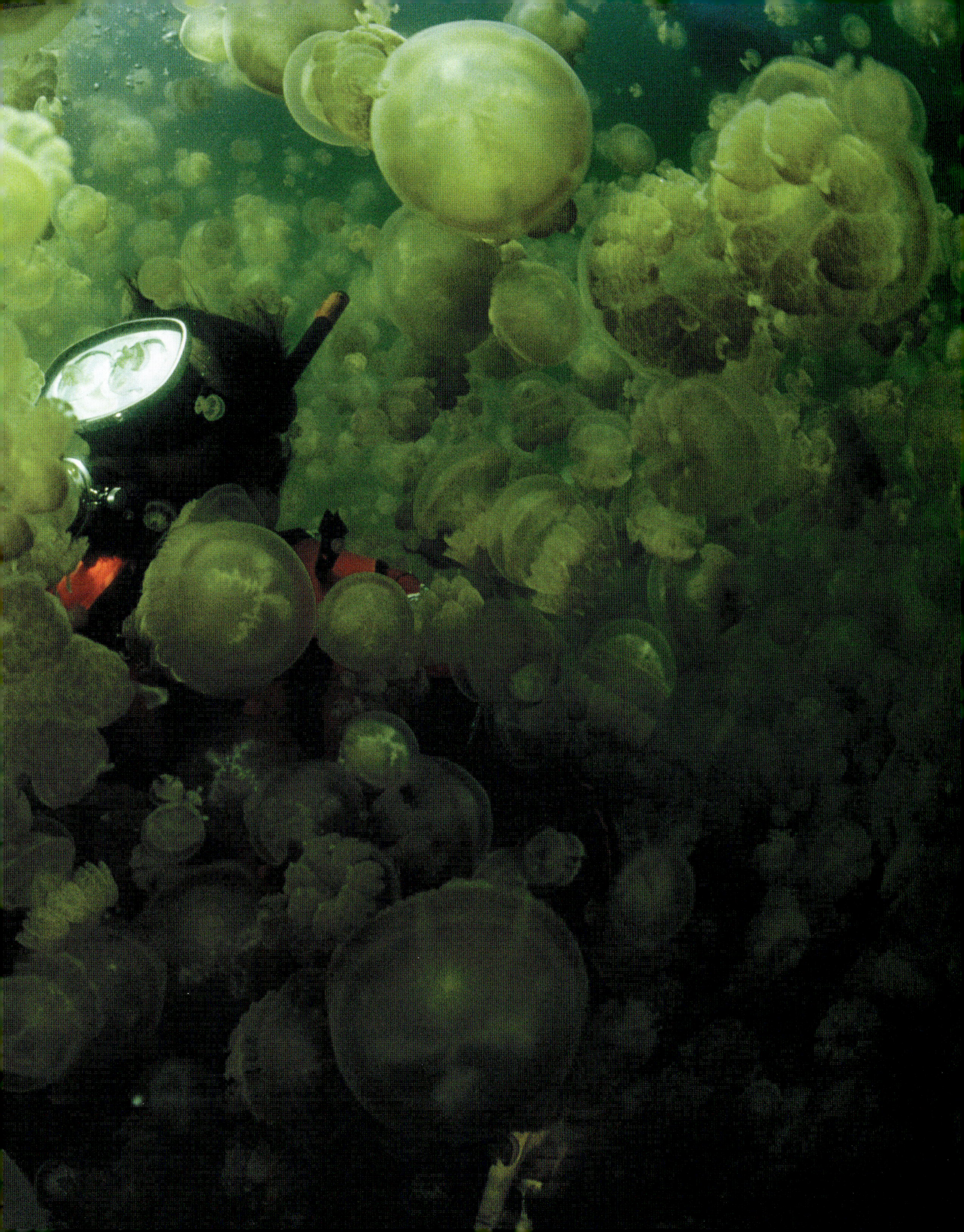

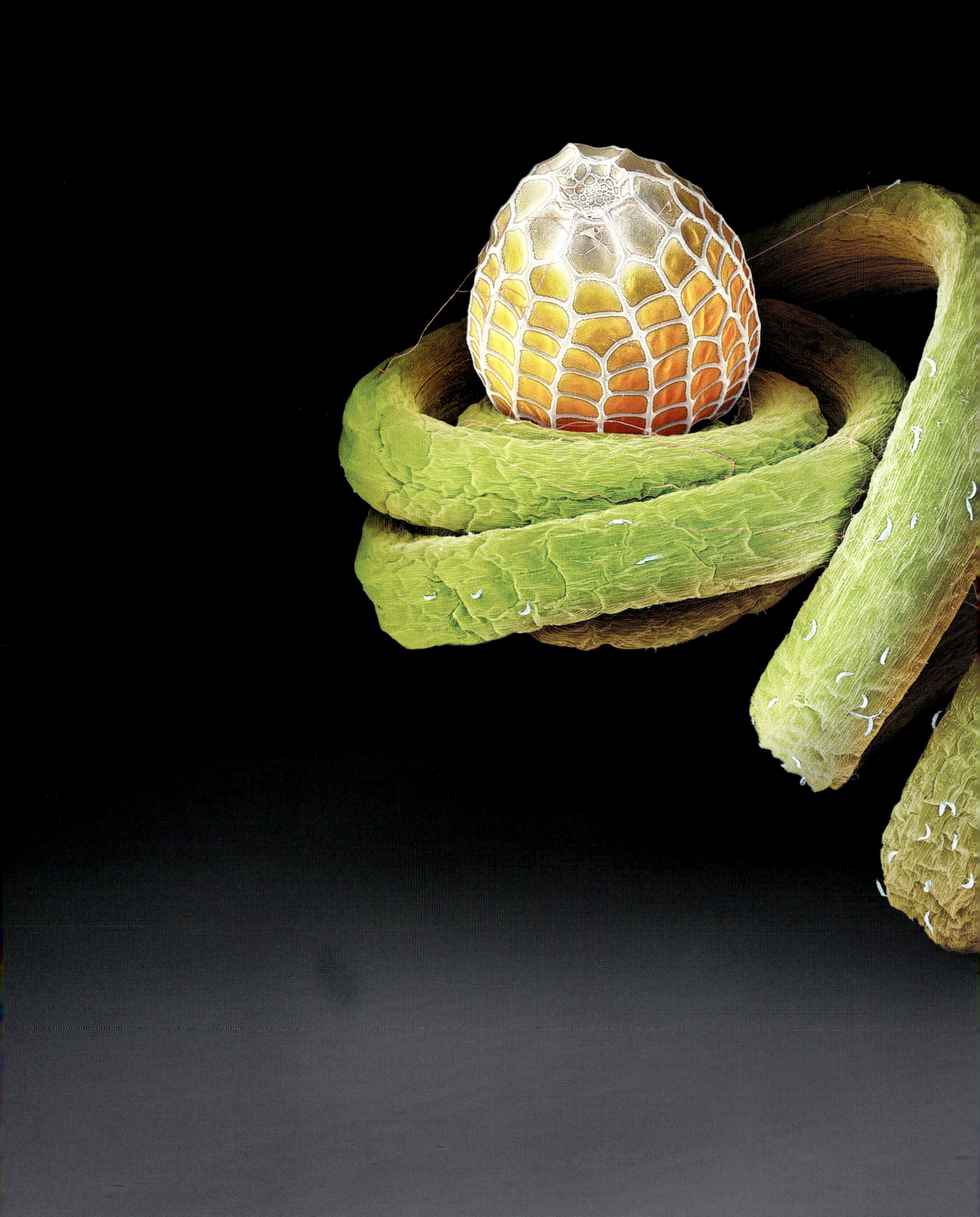

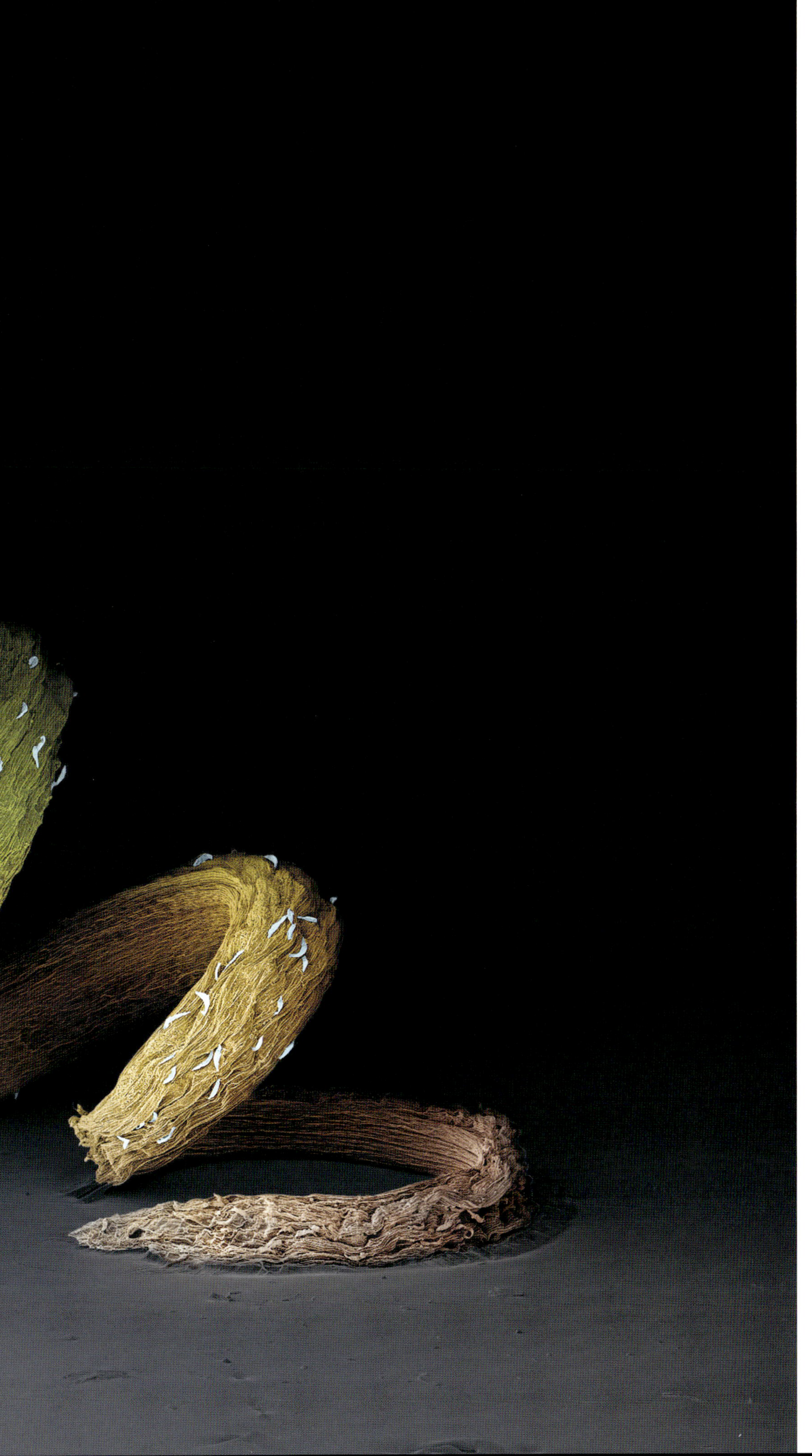

MARTIN OEGGERLI, 2010
The egg of a Julia butterfly, which measures about one millimeter in diameter, perches on a *Passiflora* plant.

ILLUSTRATING THE ABSTRACT IS NOT SO MUCH ABOUT FINDING THE MOMENT AS CREATING IT.

ROBERT CLARK, PHOTOGRAPHER

MAX AGUILERA-HELLWEG, 2004
Stacked 19th-century specimens in a Berlin, Germany, laboratory form an abstract human: hair from the head of a stillborn infant, a brain, an enlarged heart, a liver, bones, and teeth. All can be derived from a single stem cell.

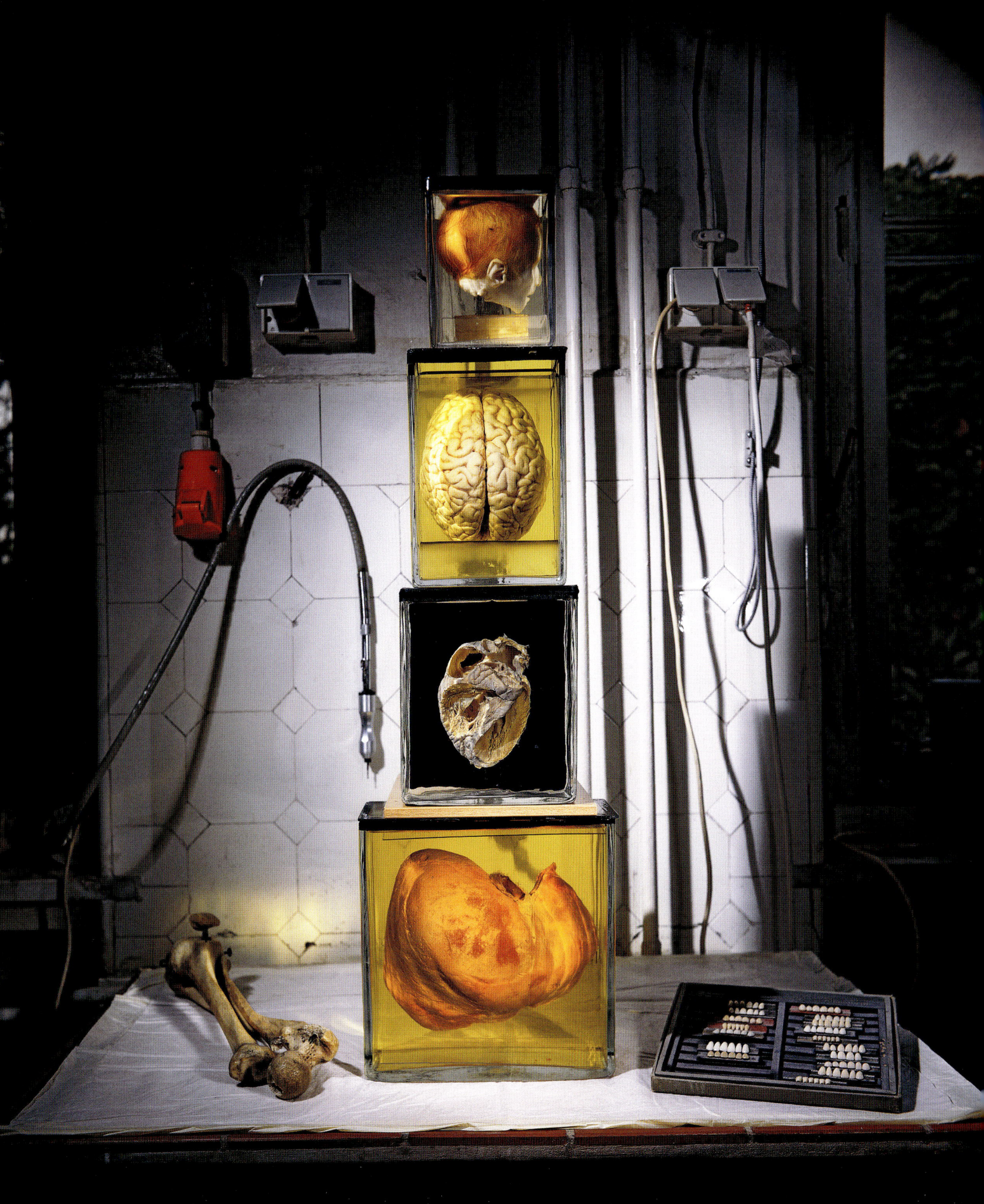

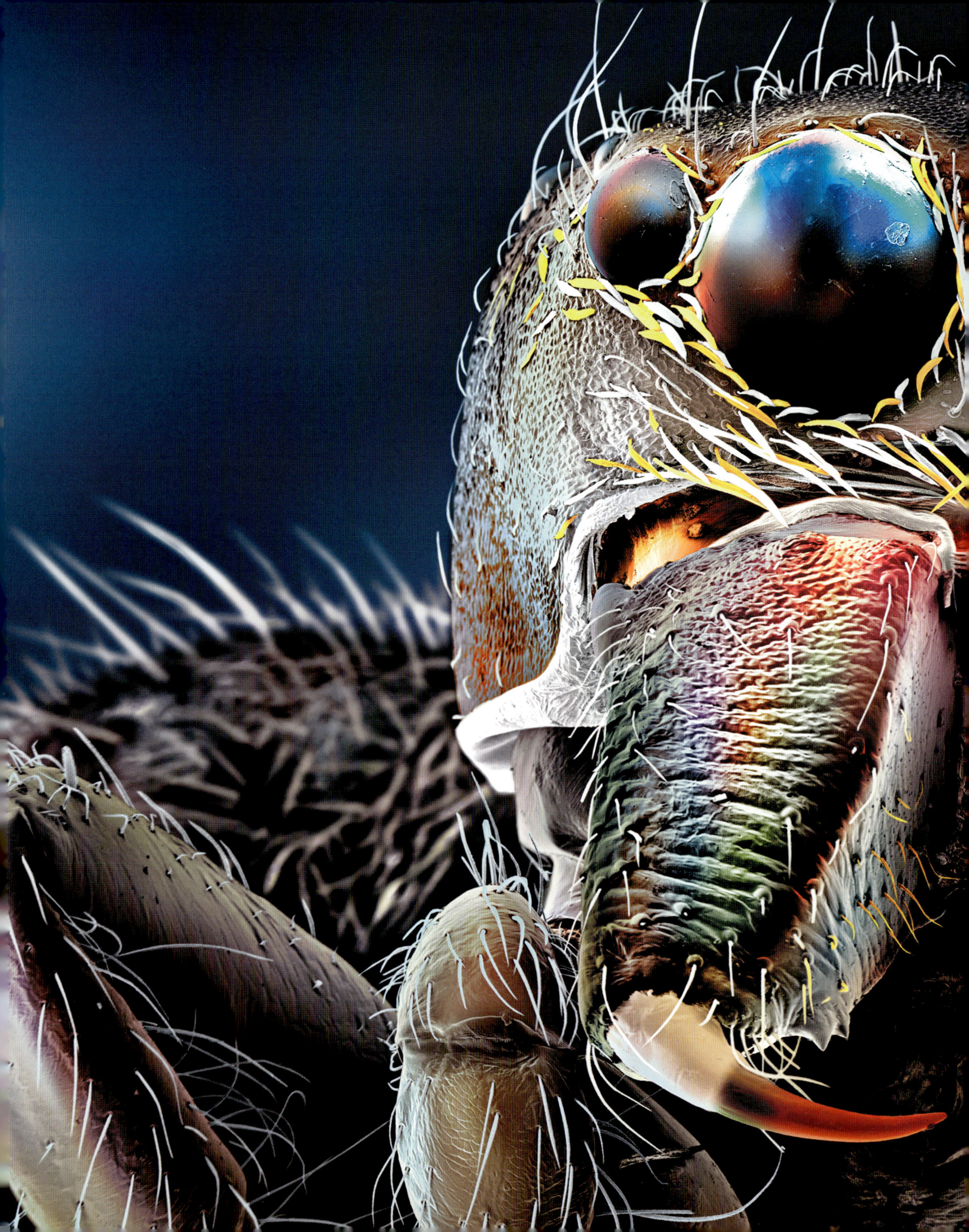

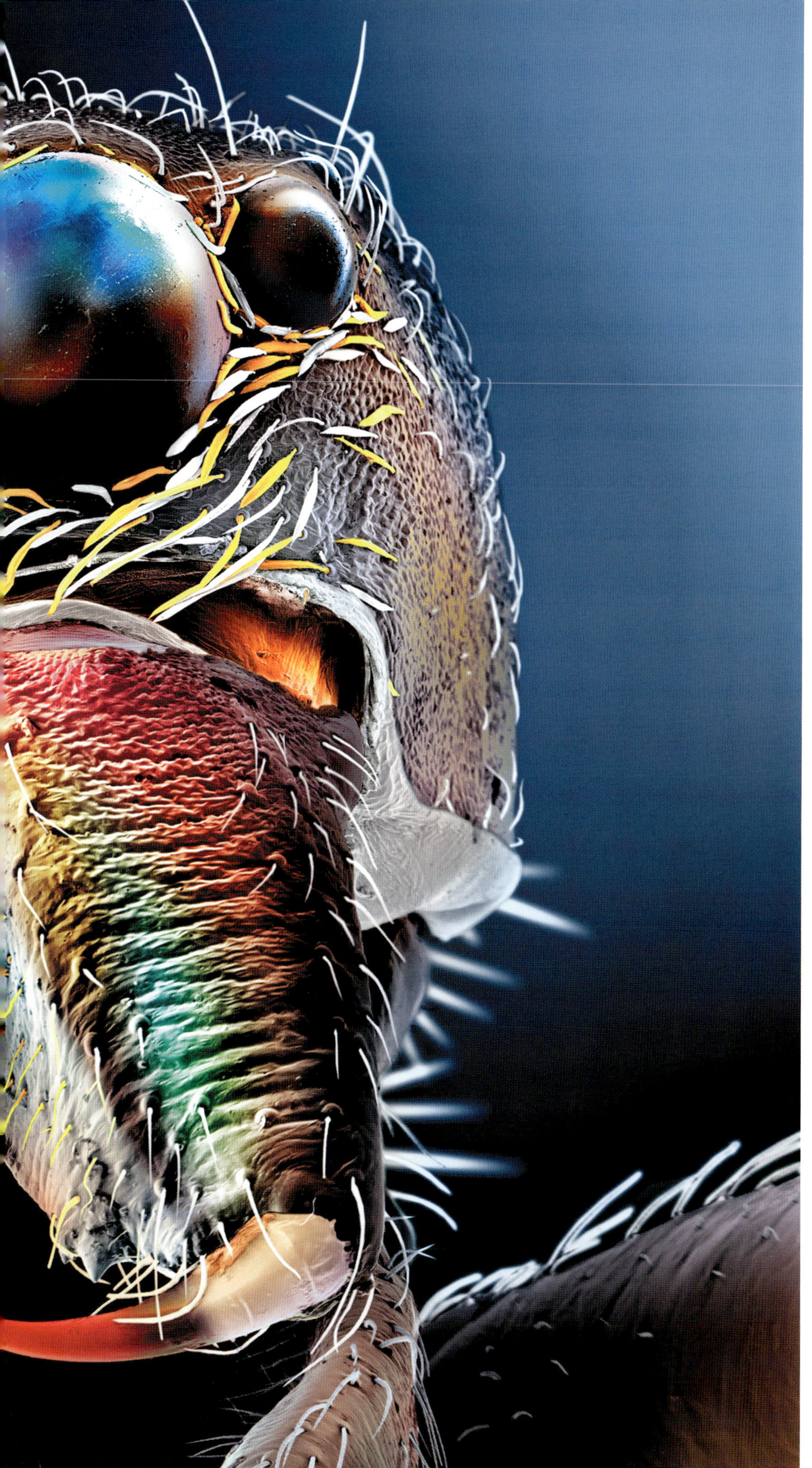

MARTIN OEGGERLI, 2015
A jumping spider—magnified here through a scanning electron microscope—has eight eyes with unique retinas that give it an almost 360-degree view of its surroundings.

FOLLOWING PAGES
REUBEN WU, 2019
Introducing artificial light in a natural environment opens the mind to another way of seeing. Here, a drone creates a circle of light over rock formations in the Bolivian Altiplano.

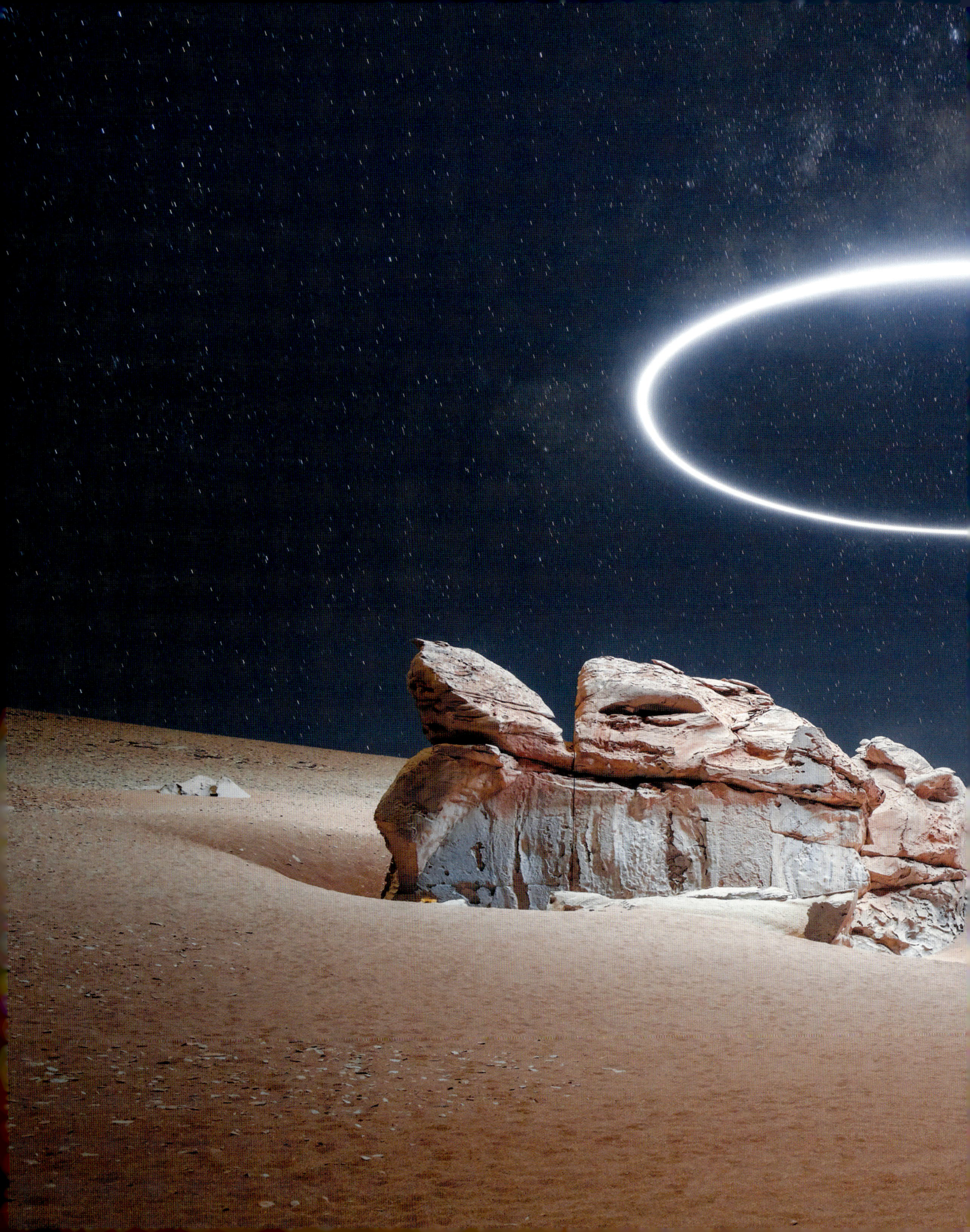

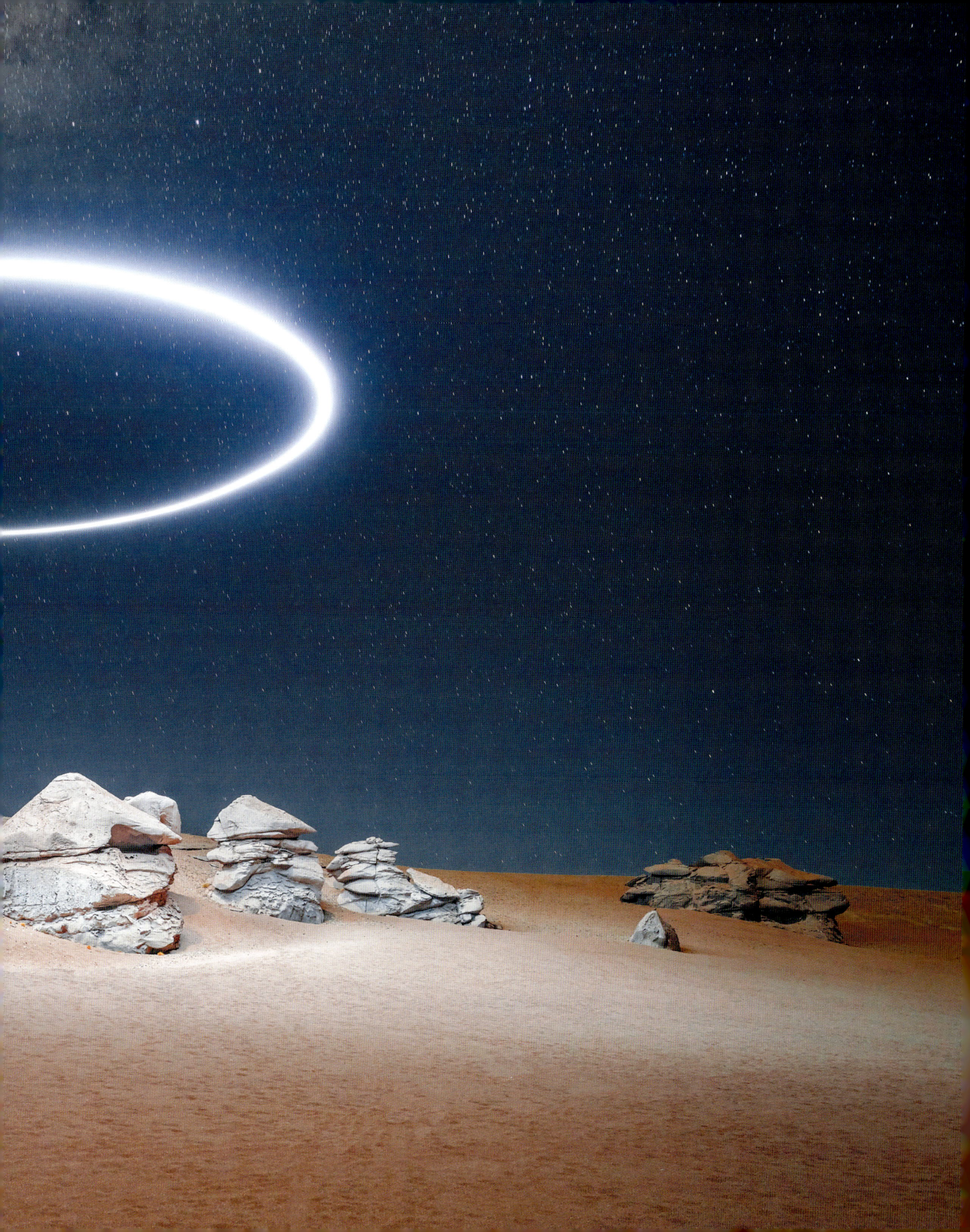

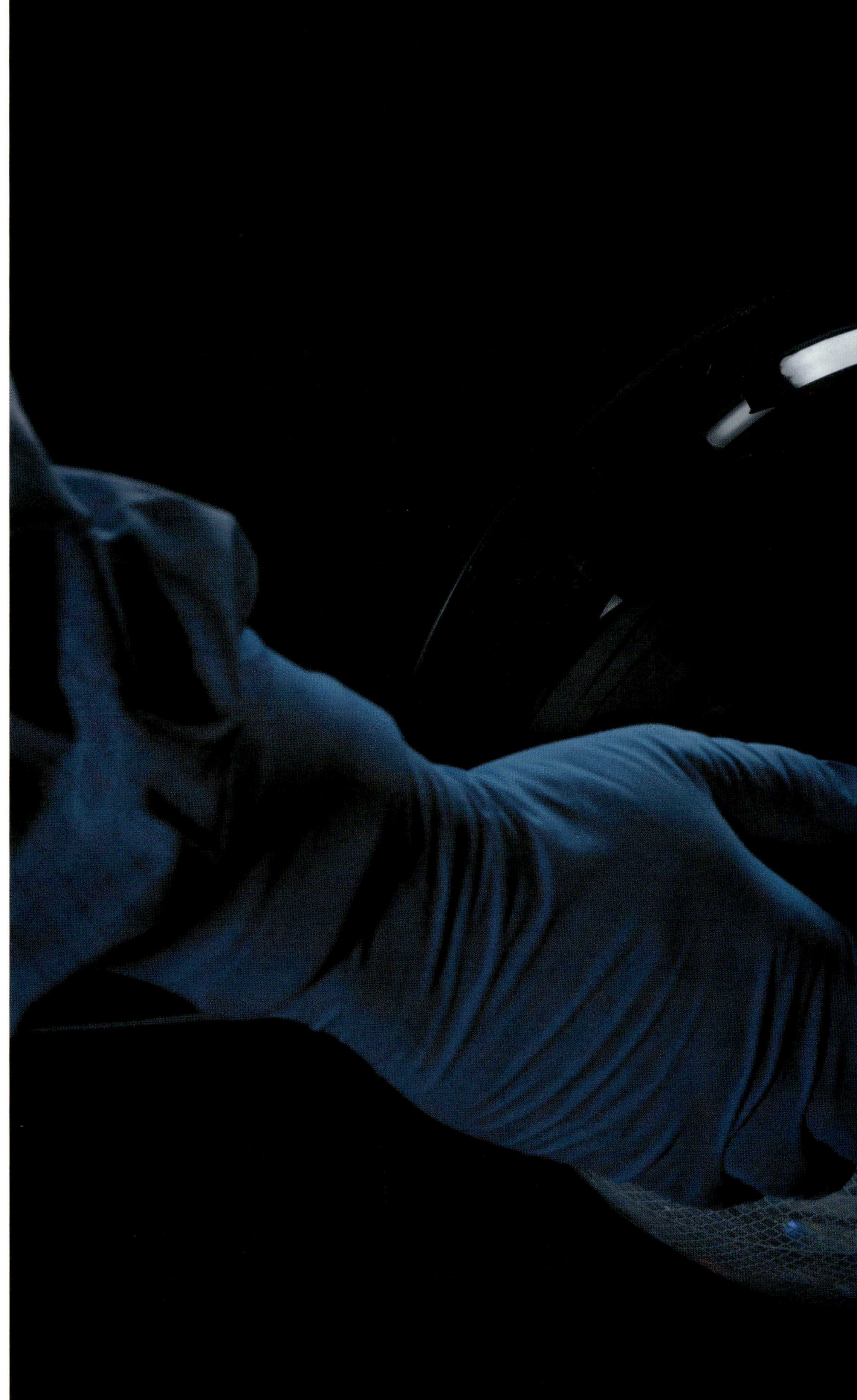

DAN WINTERS, 2021
Technicians inspect Commander Moonikin Campos, a sensor-equipped stand-in for humans used in NASA's Artemis I program, at the John F. Kennedy Space Center in Florida.

FOLLOWING PAGES
MAC STONE, 2022
A SpaceX Falcon 9 rocket streaks above a stand of bald cypress trees in Florida's Everglades.

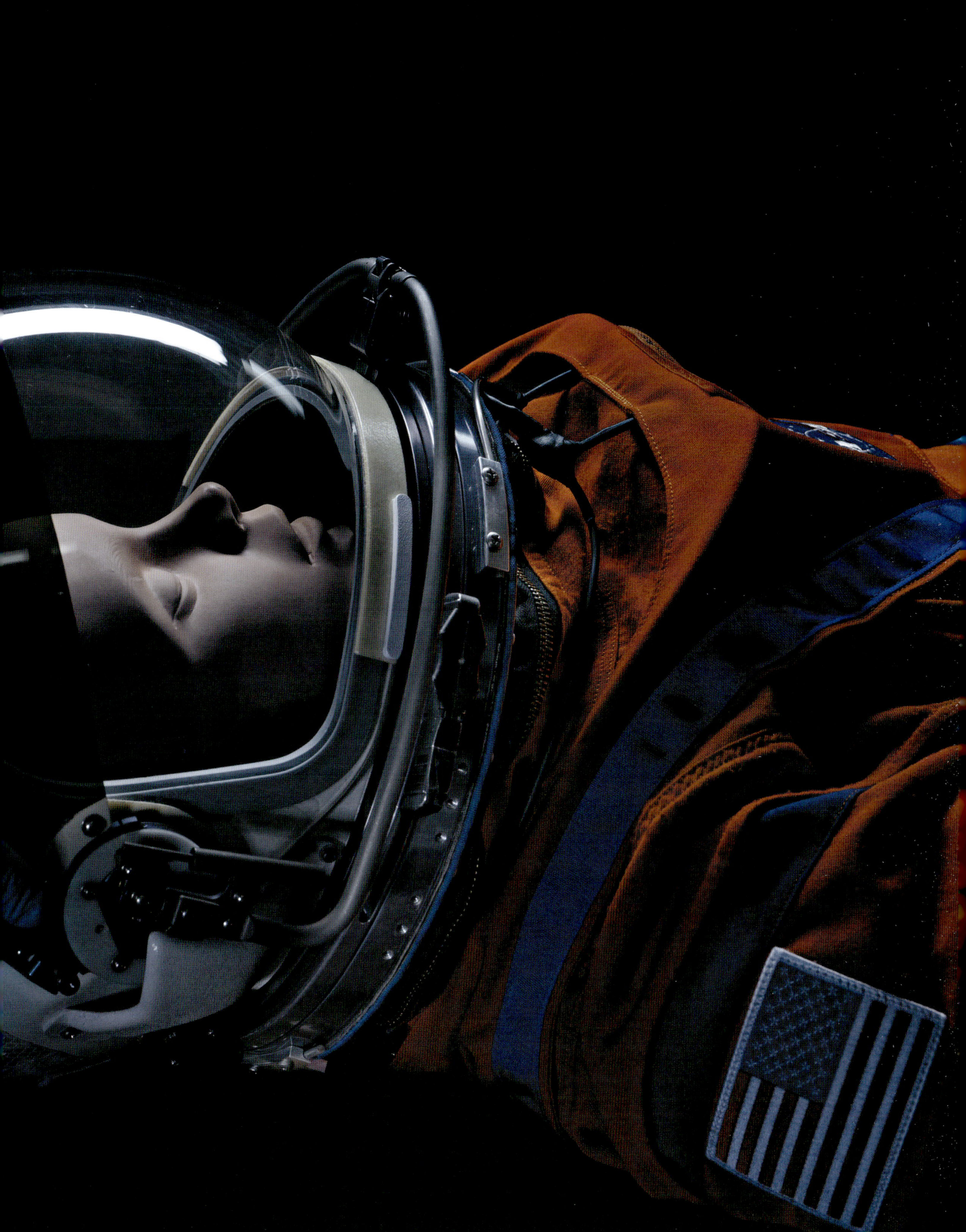

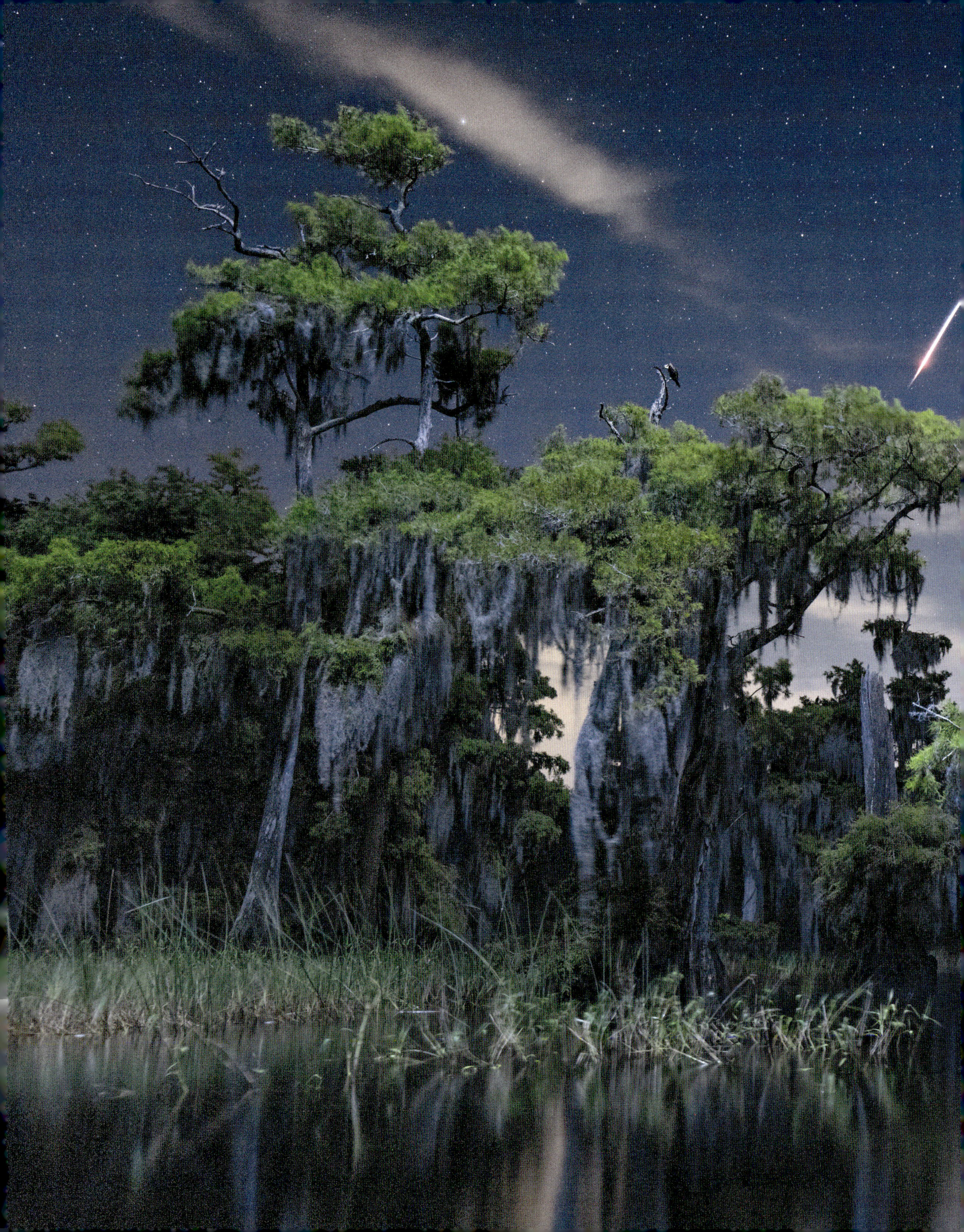

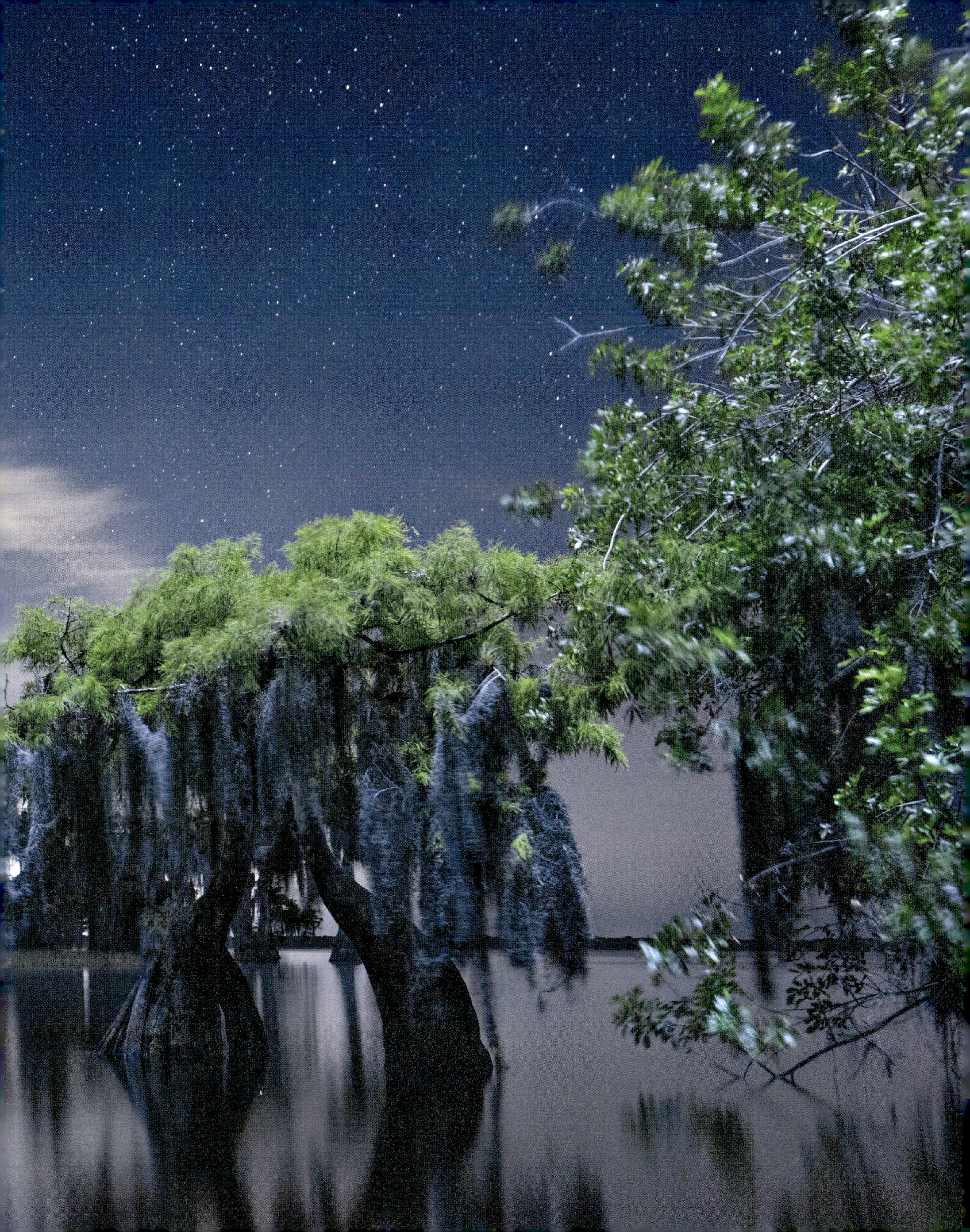

BIOGRAPHY

ANAND VARMA

IN THE WORLD OF ANAND VARMA'S CHILDHOOD, bugs and salamanders trumped elephants and sharks. "Little things were more accessible and were where I could find myself," he says. His backyard in Atlanta, Georgia, was more than a playground; it served as his first laboratory and studio. Among his early subjects was a garter snake he photographed using his father's digital camera. It wasn't so much the image of the snake that impressed as its scales: a hidden detail waiting to be revealed by the camera.

As a sophomore at the University of California, Berkeley, where he studied biology, Varma's path became illuminated when National Geographic photographer David Liittschwager approached him to collect marine specimens off the coast of Hawaii. The exercise revealed the possibility of a career that married science and photography. His first *National Geographic* story, "Mindsuckers," about parasites that cannibalize their hosts, was the cover of the November 2014 issue. Through the use of highly sophisticated cameras and techniques—some of them his own invention—Varma slows down the fast (a rain-soaked hummingbird shaking off water), speeds up the slow (the life cycle of a honeybee), and makes the invisible visible (the airflow around a hummingbird's wings in flight).

A National Geographic Explorer and World Press Photo award winner, Varma is the founder of National Geographic's WonderLab, a state-of-the-art studio in Berkeley dedicated to innovative photography and videography techniques that reveal the world we live in.

OPPOSITE TOP
ANAND VARMA, 2015
A honeybee emerges from a brood cell to start its six-week lifespan.

OPPOSITE BOTTOM
ANAND VARMA, 2012
When infected by a parasitic barnacle, a male sheep crab becomes feminized. Its abdomen widens to host a brood pouch, from which thousands of baby barnacles will eventually hatch and disperse to infect anew.

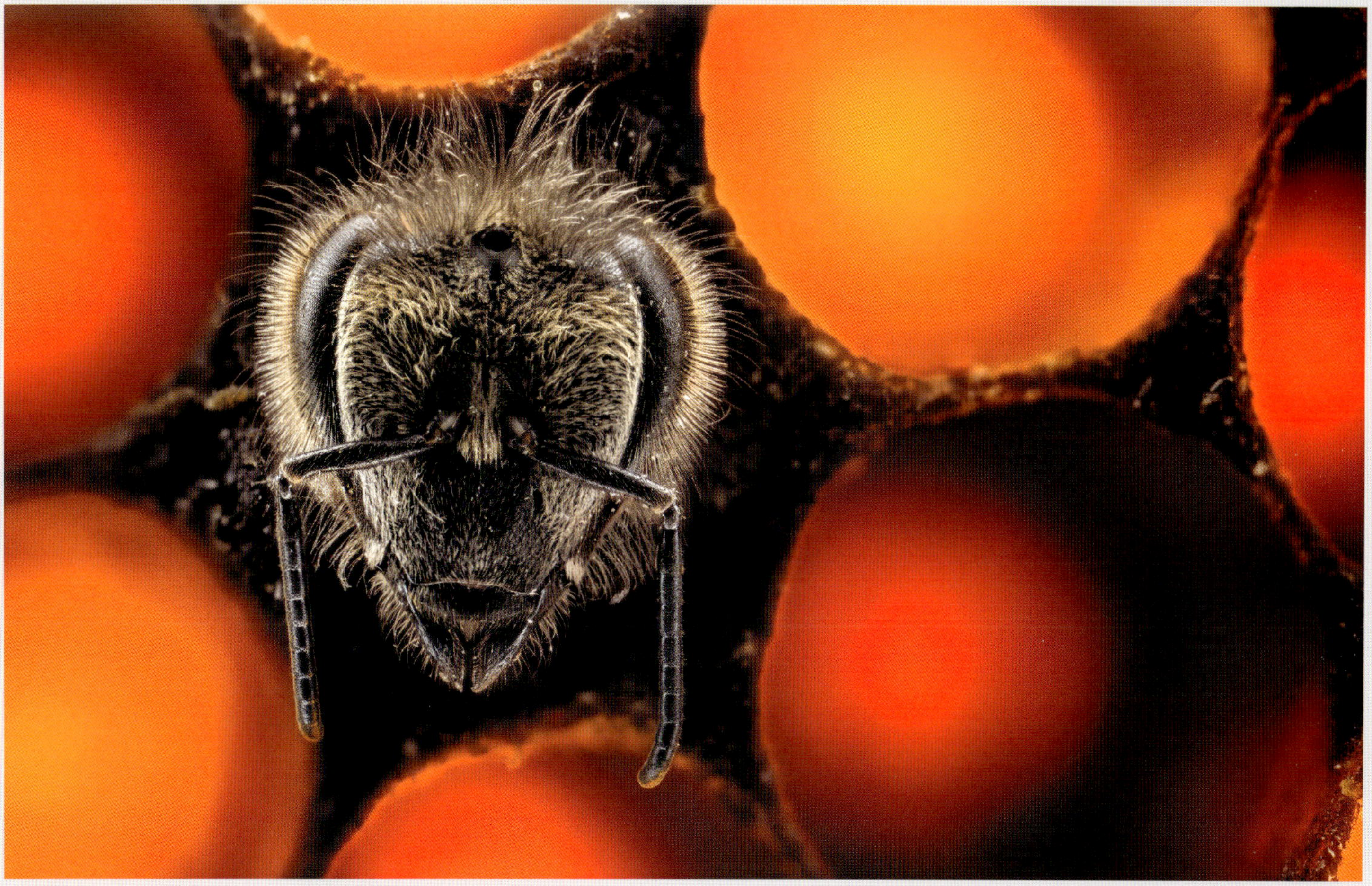

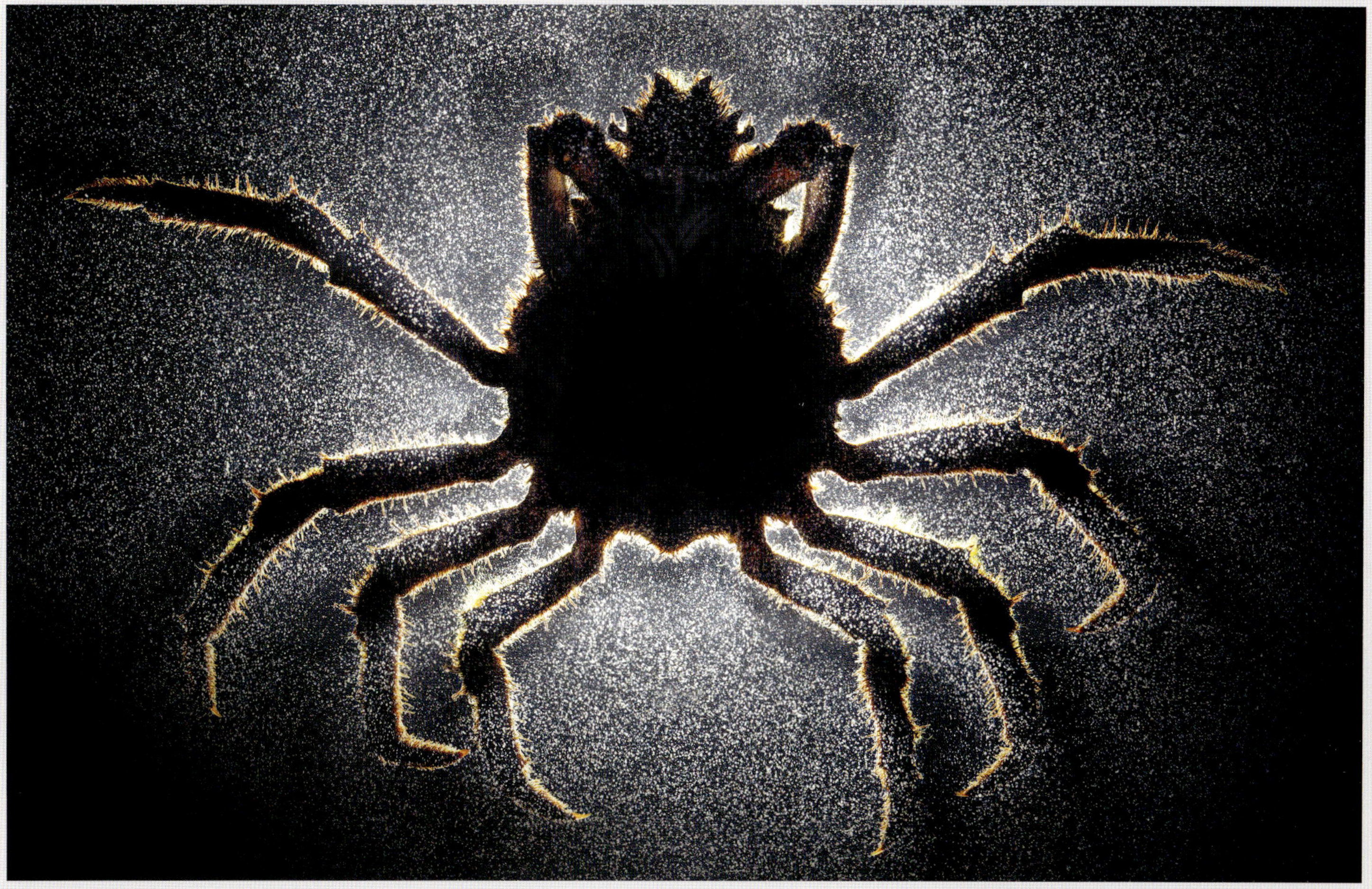

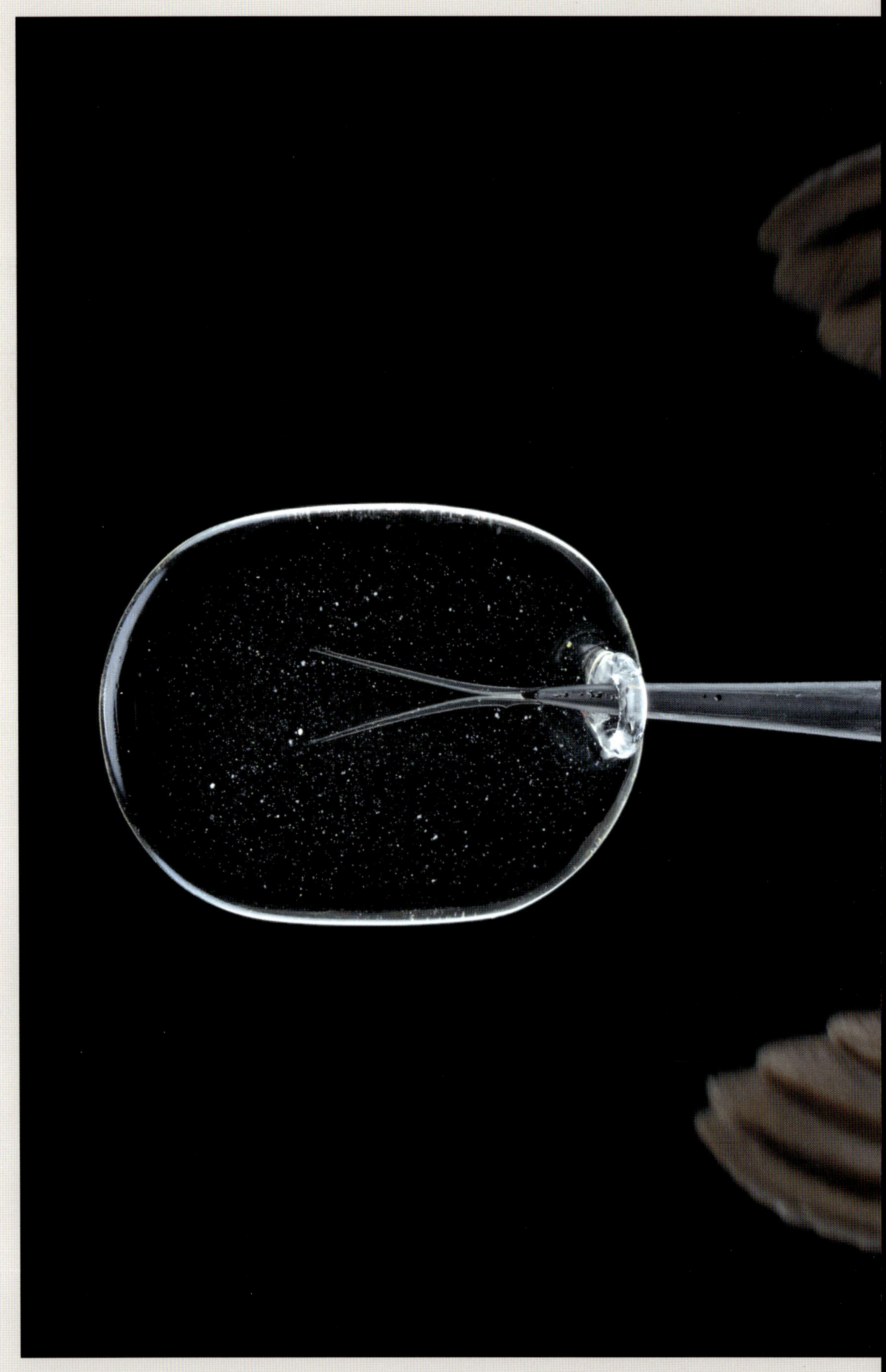

ANAND VARMA, 2016
An Anna's hummingbird drinks artificial nectar from a glass vessel, revealing its forked tongue.

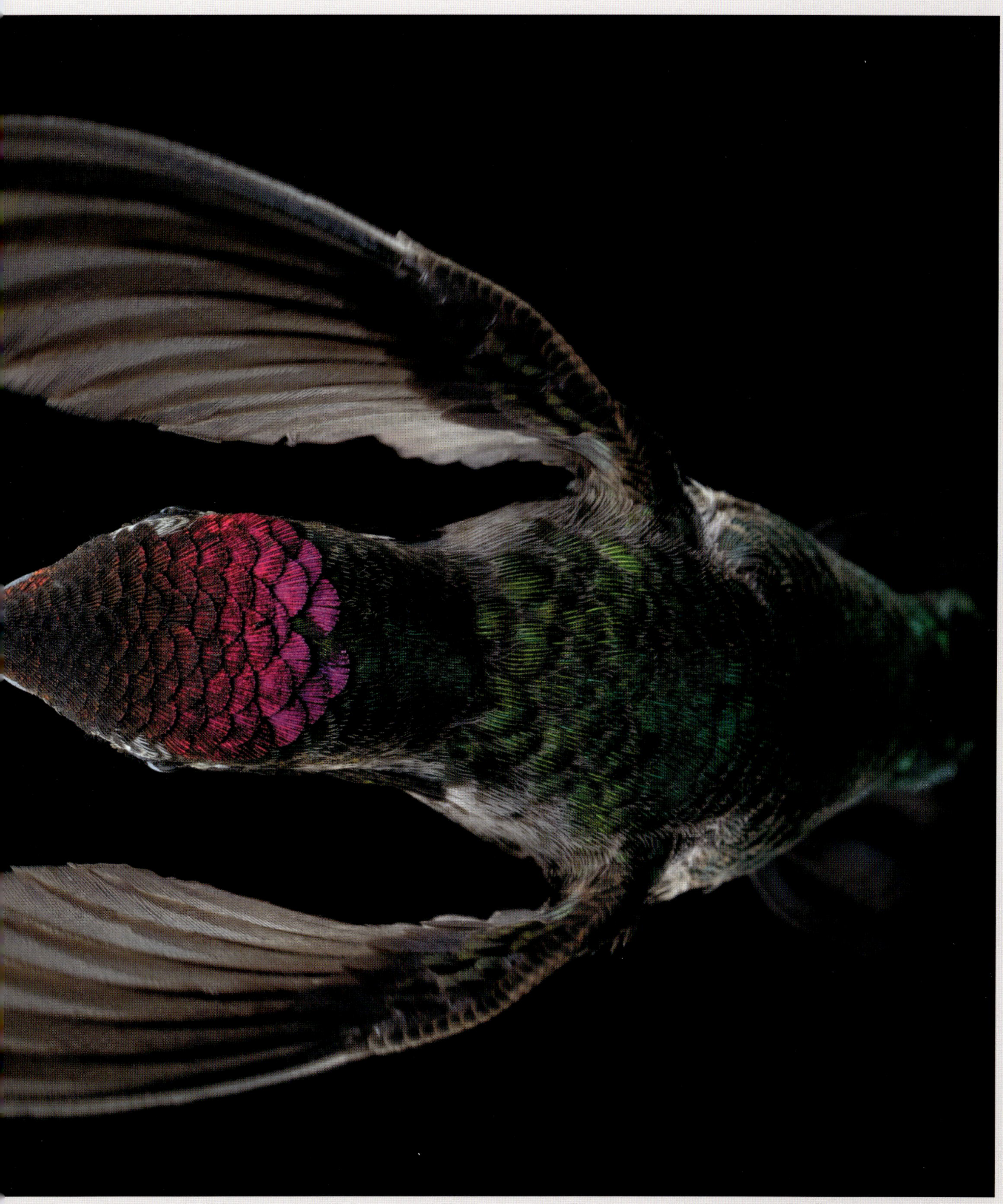

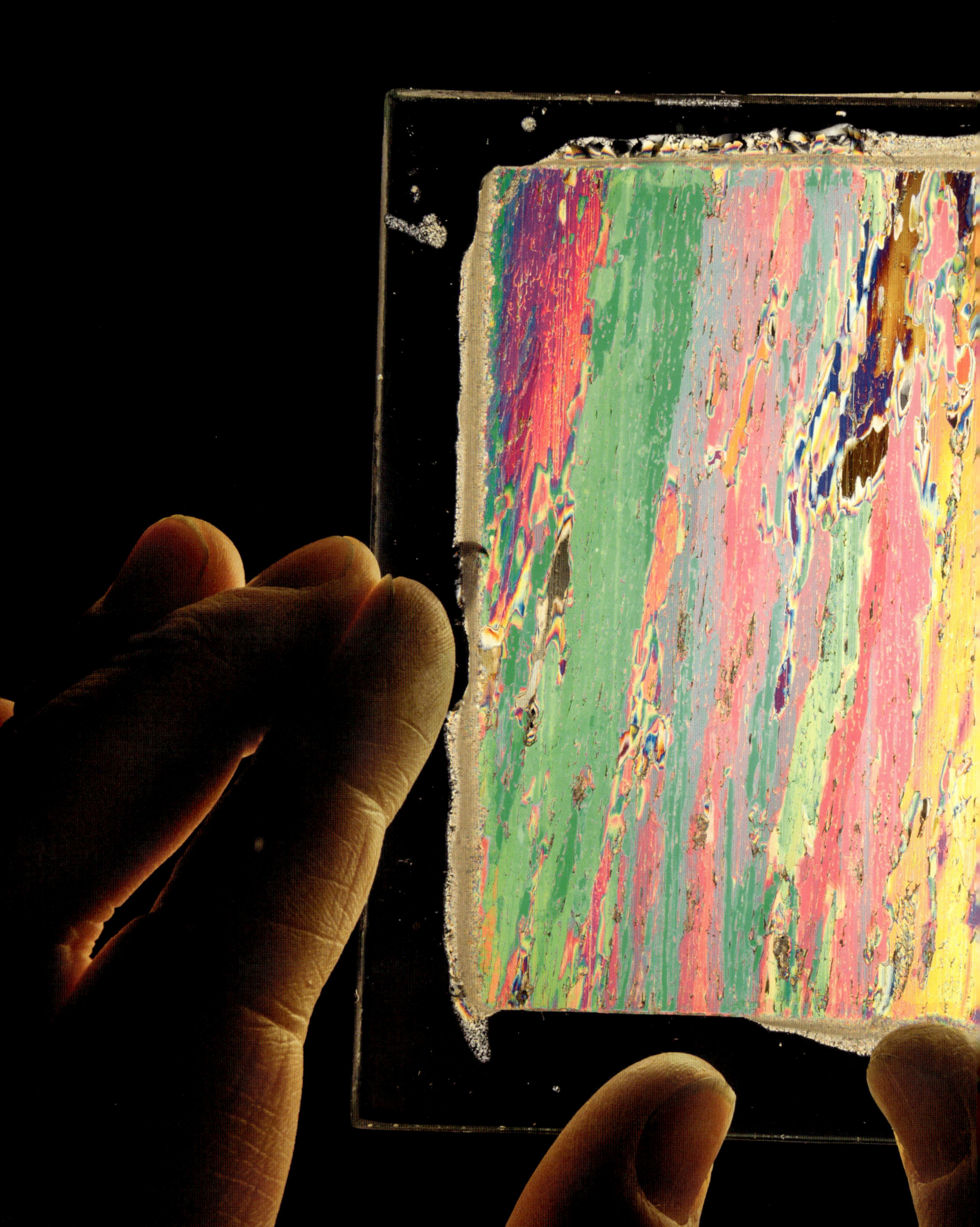

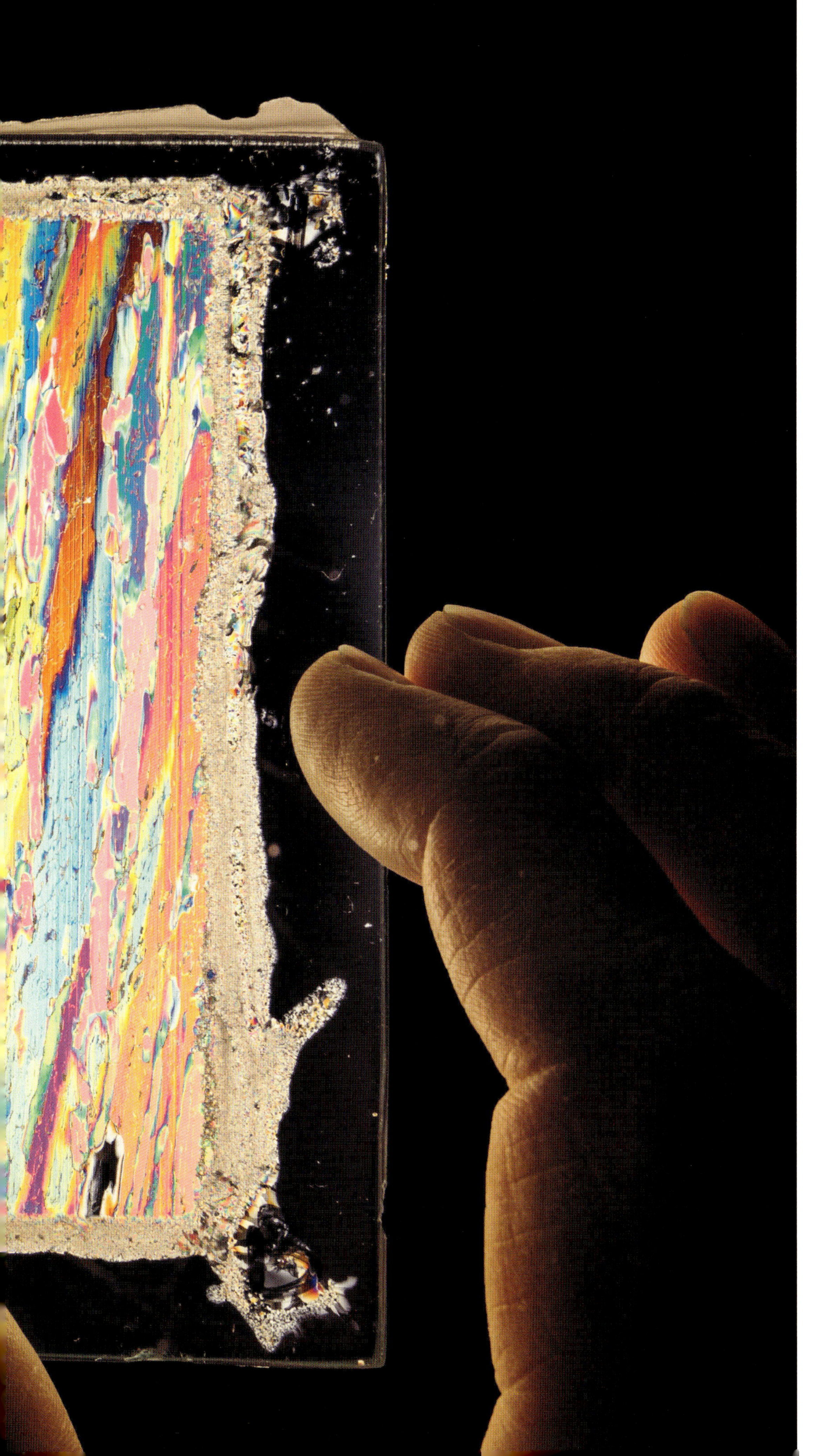

NICK COBBING, 2015
Polarized light shines through sea ice to expose tightly packed columns of crystals.

FOLLOWING PAGES
PRASENJEET YADAV, 2015
Time-lapse photography reveals a meteor over India's Sky Islands.

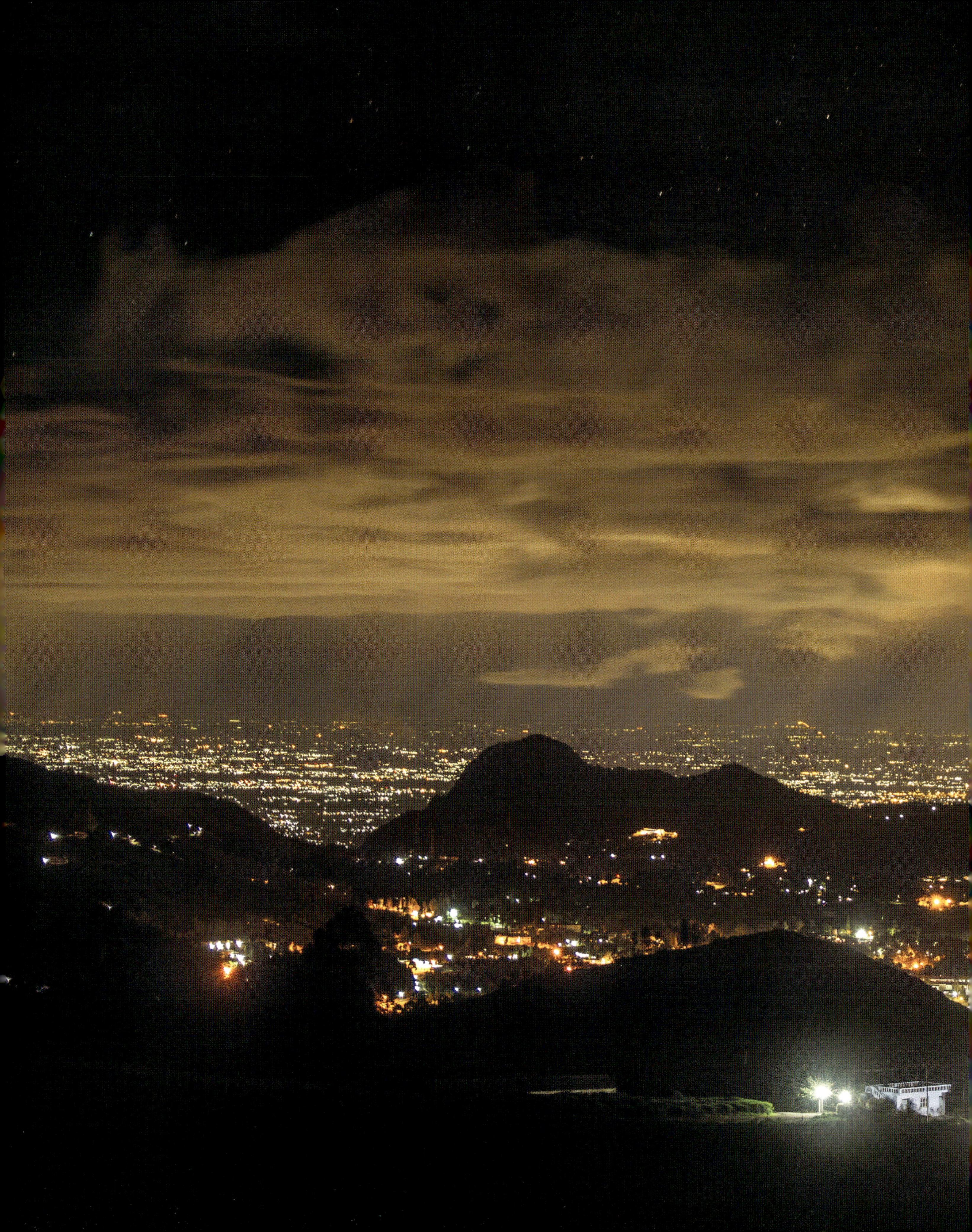

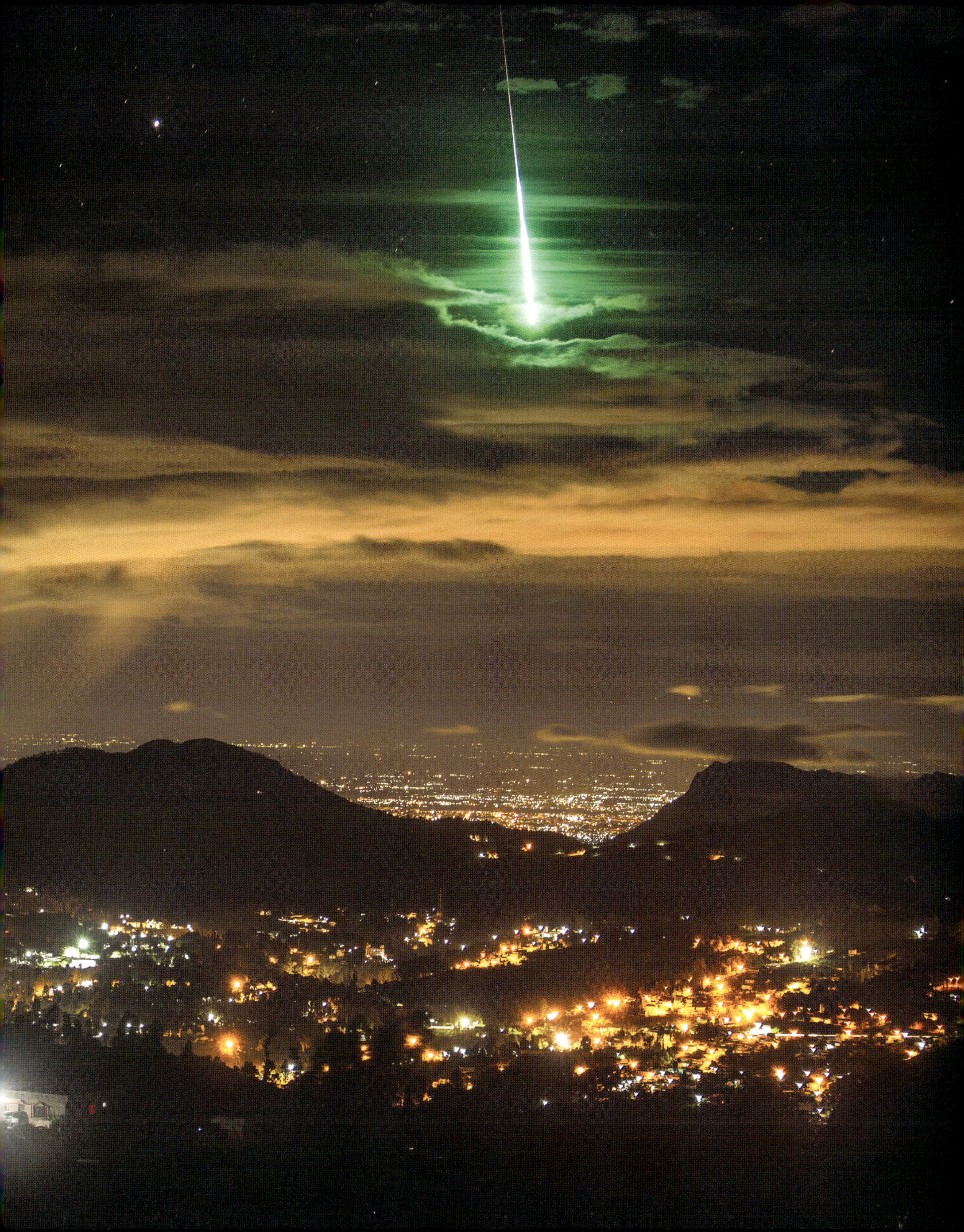

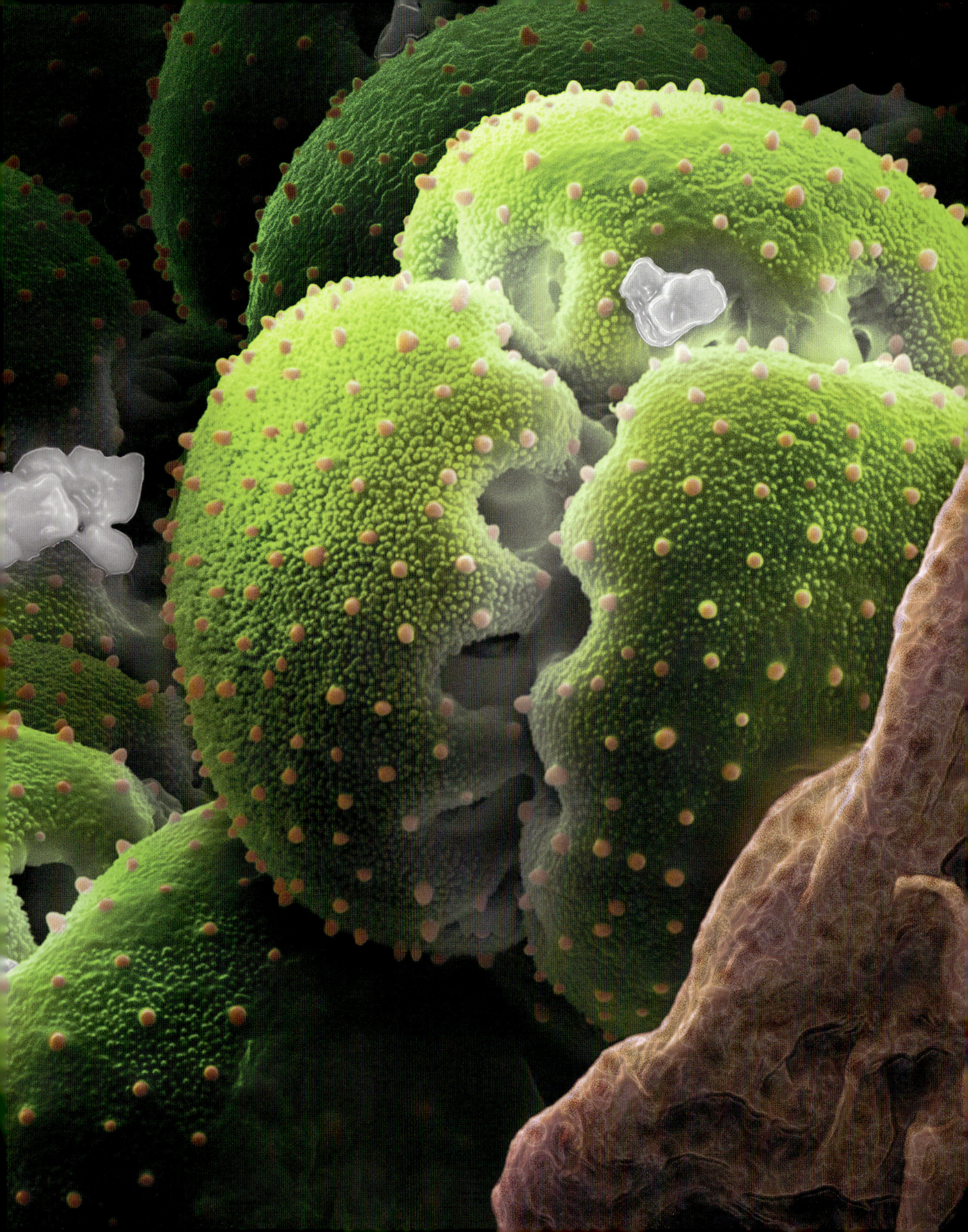

THERE IS A CRAZINESS TO SCIENCE—A WILD WONDER THAT PHOTOGRAPHY REVEALS.

MARTIN OEGGERLI, 2008
Pollen grains of a Venus flytrap

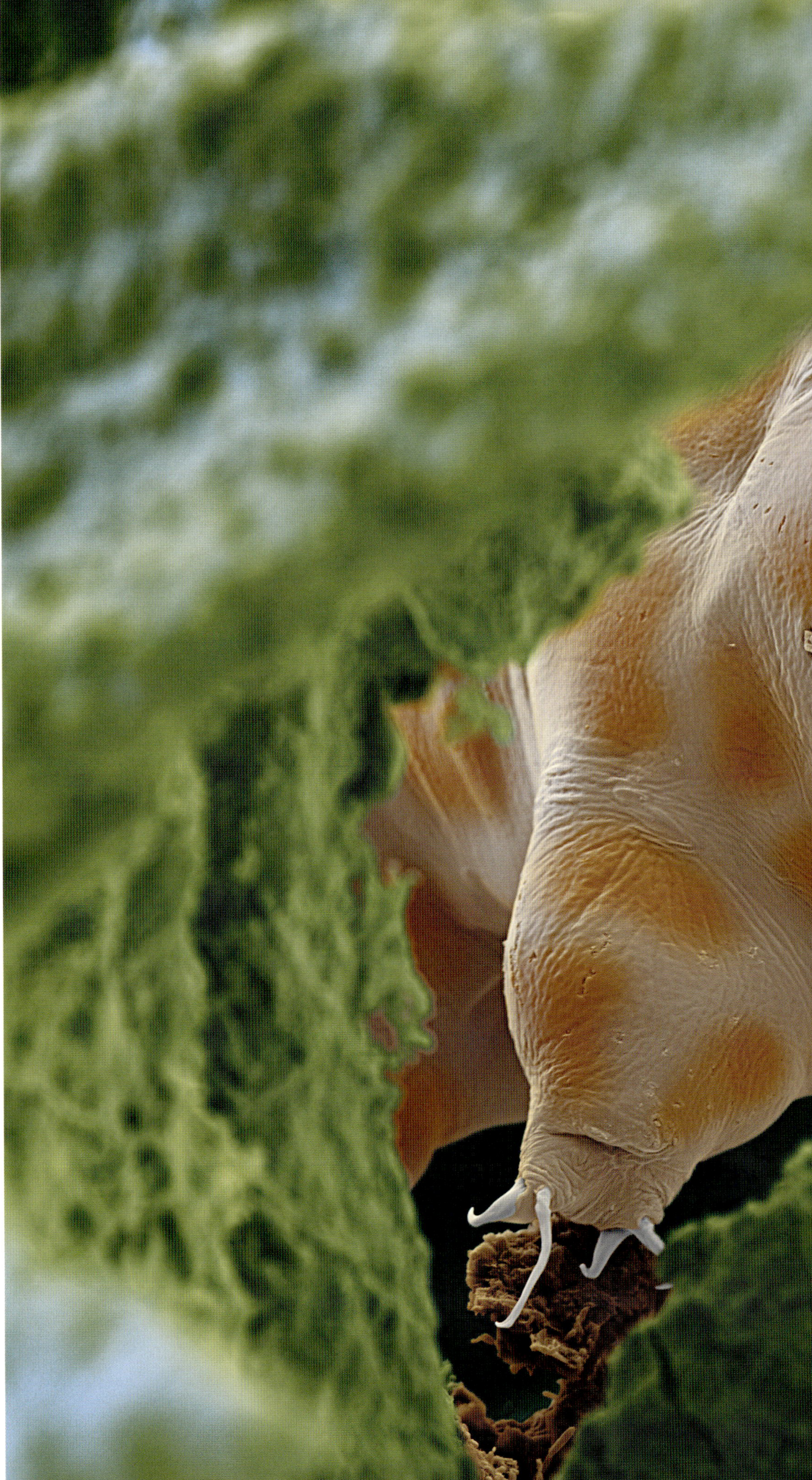

OLIVER MECKES AND
NICOLE OTTAWA, 2022
A newfound species of tardigrade, or water bear; there are more than 1,300 varieties of this eight-legged micro-animal.

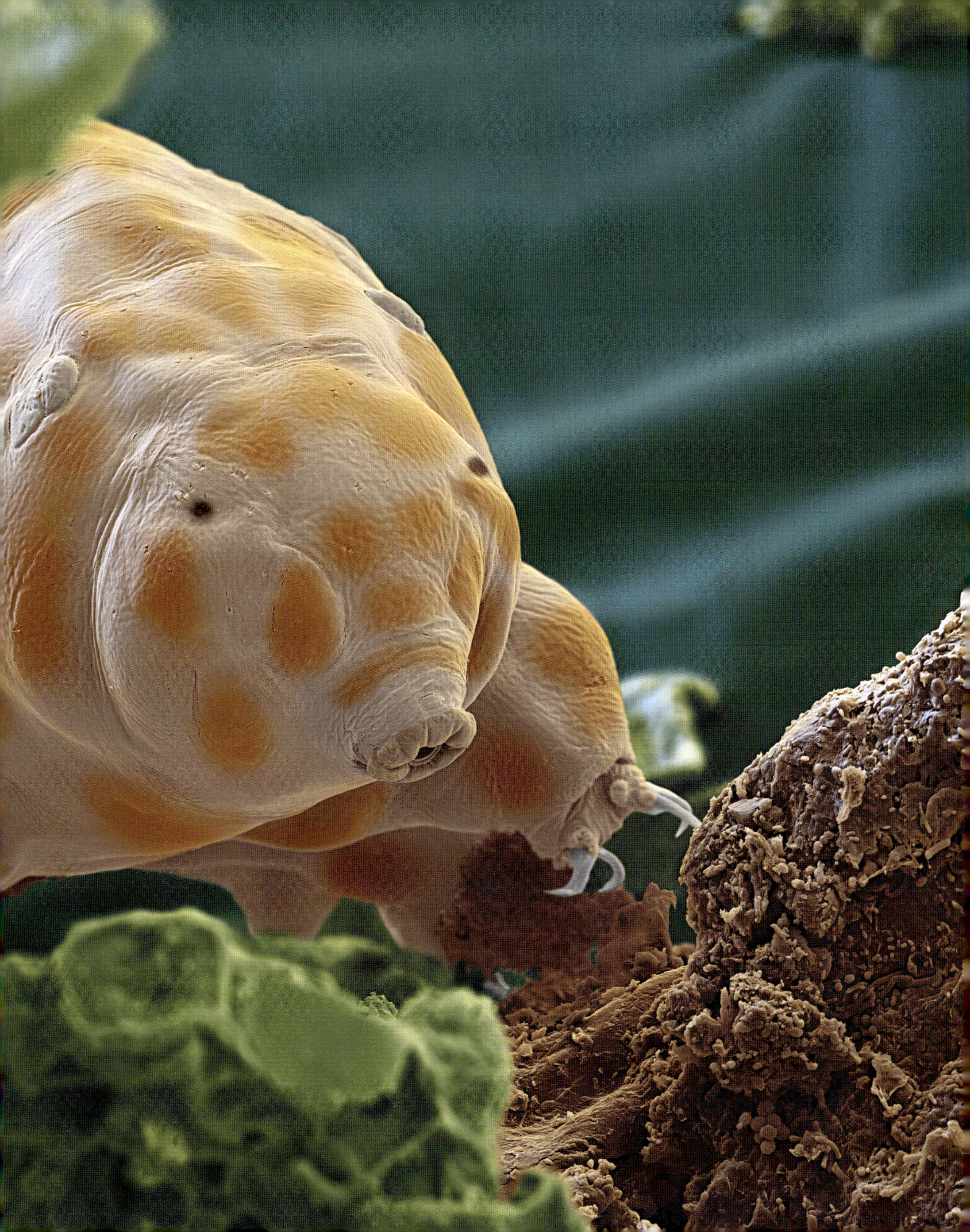

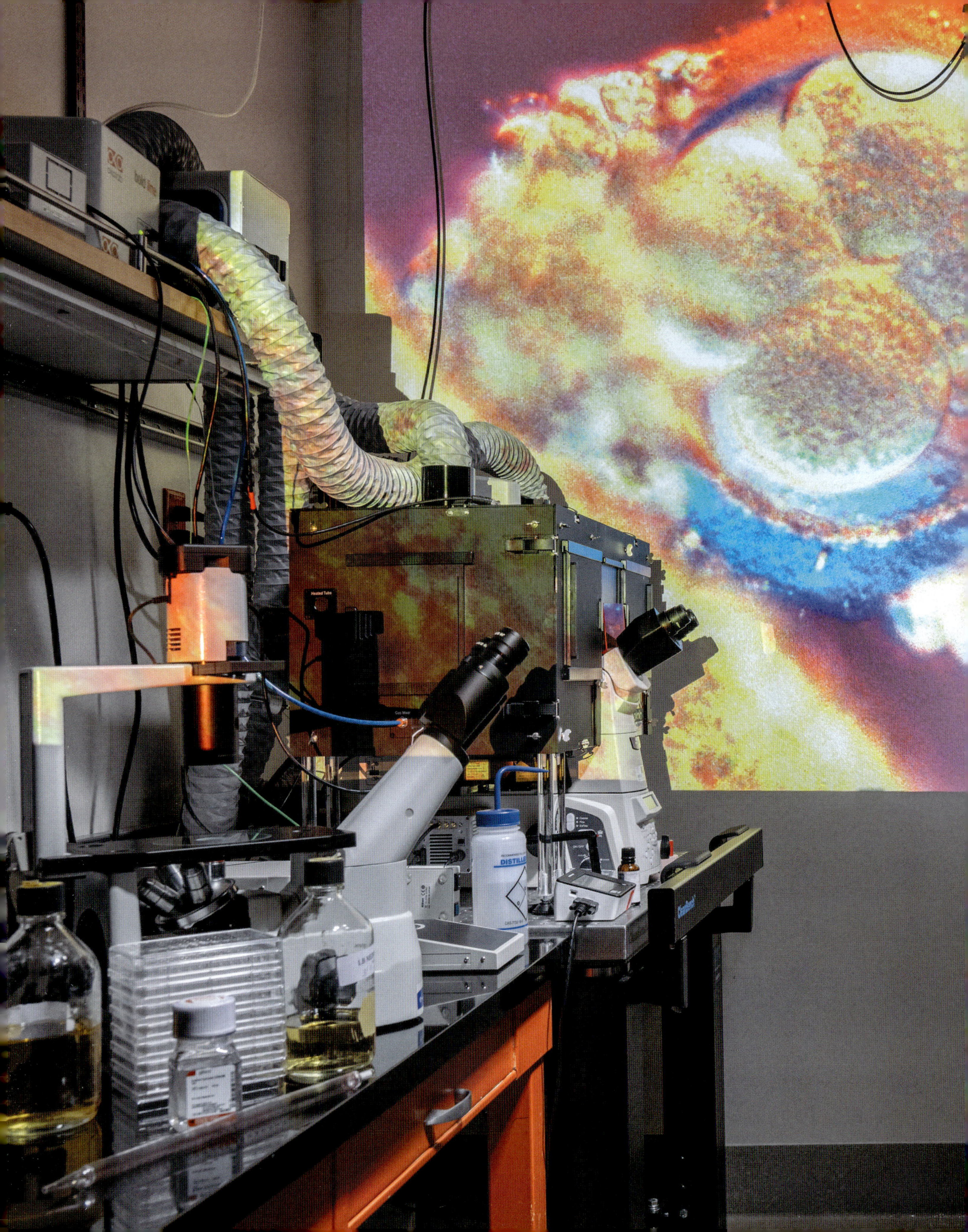

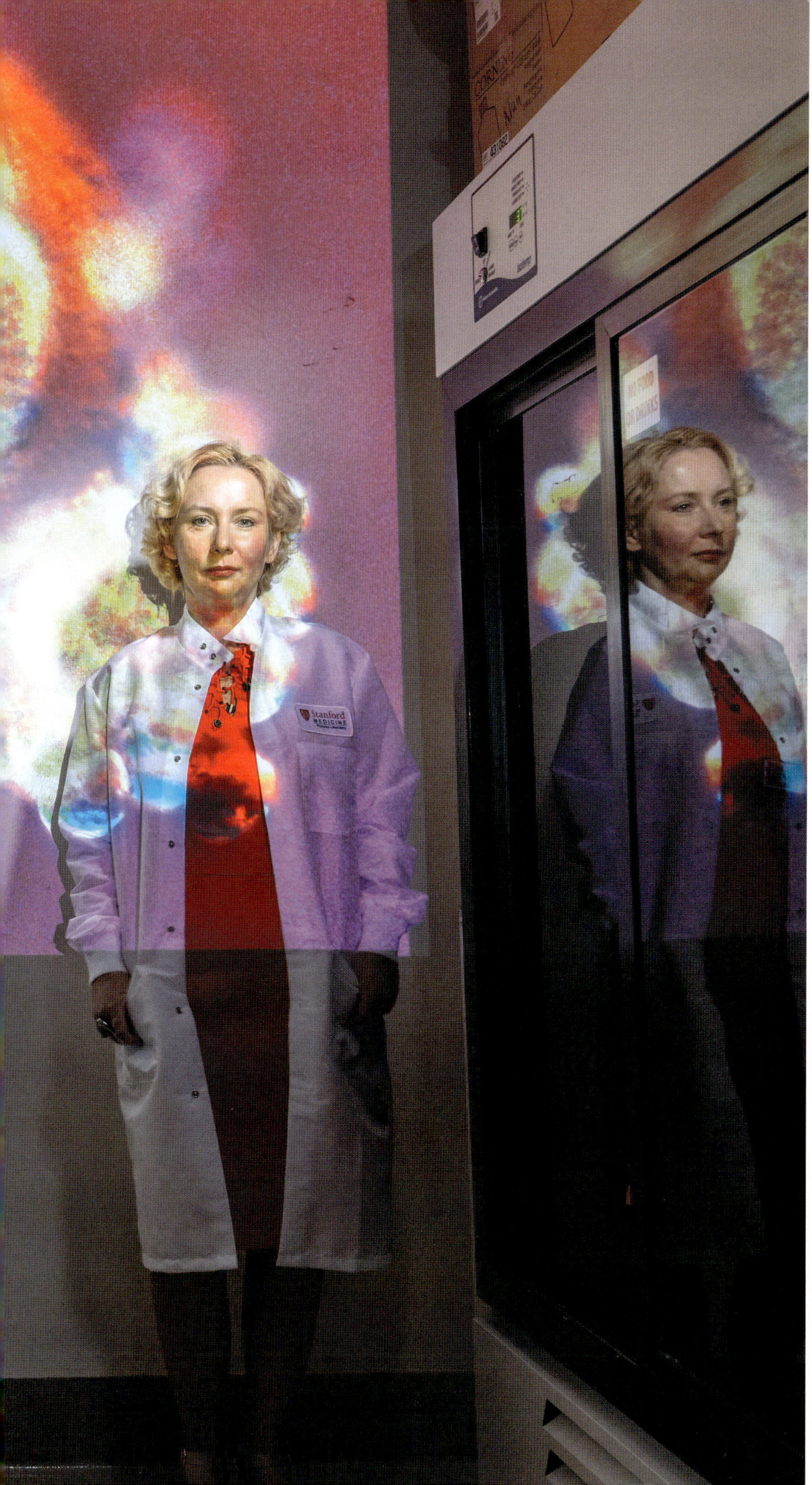

CRAIG CUTLER, 2020
Stanford University professor Joanna Wysocka stands in front of a projection of a human embryo with just eight cells. She believes that a gene known as *HERV-K* can protect embryos from viral infection and help control fetal development.

FOLLOWING PAGES
HEIDI AND HANS-JÜRGEN KOCH, 2008
A computer simulation of a spider's web projected behind a live spider

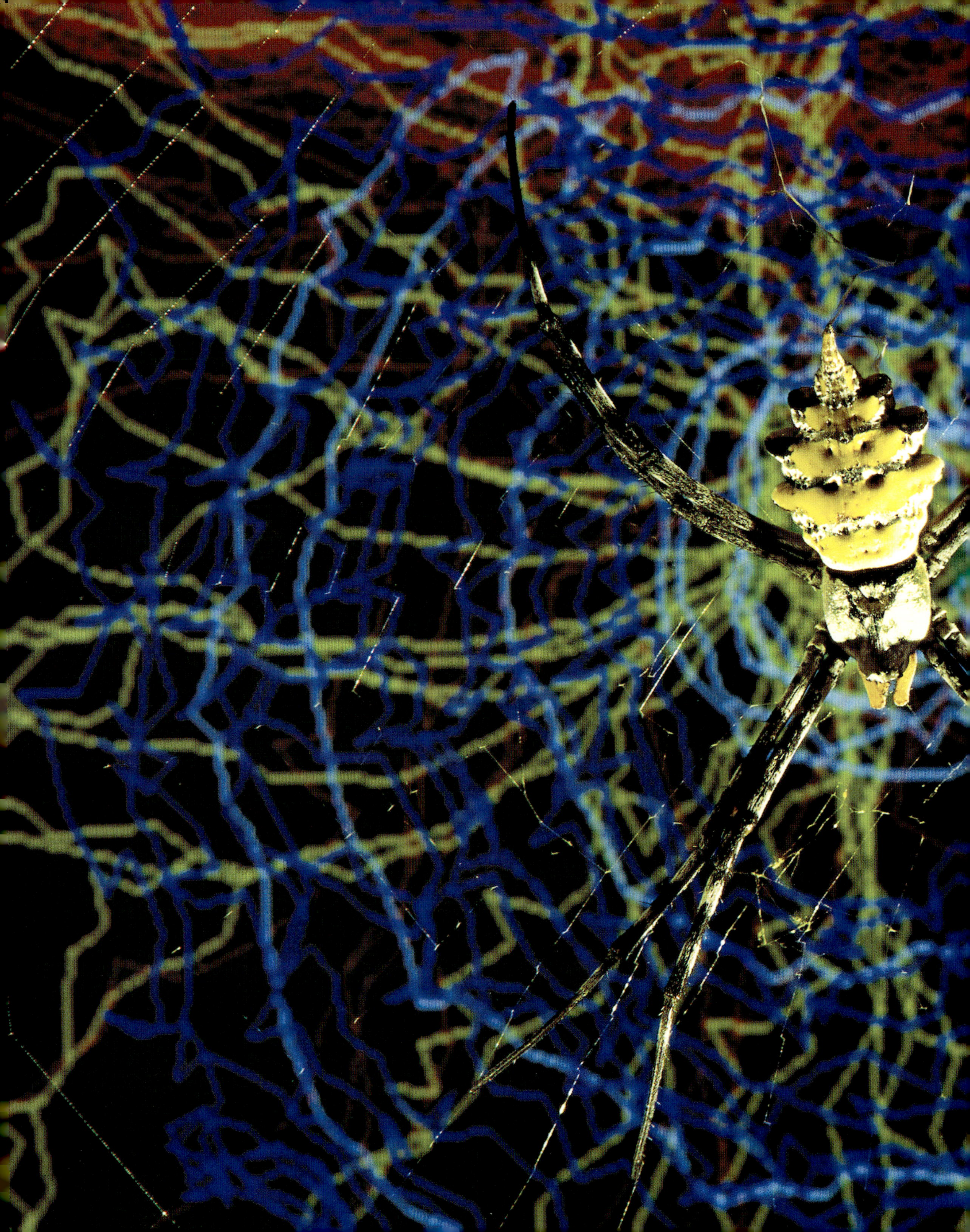

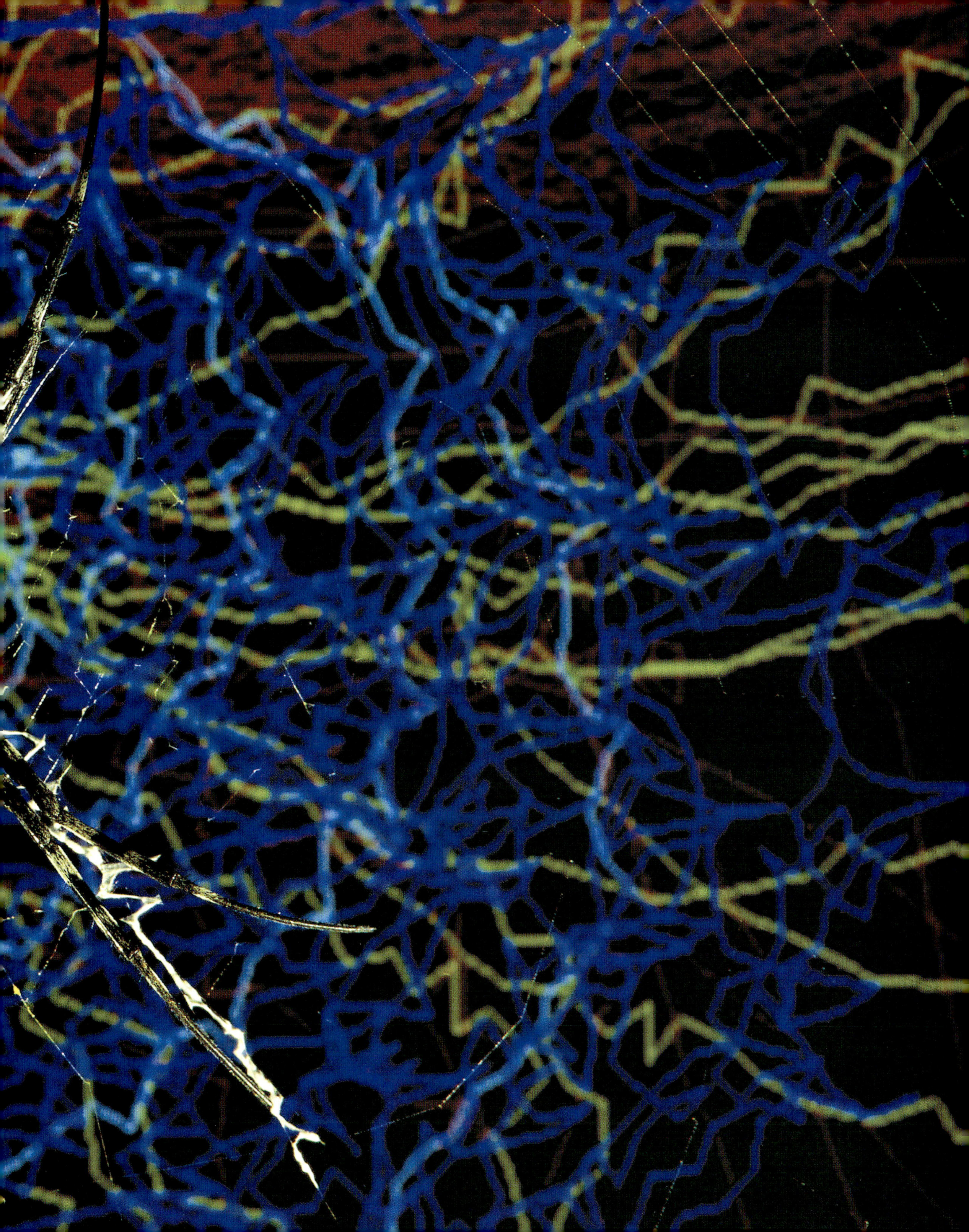

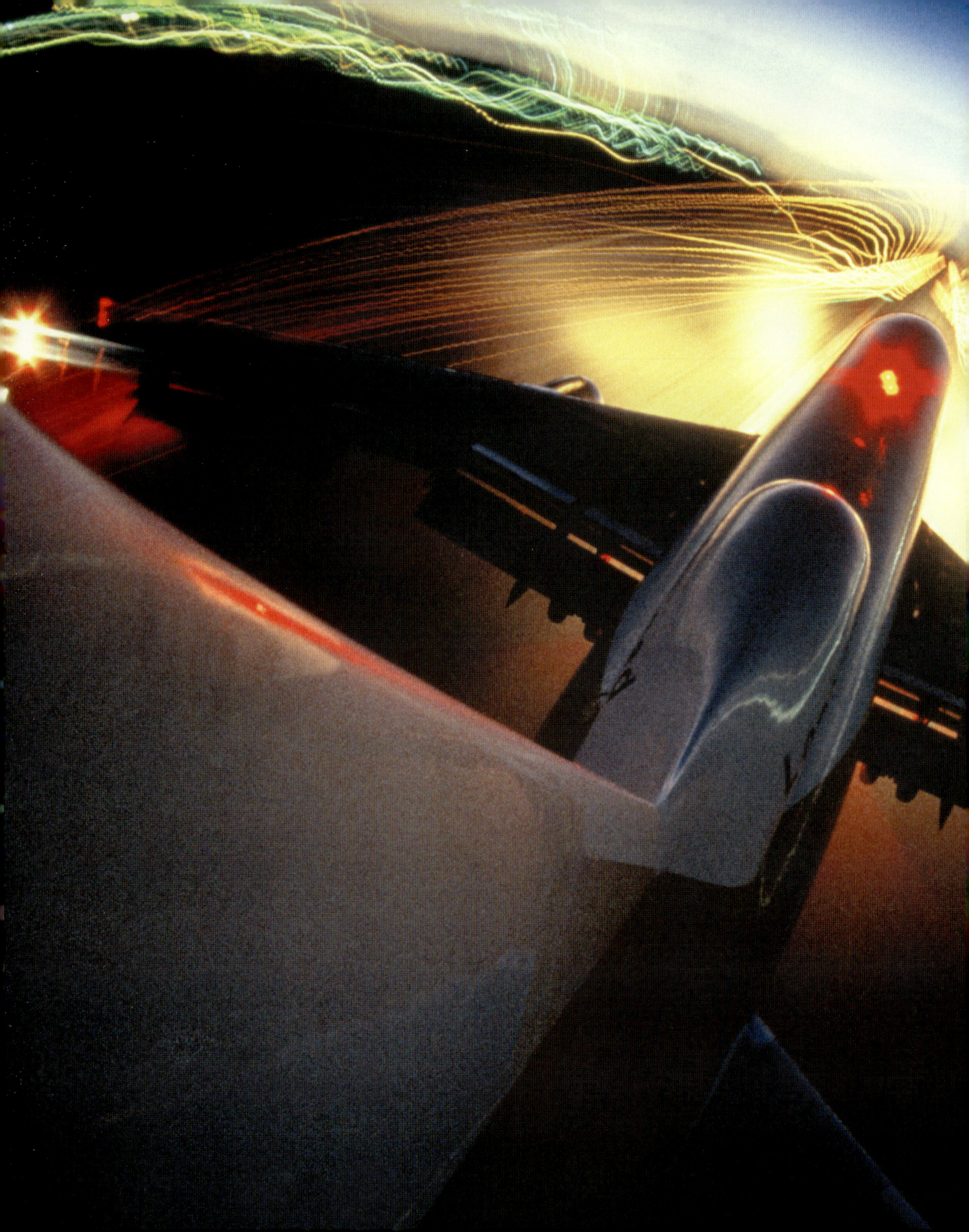

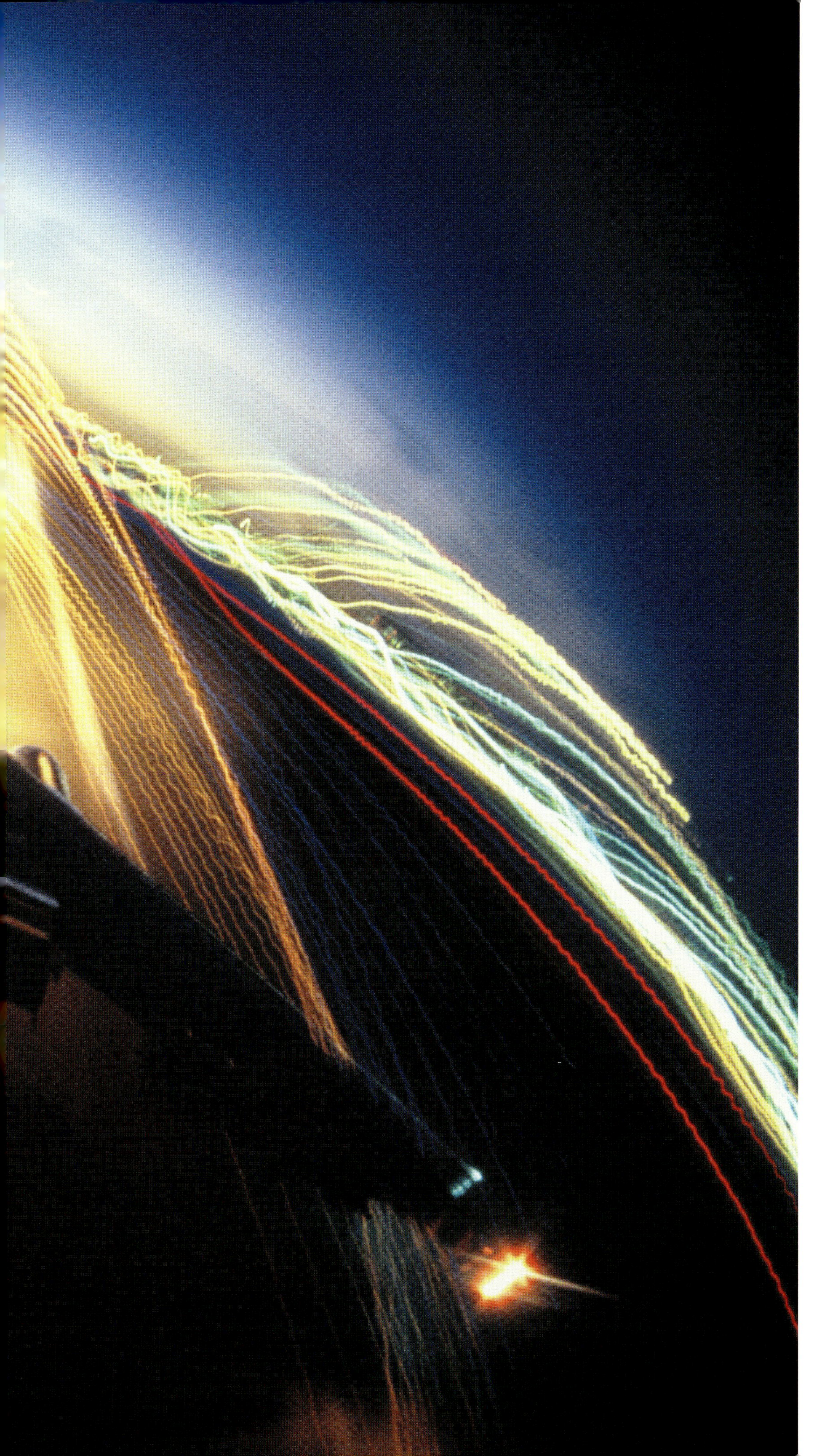

BRUCE DALE, 1977
A 23-second exposure from a camera mounted on the tail of a Lockheed TriStar jet captures the trajectory of takeoff.

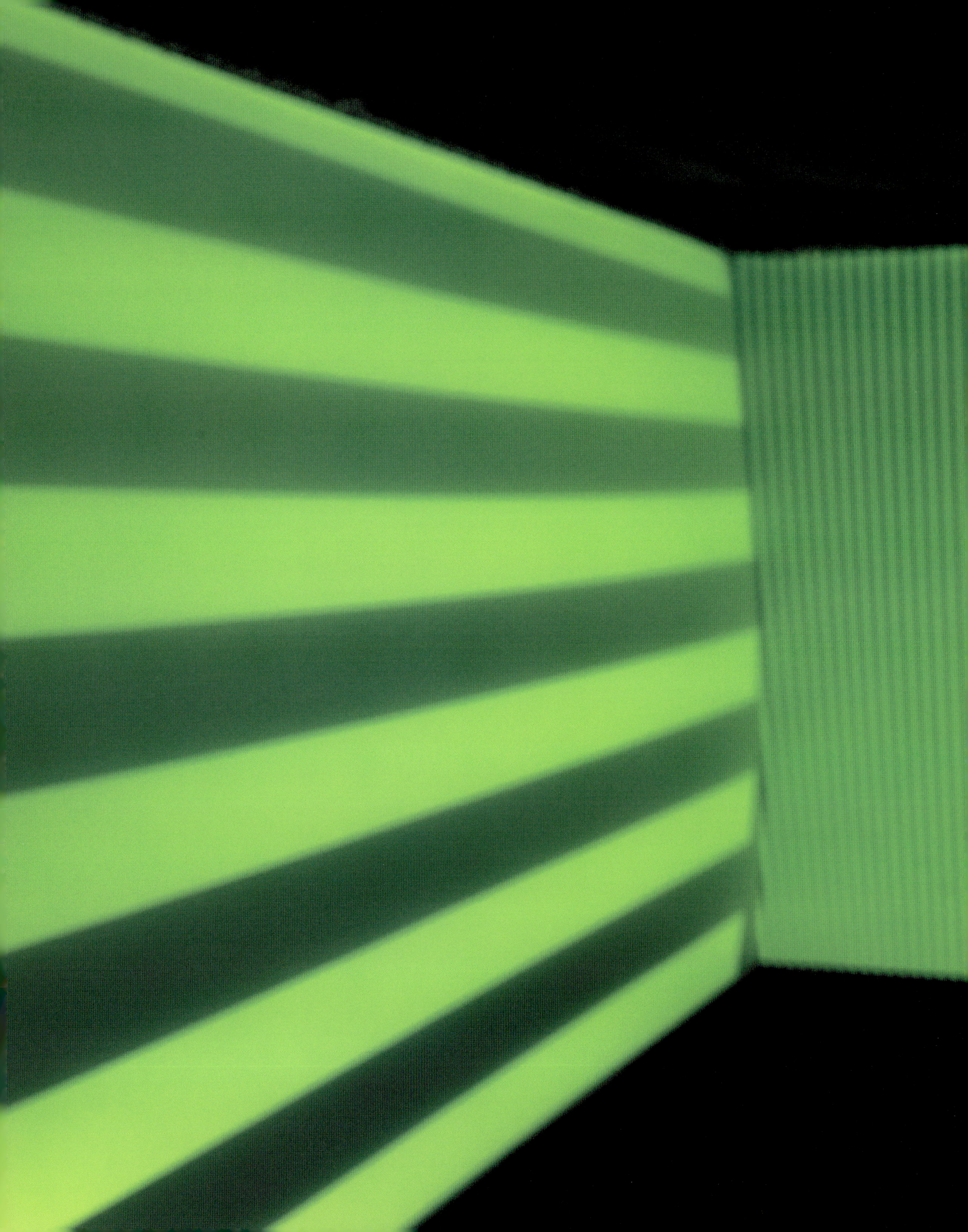

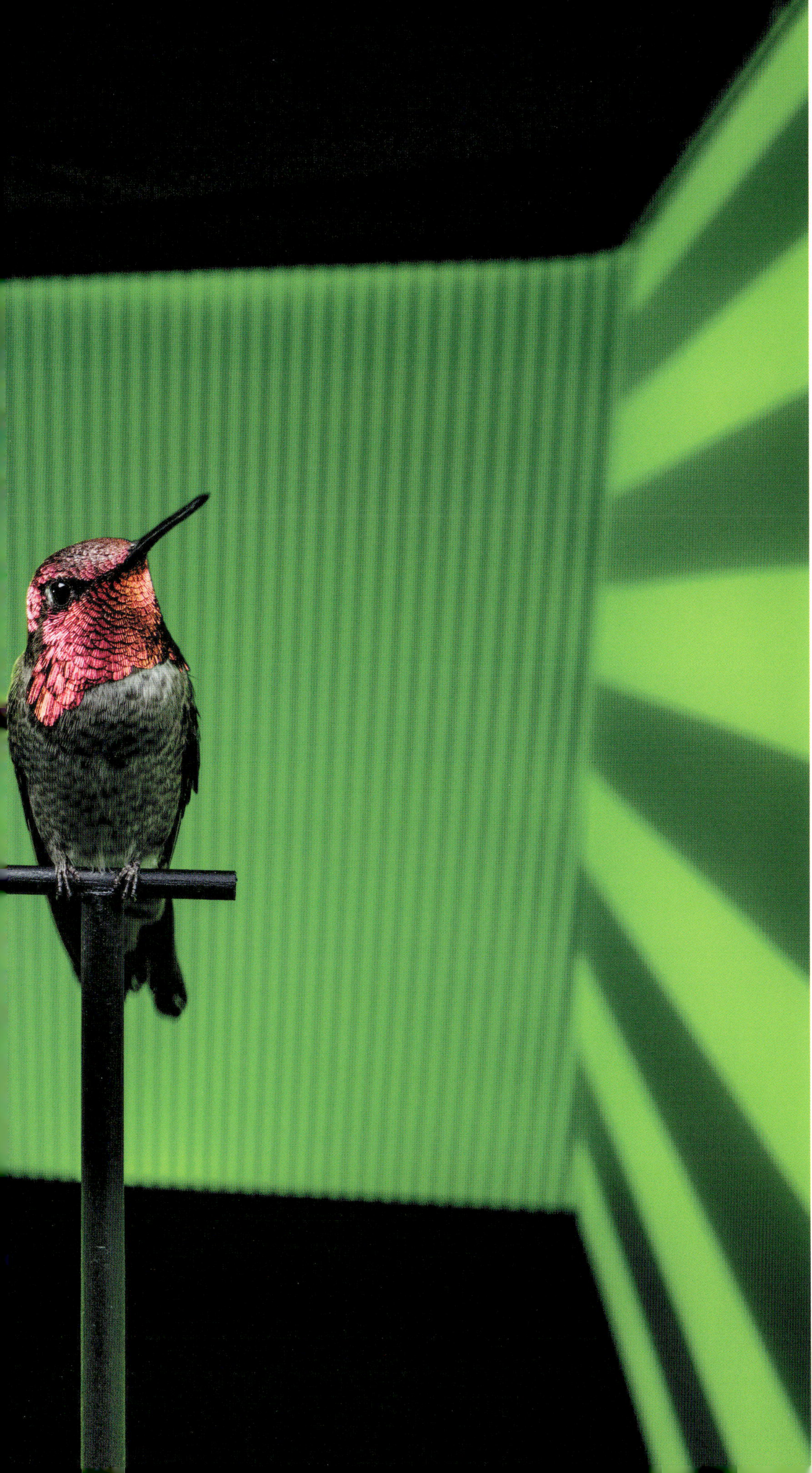

ANAND VARMA, 2016
An Anna's hummingbird inside a virtual reality tunnel used to study its visual perception

BIOGRAPHY

HELENE SCHMITZ

HELENE SCHMITZ, 2009
Macrophotography reveals the stunning details of a budding carnivorous sundew plant. Sundews are found in bogs and marshes around the world.

PAGE 412
HELENE SCHMITZ, 2009
Clockwise from top left: A butterfly senses nectar and alights on a rare California pitcher plant; upside-down blooms lure bees into an elaborate pollen chamber; a Venus flytrap snaps shut if its surface hairs are brushed twice; an Australian pitcher plant's guide hairs and cloying scent lure ants into its digestive depths.

PAGE 413
HELENE SCHMITZ, 2009
Drosera stolonifera, an Australian sundew that feasts on insects

"THEY ARE FLOWERS," photographer Helene Schmitz says of the unsettling flora she shot for a *National Geographic* story on carnivorous plants. "But they have nothing of the passive, peaceful, and serene qualities we associated with flowers, since they attract, lure, and finally devour their prey."

Schmitz, who is Swedish, also photographed a story for *National Geographic* featuring her fellow countryman Carl Linnaeus, the biologist and naturalist who brought order to the process of naming and defining different genera and species of organisms. Her subject is nature—in particular, she says, the ideas and projections we impose and how they are represented in science, art, and literature.

It is a singular vision. On the page, animal-feasting plants leap out from the plain matte backgrounds Schmitz photographs them on, glowing with beguiling menace, as in the spiky jaws of a Venus flytrap and the crimson maw of a tropical pitcher plant. "Western art and literature attributes a kind of innocence to nature," she observes. "I am interested in the more obscure sides."

Schmitz's first book, *Blow Up,* a collection of plant macrophotography, was nominated for the August Prize, which is awarded to the best Swedish book published each year. In 2006, she was named Photographer of the Year by the Swedish Environmental Protection Agency for her photographs in the book *A Passion for Systems: Linnaeus and the Dream of Order in Nature.*

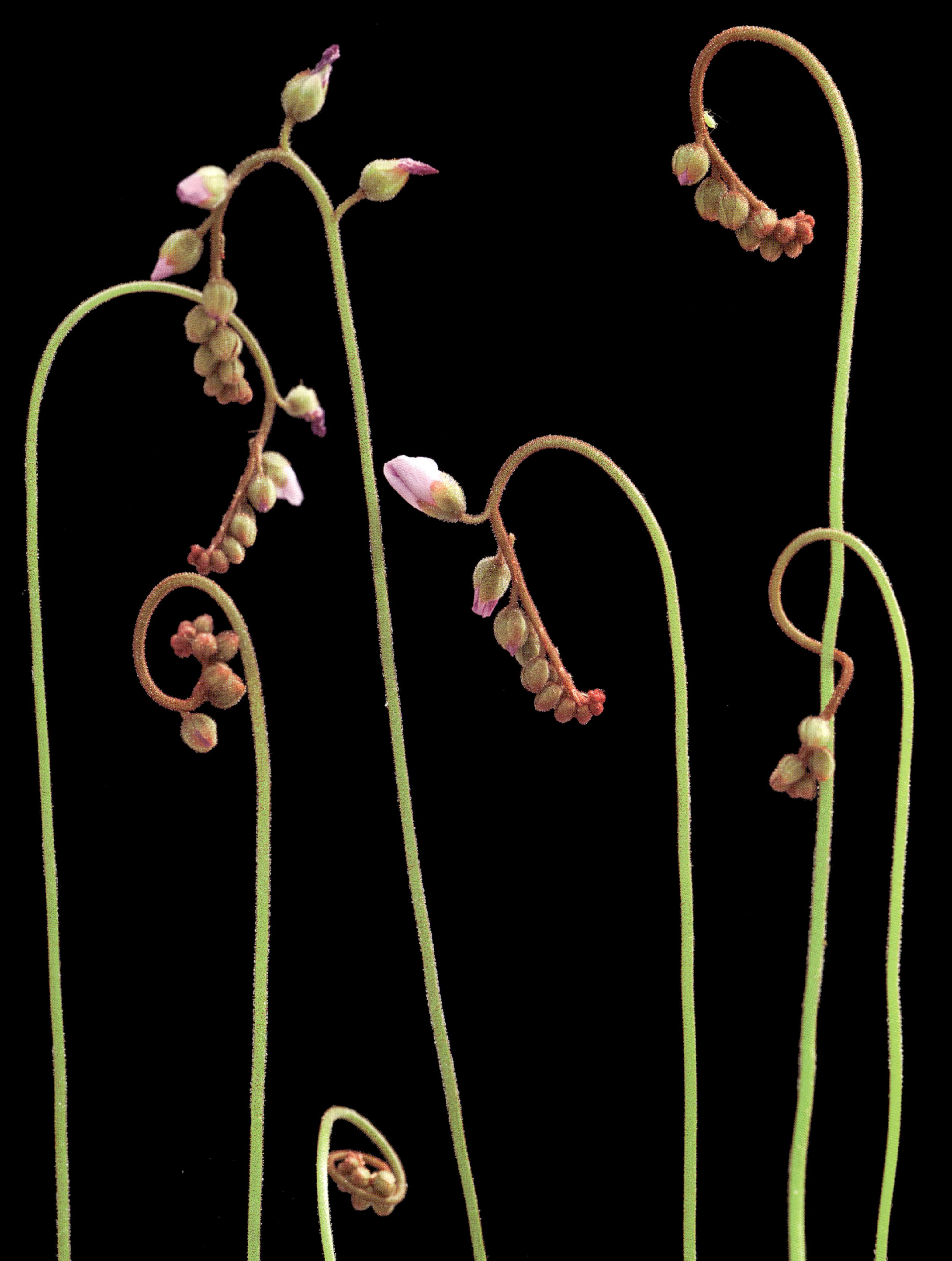

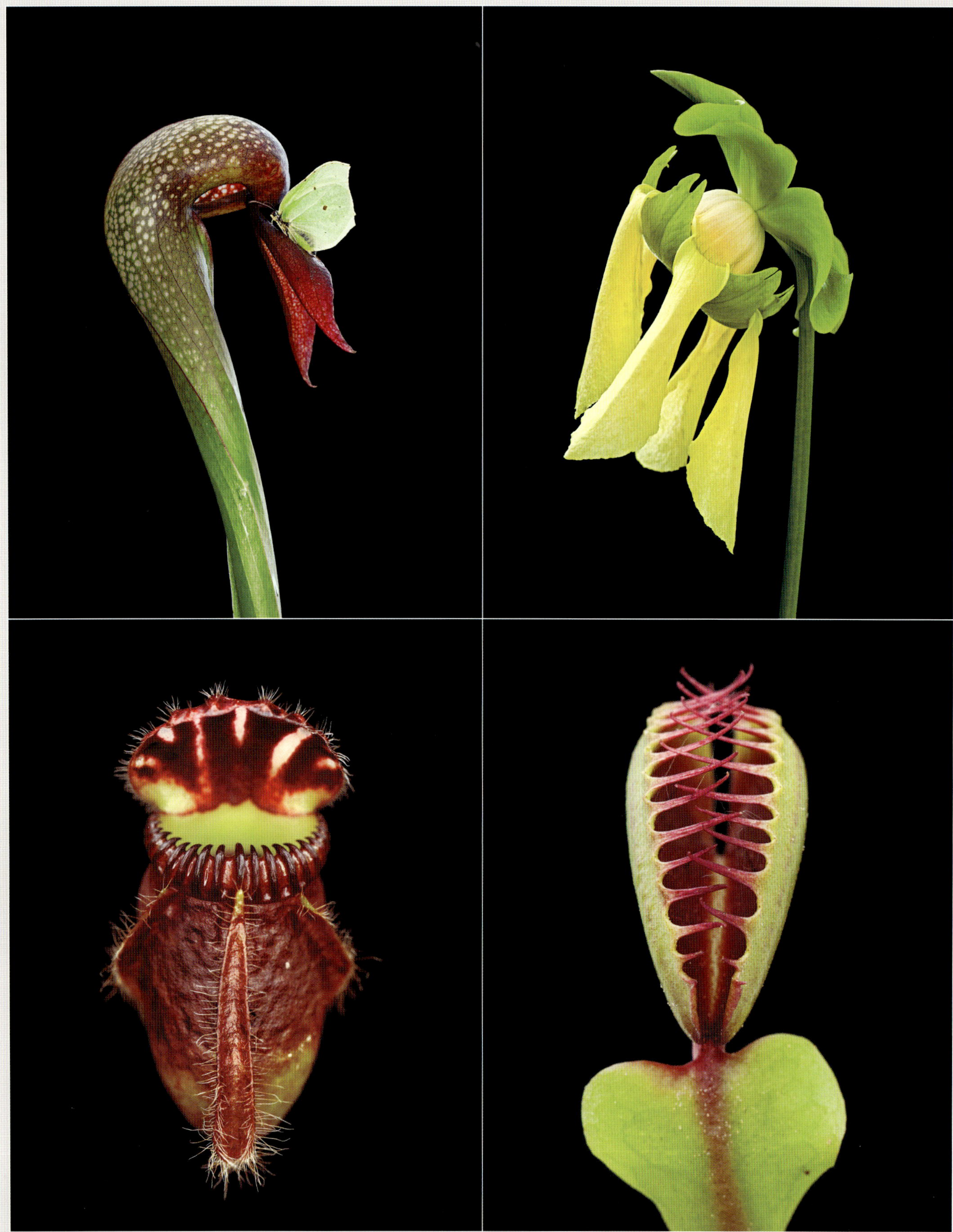

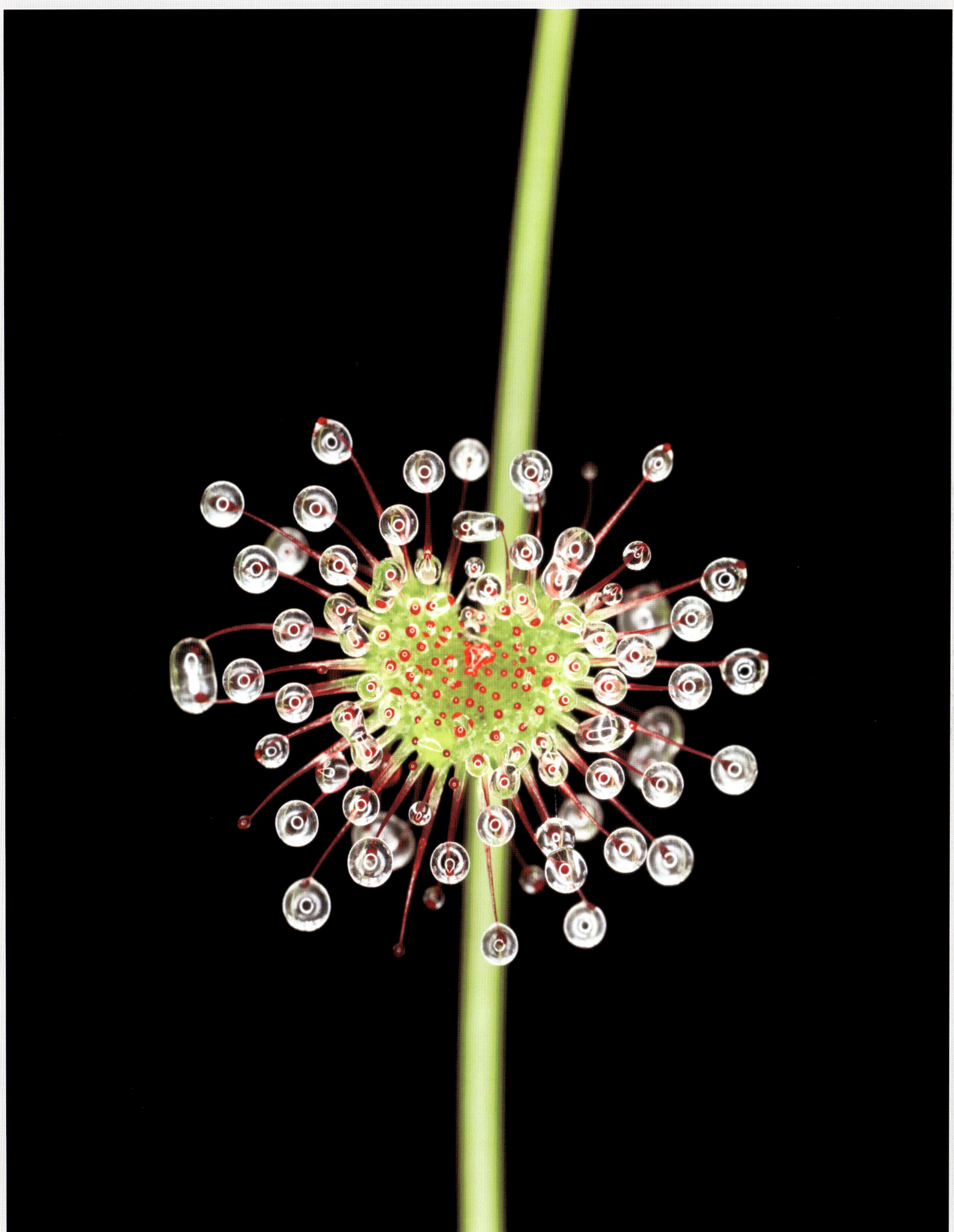

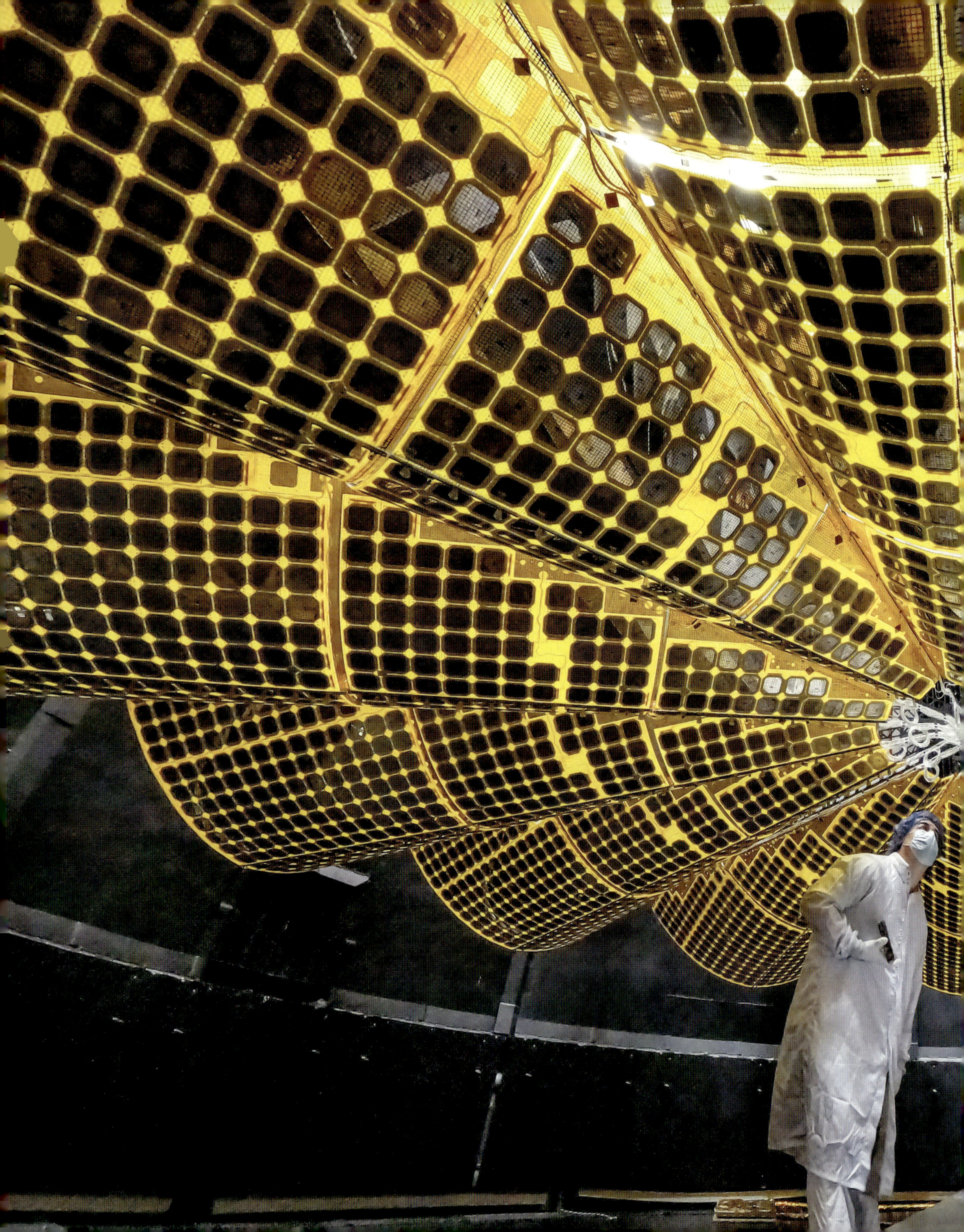

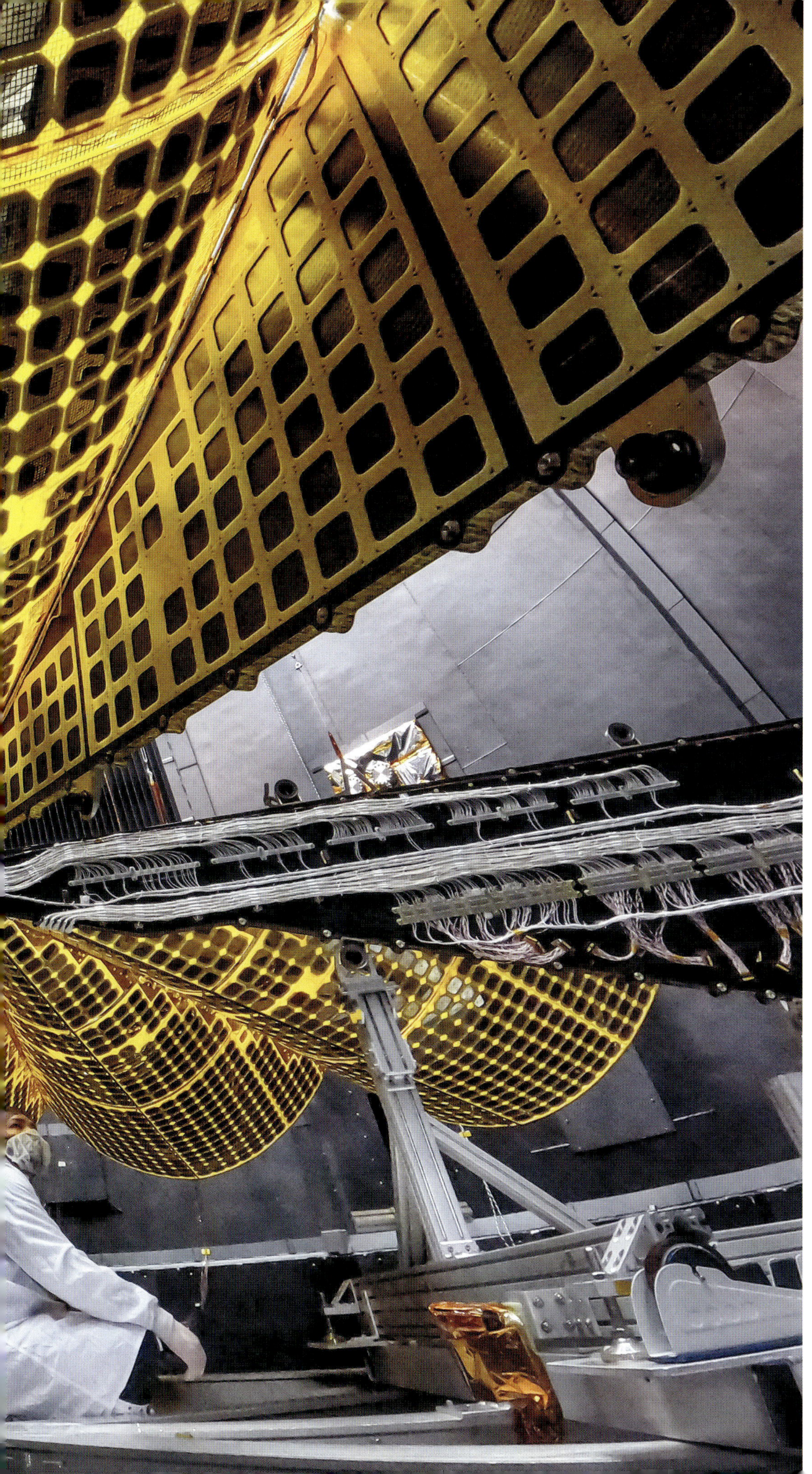

PATRICK H. CORKERY, 2021
A solar array for NASA's Lucy spacecraft unfurls as it is tested at a Lockheed Martin facility in Littleton, Colorado.

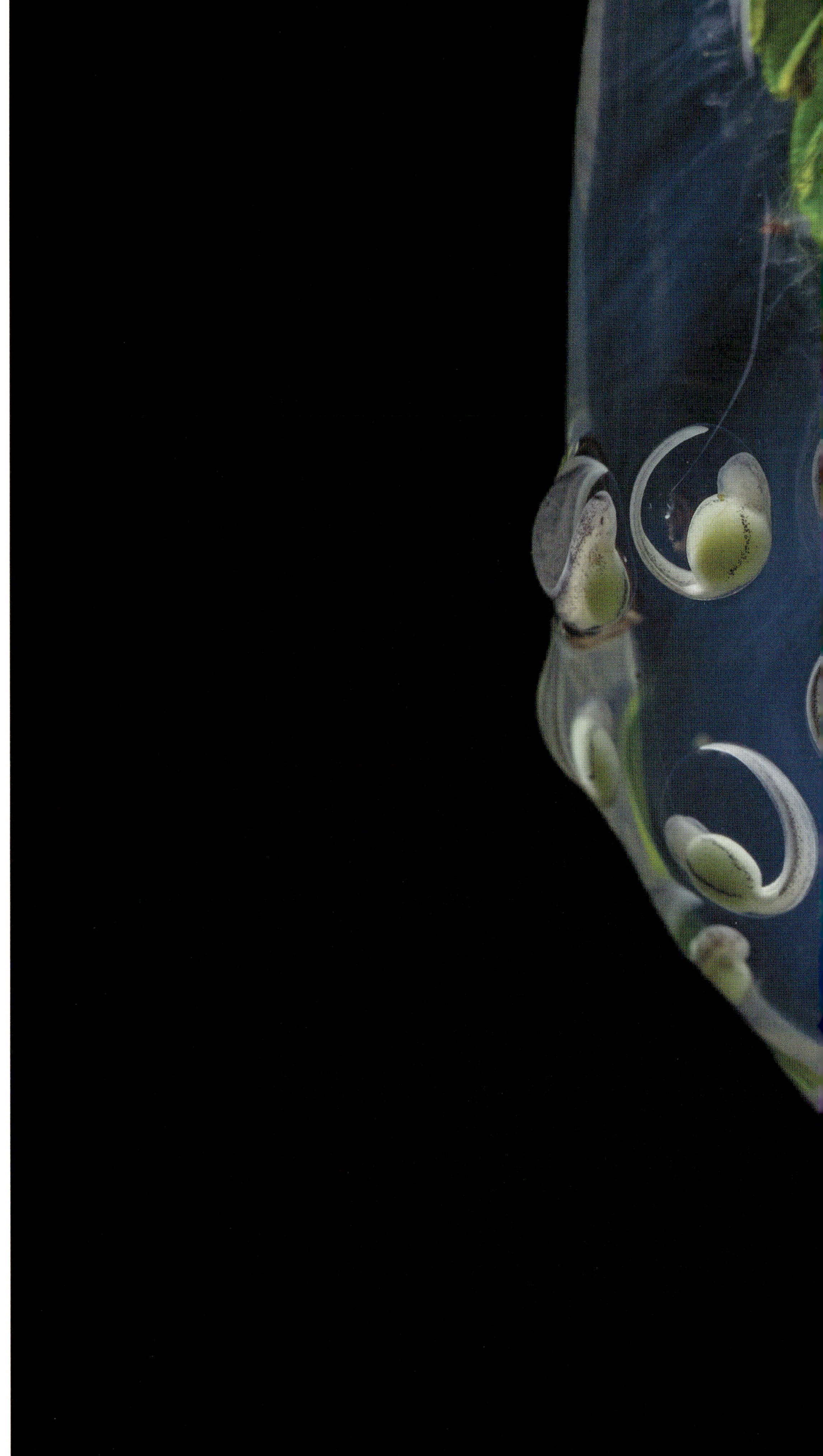

JAIME CULEBRAS, 2020
Wiley's glass frog embryos hang from the tip of a fern leaf.

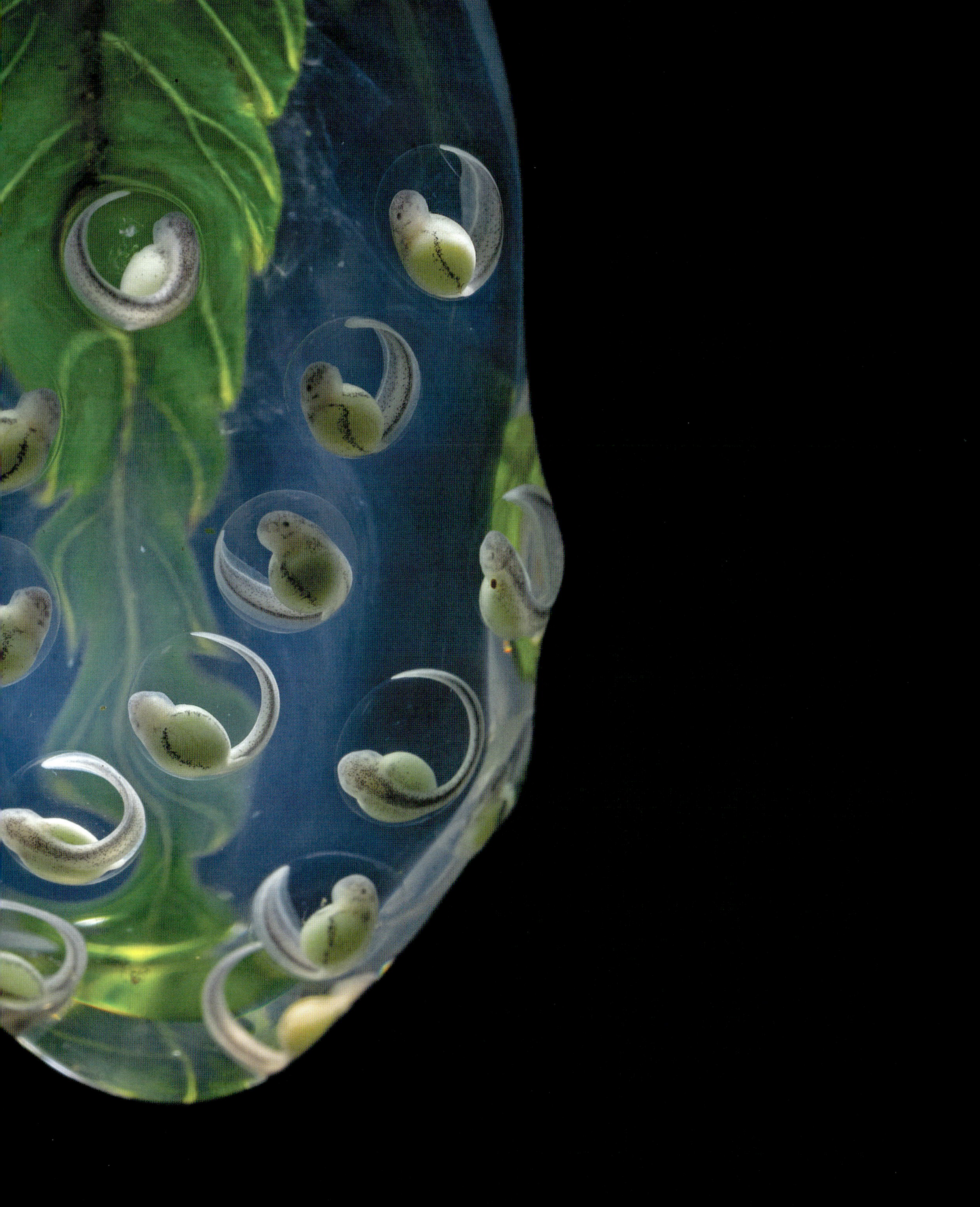

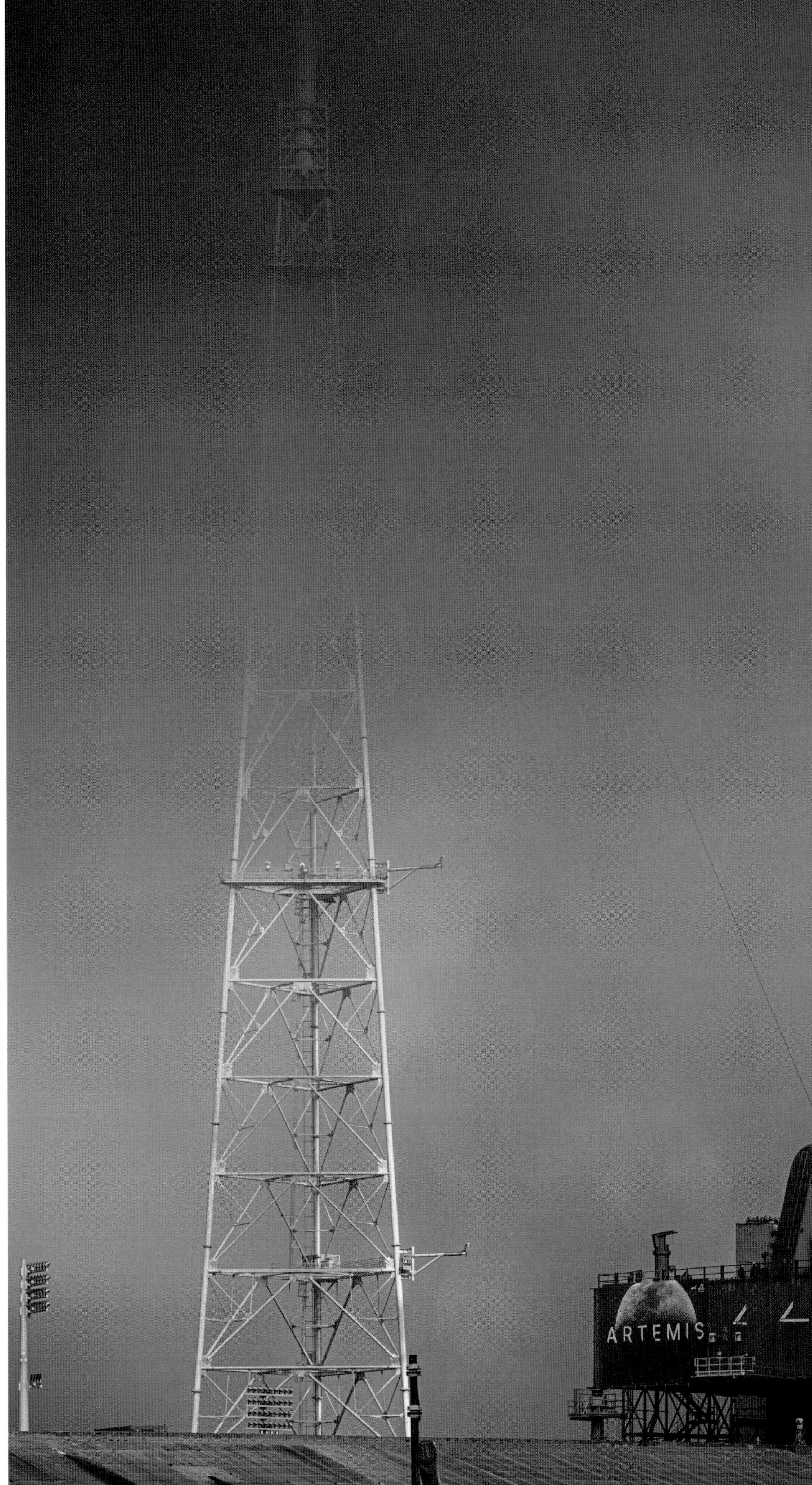

DAN WINTERS, 2022
Fog clears to reveal the Artemis I spacecraft and rocket—used in the first in a series of missions that will return humans to the moon—at Florida's John F. Kennedy Space Center.

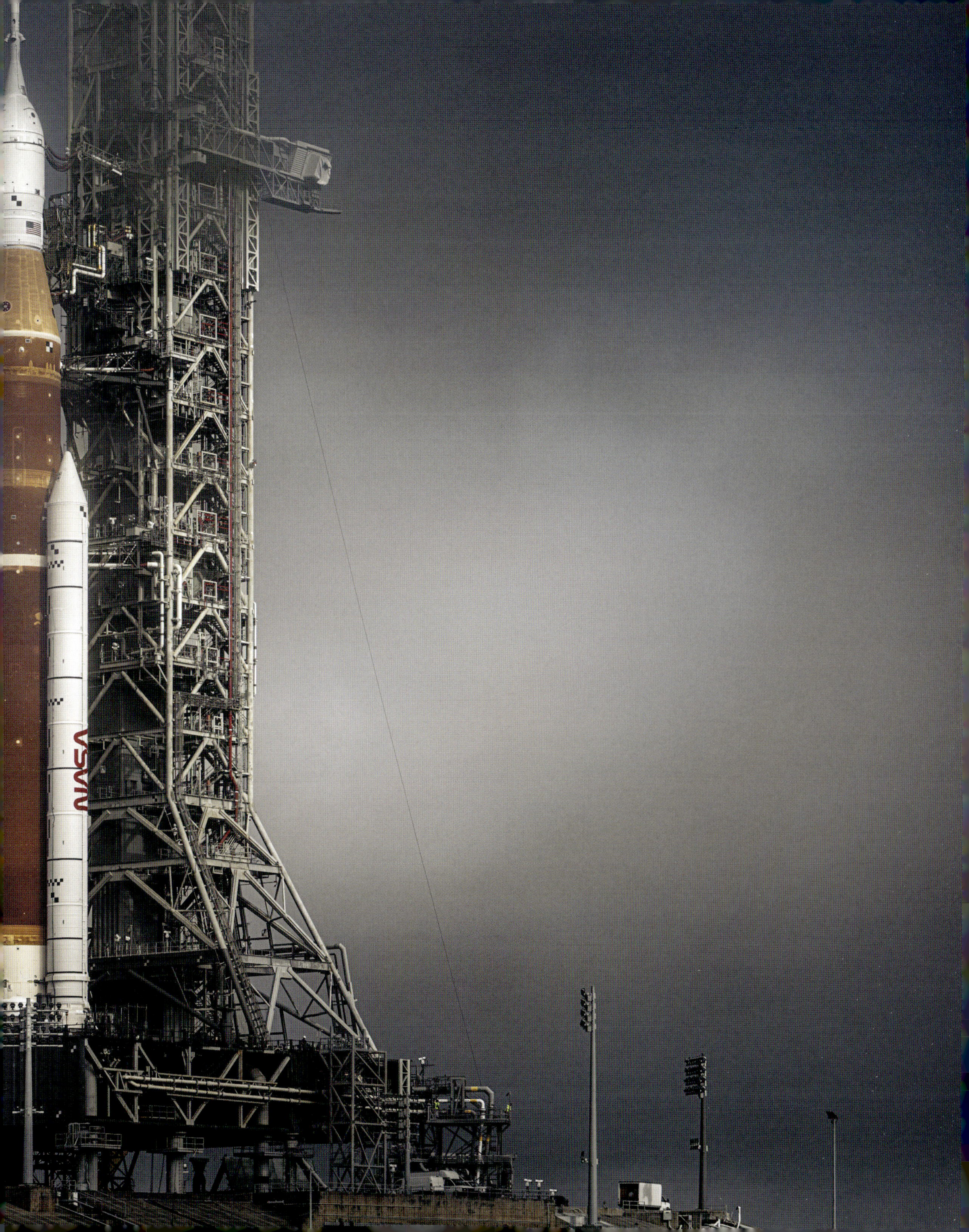
NASA

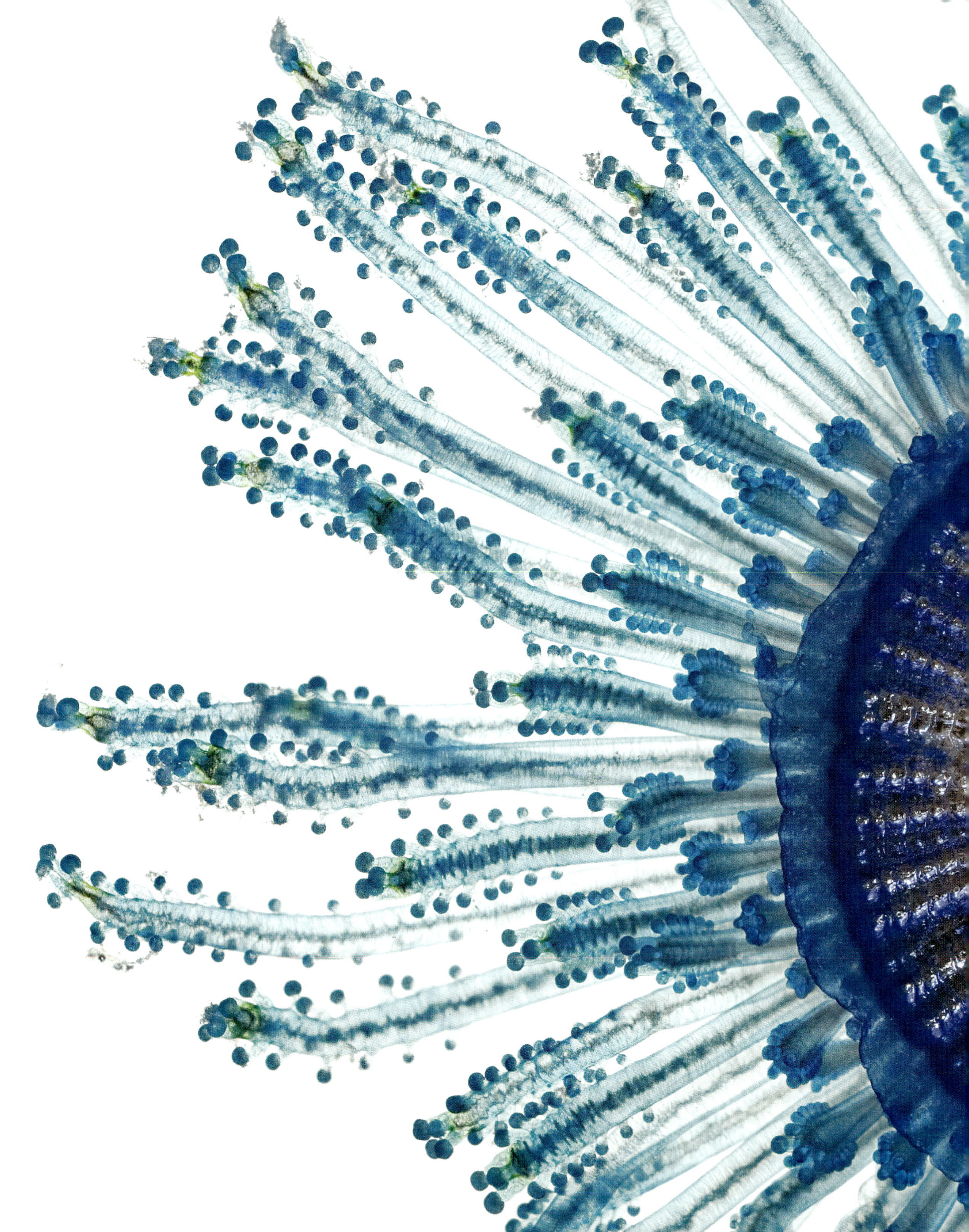

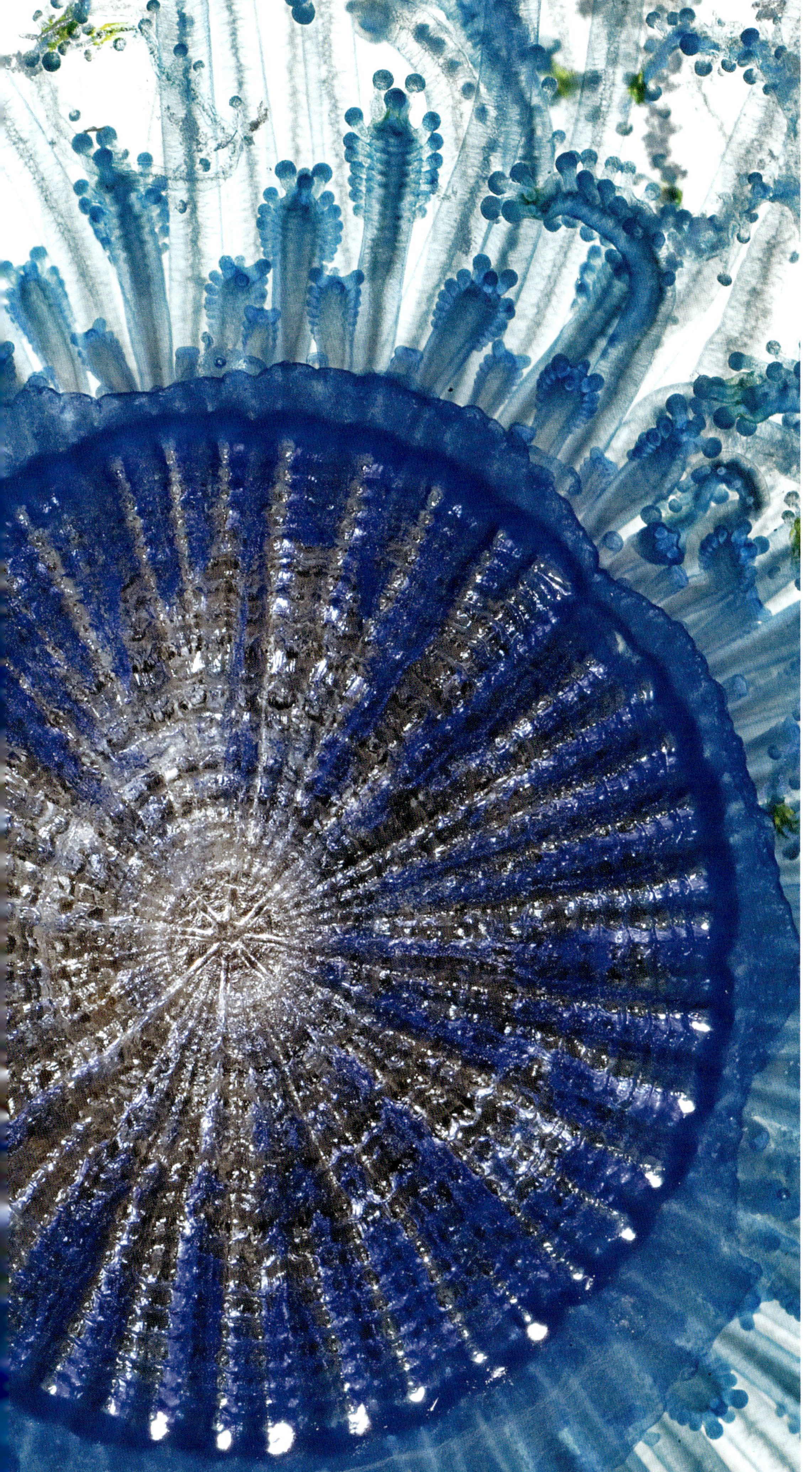

DAVID LIITTSCHWAGER, 2006
The pigment of a blue button jellyfish blocks ultraviolet rays.

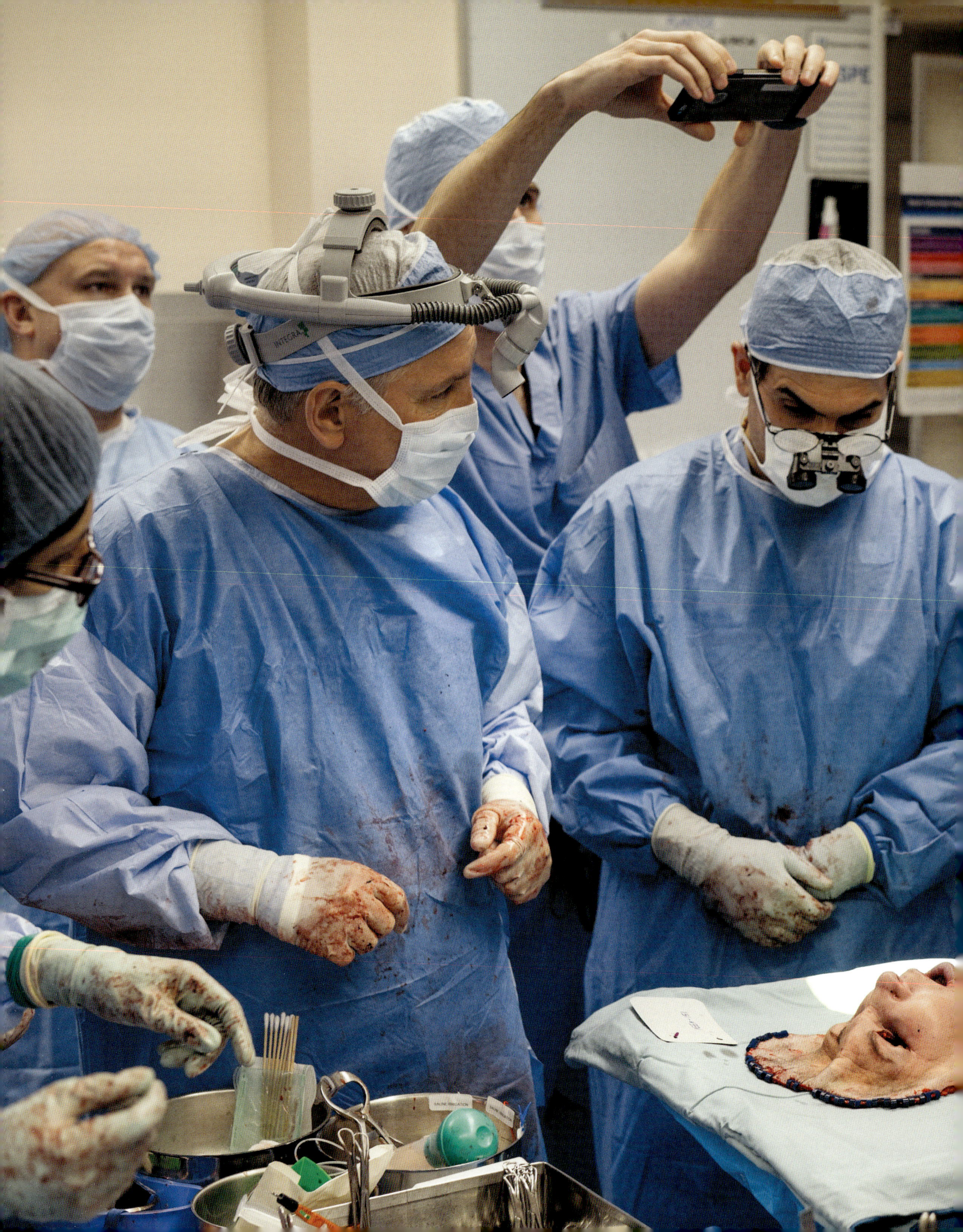

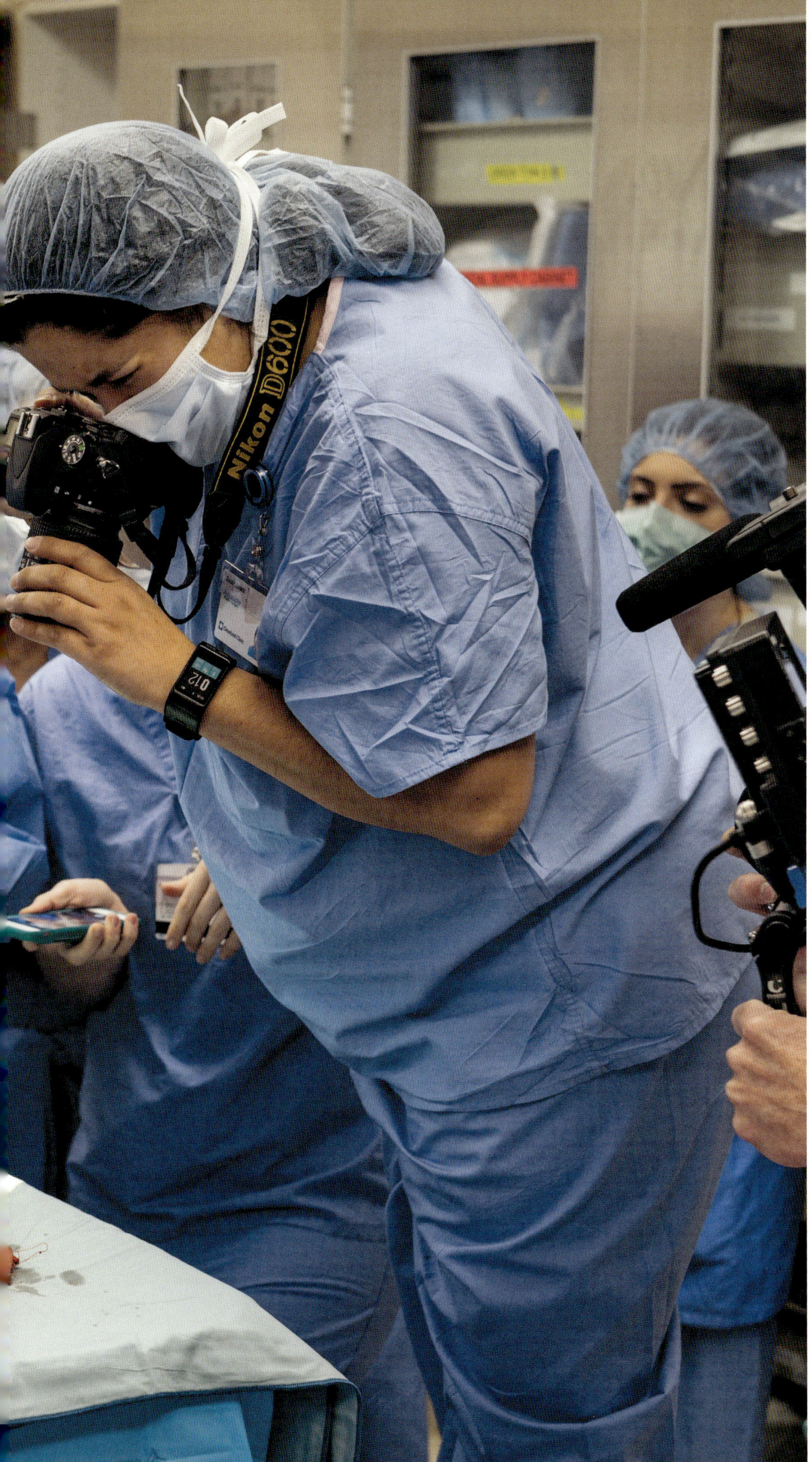

LYNN JOHNSON, 2017
Surgeons complete the intricate task of removing the face from a donor before a face transplant operation.

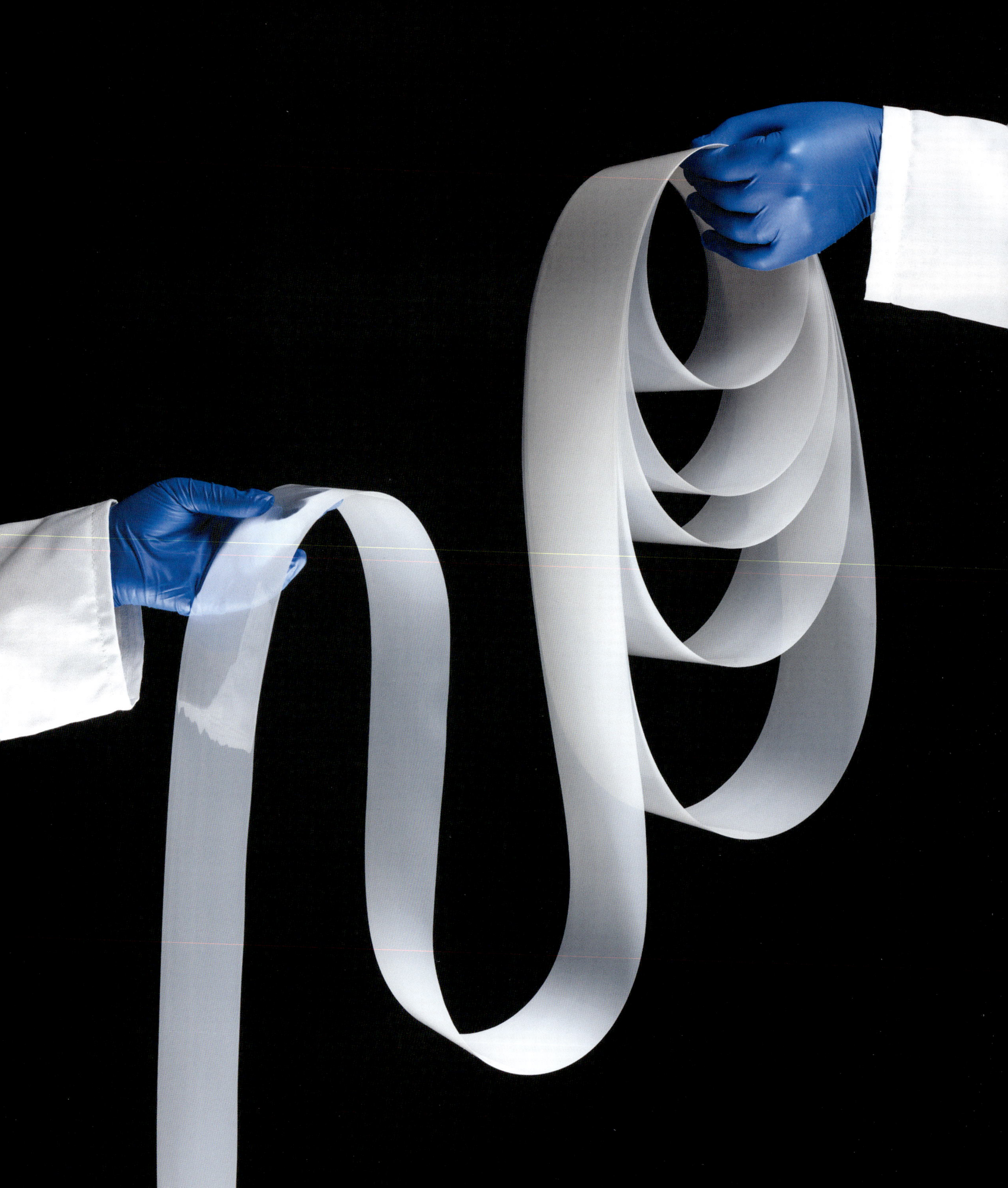

IN PHOTOGRAPHY, THE BOUNDARY BETWEEN SCIENCE AND ART CAN BLUR.

CHRISTOPHER PAYNE, 2022
Ribbon ceramics created by Corning are spooled into strips thinner than a sheet of paper. Containing the power to store vast amounts of energy, they can help combat climate change and address sustainability issues.

FOLLOWING PAGES
LAURENT BALLESTA, 2015
Seldom seen tendrils of ice-covered brine, or brinicles, leak from sea ice in East Antarctica.

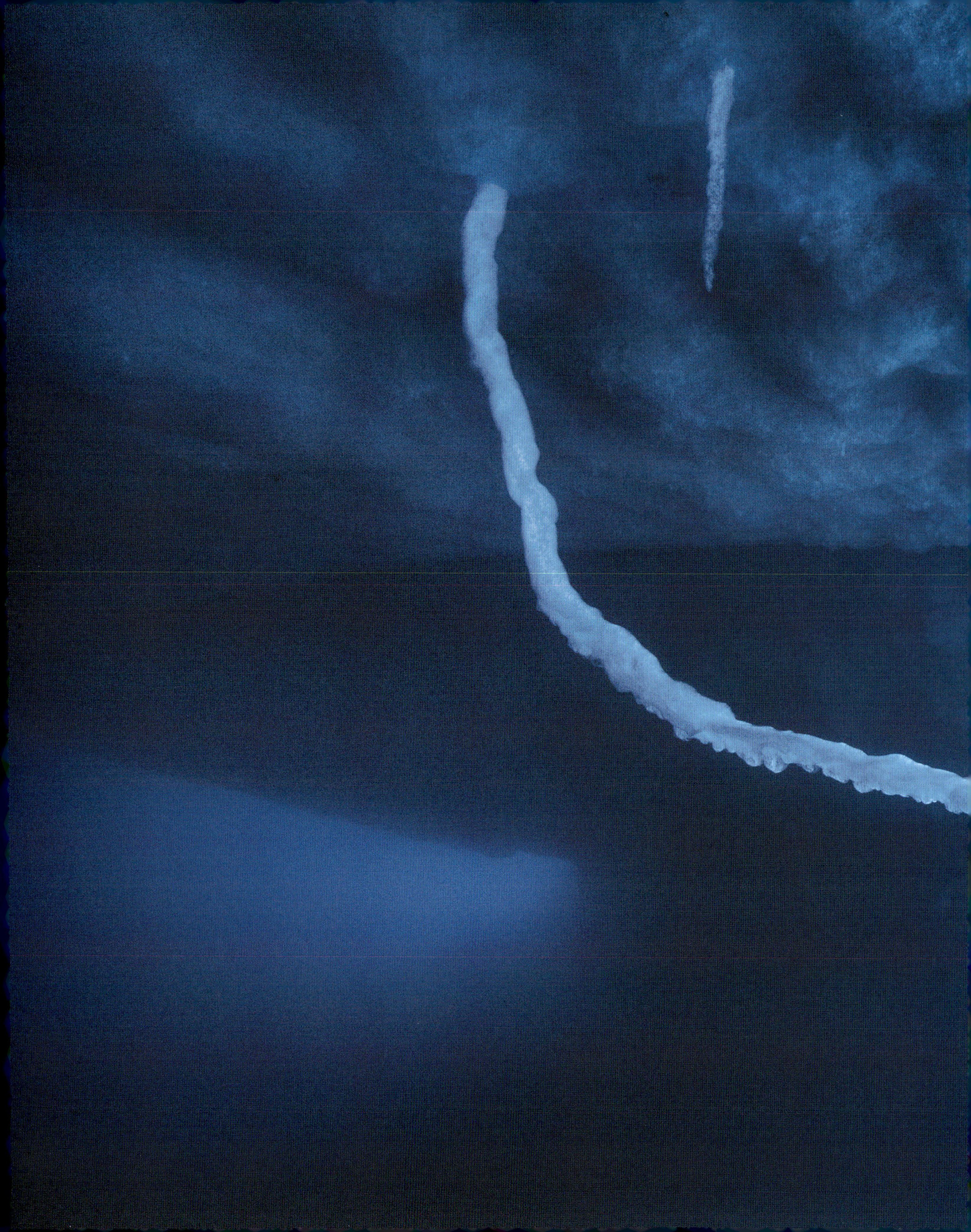

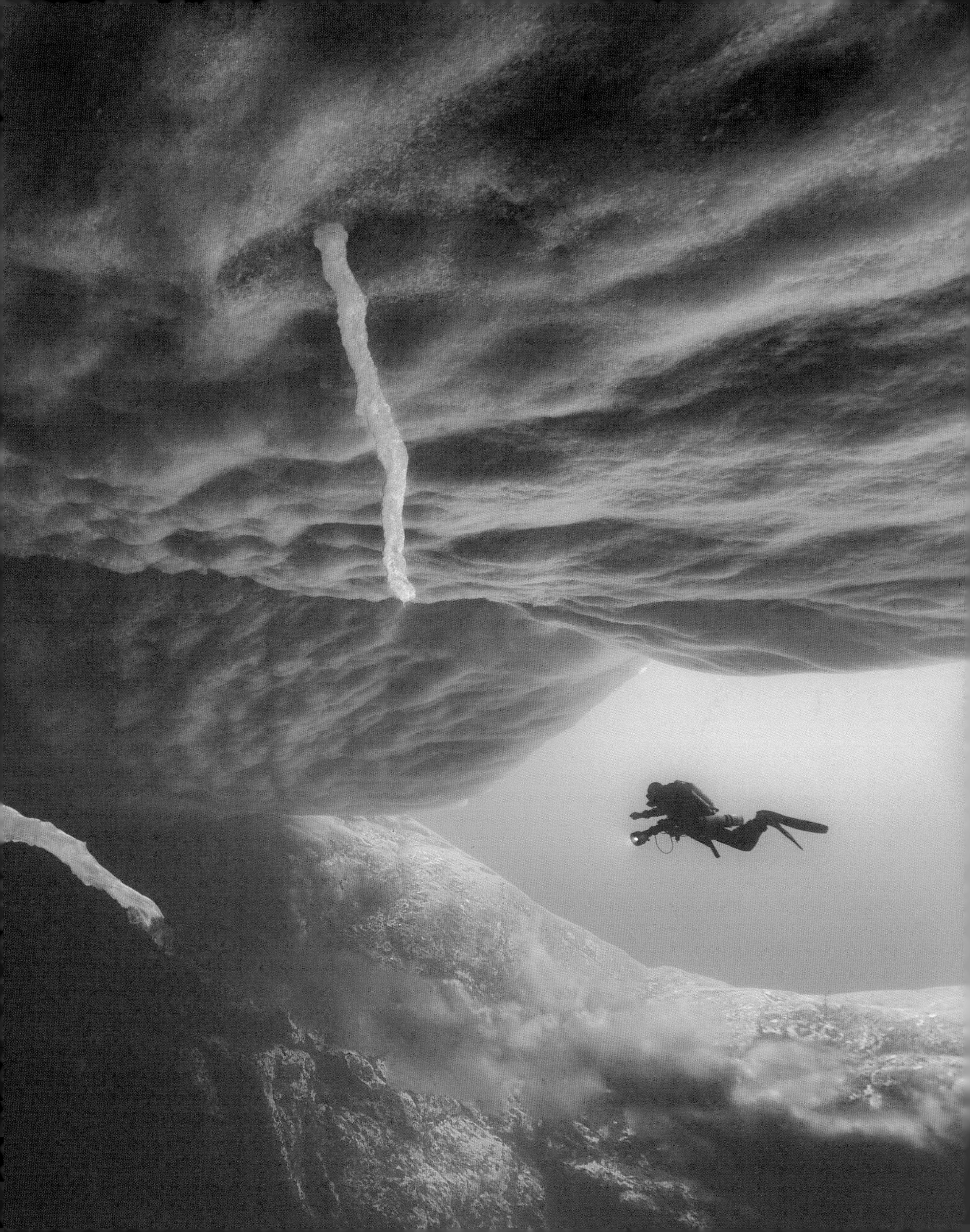

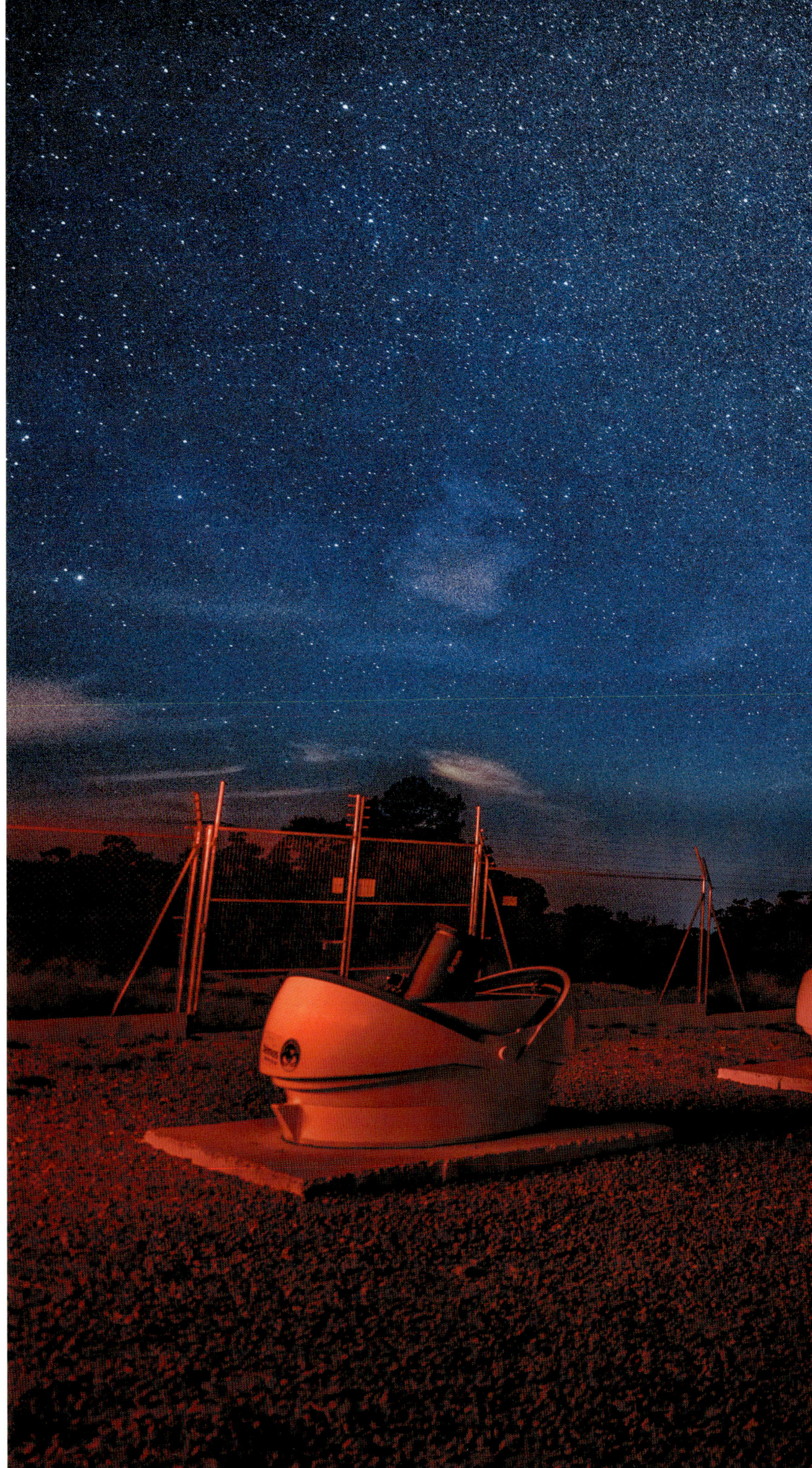

LUCA LOCATELLI, 2016
Three telescopes from the Deimos Sky Survey watch for close asteroids and human-made space debris that could harm satellites.

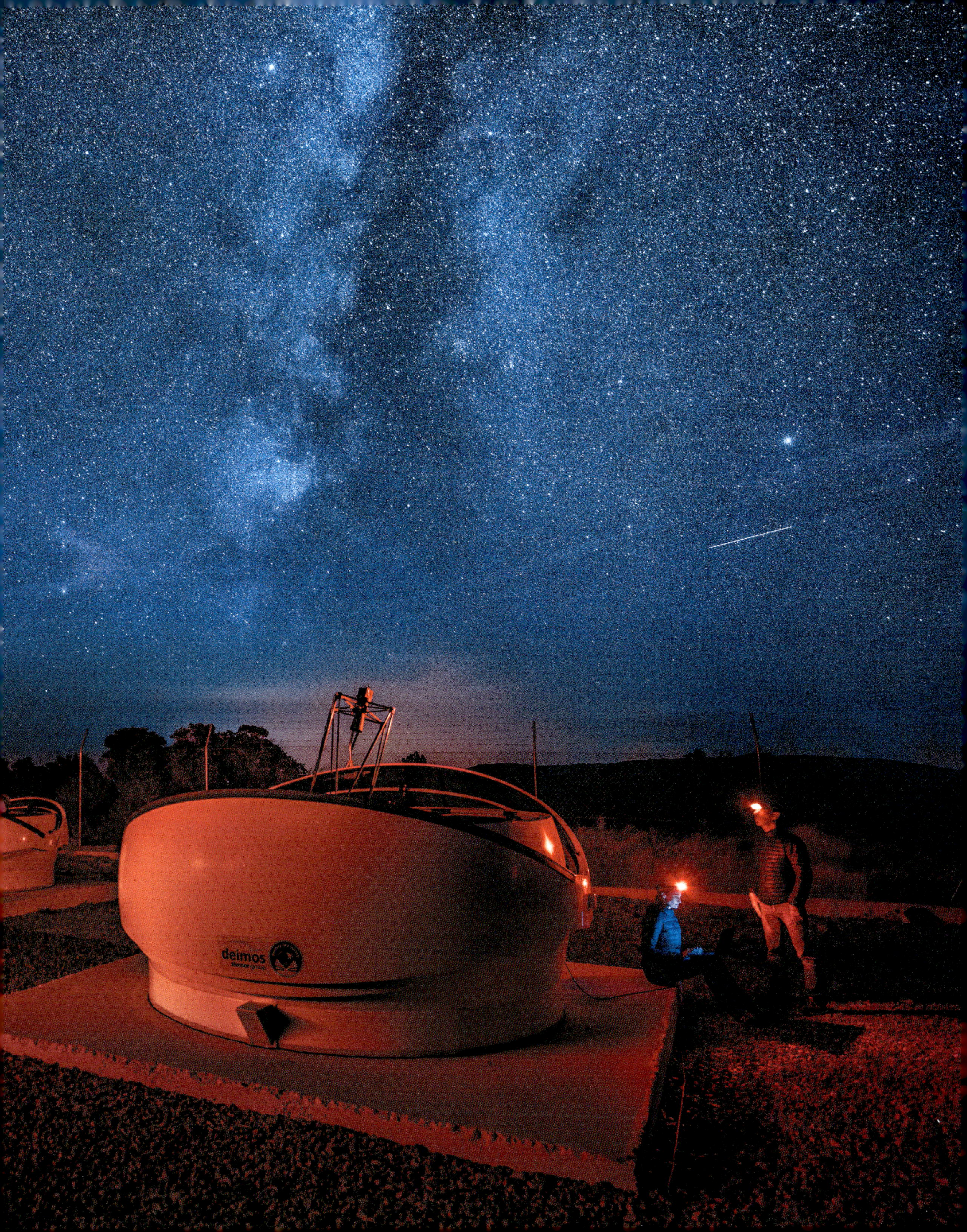
deimos

BIOGRAPHY

NICHOLE SOBECKI

IN HER WORK AS A PHOTOGRAPHER, Nichole Sobecki focuses on humanity's fraught, intimate, and ultimately unbreakable connection to the natural world. She has documented a wide variety of topics for National Geographic, including the Ebola epidemic in the Democratic Republic of the Congo, Kenya's volcanic geothermal-energy initiative, and cheetah trafficking across southern and eastern Africa. Sobecki earned access to these stories through deep, committed research. "Try and become an expert in anything you want to cover," she's observed. "Try and live in that world."

For Sobecki, expertise drives creativity, and has resulted in some of her most intimate photographs: a hunched cheetah cub hissing at an outstretched hand, a camel tugging at a Somali woman's hijab, the "superhero cool" of a fruit bat in flight. But although she begins each shoot as an outsider, she strives to become an insider. For her first *National Geographic* cover feature, 2024's "Bats: A Love Story," she adapted a nocturnal schedule to more effectively photograph the animals.

Sobecki started out as a conflict photographer. Today, she aims to portray everyday life that is neither idealized nor debased—a philosophy demonstrated in the series *Where Our Land Was,* which illuminates the human consequences of climate change in Somalia, and the collective project Everyday Africa, which uses photography to present the continent as it is. Sobecki's work has been exhibited around the world, including at the United Nations headquarters in New York City, the John F. Kennedy Center for the Performing Arts in Washington, D.C., and the Musée des Arts et Métiers in Paris. A National Geographic Explorer, she is based in Nairobi, Kenya.

OPPOSITE TOP
NICHOLE SOBECKI, 2022
Before being transferred to a research field station for further study, netted fruit bats hang from a line near the Ugandan village of Kanabu.

OPPOSITE BOTTOM
NICHOLE SOBECKI, 2022
Researchers at Brown University's Aeromechanics and Evolutionary Morphology Lab work with a Seba's short-tailed bat in Providence, Rhode Island.

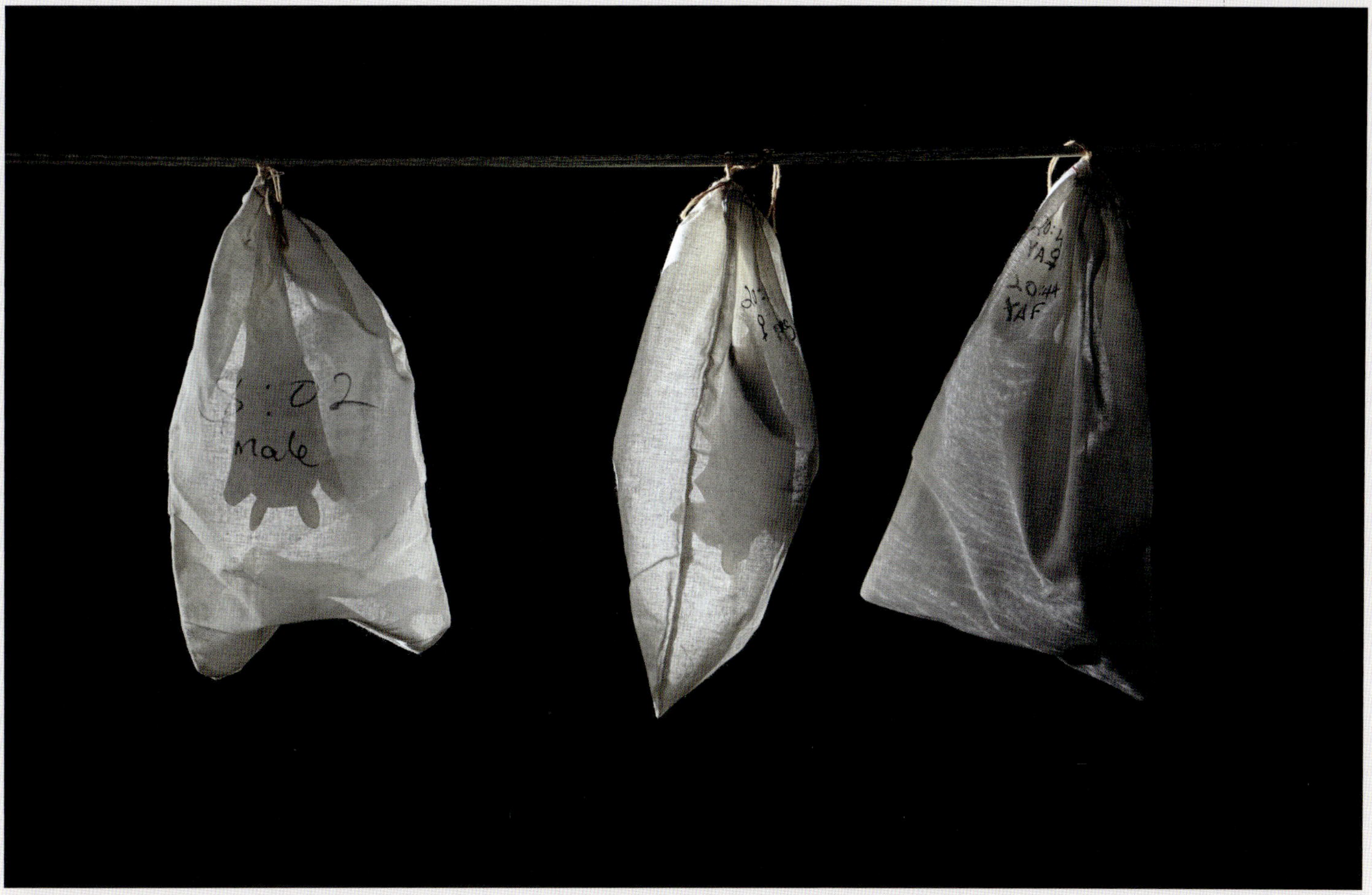

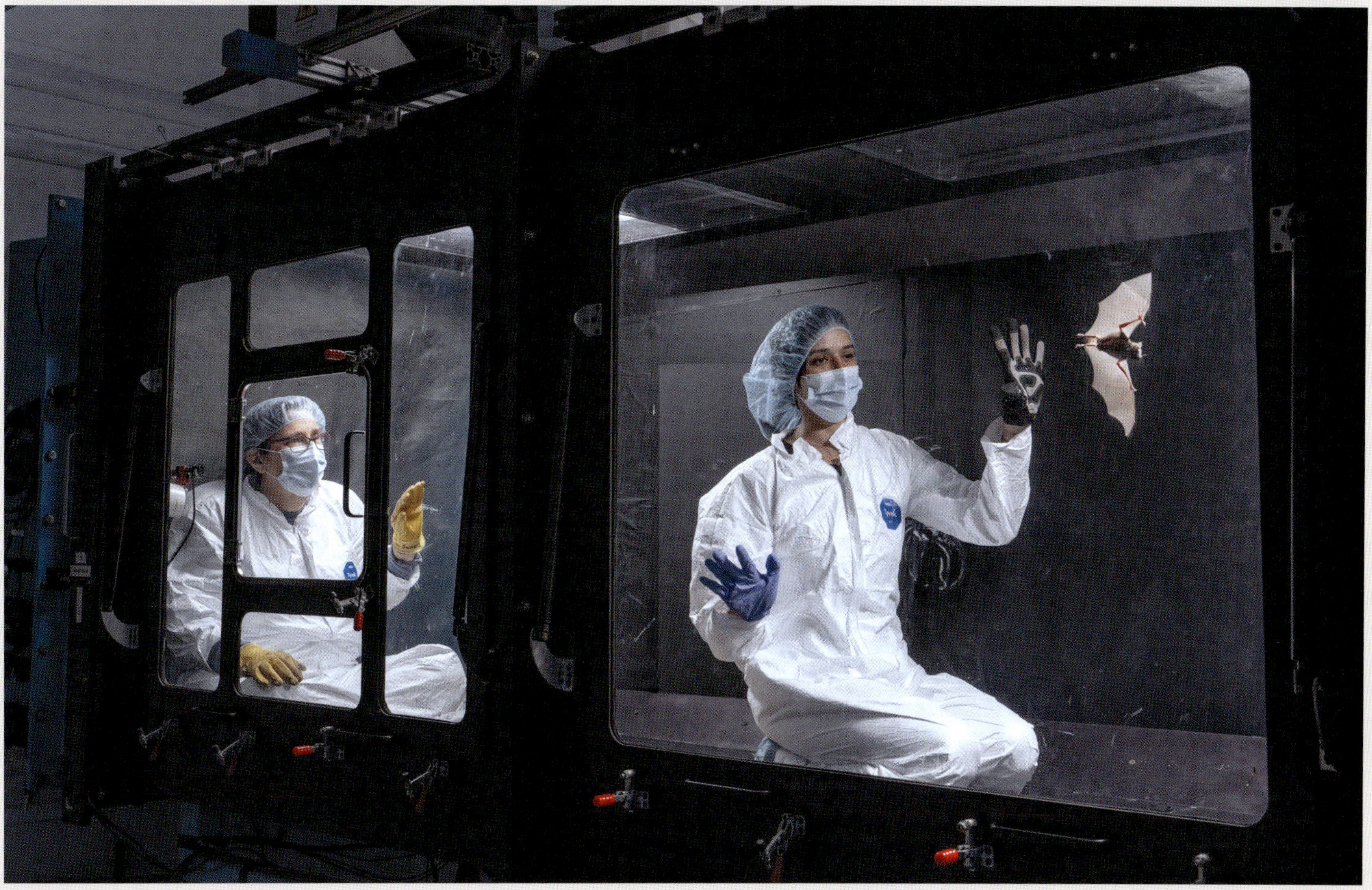

NICHOLE SOBECKI, 2022
An Egyptian fruit bat in a flight tunnel at Brown University in Providence, Rhode Island.

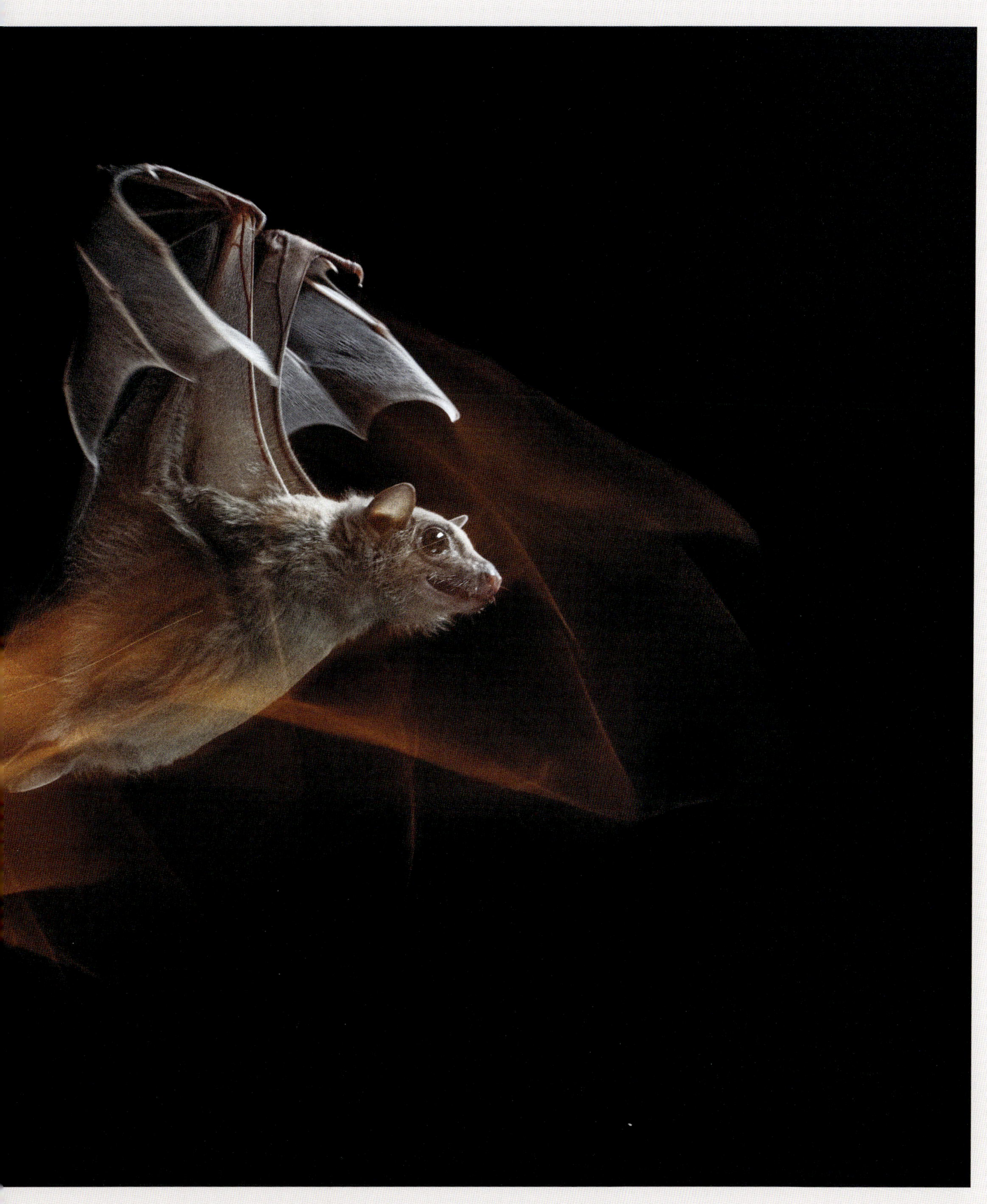

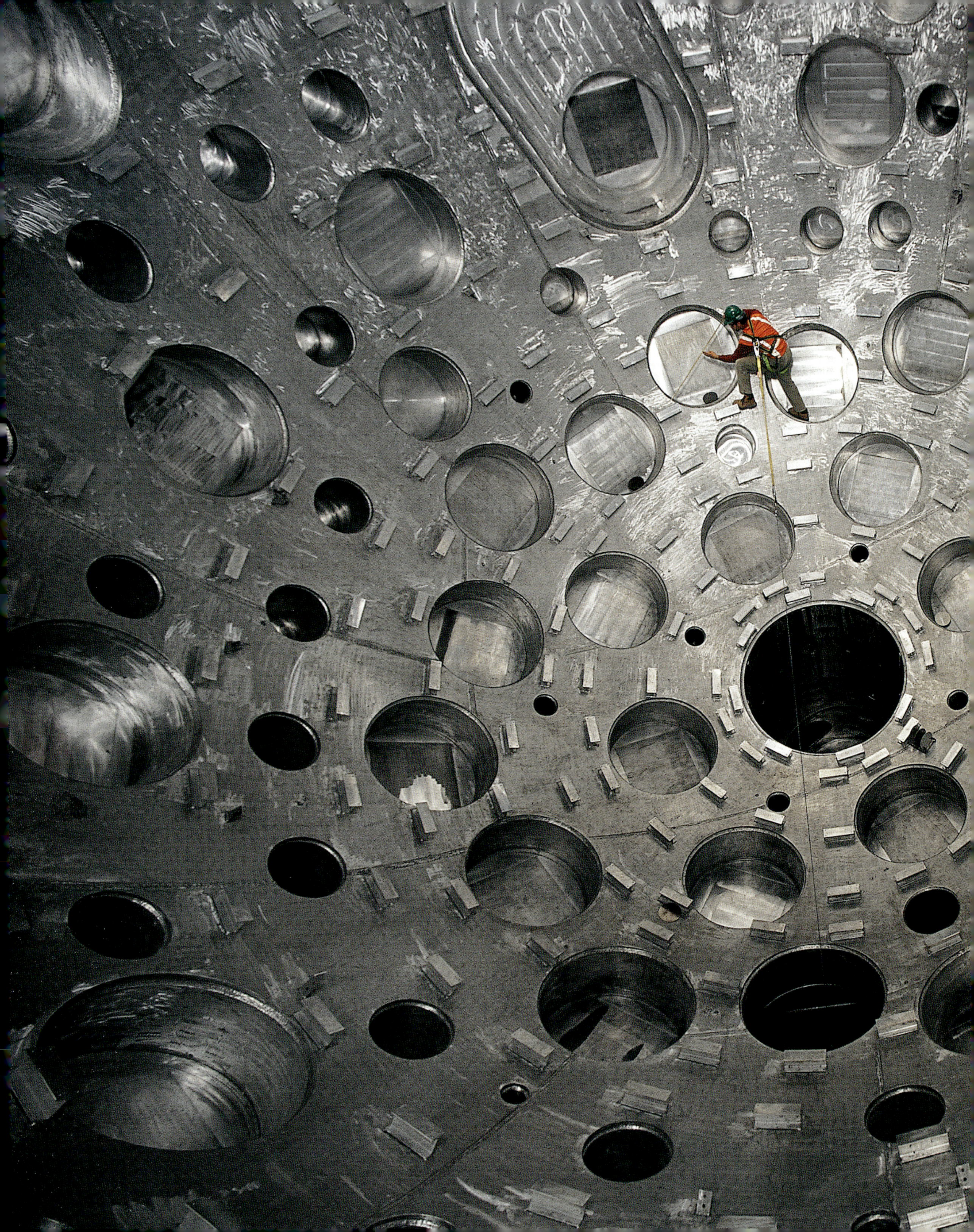

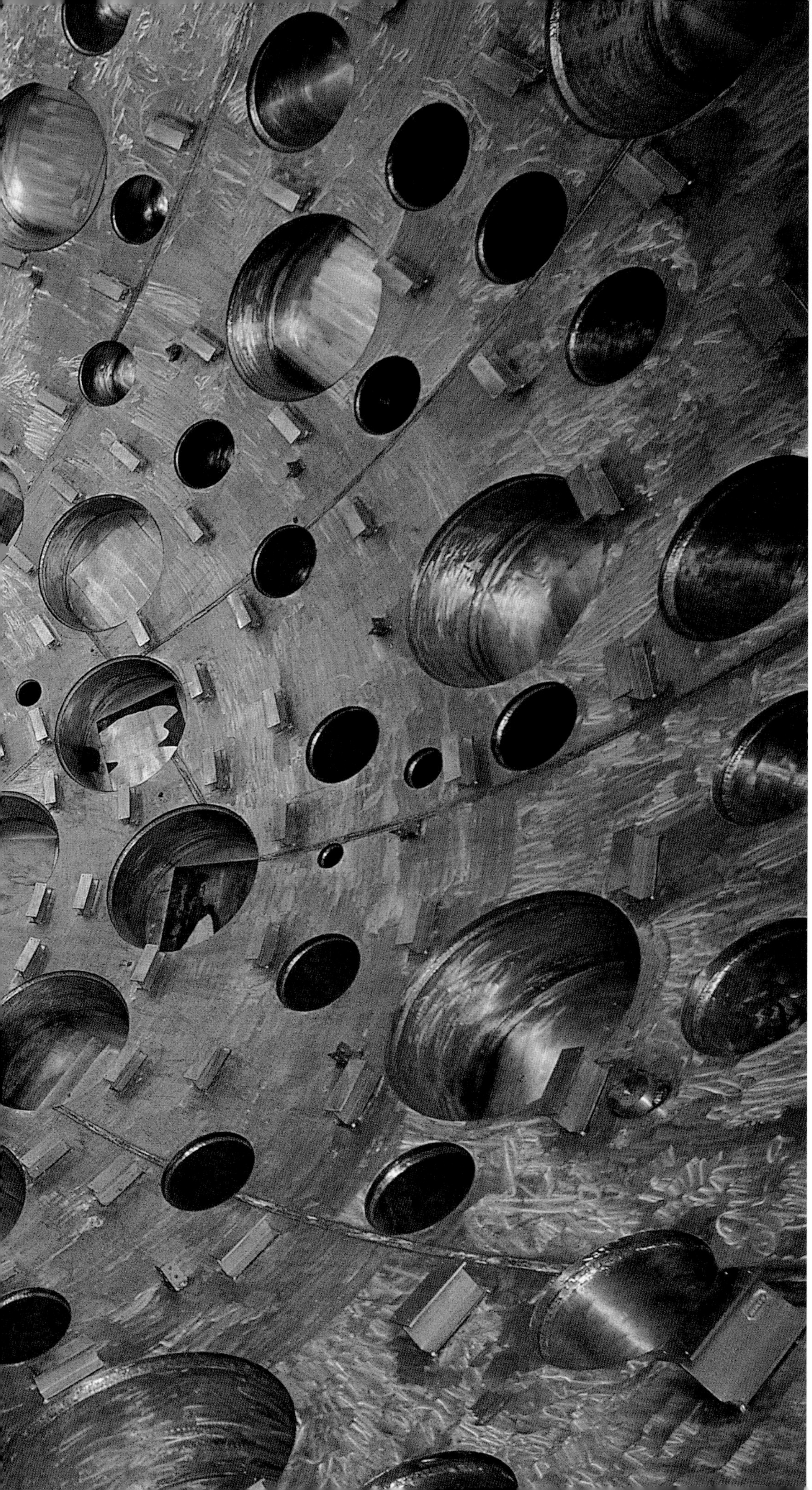

JOE MCNALLY, 2001
A target chamber, used to perform scientific experiments in high-energy physics, at the National Ignition Facility in Livermore, California

FOLLOWING PAGES
THOMAS P. PESCHAK, 2019
A conservation fieldworker radio-tracks lions in Mozambique.

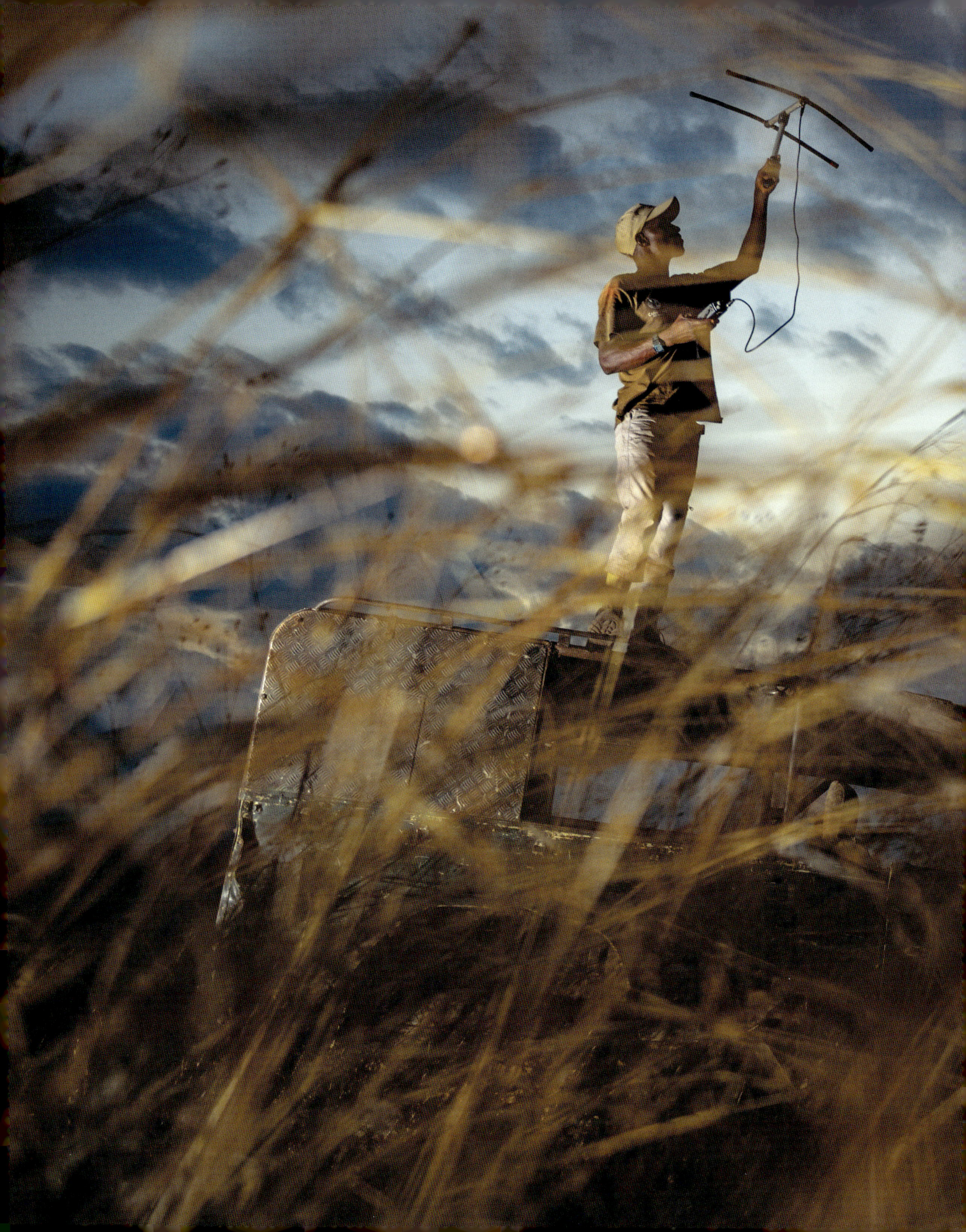

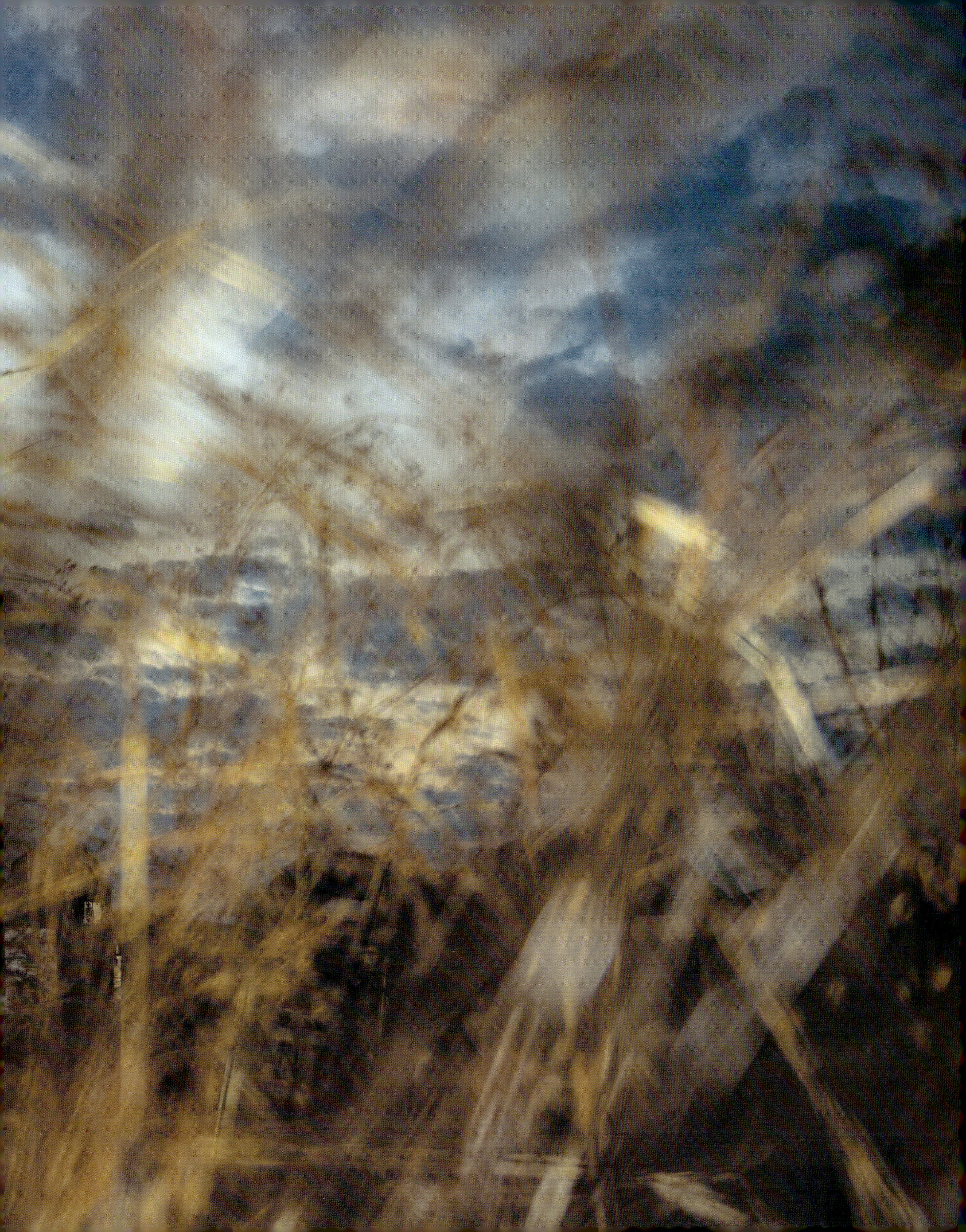

EVERY TIME WE HAVE BUILT NEW EYES TO OBSERVE THE UNIVERSE, OUR UNDERSTANDING OF OURSELVES AND OUR PLACE IN IT HAS BEEN FOREVER ALTERED.

LAWRENCE M. KRAUSS, THEORETICAL PHYSICIST

MARTIN OEGGERLI, 2008
A grain of pollen, wedged between flower petals, has missed its mark and will be unsuccessful.

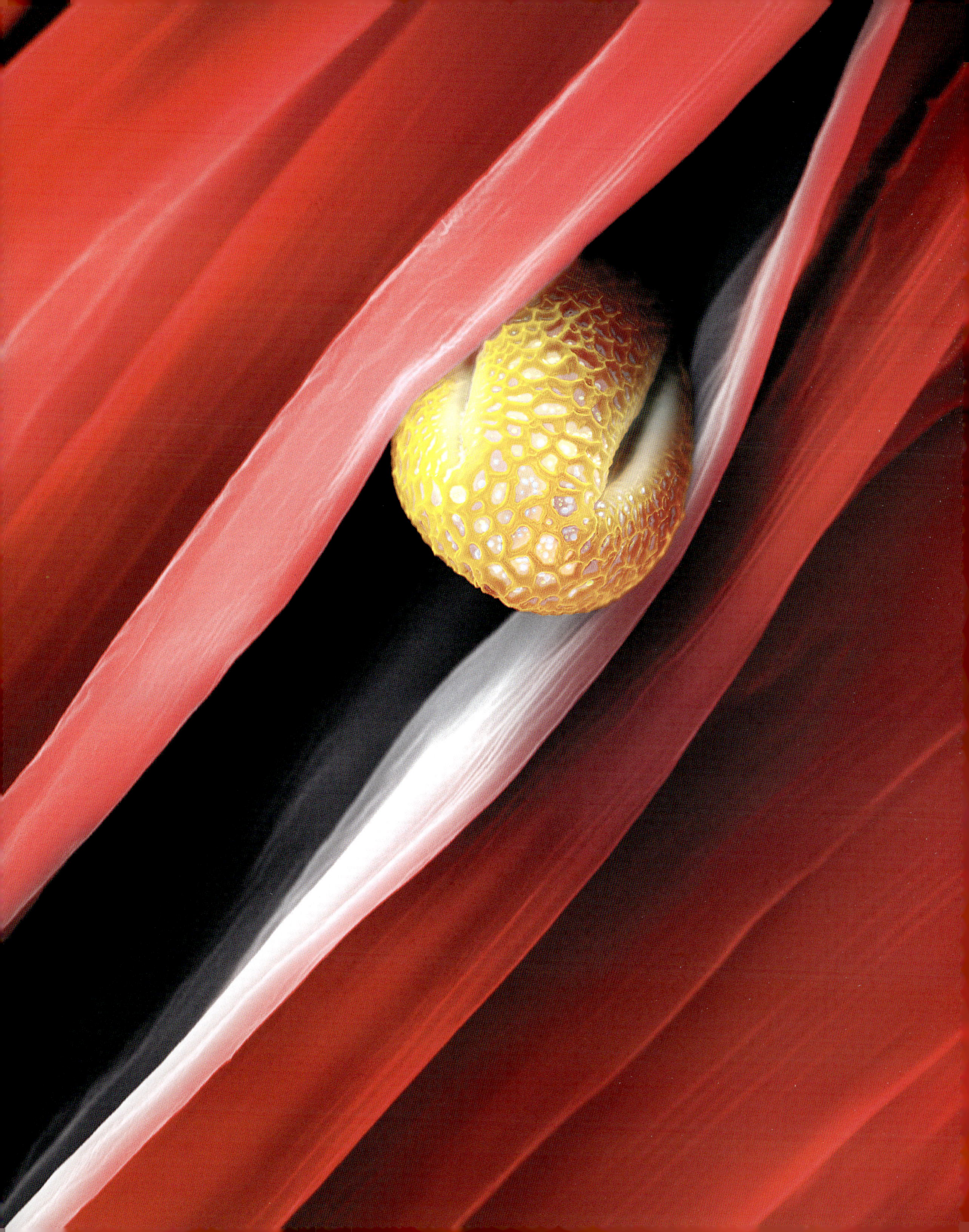

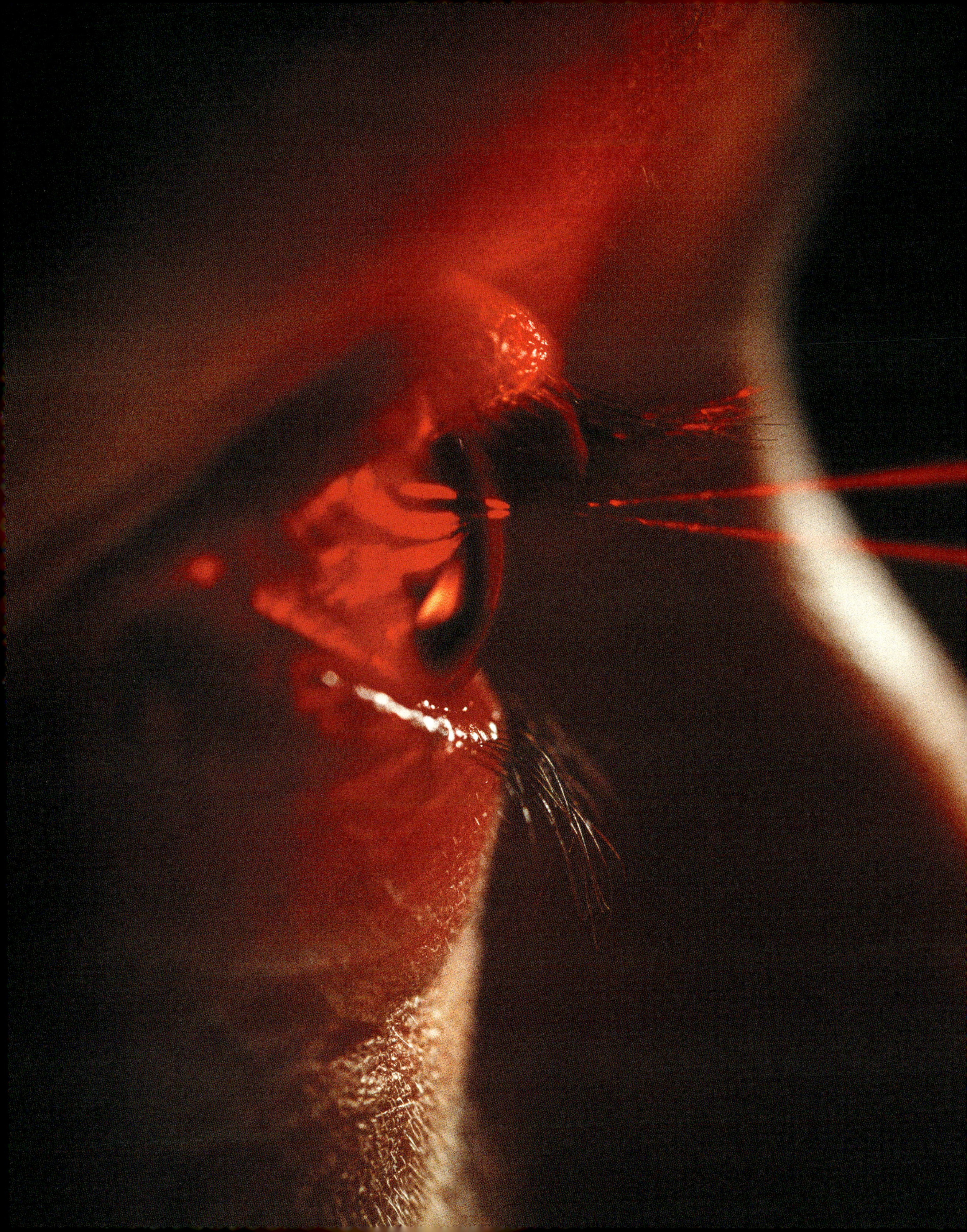

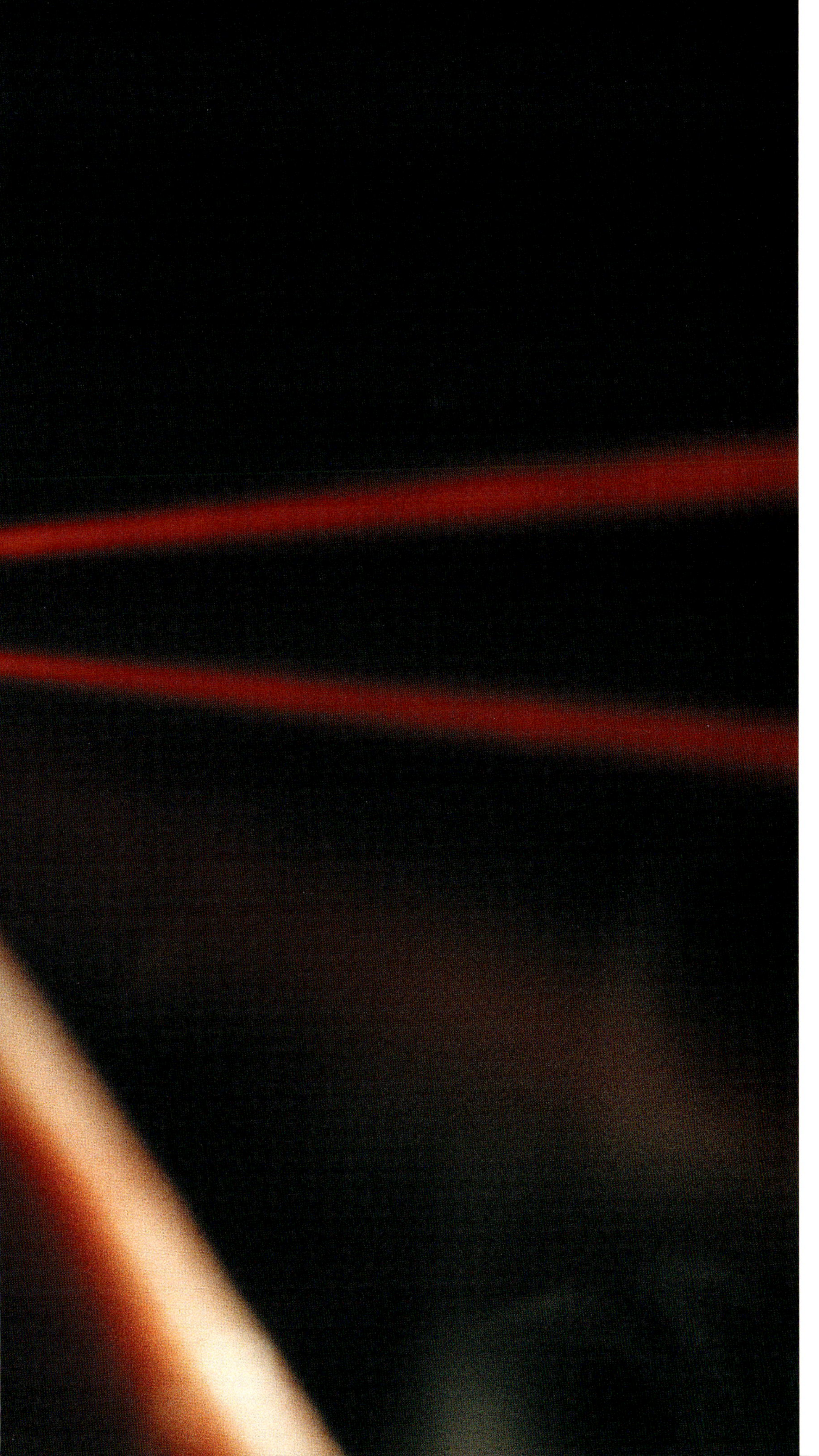

JOE MCNALLY, 1991
A laser beam cuts through the tissue of a human eye to restore sight at the New England Medical Center in Boston, Massachusetts.

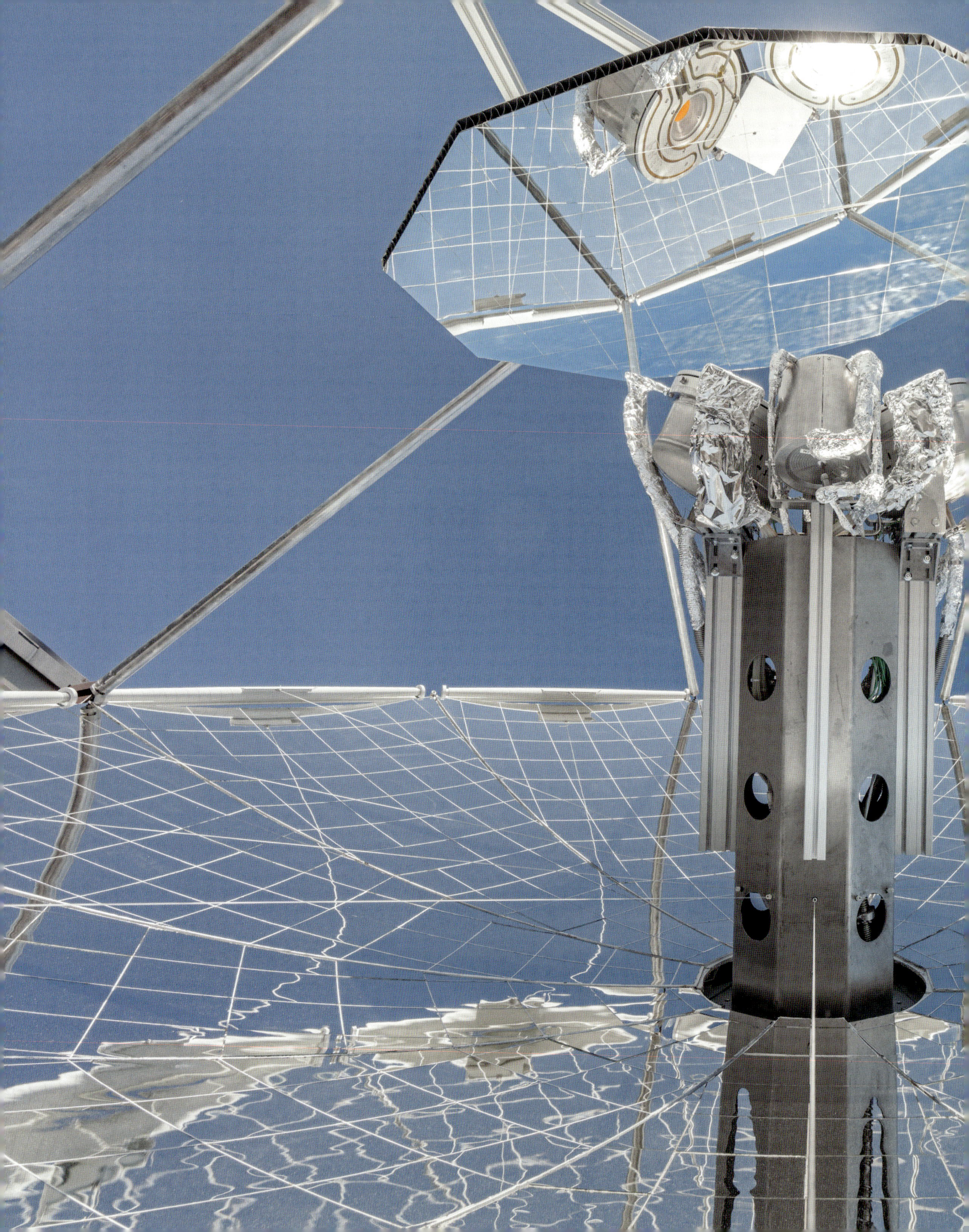

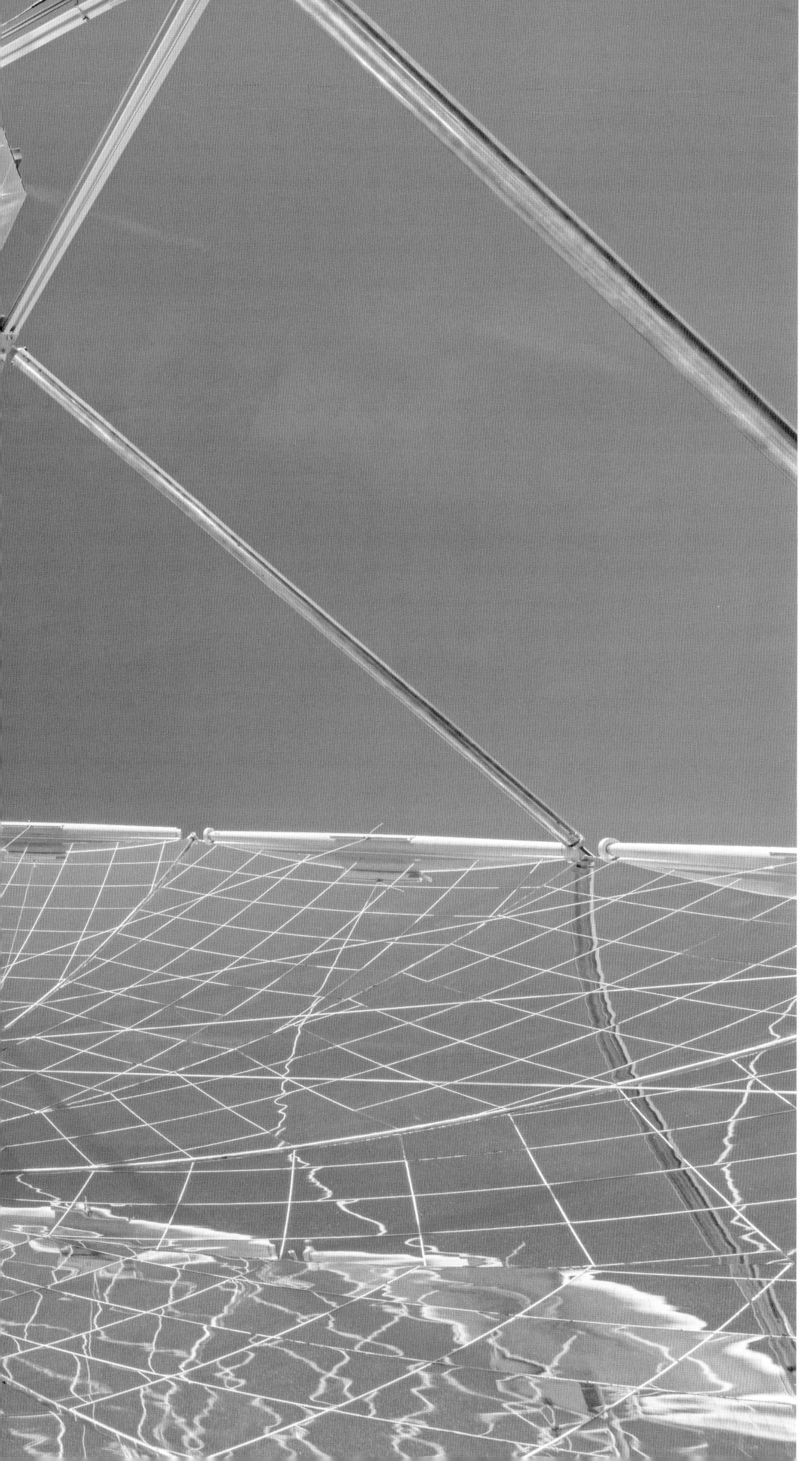

DAVIDE MONTELEONE, 2022
A solar power refinery atop a university building captures carbon dioxide and water to produce carbon-neutral jet fuel in Zurich, Switzerland.

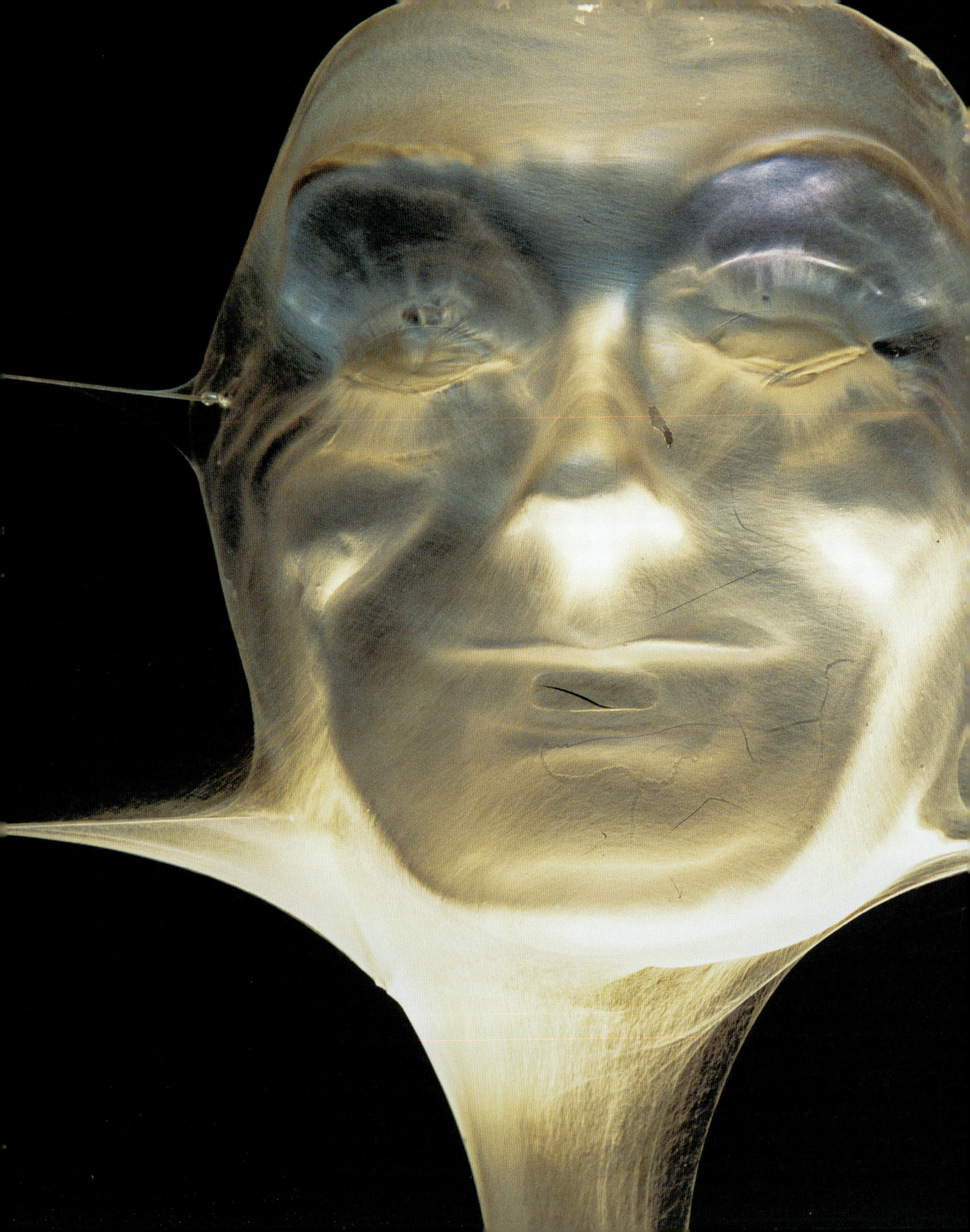

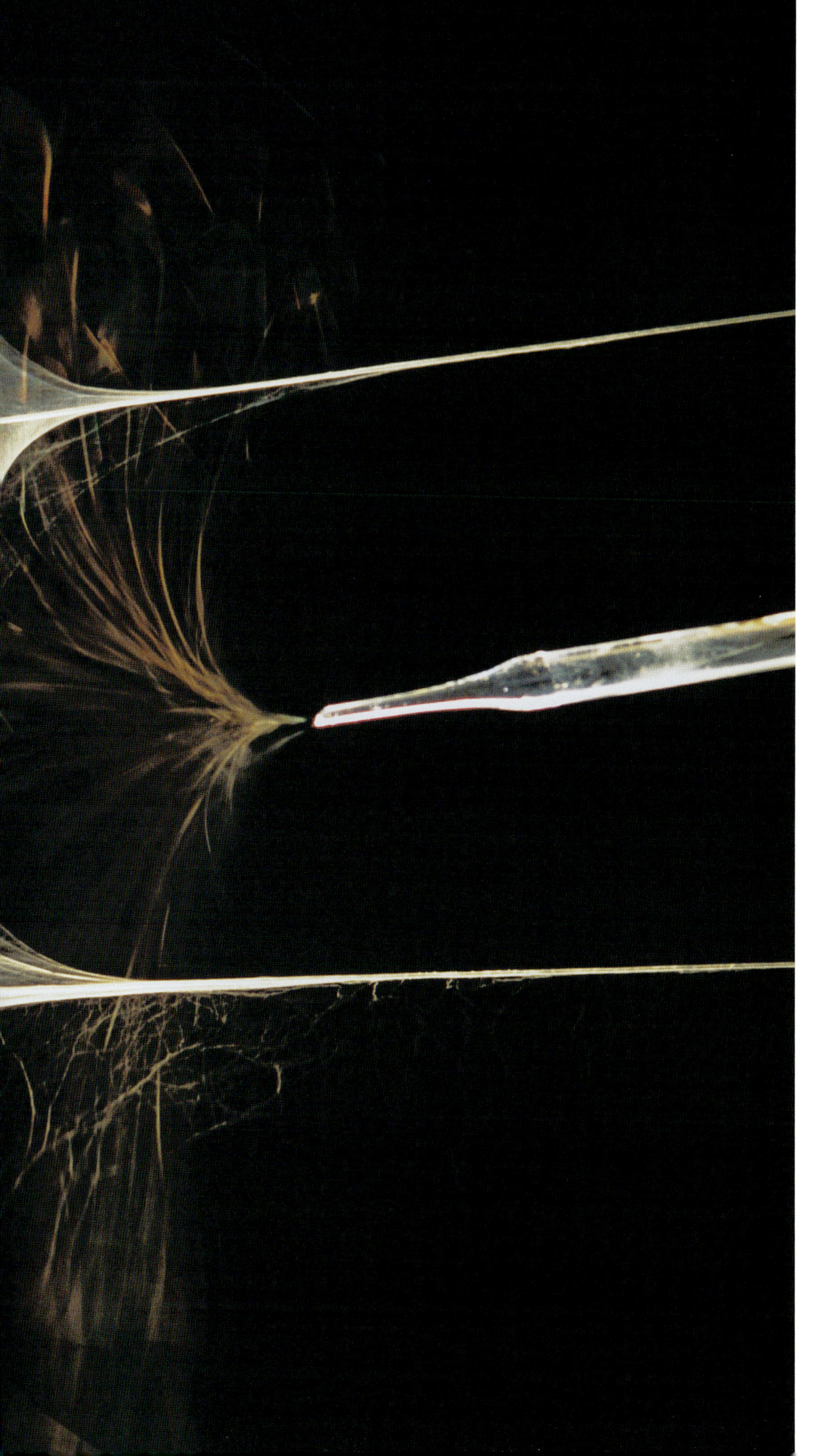

CARY WOLINSKY, 2003
In a process called electrospinning, a mask receives a spray of charged polymers that will congeal into a microfiber membrane, useful in making formfitting garments or chemically protective suits.

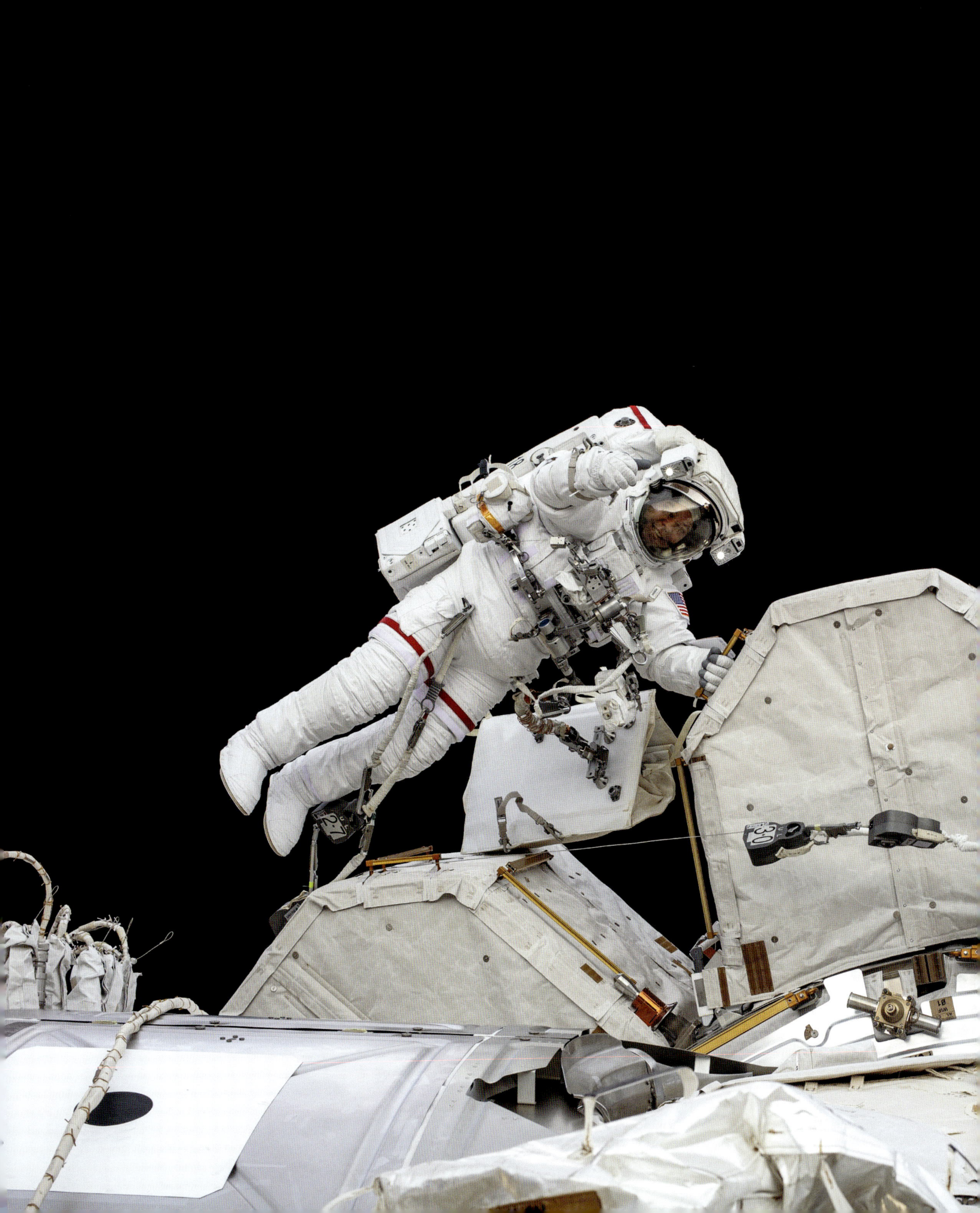

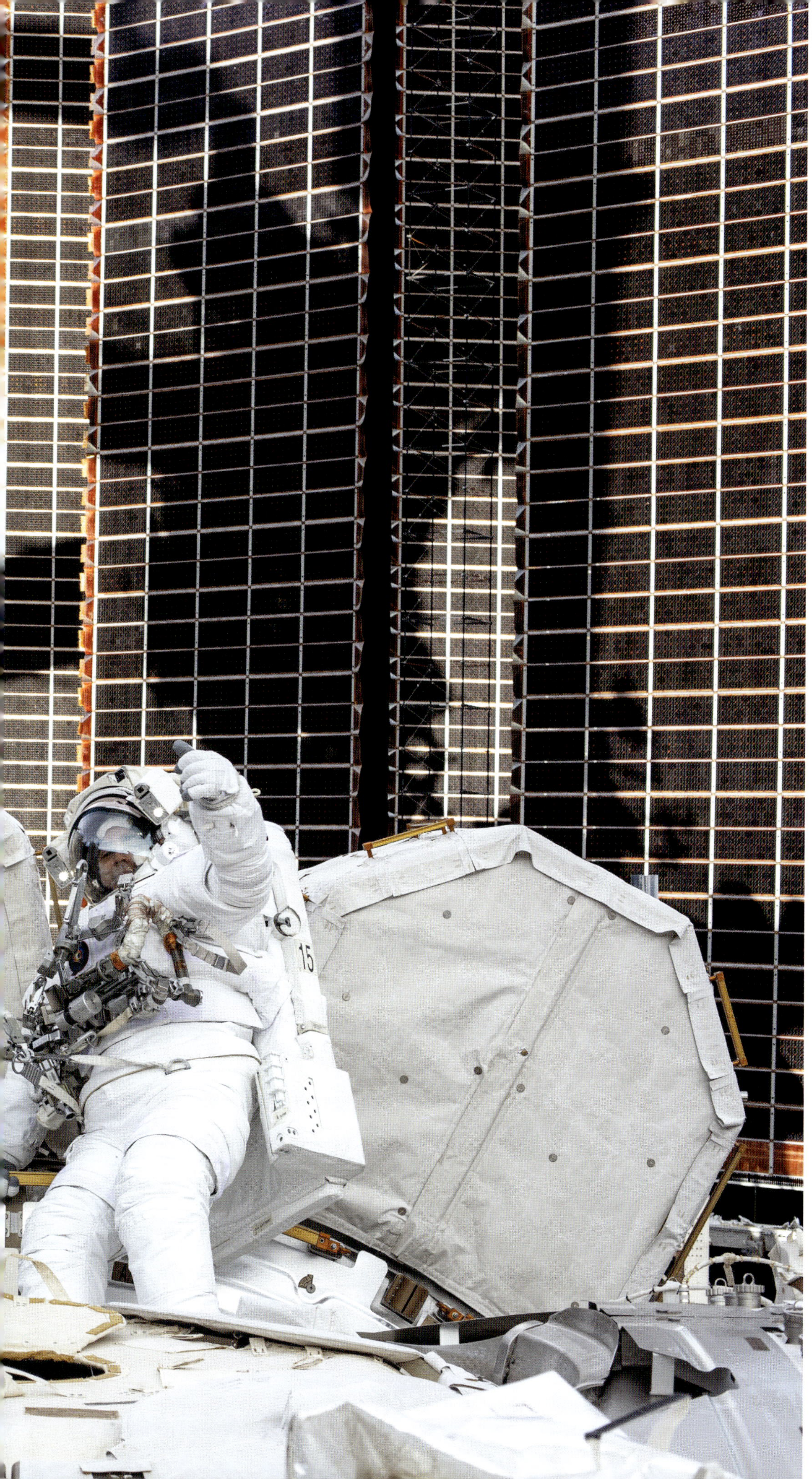

DOUGLAS HURLEY, 2020
Two astronauts conduct a space walk to install a toolbox for a Canadian Space Agency robot that services the International Space Station.

FOLLOWING PAGES
NASA, 2015
On Mars, the Curiosity rover searches for chemical evidence that the red planet once might have supported life.

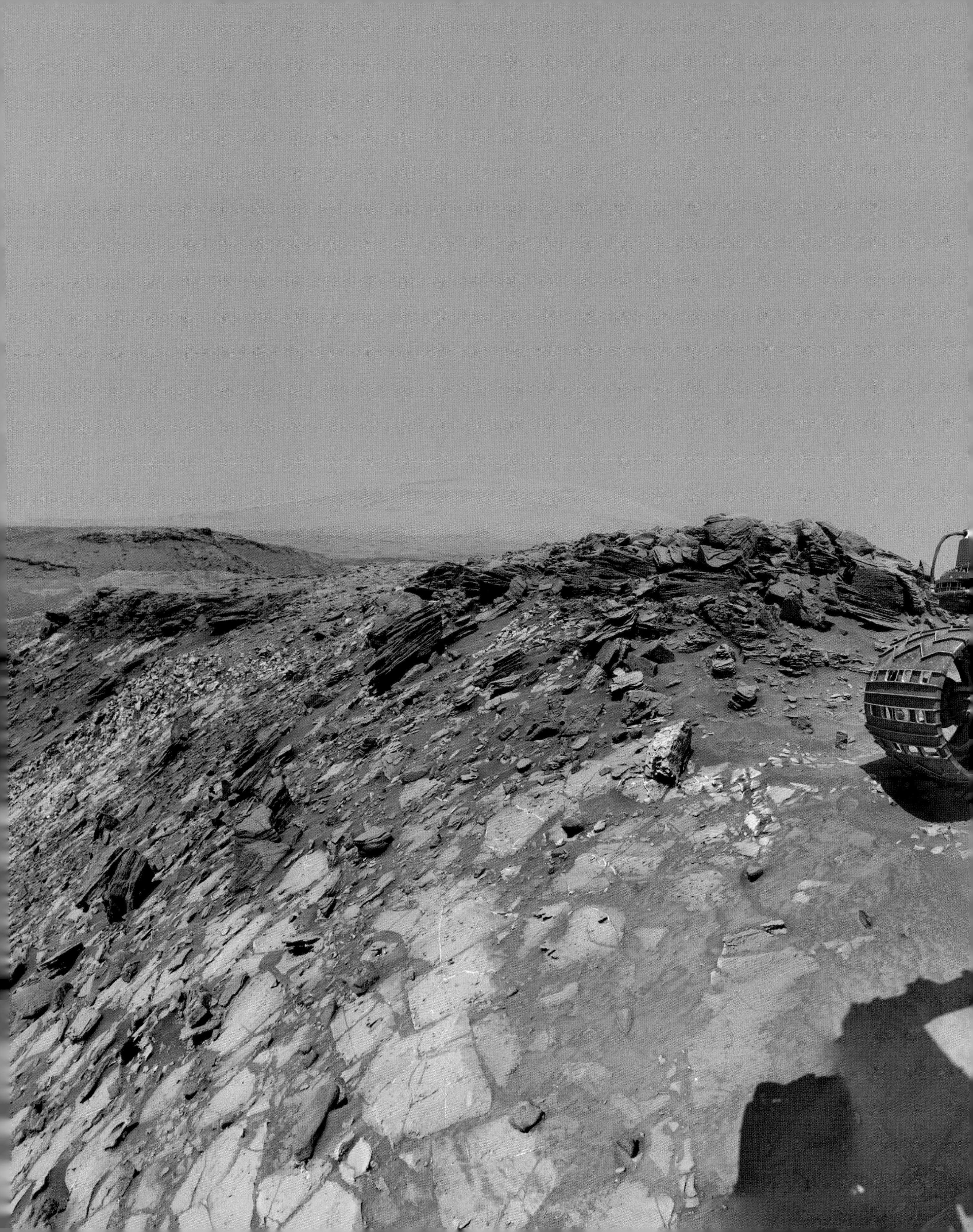

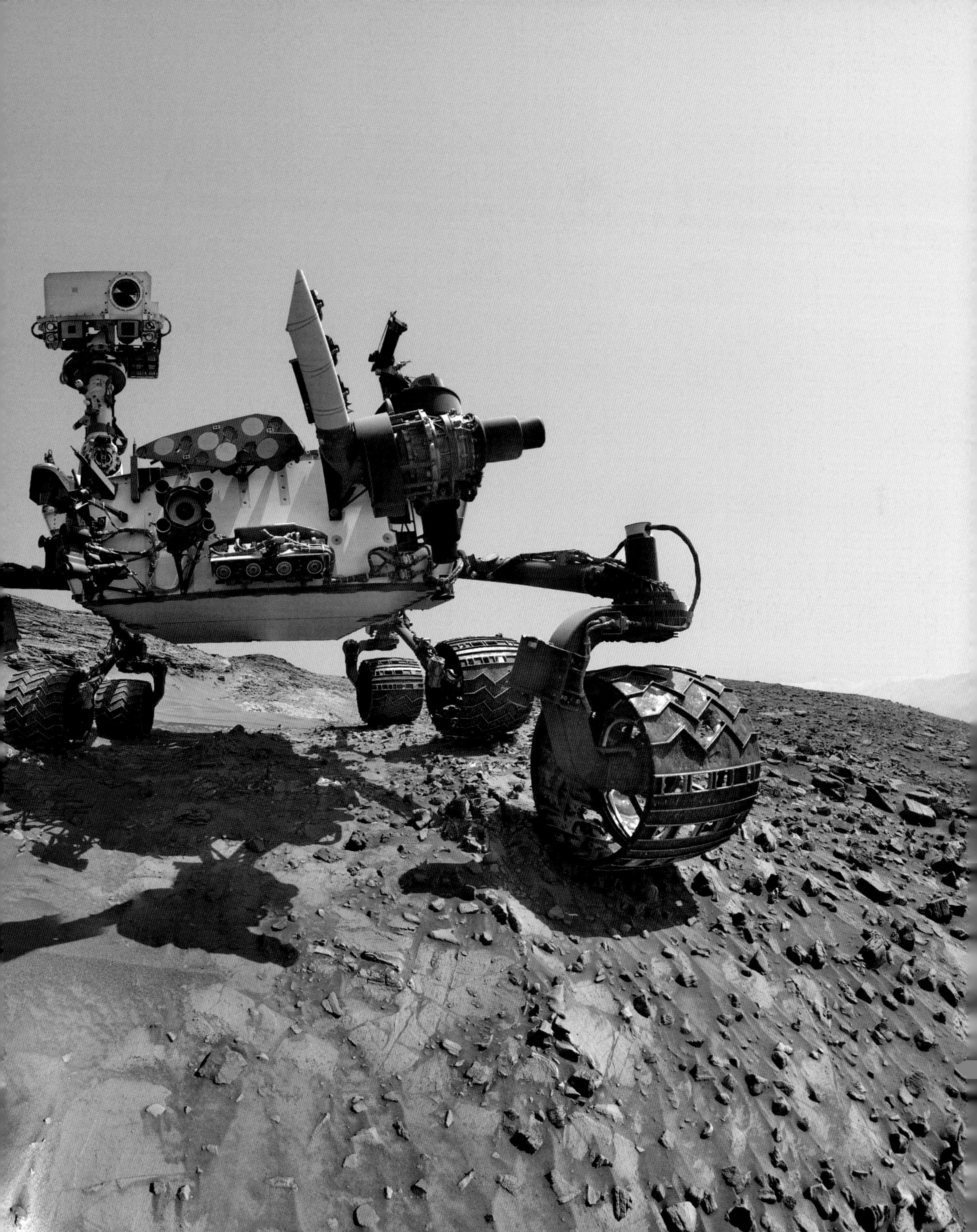

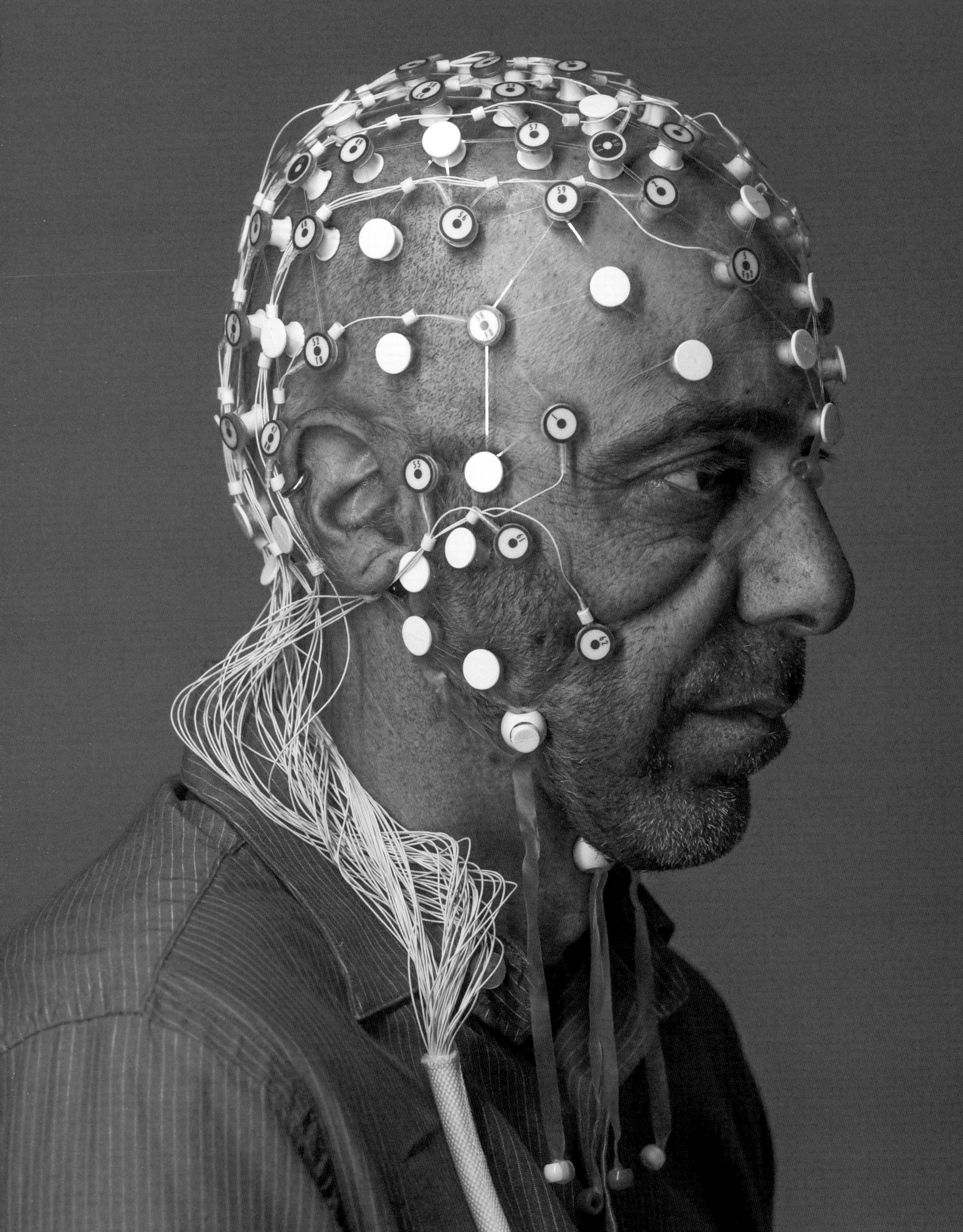

IN CONVERSATION WITH

ROBERT CLARK

Robert Clark has photographed more than 40 stories over the course of a 20-year-long association with National Geographic. His specialty is illustrative photography, which he applies to stories about science, technology, and archaeology. His tools are meticulous research, imagination, and the artistry of carefully placed lighting to portray everything from a 17th-century stoneware jug to a high-tech swimsuit based on the hydrodynamics of sharkskin.

Clark's mind is like a broadband scanner. He operates on multiple levels at once, typically while reaching for one of three (at least) cell phones fanned out in front of him. But with camera in hand, the focus is laser like. He lives in Brooklyn with his wife and daughter.

NATIONAL GEOGRAPHIC: Tell us about the first time you picked up a camera.

ROBERT CLARK: It's funny—I just moved out of my studio and actually found the first picture I ever shot. It's a Polaroid I took at Grand Lake, Colorado, when I was 14.

Once I picked up a camera, the tactile nature of it really appealed to me. I am dyslexic, so I wasn't a very good student. But I was good at tools and making stuff. My parents helped me deal with my dyslexia early on, but there was an understanding that school wasn't going to be for me.

At 16, I wanted my own camera, so my parents bought me a Nikon F2 and a 180mm lens, a 24mm lens, and an 85mm. It cost, like, $2,000. I've had a camera with me ever since.

NG: You do so many stories on science and technology. Do you have a background in these subjects?

RC: Absolutely not. I still have a hard time reading and taking in information in a "normal way," but I think being dyslexic has helped me become more visual.

NG: Your stories tend to be very complicated and difficult to illustrate. What technical skills are important in your work?

RC: When I moved to New York after working in newspapers, I had a chance to work with a few photographers who were skilled in using lighting to make complicated subjects seem simpler visually. I learned to control light to play up the things I thought were important in the picture. By using lighting to make objects more dimensional, you can focus everyone's attention. That gives me the ability to decide what people look at.

The other important thing I have is my ideas. Well, let me rephrase that. I tell young photographers that you can borrow cameras, you can rent lights. But the most important thing to have is a point of view—a reason for doing what you're doing.

NG: Did that perspective help in creating your haunting portrait of the Tollund Man [page 455]? This naturally mummified corpse, buried in a Danish bog some 2,400 years ago, has been photographed quite a bit since it was discovered in 1950.

RC: I shot the Tollund Man for a story about bog bodies. I decided to shoot him from above, an angle that I had never seen before. The body is from the Iron Age II, around 400 B.C.E., and he looks the way he does because he was preserved in peat moss and he absorbed the tannins in the soil. He was found two meters underground; the remains were so well preserved that they thought it was a new murder and took fingerprints to identify the body.

ROBERT CLARK, 2019
Vitaly Napadow, a neuroscientist at Harvard Medical School, uses electroencephalography to understand how the brain perceives pain.

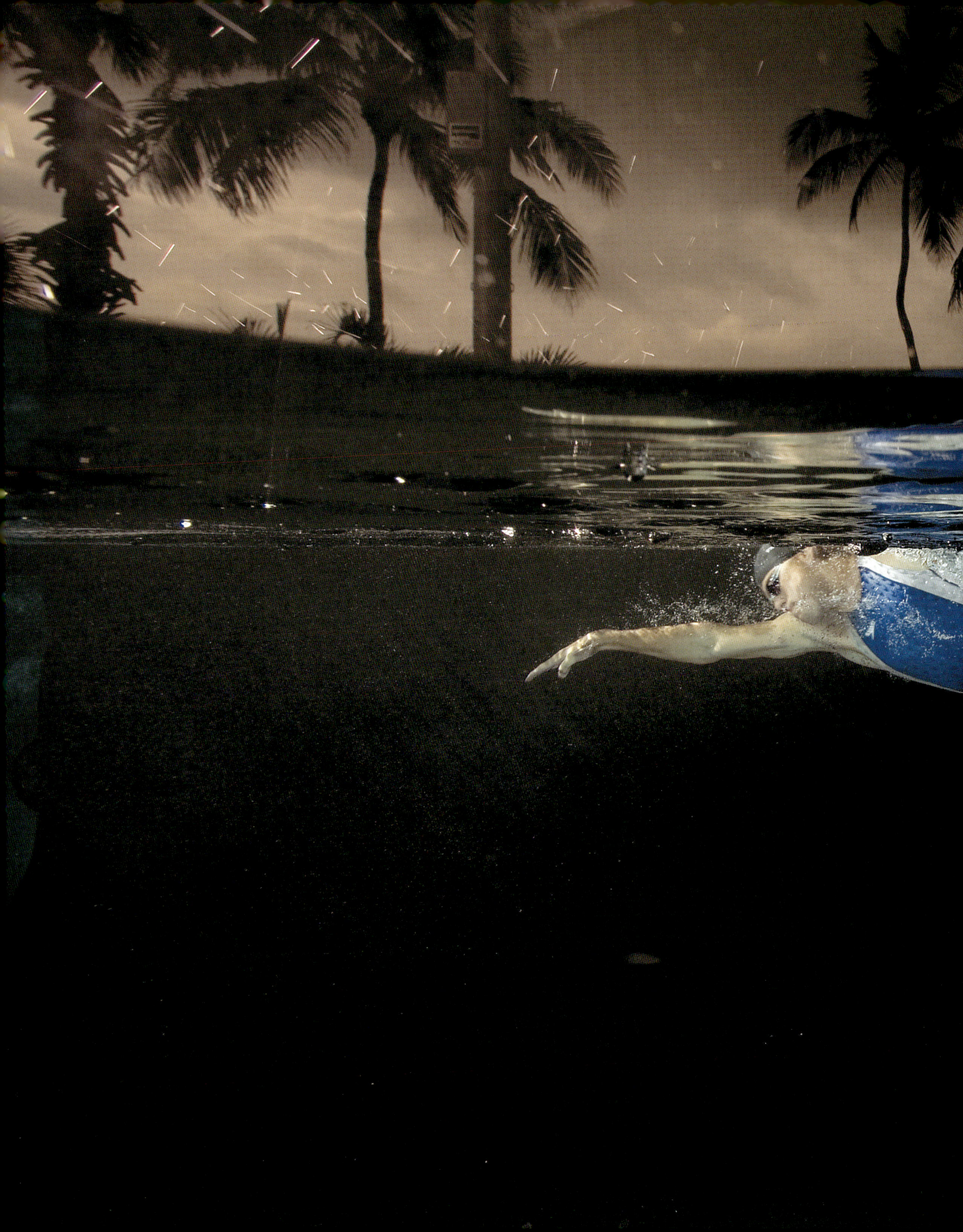

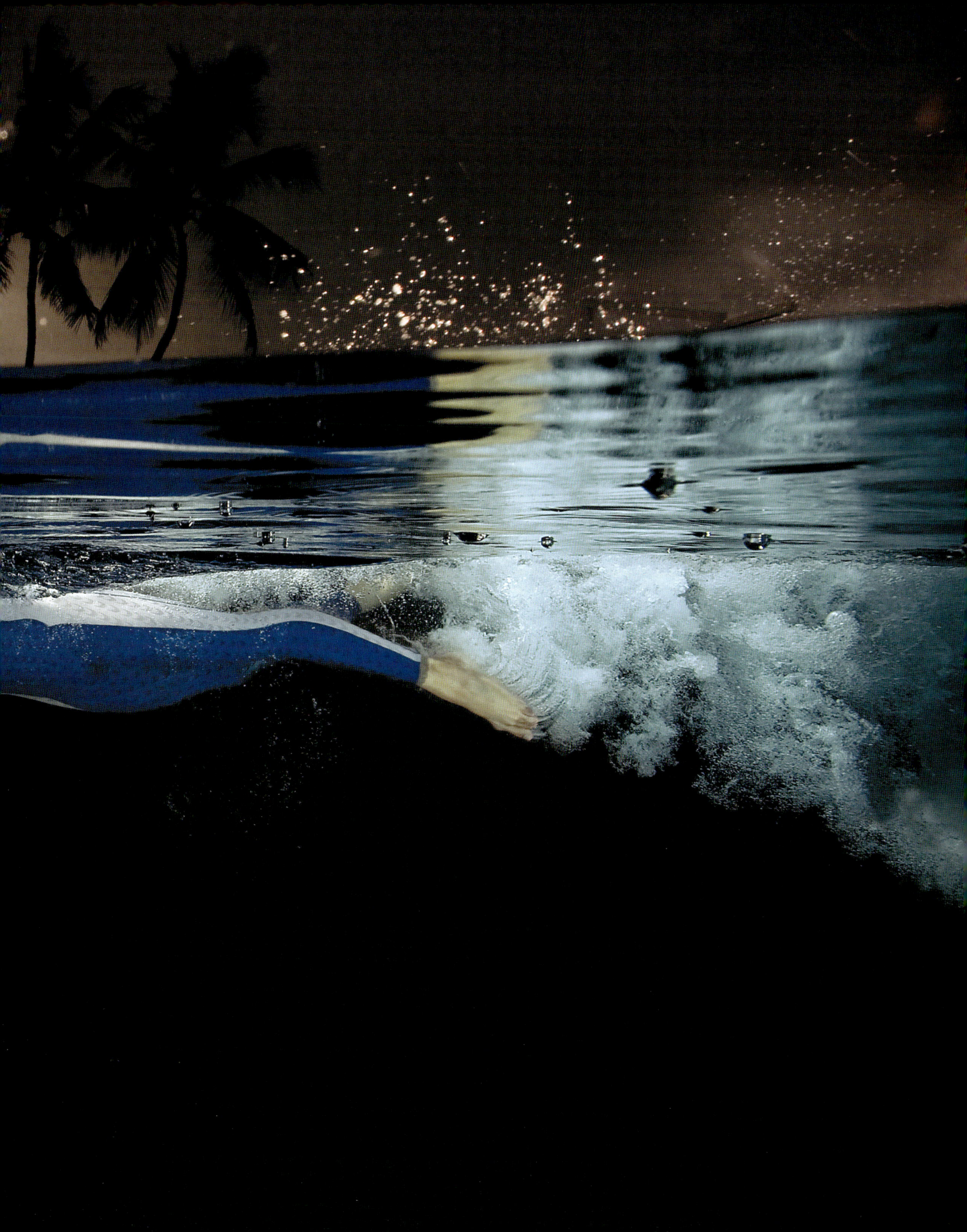

NG: How did you capture it from above?

RC: We were in the museum overnight. I took a stretch board and extended it between two ladders and took the picture from there. The light along his face was hard light, and the light in the background was soft. A director of photography—Conrad Hall, who did *In Cold Blood*—said: "Don't worry about where you put the light. Worry about where you put the shadow." It's a simple concept: You put the shadows where you don't care about the information. That idea has always helped me.

This didn't need any razzle-dazzle. It just needed to be presented in a way where people could feel his presence.

NG: He looks so peaceful.

RC: He does. I don't think he was, but it certainly gives that impression.

NG: Tell us how you captured the swimmer in the sharkskin-inspired suit [pages 452–53].

RC: That was a fun assignment. It was a piece about biomimetics: the inspiration of nature on design. That swimsuit was printed like sharkskin, since sharks move through the water with little resistance. But those suits are now illegal; you can't wear them in competitive swimming because they're practically flotation devices.

The swimmer is Olympic gold medalist Gary Hall, Jr.—one of the fastest in the world at the time. I traveled down to Fort Lauderdale with a massive piece of black velvet; I hung it in the water for the background and hardwired strobes in the bottom of the pool, with two lights above.

There are actually pictures of me swimming to do a test on the lighting. When I showed them to Gary, it looked like I was walking. He laughed at my form and said, "You might want to keep your hips up." But I knew that he would look great. I only shot 10 frames of Gary before it started to lightning and rain and we had to get out of the water. But in those frames, I had a frame that I loved.

NG: You once said that street photographers capture the moment. But what you do is create the moment.

RC: I think that's true. In almost any kind of picture I shoot, I get a really comfortable feeling in my stomach when I know I have what I wanted to capture. That's probably because I'm driven by a massive amount of insecurity. For every Geographic assignment, my first thought is, OK, how am I going to screw this up? But then you kind of pull it back, look at the story, choose an object, and break it down.

NG: Your story about the pain research lab at Harvard [page 450] offers a whole different vibe compared with other stories you've done. What happened?

RC: What happened is that digital photography has gotten so good. The lighting for that story was done with fluorescent tubes produced by a company called Asteras; you can shift them to any color you want, so I always call them "disco." In the image of the researcher, there's one tube over the camera to the left, and one more in front of him. The shadow around him is from another small hot light in front that's throwing the shadow and being filled in by the other lights.

NG: Who's the man underneath all those wires?

RC: This is a guy who studies pain at Harvard; he and his team stick pins in subjects' hands to figure out what part of the brain is firing up. Subjects can dial the level of pain up and down, from "that's annoying" to "that *really* hurts." Then they use that information to study pain meds and more.

NG: He looks like a cyborg.

RC: Yeah, that wire would normally just go down his back. But I'm making editorial choices that help explain the situation I am shooting.

NG: Is there a photograph that you're yearning to make but haven't made so far?

RC: I love birds, and have become increasingly interested in them since doing a story on the evolution of feathers. I am obsessed with crows and their intelligence. I'm planning a trip to northwestern Kansas, where over two million crows gather every year.

There are a few other things left. The Chachapoya mummies, for example—the ones that look like the Edvard Munch painting "The Scream." There are still dozens of the mummies on several mountainside ledges deep in the Cloud Forest of the Peruvian Amazon. I'd love to get up there and shoot them in situ.

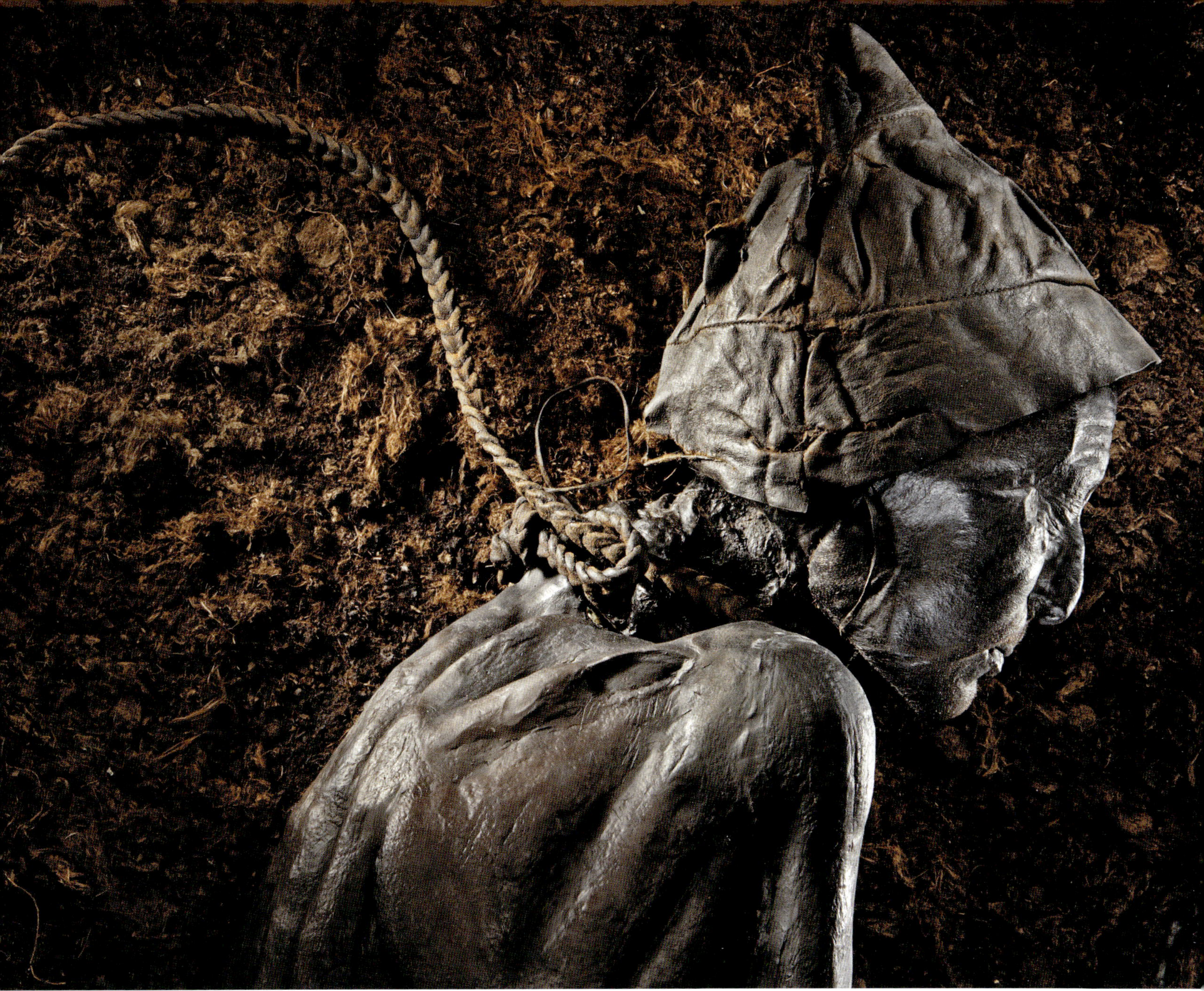

ROBERT CLARK, 2007
The remarkably well-preserved remains of the Tollund Man—mummified in a Danish bog some 2,400 years ago—are displayed in Denmark's Silkeborg Museum.

PREVIOUS PAGES
ROBERT CLARK, 2008
Olympic gold medalist Gary Hall, Jr., tests a swimsuit designed to mimic the properties of sharkskin, which by reducing the water's resistance enables the swimmer to move faster.

NG: Do you remember a time when you felt a sense of awe at what you were witnessing or trying to capture?

RC: Yes. I was doing a story on the human heart. Some guys in Germany had invented a cart—it looked like a dim sum cart—that could pump oxygenated blood through a heart removed from the human body. They took a heart from a kid who was in a motorcycle accident and got it into that machine. It was actually in the cart, beating. I was in the operating room, and I shot maybe 100 pictures of the heart pulsing in this machine before they transplanted it. I really felt like a National Geographic photographer. I was seeing the use of a technology that no one else has seen, let alone photographed.

NG: What do you hope to achieve with each photograph you take?

RC: I have learned a lot from some of the photographers who came to the magazine before me, like Cary Wolinsky and Louie Psihoyos. Their use of lighting has helped me learn to tell a story with light. Most of all, I want people to stop and ponder. William Albert Allard, who's my favorite National Geographic photographer, had the ability to capture the now. And with the stories I have shot, and the way I have shot them, I feel that I get to visit the past by photographing what once was.

ILLUSTRATIONS CREDITS

4–5, Contact Press Images; 70-1, Speleoresearch & Films; 90–1, NASA; 112, National Geographic Photo Ark, photographed at Cheyenne Mountain Zoo; 149 (UP), National Geographic Photo Ark, photographed at White Oak Conservation Center; 149 (LO), National Geographic Photo Ark, photographed at Fort Worth Zoo; 150–1, National Geographic Photo Ark, photographed at Gorongosa National Park; 186–7, Getty Images; 246–7, Contact Press Images; 260–1, Official White House photo; 316–7, courtesy Houk Gallery; 378–9, in cooperation with Pathology, University Hospital Basel, and Prüftechnik Uri; 382–3, in cooperation with Pathology, University Hospital Basel, and School of Life Sciences, FHNW, Muttenz; 398, in cooperation with Prüftechnik Uri; 404–5, Minden Pictures; 414–5, Lockheed Martin; 439, in cooperation with Pathology, University Hospital Basel, and Prüftechnik Uri; 446–7, NASA; 448–9, NASA/JPL-Caltech/MSSS.

PHOTOGRAPHER INDEX

ABOUT THE CONTRIBUTORS

JIMMY CHIN (foreword) is a National Geographic photographer, Academy Award–winning film director, renowned mountain climber, and best-selling author. His work documenting expeditions from the Sahara to the Himalaya has been featured in numerous publications, including *National Geographic,* the *New York Times Magazine, Vanity Fair, Outside* magazine, and others. His first book of photography documenting his career in the mountains, *There and Back,* became a *New York Times* best seller in 2021. His documentary film *Meru* won the Audience Award at Sundance and was shortlisted for an Academy Award; *Free Solo* won the Academy Award for Best Documentary Feature, a BAFTA Award, and seven Primetime Emmys. *Nyad,* his first scripted feature, starring Annette Bening and Jodie Foster, garnered Academy Award nominations for both actresses in 2024. Chin lives in Jackson, Wyoming, with his wife, filmmaker Chai Vasarhelyi, and their children.

CATHY NEWMAN (text) began her career writing for the *Miami News*. She joined the staff of *National Geographic* in 1978, where her 37-year-long career as a senior staff writer and editor at large enabled her to cover such diverse subjects as the Shakers, trout, beauty, the Crimea, the Seine River, and Cape York Peninsula, Australia. The author of *Perfume: The Art and Science of Scent, Women Photographers at National Geographic,* and *Fashion,* all published by National Geographic, she also edited *A Man of the World,* the memoir written by Gilbert M. Grosvenor, a fifth-generation member of the founding family of the National Geographic Society. A contributor to *The Economist, Science,* NPR.com, and *Anglers Journal,* she lives in Washington, D.C.

Since 1888, the National Geographic Society has funded more than 15,000 research, conservation, education, technology, and storytelling projects around the world. National Geographic Partners distributes a portion of the funds it receives from your purchase to National Geographic Society to support their mission to illuminate and protect the wonder of our world.

National Geographic Partners, LLC
1145 17th Street NW
Washington, DC 20036-4688 USA

Get closer to National Geographic Explorers and photographers, and connect with our global community. Join us today at nationalgeographic.org/joinus

"In Conversation With" interviews have been edited and condensed for clarity.

ISBN: 978-1-4262-2440-9

Printed in South Korea

25/QPSK/1